TAMU

CHILDREN AND YOUTH
Social Problems and Social Policy

CHILDREN AND YOUTH
Social Problems and Social Policy

Advisory Editor

ROBERT H. BREMNER

Editorial Board
Sanford N. Katz
Rachel B. Marks
William M. Schmidt

ILLEGITIMACY
AS A CHILD-WELFARE PROBLEM

Emma O[ctavia] Lundberg

and

Katharine F. Lenroot

Parts 1 and 2

ARNO PRESS
A New York Times Company
New York — 1974

Reprint Edition 1974 by Arno Press Inc.

Reprinted from copies in
  The University of Illinois Library

CHILDREN AND YOUTH
Social Problems and Social Policy
ISBN for complete set: 0-405-05940-X
See last pages of this volume for titles.

Manufactured in the United States of America

Library of Congress Cataloging in Publication Data

United States. Children's Bureau.
    Illegitimacy as a child-welfare problem, parts 1 and
2.

    (Children and youth: social problems and social
policy)
    Reprint of pts. 1 and 2 of the 1920-24 ed. published
by Govt. Print. Off., Washington, which were issued as
no. 9-10 of the Bureau's Dependent, defective, and
delinquent classes series, and as no. 66 and 75 of its
Bureau publication.
    Bibliography: p.
    1. Illegitimacy--United States. 2. Child welfare
--United States. I. Lundberg, Emma Octavia.
II. Lenroot, Katharine Fredrica, 1891-   III. Title.
IV. Series. V. Series: United States. Children's
Bureau. Dependent, defective, and delinquent classes
series, no. 9-10. VI. Series: United States.
Children's Bureau. Publication no. 66 and 75.
HQ999.U6U55 1974   362.7   74-1713
ISBN 0-405-05972-8

U. S. DEPARTMENT OF LABOR

CHILDREN'S BUREAU

JULIA C. LATHROP, Chief

ILLEGITIMACY
AS A CHILD-WELFARE PROBLEM

PART 1

A BRIEF TREATMENT OF THE PREVALENCE
AND SIGNIFICANCE OF BIRTH OUT OF WED-
LOCK, THE CHILD'S STATUS, AND THE STATE'S
RESPONSIBILITY FOR CARE AND PROTECTION

BIBLIOGRAPHICAL MATERIAL

By

EMMA O. LUNDBERG
and
KATHARINE F. LENROOT

℘

DEPENDENT, DEFECTIVE, AND DELINQUENT CLASSES SERIES No. 9
Bureau Publication No. 66

WASHINGTON
GOVERNMENT PRINTING OFFICE
1920

CONTENTS.

3

TABLES.

4

U. S. DEPARTMENT OF LABOR,
CHILDREN'S BUREAU,
Washington, December 15, 1919.

SIR: I transmit herewith the first of two studies on illegitimacy as a child-welfare problem. This report, intended in part as an introduction to the report which will follow, is a brief survey of the available statistics relating to births out of wedlock, the present rights and disabilities of the children, and the protection and guardianship by means of which public and private agencies have attempted to mitigate the handicap of illegitimate birth. The source material upon which the report is based, together with certain general references, is included.

Although the evidence available indicates that the number of children born out of wedlock in the United States is less, in proportion to population and to total births, than in European countries, the figures are sufficiently large to command attention and to arouse concern for the welfare of the children. Inadequacy of birth registration makes it impossible to secure accurate statistics, but a careful study of the data makes it fairly certain that at least 32,000 white children are born out of wedlock in the United States each year. The information presented in this report indicates that probably not more than 70 per cent of these children survive the first year of life.

This report was prepared in the Social Service Division of the Bureau. It was written by Emma O. Lundberg and Katharine F. Lenroot, and the bibliographical material for it was prepared by Ruth H. Olmsted under Miss Lundberg's supervision.

Respectfully submitted.

JULIA C. LATHROP, *Chief.*

Hon. W. B. WILSON,
Secretary of Labor.

5

ILLEGITIMACY AS A CHILD-WELFARE PROBLEM.

PART 1.

INTRODUCTORY.

Only within comparatively recent times has illegitimacy come to be recognized as a definite social problem. Yet, few topics relating to social welfare have as many ramifications or provoke as many divergent opinions. In its bearings upon social standards, especially those concerning family relationships, illegitimacy opens up a large field for discussion. It is a matter of prime importance in a consideration of social and moral prophylaxis, while in its relation to infant mortality, infant care, child abandonment and neglect, and the care of dependent children it demands the attention and concern of all who are engaged in constructive social effort. Although the problem manifests fairly regular phenomena, these vary according to the composition, customs, and social conditions of the community, and furthermore are subject to modification by social action.

The social significance of illegitimacy may be studied along two distinct lines of investigation, the first concerned with causative factors and centering in the mother and father, the second centering in the child and attempting to measure the handicaps to the child born out of wedlock and to secure the care and protection that should be afforded him. The two lines of investigation necessarily converge at many points. To a considerable extent the causative factors have an essential bearing upon the child's history and the burden of dependency imposed upon the State. Many theories have been advanced in regard to the natural endowment of the child born out of wedlock as compared with that of the child of legitimate birth, but very little authoritative information is available. Neither has there been any adequate consideration of the environmental and home influences surrounding children who are born out of wedlock, nor of the burden that is placed upon the public for the support of these children.

A consideration of illegitimacy as a problem of child welfare is in reality a study of the relation of the child born out of wedlock to his family and to the community. The detriment of illegitimate birth is neutralized in the degree to which the child is provided with normal family conditions and an equitable social attitude realized. Of equal importance with the securing of justice for children handicapped by the circumstances of their birth is the raising of moral standards and the improvement of the social conditions that are at bottom largely responsible for illegitimacy.

The close connection between birth out of wedlock and lack of proper care may be clearly shown in the case of infants. The most immediate and demonstrable effect of the disadvantages attendant upon illegitimate birth is the very high mortality rate. Little is known of the histories of the children who survive infancy, but though the influence of their birth upon their development as they grow older is less tangible and more obscured by other factors than during infancy the problem of their care is no less important. The frequent concomitants of illegitimate birth are absence of a normal home, deprivation of a mother's care, and lack of adequate support. These handicaps often result in impairment of health and vitality, dependence upon the public for support, and abnormal character development, producing in many cases waywardness and delinquency. The increasing tendency to exert every effort to conserve child life results from the recognition of the obligation of society to insure for all children a childhood as nearly normal as possible and to develop them into useful and valuable members of the community.

European countries have furnished extensive studies of various phases of the problem of illegitimacy. In Germany, where conditions have lent themselves particularly to detailed research, which has been made possible by the completeness of birth registration and the system of records for military purposes, numerous treatises have been written on the moral aspects of illegitimacy, illegitimate births as social phenomena, and the care of children born out of wedlock. In France the published studies have dealt mainly with the question of the child's right to the establishment of paternity, as a part of a campaign for recognition of this principle in law. Publications in regard to the problem in other European countries are less available, but fragmentary information indicates a special interest in the problem, usually from the point of approach of the child's birthright or his care. In Norway, especially, inquiries have been concerned with the need for the adequate support and care of children born out of wedlock. Governmental investigations and parliamentary debates culminated in the passage of the Norwegian law of 1915, which establishes inheritance rights and sets a high standard of maintenance and protection. In England and Scotland, and in Australia and New Zealand, activity in behalf of these children has mainly taken the form of efforts to lower the infant mortality rate and to provide the necessary care for the mother and child. Recently, there has been organized in England a national council [1] the aim of which is to bring about reform in the legal and social position of the unmarried mother and her child.

In the United States, with its diversity of conditions and varied State legislation, interest has been mainly local. Studies have been concerned chiefly with the numerical extent of illegitimate births in a community, the moral aspects, and the possibility of lessening the problem. Within the past few years, however, there has come an awakening of interest in illegitimacy as it affects the child. Not only has this resulted in the formation of conferences [2] for the study of the problem in a large number of cities, but also the subject has been given special attention in the proceedings of various national organizations dealing with social problems. There is a growing interest in its broader aspects as being of nation-wide concern from the point of view of child welfare, and a movement is developing for uniformity in legislation relating to the status and support of children born out of wedlock.

---

[1] The National Council for the Unmarried Mother and Her Child (and for the Widowed or Deserted Mother in Need), organized in 1918. Evelyn House, 62 Oxford St., W. I., London.

[2] For example, the Boston Conference on Illegitimacy; the Committee on Illegitimacy of the Philadelphia Conference on Parenthood; the Cleveland Conference on Illegitimacy; the Milwaukee Conference on Illegitimacy; various committees engaged in studying the problem in other cities; and the Inter-City Conference on Illegitimacy composed of representatives of these and other organizations concerned with the subject.

EXTENT OF PROBLEM.

In considering statistics of illegitimate births in various communities, differences in laws and customs and in methods of securing and compiling vital statistics must be kept in mind. In some European countries, for example, the government requires civil marriage while a part of the population holds a religious ceremony to be sufficient, with the result that the children born of the latter marriages are considered by the state to be of illegitimate birth and recorded as such. In Germany, as in some other countries, the collecting of vital statistics is an important function of the state; in Russia the records of the church supply the data on births and deaths, no doubt inadequately; in the United States the registration laws differ, and in only a small number of the States is there adequate birth registration. It is therefore necessary to consider existing data on the extent of illegitimacy in the various countries merely as approximate indications of its comparative prevalence.

Two methods of computing illegitimacy rates are used in this report. The first gives the proportion of illegitimate births to total births in a given period, and is obtained by dividing the number of illegitimate births by the total births. The second method compares the number of illegitimate births with the number of single, widowed, and divorced women of childbearing age in the community, and is obtained by dividing the number of illegitimate births by the number of such women in the population. The first method emphasizes the extent of the child-care problems involved; the second gives data relating more definitely to causative factors and to the moral and preventive sides of the problem.

PREVALENCE IN FOREIGN COUNTRIES.

European countries.

In most European countries birth registration, because of its importance in connection with military service and other governmental requirements, has been very nearly complete. Statistics of illegitimate births have been the subject of exhaustive research by students of social problems and by statistical bodies and are therefore readily available for comparative study. The data presented in the tables

10

on the numbers of births in European countries were compiled in large part from material contained in a report of an international statistical association.

Table I gives, for specified countries of Europe, comparative data on the rates of legitimate and illegitimate births based, respectively, on the total number of married women of childbearing age and the total number of single, widowed, and divorced women of the same age.

TABLE I.—*Average annual legitimate birth rate per 1,000 married women 15 to 49 years of age, and illegitimate birth rate per 1,000 single, widowed, and divorced women 15 to 49 years of age, in specified countries of Europe.*[a]

Country and period.	Legitimate live births per 1,000 married women 15 to 49 years of age.	Illegitimate live births per 1,000 single, widowed, and divorced women 15 to 49 years of age.
Austria-Hungary:		
Austria, 1908–1913	219	30
Hungary, 1906–1915	198	38
Belgium, 1908–1913	161	12
Denmark, 1906–1915	191	24
Finland, 1906–1915	239	17
France, 1910–1911	114	16
German Empire, 1907–1914	196	23
Bavaria, 1907–1914	214	31
Prussia, 1907–1914	204	21
Saxony, 1907–1914	153	36
Wurtemburg, 1907–1914	211	21
Great Britain and Ireland:		
England and Wales, 1906–1915	171	7
Ireland, 1909–1912	250	4
Scotland, 1906–1915	202	13
Italy, 1907–1914	226	14
Norway, 1907–1914	224	13
Spain, 1906–1915	218	14
Sweden, 1908–1913	196	26
Switzerland, 1906–1915	184	8
The Netherlands, 1905–1914	233	5

[a] Compiled from Annuaire International de Statistique. II. Mouvement de la Population (Europe). L'Office Permanent de l'Institut International de Statistique, La Haye, 1917. pp. 54–56.

In considering the data presented, it is important to take into account differences in methods of registration in the various countries and in legal definitions of illegitimacy, which make the figures only approximately comparable. The rates are seen to vary widely in different countries, even in those with apparently homogeneous populations and in political divisions of the same country. The number of illegitimate births per 1,000 single, widowed, and divorced women 15 to 49 years of age ranged from 4 to 38. The figures presented suggest the importance of correlating the various factors, such as racial differences, economic and social conditions, marriage customs and laws, constructive social influences, and various legal provisions in regard to the status of the child born out of wedlock. Such analysis of social causes in connection with the evidence furnished by statistics is requisite to an understanding of the real significance of the numbers of illegitimate births.

Over a period of 30 to 40 years (from about 1875 to 1915) there has been a decrease in the yearly number of illegitimate births per 1,000 single, widowed, and divorced women in Austria, Belgium, Denmark, England and Wales, Finland, the German Empire, Hungary, Italy, Norway, Scotland, Spain, Switzerland, and The Netherlands. In Ireland the illegitimate birth rate remained stationary, and in France and Sweden it fluctuated or increased.[1]

Table II gives for the specified countries of Europe, over a period of years, the proportion of illegitimate births to total births, stated in terms of per cents. This table also gives the number of illegitimate live births in each country during one year.

The percentages of illegitimate births furnish an indication of the proportion of children born out of wedlock, and the consequent problem that confronts the State in providing for their care and protection. It must be remembered that a decline in the total birth rate is likely to result in a rise in the percentage of illegitimate births, though in fact the actual number of such births may not have increased. This is illustrated by recent English vital statistics. The percentage of illegitimate births in England and Wales for 1917 was 5.6, as compared with 4.2, 4.4, and 4.8, the percentages for the three preceding years. This increase is accounted for by the large decrease in legitimate births because of war conditions. The decrease in the number of legitimate births from the number in 1914 amounted to 7.5 per cent in 1915, 11.2 per cent in 1916, and 25 per cent in 1917.[2] The number of illegitimate births, on the other hand, remained practically stationary for several years preceding the war and for the first three years of the war.[3] However, figures for 1918[4] show a considerable increase in the number of illegitimate births. In 1917 the number of illegitimate births was somewhat less than in 1916, but in 1918 there was an increase of 11.2 per cent over the preceding year. The number of legitimate births continued to decrease.

European cities.

In large centers of population social problems are massed and intensified. Because of their institutions and agencies giving maternity

---

[1] Lundberg, Emma O.: "The illegitimate child and war conditions." American Journal of Physical Anthropology, Vol. 1 (July-September, 1918). Table I on pp. 342–343.

[2] Percentages based on statistics given in Eightieth Annual Report of the Registrar-General of Births, Deaths, and Marriages in England and Wales (1917). London, 1919. p. 4.

[3] Eightieth Annual Report of the Registrar-General of Births, Deaths, and Marriages in England and Wales (1917). London, 1919. p. 4.

[4] Quarterly Return [and Annual Summary] of Marriages, Births, and Deaths Registered in England and Wales and in the Registration Counties, etc. No. 280—year 1918, p. 38. London, 1919.

TABLE II.—*Number and per cent of illegitimate births in specified countries of Europe.*[a]

Country.	Illegitimate live births, 1914.		Per cent of live births illegitimate.					
	Number.	Per cent of total live births.	Annual average, 1906–1909.	Annual average, 1910–1914.	1915	1916	1917	
Austria Hungary:								
Austria	b 102,845	11.9	12.3	b 11.9				
Hungary	63,301	8.5	9.4	9.0	9.5			
Belgium	b10,975	6.4	6.3	b 6.3				
Denmark	8,395	11.5	11.0	11.3	c 11.7	c 11.7		
Finland	6,846	7.8	6.9	7.7	8.0			
France d	b 66,000	8.8	8.9	b 8.7				
German Empire	176,270	9.7	8.7	9.4				
Bavaria	25,180	12.6	12.2	12.4				
Prussia	99,172	8.5	7.4	8.1				
Saxony	18,803	16.0	14.1	15.5				
Wurtemburg	5,737	8.6	8.3	8.6				
Great Britain and Ireland:								
England and Wales e	37,329	4.2	4.0	4.2	4.4	4.8	5.6	
Ireland f	2,943	3.0	2.6	2.8	3.1	3.0	3.1	
Scotland g	8,879	7.2	7.0	7.3	6.9	7.1	7.5	
Italy	52,813	4.7	5.1	4.8	h 4.3			
Norway	4,406	7.1	6.8	6.9	i 7.3	i 7.0	7.1	
Portugal	j 20,601	11.0	11.3	(k)				
Roumania	l 25,367	8.1	9.2	(k)				
Russia in Europe m	118,159	2.3	2.3	(k)				
Spain	28,858	4.7	4.6	4.8	5.0	n 5.3		
Sweden	o 20,481	o15.8	13.3	o 15.1				
Switzerland	4,341	5.0	4.4	4.7	4.6	p 4.4		
The Netherlands	3,728	2.1	2.1	2.1	2.2	q 2.2		

a Except where otherwise noted, figures are based on statistics of live births reported in Annuaire International de Statistique. II. Mouvement de la Population (Europe). L'Office Permanent de l'Institut International de Statistique, La Haye, 1917. pp. 40–53.

b Number given for 1913; average based on four-year period 1910–1913.

c Statistisk Aarbog [Danmark], 1917. Statistiske Departement. København, 1917. p. 18.

d Figures for 1910–1913 are based on statistics in Annuaire Statistique, 1916, 1917, 1918. Résumé Rétrospectif.—Divers Pays., pp. 11*–12*. Ministère du Travail et de la Prévoyance Sociale. Statistique Général de la France, Paris, 1919. (Numbers given only in thousands.)

e Seventy-seventh (1914), Seventy-eighth (1915), Seventy-ninth (1916), and Eightieth (1917) Annual Reports of the Registrar-General of Births, Deaths, and Marriages in England and Wales. London, 1915–1919.

f Fifty-first (1914), Fifty-second (1915), Fifty-third (1916), and Fifty-fourth (1917) Annual Reports of the Registrar-General for Ireland. Dublin, 1915–1918. Annual average for 1906–1909 derived from Supplement to the Forty-seventh Report of the Registrar-General for Ireland, containing summaries for the years 1901–1910, p. xiv.

g Fifty-ninth (1913), Sixtieth (1914), Sixty-first (1915), Sixty-second (1916), and Sixty-third (1917) Annual Reports of the Registrar-General for Scotland. Edinburgh, 1916–1919.

h Annuario Statistico Italiano, Seconda Serie, Vol. VI. Anno 1916. Roma, 1918. p. 31.

i Statistisk Aarbok or Kongeriket Norge, 38te Årgang, 1918. Statistiske Centralbyrå. Kristiania, 1919. pp. 8–9.

j Number given for 1910—the only figure available during the period 1910–1914.

k No average given as figures are not available for a period of four years.

l Number given for 1912.

m Excluding Finland and Poland. Number given for 1909; no later figures available.

n Anuario Estadístico de España. Año IV–1917. Ministerio de Instrucción Pública y Bellas Artes. Dirección General del Instituto Geográfico y Estadístico. Madrid, 1918. p. 41.

o Statistisk Årsbok för Sverige. Femte Årgången, 1918. Kungl. Statistiska Centralbyrån. Stockholm, 1918. p. 46.

p Annuaire Statistique de la Suisse. 1917—26e année. Bureau Fédéral de Statistique. Berne, juillet 1918. pp. 17, 19.

q Annuaire Statistique de la Ville d'Amsterdam. Publié par le Bureau Municipal de Statistique. 14ième Année, 1917. Amsterdam, 1919. p. 54.

care and providing for children who must depend upon the public for support, these cases gravitate to the cities. Unquestionably the city, by reason of economic and social conditions inherent in congested areas, also produces an undue proportion of births out of wedlock and of child dependency. A comparison of the percentages of illegitimate births in large cities with those in the entire population of a country [1] gives striking evidence of the abnormal situation in large population centers. In Table III are given the proportions of illegitimate to total births over a quinquennial period for 38 of the large cities of Europe.

TABLE III.—*Average annual per cent of illegitimate births in European cities, 1905 to 1909.*[a]

City.[b]	Population, 1909.	Per cent of live births illegitimate, 1905-1909.	City.[b]	Population, 1909.	Per cent of live births illegitimate, 1905-1909.
Amsterdam	567,000	4.4	Lyon	472,000	22.2
Barcelona	547,000	6.6	Manchester	655,000	3.8
Belfast	387,000	3.4	Marseilles	517,000	[c]17.2
Berlin	2,107,000	18.1	Milan	594,000	9.5
Birmingham	564,000	2.6	Moscow	1,452,000	24.0
Breslau	503,000	18.8	Munich	571,000	27.8
Bristol	378,000	3.2	Naples	612,000	9.7
Budapest	823,000	26.3	Odessa	467,000	[d]14.0
Christiania	233,000	[c]13.6	Paris	2,760,000	25.5
Cologne	472,000	11.9	Petrograd	1,596,000	20.2
Copenhagen	450,000	25.5	Prague	467,000	[c]28.7
Dresden	546,000	19.4	Riga	356,000	[c]6.3
Dublin	398,000	3.1	Rome	534,000	16.5
Edinburgh	355,000	8.5	Rotterdam	415,000	4.0
Frankfort on the Main	367,000	13.8	Sheffield	463,000	[c]4.3
Glasgow	872,000	7.0	Stockholm	340,000	33.5
Hamburg	888,000	13.6	Turin	392,000	11.4
Leipzig	538,000	19.2	Vienna	2,064,000	30.1
London	4,834,000	3.5	Warsaw	746,000	9.1

a Based on statistics published in Statistique Démographique des Grandes Villes du Monde pendant les années 1880-1909. Première partie—Europe. Publiée à l'occasion de la XIIIe Session de l'Institut International de Statistique à la Haye, Septembre 1911. Communications Statistiques, publiées par le Bureau municipal de Statistique d'Amsterdam, No 33, 1911. pp. 1-137.
b With the exception of Stockholm and Christiania, all the cities are of 350,000 population or over.
c Average per cent for five-year period 1904-1908.
d Average per cent for five-year period 1904-1908. As illegitimate births are included all births whose status as to legitimacy is unknown.

The differences in the percentages of illegitimate births in large cities and in entire countries [2] may be illustrated by comparing the percentage for the German Empire with the cities within its borders. For the period 1906-1909, the annual average for the German Empire was 8.7 illegitimate in every 100 live births. During the period 1905-1909, the percentages for the eight cities within the Empire having a population of 350,000 or over ranged from 11.9 to 27.8. Similarly, in France during the selected periods the average annual percentage for the whole country was 8.9, while the percentages for the three largest cities were 17.2, 22.2, and 25.5, respectively. During the time periods specified, the percentage for Sweden was 13.3 with apparently an enormous concentration of the problem in Stockholm, the metropolis, producing a percentage of 33.5; for Denmark the general percentage was 11, as compared with 25.5 in Copenhagen; for Norway 6.8, as compared with 13.6 in Christiania; for

Austria 12.3 and for Hungary 9.4, the three large cities within the Empire having percentages ranging from 26.3 to 30.1. The general percentage for Italy was 5.1, and the percentages for its four large cities from 9.5 to 16.5. For Russia a general percentage of only 2.3 was reported, while the percentages in the five large cities were from 6.3 to 24. How much reliance may be placed on the Russian figures is problematic.

In the other countries for which comparative data were secured, the percentages of illegitimate births, both for cities and entire countries, were much lower than in the cases above cited; but a similar difference occurred between city and entire country, except in England and Wales, where the city rates were lower. During the specified periods, in England and Wales the average annual percentage was 4, while in London it was only 3.5, and in the three largest manufacturing cities and the port of Bristol the percentages ranged from 2.6 to 4.3. Ireland had an average of only 2.6, while Dublin and Belfast had percentages of 3.1 and 3.4. Scotland, with an average of 7, had percentages of 7 and 8.5 in Glasgow and Edinburgh. In Spain the general average was 4.6, with a percentage of 6.6 in Barcelona. The Netherlands had the lowest average of any European country, 2.1, but in Rotterdam and Amsterdam the percentages were 4 and 4.4, respectively.

Comparative percentages of illegitimate births for any considerable number of European cities were not available for a later period than 1905-1909. As showing the variation in rates from year to year, and particularly the situation during the years when war conditions prevailed, the figures for Berlin, Paris, and London are of interest. In Berlin the percentages of illegitimate births were as follows:[1] 1913, 23.3; 1914, 22.6; 1915, 22.2; first five months of 1916, 23.8. These rates are considerably higher than the average rate, 18.1, shown in Table III for the period 1905-1909. In Paris[2] the percentages of illegitimate births were: 1912, 23.8; 1913, 26.5; 1914, 23.9; 1915, 26.8; 1916, 30.8; 38 weeks of 1917, 31.7. The average rate in Paris for the period 1905-1909 was 25.5. The percentages of illegitimate births in London were: 1914, 4.5; 1915, 4.8; 1916, 5.4; 1917, 6.8; 1918, 8.[3] For 1905 to 1909 the average rate in London was 3.5.

[1] Percentages derived from data given in Guradze, Dr. Hans: " Säuglingssterblichkeit, Geburtenhäufigkeit, Eheschliessungen und Gesamtsterblichkeit in Berlin während des Krieges." Jahrbücher für Nationalökonomie und Statistik. Oktober 1916. Jena. p. 550.
[2] Pinard, M. A.: " De la Protection de l'enfance pendant la troisième année de guerre dans le camp retranché de Paris." Bulletin de l'Académie de Médecine. 3e Série—Tome lxxviii. No. 49. Séance du 18 Décembre 1917. p. 776.
Percentage for 1913 derived from Annuaire Statistique de la Ville de Paris, XXXIVᵉ Année—1913. Paris, 1917. p. 112.
[3] Derived from Quarterly Return and Annual Summary of Marriages, Births, and Deaths Registered in England and Wales and in the Registration Counties, etc. Published by Authority of the Registrar-General. Nos. 264, 268, 272, 276, and 280—years 1914-1918. London.

Other countries.

The situation in Australia and New Zealand is of especial interest, since conditions in these countries are somewhat similar to those existing in the United States. Table IV gives, for the Commonwealth of Australia and its component States and for the Dominion of New Zealand, the number of illegitimate births in one year, and the percentages of illegitimate births for a series of years.

TABLE IV.—*Number and per cent of illegitimate births in Australia and New Zealand.*

Country and State.	Illegitimate live births, 1914.		Per cent of live births illegitimate.				
	Number.	Per cent of total live births.	Annual average, 1905–1909.	Annual average, 1910–1914.	1915	1916	1917
Australia a	7,263	5.3	6.2	5.6	5.1	4.8	4.9
New South Wales	2,836	5.3	6.9	5.7	5.0	4.7	4.7
Victoria	2,015	5.6	5.7	5.8	5.7	5.2	5.5
Queensland	1,148	5.8	7.4	6.2	5.4	5.1	5.0
South Australia	500	3.9	4.2	4.3	4.0	3.8	4.0
Western Australia	388	4.2	4.3	4.3	4.2	3.8	4.2
Tasmania	355	5.9	5.5	5.3	5.3	5.1	5.3
Northern and Federal Territories	b 21						
New Zealand c	1,302	4.6	4.5	4.3	4.1	4.0	4.1

a Except for 1905–1909, averages based on statistics in Population and Vital Statistics, Bulletin No. 35, Commonwealth Demography, 1917 and Previous Years. Commonwealth Bureau of Census and Statistics, Melbourne, 1918. pp. 30, 31.
Averages for 1905–1909 based on statistics in Official Year-Book of the Commonwealth of Australia Containing Authoritative Statistics for the Period 1901–1916, etc. No. 10—1917. Melbourne. pp. 159, 162.
b Numbers too small upon which to base a per cent.
c Statistics of the Dominion of New Zealand. Population and Vital Statistics, in Volume I for each year from 1905 to 1917. Wellington, 1906–1918.

It will be seen that the percentages of illegitimate births for Australia and New Zealand almost uniformly indicate a slight but persistent decline. The percentages in 1916 were approximately the same as in England and Wales for the same year.

Comparing the number of births out of wedlock with the number of single, widowed, and divorced women in the population, the rate in England and Wales is lower than in the Australian States and in New Zealand, all of them being low as compared with most European countries. For the year 1911 the following rates represent the illegitimate births per 1,000 single, widowed, and divorced women 15 to 45 years of age:[1]

Australia :
```
    Queensland _____ 15.5
    New South Wales_____ 14.5
    Western Australia_____ 14.0
    Tasmania _____ 11.9
    Victoria _____ 10.5
    South Australia_____  8.5
New Zealand_____  9.2
```

[1] Victorian Year Book, 1916–1917. Melbourne, 1918. p. 331.

The rate for England and Wales during the same year for women of this age group was 8.[1]

Australian statistics show a larger percentage of illegitimate births in cities than in country districts. In New South Wales, in 1916, the percentage of illegitimate births in Sydney was 6.4, as compared with 3.7 in the remainder of the State.[2] The proportion of illegitimate births in the city of Melbourne and suburbs in 1916 was greater than in the other urban and rural districts of Victoria, the lowest percentages prevailing in the country districts.[3] In South Australia the percentages of illegitimate births in 1916 were 6.2 for the metropolitan area and 3.9 for the State as a whole.[4] In Western Australia the percentage of illegitimate births in Perth and its suburbs, in 1916, was 4.5, as compared with 3.7 for the State as a whole.[5] The percentages in the two cities of Tasmania—Hobart and Launceston—in 1914, were 9.7 and 11, respectively, as compared with 3.3 in country districts.[6]

Without a comprehensive understanding of the customs and laws, the conditions surrounding child life, and the completeness of birth registration, it is impossible to evaluate the statistics on illegitimate births in oriental countries. The illegitimacy rate in Japan, according to official statistics,[7] is practically the same as that found in France, Germany, and Hungary. In 1915, 8.7 per cent of all births in Japan were reported as illegitimate. The average for 1905 to 1909 was 9.2, and for 1910 to 1914, 9.1. Information is not available as to the effect illegitimate birth may have upon the lives of the 150,000 children born out of wedlock in Japan each year.

The effect of racial differences and variations in social customs upon the illegitimacy rate is indicated by the statistics for the Union of South Africa excluding the Orange Free State.[8] In 1914, 2.2 per cent of the births among the white population were illegitimate, while the percentage of illegitimate births among the Bantus was 11.2 and among the mixed and other colored races 30.8. No information is available as to the completeness of birth registration, nor in regard to social customs and standards.

---

[1] Seventy-fourth Annual Report of the Registrar-General of Births, Deaths, and Marriages in England and Wales, 1911. London, 1913. p. xxvi.

[2] Official Year Book of New South Wales, 1917. Sydney, 1918. p. 82.

[3] Victorian Year Book, 1916–17. Melbourne, 1918. p. 331.

[4] South Australia, Statistical Register, 1916–17. Part I—Population. Adelaide, 1917. p. 9.

[5] Percentages derived from Statistical Register of Western Australia for 1916 and Previous Years. Part I.—Population and Vital Statistics. Perth, 1918.

[6] Statistics of the State of Tasmania for the year 1914–15. Part III. Vital and Meteorological. Tasmania, 1915. p. 151.

[7] Mouvement de la Population de l'Empire du Japon. Cabinet Impérial, Bureau de la Statistique Générale. Reports for 1905 to 1915. Tokio.

[8] Figures derived from Statistical Year-Book of the Union of South Africa, No. 3—1914–15. Pretoria, 1916. pp. 16–27.

Statistics were available for three Central American and three South American countries. In Costa Rica,[1] Guatemala,[2] and San Salvador,[3] the percentages of illegitimate births ranged from 23.4 to 54.5. In Uruguay[4] 21.9 per cent of all births in 1916 were illegitimate, and in Chile[5] the percentage in the same year was 38.1. In Venezuela[6] the average percentage for 1910 to 1912, the years for which statistics were available, was considerably higher. These figures for Central and South America should be studied in relation to the composition of the populations of the various countries, the marriage laws and customs that prevail, and the bearing that illegitimacy has upon child welfare.

Separate figures for the Latin population and the Indians were available for Guatemala in 1912 and for San Salvador in 1914. In the former country the percentage of illegitimate births among the Latin population was 6.6 per cent higher than the percentage among the Indians, and in the latter country 8 per cent higher.

PREVALENCE IN THE UNITED STATES.

Registration of illegitimate births.

The purposes of birth registration in this country include mainly the collection of vital statistics, the safeguarding of the health of infants, the establishment of parentage for support and inheritance, the proof of age for the proper enforcement of education and child labor laws, and, more recently, the determination of age in connection with military service. Registration as an aid in the prevention of infant mortality and as an infant welfare measure is of even greater importance for children born out of wedlock than for others. Often, too, the legal rights of a child of illegitimate birth may depend on registration as much as do the rights of a child of legitimate birth, and there is as great need for accurate proof of age for purposes of protection against premature work and for assuring the child's education. There appears to be little difference of opinion as to the necessity for registering the births of children born out of wedlock.

---

[1] Percentage derived from statistics in República de Costa Rica, América Central, Anuario Estadístico, Año 1917—Tomo Vigesimoprimero. Dirección General de Estadística, San Jose, 1918. p. xxi.

[2] Percentage derived from statistics in Boletín de la Dirección General de Estadística. Año 1. Núm. 1 (Noviembre de 1913), Guatemala, C. A. p. 143.

[3] Percentage derived from statistics in Anuario Estadístico de la República de el Salvador, 1914. Correspondiente A. Dirección General de Estadística, San Salvador, 1915. p. 25.

[4] Percentage derived from statistics in Anuario Estadístico de la República Oriental del Uruguay, Año 1916—Libro XXVI. Director General de Estadística, Montevideo, 1918. p. 36.

[5] Percentage derived from statistics in Statistical Abstract of the Republic of Chile, Central Statistics Bureau, Santiago de Chile, 1917. p. 10.

[6] See Anuario Estadístico de Venezuela, 1910 to 1912. Dirección General de Estadística, Caracas, 1913–1915.

But there is much controversy as to the method by which these
shall be so recorded as best to safeguard the child's legal stat
property rights and at the same time protect him against any s

The birth registration law recommended by the United
Bureau of the Census requires that the birth certificate shall state
"whether legitimate or illegitimate," "full name of father," and
"maiden name of mother." The registration laws or regulations of
20 States contain these provisions—Alabama, Arizona, Colorado,
Florida, Idaho, Iowa, Kentucky, Louisiana, Michigan, Montana, Nebraska, North Dakota, Oklahoma, Pennsylvania, Texas, Utah, Vermont, Washington, Wisconsin, and Wyoming.

In 6 States—Delaware, Missouri, Nevada, Ohio, Tennessee, and
Virginia—the law prohibits entry of the name of the father of a child
of illegitimate birth, and in Oregon the provision requiring that the
"full name of father" be recorded, contained in the law of 1915, has
been omitted in the amendatory law of 1917. In Georgia, Massachusetts, Minnesota, and New York the father's name may be entered
only by his consent; however, in Minnesota the name must be entered
after paternity is established. The Illinois law prohibits the recording of the names or other identifying data in regard to the father or
the mother without their consent. In the District of Columbia "it
shall in no case be necessary for any physician, midwife, or other person to report any fact or facts whereby the identity of the father or
of the mother or of the child born shall be disclosed"; the provision
in North Carolina is similar, except that such entry is forbidden.
In all the above States except Massachusetts there is required a statement as to legitimacy; in Illinois the law provides for the items included in the standard certificate of birth, but the certificate form
used for recording births does not include this entry; a special law
governs birth registration in New York City, and this law does not
require information as to legitimacy of birth. In the remaining 15
States there is no specific provision in the law regarding entry of
legitimacy or illegitimacy of birth; but in most cases the birth-certificate form provides for the checking of this fact.

The question of registration is closely connected with the legal
determination of paternity. There are some who hold that no record
should be made either of the mother's or of the father's name. As
indicated, only two States and the District of Columbia have incorporated this idea in legislation. It may be assumed that the data
in regard to the mother are considered of importance in measures
for the protection of the child. Certainly, without this information
efforts looking to the prevention of infant mortality and for protection of children are greatly handicapped. It becomes an issue as to
whether the greater emphasis should be placed on safeguarding the
mother's name or on protecting the child's life.

The identity of the mother is beyond question, whereas the identity of the father is not. As it now exists in the United States, the birth registration machinery is entirely inadequate as a means of determining paternity. In the absence of judicial determination of paternity, there is some question as to the value of the registration. The point may well be made, however, that the law should recognize no distinction in the responsibility of the parents of the child born out of wedlock. In order to safeguard the property rights of the child and for the purpose of holding the father liable for support, it is necessary that paternity should be determined legally and in as large a proportion of cases as possible.

Together with efforts to secure complete and accurate birth registration must go concern that no record shall be so used that the child's future happiness may be in any way endangered. In some communities, either by law or by regulations of the health department or the bureau of vital statistics, it is provided that only persons who can show a legitimate interest in the information may be permitted access to birth records. Experience in cities where this rule is not in force would indicate the necessity for preventing the use for malicious purposes of records relating to births out of wedlock. It is often of vital importance to the individual child that transcripts of birth records used for school, employment, and other purposes should contain no information which will indicate birth status. New York City has set an example by omitting on transcripts for school and employment purposes information in regard to parentage.

Statistics for States.

The inadequacy of birth registration data in this country is evidenced by the fact that for only 16 States and 20 of the 62 cities having in 1915 populations of 100,000 or over could figures on illegitimate births be secured from reports of State or city departments. In 19 States[1] from which no statistics could be secured the law or regulations relating to birth registration require the reporting of the fact of legitimacy or illegitimacy on the birth certificate.

Because the failure to register probably affects the accuracy of figures on illegitimate births to an even greater extent than those on legitimate births, and the entry of incorrect information on the birth certificate further invalidates these statistics, only a minimum statement is possible of the percentage of births that occur out of legal wedlock. Some indication of the inadequacy of the figures cited

---

[1] Arizona, Colorado (figures later than 1910 could not be secured), Delaware, Florida, Georgia, Idaho, Illinois. Kentucky, Nebraska, New York, North Carolina, North Dakota, Ohio, Oregon, Tennessee, Texas, Virginia, Washington, and Wyoming.

is given by the fact that only 8 of the States and 11 of the cities from which statistics on illegitimate births were secured were included by the Bureau of the Census in the birth registration area in 1915 as having birth registration 90 per cent or more complete. A further difficulty is occasioned by the lack of uniformity in the inclusion or exclusion of stillbirths and the failure, in many instances, to indicate whether or not the figures include stillbirths. This is particularly true of figures relating to illegitimate births.

TABLE V.—*Legitimate birth rate per 1,000 married women 15 to 44 years of age, and illegitimate birth rate per 1,000 single, widowed, and divorced women 15 to 44 years of age, in 16 States of the United States, 1915.*

State.	Estimated number of married women 15 to 44 years of age.[a]	Live births reported as legitimate.[b]		Estimated number of single, widowed, and divorced women 15 to 44 years of age.[a]	Live births reported as illegitimate.[b]	
		Number.	Per 1,000 married women 15 to 44 years of age.		Number.	Per 1,000 single, widowed, and divorced women 15 to 44 years of age.
Alabama:						
White [c].............	183,400	31,122	169.7	108,700	302	2.8
Negro.............	139,000	14,892	107.1	98,500	2,448	24.9
Connecticut [d].............	159,200	31,554	198.2	137,600	356	2.6
Indiana.............	399,200	60,969	152.7	256,000	881	3.4
Maryland:						
White [c].............	146,200	25,504	174.4	124,200	622	5.0
Negro.............	33,200	4,946	149.0	27,900	1,295	46.4
Massachusetts [c].............	464,500	91,286	196.5	468,100	2,108	4.5
Michigan.............	415,300	79,737	192.0	278,500	1,363	4.9
Minnesota.............	261,800	54,116	206.7	245,100	1,117	4.6
Missouri.............	483,400	70,039	144.9	332,500	1,504	4.5
Nevada.............	13,800	1,278	92.6	6,300	12	1.9
New Hampshire.............	56,400	9,919	175.9	44,600	84	1.9
Pennsylvania.............	1,134,100	214,613	189.2	854,100	4,448	5.2
Rhode Island.............	78,400	13,772	175.7	75,300	215	2.9
South Dakota.............	88,400	13,543	153.2	58,800	107	1.8
Utah.............	55,600	12,874	231.5	36,200	109	3.0
Vermont.............	47,400	7,726	163.0	31,900	149	4.7
Wisconsin.............	302,200	57,174	189.2	259,300	840	3.2
Eight States in birth registration area[f]..	2,617,100	502,723	192.1	2,135,200	9,840	4.6
Total (exclusive of the Negroes in 2 States)[g].............	4,289,300	775,226	180.7	3,317,200	14,217	4.3

[a] Number of women estimated as for July 1, 1915, from U. S. Census figures for 1910 and U. S. Census estimated population as of July 1, 1915. For Connecticut and Massachusetts the estimates are for July 1, 1914, since the numbers of illegitimate births were secured for 1914. It was assumed that the number of married women and of single, widowed, and divorced women 15 to 44 years of age would represent the same percentages of the total population in 1915 as they represented in 1910. Estimates are expressed in even hundreds.
    See Thirteenth Census of the United States, 1910, Vols. II and III, Population Reports by States. Washington, 1913. Also, U. S. Bureau of the Census Bulletin 138. Estimates of the Population of the United States, 1910–1917, including results of the State enumerations made in 1915. Washington, 1918.
    [b] Except for the State of Massachusetts, information was furnished by State departments of health and bureaus of vital statistics. In some States it was impossible to tell with absolute certainty whether or not stillbirths were included in the number of births, and this was especially true in the case of illegitimate births.
    [c] Includes a small number belonging to other races than white and Negro.
    [d] Figures for 1914; figures for 1915 not available.
    [e] Figures for 1914; compiled by the U. S. Children's Bureau from original records.
    [f] In 1915: Connecticut, Massachusetts, Michigan, Minnesota, New Hampshire, Pennsylvania, Rhode Island, Vermont. See U. S. Bureau of the Census: Birth Statistics for the Registration Area of the United States, 1915. First Annual Report. Washington, 1917. p. 9.
    [g] The Negro populations and births of Alabama and Maryland were excluded, since they comprised more than 10 per cent of the total population of each of these States.

The incompleteness of birth registration in the United States renders impracticable any attempt at comparison with foreign figures, though the evidence would seem to indicate that there is a smaller proportion of births out of wedlock among the white population in this country than in most of the European countries.

In order to secure fairly comparable figures for the United States, it is necessary to treat separately the figures for the white and for the Negro population of the States in which Negroes formed more than 10 per cent of the total population. Illegitimacy among Negroes is a phenomenon which must be studied by itself in its relation to the social and economic conditions surrounding the race at the present time and in their past history. Unfavorable economic conditions and lack of educational opportunities have resulted in laxness of marriage relations among the Negroes of many localities, and consequently in a high illegitimacy rate. However, illegitimacy as it prevails among the Negroes in these localities is not comparable with the same condition among the white population. Regardless of the status of colored children, they are usually provided for by the mother or her relatives, and a child born out of wedlock has very much the same advantages and disadvantages as a child born in lawful marriage. Therefore, in the discussion of comparative data presented in Tables V, VI, and VII there have been excluded the Negro population and the Negro births in the two States included in which Negroes comprise one-tenth or more of the entire population. Sufficient data were not available for an adequate discussion of illegitimate births among Negroes.

The average legitimate birth rate per 1,000 married women of childbearing age in the 16 States represented, excluding the Negroes in Alabama and Maryland, was 180.7. The average illegitimate birth rate per 1,000 single, widowed, and divorced women of the same age was 4.3. For the 8 States which were in the birth registration area in 1915 the legitimate birth rate was 192.1 and the illegitimate, 4.6.

There seems to be no close relation between legitimate and illegitimate birth rates. Seven States had legitimate birth rates above the average. The illegitimate birth rate in 4 of these States was above the average and in 3 below. Of the 9 States having legitimate birth rates below the average, 3 had illegitimate rates above the average, and 6 below.

Neither does there appear to be a definite relation between the illegitimacy rate and the percentage of unmarried women among all women of childbearing age. In the 16 States for which the analysis was made the average percentage of women 15 to 44 years of age who were single, widowed, or divorced was 43.6 (exclusive of the Negro population in 2 Southern States). Of 7 States where tho percentage was above the average, 3 had illegitimate birth rates above and 4 had rates below the general illegitimate birth rate. In Vermont, where the illegitimate birth rate was relatively high, only 40.2 per cent of the women of childbearing age were unmarried. On⁹ the other hand, in Connecticut, where the illegitimacy rate was low, 46.4 per cent of the women 15 to 44 years of age were unmarried.

The percentages of illegitimate births in the States from which figures were obtained are given in Table VI.

TABLE VI.—*Number and per cent of illegitimate births in 16 States of the United States.*

State.	Live births in 1915.[a]			Per cent of live births reported as illegitimate.[a]			
	Total.	Reported as illegitimate.		Annual average, 1910–1914.	1916	1917	1918
		Number.	Per cent.				
Alabama:							
White	31,424	302	1.0		0.9	0.9	
Negro	17,340	2,448	14.1		13.7	12.8	
Connecticut	b 31,910	b 356	b 1.1	1.0			
Indiana	61,850	881	1.4	1.6	1.5	1.4	
Maryland:							
White	26,126	622	2.4	c 2.3			
Negro	6,241	1,295	20.7	c 15.2			
Massachusetts	d 93,394	d 2,108	d 2.3				
Michigan	81,100	1,363	1.7	e 1.6			
Minnesota	55,233	1,117	2.0	f 2.0	1.9	1.8	
Missouri	71,543	1,504	2.1	g 2.4	2.2	2.4	2.3
Nevada	1,290	12	.9	h .8	.1.9	1.0	.3
New Hampshire	10,003	84	.8	h 1.0			
Pennsylvania	219,061	4,448	2.0				
Rhode Island	13,987	215	1.5	1.5	1.3	1.2	
South Dakota	13,650	107	.8	.8	.9	.9	
Utah	12,983	109	.8	g .7	.7	.7	
Vermont	7,875	149	1.9	1.7	1.4	1.8	
Wisconsin	58,014	840	1.4	1.5	1.6	1.5	

a Except for the State of Massachusetts, information was furnished by State departments of health and bureaus of vital statistics. In some States it was impossible to tell with absolute certainty whether or not stillbirths were included in the number of births; this was especially true in the case of illegitimate births.
b Figures for 1914; figures for 1915 not available.
c Average based on 3-year period 1912-1914; statistics not given for white and colored separately prior to 1912.
d Figures for 1914; compiled by the U. S. Children's Bureau from original records.
e Average based on 2-year period 1913-1914. Reports previous to 1913 included stillbirths in illegitimate births, and it was impossible to obtain the number of illegitimate live births.
f Average based on 2-year period 1913-1914.
g Average based on 4-year period 1911-1914.
h Average based on 3-year period 1912-1914.

The population of the 16 States included in Table VI, exclusive of the Negro population in Alabama and Maryland, represented, in 1915, more than one-third of the total population of the country, exclusive of the Negro population of the 14 States and the District of Columbia, in which Negroes formed as much as 10 per cent of the population.[1] The percentage of illegitimate among the total births in these 16

[1] Population estimated as for July 1, 1915, except that for Connecticut and Massachusetts the estimates are for July 1, 1914.

States in 1915 was 1.8.[1] Eight of the States—Connecticut, Massachusetts, Michigan, Minnesota, New Hampshire, Pennsylvania, Rhode Island, and Vermont—were included in the birth registration area in 1915; in that year the percentage of illegitimate births in these States was 1.9. Grouping the States geographically, the percentage was lowest in the sparsely settled Western States, the average for Nevada, South Dakota, and Utah, in 1915, being 0.8. In the 5 Middle Western States the rate was 1.7, in the 1 Middle Atlantic State 2, and in the 5 New England States 1.9. The rate in the 2 Southern States, excluding births to Negroes, was 1.6. It may be questioned, however, whether these rates would have been relatively the same if birth registration had been equally complete in all sections and if data had been available for the whole country. In this connection it is significant that the 5 New England States and the Middle Atlantic State were all in the birth registration area, and that the rates for these sections were comparatively high.

Statistics for cities.

In the 20 cities for which statistics were secured, the percentages of births out of wedlock in 1915 varied from 1.2 to 6.1, excluding the births to Negroes in 2 cities. The percentages of illegitimate births among the Negroes in Baltimore, Washington, and Philadelphia were, in 1915, 24.5, 19.5, and 16.4,[2] respectively. No figures were obtainable for cities farther south. Although possible differences in the accuracy of registration may affect these comparative percentages, the low percentage in Philadelphia, where in 1910 one-eighteenth of the population was Negro, as compared with Baltimore, having one-sixth Negro, and Washington, almost one-third Negro, suggests a better condition among the colored population in cities and States where the race is more dispersed, and where Negroes live under more favorable economic and social conditions.

The difference in the extent of the problem in cities and in less congested areas is brought out by comparison of the percentages of illegitimate births in States as a whole and in their large centers of population. As has been pointed out in the discussion of the European statistics, the preponderance in the number of illegitimate births in large cities is due largely to the position of the city as a refuge and as a center for hospital and other types of care. It is probable, however, that conditions of life in a city are a considerable

---

[1] Total births, exclusive of Negro births in Alabama and Maryland, 789,443; reported as illegitimate, 14,217. For 2 States, figures were for 1914.

[2] See footnote i, p. 25.

Table VII.—*Number and per cent of illegitimate births in 20 cities of the United States having more than 100,000 population.[a]*

City.	Live births in 1915.			Per cent of live births reported as illegitimate.			
	Total.	Reported as illegitimate.		Annual average, 1910–1914.	1916	1917	1918
		Number.	Per cent.				
Baltimore:							
White...................	11,460	359	3.1	3.8	2.6	2.1	....
Negro..................	2,174	533	24.5	23.3	22.7	21.6	....
Boston.........................	19,725	800	4.6	4.1	....	....	....
Buffalo........................	12,683	263	2.1	b 2.0	2.2	2.5	1.8
Cincinnati c.................	7,804	299	3.8	3.7	....	....	....
Cleveland	16,623	386	2.3	2.3	....	....	1.2
Denver........................	3,703	105	2.8	d 3.0	2.9	3.6	....
Detroit........................	21,088	547	2.6	e 2.7	....	....	....
Grand Rapids.................	3,157	117	3.7	e 2.7	....	....	....
Kansas City c.................	5,418	329	6.1	f 6.1	6.2	7.9	8.2
Milwaukee g	11,278	292	2.6	2.6	2.8	2.6	....
Minneapolis	8,529	365	4.3	b 4.4	4.0	4.0	3.8
Newark	10,955	152	1.4	1.5	1.3	1.1	....
New York h	141,256	1,703	1.2	1.4	1.1	1.0	....
Philadelphia i................	40,849	1,122	2.7	j 2.5	2.4	2.3	....
Pittsburgh	16,139	490	3.0	k 3.6	....	....	....
Providence	5,835	123	2.1	2.2	1.7	2.1	....
St. Louis c...................	14,143	529	3.7	f 4.3	3.9	3.6	3.6
St. Paul......................	5,291	272	5.1	4.5	4.5	5.0	....
Toledo	4,495	118	2.6	b 2.5	1.7	1.8	....
Washington:							
White	4,872	110	2.3	2.1	1.6	2.3	....
Negro	2,195	427	19.5	20.9	18.2	18.8	....

a Statistics furnished by State or city departments of health or bureaus of vital statistics, except for Boston, where the statistics for the period 1910–1914 were compiled by the U. S. Children's Bureau from original records.

b Average based on two-year period 1913–1914; no previous statistics of illegitimate births.

c Separate statistics for white and Negro births not available. In 1910, the population of Cincinnati was 5.4 per cent Negro, of Kansas City 9.5 per cent, of St. Louis 6.4 per cent.

d Average for the period 1912–1914.

e Average based on two-year period 1913–1914. Reports previous to 1913 included stillbirths in illegitimate births, and it was impossible to obtain the number of illegitimate live births.

f Average based on four-year period 1911–1914.

g Includes stillbirths. The percentages would have been slightly lower had stillbirths been excluded.

h New York City is a center of maternity care for surrounding territory, and the percentage of illegitimate births would be expected to be high. Workers in touch with the local situation suggest that the low rates shown by these figures may be due to the fact that large numbers of unmarried mothers when entering a hospital claim to be married. One reason for this may be the provision of the New York law which makes the inquiry into paternity compulsory in cases in which the child is chargeable to a county, city, or town, and which in such cases requires the mother, under penalty, to disclose the name of the father. (Bender's Penal Law and Code of Civil Procedure, 1918, secs. 840, 856.)

i In 1910, 5.5 per cent of the population was Negro. The percentages of illegitimate births, including stillbirths, among the Negroes were: 1915, 16.4; 1916, 13.4; 1917, 13.6. The percentages among the whites were: 1915, 2.1; 1916, 1.8; 1917, 1.6.

j Rate for 1914; no previous statistics of illegitimate births.

k Average based on reports for four years—1910, 1911, 1913, and 1914.

factor in producing the high rate. The 1915 rates for the States and cities for which comparable statistics were secured were as follows:

Maryland:
    White _____ 2.4
    Colored _____ 20.7
    Baltimore—
        White _____ 3.1
        Colored _____ 24.5
Massachusetts [1]_____ 2.3
    Boston [1]_____ 3.9

_____

[1] For 1914.

Minnesota _____ 2. 0
    Minneapolis _____ 4. 2
    St. Paul _____ 3. 7
Missouri _____ 2. 1
    Kansas City _____ 6. 1
    St. Louis _____ 3. 7
Pennsylvania _____ 2. 0
    Philadelphia _____ 2. 7
Rhode Island _____ 1. 5
    Providence _____ 2. 1

Estimated number of illegitimate births.

Although the available statistics are meager, an attempt was made to approximate roughly the total number of illegitimate births in the United States each year. It was impracticable to arrive at such an estimate by the method based on the total number of live births in the United States, since incomplete birth registration makes it impossible to obtain, for the country as a whole, statistics having any degree of accuracy. Hence, the estimate was based on the number of single, widowed, and divorced women of child-bearing age. In the United States in 1915 the estimated number of single, widowed, and divorced white women 15 to 44 years of age was 8.769,000.[1] In the 16 States for which figures of illegitimate births were obtained the rate per 1,000 single, widowed, and divorced white women of child-bearing age may be estimated as at least 3.7.[2] Applying this ratio to the estimated population given above gives 32,400 as an estimated number of illegitimate white births in the United States each year. It must, of course, be remembered that this figure is an estimate based on only a part of the country; it is improbable, however, that the true figure is below it. Indeed it may safely be considered as a minimum estimate because of incompleteness of birth registration and erroneous registration of illegitimate as legitimate births.

Because of the recognized inadequacy of birth registration in a considerable part of the United States, another estimate was made based on data from States included in the birth-registration area in 1915. By the method described above the rate for white unmarried

---

[1] The number of single, widowed, and divorced white women 15 to 44 years of age on July 1, 1915, was estimated by projecting the annual increase in this group between 1900 and 1910, using the arithmetical method. Strictly speaking, the figures for " white women " refer to women of all races other than Negro. The figure 8,769,000 includes approximately 0.2 per cent of Indians, Chinese, and Japanese.

[2] The rate per 1,000 white and Negro women in the group specified, exclusive of the Negro women in two States, was found to be 4.3. (See Table V, p. 21.) The rate per 1,000 white women in this group can be found by assuming, in the absence, for most of the States, of illegitimate births classified by color, that the ratio between the white and Negro illegitimate birth rates was the same as that in the area of good birth registration, Maryland and Philadelphia combined, where illegitimate births are classified by color. (Maryland was not in the birth registration area in 1915 but was admitted in 1916.) Applying this ratio to the respective white and Negro populations in the group specified results in the figure of 3.7 for the white unmarried female population of child-bearing age.

women of childbearing age in these States may be estimated as 4.[1] This rate, applied to the number of single, widowed, and divorced white women of childbearing age in the United States, gives a total of 35,100 illegitimate white births. It must be borne in mind that States in the birth registration area have a disproportionate urban population among which the illegitimate birth rate is high. Nevertheless, this figure may be regarded as an understatement because of errors and omissions of registration of illegitimate births even in States included in the birth-registration area.[2]

---

[1] The rate per 1,000 white and Negro women in the group specified was 4.6; the correction has been made on the same basis as described in note 2, p. 26.

[2] A careful study of records of social agencies in Boston added one-eighth to the number of illegitimate births registered as such in the city. Similar estimates for Negroes would be subject to a much greater percentage of error than are estimates for whites, first, because of inadequate registration in areas where the Negro population is largest, and secondly, because of special conditions affecting Negroes. Such an estimate, if made, should of course be accompanied by a full discussion of the history of the problem and of the difficulties involved in setting up new standards of family morality in place of those existing under slavery conditions.

INFANT MORTALITY.

Infant mortality statistics are an index not merely of the number of infants who fail to survive their first year, but of the conditions surrounding infancy and early childhood. The significance of the infant mortality rate is not alone in the sacrifice of infant life, but perhaps of even greater social import are the impaired physical development, hardship, and social handicap likely to be the lot of many who survive. The unfavorable conditions surrounding children born out of wedlock are clearly shown by the fact that the infant mortality among them is invariably found to be far in excess of the mortality among infants born in wedlock. Most European countries recognize the significance of the relation between illegitimate birth and infant mortality and furnish comparative statistics on the deaths of infants of illegitimate and of legitimate birth. Table VIII gives for 13 European countries the infant mortality rates among children of illegitimate and of legitimate birth, and the relative differences between the mortality rates among infants born in wedlock and those born out of wedlock.

TABLE VIII.—*Average infant mortality rates for legitimate and illegitimate births in specified countries of Europe, 1910 to 1914.*

Country.	Annual average number of deaths under one year per 1,000 live births.		
	Illegitimate.[a]	Legitimate.[a]	Relative difference.[b]
Austria	247	188	1.3
Belgium	213	136	1.6
Denmark	167	90	1.9
England and Wales	208	104	2.0
Finland	175	106	1.7
France	221	111	2.0
German Empire	256	154	1.7
Bavaria	250	187	1.3
Prussia	271	151	1.8
Saxony	233	167	1.4
Wurtemburg	215	150	1.4
Italy	223	134	1.7
Norway	122	62	2.0
Scotland[c]	223	120	1.9
Sweden	109	66	1.7
Switzerland	169	99	1.7
The Netherlands	233	102	2.3

a Derived from statistics in Annuaire International de Statistique. II. Mouvement de la Population (Europe). L'Office Permanent de l'Institut International de Statistique, La Haye, 1917, pp. 158–160. Annual average for the quinquennial period 1910–1914 in all countries with the following exceptions: Austria, France, Scotland, and Sweden, 1909–1913; Belgium, 1908–1912.
b Rate in column 1 divided by rate in column 2.
c Mackenzie, W. Leslie, M. D.: Scottish Mothers and Children, being Vol. III of Report on the Physical Welfare of Mothers and Children. The Carnegie United Kingdom Trust, East Port, Dunfermline, 1917. p. 133. Annual average 1909–1913.

The infant mortality rate among infants born out of wedlock is without exception higher than among other infants, ranging from 1.3 to 2.3 times that found among infants of legitimate birth. The four countries having the lowest infant mortality among children of legitimate birth—Norway, Sweden, Denmark, and Switzerland— also had the lowest mortality among infants born out of wedlock. Nevertheless, in these countries the illegitimate infant mortality rates were from 1.7 to 2 times as high as the rates among infants of legitimate birth. The countries showing the lowest relative difference between illegitimate and legitimate infant mortality rates—Austria, Belgium, and three States of the German Empire—had extremely high infant mortality among infants of both legitimate and illegitimate birth.

In Norway the infant mortality rate among infants born in wedlock during the quinquennial period 1910–1914 was only 62, whereas the corresponding rate for infants born out of wedlock was 122. As an argument for the passage of the Norwegian law relating to " children whose parents have not married each other," the Government made an exhaustive study of the infant mortality among these children. The conditions imposed by the law passed in 1915 are expected to effect radical changes in this respect, through insuring for the children born out of wedlock maternal care and adequate support either by the parents or by the State. In an article on this measure the author of the Norwegian law says:[1]

This demand for the increasing of a father's duties to his illegitimate child was considerably strengthened by the result of the official investigation into the economic and social position of unmarried mothers and their children. Those investigations * * * presented a dark picture of the existing conditions, especially in regard to stillbirths and infant mortality. It was stated that the stillbirths in the years 1891–1900 amongst the illegitimate children were 164 to 165 compared with 100 stillbirths among the legitimate children. The district doctors stated the reasons for this to be—besides venereal disease in several towns—unsatisfactory obstetrical help, concealment of birth, and the mother's needy position during pregnancy. * * * A still graver impression is produced by the investigation of the mortality of children born out of wedlock. It is stated that the mortality of illegitimate children in proportion to that of the legitimate ones is in the first month of life 195 to 100; in the second month of life 239 to 100; in the third month of life 274 to 100—nearly three times as great.

The annual report of the registrar-general of England and Wales shows for the year 1915[2] a mortality rate among infants born in wedlock of 105 per 1,000 births, and a mortality rate of 203 per 1,000

---

[1] Castberg, J.: " The children's rights laws and maternity insurance in Norway." Journal of the Society of Comparative Legislation. (New Series.) Vol. XVI, Pt. 2 (1916). pp. 290–291. London.
[2] Seventy-eighth (1915), Seventy-ninth (1916), and Eightieth (1917) Annual Reports of the Registrar-General of Births, Deaths, and Marriages in England and Wales. London, 1917–1919. p. 41.

births for infants of illegitimate birth. During the year 1916 the infant mortality among babies of legitimate birth was reduced to 87, while the rate among babies of illegitimate birth was 183. In 1917 the rates showed an increase to 90 for children of legitimate birth and to 201 for those born out of wedlock. The registrar-general has persistently called attention to the meaning of these comparative infant mortality rates, and there is evidence that public opinion in England has been aroused to a realization of the necessity for correcting the existing conditions by providing through legislative action and constructive social measures better protection, support, and care for these infants.

In the Report on the Physical Welfare of Mothers and Children in Scotland Dr. W. Leslie Mackenzie, after discussing the difficulties surrounding unmarried mothers, says in regard to their children:[1]

In many respects it is less difficult to make provision for the mothers than for the annual crop of 8,600 children. The mothers, however they are provided for, can at least fight for their lives and often attain to a passable living. The newborn infant can do nothing for himself. He hangs on the service of others. Within hours of his birth he may be taken from his mother's breast and put among those whose skill is often no substitute even for an unskilled mother's care. He may pass from hand to hand and from place to place. Besides the risks he has encountered in coming to birth, he encounters a thousand others that fall only to the children of the unmarried. If, starting from the same line, he loses in the race with his legitimate fellows, it is from no fault of his own. He has not sinned, but he comes short of the glory. That is the tragedy of the unmarried mother's child.

In New South Wales[2] the infant mortality rate among children born out of wedlock in 1916 was 145.9, as against 63.9 for children of legitimate birth. For the years 1906–1915 the rate for the former was 170.4, and for the latter 68.1. In his report for 1917,[3] the president of the State Children Relief Board discusses the desirability of providing special homes for babies with mothers, both for the sake of the mother's training in infant care and of her moral development and for the safeguarding of the life of the child during the first critical period of infancy. In the State of Victoria the discrepancy between the mortality rate of infants born out of wedlock and of those of legitimate birth is even greater than in New South Wales. The report of the Government statistician sums up the situation thus:[4]

---

[1] Mackenzie, W. Leslie, M. D.: Scottish Mothers and Children, being Vol. III of Report on the Physical Welfare of Mothers and Children. The Carnegie United Kingdom Trust, East Port, Dunfermline, 1917. p. 131.

[2] State Children Relief Board: Report of the President, Alfred William Green, for the Year Ended 5 April, 1917. Sydney, 1918. p. 26.

[3] State Children Relief Board: Report of the President, Alfred William Green, for the Year Ended 5 April, 1917. Sydney, 1918. p. 24.

[4] Victorian Year Book, 1916–17. Melbourne, 1918. pp. 349, 350.

On the average of the past eight years, 185 in every 1,000 illegitimate infants died within a year, as against 66 in every 1,000 legitimate children. It is thus seen that the chance of an illegitimate child dying before the age of 1 year is nearly three times that of the legitimate infant. * * * The rates for 1916 show that of every 1,000 children born out of wedlock 61.2 died from diarrheal diseases within a year as compared with 16.6 deaths per 1,000 legitimate infants from the same cause. Owing to a larger proportion of the former children being deprived of breast food, a higher mortality from these diseases might be expected among them than among legitimate infants, but the striking differences in the death rates from this cause and from the chief respiratory diseases would indicate considerable neglect in the rearing of illegitimate infants.

With the exception of full statistics for German cities, there is little information available in regard to the comparative mortality rates of children of illegitimate and of legitimate birth in cities. The figures for several German cities may be of especial interest in view of the efforts that are reported to have been made to reduce the mortality of children born out of wedlock.

TABLE IX.—*Infant mortality rates for legitimate and illegitimate births in five German cities of over 300,000 population, for specified periods.*

City.	Annual average number of deaths under 1 year per 1,000 live births.				Deaths under 1 year per 1,000 live births.			
	1904–1908 a		1909–1913		1904		1913	
	Illegitimate.	Legitimate.	Illegitimate.	Legitimate.	Illegitimate.	Legitimate.	Illegitimate.	Legitimate.
Berlin b..........................	255.1	167.1	211.0	138.7	c 285.6	c 189.8	197.5	120.4
Dresden d.........................	210.8	169.0	158.7	126.0	233.7	182.6	144.5	107.9
Frankfort on the Main e...........	304.8	123.8	f 218.2	f 100.7	335.0	133.0	g 192.8	g 85.9
Leipzig h.........................	289.3	184.0	232.8	150.0	334.3	222.5	194.1	127.3
Munich i..........................	222.5	205.3	169.7	158.4	230.8	228.4	146.9	134.9

a Keller, Prof. Dr. Arthur, und Klumker, Chr. J.: Säuglingsfürsorge und Kinderschutz in den europäischen Staaten. I. Band. Erste Hälfte. "Deutschland," von Arthur Keller. Berlin, 1912. p. 105.

b Figures for 1909–1913 and for the year 1913 derived from Statistisches Jahrbuch der Stadt Berlin. 32. Jahrgang—enthaltend die Statistik der Jahre 1908 bis 1911, sowie Teile von 1912. Statistisches Amt der Stadt Berlin, 1913. Gross Berlin, Statistische Monatsberichte. Statistisches Amt der Stadt Berlin, 1910, 1911, 1912, 1913. (Summary of deaths for 1910, 1911, 1912, in III. Jahrgang. 1912. Heft XII. p. 2.) Figures for 1905 derived from Statistisches Jahrbuch deutscher Städte. Vierzehnter Jahrgang. Statistisches Amt der Stadt Breslau. 1917. pp. 60–61.

c Rates for 1905.

d Figures for 1909–1913, and for the years 1904 and 1913, derived from Statistisches Jahrbuch der Stadt Dresden, 1909, p. 45; 1910, p. 11; 1911, p. 10; 1912, p. 10; Statistisches Amt der Stadt Dresden, 1910–1913. Monatsberichte des Statistischen Amtes der Stadt Dresden, 1904; 1913, p. 209.

e Figures for the years 1904 and 1912 and for the period 1909–1912 derived from Statistiches Handbuch der Stadt Frankfurt am Main; Erste Ausgabe, enthaltend die Statistik bis zum Jahre 1905/06; Statistisches Amt; Frankfurt am Main, 1907; pp. 49, 55. Statistische Jahresübersichten der Stadt Frankfurt am Main; 4–7 Ergänzungshefts zum "Statistischen Handbuch der Stadt Frankfurt am Main. Erste Ausgabe." 1909/1910 and 1910/1911, pp. 13, 14; 1911/1912, pp. 27, 28; 1912/1913, pp. 13, 14. Statistisches Amt. Frankfurt am Main, 1910–1913.

f Averages for 1909–1912.

g Rates for 1912.

h Figures for 1909–1913 and for the years 1904 and 1913 derived from Statistisches Jahrbuch der Stadt Leipzig. 2. Jahrgang. 1912. Statistisches Amt. Leipzig, 1914. pp. 43, 56. Statistisches Monatsberichte der Stadt Leipzig. V. Jahrgang. Jahresübersichten, 1913, p. 2. Statistisches Amt. Leipzig.

i Figures for the years 1904 and 1911, and for the period 1909–1911 derived from: Münchener Jahresübersichten für 1908. I. Teil, p. 6*; für 1911, p. 7. Statistisches Amt der Stadt München, 1909, 1913. Figures for 1912 and 1913 derived from Mataré, Franz: "Die Geburten und die Säuglingssterblichkeit in München während der Kriegsjahre, 1915, 1916 und 1917." Zeitschrift für Bevölkerungspolitik und Säuglingsfürsorge. Band 11 (Juni 1919), p. 10.

The figures in Table IX show a marked reduction in infant mortality both among children born in wedlock and among those of illegitimate birth. During the period 1904–1908 legitimate infant mortality rates in the five cities specified ranged from 123.8 to 205.3, while the rates for children of illegitimate birth ranged from 210.8 to 304.8. For the later period, 1909 to 1913, the mortality rates for infants born in wedlock ranged from 100.7 to 174.4, while for infants of illegitimate birth the rates ranged from 158.7 to 232.8. Figures for the first and last years of the ten-year period 1904–1913 indicate still more markedly the reduction that has taken place in infant mortality. In Frankfort on the Main the mortality rate for infants of legitimate birth was 133 in 1904; in 1912[1] the rate was 85.9. The mortality rate for infants of illegitimate birth in Frankfort on the Main was 335 in 1904 and 192.8 in 1912. In Leipzig the mortality rate for infants born in wedlock was 222.5 in 1904 and 127.3 in 1913; the rate for infants of illegitimate birth was 334.3 in 1904 and 194.1 in 1913.

The decline in mortality among infants of legitimate and of illegitimate birth was in approximately the same ratio, so that the relative differences between the mortality rates remained practically unchanged except in Frankfort on the Main where the relative difference between the mortality rates among infants of illegitimate and of legitimate birth was 2.5 in the period 1904–1908 and 2.2 in the subsequent period. The city of Munich showed the lowest relative difference between the rates for the two classes of infants—1.1 for both periods.

More recent figures for Leipzig show mortality rates for infants of illegitimate birth of 202 in 1914 and 174 in 1915, as compared with rates of 101 and 125, respectively, for infants born in wedlock.[2] In Munich the comparative rates for infants of illegitimate and of legitimate birth, respectively, for the period of 1914–1917 were as follows: 1914, 149.2 and 145.9; 1915, 156.2 and 145.9; 1916, 140.2 and 129.9; 1917, 166.1 and 132.1.[3]

The data would seem to refute the claims that have been made, for example, in regard to Leipzig,[4] to the effect that infant mortality among infants born out of wedlock had been reduced below the rate among other infants. That the mortality of infants of illegitimate birth has been reduced in the cities specified in approximately the same proportion as the mortality among infants of more fortunate

---

[1] Figures for 1913 not available.

[2] Hanauer, Dr. W.: "Die Fürsorge für uneheliche Kinder und der Krieg." Zeitschrift für Bevölkerungspolitik und Säuglingsfürsorge. Band 10 (August, 1918), p. 205.

[3] Mataré, Franz: "Die Geburten und die Säuglingssterblichkeit in München während der Kriegsjahre 1915, 1916 und 1917." Zeitschrift für Bevölkerungspolitik und Säuglingsfürsorge. Band 11 (Juni 1919), p. 10.

[4] Gorst, Sir John E.: The Children of the Nation. London, 1906. p. 24.

circumstances, and that the reduction has been so considerable, does, however, show forcibly the effect of the special measures that have been undertaken under the guardianship system for the protection, through health supervision and otherwise, of all children born out of wedlock.

Also significant of the efforts to lower infant mortality in the cities included in Table IX is the fact that the infant mortality rates among children of illegitimate birth were lower in these cities than in the country as a whole. The infant mortality rate among children born out of wedlock was 256 for the German Empire during the period 1910–1914,[1] while the rates in the five cities ranged from 159 to 233 for the period 1909–1913. Among infants of legitimate birth, also, the infant mortality in the cities, with the exception of Munich, was lower than the rate for the country as a whole.

In England and Wales the infant mortality, both for children born in wedlock and for those of illegitimate birth, was considerably higher in urban than in rural districts. Table X shows the rates for the two periods, 1912–1914 and 1915–1917.

TABLE X.—*Average infant mortality rates for legitimate and illegitimate births in urban and rural districts of England and Wales, 1912 to 1917.*

Administrative area.	Annual average number of deaths under 1 year per 1,000 live births.					
	1912–1914 a			1915–1917 b		
	Illegitimate.	Legitimate.	Relative difference.c	Illegitimate.	Legitimate.	Relative difference.c
England and Wales	200.4	98.3	2.0	195.8	94.1	2.1
All urban districts	214.5	102.3	2.1	208.6	97.8	2.1
London	235.9	95.0	2.5	256.0	94.4	2.7
County boroughs	231.0	112.6	2.1	218.2	106.2	2.1
Other urban districts	190.6	94.9	2.0	182.0	90.4	2.0
Rural districts	149.6	81.5	1.8	148.2	78.9	1.9

a Averages derived from yearly rates given in Seventy-fifth (1912), Seventy-sixth (1913), and Seventy-seventh (1914) Annual Reports of the Registrar-General of Births, Deaths, and Marriages in England and Wales. London, 1914–1916. pp. 75, 77.

b Averages derived from yearly rates given in Seventy-eighth (1915), Seventy-ninth (1916), and Eightieth (1917) Annual Reports of the Registrar-General of Births, Deaths, and Marriages in England and Wales. London, 1917–1919. pp. 41, 43.

c Rate in column 1 divided by rate in column 2.

During both periods the highest rates among infants born out of wedlock were in London, the mortality being lower in smaller towns than in large cities, and lowest of all in rural districts. Among infants born in wedlock the mortality rates followed the same general tendency, except that in London they were lower than in the county boroughs. The relative difference between the infant mortality

[1] See Table VIII, p. 28.

among infants born out of wedlock and among infants of legitimate
birth was greatest in London, the rate among the former being 2.5
times that among the latter in the first period, and 2.7 times as great
in the second period. The relative difference was less for rural than
for urban districts, in the former being 1.8 and 1.9, respectively, in
the two periods. as compared with 2.1 for all urban districts in both
periods.

Figures from Norway give the following comparative infant
mortality rates for children of illegitimate and of legitimate birth
during the period 1901–1905 : [1]

	Illegiti- mate.	Legiti- mate.
Cities	208. 4	92. 6
Rural	110. 1	67. 7

Here again we find a startling difference between the rates in city
and in rural districts, with the mortality rate among infants born
out of wedlock 2.3 times as high as the rate among infants born in
wedlock in cities, and 1.6 times as high in rural districts. It will
be noted that these rates are considerably higher than the rates
shown for the country as a whole for a later period, 1910 to 1914. [2]

For Denmark the situation appears to be reversed, the ratio of
infant mortality among children of illegitimate birth to that among
those born in wedlock being highest in rural districts and lowest in
the city of Copenhagen. The average yearly infant mortality rates
in Denmark were as follows : [3]

	Illegiti- mate.	Legiti- mate.
Copenhagen	Boys, 242	146
	Girls, 213	112
Province cities	Boys, 263	140
	Girls, 217	109
Country districts	Boys, 220	107
	Girls, 191	85

In Sweden, on the other hand, the mortality rate among infants
born out of wedlock in 1909 was 144 in the city of Stockholm, as
compared with 106 in the entire country. [4] The infant mortality rate
among children of legitimate birth during that year was 75 in
Stockholm and 67 in the entire country. The infant mortality rate
for children born out of wedlock was, therefore, both numerically

---

[1] Keller, Prof. Dr. Arthur, und Klumker, Chr. J.: Säuglingsfürsorge und Kinderschutz
in den europäischen Staaten. I. Band. Erste Hälfte. "Norwegen," von Axel Johannessen. Berlin, 1912. pp. 569, 570.

[2] Table VIII. p. 28.

[3] Keller, Prof. Dr. Arthur, und Klumker, Chr. J.: Säuglingsfürsorge und Kinderschutz
in den europäischen Staten. I. Band. Erste Hälfte. "Dänemark," von Pool Heiberg.
Berlin, 1912. p. 61.

[4] Ibid., "Schweden," von J. E. Johansson. Berlin, 1912. p. 752.

and proportionally, lower outside Stockholm. The high infant mortality among children born out of wedlock in Stockholm, as well as in other large cities that are centers for care of the helpless, may be attributed largely to the high infant mortality in institutions.

Figures on comparative mortality rates among infants bòrn out of wedlock are not obtainable for the United States as a whole or for any of the States. It is clear, however, that each year a considerable proportion of these infants die because of the especially hazardous conditions under which they come into the world. Neither State nor city departments of health nor bureaus of vital statistics have as yet recognized in their reports the importance of illegitimate birth as a factor in infant mortality. So far as could be discovered, the only published sources of information on mortality among infants born out of wedlock are the figures in the report of the Health Department of the City of Boston for the year 1915; similar data in earlier reports of the Newark, N. J., Health Department, and an analysis of mortality among infants of illegitimate birth in the 1913 report of the Health Officer of the District of Columbia, the figures covering the year 1912.

The alarming conditions that may be disclosed by analysis of infant mortality statistics in this country are indicated in the figures secured in a study of illegitimate births in Boston,[1] and the situation discovered in the study of infant mortality in Baltimore.[2] In Boston, it was found that in 1914 the infant mortality rate among children of legitimate birth was 95, while infants born out of wedlock died at the rate of 281 per 1,000; hence, the mortality rate among infants of illegitimate birth was 3 times as great as among infants born in wedlock. In Baltimore, white children of legitimate birth died at a rate of 95.9, while the infant mortality rate for white children of illegitimate birth was 315.5, or 3.3 times as great.

The 1913 report of the Health Officer of the District of Columbia showed infant mortality rates for the calendar year 1912 of 79.7 for white infants of legitimate birth and 302.7 for white infants born out of wedlock. The report calls attention to the difficulty involved in drawing trustworthy inferences from the records because of the incompleteness of registration of illegitimate births.[3]

---

[1] U. S. Children's Bureau: Illegitimacy as a Child-Welfare Problem, Part 2: A study of original records in Boston and the State of Massachusetts, by Emma O. Lundberg and Katharine F. Lenroot. Dependent, Defective, and Delinquent Classes Series No. —, Bureau Publication No. —. (In press.)

[2] Study by the U. S. Children's Bureau of infant mortality in Baltimore. (In preparation.)

[3] Report of the Health Officer of the District of Columbia, 1913. Washington, 1914. pp. 12–13.

THE CHILD'S STATUS AND RIGHT TO SUPPORT.

The natural consequence of the legal recognition of the married state as a necessary ordinance for the future of the race and the upbringing of children was that children were placed in a different status according as they were born within or outside the legal relationship. The institution of private property and inheritance rights accounted in part for the prestige of the child born in wedlock, since descent on the father's side could be traced only for such children. When the religious element entered in as a means of building up and safeguarding the family relationship the mother of a child born outside marriage, and also the child, suffered not only economic disadvantages but were stigmatized by society. In an effort to stamp out infanticide by unmarried mothers, which was alarmingly prevalent because of the hardships they had to face, church and state sought to prevent illegitimacy by drastic means. Mothers of children of illegitimate birth were severely punished, and the children were treated with disdain and deprived of civil and ecclesiastical rights.

Extra-marital unions throughout civilized time have been held to be inimical to the interest of society and of the child born as a result of such relationships, and various penalties have been provided by modern law; but the social and legal theory has gradually developed that the children are innocent of wrongdoing, and that they are entitled to the benefits enjoyed by children of more fortunate birth. It is recognized that children born without the possibility of a normal home are likely to suffer special hardships, and that they must be protected with especial care from injurious influences.

Society early imposed upon the mother, as the child's natural caretaker, the duty of providing for its maintenance. The provision of the Napoleonic Code forbidding inquiry into paternity was until recent years the law in France and other Latin countries. Recognition of the father's responsibility is still partial and incomplete, but there is increasing agitation for placing all children in an equal status in relation to both parents. Where the parents can not or will not fulfill their duties, the interests of society demand that the State must render to the child the care and protection necessary to its proper development.

36

Legal provisions concerning the child born out of wedlock deal with the legal status of the child, the determination of paternity, and the method of securing support from the father. In addition there have been special measures enacted for the safeguarding by the State of children of illegitimate birth, by virtue of their status, and children born out of wedlock are very considerably affected by State laws for the protection of children who become dependent. These protective measures are included in the later discussion of care and guardianship.

American legislation [1] dealing with children of illegitimate birth was enacted at an early period and was based largely upon the English law. In England the child born out of wedlock is still, so far as property rights are concerned, filius nullius—the child of nobody. Under the poor law, however, the mother has been held responsible for the child's support, and under other legislation the father may be compelled to contribute.

In the United States the child of illegitimate birth has been practically legitimized with respect to the mother—the relation of the mother and child born out of wedlock approximating the relation of mother and lawful child. The most important change involved in accomplishing this has been with respect to inheritance. Under the laws of some of the States and, in the absence of a statute, under judicial decisions the mother is charged with the maintenance of her child of illegitimate birth, and under the desertion and nonsupport laws she may be prosecuted for neglect to support the child.

The full legal relation of parent and child is not commonly recognized as existing between the father and his child born out of wedlock, though there has recently been some advanced legislation dealing with this subject. The responsibility of the father is usually recognized by the laws relating to compulsory support, but most of the States recognize only a partial obligation of the father to support his child born out of wedlock. In 12 States [2] the desertion and nonsupport laws are made applicable to the child of illegitimate birth, to the end that the father may also be prosecuted for neglect

---

[1] For a detailed analysis of the legal status of the child of illegitimate birth, see U. S. Children's Bureau: Illegitimacy Laws of the United States and Certain Foreign Countries, by Ernst Freund. Legal Series No. 2, Bureau Publication No. 42. Washington, 1919.

[2] California : Penal Code 1915, sec. 270 as amended by Laws 1917 ch. 168 ; sec. 270b, 270d, 271, 271a, 273h. Colorado : Laws 1911 ch. 179 secs. 1–10. Delaware : Revised Code 1915 secs. 3034–3046, 3088. Massachusetts : Laws 1911 ch. 456, secs. 1–4 ; 5, 6 as amended by Laws 1918 ch. 257 secs. 453, 454 ; 7 ; 8 as amended by Laws 1912 ch. 310 (made applicable by Laws 1913 ch. 563 sec. 7). Minnesota : Laws 1917 ch. 213 (made applicable by Laws 1917 ch. 210). Nebraska : Revised Statutes 1913 secs. 8614–8616. Nevada : Revised Laws 1912 sec. 766. New Hampshire : Laws 1913 ch. 57 sec. 1. Ohio : General Code 1910, secs. 13008–13017 ; 13018 as amended by laws 1913 p. 913 ; 13019 as amended by Laws 1911 p. 115 ; 13020, 13021. Pennsylvania : Laws 1917, No. 145 secs. 1–3 ; No. 290 secs. 1–6. West Virginia : Laws 1917 ch. 51 secs. 1–9. Wisconsin : Statutes 1917 secs 4587c.1–4587c.6, 4587d.

to support it, presumably after paternity is established. The Minnesota law of 1917 makes the person adjudged father liable to all the obligations imposed by law upon the father of a child of legitimate birth, and the Massachusetts law of 1913 makes the father who neglects or refuses to contribute reasonably to the support of the child liable to all the penalties and orders provided in the case of legitimate parents. The law passed in North Dakota in 1917 [1] goes further than any other in this country, declaring that every child is the " legitimate child " of its natural parents, and as such is entitled to support and education to the same extent as if he had been born in lawful wedlock. The child inherits from both parents and from their kindred. However, action to establish paternity must be brought by the mother within a year of the child's birth. In a few States a right of inheritance from the father follows upon adjudication of paternity. In other States inheritance from the father comes only upon acknowledgment or legitimation, while in almost half the States there is no provision for inheritance from the father. [2]

Recent social legislation in the United States has, specifically or by implication, included children of illegitimate birth within the scope of its provisions. One State, Nevada,[3] includes children of illegitimate birth among those entitled to benefit under the workmen's compensation act. Eight States [4] extend the act to acknowledged children of illegitimate birth; three,[5] to children legitimized prior to the injury; and one [6] includes children of illegitimate birth if they were a part of the decedent's household at the time of his death. In some other States the courts have held that children of illegitimate birth were entitled to benefit under the compensation act if they were being actually supported by the father as a member of his family at the time of his death.[7]

The tendency of the courts to hold that children born out of wedlock should not be made to suffer from the wrongdoing of their

---

[1] Laws 1917 ch. 70 secs. 1–4.

[2] For text of illegitimacy laws, see U. S. Children's Bureau: Illegitimacy Laws of the United States and Certain Foreign Countries, by Ernst Freund. Legal Series No. 2, Bureau Publication No. 42. Washington, 1919.

[3] Laws of 1913 ch. 3, sec. 26 as amended by Laws 1917 ch. 233.

[4] Idaho : Laws 1917 ch. 81 sec. 14 ; Indiana : Laws 1915 ch. 106 sec. 38 ; Kentucky : Laws 1916 ch. 33 sec. 11 ; Louisiana : Laws 1918 No. 38 ; New Mexico. Laws 1917 ch. 83 sec. 12 (j and k) ; New York : Birdseye Consolidated Laws (2d ed.) 1917 ch. 67 sec. 3 ; Virginia : Laws 1918 ch. 400 sec. 40 ; Vermont : General Laws 1917 sec. 5759.

[5] Montana : Laws 1915 ch. 96 sec. 6p ; Oregon : Laws 1913 ch. 112 sec. 14 as amended by Laws 1917 ch. 288 ; Washington : Laws 1917 ch. 120 sec. 1.

[6] New Jersey : Laws 1911 ch. 95 sec. 12 as amended by Laws 1914 ch. 244.

[7] Connecticut : Piccinim v. Connecticut Light and Power Co. (Apr. 16, 1919) 106 Atlantic 330.

Maine : Scott's Case (Nov. 12, 1918) 104 Atlantic 794.

Michigan : Roberts et al v. Whaley et al (June 2, 1916) 158 Northwestern 209.

parents is illustrated in the Connecticut decision. The court held as follows:

> The children's position in that household was a very different one [from that of their mother]. They were not only innocent of their parents' wrongdoing, but their father, in caring for them, was acting in obedience to the mandate of the law. It was alike his moral and legal duty to maintain them. * *. *
>
> There is nothing in their own conduct that calls for punishment, and we are unable to discover how the cause of morality is to be advanced by the treatment of innocent children, although born of illicit relations, as so far outcasts from the social and legal pale that they are to be denied the benefit of those beneficial provisions which our law has adopted for the care, welfare, and maintenance of those who, helpless of themselves, are dependent * * * upon the labor of others engaged in industrial pursuits.

By the end of 1919, 39 States had adopted mothers' pension laws. Two of these States—Michigan and Nebraska—specifically make provision for aid to " unmarried mothers," while one State—Wisconsin— provides for a " mother without a husband." In Indiana, Maine, Massachusetts, New Hampshire, North Dakota, and Washington, where the law applies to any mother with dependent child or children, and in Colorado, where it is made applicable to " any parent or parents," it would seem possible to extend the benefits of such laws to the mother of a child of illegitimate birth; yet these States impose such restrictions as to character as may be interpreted to preclude such mothers.[1] In 29 States the benefits of the law extend only to mothers of children born in wedlock.

The Federal act providing for allotments, allowances, and compensation to dependents of soldiers and sailors includes children born out of wedlock among the beneficiaries, if support has been ordered by court or if the child has been acknowledged by the father.[2]

The determination of the paternity of children born out of wedlock is usually provided for only in connection with securing support from the father. This is due to the fact that the relation of the father to his child is generally limited to the one obligation— that of contributing to the child's maintenance. The importance of the determination of paternity in connection with birth registration has already been pointed out. Where rights of inheritance from and through the father are given children born out of wedlock the

---

[1] Colorado : Laws 1913 p. 694 ; Indiana : Laws 1915 ch. 95; Maine : Laws 1917 ch. 222 as amended by Laws 1919 ch. 17 ; Massachusetts : Laws 1913 ch. 763 sec. 104 ; Michigan : Compiled Laws 1915, sec. 2017 ; Nebraska : Laws 1919 ch. 221 sec. 2 ; New Hampshire : Laws 1915 ch. 132 ; North Dakota : Laws 1915 ch. 185 ; Washington : Laws 1915 ch. 135 as amended by Laws 1919 ch. 103 ; Wisconsin : Statutes 1917 sec. 573f.5 as amended by Laws 1919 ch. 251.

[2] 40 U. S. Statutes at Large (65th Congress), p. 404, sec. 205 ; p. 610, sec. 200.

establishment of paternity has still another value apart from that involved in the immediate need for support.[1]

No one of the United States has made proceedings for establishing paternity compulsory in every case.[2] There is a strong feeling that a mother who does not need assistance from the father and who does not wish to disclose his identity should not be compelled to do so. On the other hand, the movement for complete birth registration including the names of both parents, as a matter of justice to the child and for more adequate protection of children handicapped by the circumstances of their birth, may result in more general requirements for the determination of fatherhood.

Legislation in the United States compelling the father to contribute to the support of his child born out of wedlock[3] originated in the desire to protect the public from the necessity of supporting such children rather than from concern for their welfare. While this principle had been somewhat modified in favor of the mother and the child, few radical changes were made until recent years. Within the last decade there has been a marked change in social emphasis, the child's welfare being made the predominant consideration, accompanied by the recognition of the State's responsibility. Laws in accordance with this trend have already been enacted in some States, and in a number of others bills embodying radical changes have been given serious consideration.

The present law of Oregon[4] is an illustration of a liberal type of provision for the child's maintenance, not yet very common in the United States. The law makes the father chargeable for the expenses incurred by a county or by the mother for the lying-in and attendance of the mother during her sickness and states that "the judgment of the court providing for the maintenance of such child by the father shall be in yearly sum not less than $100 nor more than $350 for the first two years, and not less than $150 nor more than $500 for each succeeding year until the child reaches the age of 14 years."

The laws of the Scandinavian countries relating to children born out of wedlock are recognized as setting standards in advance of those prevailing in most countries. The Norwegian law which became effective January 1, 1916, gives a child born out of wedlock the

---

[1] For a discussion of the value of an early adjudication of paternity *see* Hart, Hastings II.: The Registration of Illegitimate Births; a preventive of infant mortality. Department of Child-Helping, Russell Sage Foundation, New York City, March, 1916.

[2] The laws of five States—New Jersey, New York, North Carolina, South Carolina, and Tennessee—contain provisions requiring the mother, under penalty, to disclose the name of the father in cases in which the child is likely to become a public charge.

[3] For a detailed discussion of support provisions, *see* U. S. Children's Bureau: Illegitimacy Laws of the United States and Certain Foreign Countries, by Ernst Freund. Legal Series No. 2, Bureau Publication No. 42. Washington, 1919.

[4] Laws 1917 ch. 48 sec. 5.

same right of inheritance that is given a child of legitimate birth. The responsibility for maintenance is placed upon both parents in accordance with the economic status of the one most favorably situated.[1] The law requires the compulsory reporting of pregnancy by the physician or midwife consulted and of the birth of a child out of wedlock by the physician or midwife or by the mother. Upon receipt of the notice the local police authority reports to the superior magistrate, who issues a citation upon the man named as father. If the alleged father does not admit paternity, he must make application for an action of paternity or else be held liable as the father.

The Swedish law[2] which went into effect January 1, 1918, gives no right of inheritance from the father except in the case of "betrothal children," but places the responsibility for support on both parents. The economic circumstances of both are to be taken into account. The mother is given the custody and legal guardianship of the child, unless otherwise ordained by the court. The parent not having the care of the child is to meet the expenses of his maintenance. A woman with child out of wedlock must report her condition to the "guardian official" of the parish or to the person commissioned by him. Immediately upon receipt of such report or of information that a child has been born out of wedlock, the guardian official must designate a suitable man or woman as guardian of the child. It is made the duty of the guardian to assist the mother with counsel and information, and to see that the child's rights and welfare are properly safeguarded. It is especially incumbent upon him to see that steps are taken immediately for the determination of paternity and status and for insuring the child's support. In the trial the burden of proof is on the complainant, and not on the alleged father, as in Norway, unless formal acknowledgment of paternity has been made previously. The guardian is to assist in fixing the amount of support and in securing payments.

The Minnesota law of 1917 is the most practical and far-reaching yet enacted in the United States, and embodies in large part the features of the best foreign laws, in so far as they were considered applicable to conditions in this country. It includes an emphatic declaration of the State's responsibility for the welfare of children born out of wedlock.[3]

This chapter shall be liberally construed with a view to effecting its purpose, which is primarily to safeguard the interest of illegitimate children and secure for them the nearest possible approximation to the care, support,

---

[1] U. S. Children's Bureau: Norwegian Laws Concerning Illegitimate Children: Introduction and translation by Leifur Magnusson. Legal Series No. 1, Bureau Publication No. 31. Washington, 1918.

[2] Svensk Författningssamling. 1917. N:r. 376. Lag om barn utom äktenskap: given Stockholms slott den 14 juni 1917.

[3] Laws 1917 ch. 210 amending General Statutes 1913 by adding sec. 3225(d).

and education that they would be entitled to receive if born of lawful marriage, which purpose is hereby acknowledged and declared to be the duty of the State.

In accordance with the authority given under the law, the State Board of Control of Minnesota on October 19, 1918, adopted the following "Resolution governing the policy of the state board of control in illegitimacy proceedings":

Whereas chapter 194 of the General Laws of 1917 places certain responsibilities upon the State Board of Control for the protection of illegitimate children, and

Whereas chapter 210 of the General Laws of 1917 provides that the father of an illegitimate child shall be subject to the same responsibility as though the child were born to him in lawful wedlock: Now, therefore, be it

Resolved, That the following statement of policy shall be adopted by the State Board of Control in making provision for the care and education of illegitimate children:

1. The State Board of Control will not be a party to any agreement for the mere purpose of releasing an action begun or threatened, by the payment of a small sum of money. There must be an admission of paternity and an agreement to assume full paternal responsibility. If the defendant or the prospective defendant denies his paternity, his remedy lies in a proper defense at the hearing in court, which hearings should always be held in private for the protection of all persons concerned.

2. The State Board of Control does not regard any man as wronged who has had relations with a girl at a time when he could be the father of a child born to her, if he is made to bear the paternal responsibility, even though other men have had relations with the girl at or about the same time. In such cases if the defendant refuses to assume responsibility, the interests of the child demand that a jury shall pass upon the question of paternity. Under such conditions the defendant will have full opportunity to establish his defense.

3. Because of the very large death rate among children born out of wedlock, the State Board of Control has ruled that such children must be nursed by their mothers for a period of at least three months, and as long thereafter as possible. There are properly equipped hospitals in the Twin Cities which will receive women for this full term of maternity care and afford the mother and child full protection as well as aid and assistance at a reasonable cost. The board has licensed a number of such hospitals and will furnish a list on application.

4. In making settlements, full consideration should be given to the circumstances of the defendant; but the standard should be that care which he would be able to give his children born in lawful wedlock. An infant can not be maintained properly on much less than $20 a month, and the cost increases as the infant grows older.

5. If a lump-sum settlement is desired, the entire amount may be deposited with the State Board of Control as trustee, and any unexpended surplus returned, should the child die. A minimum lump-sum settlement should be in the neighborhood of $3,000.

6. The question of adopting the child out with an approved family must abide the circumstances of the case. Adoption can not be considered until after the nursing period, and then only if it seems necessary under all the circumstances.

7. All matters relating to illegitimacy should be treated confidentially, and all parties should be protected from unnecessary publicity. The child's interest is in all cases paramount.

PROTECTION AND GUARDIANSHIP.

THE BEGINNINGS OF CARE.

The earliest provisions for the care of children who had been abandoned was occasioned by the prevalence of infanticide. Because of social disorder and hardship, infanticide by exposure was of frequent occurrence in ancient times. Evidence indicates that much of this early abandonment of children may be attributed to the difficulties experienced by unmarried mothers. In an effort to prevent deaths resulting from exposure of infants, the church early took steps for rescuing and caring for children left at the church doors. Foundling hospitals appear to have been established in Italy as early as the sixth century. In the Middle Ages foundling hospitals existed in all the large cities of western Europe. An institution which is considered the origin of the modern foundling asylum was established by St. Vincent de Paul, in 1638, for the foundlings of Paris. The first tour[1] reported was that in the hospital built in Rome at the end of the twelfth century by Pope Innocent the Third, at the entrance of which was placed a cradle where a child could be deposited secretly. The custom has continued to this day in Italy, and also in Spain and in Portugal. The tours were officially introduced into France in 1811, in order to combat the increasing prevalence of infanticide. Their establishment was, strangely enough, coincident with the first decree relating to the establishment of the Assistance Publique. They were abolished in France in 1862, after it became evident that this supposed preventive of infant deaths in reality resulted in the death of an alarming proportion of the abandoned children. In Belgium, as in France, tours were introduced in 1811; they were eliminated in 1860.

Although foundling asylums were early condemned in France, it was not until 1904 that this system was largely displaced through the granting of aid to mothers in order that they might care for their children; and the development of the principle that all children

---

[1] The tour, or turn-box, was usually a box, one side of which is left open, fixed in a revolving cylinder in the outer wall of the foundling hospital. Anyone wishing to leave a child placed it in the receptacle, ringing a bell and going away unseen, while the hospital attendant, from within, turned the box and received the infant.

less than 13 years of age under the guardianship of the State, whose physical and mental condition makes it desirable, must be boarded out in country districts. In Germany foundling asylums were early abolished. Abandoned children are cared for directly by the local authorities, being boarded out or placed in institutions. In Italy foundling asylums have continued. In Austria the foundling hospitals are local public institutions. Here the development has been toward providing home care. If the mother comes to the hospital with the child, she may remain four months as a nurse. When a child is two months old he is sent from the foundling hospital to a home that has been certified. An allowance is paid to the foster family, and the care is supervised by a medical officer. The founder of the Foundling Hospital of London, incorporated in 1739, stated that its object was " to prevent the frequent murders of poor miserable children at their birth, and to suppress the inhuman custom of exposing newborn infants to perish in the streets."[1] Public funds were provided for the extension of this care, and local receiving places established, until the evils connected with the system became so flagrant that the House of Commons withdrew its support. Regulations of the methods by which children may be received have greatly reduced the numbers cared for annually. The children must be first children of unmarried mothers. As soon as possible after entering the institution they are sent to homes in the country, there to remain until they are four or five years old. At 14 the boys are usually apprenticed as mechanics for seven years, and at 16 the girls are apprenticed as servants for four years.

In the United States foundling asylums are still common in the larger cities, the majority of the children received being infants. The effort in the best of these institutions is to keep the mother with the child during the first months of life. The mothers who enter the institution with their infants also act as wet nurses to infants who have been abandoned. The children are given for adoption or otherwise placed out from these hospitals, often with very inadequate protection. In many cases the absence of records in regard to the origin and disposition of these children and the indiscriminate receiving and giving out of foundlings are very serious evils. In the present era of child care this condition is an anomaly. Studies of the mortality of infants placed in these institutions have revealed an alarming situation. It is a hopeful sign that the institutions themselves are coming to realize the causes and meaning of the high mortality among the infants placed in their charge.

---

[1] The Encyclopædia Britannica, 11th ed. "Foundling hospitals," Vol. X, p. 747. Cambridge, 1910.

MATERNITY CARE AND ASSISTANCE TO MOTHER AND CHILD.

Of more recent origin, and indicating a better appreciation of the principles of child welfare, are the maternity homes and similar institutions providing not only maternity care but also giving the mother necessary attention and assistance for a period preceding the birth of the child, keeping the mother and child during a considerable portion of the nursing period, and giving advice and supervision after discharge from the home in an effort to keep mother and child together. Numerous homes of this character have been established in the larger cities of the United States, either as adjuncts of hospitals or as independent institutions. Homes that are the outgrowth of two nation-wide organizations, the Florence Crittenton Missions and the Salvation Army Maternity Homes, are to be found in a large number of cities. Care is given for a period preceding confinement, and the mothers and their children are kept for a considerable period of time. There are many other institutions established for a similar purpose.

In addition to this type of care, certain agencies give special attention to work with unmarried mothers and their children, assisting the mother to find a home and to care for her child, and securing employment for the mother where she can keep her child with her. An agency that was engaged in this work for mothers and infants for 40 years gives the following among the important factors in successful work with these cases:[1]

Careful study of the patient, her family, heredity, previous employment, physical condition, her own needs and desires.

The elimination of feeble-minded women or those unfit in any way to care for the child.

Cooperation with other societies in regard to these latter cases.

Following up the case so that we know exactly what becomes of the patient and her infant. To safeguard the child at this period is a necessity, and we are obliged to watch it most constantly and carefully. Without this supervision it would in many cases not survive at all.

In England private effort is at the present time being directed toward the provision of care and training for the mothers before and after confinement, and the founding of hostels where they may board, going daily to work and tending their babies at night. It is recognized that in almost every case of illegitimacy the mother is in need of some assistance, and that each infant needs to be carefully watched. The announced program of the recently organized National Council for the Unmarried Mother and Her Child[2] indicates that the estab-

---

[1] Clarke, Lilian Freeman: The Story of an Invisible Institution; forty years' work for mothers and infants. [The Society for Helping Destitute Mothers and Infants, Boston.] Part IV, pp. 10–11. Boston, 1918.

[2] Report of National Council for the Unmarried Mother and Her Child. London, 1919.

lishment of hostels for the care of mothers and infants is one of the important measures advocated for the reduction of the high death rate among infants of illegitimate birth.

The system of home visiting for the purpose of following up registered births and giving assistance to mother and infant where needed is in use in a number of cities of the United States. Because of the difficulties involved it has not always been found practicable to include the illegitimate births in this home visiting, and the high mortality rate among these infants is therefore not affected. In England the inclusion of infants of illegitimate birth is apparently a recognized part of the working of the notification of births (extension) act, which was passed in 1915. The following statement by Dr. Leslie describes the method in a city which he says may be taken as an example of efficient work under this act:[1]

Huddersfield is a town of 100,000 inhabitants and was one of the first to adopt the Notification of Births Act: 95 per cent of the births are notified to the Medical Officer of Health within forty-eight hours, and women doctors visit the homes with the utmost possible dispatch. Notifications are sent every Monday to the voluntary lady health visitors, who visit the homes and report on the conditions present. If a baby does not thrive, and is not already under medical care, the fact is at once reported to the Medical Officer of Health, who immediately takes action. The result has been an enormous reduction of infant mortality in that city.

In the 1915–16 report of the Local Government Board of England and Wales, Sir Arthur Newsholme, after calling attention to the high mortality rate among infants of illegitimate birth, points out the great need for increased supervision of the welfare of these children:[2]

The aim should be, whenever practicable, to prevent the separation of the mother from her infant during the first year after birth. This has important moral value as well as value in securing continued parental care. There is large scope for increased voluntary work in this connection. Institutions for the reception of infants, especially of illegitimate infants, generally experience a very heavy death rate. A system of home visiting of the mothers or foster-mothers, adequately supervised, in most instances is preferable to such institutions.

The effect of war conditions in emphasizing the importance of public protection of infancy is seen in France in the order of 1916,[3] by which the Assistance Publique of the Department of the Seine was empowered to grant assistance to mothers until the children

---

[1] Leslie, R. Murray, M. D.: "Infant welfare in war time." The Child, Vol. VI (October, 1915), p. 13. London.

[2] Forty-fifth Annual Report of the Local Government Board (England and Wales), 1915–16. Supplement in continuance of the report of the medical officer of the board for 1915–16, containing a report on child mortality at ages 0–5, in England and Wales. London, 1916. pp. 93, 94.

[3] Raimondi, R., M. D.: "Four years of infant welfare work during war time in France." Maternity and Child Welfare, Vol. II (September, 1918), p. 305. London.

had reached three years of age, instead of two years, as formerly. In the very month the war began, this assistance had been raised from 20 francs to 30 francs a month. Since April, 1918, in the Department of the Seine, mothers who nurse their babies have been granted a premium for breast feeding, amounting to 200 francs a year.[1] The payments are made quarterly by women visitors of the Assistance Publique after a doctor has certified that the mother breast feeds the infant. For mothers who do not breast feed their babies, a bonus is given for regular attendance at the infant consultations and is paid to the mothers when the child is a year old.

The awakening to the importance of the protection of infancy that came as a result of war conditions is reflected in a report made by the committee on public health of the Italian Commission for the Study of Measures Necessary for the Period of Transition from War to Peace.[2] The report urged the need not only "to improve, coordinate, and develop the already existing provisions for the benefit of mothers and children, and to give a permanent character to the temporary measures brought about by the war, but also, upon completion of the urgent government work, to take new and energetic measures for the purpose of making secure the lives of the mothers and children of Italy."

As one of the fundamental concepts to which laws intended for the protection of childhood should conform, the committee specifies that the work of assistance and social provision should apply equally to all mothers and children needing material and moral aid, and that "the old, confusing, and obnoxious classifications of abandoned, mistreated, natural, legitimate, illegitimate, adulterine" children and mothers should be abolished. The enactment of a law on inquiry into paternity is considered essential to the protection contemplated.

The committee recommends that legislative reforms begin with the foundling asylums, and that these asylums require all mothers, whether married or not, to nurse their own children for one year, except those absolutely unable to do so. The mothers are to be given the choice either of a monthly allowance paid by the foundling asylums, or of maintenance with their children in the asylums, which in such cases shall be called "mothers' asylums." The committee further recommends that the "immoral and criminal methods of admission of children to foundling asylums, such as reception rooms, turn-boxes, and direct admission without documents" be abolished.

---

[1] Revue Philanthropique, Tome XXXIX (Avril 1918), p. 187. Paris.
[2] Tropeano, Prof. Guiseppe: "Assistenza e Previdenza Sociale per la Maternità e per l'Infanzia" [Social assistance and provision for motherhood and childhood]. Rassegina della Previdenza Sociale, gennaio, 1919, pp. 54–63.

In outlining the needed reorganization of foundling asylums, it is proposed that the children of unmarried adult women should not be admitted to foundling asylums even after the first year of nursing, but that instead adult mothers under 30 years of age should receive nursing pay and a premium for having recognized the child, and that those over 30 should receive nursing pay or should simply be admitted to institutions giving assistance to mothers. The children of mothers under the age of majority may be admitted under certain conditions. It is recommended that all communes having turn-boxes or reception houses establish instead centers of free assistance to children.

With similar concern for the protection of infancy, a law recently placed on the statute books of the State of Maryland [1] forbids the separation of mother and child within six months after the child's birth, unless authorities specified certify that the physical condition of the mother makes it impossible for her to care for her child. Provision of funds for maintenance that will enable her to do this is left to private effort. It is significant that the mothers' pension law of Maryland passed in 1916 by inference excludes unmarried mothers from the benefits of the act.[2] A North Carolina law enacted in 1917 also prohibits the separation of a child under six months of age from its mother or the surrender of the child by the mother, unless consent has been obtained from the clerk of the superior court and the county health officer.[3] This State, by the end of 1918, had not passed a mothers' pension law.

In Minnesota, joint resolutions by the State board of control and the State board of health [4] similarly forbid the removal of infants from their mothers:

Whereas the death rate of infants under one year of age is considerably higher among those infants who are artificially fed;

Whereas the health and well-being of infants under one year of age is dependent in large measure upon proper nursing at the breast by the mother: Now, therefore, be it

Resolved, By the State Board of Health and by the State Board of Control that no patient shall be received by any person or at any hospital or institution licensed by or under the supervision of either of said boards on any basis other than that the mother shall nurse her own child so long as she shall remain under the care of said person, hospital, or institution.

Provided, That where nursing by the mother is impossible for any physical reason, exception to the above rule may be made by the State board of health, or by the State board of control acting upon proper medical advice.

---

[1] Laws 1916, ch. 210, amending Annotated Code of the Public General Laws, vol. 3 (1914), art. 27, by adding secs. 484-488. North Dakota in 1919 passed a law (Laws 1919 ch. 77) practically identical with that of Maryland.

[2] Laws 1916, ch. 670.

[3] Laws 1917, ch. 59.

[4] Adopted by the State Board of Control July 19, 1918, and by the State Board of Health July 31, 1918.

These regulations undoubtedly are designed primarily to counteract the practice of certain institutions of parting mother and child within a short time after birth, with the resulting high mortality attributable to lack of proper food and care. It is evident that no such restriction can be enforced arbitrarily, and each of the regulations cited makes allowance for consideration of individual circumstances. It is also clear that a measure of this kind, in order to bring the benefit intended, must carry with it adequate provision for assistance to mothers who without such aid would be unable to care for their children.

CARE OF CHILDREN IN INSTITUTIONS AND FAMILY HOMES.

For children who have been deprived of normal homes, care and upbringing must be provided by public or private institutions or agencies. Various types of institutions and agencies for the care of orphan and destitute children meet with the problem of the child born out of wedlock. In some cases such children represent only a minority of the total under care, while in others most of the wards are children born out of wedlock.

In the modern development of the foundling hospital, children are kept in the institution only until a home can be found for them. They return to the hospital only when in need of medical treatment or pending placement in a new home. If they are in poor physical condition when received, they are not boarded out until their condition has been remedied. The hospital is the center of supervision for the children boarded out by it.

Orphanges and schools for dependent children vary from poorly equipped congregate institutions to institutions which provide the highest grade of training and also afford an approximation of home life through the plan of caring for the children in small groups. Some of these institutions keep each child for a period of time and then find free homes for as many of their charges as possible. Others keep the children until they are of an age to be self-supporting, having given them a well-rounded education, particularly along vocational lines.

There has been in the United States a rapid development of societies whose function it is to supply family care for children who have been deprived of their homes or who have never had homes of their own. Methods of receiving and placing children differ with the various societies, and not all hold to the recognized standards. Some of these agencies place children only in homes where they are taken free of charge, and into which they are sometimes legally adopted. Other agencies use boarding homes to a large extent, paying stipulated amounts for the care of the children. Although there has been considerable controversy as to whether the institution or the family home is the better adapted to the care of dependent children, the present tendency is more and more toward placing normal children in family homes, especially those who must remain permanently under the care of others than their own relatives. The White House Conference on the Care of Dependent Children, comprising representatives of the leading religious bodies and men and women actively engaged in child-caring work, indorsed the use of carefully selected family homes for normal children who must be removed from their own homes, or who have no homes.[1]

PUBLIC SUPERVISION AND CARE.

The history of the child-welfare movement shows that the State has become increasingly active in taking measures to protect children who are not given the necessary care by their parents. Measures providing for the care of infants born out of wedlock are probably responsible for many of the beginnings of general infant-welfare work. State protection or guardianship over children of illegitimate birth has been undertaken, either directly by virtue of their status, or indirectly through supervision over agencies and institutions caring for dependent children and over homes in which such children are placed.

In Norway,[2] the State holds that the mother and child must be protected and sets in motion its machinery to the end that the necessary attention shall be given the mother before and during her confinement, and support secured for the maintenance of the child. If this support can not be secured from the father, the State supplies assistance, making especial provision for maternal care.

In Sweden the guardian appointed for every child born out of wedlock for the protection of the child's rights and welfare, besides seeing that steps are taken for the determination of paternity and the securing of support, assists in the collecting and managing of the support payments, and when necessary may make application for the appointment of a trustee of the child's property. The guardian represents the child in court and may call upon the police authorities to make the preliminary investigations and assist in the enforcement of support payments. The guardianship remains in force until

---

[1] Proceedings of the Conference on the Care of Dependent Children, held at Washington, D. C., Jan. 25, 26, 1909. Government Printing Office, Washington, 1909.

See also U. S. Children's Bureau: Minimum Standards for Child Welfare Adopted by the Washington and Regional Conference on Child Welfare, 1919. Conference Series No. 2, Bureau Publication No. 62. Washington, 1919.

[2] U. S. Children's Bureau: Norwegian Laws Concerning Illegitimate Children: Introduction and translation by Leifur Magnusson. Legal Series No. 1, Bureau Publication No. 31. Washington, 1918.

the child is 18 years of age, unless terminated by the guardian official who has supervision over the guardian's activities and may, if occasion arises, relieve him and appoint a new guardian. If the mother changes her residence the transfer of guardianship is provided for. The law authorizes the reimbursement of guardians.[1]

In Germany a movement to secure the appointment of public guardians for dependent children was begun in 1886. A national society, entitled "Deutsche Gesellschaft für Berufsvormundschaft," was organized for the extension of this system. A Federal law of the German Empire was secured, providing for the appointment of public guardians whose duty it was to see that the laws with regard to dependent children were strictly enforced and that they received the benefit from money allotted for their maintenance. The methods differ in various States and cities, but children of illegitimate birth are usually included under the guardianship more generally than other children. In some States and cities only children maintained by public funds are placed under guardianship, other States extending the supervision to all children born out of wedlock, whether or not supported by public funds. Leipzig was the first city to institute a system by which doctors and nurses were appointed and paid to supervise the care of all children born out of wedlock. Similar measures were later taken in other large cities.[2] Statistics of the guardians' court of Leipzig for the years 1911–1913 [3] show that in 1913 there were 10.188 wards of the court who were of illegitimate birth. Of these in 1913, 1,382 were under 1 year: 1,113, 1 year; 3,078, 2 to 5 years; 3,893, 6 to 13 years; 524, 14 to 16 years; and 198, 17 to 20 years. In comparison, only 528 children born in wedlock were under guardianship in 1913.

One of the chief functions of the public guardian is to secure support from the father. This is accomplished in a considerable percentage of cases. As soon as an illegitimate birth is registered it is reported to the public guardian. In many cities supervision and medical and nursing care, at first provided only for particular classes of children, have been extended to cover all children born out of wedlock. Early in the year 1918 it was reported that an important extension had been made in the work of public guardianship in Berlin and over 200 other large cities. through raising the age of guardianship for children of illegitimate birth from 6 years to 14 years, and in a number of cities to 21 years.[4] It was pointed

[1] Svensk Författningssamling. N:r. 376. Lag om barn utom äktenskap: given Stockholms slott den 14 juni 1917. Secs. 13, 15, 16, 17.

[2] Infant Welfare in Germany during the War. Report prepared in the Intelligence Department of the Local Government Board (England and Wales). London, 1918. p. 22.

[3] Schöne. Dr. Walter: "Die Leipziger Mündelstatistik." Zentralblatt für Vormundschaftswesen, Jugendgerichte und Fürsorgeerziehung. VII. Jahrgang (25. Januar. 1916). pp. 229–231.

[4] Vorwärts, 3 Jan. 1918.

out as an explanation of this measure that guardianship by the city until the age of 6 had resulted in considerable advantages to the children which should be assured after the age of 6—even greater protection being needed after than before that age. The willingness of the father to pay for the child's support often disappears as the child grows older. Also the care of the child's health and the general supervision exercised by the guardian must be continued in order to safeguard him from physical, moral, and mental harm, help being particularly needed when the child faces the choice of a vocation and should have aid in finding apprenticeship or training.

A number of guardianship committees in Austria-Hungary and Switzerland were affiliated with the German society for the extension of public guardianship. Indicative of the emphasis on child welfare that resulted from war conditions, an imperial order was issued in Austria, October 12, 1914,[1] establishing an office called " over-guardian." Regulations of June 24, 1916, provide that [2]—

In compliance with the recommendation made by a community or other corporate body establishing the office of " over-guardian " the president of the provincial or district court may order, in agreement with the political authorities, that the over-guardian permanently assume the guardianship of all or of certain groups of illegitimate children in the district, who have no legal representative.

* * * The over-guardian may be charged with certain specific rights and duties of a guardian, such as supervision of the child, collection of money paid for the child's support; also investigation of conditions among relatives, and with similar duties of a legal representative.

In February, 1919, the Provisional National Assembly of Austria passed a law bringing under the supervision of the State all children born out of wedlock, whether or not in the care of their natural parents. The law also applies to children of legitimate birth cared for by others than their parents. The supervision is placed in the public guardianship offices or in special offices created for the purpose. Reporting is required within 3 days after the reception of a child or within 11 days after the birth of a child out of wedlock. The children continue under supervision until the age of 14 years.[3]

The law of France providing for the protection of children by the department of public assistance [4] does not specifically include as wards of the department children born out of wedlock except as they

---

[1] Reichsgesetzblatt für die im Reichsrate vertretenen Königreiche und Länder. Jahrgang 1914. Nr. 276. pp. 1122 ff. Wien, 1914.

[2] Soziale Rundschau, XVII. Jahrgang (Juli–August 1916), II. Teil. Nr. 9. pp. 93–96. Regulation of June 24, 1916, for the administration of the order of Oct. 12, 1914, establishing the office of over-guardian.

[3] Zampis, Dr. Ernst : " Der Schutz der Ziehkinder und unehelichen Kinder." Zeitschrift für Kinderschutz und Jugendfürsorge. XI. Jahrgang (Juli 1919). pp. 153–159.

[4] Law of June 27, 1904, on assistance to dependent children. Bulletin des Lois, 1904. No. 2575.

come under the definition of "assisted children." These comprise: 1. Children whose mothers can not maintain or educate them owing to insufficient means, and for whom temporary aid is granted to prevent their becoming neglected. 2. Children in public institutions, admitted temporarily because lacking means of support owing to the presence in a hospital or in a house of detention of the father, mother, or grandparents. 3. Children whose custody has been intrusted to the department of public assistance by the courts. 4. Children placed under the guardianship of the department and called wards of public assistance, comprising foundlings, children who have been neglected, poor orphans, ill-treated children, and deserted or morally neglected children. It is evident that there are included under this guardianship large numbers of children born out of wedlock. Special provision is made for receiving such children as wards of the department, under official secrecy, in depots provided for the purpose. In these cases, however, the person presenting the child is informed that the mother, if she keeps the child, may receive the assistance provided under the law and immediate aid if necessary. This aid is granted in order to allow a poor mother to keep and maintain her child or place him with a nurse. The amount and condition of relief are determined by the general council, and assistance may be suspended if the mother ceases to give, or cause to be given, the care necessary for her child.

In England the reports of the registrar-general and of the local government board, as well as the discussions of voluntary organizations, have continually emphasized the need for increased supervision of infants born out of wedlock, particularly because of its importance in decreasing the disproportionately high mortality among these children. The following recommendations are made in the last annual report of the local government board:[1]

(1) Whenever practicable the mother and the child must be kept together—the mother, if possible, undertaking the care of the child.

(2) If it is not feasible to keep mother and infant together, carefully selected foster mothers should be paid an adequate sum to cover the careful maintenance of the infant, supplementing what the mother can pay for this purpose.

(3) When such foster mothers are employed, it should be a condition of their employment that they register any change of address with the medical officer of health and that they take the infant for inspection periodically to the nearest child-welfare center. In addition, fairly frequent visits by health visitors should be organized.

(4) Unless this is unavoidable, it is not desirable to collect a considerable number of illegitimate or other infants under six months of age in an institution. When this becomes necessary, the most rigid hygienic precautions are needed if excessive mortality is to be avoided.

---

[1] Forty-seventh Annual Report of the Local Government Board (England and Wales), 1917–18. Supplement containing the report of the Medical Officer for 1917–18, pp. xxxi–xxxii. London, 1918.

(5) If such an institution is necessary, the mothers should, whenever this is practicable, live with their children, possibly going out to work during the day and returning at night.

Two measures that mark an era in child-welfare legislation were passed by France and Italy while these countries were in the midst of the world war. The French law creating the " wards of the nation "[1] and the Italian " war orphan " law[2] were both enacted in July, 1917. They are drawn along very similar lines. France adopts as wards of the nation children who have been deprived of their natural guardians as a result of the war. Italy, though not declaring the children adopted by the nation, assumes their protection and assistance. Coupled with the assertion of the State's ultimate responsibility for the welfare of these children, is a recognition of the rights of the family and the desirability of conserving family ties wherever possible.

Children who in consequence of the war have lost father, mother, or other person who was their chief support, and those children whose parent or other guardian, as a result of the war, has become incapacitated from earning a livelihood, are taken under the protection of the State. The French law specifies that the incapacity for work on the part of the parent or guardian may be total or partial. The State's responsibility, in both countries, continues during the child's minority. The Italian law covers also persons of any age handicapped by mental incompetence. Children of illegitimate birth are included among those benefiting by the law, in France by implication and in Italy by specific definition.

The administration of the law is placed in both countries in the hands of national, provincial, and local organizations created for the purpose. Existing agencies and institutions for the care and education of children are recognized and utilized, their activities in behalf of children covered by the law being carefully supervised. The responsibility of the State for the material support, education, and moral upbringing of its wards is emphasized over and over again. In both countries material aid is granted in cases where the family income is insufficient, the laws providing that the children shall, as far as possible, be brought up in their own homes. These acts are a recognition of the obligation of the State to secure for every child, regardless of his status, the opportunity for normal development through giving him home care or, if that is impossible, through supervision of institutional care, safeguarding his health and moral development and providing him with educational advantages.

---

[1] Law of July 27, 1917, establishing the " wards of the nation." Journal Officiel, 29 juillet 1917. Paris.

[2] Law No. 1143, July 18, 1917, for the protection and assistance of war orphans. Gazzetta Ufficiale, 27 luglio, 1917.

In the United States, with the exception of Minnesota, the supervision or guardianship of the State over children born out of wedlock occurs as an incidental feature of State control or supervision over agencies or institutions caring for dependent children and over homes in which such children are placed. In many States the law provides that the State board of charities or similar body shall inspect and license maternity boarding homes and lying-in hospitals, usually requiring approval of health conditions by the State or local board of health. Institutions caring for or placing out children are subject to State supervision. In many States all institutions or associations, whether public or private, which receive or care for children must report to the State board, and are investigated periodically. In Minnesota and in New Jersey the State board has general supervision over all children who are placed in family homes. Agencies placing children in foster homes must notify the board, and the homes are visited by agents of the State board, which may order the transfer of a child if the home is unsuitable. In Massachusetts the board must receive notice within two days of the reception of an infant under 2 years of age by any person not related by blood or marriage, also of the reception of such an infant for the purpose of adoption or procuring a home, and of discharge.

Provisions for State supervision relating specifically to children born out of wedlock are less common. The laws of Massachusetts require that any person receiving a child under 3 years of age, if he has reason to believe him to have been born out of wedlock, must notify the State board of charity, which has powers of inspection and removal. The board may receive from the mother, for the purpose of placing for adoption, a child born out of wedlock who is under 2 years of age.

The laws enacted in Minnesota in 1917 place upon the State more definite responsibility for the welfare of children born out of wedlock. The statutes provide that [1]—

It shall be the duty of the board of control when notified of a woman who is delivered of an illegitimate child, or pregnant with child likely to be illegitimate when born, to take care that the interests of the child are safeguarded, that appropriate steps are taken to establish his paternity, and that there is secured for him the nearest possible approximation to the care, support and education that he would be entitled to if born of lawful marriage. For the better accomplishment of these purposes the board may initiate such legal or other action as is deemed necessary; may make such provision for the care, maintenance and education of the child as the best interests of the child may from time to time require, and may offer its aid and protection in such ways as are found wise and expedient to the unmarried woman approaching motherhood.

---

[1] Laws 1917, ch. 194, sec. 2.

Under the Minnesota juvenile court act passed in 1917, a child of illegitimate birth is declared to be "dependent" within the meaning of that act. This gives the juvenile court the power to place him under legal guardianship upon proof of illegitimacy.[1]

In the United States the handicap of the child born out of wedlock is defined almost entirely by the lack of normal home conditions, rather than by any civic or social disabilities. The child of illegitimate birth often suffers great injustice through being deprived of the care that is his due. Society is forced to bear a burden that properly belongs to the child's parents. Sentiment has ruled largely in the treatment of these cases, often with the result that the emphasis has been placed upon saving the mother from the social consequences, especially if her status or that of her family is likely to be affected. Most often there has been little recognition of the importance of the father as a factor and of his liability for the support of the child.

With the growing concern of social agencies to render permanent help and to deal in a larger way with this whole problem, it is now being considered from a new angle with the child as the central factor. Of increasing interest is the question as to whether in being separated from the mother the child is not deprived of something that society can not replace even with the best care it can provide, and whether this most important consideration may not outweigh all others.

The care of children born out of wedlock in this country has been assumed merely as a part of the general policy of social provision for those in need of special care. Social agencies have become more and more conscious of the large proportion of their work that may be attributed to illegitimacy. They have begun to question whether society has not a peculiar responsibility toward these children who from birth are deprived of normal home life.

---

[1] Laws 1917, ch. 397, sec. 1.

BIBLIOGRAPHICAL MATERIAL ON ILLEGITIMACY AS A CHILD-WELFARE PROBLEM.

(The publications listed are for the most part in the library of the United States Department of Labor.)

BIBLIOGRAPHICAL MATERIAL ON ILLEGITIMACY AS A CHILD-WELFARE PROBLEM.

SOURCE MATERIAL.

STATISTICAL DATA RELATING TO BIRTHS OUT OF WEDLOCK.[1]

UNITED STATES.

STATES.

Alabama.

Annual Report of the State Board of Health of Alabama. 1917. Montgomery, 1918.
> Births, by race and counties, p. 70.

Connecticut.

Bureau of Vital Statistics of the State of Connecticut. Sixty-seventh Registration Report of Births, Marriages, Divorces and Deaths, 1914. Public Document No. 9. Hartford, 1915.
> Births, by sex and counties, 1914; by counties, 1905–1914; pp. 198, 199. Rates, by counties, 1914, p. 199.

Indiana.

Thirty-fifth Annual Report of the Indiana State Board of Health. 1916.
> Births, by counties, sex, nativity and color of mother, pp. 405, 406.

Maryland.

Annual Report of the State Board of Health of Maryland, 1915. Baltimore, 1918.
> Births, by race and counties, and illegitimacy rates, p. 19.

Michigan.

Forty-ninth Annual Report of the Secretary of State on the Registration of Births and Deaths, Marriages and Divorces in Michigan for the Year 1915. Lansing. 1918.
> Births by counties, 1915, pp. 92, 93; by cities, 1915, pp. 94, 95.

Minnesota.

Seventh Biennial Report (New Series) of the State Board of Health and Vital Statistics of Minnesota. 1916–1917. St. Paul. 1918.
> Births, by counties, 1913–1917, pp. 49–50; illegitimacy rates per 1,000 live births, 1913–1917, for State, St. Paul, Minneapolis, Duluth, pp. 45–46, 51.

Missouri.

Thirty-sixth Annual Report of the State Board of Health of Missouri. 1918. Bureau of Vital Statistics, 1917–1918. Jefferson City.
> Births, by counties, 1917, pp. 216–218; 1918, pp. 381–383. Number and per cent of illegitimate births in cities of over 10,000 inhabitants, 1917, p. 225; 1918, p. 390.

---

[1] Only recent reports containing statistical data on illegitimate births and deaths are listed. Statistics for cities of less than 100,000 population are not included.

Nevada.

Biennial Report of the State Board of Health for the Period Ending December 31, 1918.   Carson City, 1919.
> Births, p. 29.

New Hampshire.

Twenty-fifth Report (Eleventh Biennial) Relating to the Registration and Return of Births, Marriages, Divorces and Deaths in New Hampshire, 1914 and 1915.   Concord, 1916.
> Births, by age, nationality, residence, and occupation of mother; by order of birth; p. 309.

Pennsylvania.

Tenth Annual Report of the Commissioner of Health for the Commonwealth of Pennsylvania, 1915.   Harrisburg, Pa., 1918.
> Births, 1915, native and foreign, for the entire State, for municipalities having more, and for those having less than 5,000 population, and for the total rural area exclusive of all municipalities, p. 643.

Rhode Island.

Sixty-fifth Report Relating to the Registry and Return of Births, Marriages and Deaths, and of Divorce, in the State of Rhode Island, 1917.   Providence, 1918.
> Births, by town, ratio to population; sex and color; nativity of parents, age of mother; pp. 48, 49.

South Dakota.

Twelfth Annual Report, Division of Vital Statistics, Department of History, State of South Dakota, 1917.
> Births, by counties, sex, age of parents, p. 7.

Utah.

Report of the State Board of Health of Utah for the Biennial Period Ending December 31, 1914.
> Births, by sex and counties, pp. 73, 74.

Vermont.

Twenty-first (Eleventh Biennial) Report of the State Board of Health of the State of Vermont from January 1, 1916, to December 31, 1917.   Rutland, 1918.
> Births, by months, sex, counties, pp. 131, 209.

Wisconsin.

Twenty-sixth Report of the State Board of Health of Wisconsin, for the Term Ending June 30, 1916, with Report of the State Bureau of Vital Statistics for the Calendar Years of 1914 and 1915.   Madison, 1917.
> Births, by sex and counties, 1914, pp. 174, 175; 1915, pp. 178, 179.

Porto Rico.

Report of the Governor of Porto Rico to the Secretary of War.   Fiscal year ended June 30, 1917.   Washington, 1917.
> Births, by sex and color, July, 1916–June, 1917, p. 212.

Informe Anual del Departamento de Sanidad de Puerto Rico.   Año Fiscal de 1917–18.   San Juan, P. R. 1918.
> Births, by sex and color, July, 1917–June, 1918, p. 221; stillbirths, p. 236.

CITIES.

Baltimore.

Annual Report of the Sub-Department of Health, 1917.   Department of Public Safety.
> Births, by race, p. 15.

Boston.

Forty-fourth Annual Report of the Health Department of the City of Boston, 1915. Boston, 1916.

Births and infant mortality, by color, ward residence, nativity of white mothers, pp. 144–145.

Buffalo.

Annual Report of the Department of Health, Buffalo, N. Y., for the Year Ending December 31, 1918.

Births, p. 63.

Cincinnati.

Annual Report for the Year 1915, Department of Health.

Births, by months, p. 34.

Cleveland.

Annual Report of the Division of Public Health, Department of Public Welfare of the City of Cleveland, 1915.

Births, by nativity of mother, month of birth, Table No. 10, p. 217.

Detroit and Grand Rapids.

Forty-ninth Annual Report of the Secretary of State on the Registration of Births and Deaths, Marriages and Divorces in Michigan for the Year 1915. Lansing, 1918.

Births, 1915, p. 94.

Kansas City.

Thirty-sixth Annual Report of the State Board of Health of Missouri, 1918. Bureau of Vital Statistics, 1917–1918. Jefferson City.

Births, 1917, p. 225 ; 1918, p. 390.

Milwaukee.

Forty-first Annual Report of the Commissioner of Health of the City of Milwaukee, 1917.

Births, by occupation and age of mother, 1908–1917, p. 84.

Minneapolis.

Seventh Biennial Report (New Series) of the State Board of Health and Vital Statistics of Minnesota, 1916–1917. St. Paul, 1918.

Illegitimacy rates per 1,000 live births, 1913–1917, p. 51.

Annual Report of the Department of Health, Minneapolis, Minnesota, for the Year Ending 1918.

Births, by sex, according to ward, 1918, p. 37.

Newark.

Annual Report of the Department of Health (Department of Public Affairs), City of Newark, 1917.

Births, by ward, nativity of mother, p. 162. Analysis of unmarried mother cases : Supervision, grade and age at which mother left school, occupation and wages, age at birth of child, nativity, mother's parents living or dead, pp. 147–150.

New York.

Annual Report of the Department of Health of the City of New York for the Calendar Year 1917.

Births " apparently illegitimate," by months, 1917, pp. 64, 65.

Philadelphia.

Vital Statistics of Philadelphia. Reprint from the Annual Report of the Bureau of Health of the Department of Public Health and Charities for the Year 1917. Philadelphia, 1918.

Live births and stillbirths, by sex, order of birth, attendant at birth ; color and nativity of parents ; residence of father ; age and occupation of mother ; pp. 38–48.

Pittsburgh.

Annual Report of the Department of Public Health, City of Pittsburgh, 1915.
Births, p. 35.

Providence.

Sixty-fifth Report Relating to the Registry and Return of Births, Marriages, and Deaths, and of Divorce, in the State of Rhode Island, 1917. Providence, 1918.
Births, by town, ratio to population, sex and color, nativity of parents, and age of mother, pp. 48, 49.

St. Louis.

Thirty-sixth Annual Report of the State Board of Health of Missouri, 1918. Bureau of Vital Statistics, 1917–1918. Jefferson City.
Births, 1917, p. 225 ; 1918, p. 390.

St. Paul.

Seventh Biennial Report (New Series) of the State Board of Health and Vital Statistics of Minnesota, 1916–1917. St. Paul, 1918.
Illegitimacy rates per 1,000 live births, 1913–1917, p. 51.

Annual Report of the Bureau of Health, Department of Public Safety of the City of St. Paul, 1917.
Births, by months, nativity of parents, ward of residence of mother, pp. 36, 38.

Washington (District of Columbia).

Report of the Health Officer of the District of Columbia, 1913. Washington, 1914.
Births and stillbirths, by race, 1906–1912, and by age of mother ; infant mortality, by race, 1912 ; pp. 11–13.

Annual Report of the Commissioners of the District of Columbia, Year Ended June 30, 1918. Vol. III. Report of the Health Officer. Washington, 1918.
Births and stillbirths, by race, rate per 1,000 population, percentage of all births (1906–1917), age of mother (1911–1917), p. 10 ; births, by race (1896–1917), p. 200.

EUROPEAN COUNTRIES.

General.

Annuaire International de Statistique. II. Mouvement de la Population (Europe). L'Office Permanent de l'Institut International de Statistique. La Haye, 1917.
Births and infant mortality in European countries, 1876–1915 : Number of illegitimate live and stillbirths ; number of illegitimate births per 10,000 births—Table D 2 ; legitimate and illegitimate birth rates per 1,000 married women, and per 1,000 single, widowed, and divorced women, respectively, 15 to 49 years of age—Table D 3 ; plural births—Table D 4 ; infant mortality—Table E 7.

Annuaire Statistique des Grandes Villes Européennes. Prof. Dr. Gustave Thirring. Publié à l'Appui Moral de l'Institut International de Statistique par la Municipalité de Budapest. 1e année—1e partie. III. Mouvement de la Population. Budapest, 1913.
Births in 143 European cities, 1906, pp. 64–66 ; per cent of illegitimate births in 139 European cities, 1906, p. 67 ; infant mortality in 112 European cities, 1906, pp. 86–87.

Statistique Démographique des Grandes Villes du Monde pendant les années, 1880–1909. Première partie—Europe. Publiée à l'occasion de la XIIIe Session de l'Institut International de Statistique à la Haye, Septembre 1911. Communications Statistiques publiées par le Bureau municipal de Statistique d'Amsterdam, N°. 33. Amsterdam, 1911.
Births, 1880–1909, in 93 European cities having more than 100,000 population in 1909, pp. 52–137 ; legal requirements relating to registration of stillbirths in various countries of Europe, pp. 162–164.

Austria-Hungary.

Österreichisches Statistisches Handbuch nebst einem Anhange für die gemein-
samen Angelegenheiten der Österreichisch-Ungarischen Monarchie. K. K.
Statistische Zentralkommission. XXXIV. Jahrgang. 1915. Wien, 1917.
(Vol. XXXV, 1916–1917, gives illegitimate birth and death statistics through
1913, but does not give all the data contained in Vol. XXXIV.)

Births, 1896–1913, p. 41 ; births, 1913, by States, p. 47 : by age of mother, p. 48 ;
by occupation of mother, p. 49. Deaths, 1909–1913, of children under 5, p. 54 : of
children under 5, 1913, by year of birth, p. 58 ; deaths of children under 5 per 1,000
children born each year, 1901–1912, by year of birth and age to which survived. p. 60.

Annuaire Statistique Hongrois. Nouveau Cours, XIX—1911. L'Office Central
de Statistique du Royaume de Hongrie. Traduction Officielle. Imprimerie
de la Société Anonyme Athenaeum. Budapest, 1913.

Births, live and stillborn, 1891–1911. Hungarian, Croatian-Slavonic, and for the
Kingdom, pp. 27–28 ; births, and per cent illegitimate, 1911, by age, race, and religion
of mother, pp. 39–41 ; live births, 1911, by language of parents, pp. 41–42.

Belgium.

Annuaire Statistique de la Belgique et du Congo Belge. Quarante-quatrième
année—1913. Ministère de l'Intérieur, Bruxelles, 1914.

Births, by provinces, with per cent illegitimate ; legitimate and illegitimate birth
rates per 100 inhabitants, per 100 married women, and per 100 single, widowed, and
divorced women, respectively, 15 to 45 years, 1861–1912 ; p. 129.

Denmark.

Statistisk Aarbog [Danmark], 1917. (Statistiske Departement.) København,
1917.

Births, 1907–1916, p. 18 ; confinements by age and civil condition of mothers (married and unmarried), annual average for 1911–1915, p. 20.

Keller, Professor Dr. Arthur, und Klumker, Chr. J.: Säuglingsfürsorge und
Kinderschutz in den europäischen Staaten. I. Band. Erste Hälfte. " Statistik der Säuglingssterblichkeit in Vergangenheit und Gegenwart in Dänemark," von Pool Heiberg. Berlin, 1912.

Per cent of illegitimate births, 1860–1905, in cities and rural districts and for
Denmark as a whole ; annual average infant mortality rates, 1901–1905, in cities
and rural districts and for the country as a whole ; p. 61.

Finland.

Statistisk Årsbok för Finland. Ny Serie Femtonde Årgången, 1917. Helsing-
fors, 1918.

Number and per cent of illegitimate births, 1751–1915, pp. 65–66 ; number and
per cent of illegitimate births, 1915, in cities and rural districts, by provinces, p. 69 ;
by month of birth, p. 70. Infant mortality rates, 1907–1915, in cities and rural districts, and, 1901–1915, for entire country, p. 74.

France.

Annuaire Statistique. Trente-cinquième volume—1916, 1917, 1918. Résumé
Rétrospectif.—Divers Pays. Ministère du Travail et de la Prévoyance
Sociale. Statistique Générale de la France. Paris, 1919.

Number of births and rate per 1,000 inhabitants, 1913, pp. 11*–12*.

Annuaire Statistique de la Ville de Paris. XXXIVᵉ année—1913. Préfecture
de la Seine, Direction des Affaires municipales. Paris, 1917.

Births and infant mortality in Paris, 1913, pp. 108–113, 129, 132–133.

Pinard, M. A.: " De la Protection de l'enfance pendant la troisième année de
guerre dans le camp retranché de Paris." Bulletin de l'Académie de Médecine. 3ᵉ serie—Tome lxxviii. No. 49. Séance du 18 Décembre 1917.

Number and per cent of illegitimate births during the war (1914–1916, and 38
weeks of 1917) compared with 1912, pp. 774–776.

Germany.

Statistisches Jahrbuch für das Deutsche Reich. 37. Jahrgang. 1916. Berlin, 1916.

> Births, and per cent illegitimate, 1914, by cities and States, and for the German Empire, 1911–1914, p. 5; births and per cent illegitimate, 1865–1914, p. 6; births, 1914, by month of birth, p. 7; infant mortality, 1912–1914, by cities and States, p. 10.

Keller, Arthur: "Erfolge der Säuglingsfürsorge." Zeitschrift für Saüglingsschutz. III. Jahrgang (September 1911).

> Mortality during first month of life and during second to twelfth months in European countries, Japan, Australia, and New Zealand, 1901–1905, p. 275; mortality during first month in European countries and in Japan, 1901–1905, p. 277.

Keller, Professor Dr. Arthur, und Klumker, Chr. J.: Säuglingsfürsorge und Kinderschutz in den europäischen Staaten. I. Band. Erste Hälfte. "Deutschland," von Arthur Keller. Berlin, 1912.

> Per cent of illegitimate births for various German States, 1901–1908, p. 113; infant mortality in Germany, 1901–1910, p. 102. Infant mortality in the German States and cities, 1910, p. 103; infant mortality in German cities having more than 100,000 population, 1904–1908 (five-year average), p. 105; infant mortality in Prussia, 1876–1910, p. 108; and in other States, 1901–1908, pp. 113–114; infant mortality in Berlin, 1876–1909, p. 114, and in Charlottenburg, 1876–1910, p. 116; stillbirths in Prussia, in cities and rural areas, 1902–1910, p. 115; infant mortality in Hamburg, 1893–1910, pp. 270–271.

Statistischse Jahrbuch deutscher Städte. 19. Jahrgang. Statistisches Amt der Stadt Breslau, 1913.

> Births and infant mortality in German cities, 1910, pp. 46–49; illegitimacy birth rates per 1,000 population, pp. 67–68.

Statistischse Jahrbuch der Stadt Berlin. 32. Jahrgang, enthaltend die Statistik der Jahre 1908 bis 1911; sowie Teile von 1912. Im Auftrage des magistrats herausgegeben von Prof. Dr. H. Silbergleit. Statistisches Amt der Stadt Berlin. 1913.

> Legitimate and illegitimate birth rates in Berlin, per 1,000 inhabitants, and per cent of births illegitimate, 1906–1911, pp. 104*–105*; birth rates by months, 1906–1910, pp. 116*–117*; institution births, 1910, p. 120*; births by age of mother, p. 121*, and by occupation of mother, 1910, p. 124*; number of infants surviving to specified months in first year of life, per 1,000 births, 1882–1911, pp. 174*–176*; deaths of children under 5 years of age, by age at death, 1910, p. 179*, and by age at death and cause of death, 1909–1910, pp. 180*–181*; deaths of infants under 1 year by age at death and type of feeding, and by age at death, cause of death and type of feeding, 1909–1910, pp. 182*–185*, 190*–193*, 209*–212*; deaths of children under 10 years of age, by calendar month of death and age at death, 1910, pp. 196*; number and proportion of infants under 1 year surviving to specified months, 1909–1911, pp. 199*–201*.

Gross Berlin, Statistische Monatsberichte. IV. Jahrgang. 1913. Statistisches Amt der Stadt Berlin.

> Births and infant deaths in Berlin and suburbs. Monthly figures, 1913.

Guradze, Dr. Hans: "Säuglingssterblichkeit, Geburtenhäufigkeit, Eheschliessungen und Gesamtsterblichkeit in Berlin während des Krieges." Jahrbücher für Nationalökonomie und Statistik. III. Folge. 52. Band. Oktober 1916. Jena.

> Live births in Berlin, 1913–1916, by month of birth, p. 550.

Statistisches Jahrbuch der Stadt Dresden für 1912. 14. Jahrgang. Statistisches Amt der Stadt Dresden. 1913.

> Births in Dresden, and total and illegitimate births per 1,000 inhabitants, 1889–1912, p. 10; births and infant deaths by month, 1912, p. 10; number and per cent of legitimate and illegitimate confinements, confinements per 1,000 married women

under 50 and per 1,000 unmarried and widowed women 15 to 50 years of age, 1892–1912, p. 11; illegitimate confinements, 1912, by occupation of mother, by number of previous illegitimate confinements, and by age of mother, pp. 12–13; by age of father and age of mother, 1912, p. 12; illegitimate births, 1895–1908, and number and per cent of boys and girls living at end of 5 calendar years and not legitimated, p. 14; infant deaths, by age at death, 1912, p. 19.

Monatsberichte des Statistischen Amtes der Stadt Dresden auf das Jahr 1913. 36. Jahrgang.

Births and infant deaths in Dresden; infant deaths by cause of death, by age at death, and type of feeding. Monthly figures, 1913.

Statistisches Handbuch der Stadt Frankfurt am Main. Erste Ausgabe, enthaltend die Statistik bis zum Jahre 1905–06. Statistisches Amt. Frankfurt am Main, 1907.

Births in Frankfort on the Main, 1891–1905; total and illegitimate birth rates per 1,000 inhabitants, 1891–1905, p. 49; deaths of children under 1 year and 1 to 5 years of age, 1906, p. 50; deaths of children under 1 year and under 5 years of age, by cause of death, 1901–1905, p. 55.

Statistische Jahresübersichten der Stadt Frankfurt am Main. Ausgabe für das Jahr 1912–13. Statistisches Amt. Frankfurt am Main, 1913.

Births, and total and illegitimate birth rates per 1,000 inhabitants, 1912, p. 14; infant deaths, and deaths under 5 years of age, 1912, p. 13.

Statistisches Jahrbuch der Stadt Leipzig. 2 Jahrgang. 1912. Statistisches Amt. Leipzig, 1914.

Births in Leipzig, 1912, by month of birth, p. 42; number and per cent of illegitimate births, 1872–1912, pp. 43, 44; births by age of mother, 1912, p. 45; infant deaths and infant mortality rates, 1902–1912, by month of death, p. 56; infant deaths, 1912, by age at death and by cause of death, p. 57.

Statistische Monatsberichte der Stadt Leipzig. V. Jahrgang. 1913. Jahresübersichten. Statistisches Amt. Leipzig.

Births and infant mortality in Leipzig, 1903–1913, p. 2.

Münchener Jahresübersichten für 1911. Statistiches Amt der Stadt München. " Mitteilungen," Band XXIV. Heft 2. München, 1913.

Births in Munich, birth rates, legitimate and illegitimate, per 1,000 inhabitants, and per cent of births illegitimate, 1871–1911, p. 6; births and infant deaths, 1896–1911, and in each month of 1911, p. 7; births, 1911, by age of mother, civil condition, residence, p. 7.

Mataró, Franz: " Die Geburten und die Säuglingssterblichkeit in München während der Kriegsjahre 1915, 1916 und 1917." Zeitschrift für Bevölkerungspolitik und Säuglingsfürsorge. Band 11 (Juni 1919), pp. 7–15. Leipzig.

Births and infant mortality, 1910–1917, p. 10.

Great Britain and Ireland.

Eightieth Annual Report of the Registrar-General of Births, Deaths, and Marriages in England and Wales, 1917. London, 1919.

Discussion of illegitimate birth statistics, 1917, pp. xxiii–xxiv; illegitimate birth rates, 1876–1917, per 1,000 total births, per 1,000 total population, per 1,000 unmarried and widowed women 15 to 45 years, and compared with rates for 1876–1880 taken as 100, p. xxiv; births per 1,000 total population, 1917, by sections and urban and rural districts, p. xxiv; births, p. 4; birth rates, per 1,000 total population, per 1,000 single and widowed women 15 to 45 years, and per 1,000 total births, 1851–1917, p. 5; births and infant deaths, 1917, according to sections and urban and rural districts, pp. 82–114. Infant mortality, 1917, per 1,000 births, by age at death and cause of death, with mortality per cent illegitimate based on mortality of legitimate infants as 100, p. xliii; infant mortality, 1911–1917, per 1,000 births due to syphilis, p. lix; infant mortality, 1906–1917, p. 5; infant mortality, 1917, by age to death and cause of death, pp. 41–42; by age at death and cause of death, according to urban and rural districts, pp. 43–47.

Seventy-fourth Annual Report of the Registrar-General of Births, Deaths, and Marriages in England and Wales, 1911. London, 1913.

Births, and lowest and highest groups of mortality among infants born out of wedlock, by age at death and cause of death, according to occupation of mother, pp. xlv-xlvi; percentage at various ages of total excess of mortality among infants born out of wedlock, 1906–1911, p. xlvi; percentage excess of mortality at various ages, 1906–1911, p. xlvii; births, and mortality by age at death and cause of death, according to occupation of mother, pp. 90–93.

Quarterly Return of Marriages, Births, and Deaths Registered in England and Wales and in the Registration Counties; and of Births, Deaths, and Notified Cases of Infectious Disease in Certain Large Towns. Published by authority of the Registrar-General. No. 280—Year 1918. London, 1919.

Births for last quarter of 1918, and for 1917 and 1918, in London and the other registration counties, pp. 6, 38.

Fifty-fourth Detailed Annual Report of the Registrar-General for Ireland Containing a General Abstract of the Numbers of Marriages, Births, and Deaths Registered in Ireland during the Year 1917. Dublin, 1918.

Births, 1917, by provinces according to per cent and rate per 1,000 population, 1917, pp. x–xi; births, by provinces and counties, pp. 2–11.

Supplement to the Forty-seventh Report of the Registrar-General of Marriages, Births, and Deaths in Ireland, Containing Decennial Summaries of the Returns of Marriages, Births, Deaths, and Causes of Death in Ireland, for the Years 1901–1910. London, 1913.

Number and per cent of illegitimate births registered, 1901–1910, by provinces and urban and rural districts, p. vii; per cent of illegitimate births in each year of the period, by provinces, p. xiv; number and per cent of illegitimate births by provinces and civic and rural counties, p. xv; illegitimate births, 1901–1910, by provinces, counties, and unions, pp. 14–18.

Sixty-third Annual Report of the Registrar-General for Scotland, 1917. Edinburgh, 1919.

Births and per cent illegitimate, 1917, for country, larger burghs, smaller burghs, and county districts, pp. lxix–lxxvii; births, 1917, and legitimate and illegimitate birth rates per 1,000 unmarried women and widows aged 15 to 45, by counties, larger burghs, and the entire country, p. lxxviii; births, 1917, in registration districts, pp. 1–41; corrected births by burghs and county districts, pp. 78–106.

Report of the Inter-Departmental Committee on Physical Deterioration. Vols. I, II, III. London, 1904.

High mortality of children born out of wedlock referred to in Vol. II, Minutes of Evidence (see Index, Vol. III); relative incidence of infant mortality among legitimate as compared with illegitimate infants, in London and certain rural counties, as shown by average rates of death under 1 year from various causes, per 1,000 births, infant deaths by age at death, proportional age incidence of deaths at the several age groups to 160 deaths at all ages under 1 year, and deaths per 1,000 births at the several age groups, 1902—data submitted by Dr. Tatham, Vol. I, App. VA, II and III, pp. 133–137; percentages of illegitimate births and infant mortality in Glasgow, 1898–1902—data submitted by Dr. Chalmers, Vol. III, App. XI, Table D, p. 26; infant mortality in Manchester, 1891–1902—data submitted by Dr. Niven, Vol. III, App. XII, V, p. 49. Births and infant deaths in Blackburn, Preston, and Burnley, 1903, by occupation of mother—data submitted by Miss A. M. Anderson, H. M. Principal Lady Inspector of Factories, Vol. I, App. V, pp. 121–122.

Thirty-ninth Annual Report of the Local Government Board (England and Wales), 1909–1910. Supplement to the report of the board's Medical Officer containing a report by the Medical Officer on infant and child mortality. London, 1910.

Proportion of illegitimate to legitimate births in England and Wales, 1881–1885 and 1906–1908, p. 46; relative mortality figures for infant mortality in certain registration counties, 1898–1907, compared with relative corrected illegitimate birth-rate figures, 1901, p. 47.

Forty-seventh Annual Report of the Local Government Board (England and Wales), 1917–1918. Supplement containing the report of the Medical Officer for 1917–1918. London, 1918.

Infant mortality in England and Wales in 1916: Reasons for excessive mortality among illegitimate infants, proportionate excess over legitimate infant mortality at specified ages, comparison with legitimate infant mortality by cause of death and by occupational groups of mothers, pp. xxix–xxxii.

City of Birmingham, Report of the Medical Officer of Health for the Year, 1918.

Births, illegitimate, 1915–1918 ; suggestions by Mr. Robert Parr in regard to method of determining paternity and registration of births ; pp. 7–10. Infant mortality, 1918 ; death rate per 1,000 births ; p. 63. Causes of death, p. 64.

Newman, George, M. D.: Infant Mortality: A social problem. Methuen & Co., London, 1906.

Comparison of deaths per 1,000 births at the several age periods under one year in London and certain rural counties in 1902 (summary of data given in " Report of the Inter-Departmental Committee on Physical Deterioration, 1904 "), pp. 15–17 ; birth rates and infant mortality, pp. 211–216.

Newsholme, Arthur, M. D., and Stevenson, T. H. C., M. D.: " The decline of human fertility in the United Kingdom and other countries as shown by corrected birth rates." Journal of the Royal Statistical Society, Vol. LXIX— Year 1906, pp. 34–87. London, 1906.

Illegitimate birth rates, 1881 and 1903, in England and other countries, pp. 50–60 ; corrected and relative corrected birth rates in metropolitan (London) boroughs, pp. 67–68. Crude and corrected illegitimate birth rates: United Kingdom—England and Wales (1861–1901) and selected urban and rural districts (1881 and 1901), territorial subdivisions of Scotland, counties of Ireland, counties of England and Wales, and towns of United Kingdom (1881 and 1901) : Australasia (1881 and 1901), and certain foreign countries and cities (1880 and 1900) ; pp. 72–83.

Nixon, J. W.: " Some factors associated with the illegitimate birth-rate." Journal of the Royal Statistical Society, Vol. LXXVII—Year 1913–14, pp. 852–862.

Birth rates in England and Wales, 1876–1911, per 1,000 total births, per 1,000 unmarried and widowed women 15 to 45 years, per 1,000 total population (together with per cents based on rates for 1876–1880 taken as 100) ; number of illegitimate births in England and Wales, 1901–1911 ; illegitimate birth rates in urban and rural districts in England and Wales, 1911 ; map showing illegitimate birth rates in the counties of England and Wales ; Australian statistics, 1910–1912, for age periods and for illegitimate births and births in first six months of marriage ; problem as related to domestic servants, housing, number of unmarried women in employment, and proportion of unmarried men to unmarried women.

Italy.

Annuario Statistico Italiano. Seconda Serie. Vol. VI—Anno 1916. Roma, 1918.

Illegitimate births, 1915, acknowledged and unacknowledged, p. 31 ; per cent of illegitimate births and per cent acknowledged, 1910–1914 and 1915, p. 31 ; births, 1915, by provinces, with number acknowledged and per cent illegitimate, 1910–1914 and 1915, p. 32 ; infant mortality, 1914, by cause of death, p. 49.

Statistica delle Cause di Morte. Nell' anno 1914. Roma, 1917.

Infant mortality, 1914, in first and in subsequent months, 1912–1914, p. xlviii ; mortality of children under 5 years, p. xlviii ; infant mortality, 1912–1914, by cause of death, p. xlix ; deaths, 1914, of children under 5 years of age, by age at death and cause of death, p. 82.

Norway.

Statistisk Aarbok for Kongeriket Norge. 38te Årgang. 1918. Statistiske Centralbyrå. Kristiania. 1919.

Number and per cent of illegitimate births, 1891–1917, pp. 8–9 ; births, 1916, by prefectures, with per cents for the Kingdom, 1914–1916, p. 10.

Keller, Professor Dr. Arthur, und Klumker, Chr. J.: Säuglingsfürsorge und Kinderschutz in den europäischen Staaten. I. Band. Erste Hälfte. "Norwegen," von Axel Johannessen. Berlin, 1912.

Births, and legitimate and illegitimate birth rates per 1,000 inhabitants, and per 1,000 live births, 1801–1905; birth rates, per 1,000 unmarried women, for Norway, 1861–1900, and for cities and rural districts, 1871–1875, 1901–1905, 1875, 1890, 1900; births, infant deaths, infant mortality rates, 1876–1905, in cities and rural districts; mortality among infants of illegitimate birth compared with that among infants of legitimate birth; pp. 566–579.

Portugal.

Anuario Estatístico de Portugal. 1908, 1909 e 1910. Vol. I. Lisboa, 1914.

Births, 1906–1910, by districts, p. 57.

Roumania.

Buletinul Statistic al Romaniei. Seria III. Anul XI—1911–1912. Publicat de Serviciul Statisticei Generale din Ministerul Agriculturii și Domeniilor. Bucarest, 1911.

Births, 1910, 1911, by territorial divisions, and by cities and rural districts, pp. 266, 275, 654, 662; legitimate and illegitimate birth rates per 1,000 married women and per 1,000 unmarried women, respectively, 15 to 49 years, in specified countries of Europe, 1876–1905, p. 295; births, 1909, 1910, 1911, pp. 223, 533; births, April, 1910, to December, 1911, by month of birth and by urban and rural districts, pp. 87, 157, 223, 281, 447, 531, 533.

Serbia.

Annuaire Statistique du Royaume de Serbie. Douzième Tome—1907 et 1908. Statistique d'Etat du Royaume de Serbie. Belgrade, 1913.

Births, by departments, and by month of birth, 1907 and 1908, pp. 87–90; births, 1809–1908, p. 101; births by occupations of parents, 1907 and 1908, pp. 93–94; per cent of illegitimate births by departments, 1907 and 1908, and for whole country, 1898–1907, pp. 97–98; confinements in each department, 1907 and 1908, and for country as a whole, 1905–1908, by single and plural births and whether in cities or villages, pp. 112–113; births, 1907 and 1908, in cities and in villages, by order of birth, pp. 114–115.

Spain.

Anuario Estadístico de España. Año IV—1917. Ministerio de Instrucción Pública y Bellas Artes. Dirección General del Instituto Geográfico y Estadístico. Madrid, 1918.

Number and per cent of illegitimate births, and legitimate and illegitimate birth rates per 100 inhabitants, 1908–1916, p. 41.

Sweden.

Statistisk Årsbok för Sverige. Femte Årgången, 1918. Kungl. Statistiska Centralbyrån. Stockholm, 1918.

Births and per cent illegitimate, 1821–1916, for cities and rural districts, p. 33; per cent of births illegitimate and rates per 1,000 population, pp. 36–37; per cent of births illegitimate, 1901–1914, by cities, p. 38; number and per cent of illegitimate confinements, and rate per 1,000 unmarried women 20 to 45 years, 1751–1914, p. 44; confinements per 1,000 married and per 1,000 unmarried women in each age group, 1871–1914, p. 45; births and per cent illegitimate, 1751–1914, and birth rates per 1,000 inhabitants, p. 46; infant mortality, 1801–1914, p. 47.

Keller, Professor Dr. Arthur, und Klumker, Chr. J.: Säuglingsfürsorge und Kinderschutz in den europäischen Staaten. I. Band. Erste Hälfte. " Schweden: Die Sterblichkeit im Säuglingsalter," von J. E. Johansson. Berlin, 1912.

Per cent of illegitimate births and infant mortality, 1801–1909, for Stockholm and for Sweden as a whole; mortality among infants of illegitimate birth in proportion to that among infants of legitimate birth, for Stockholm and for the country as a whole, p. 752.

Sweden: Historical and Statistical Handbook. By order of the Swedish Government, edited by J. Guinchard. 2d Edition—English Issue. First Part, Land and People. Stockholm, 1914.

Number of mothers of children born in wedlock per 1,000 married women 15 to 45 years, and number of mothers of children born out of wedlock per 1,000 unmarried women 20 to 45 years, 1751–1910, p. 134; number of mothers, 20 to 45 years, of children born out of wedlock, 1751–1910, compared with other European countries, 1891–1900, p. 161; map of Sweden showing illegitimate birth rates, 1901–1910, per 1,000 unmarried women and widows 20 to 45 years, by provinces, p. 160; decline in marriage, p. 131; Stockholm's illegitimate birth rate, p. 163; infant mortality rate, 1901–1910, p. 141.

Switzerland.

Annuaire Statistique de la Suisse. 1917—26° année. Bureau fédéral de Statistique. Berne, juillet 1918.

Births and birth rates per 1,000 single women of childbearing age, 1916, by cities and urban districts, p. 17; birth rates per 1,000 single women of childbearing age, and births by residence of mother, for cantons, 1916, and for country as a whole, 1907–1916, p. 19; deaths in the first month of life, 1916, by cantons, p. 22; infant deaths and infant mortality rates, 1876–1916, p. 23.

The Netherlands.

Bijdragen tot de Statistiek van Nederland. Nieuwe Volgreeks. No. 221. Statistiek van den loop der bevolking in Nederland over 1914. Centraal Bureau voor de Statistiek. 's-Gravenhage, 1915.

Number and per cent of illegitimate births, 1848–1914, p. xi; per cents of births illegitimate, 1848–1914, with per cents based on the number for the year 1848–49 as 100, p. xii; per cent of illegitimate births, 1850–1914, by provinces, p. xiii; births, 1910–1914, by attendant at birth, p. xvi; births, 1914, by provinces and population of communes, pp. 2–55; births, 1914, by attendant at birth, for provinces and for communes grouped according to population, and for the Kingdom, 1909–1914, pp. 62–63; deaths under 1 year, 1914, by provinces and for the Kingdom, 1905–1914, p. xxxii; deaths under 1 year of age, 1913–14, by age at death and place of birth, pp. 66–69.

Annuaire Statistique de la Ville d'Amsterdam. Publié par le Bureau Municipal de Statistique. 14ième Année, 1917. Amsterdam, 1919.

Per cent of births, 1912–1916, for cities and the Kingdom, p. 54.

OTHER COUNTRIES.

AUSTRALASIA.

Australia.

Population and Vital Statistics. Bulletin No. 35. Commonwealth Demography, 1917 and previous years. Commonwealth Bureau of Census and Statistics, Melbourne, 1918.

Statistics by States and Territories: Births, single and plural, 1917, p. 28; number and per cent of illegitimate births, 1907–1917, and masculinity, p. 30; births, 1917, in public institutions and elsewhere, p. 31; number and per cent of illegitimate births registered in each month of 1917, p. 35; births, 1917, by age of mother, by birthplace of child, and by birthplace of mother, pp. 37–79; interval between birth and registration, 1917, p. 90.

Official Year Book of the Commonwealth of Australia; containing authoritative statistics for the period 1901–1916 and corrected statistics for the period 1788–1900. No. 10—1917. Commonwealth Bureau of Census and Statistics, Melbourne.

Masculinity of ex-nuptial births registered in Commonwealth, 1905–1915, by States and Territories; masculinity of births in various European countries, 1887–1891; number and per cent of ex-nuptial births registered in the Commonwealth, 1905–1915, by States and Territories; number of births per 1,000 of mean population, 1905–1915; number of births per 1,000 unmarried and widowed women 15 to 45 years, in the Commonwealth and in various countries of Europe, 1880–1882, 1890–1892, 1900–1902; births, single and plural, by birthplace of mother and by age of mother, 1915; interval between birth and registration, 1915, and average for each year, 1911–1915; pp. 161–165, 173, 174.

New South Wales, State Children Relief Board. Report of the President, Alfred William Green, for the Year Ended 5 April, 1917. Sydney, 1918.
    Births, 1915, 1916; infant deaths and infant mortality rates, 1895–1916; pp. 25, 26.

The Official Year Book of New South Wales, 1917. Published by authority of the Government of New South Wales, Sydney, 1918.
    Number and per cent of illegitimate births for the metropolis and the remainder of the State, 1880, 1890, 1900, 1905, 1910, 1915, and 1916, p. 82; masculinity of births, 1870–1916, pp. 81, 82; plural births, 1916, p. 83; infant mortality, 1916, by age at death, for the metropolis and the remainder of the State, pp. 88, 89; infant mortality, 1916, by cause of death, p. 109; deaths under 1 year and under 5 years, and death rates, 1911–1915 and 1916, p. 90.

Queensland, Vital Statistics, 1915. Fifty-sixth Annual Report of the Government Statistician. Brisbane, 1916.
    Births, and legitimate and illegitimate birth rates per 1,000 married women and per 1,000 unmarried women, respectively, 15 to 45 years, at ten-year intervals, 1861–1911; births. 1915, compared with other Australian States; per cent of illegitimate births, 1906–1915; p. XIII.

South Australia, Statistical Register, 1917–18. Part III.—Population and Vital. Adelaide, 1918.
    Number and per cent of illegitimate births, metropolitan area and State, 1908–1917, pp. 21–22.

Statistics of the State of Tasmania for the Year 1917–18. Part III. Vital and Meteorological. Tasmania, 1918.
    Births, 1917, in cities and in country districts; per cent of illegitimate births, 1916 and 1917, in cities and in country districts; p. 149.

Statistical Register of the State of Victoria, 1915. Part IV. Vital Statistics, etc. Melbourne, 1917.
    Births, 1915, in metropolitan, urban and rural districts, p. 11; births, 1906–1915, p. 12; single and plural births, 1915, by age of mother and by birthplace of mother, pp. 13–15; deaths of children under 5 years. 1915, by cause of death and age at death, p. 46.

Victorian Year-Book, 1916–17. Melbourne, 1918.
    Births, 1916; per cent of illegitimate births, 1910–1916: per cent of illegitimate births, 1916, compared with per cents in various countries and in other States of Australia; births and birth rates per 1,000 single women 15 to 45 years, 1891, 1901, 1911; birth rate, 1911, compared with rates in various countries and in other States of Australia; proportion of illegitimate births in town and country, 1916, and average for 1907–1912; infant mortality rates from various causes, 1904–1908, 1909–1913, 1916; pp. 330, 331, 349, 350.

Statistical Register of Western Australia for 1916 and Previous Years. Part I. Population and Vital Statistics. Perth, 1917.
    Births in each month and quarter, 1916; births, 1907–1916, in the State and in Perth and suburbs; p. 5.

New Zealand.

Statistics of the Dominion of New Zealand for the Year 1917. Vol. I: Blue Book. Population and Vital Statistics. Law and Crime. Wellington, 1918.
    Births, 1917, by registration districts, pp. 32–33; by provincial districts, p. 35; by age of mother, p. 38.

CENTRAL AND SOUTH AMERICAN COUNTRIES.

Chile.

Statistical Abstract of the Republic of Chile. Central Statistics Bureau. Santiago de Chile, 1918.
    Births, and number legitimate and illegitimate per 1,000 births, 1917, by provinces, p. 13; births, and number legitimate and illegitimate per 1,000 births, 1848–1917, p. 13.

Anuario Estadístico de la República de Chile. Vol. 1. Demografía. Año 1917. Santiago de Chile, 1918.

Births, and number legitimate and illegitimate per 1,000 births, 1917, by provinces, and for the Republic, 1913–1917, p. 26 ; births and number legitimate and illegitimate per 1,000 births, 1848–1917, p. 73.

Costa Rica.

República de Costa Rica, América Central. Anuario Estadístico. Año 1917— Tomo Vigesimoprimero. Dirección General de Estadística, San Jose, 1918.

Number and per cent of illegitimate births, 1917, by provinces, p. xxi.

Guatemala.

Boletín de la Dirección General de Estadística. Año 1. Núm. 1. Noviembre de 1913. Ministerio de Fomento, República de Guatemala, C. A.

Births, 1912, p. 149 ; by departments and race, p. 143.

San Salvador.

Anuario Estadístico de la República de el Salvador, 1914. Correspondiente A. Dirección General de Estadística, San Salvador, 1915.

Births in each department, 1914, by race, and per cent of births illegitimate, 1914, p. 25.

Uruguay.

Anuario Estadístico de la República Oriental del Uruguay. Año 1916—Libro XXVI. Director General de Estadística, Montevideo, 1918.

Number and per cent of illegitimate births and rate per 1,000 inhabitants, 1876– 1916, p. 17 ; births, 1916, in each department, and by months, 1916, p. 36.

Venezuela.

Anuario Estadístico de Venezuela, 1912. Ministerio de Fomento, Dirección General de Estadística. Caracas, 1915.

Illegitimate births, acknowledged and unacknowledged, in each section, 1912, p. 25 ; births, in each section, 1912, by age and civil condition of mother and father, p. 27.

JAPAN.

Mouvement de la Population de L'Empire du Japon, pendant l'an IV de Taisho— 1915. Cabinet Impérial. Bureau de la Statistique Générale. Tokio, 1918.

Births, legitimate, illegitimate, and acknowledged, in each district, 1915, pp. 62–63 ; deaths of legitimate, illegitimate, and acknowledged children under 5 years of age, by age at death and by provinces, pp. 110–117.

SOUTH AFRICA.

Statistical Year-Book of the Union of South Africa. No. 3—1914–15. Published under authority of the Minister of the Interior. Pretoria, 1916.

Cape of Good Hope : Number and per cent of illegitimate births to Europeans, 1910–1914, p. 7 ; births, 1914, by race, district, and urban and rural areas, pp. 8–17.

Natal : Number and per cent of illegitimate births to Europeans, 1913–1914, in urban and rural areas, p. 19 ; births, 1914, by race, district, and urban and rural areas, pp. 20, 21.

Transvaal : Number and per cent of illegitimate births to Europeans, 1909–1914, in urban and rural areas, p. 23 ; births, 1914, by race, district, and rural areas, pp. 24–25.

Orange Free State : Number and per cent of illegitimate births to Europeans, 1910– 1914, in urban and rural areas, p. 26 ; births to Europeans, 1914, in each district, and in urban and rural areas, p. 27.

LEGISLATION.[1]

UNITED STATES.

U. S. Children's Bureau. Illegitimacy Laws of the United States and Certain Foreign Countries, by Ernst Freund. Legal Series No. 2, Bureau Publication No. 42. Washington, 1919.

Analysis of legislation; comparative chart; legal index; text of laws of the United States; includes also laws of France, Germany, and Switzerland.

Illinois.

" The Illegitimacy Bill (House Bill 620)." The Institution Quarterly, Vol. IX (Mar. 31, 1918), pp. 72–73.

Discussion of provisions of bill introduced in 1917.

Bowen, Louise de Koven: Some Legislative Needs in Illinois. Juvenile Protective Association of Chicago, 1914.

Changes needed in " bastardy law," pp. 5–7.

Kansas.

The Kansas State Board of Health, Bulletin. Handbook of Child Hygiene. Vol. XIV. Nos. 8 and 9 (August and September, 1918). Topeka.

The Kansas law relating to children born out of wedlock, pp. 151–152.

Massachusetts.

Report on Criminal Remedies in Massachusetts for Failure to Furnish Support. Committee on Law and Procedure of the Association of Justices of District, Police and Municipal Courts of Massachusetts. Report No. 7. August, 1916. " Illegitimate Children Act (St. 1913, c. 563)," pp. 37–48.

Discussion of interpretation of law and method of enforcement.

Manual of Laws Relating to Illegitimacy in Massachusetts. Compiled by Boston Conference on Illegitimacy.

Brief survey of European legislation; summary of Massachusetts statutes on illegitimacy with related laws.

Probation Manual. The Commission on Probation. " Illegitimate Children " (Acts of 1913, Chapter 563)," pp. 47–49. Court House, Boston, Mass. July, 1916.

Jurisdiction; payment of confinement expenses; care and support of child; penalty for neglect.

Minnesota.

Report of the Minnesota Child Welfare Commission; with bills recommended and synopses of all changes from present law. 1917. St. Paul, Minn.

Laws recommended for the protection of children born out of wedlock, pp. 9, 13, 14, 22, 23, 42–57, 62.

Hodson, William W.: A Compilation of the Laws of Minnesota Relating to Children, 1919. The State Board of Control. St. Paul, Minn.

Laws relating to children born out of wedlock, pp. 10, 45, 47, 51, 52, 61, 160–164.

Resolution Governing the Policy of the State Board of Control in Illegitimacy Proceedings. Adopted by the State Board of Control, October 19, 1918. (Leaflet distributed by State Board of Control, St. Paul.)

Establishment of paternity; settlement; maternity and infant care.

Merrill, Galen A.: " The new child welfare laws—their relation to the dependent child." Quarterly of the State Board of Control, St. Paul, Minnesota, Vol. XVII (August, 1917), pp. 22–29, 33, 36, 37, 39, 40.

New laws framed by Child Welfare Commission for protection of children of illegitimate birth. Discussion.

---

[1] References to original statutes are not included in this list.

Missouri.

Missouri Children's Code Commission; a complete revision of the laws for the welfare of Missouri children. Second edition, January, 1917.

Care and support of children born out of wedlock; present handicaps of child; proposed legislation; pp. 9–14, 16, 58–62, 76, 77, 79, 80, 82–85, 94–98.

Report of the Missouri Children's Code Commission; a complete revision of the laws for the welfare of Missouri children. 1918.

Proposed legislation to establish paternity and insure support and right of inheritance; certificate of birth; pp. 20–24, 84, 85, 87–93, 195–198.

New York.

Palzer, Nathaniel J.: Handbook of Information on Non-Support, Desertion and Illegitimacy. The Charity Organization Society of the City of New York, 1916.

Brief explanation of organization and procedure in courts having jurisdiction over nonsupport, desertion and illegitimacy, prepared for the use of social workers in New York State.

North Carolina.

Child Welfare in North Carolina; an inquiry by the National Child Labor Committee for the North Carolina Conference for Social Service. Under the direction of W. H. Swift. National Child Labor Committee, New York, 1918.

Legislation relating to "illegitimate children," pp. 260–263.

Oklahoma.

Child Welfare in Oklahoma; an inquiry by the National Child Labor Committee for the University of Oklahoma. Under the direction of Edward N. Clopper. National Child Labor Committee, New York, 1917.

Legislation relating to illegitimacy, pp. 210, 211, 222, 226–231, 238, 245.

Pennsylvania.

MacCoy, W. Logan: The Law of Pennsylvania Relating to Illegitimacy. (From the Philadelphia Conference on Illegitimacy: Report of Sub-committee on Legal Aspects.) Reprinted from the Journal of the American Institute of Criminal Law and Criminology, Vol. VII. (November, 1916), pp. 505–529.

Procedure and trial; enforcement of orders of support; birth registration; recommendations.

FOREIGN.

General.

Bommezijn, Adriaan Baltus: Het Onderzoek naar het Vaderschap. Leiden, 1909.

Inquiry into paternity, historical and legal. Laws of France, Germany, Norway, Switzerland; comparison of laws of Holland and Germany; arguments against law permitting inquiry.

Keller, Professor Dr. Arthur, und Klumker, Chr. J.: Säuglingsfürsorge und Kinderschutz in den europäischen Staaten. I. Band. Zweite Hälfte. Berlin, 1912.

Social-legal provisions: Discussion of laws relating to guardianship and illegitimacy in Denmark, Germany, France, Great Britain, Netherlands, Norway, Austria-Hungary, Portugal, Russia, Finland, Sweden, Switzerland, United States. Vol. I, Part II, pp. 877–1188.

Laws and provisions relating to protection of children and care of mothers: Text of laws of Belgium, Denmark, Germany, France, Great Britain, Italy, Luxemburg, Norway, Austria-Hungary, Spain, Sweden, Switzerland. Vol. I, Part III, pp. 1193–1492.

Mackellar, Sir Charles: The Treatment of Neglected and Delinquent Children in Great Britain, Europe, and America, with Recommendations as to Amendment of Administration and Law in New South Wales. Sydney, 1913.

The law relating to maintenance of children born out of wedlock in England, Scotland, Germany, Australia, and New Zealand, pp. 89, 90, 194–197.

Meister, Dr. R.: "Das Recht des unehelichen Kindes; ein geschlichtlicher Ueberblick." Zeitschrift für Säuglingsschutz. III. Jahrgang (September 1911), pp. 264–272.

The law relating to children born out of wedlock; ancient history; Middle Ages in Germany; modern laws of France and Germany.

Monteros, F. Espinosa de los: Die rechtliche Stellung der unehelichen Kinder nach dem deutschen bürgerlichen Gesetzbuch und den spanischen Código civil. Borna—Leipzig, 1909.

Definition of illegitimacy, and legal rights of child, according to the German and Spanish Civil Codes; inheritance.

Nagórski, Dr. iur. Sigmund: Das Rechtsverhältnis des unehelichen Kindes zu seinem Erzeuger, nach deutschem und französischem Recht in geschichtlicher und rechtsvergleichender Darstellung. Zürich—Selnau, 1908.

Discussion of German and French laws on: Legal proof of fatherhood; status and family relations of child; his title to maintenance.

Austria.

Zampis, Dr. Ernst: "Der Schutz der Ziehkinder und unehelichen Kinder." Zeitschrift für Kinderschutz und Jugendfürsorge. XI. Jahrgang (Juli 1919), pp. 153–159.

Law of Feb. 4, 1919, and regulations bringing under State supervision placed-out children and all children of illegitimate birth.

France.

Bernard, René: De la Légitimation des Enfants Adultérins ou Incestueux. Lois du 30 Décembre 1915 et du 7 Avril 1917. Rennes, 1918.

Legal development of legitimation: Before the Civil Code up to Law of April 7, 1917; in comparative law.

Brun, François: La Recherche de la Paternité. Commentaire théorique et pratique de la Loi du 16 Novembre 1912. Suivi d'un Essai de Législation comparée. Paris, 1913.

Ancient law; legislation of the Revolution; the Civil Code, criticism of Civil Code; law of November 16, 1912. Appendix: Comparative study of legislation in other countries.

Lévy, Édouard: Traité Pratique de la Légitimation des Infants Naturel Simples, Incestueux ou Adultérins. Préface de M. Albert Wahl. Librairie de la Société du Recueil Sirey. Paris, 1919.

Discussion of methods of legitimation.

Rigaud, Louis: La Recherche de la Paternité. Loi du 16 Novembre 1912 et Jurisprudence Antérieure. Paris et Reims.

Origin and consequence of prohibition of inquiry into paternity in French law.

Wahl, Albert: La Recherche de la Paternité. D'après la Loi du 16 Novembre 1912. (Extrait de la Revue trimestrielle de Droit Civil. Janvier–Février–Mars 1913.) Paris, 1913.

Legal action to establish paternity; cases where action is allowable; powers of the judge; limits of refusal; competency and procedure; effects.

Germany.

Behrends, H.: "Zwei Karten über die Rechtstellung des unehelichen Kindes in Europa und im Deutschen Reiche vor dem 1. Januar 1900." Zeitschrift für Säuglingsschutz. III. Jahrgang (September 1911), pp. 280–284.

Two systems of legal status of the child of illegitimate birth in Europe and German Empire.

Great Britain and Ireland.

Hooper, Wilfrid: The Law of Illegitimacy; a treatise on the law affecting persons of illegitimate birth, with the rules of evidence in proof of legitimacy and illegitimacy; and an historical account of the bastard in mediæval law. Sweet & Maxwell, Ltd., London, 1911.

Lushington, Guy: The Law of Affiliation and Bastardy. (Third edition, Henry Delacombe Roome.) Butterworth & Co.; Shaw & Sons, London, 1916.
Statutes, England and Wales.

Parr, Robert J.: Beyond the Law; some facts on illegitimacy in Ireland. 40, Leicester Square, London, W. C., 1909.
Restriction of English law in Ireland; extension recommended.

Royal Commission on the Poor Laws and Relief of Distress, Report. Part VIII, Chapter 4. (Parliamentary paper. Cd. 4499.) Wyman and Sons, Ltd., London, 1909.
Maintenance orders for support of children born out of wedlock, pp. 558–563.

Norway.

Castberg, J.: "The children's rights laws and maternity insurance in Norway." Journal of the Society of Comparative Legislation. (New Series), Vol. XVI, 1916, pp. 283–299. London.
The status of children of illegitimate birth; the objects of the law; statistics; affiliation proceedings; maternity insurance.

U. S. Children's Bureau. Norwegian Laws Concerning Illegitimate Children: Introduction and translation by Leifur Magnusson. Legal Series No. 1, Bureau Publication No. 31. Washington, 1918.
Early legislation; reforms; legislative history of the Acts of 1915; text of law.

Wiesener, G.: Barnelovene av 10. April 1915 og Pleiebarnloven av 29. April 1905. Kristiania.
Text of law relating to children born out of wedlock; discussion of interpretation and purpose of legislation.

METHODS OF CARE.[1]

Bosnynák, Zoltán de, et Edelsheim-Gyulai, Cte. L.: Le Droit de l'Enfant Abandonné et le Système Hongrois de Protection de l'Enfance. Imprimerie de la Société Anonyme Athenæum, Budapest, 1909.
The right of the child to State protection in Hungary; placing-out of mother and child in adoptive homes; colony system of care for mother and child.

Carnegie United Kingdom Trust, The. Report on the Physical Welfare of Mothers and Children. Four Volumes. East Port. Dunfermline, 1917.

Vol. I. England and Wales, by E. W. Hope, M. D.
Introductory statement of problem, pp. xv–xvi: dangers to the "illegitimate infant"; mortality rate, pp. 6, 48, 49, 64; methods of care, pp. 49–51.

Vol. III. Scotland, by W. Leslie Mackenzie, M. D.
"Provision for the unmarried mother": Types of unmarried mothers; provision in Edinburgh; in Glasgow; small homes for children; personal histories, showing type of care given; criminal aspects; suggestions for remedy; pp. 115–130.
"The unmarried mother's child": Number and distribution of births; infant mortality rates, 1899–1913; immediate destiny of child; later history; pp. 131–143.

Vol. IV. Ireland, by E. Coey Bigger, M. D.
Statistics of illegitimacy, p. 47; "bastardy law" of Ireland; guardianship and care; pp. 61, 62.

Conference on the Care of Dependent Children, held at Washington. D. C. January 25, 26, 1909, Proceedings. Senate Document No. 721, Government Printing Office, Washington. 1909.
Papers and discussion relating to care of dependent children; conclusions.

---

[1] See also citations under Reports of Agencies, Institutions, and Courts and under General References.

Engel, Sigmund: The Elements of Child-Protection. (Translated from the German by Dr. Eden Paul.) The Macmillan Company, New York, 1912.

The problem of the child of illegitimate birth in Europe, pp. 15, 16; rights of survival, pp. 47, 48; protection of the child, legal disabilities and reforms, delinquency, pp. 90–105; evolution of methods of care of foundlings, pp. 64, 71, 154.

Folks, Homer: The Care of Destitute, Neglected, and Delinquent Children. The Macmillan Company, New York & London, 1902.

Historical survey of State and city care of dependent children; private charities caring for destitute children.

Hanauer, Dr. W.: "Die Fürsorge für uneheliche Kinder und der Krieg." Zeitschrift für Bevölkerungspolitik und Säuglingsfürsorge. Band 10 (August 1918), pp. 201–207.

Support of children of illegitimate birth during the war; public guardianship system in Berlin, Leipzig, and the municipalities of Saxony; infant mortality in Leipzig, 1912–1915.

Hart, Hastings H.: Preventive Treatment of Neglected Children. Charities Publication Committee, Russell Sage Foundation, New York, 1910.

Foundling homes and asylums; relation between problem of delinquency and method of treatment of unmarried mother and her child; pp. 73, 74.

Hoffa, Dr. Theodor: "Offene und geschlossene Fürsorge für Haltekinder und Uneheliche." Zeitschrift für Säuglingsschutz. IV. Jahrgang (Oktober 1912), pp. 423–437.

Provision for children born out of wedlock, in homes and in asylums, in Barmen.

Keller, Professor Dr. Arthur, und Klumker, Chr. J.: Säuglingsfürsorge und Kinderschutz in den europäischen Staaten. I. Band. Erste Hälfte. Berlin, 1912.

Social-hygienic provisions: Articles dealing with illegitimacy, foundlings, abandoned children, placing-out, and guardianship in European countries. Vol. I, Part I, pp. 3–874.

Keller, Dr. Arthur, und Reicher, Dr. Heinrich: Die Fürsorge für uneheliche Kinder. Leipzig und Wien, 1909.

Systems of care in European countries for children born out of wedlock; connection between infant mortality and neglect; discussion of foundling hospitals; laws for protection of child; desirability of public guardianship.

Local Government Board (England and Wales). Report prepared in the Intelligence Department: Infant Welfare in Germany during the War. London, 1918.

Vital statistics before the war; guardianship and care; separation allowances; imperial maternity grants; pp. 6, 21–24, 29, 34.

——— Forty-fifth Annual Report, 1915–16. Supplement in continuance of the report of the Medical Officer of the board for 1915–16, containing a report on child mortality at ages 0–5, in England and Wales. London, 1916.

The supervision of children of illegitimate birth in foster homes, pp. 93, 94.

——— Forty-seventh Annual Report, 1917–18. Supplement containing the report of the Medical Officer for 1917–18. London, 1918.

Causes of high infant mortality among children born out of wedlock; rates according to ages of infants and occupations of mothers; lack of parental care; conditions of care necessary for child, pp. xxix–xxxii.

Maxfield, Francis N.: "The social treatment of unmarried mothers." The Psychological Clinic. Vol. IX (December 15, 1915), pp. 210–217.

Discussion of working principles of Social Service Department of University Hospital, Philadelphia.

National Baby Week Council, Report, 1917. Abstracts of papers of the Conference. London.

Papers on: "The problem of illegitimacy" and "The care of the unmarried mother and her child," pp. 51–53.

National Conference on Infant Welfare, Held at Kingsway Hall, London, on July 1st, 2nd and 3rd, 1919, Report of the Proceedings. National League for Health, Maternity and Child Welfare. 4, Tavistock Square, London, W. C, 1, 1919.

> Cox, Adelaide: The unwanted babe, pp. 184–191.
> Gotto, Mrs.: Parental responsibilities in relation to illegitimacy, pp. 167–176.
> Kensington, Bishop of: The illegitimate child, pp. 140–145.
> Nott–Bower, Lady: The destitute unmarried mother, pp. 135–140.
> Parr, Robert: The legal position of the unmarried mother, pp. 145–149.
> Routh, Amand, M. D.: Causes of ante-natal, intra-natal, and neo-natal mortality, pp. 8–19.
> Whitley, William F. J., M. D.: Criminal abortion and abortifacients, with special reference to illegitimacy, pp. 176–183.
> Discussion, pp. 149–166, 191–199.

National Council for the Unmarried Mother and Her Child (and for the Widowed or Deserted Mother in Need), Report. Evelyn House, 62, Oxford Street, W. I. London, 1919.

> Origin and aims of the Council; findings of special committee. Recommendations adopted: Welfare measures for all mothers; finance; legal recommendations. Births, 1906–1918; infant mortality, 1906–1917. Action taken in other countries.

Revue Philanthropique. Tome XXXIX (Avril 1918), p. 187. Paris.

> Maternity care and assistance.

Royal Commission on the Poor Laws and Relief of Distress, Report. Part VIII, Chapter 4. (Parliamentary paper, Cd. 4499.) Wyman and Sons, Ltd., London, 1909.

> Treatment of unmarried mothers; mothers in workhouses; pp. 563–566.

Schöne, Dr. Walter: "Die Leipziger Mündelstatistik." Zentralblatt für Vormundschaftswesen, Jugendgerichte und Fürsorgeerziehung. VII. Jahrgang (25. Januar. 1916). pp. 229–231.

> Guardianship methods; statistics.

Slingerland, William H.: Child Welfare Work in California; a study of agencies and institutions. Department of Child-Helping, Russell Sage Foundation, New York, 1915.

> Institutions for combined care of mothers and children, pp. 122–127; illegitimacy as a cause of dependency, p. 196.

——— Child Welfare Work in Pennsylvania; a co-operative study of child-helping agencies and institutions. Department of Child-Helping, Russell Sage Foundation, New York, 1915.

> Institutions for combined care of mothers and children, pp. 214–221.

——— A Child Welfare Symposium. Edited by William H. Slingerland. Supplement to Child Welfare Work in Pennsylvania. "The problem of the illegitimate child," by Mrs. Henry Finkelpearl, pp. 19–23. Department of Child-Helping, Russell Sage Foundation, New York, 1915.

> Disposition of 100 infants admitted to the Pittsburgh Home in 8 years; their parentage; institutional care.

——— Child Welfare Work in Oregon; a study of public and private agencies and institutions for the care of dependent, delinquent and defective children. For the Oregon Child Welfare Commission. July Bulletin, Extension Division, University of Oregon, 1918.

> Private institutions caring for unmarried mothers and children, pp. 51–56.

State Children Relief Board, New South Wales. Report of the President, Alfred William Green, for the Year Ended 5 April, 1915. Sydney, 1915. (Legislative Assembly.)

> Homes for babies with mothers; their object and results; pp. 34–39.

Swedish Poor Laws and Charities. Prepared by Axel Hirsch for The Swedish Poor Law Reform Association. Stockholm, 1910.

Establishment of infants' homes for the care of unmarried mothers and their babies ; the foundling home in Stockholm ; p. 30.

Tropeano, Prof. Guiseppe: "Assistenza e Previdenza Sociale per la Maternitâe per l'Infanzia." Rassegina della Previdenza Sociale, gennaio, 1919, pp. 54–63.

Report of Committee on Public Health of the Commission for the Study of Measures Necessary for the Period of Transition from War to Peace. Discussion of need for social assistance and provision for motherhood and childhood.

Tugendreich, Dr. Gustav: Die Mutter und Säuglingsfürsorge. Kurzgefasstes Handbuch. Mit Beiträgen von J. F. Landsberg, und Dr. med. W. Weinberg. Stuttgart, 1910.

History of status of unmarried mother and her child, pp. 17–19 ; history of care of children born out of wedlock, pp. 22–24 ; guardianship, pp. 24, 25, 412, 413 ; comparison of birth rates, legitimate and illegitimate, among all women, 15 to 50 years, 1896–1905, in various countries, and by age groups, pp. 33, 34 ; influence of illegitimacy on infant mortality rate, pp. 78–80 ; legal status and care of unmarried mothers and their children, pp. 91–93, 108–111, 127 ; legitimation, pp. 94–97 ; maternal rights and duties, pp. 112, 113 ; duties of father to provide support, pp. 113–118 ; percentage of illegitimate births in Berlin institutions, p. 348 ; infant mortality in foundling asylums, pp. 390–392.

U. S. Children's Bureau. Governmental Provisions in the United States and Foreign Countries for Members of the Military Forces and their Dependents. Miscellaneous Series No. 11, Bureau Publication No. 28, Washington, 1917.

Separation allowances, pensions, and maternity benefits in Austria, France, Germany, Great Britain and British colonies, Italy, Netherlands, Russia, and United States, pp. 27, 34, 40, 49, 61, 68, 69, 72, 114, 115, 117, 118, 131, 132, 137, 140, 141, 143, 145, 149, 155, 164–166, 168–170, 172, 173, 186, 197, 204, 214, 230.

————— Standards of Child Welfare: a report of the Children's Bureau Conferences. May and June, 1919. Conference Series No. 1, Bureau Publication No. 60. Washington, 1919.

Care of children of illegitimate birth, pp. 308, 360, 361, 425, 442.

————— Minimum Standards for Child Welfare Adopted by the Washington and Regional Conferences on Child Welfare, 1919. Conference Series No. 2, Bureau Publication No. 62. Washington, 1919.

Care of children born out of wedlock, p. 12.

REPORTS OF AGENCIES, INSTITUTIONS, AND COURTS.[1]

UNITED STATES.

Boston.

Boston Children's Aid Society, Annual Reports.

Report of work with unmarried mothers: 1912, pp. 9–13 ; 1913, pp. 14–16 ; 1914, pp. 14–19 ; 1915, pp. 14–17 ; 1916, p. 18 ; 1917, pp. 6, 7, 17, 18 ; 1918, pp. 10–12.

Boston City Hospital. Department of Medical-Social Work, Annual Reports.

Report of work with unmarried mothers: 1914–1916, pp. 17–18 : 1917–1918, pp. 21–24 ; 1918–1919, pp. 6–7.

————— Russell, Bess Lynde: A year's study of the maternity ward at the Boston City Hospital. Reprinted from the Boston Medical and Surgical Journal, Vol. CLXXX (May 1, 1919), pp. 487–495.

Number of cases, pp. 5–6 ; comparison of ages of mothers of children born out of wedlock, with all mothers cared for, pp. 10–12 ; illustrative cases, pp. 20–22 ; analysis of illegitimacy cases, pp. 24–25 ; suggestions, pp. 27–28.

---

[1] It is not possible to present a complete list of reports of agencies concerned in whole or in part with the care of children born out of wedlock. The reports here listed may serve as an indication of sources of such material.

Florence Crittenton League of Compassion, Annual Report for 1914. Boston.
> Statistical summary, p. 14. Constitution and by-laws, pp. ii–vi.

Society for Helping Destitute Mothers and Infants. Reports Boston.
> Method of work for mothers and infants: 1914, pp. 7–15, 20–22; 1914–15, pp. 5–17, 22–24; 1915–16, pp. 9–16, 18–23; 1916–17, pp. 7–14, 16–21.

——— Clarke, Lilian Freeman: The Story of an Invisible Institution; forty years' work for mothers and infants. Reprints from The Outlook. Press of Geo. H. Ellis Co., Boston.
> History of Boston Society for Helping Destitute Mothers and Infants. In four sections: " I. How it began: Susan Dimock [1873]. II. First Days: What we learned. III. What more we learned: How not to do it. Not classification: Discrimination. IV. How to do it; hospital work; the care of the infant."

Talitha Cumi Maternity Home and Hospital. New England Moral Reform Society, Boston, Annual Reports.
> Method of work and analysis of cases: 1914, pp. 14–25; 1915, pp. 17–23.

California.

State Board of Control, Report of the Children's Department for the Period Beginning July 1, 1916, and Ending July 1, 1918. Sacramento, 1919.
> Agencies caring for unmarried mothers and their children; study of 153 cases; the need of greater protection; pp. 29, 30.

State Board of Charities and Corrections of the State of California. Eighth Biennial Report, from July 1, 1916, to June 30, 1918. Sacramento, 1918.
> Rescue homes: Number licensed, p. 47; movement of population, disposition of babies, pp. 140–141.

——— Surveys in Mental Deviation in Prisons, Public Schools, and Orphanages in California. 1918. "The intelligence of orphan children and unwed mothers in California charitable institutions," by J. Harold Williams, pp. 46–82.
> Results of tests of 12 unwed mothers, in private institutions; close relation of dependency and illegitimacy to mental condition.

Chicago.

The Municipal Court of Chicago. Tenth and Eleventh Annual Reports, for the Years December 6, 1915, to December 2, 1917. Inclusive.
> " Bastardy " cases, 1916–1917, domestic relations court, pp. 107–108; conditions due to war, p. 112; the psychopathic laboratory "bastardy" cases, pp. 233–238.

——— Report of the Domestic Relations Branch, 1917, by Judge John Stelk. Chicago, 1917.
> Support of children of illegitimate birth, pp. 14, 42, 48, 50; report of work of social service department, p. 112; cases considered and disposed of in court, pp. 113–115, 126; report of Woman's Protective Association, pp. 128, 129; the present "bastardy law" and necessary changes, pp. 148–163.

——— Report of the Psychopathic Laboratory for the Years May 1, 1914, to April 30, 1917.
> Study of 117 girls and 7 men involved in "bastardy cases": chronological age; mental age; years at school; grade; pp. 126–131.

Cleveland.

The Second Social Year Book: the human problems and resources of Cleveland, sixth city. The Cleveland Federation for Charity and Philanthropy. December, 1916.
> The work of agencies dealing with unmarried mothers, pp. 19, 22, 27, 89, 90.

Social Service at Home During the War Years. The Welfare Federation of Cleveland, April, 1919.
> Summary of work of agencies dealing with unmarried mothers, 1917–1918, pp. 24, 25.

Columbus.

A Study of the Social Service Field by The Social Service Bureau of the Columbus [Ohio] Chamber of Commerce. February 15, 1917, to April 30, 1918.
    Study of the births in 1916; agencies caring for the mothers; age, nativity, and
    previous occupation of mother; pp. 115–117, 59–62.

Kansas City.

Board of Public Welfare of Kansas City, Missouri, Seventh Annual Report,
April 20, 1915–April 19, 1916.
    Private homes caring for unmarried mothers; number receiving care; pp. 48, 49.

Massachusetts.

State Board of Charity of Massachusetts. Thirty-eighth Annual Report, for
the Year Ending November 30, 1916. Part I. Boston.
    After-care of women and children discharged from State Infirmary, p. 150; classifi-
    cation of admissions, p. 156; legal work, pp. 158–161; " the married woman with the
    illegitimate child," p. 151; summary of infants under 2 years reported to State Board
    of Charity, p. 185.

——— Thirty-ninth Annual Report, for the Year Ending November 30, 1917.
Part I. Boston.
    Classification of mother-and-baby cases by legal status, p. 145; after-care of women
    and children discharged from State Infirmary, pp. 146–148; summary of infants under
    2 years reported to State Board of Charity, p. 173.

——— Fortieth Annual Report, for the Year Ending November 30, 1918.
Part I. Boston, 1919.
    Classification of women admitted to the State Infirmary in 1918, p. 119; number
    of illegitimate births, p. 120; data concerning 50 girls under supervision from three to
    five years, pp. 121–124; number and per cent illegitimate of dependent children
    received as State minor wards, and the chief causes for acceptance, pp. 129–130;
    infants under 2 years of age reported to the State Board of Charity, according to the
    number and sex in each boarding home, pp. 147–149.

Massachusetts Society for the Prevention of Cruelty to Children, Annual
Reports. Boston.
    Inadequate provision made for children born out of wedlock: 1911, pp. 35–36; 1912,
    p. 22; 1917. p. 29.

Michigan.

Michigan State Board of Corrections and Charities, Twenty-fourth Biennial
Report, 1917–1918.
    Maternity hospitals: Births, and infant mortality; disposition of babies; rules and
    regulations adopted by the State Board of Corrections and Charities for the govern-
    ment of maternity hospitals; pp. 111, 112, 116–119. Children in institutions: Admis-
    sions and placements, pp. 136–139.

Milwaukee.

The Juvenile Protective Association, Report, October, 1919.
    Illegitimacy cases, pp. 14, 15; special research, pp. 8, 11.

Minnesota.

State Board of Control. Report of the Children's Bureau. St. Paul, 1918.
    Unmarried mothers and their children; support of child; general principles of the
    Bureau; forms to be used in case work; statistics; pp. 9–12.

——— Ninth Biennial Report. Period ended July 31, 1918. St. Paul.
    Report of the Children's Bureau, 1918, pp. 37–39.

Montana.

Bureau of Child and Animal Protection of the State of Montana, Ninth Biennial
Report for the Years 1917, 1918. Helena.
    Florence Crittenton Home cases; prosecution; home-finding; pp. 16, 17.

New Hampshire.

Children's Commission, Report to the Governor and Legislature, January, 1915. Concord, New Hampshire, 1914.
The children of feeble-minded women, p. 97; New Hampshire laws relating to illegitimacy, p. 121; desertion, p. 30; birth registration, p. 69.

New York.

State Board of Charities, Fifty-second Annual Report, for the Year 1918. Albany, 1919.
Number of children of illegitimate birth committed to orphan asylums and homes for children, with causes for commitment, p. 100; number cared for in orphan asylums during year, p. 106.

State Charities Aid Association of New York, Annual Reports. New York City.
Report of subcommittee on assisting and providing situations for mothers with babies: 1914, pp. 70–76; 1915, pp. 66–71; 1916, pp. 33–38; 1917, pp. 32–36.

Court of Special Sessions of the City of New York, Annual Report for the Year Ending December 31, 1918.
"Bastardy" proceedings: Dispositions of cases, pp. 17, 22, 28, 32, 37, 41; use of probation, pp. 10, 11, 47, 52, 55, 58, 61, 64, 67; funds collected, p. 53.

Free Synagogue Child Adoption Committee, Annual Report, 1916–1917. "The illegitimate child," by Dr. Chas. Gilmore Kerley, pp. 15–16.
Discussion of environment and heredity in relation to care and development of children of illegitimate birth.

Ohio.

Ohio Board of State Charities, First Report of the Children's Welfare Department. The Ohio Bulletin of Charities and Correction, Vol. 21 (August, 1915), pp. 22, 23.
Infant mortality rate of children of illegitimate birth in institutions; need of homes for mothers and children.

Philadelphia.

Children's Bureau [Philadelphia]. Annual Reports, published in "Co-operation" (monthly).
1913. Number of children of illegitimate birth under care; committee appointed to reorganize work. Vol. I (September, 1914), pp. 5, 16.
1914. Work of department for mothers with children. Vol. III (November, 1915), pp. 4, 5, 9, 10.
1915. Legitimacy of children. Vol. IV (December, 1916), pp. 2, 3, 8.

The Municipal Court of Philadelphia. Second Annual Report, 1915. "Court work with illegitimate families," by Louise Stevens Bryant, pp. 54–103.
Procedure in court cases; study of 355 "illegitimate families;" color, age, nationality, mentality, occupation, social relationship of parents; the children. Recommendations. Tables.

—— Third Annual Report, 1916.
Procedure in cases, Women's Division of the Criminal Probation Department, pp. 104–121. Study of 381 cases: Nativity and race; conjugal condition; occupation and wage; the child's age; care; court disposition of cases. Further legislation recommended. Tables, pp. 221–247.

—— Fourth Annual Report, 1917.
Unmarried mothers' cases in probation department; weekly orders for support; legislation; pp. 158–160, 184, 223, 224.

South Carolina.

State Board of Charities and Corrections of South Carolina. The Quarterly Bulletin, Vol. V (March, 1919), pp. 24–26, 30, 31, 33–35.
Institutions caring for unmarried mothers.

CANADA

Alberta.

Neglected Children of the Province of Alberta, Annual Reports of the Superintendent. Department of Attorney General. Edmonton.

 1915. Provision for child of illegitimate birth (Sections 242a and 242b of the Criminal Code), pp. 36, 37.

 1916. Number under care; the father's responsibility; custom among the foreign population of arranging forced marriages; pp. 68, 69.

 1917. Number under care; the State's responsibility; p. 9.

Manitoba.

Public Welfare Commission of Manitoba, Second Interim Report. Printed by order of the Legislative Assembly of Manitoba, February, 1919. Winnipeg.

 Study of hospital cases of unmarried mothers: Nationality, age, occupation and mentality; infant mortality; pp. 91–94, 109, 110. Care of feeble-minded girls, p. 127. Recommendations of commission, p. 146.

Ontario.

Neglected and Dependent Children of Ontario, Annual Reports of Superintendent. Printed by order of the Legislative Assembly of Ontario. Toronto.

 Number of children of illegitimate birth under care: 1913, 1914, 1915, p. 9.

Saskatchewan.

Neglected and Dependent Children of the Province of Saskatchewan, Annual Reports of the Superintendent. Regina.

 Provision in foster homes for children born out of wedlock: 1915, p. 22; 1917, pp. 19, 20.

INVESTIGATIONS.

UNITED STATES.

Kammerer, Percy Gamble: The Unmarried Mother; a study of five hundred cases. Introduction by Dr. William Healy. Little, Brown, and Company, Boston, 1918.

 Introductory discussion of psychological factors. A study of 500 case records, with especial attention to hereditary and environmental factors. A brief treatment of general aspects of the problem; statistical data.

U. S. Children's Bureau. Illegitimacy as a Child-Welfare Problem, Part 2: A study of original records in Boston and the State of Massachusetts, by Emma O. Lundberg and Katharine F. Lenroot. Dependent, Defective, and Delinquent Classes Series No. —, Bureau Publication No. —. (In press.)

 Illegitimate births in one year: Infant mortality; the child's parentage; the care of the child. Children under care of social agencies: Extent of problem: the dependent child of illegitimate birth; the child's heritage and possibilities of parental care. Legal action for support. Births in Massachusetts. Children under care of State agencies and institutions for the dependent, delinquent, and mentally defective. Adoptions.

——— Infant Mortality: Results of a field study in New Bedford, Mass., based on births in one year, by Jessamine S. Whitney. Infant Mortality Series No. —, Bureau Publication No. —. (In press.)

 Mortality of infants of illegitimate birth; confinement care; disposition of infants; boarding homes; court action; age, occupation, and nationality of mother: pp. ——.

Baltimore.

Walker, George, M. D.: The Traffic in Babies; an analysis of the conditions discovered during an investigation conducted in the year 1914. The Norman, Remington Co., Baltimore, 1918.

 Investigation of institutions; interviews with physicians, nurses, midwives, and social workers; institutional and city data on mortality of infants; investigation of boarding homes.

Boston.

Studies of the Boston Conference on Illegitimacy. September, 1914.
Reports of studies by groups of the conference on: Massachusetts "bastardy laws".; syphilis and gonorrhea; feeble-mindedness; public opinion; normal girls; data for Boston, 1913. Recommendations.

Chicago.

Bowen, Louise de Koven: A Study of Bastardy Cases; taken from the Court of Domestic Relations in Chicago. Juvenile Protective Association of Chicago, 1914.
Study of 163 cases; histories of mothers and fathers; court verdicts; needed amendments to the Illinois law.

Guild, Arthur Alden: Baby Farms in Chicago; an investigation made for the Juvenile Protective Association, 1917.
Conditions found in homes investigated; mental and physical condition of children; data concerning parents. Results following investigation. Recommendations.

Moore, Howard: The Care of Illegitimate Children in Chicago. Juvenile Protective Association of Chicago, December, 1912.
Hospital statistics; disposition of children; analysis of 590 cases reported to the health department. Recommendations regarding registration, adoption, placing-out, amendment of "bastardy law."

Cincinnati.

Trounstine, Helen S.: Illegitimacy in Cincinnati. Studies from the Helen S. Trounstine Foundation, Vol. 1, September 1, 1919.
Extent of illegitimacy; data concerning 666 unmarried mothers; fathers; disposition of child; the law; the courts; the work of social agencies.

Cleveland.

The Unwed Mother and her Child; reports and recommendations of the Cleveland Conference on Illegitimacy and its committees. The Cleveland Federation for Charity and Philanthropy, Cleveland, Ohio, July, 1916.
Study of 175 birth certificates; the courts and illegitimacy; the menace of the feeble-minded. Recommendations.

Children's Committee of the Cleveland Humane Society, Report. 1914–1915. (Manuscript.)
100 cases studied. Recommendations of committee.

Milwaukee.

Drury, Louise: Unmarried mother and her child. Proceedings of the Wisconsin State Conference of Social Work, 1918, pp. 61–68.
Report of investigation in 1916–17 by the Milwaukee Conference on Illegitimacy. Study of 362 cases: Agencies caring for unmarried mothers and their children; status of mothers; classification of mothers, according to mentality and character; the father; dispositions of infants. Recommendations.

Illegitimacy in Milwaukee: a study made by the Juvenile Protective Association, 1915. (Manuscript.)
282 cases studied; occupation and age of mother; disposition of children.

St. Louis.

Mangold, George B., and Essex, Lou R.: Illegitimate Births in St. Louis. The School of Social Economy of Washington University, Report Number 4. St. Louis, 1914.
Analysis of data on 2,082 birth certificates; residence, age, and occupation of mother; previous births; place of confinement. Missouri laws.

FOREIGN.

Dingwall-Fordyce, A., M. D.: The Illegitimate Baby in Peace and War. Infants' Edinburgh Home, 5, Admiral Terrace. Edinburgh.

Infants born in the Royal Maternity Hospital, Edinburgh, January 1 to June 30, 1911, and their history for three years. Discussion of child's heredity; effect on illegitimacy rate of giving aid to mothers and children. Existing statutory regulations; prospects of improved conditions; after-care in homes connected with hospital.

Lange, Dr. Auguste: Die unehelichen Geburten in Baden. Eine Untersuchung über ihre Bedingungen und ihre Entwicklung. Karlsruhe i. B., 1912.

Conditions affecting illegitimate births in agricultural and industrial districts of Baden; population of marriageable age; accessory conditions of marriage; statistical tables.

Prenger, Dr. Georg: Die Unehelichkeit im Königreich Sachsen. Leipzig und Berlin, 1913.

Illegitimacy in the districts of Saxony according to city and rural; comparison with other States; stillbirths; infant mortality. Statistics of Dresden: Legitimation; occupation and age of mother; prenuptial pregnancies.

Rauhe, Dr. C.: Die unehelichen Geburten als Sozialphänomen. Ein Beitrag zur Bevölkerungsstatistik Preussens. München, 1912.

Analysis of types and causes of illegitimate births and the various methods of measuring the birth rate; historical and geographical survey of illegitimacy in Prussia; statistics.

Spann, Othmar: Die unehelichen Mündel des Vormundschaftsgerichtes in Frankfurt am Main. Dresden, 1909.

Statistical study of cases of illegitimacy in the guardianship court, 1885–1905; comparison of condition of children under eight forms of care; relation between form of care and mortality.

Speich, Th. Rud.: Die unehelichen Geburten der Stadt Zürich. Glarus, 1914.

Comparison of illegitimate births in Zürich with other cities and countries; study of the mothers, 1904–1910; the children, 1904–1906; infant mortality, and conditions of care; the fathers, 1908–1912.

GENERAL REFERENCES.

BOOKS AND PAMPHLETS.

The Encyclopædia Britannica; a dictionary of arts, sciences, literature and general information. Eleventh edition. Cambridge, England: at the University Press; New York. 1910.
Bastards, Vol. III, pp. 499–500.
Foundling Hospitals, Vol. X, pp. 746–747.
Illegitimacy, by Thomas Allan Ingram, Vol. XIV, pp. 301–304.
Legitimacy and legitimation, Vol. XVI, pp. 378–379.

The Catholic Encyclopedia; an international work of reference on the constitution, doctrine, discipline, and history of the Catholic church. Robert Appleton Company, New York.
Illegitimacy, by John A. Ryan, Vol. VII, pp. 650–653.
Foundling Asylums, by John A. Ryan, Vol. VI, pp. 159–160.
Legitimation, by W. Fanning, Vol. IX, pp. 131–132.

The Jewish Encyclopedia; a descriptive record of the history, religion, literature, and customs of the Jewish people from the earliest times to the present day. Funk & Wagnalls Co., New York & London, 1916.
Bastard, by Lewis N. Dembitz, Vol. II, p. 587.
Illegitimacy, by Julius H. Greenstone, Vol. VI, pp. 559–560.
Foundling, by Julius H. Greenstone, Vol. V, pp. 440–441.

The New Dictionary of Statistics; a complement to the fourth edition of Mulhall's "Dictionary of Statistics." Augustus D. Webb. George Routledge and Sons, Limited, London; E. P. Dutton & Co., New York, 1911.
Statistics of illegitimate births in different countries, pp. 70–76; infant mortality among children born out of wedlock, pp. 195, 207.

The New Encyclopedia of Social Reform. William D. P. Bliss, editor-in-chief. Funk & Wagnalls Co., New York & London, 1908.
Illegitimacy, by Albert Leffingwell, pp. 594–596.

Anthony, Katharine: Feminism in Germany and Scandinavia. Henry Holt & Co., New York, 1915.
Illegitimacy in Germany, Sweden, Norway; the "Mutterschutz" movement; maternity insurance for unmarried mothers; protection of children born out of wedlock in Norway; general discussion of illegitimacy; pp. 83–116, 133–141, 142–168.

Bailey, William B.: Modern Social Conditions; a statistical study of birth, marriage, divorce, death, disease, suicide, immigration, etc., with special reference to the United States. The Century Co., New York, 1906.
Birth statistics of children born out of wedlock in foreign countries, pp. 119–128; stillbirths, p. 132; infant mortality, pp. 321, 322, 324, 325.

Barrett, Kate Waller, M. D.: Some Practical Suggestions on the Conduct of a Rescue Home. National Florence Crittenton Mission, Washington, D. C.
Discussion of management of home and methods of care.

Bowen, Louise de Koven: Safeguards for City Youth at Work and at Play. With a preface by Jane Addams. The Macmillan Company, New York, 1914.
Study of "bastardy" court cases by Juvenile Protective Association of Chicago, pp. 131–154; Norwegian law, p. 225.

Calhoun, Arthur W.: A Social History of the American Family from Colonial Times to the Present. The Arthur H. Clark Company, Cleveland.

> Vol. I. Colonial period. Published 1917.
>
>> Medieval position of women, pp. 15–20; influence of the Reformation on attitude toward marriage, pp. 21–28; "bundling" in New England, pp. 129–132. Puritan attitude on sex irregularities, pp. 39, 81, 132–142, 149; illegitimate births in Pennsylvania, p. 204; clandestine marriages, p. 211; conditions in southern colonies, pp. 313–323.
>
> Vol. II. From Independence through the Civil War. Published 1918.
>
>> Conditions in the South, pp. 204–208, 354; sex and family relations among the Negroes, pp. 243–279.
>
> Vol. III. Since the Civil War. Published 1919.
>
>> Miscegenation in the South, pp. 27–38; the negro family, pp. 39–50; deterioration in New England villages, p. 81; baby farming, p. 141; modern family aspects, pp. 211, 217, 222, 260, 278, 289, 311.

Fleagle, Fred K.: Social Problems in Porto Rico. D. C. Heath & Co., Publishers, Boston, New York, Chicago, 1917.

> Number of persons of illegitimate birth in the Island of Porto Rico, as given by the census of 1899 and that of 1910, white and colored, pp. 30–32.

Goddard, Henry Herbert: Feeble-mindedness; its causes and consequences. The Macmillan Company, New York, 1914.

> The part feeble-mindedness plays in problems of sexual immorality, pp. 13–15, 497–499.

Goodsell, Willystine: A History of the Family as a Social and Educational Institution. The Macmillan Company, New York, 1915.

> Discussion of family relationship: Among the Hebrews, Greeks, and Romans, pp. 56, 60, 95, 118, 121; in the Middle Ages, in the Renaissance, and in England in the nineteenth century, pp. 183, 249–251, 253, 254, 268–271, 443.

Hall, W. Clarke: The State and the Child. Headley Bros., Publishers, Ltd., London, 1917.

> The main cause of high mortality, degeneracy, and crime among children born out of wedlock; historical sketch; State care recommended; pp. 132–144.

Hart, Hastings H.: The Registration of Illegitimate Births; a preventive of infant mortality. Department of Child-Helping, Russell Sage Foundation, New York City, March, 1916.

> Statistics of States; questions of registration; causes of excessive mortality; measures to lower mortality rates.

Healy, William: Mental Conflicts and Misconduct. Little, Brown, and Company, Boston, 1917.

> Cases showing mental conflicts concerning parentage, pp. 47, 73, 74, 213–217.

Heath, H. Llewellyn: The Infant, the Parent, and the State; a social study and review. P. S. King & Son, London, 1907.

> Illegitimate births and infant mortality in England and Wales; legal position of children born out of wedlock; pp. 168–183.

Hoffman, Frederick L.: Race Traits and Tendencies of the American Negro. Publications of American Economic Association, 1896, Vol. XI, pp. 1–329.

> Laxity of morals among the Negro race, pp. 202–208, 235–241.

Horn, Dr. G.: "Zur Geschichte des Findelwesens." Zeitschrift für Säuglingsschutz. III. Jahrgang (September 1911), pp. 260–263.

> Development of care of abandoned children in France.

Howard, George Elliott: A History of Matrimonial Institutions; chiefly in England and the United States, with an introductory analysis of the literature and the theories of primitive marriage and the family. Three volumes. The University of Chicago Press, Chicago; T. Fisher Unwin, London, 1904.

Analysis of the literature and the theories of primitive matrimonial institutions, Vol. I, Part I. Matrimonial institutions in England, Vol. I, Part II. Matrimonial institutions in the United States, Vol. II, Part III. Penalties for violation of moral code in New England, Vol. II, pp. 109–200; clandestine contracts and the law, Vol. II, p. 212; problems of marriage and the family, Vol. III, Ch. XVIII.

Leffingwell, Albert, M. D.: Illegitimacy and the Influence of Seasons upon Conduct; two studies in demography. Swan Sonnenschein & Co., London; Charles Scribner's Sons, New York, 1892.

Prevalence of illegitimacy in Great Britain and Ireland since 1879; comparison for England, Scotland, and Ireland; inquiry as to causes; age and social condition of mother; infant mortality; influence of seasons upon birth rates.

Mangold, George B.: Problems of Child Welfare. The Macmillan Company, New York, 1914.

Mortality rate among infants born out of wedlock, p. 50; relation between delinquency and abnormal home conditions of children of unmarried mothers, pp. 353, 354; studies of unmarried mothers in St. Louis and Baltimore and causes of illegitimacy, p. 426. Present care and recommendations: State authority; registration of births; responsibility of father; supervision of maternity homes; keeping mother and child together; pp. 444–447.

Richmond, Mary E.: Social Diagnosis. Russell Sage Foundation, New York, 1917.

Case work involving problems of illegitimacy, pp. 95, 144, 190–192; questionnaire regarding an unmarried mother, prepared by Mrs. Ada Eliot Sheffield, pp. 413–419.

Royal Commission on the Care and Control of the Feeble-minded. The Problem of the Feeble-minded; an abstract of the Report. With an introduction by the Rt. Hon. Sir Edward Fry, G. C. B., and contributions by Sir Francis Galton, Rev. W. R. Inge, Professor Pigou, Miss Mary Dendy. P. S. King & Son, London, 1909.

Mental defect and illegitimacy, pp. 19–23; segregation, pp. 81–85.

Slingerland, William H.: Child-Placing in Families; a manual for students and social workers. Russell Sage Foundation, New York, 1919.

Illegitimate birth rates in Germany and Austria; status in Missouri, and the proposed code; results of social ostracism; social program; pp. 33, 34, 89, 90, 158, 159, 165–177.

Tredgold, A. F.: Mental Deficiency (Amentia). 2nd Edition. William Wood & Company, New York, 1914.

Question of illegitimacy as a cause of amentia, p. 55; propagation of aments, pp. 450–454.

U. S. Children's Bureau. A Social Study of Mental Defectives in New Castle County, Delaware, by Emma O. Lundberg. Dependent, Defective, and Delinquent Classes Series No. 3, Bureau Publication No. 24. Washington, 1917.

Relation between mental defect and illegitimacy, pp. 14, 15, 23, 26, 35.

—— Mental Defect in a Rural County; a medico-psychological and social study of mentally defective children in Sussex County, Delaware. A study made through the collaboration of the United States Public Health Service and the Children's Bureau, by Walter L. Treadway, M. D., and Emma O. Lundberg. Dependent, Defective, and Delinquent Classes Series No. 7, Bureau Publication No. 48. Washington, 1919.

Illegitimacy and mental defect, pp. 33, 47, 48, 56–60, 62, 64, 75, 81–83, 85, 87, 88, 90.

Werner, Oscar Helmuth: The Unmarried Mother in German Literature; with special reference to the period 1770–1800. Columbia University Press, New York, 1917.

Popularity of theme of unmarried mother during " storm of stress " period; extent of, and punishment for, infanticide; traditional status of the unmarried mother; conflict with church; punishments; revolt; cause of widespread illegitimacy.

Westermarck, Edward: The History of Human Marriage. Macmillan and Co., London and New York, 1894.
Marriage customs and family relationships among various tribes; special references to illegitimacy; pp. 16, 32, 60–66, 69, 70.

CONFERENCE PROCEEDINGS.

American Association for Study and Prevention of Infant Mortality:
Transactions, 1911:
Hart, Hastings H.: The illegitimate child, pp. 34–38.
Recommendations for prevention of high mortality rate among infants of illegitimate birth.

Transactions, 1913:
Babbitt, Ellen C.: The foundling asylum and the unmarried mother, pp. 363–365.
Influence of method of hospital care and after-supervision upon unmarried mothers in their later care of children.

Transactions, 1914:
Mason, Mary R.: Report of the sub-committee for assisting and providing employment for mothers with children, State Charities Aid Association, New York, pp. 339–340.
Report of work and aim of committee.

American Prison Association:
Proceedings of Annual Congress, 1910:
Abstracts of papers of the Eighth International Prison Congress:
Correvon, Gustave: Children born out of wedlock, pp. 396–398.
Recent legislation in Switzerland; inheritance and support.

Joly, Henri: Illegitimate children, pp. 398–399.
Children of illegitimate birth in reform schools in France; provision for guardianship by law.

Neander, Paul: Children born out of wedlock, pp. 394, 395.
Recommendations for protection and care in Russia.

Szilagyi, Arthur Charles: Illegitimate children, pp. 399–401.
Increase of illegitimacy in Hungary; recommended legislative and administrative measures.

Resolutions on measures for protection of children born out of wedlock, passed by Eighth International Prison Congress, p. 265.
Proceedings of Annual Congress, 1911:
Henderson, Dr. Charles R.: Discussion, pp. 202–203.
Illegitimacy and crime; administration of "bastardy laws."

Wines, Dr. F. H.: Discussion, pp. 203–205.
Effect of Swedish law on number of children born out of wedlock.

Inter-City Conference on Illegitimacy:
Reports of Committees at Annual Meeting, Atlantic City, June 7, 1919. (Multigraphed.)
Drury, Louise: Results of the study on registration of vital statistics.
Jewell, Helen M.: Legislation in 1919.

National Conference of Catholic Charities:
Proceedings, 1918:
Keegan, Rev. Robert F.: Policies of public and private agencies in dealing with illegitimacy, pp. 159–168.
Present laws in Norway, Minnesota, and Illinois; proposed legislation in Illinois; Catholic teaching concerning the child, the mother, and moral problems involved.

National Conference of Catholic Charities—Continued.
  Proceedings, 1918—Continued.
    Kennedy, James F.: Discussion on illegitimacy, pp. 171 174.
      The Illinois law; care of mother and child in a foundling hospital; legislation relating to maternity hospitals.

    Warren, George L.: Discussion on illegitimacy, pp. 168–171.
      Method of care in Connecticut.

National Conference of Charities and Correction:
  Proceedings, 1910:
    Barrett, Kate Waller: The unmarried mother and her child, pp. 96–100.
      Method of care to promote the physical welfare of the child and the moral stability of the mother.

  Proceedings, 1913:
    Gates, W. Almont: Caring for dependent children in California, pp. 306–311.
      Problems of child abandonment and illegitimacy.

  Proceedings, 1915:
    Fernald, Walter E., M. D.: What is practical in the way of prevention of mental defect, pp. 289–297.
      State registration; supervision of feeble-minded outside of institutions; formal commitment and permanent segregation of those who are likely to transmit their defects.

    Jones, Cheney C.: The relation of private societies to juvenile courts and to State bureaus of protection, pp. 149–163.
      Cooperation between private societies, juvenile courts, and State bureaus, in dealing with illegitimacy, p. 161.

    Knox, J. H. Mason, M. D.: Infant mortality, pp. 133, 134.
      Infant mortality as related to institutional care, foster home care, and care by mother in a boarding home.

    Lawton, Ruth W., and Murphy, J. Prentice: A study of results of a child-placing society, pp. 164–174.
      Research into methods of treatment of unmarried mothers, p. 166.

    Case-work problems of illegitimacy:
      Curry, H. Ida: A girl with a second or third illegitimate child, pp. 115–117.

      Donahue, A. Madorah: A case of illegitimacy, where mother and baby have been dealt with separately, pp. 121–126.

      Newman, Herman: The unmarried mother of border-line mentality, pp. 117–121.

      Shuman, Mrs. Cora V.: The good girl with a first baby, who is not feeble-minded, pp. 114, 115.

National Conference of Social Work (formerly National Conference of Charities and Correction):
  Proceedings, 1917:
    Donahue, A. Madorah: The case of an unmarried mother who has cared for her child, and succeeded, pp. 282–284.

    Fisher, Harry M.: The legal aspects of illegitimacy, pp. 294–299.
      Present "bastardy law" in Illinois; pending legislation.

    Lundberg, Emma O.: Illegitimacy in Europe as affected by the war, pp. 299–304.
      Effect upon number of births, status of child, and his right to support; special measures for child care.

    Parmenter, Mrs. Laura S.: The case of an unmarried mother who has cared for her child and failed, pp. 285–287.

National Conference of Social Work—Continued.
Proceedings, 1917—Continued.
Weidensall, Jean: The mentality of the unmarried mother, pp. 287–294.
Comparison of groups of patients tested in psychological clinic of Cincinnati General Hospital.
Discussion on illegitimacy, pp. 304–307.
Proceedings, 1918:
Davis, Otto W.: Children of unmarried and of illegitimate parents: Recent legislation in Minnesota and elsewhere, pp. 94–101.
Legislation in Norway, Massachusetts, Minnesota, and North Dakota.
Jones, Cheney C.: A tentative outline for a study on illegitimacy, pp. 91–94.
Proposed outline for the National Conference programs.
Watson, Mrs. Frank D.: The attitude of married parents and social workers toward unmarried parents, pp. 102–108.
Constructive social measures; standards of parenthood: education.
Proceedings, 1919:
Sheffield, Mrs. Ada Eliot: Program of the Committee on Illegitimacy— Committee Report.
Five divisions of the program: I. Prenatal, obstetrical, and convalescent care; II. After-care; III. The unmarried mother as human material; IV. Enactment and enforcement of laws; V. Construction and education.
State Conference Proceedings:
Indiana State Conference of Charities and Correction. Proceedings, 1913.
Clark, S. Ethel: What Indiana is doing for the unmarried mother, pp. 376–379; discussion, pp. 379–386.
Supervision of Board of State Charities over maternity homes and child-caring institutions.
——— Proceedings, 1917, in Indiana Bulletin of Charities and Correction, June, 1918.
Barrett, Kate Waller: The unmarried mother as a community problem, pp. 189–194.
Brief survey of European methods of care; the Maryland law forbidding separation of mother and child for six months; foundlings cared for by Florence Crittenton Home; consequent reduction in mortality rate; the protection of the child; the father; the mother; keeping mother and child together.
Minnesota. First State Conference of Child Welfare Boards with the Board of Control. Proceedings, May 9 and 10, 1919. St. Paul, Minnesota.
Hodson, William: The problem of illegitimacy, pp. 92–96.
General principles relating to care of mother, establishment of paternity, paternal responsibility, custody of child.
Missouri Conference for Social Welfare, 1917:
Mangold, George B.: The care of illegitimate children, pp. 55–57.
Inadequate legal provision for child's support by father.
Ohio State Conference of Charities and Correction, 1917, in Ohio Bulletin of Charities and Correction, June, 1918:
Murphy, J. Prentice: The unmarried mother and her child, pp. 50–54.
Extent of the problem; treatment of the mother; responsibilities of social agencies in principles of treatment; inadvisability of rigid rules and methods.
Wisconsin State Conference of Social Work, Proceedings, 1918.
Drury, Louise: Unmarried mother and her child, pp. 61–68.
Report of investigation by the Milwaukee Conference on Illegitimacy; Findings and recommendations.

PERIODICAL LITERATURE.

UNITED STATES.

American Academy of Political and Social Science, Annals, Vol. 77 (May, 1918).
  Social Work with Families:
  Murphy, J. Prentice: The foster care of neglected and dependent children,
    pp. 117–130.
    Need of careful case work with unmarried mothers by social agencies, p. 122.
  Watson, Amey Eaton: The illegitimate family, pp. 103–116.
    Outline for minimum investigation; individualization of treatment.
American Journal of Physical Anthropology:
  Lundberg, Emma O.: The illegitimate child and war conditions. Vol. I
    (July–September, 1918), pp. 339–352.
    European statistics; changes in legal status and care.
American Journal of Sociology, Vol. XVII:
  Henderson, Charles R.: Infant welfare: Methods of organization and ad-
    ministration. Series of articles—
    Italy. November, 1911, pp. 289–302.
      Institutional care and preventive work.
    France. January, 1912, pp. 458–477.
      Provision for poor mothers; history of laws.
    Germany. March, 1912, pp. 669–684.
      High mortality rate; professional guardianship by city poor relief board.
    Germany and Belgium—General Conclusions. May, 1912, pp. 783–803.
      Women supervisors in German cities; law in Belgium; summary of prin-
    ciples derived from experience.
Catholic Charities Review, The:
  Editorial. The Maryland law against abandonment of babies, Vol. I (De-
    cember, 1917), p. 303.
    Reduction in infant mortality rate in asylums as a result of this law.
  Keegan, Rev. Robert F.: The problem of illegitimacy. Vol. II (November,
    1918), pp. 266–269.
    Legislation in Norway and Minnesota; bill presented in Illinois legislature;
    economic aspect; moral problem.
Forum, The:
  Mangold, George B.: Unlawful motherhood. March, 1915, pp. 335–343.
    Prevalence in the United States; age and occupation of the mothers.
Journal of the American Institute of Criminal Law and Criminology:
  Borosini, Victor von: The problem of illegitimacy in Europe. Vol. 4 (July,
    1913), pp. 212–236.
    Comparison of birth and death rates in different countries; methods of care in
    German cities, and in France and Italy; laws of European countries.
Mental Hygiene:
  Murphy, J. Prentice: Illegitimacy and feeble-mindedness. Vol. I (October,
    1917), pp. 591–597.
    Different principles involved in treatment of mothers of normal and of defective
    mentality; separation of mother and child; State supervision.
National Humane Review, The:
  Lundberg, Emma O.: A square deal for children born out of wedlock.
    January, 1920, p. 9.
  Morgan, Eugene: Safeguarding the rights of illegitimate children. April,
    1919, pp. 66, 67.
    Proposed legal reforms for establishment of paternity and support of child.

Survey, The:

Editorial. The feeble-minded woman of childbearing age. Vol. 32 (June 6, 1914), p. 251.

Addams, Jane: Disturbing conventions. Vol. 37 (October 7, 1916), pp. 1–5.
Indications of a modified point of view regarding the traditional conventions.

Bryant, Louise Stevens: For unmarried mothers. Vol. 33 (October 24, 1914), pp. 95–96.
Recent decisions made by judge of Municipal Court in Philadelphia, for child's support by his father.

DeVilbiss, Lydia Allen, M. D.: Who is the father? Vol. 41 (March 29, 1919), pp. 923–924.
Proposed law for Kansas; recent legislation in Massachusetts, Minnesota, North Dakota, and Missouri.

Emerson, Francis V.: The place of the maternity home. Vol. 42 (August 30, 1919), pp. 772–774.
Value to unmarried mothers of training and prenatal care given by maternity homes; placement and follow-up work.

Lane, Winthrop D.: Just flickerings of life. Vol. 36 (May 6, 1916), pp. 157–162.
Baltimore Vice Commission findings regarding traffic in babies.

Murphy, J. Prentice: Mothers and — mothers. Vol. 42 (May 3, 1919), pp. 171–176.
Need of conscientious case work with the unmarried mother; flexibility of treatment; economic phase.

Ottenberg, Louis: Fatherless children of the National Capital. Vol. 33 (January 30, 1915), pp. 459, 460.
Illegitimacy statistics for 1913; necessity for stricter legislation; supervision; compulsory support of child by father.

Walsh, Elizabeth S.: Keeping mothers and babies together. Vol. 39 (November 3, 1917), p. 123.
Discussion of Maryland law; reduction in infant mortality rate.

FOREIGN.

Child, The (London):

Editorials and articles:

The illegitimate child. Vol. V (August, 1915), pp. 674–675.
The affiliation orders act, 1914.

War and vital statistics. Vol. VIII (January, 1918), pp. 209–210.
Effect of war on rate of illegitimacy.

The illegitimate child. Vol. VIII (September, 1918), pp. 573–576.
Norwegian statute, 1915.

Nota bene. Vol. IX (November, 1918), p. 80.
Origin and aims of the National Council for the Unmarried Mother and Her Child. Births in England and Wales, 1906–1918 (first half of 1918).

The unmarried mother. Vol. IX (March, 1919), pp. 283–286.
Aims of National Council for the Unmarried Mother and Her Child.

Memoranda. Vol. IX (March, 1919), pp. 269, 270.
The affiliation orders act, 1918; increased weekly sum for support of child, p. 270.

Maternity and Child Welfare. Vol. IX (April, 1919), pp. 305–307.
Circular, M. & C. W., 5, issued by Local Government Board, concerning regulations of August 9, 1918, providing support for mother and child in a home, p. 306.

Child, The (London)—Continued.

Adler, D.: The unmarried mother and her child. Vol. VIII (September, 1918), pp. 584–585.

Infant mortality rate of children of illegitimate birth in 1916; causes; remedies; economic phase; reform of the "bastardy" act and affiliation orders act.

Burns, The Rt. Hon. John: Infant life protection. Vol. II (August, 1912), pp. 915–928.

Infant mortality, a century ago, in foundling hospitals in Paris, Dublin, and London; present rate in London; p. 917.

Ewart, R. J., M. D.: The aristocracy of birth. Vol. II (November, 1911), pp. 104–109.

Relation between illegitimacy and excess of female population; infant mortality; child of poor stock; p. 108.

Leslie, R. Murray, M. D.: Infant welfare in war time. Vol. VI (October, 1915), pp. 9–17.

Rate of illegitimate births declining in England; low rate in London; p. 13.

Wakefield, Col. Charles Cheers, Bart.: The care of the unmarried mother and her child. Vol. IX (March, 1919), pp. 241–244.

Work of the National Council for the Unmarried Mother and Her Child. Act of 1918 authorizing the opening of hostels and crèches for unmarried mothers; present infant mortality rate.

Contemporary Review, The (London and New York):

Barnes, Annie E.: The unmarried mother and her child. Vol. 112 (November, 1917), pp. 556–559.

Changes in methods of provision; lack of good foster homes; new social ideas; suggested activity for proposed ministry of health.

Eugenics Review, The (London Quarterly):

Darwin, Major Leonard: Divorce and illegitimacy. Vol. IX (January 1918), pp. 296–306.

Discussion of matrimonial clauses bill; effect on illegitimacy. Discussion of Norwegian law; effect of law on inheritance.

Journal of the Royal Statistical Society (London):

Mallet, Sir Bernard: Vital statistics as affected by the war. Vol. 81 (January, 1918), pp. 1–36.

Illegitimate births in Great Britain, 1913–1916, pp. 13, 14.

Maternity and Child Welfare (London):

Special articles on "The illegitimate child":

(1) Morant, H. M.: Federation of effort. Vol. I (September, 1917), pp. 384–387.

A clearing house; specialized study; need of hostels for mothers and babies.

(2) Ellis, Louise: The child's claim. Vol. I (October, 1917), pp. 427, 428.

The right to life; the right to support; appointment of overseers.

(3) Gray, Almyra: Some suggestions for the solution of the problem. Vol. I (December, 1917), pp. 523–526.

The need for action; improvement of laws; voluntary agencies combined with State action.

(4) Cox, Adelaide: The case of the mother. Vol. I (December, 1917), pp. 526–528.

Work of the women's social department of the Salvation Army.

(5) Hartley, C. Gasquoine: The protection of the child of the unmarried mother. Vol. II (January, 1918), pp. 3–6.

A new moral attitude; mother's ability to care for child; guardianship.

Maternity and Child Welfare (London)—Continued.

Special articles on "The illegimate child"—Continued.

(6) Crane, R. Newton: The need of legal reform. Vol. II (March, 1918). pp. 83–85.

Reform, an obligation of the State; what other countries have done.

Editorials and articles:

Homes for illegitimate children. Vol. I (September, 1917) pp. 423–424.

Directory of homes.

Expectation of life of the child born out of wedlock. Vol. I (October, 1917), pp. 453–454.

Infant mortality in Hampstead, 1907–1916, and in New South Wales, 1904–1914; justice to the child; separation allowances granted unmarried wives of soldiers and sailors. A proposed welfare scheme.

Concerted action on behalf of the unmarried mother. Vol. I (November, 1917), pp. 499–501.

Meeting of Child Welfare Council, October 18, 1917; infant mortality; wards of the court; hostels for mothers and children.

Syphilis and the illegitimate child. Vol. I (November, 1917), p. 501.

Infant mortality rate from syphilis over all areas (urban and rural), 1906–1910.

Illegitimate fatherhood. Vol. I (December, 1917), pp. 554–555.

Contributions toward support of child.

The value of fatherhood. Vol. II (March, 1918), pp. 93–94.

The English law; rates, by months, of mortality among infants born out of wedlock, compared with rates for children of legitimate birth.

Adoption of children. Vol. II (April, 1918), pp. 136–137.

Western Australian statute, 1916.

The unmarried mother and her child. Circulars issued by the National Council. Vol. II (October, 1918), p. 351.

Extension of treasury grant by Local Government Board to keep mother and child together; need of combating restrictions against the unmarried mother.

National Council for the Unmarried Mother and Her Child. Vol. II (November, 1918), p. 400.

Resolutions and legal recommendations passed at quarterly meeting, October 22, 1918.

Hostels for unmarried mothers. Vol. II (December, 1918), p. 437.

Two hostels opened.

The care of the illegitimate child. Vol. III (February, 1919), pp. 58–59.

Baby week conference, July, 1919; proposed legislation.

The work of the National Council for the Unmarried Mother and Her Child. Vol. III (February, 1919), pp. 61–63.

The aims of the National Council; addresses at the Mansion House meeting, January 28, 1919. Birth rates, 1910–1918; infant mortality, 1910–1917.

Provision for the unmarried mother in Bristol; Grove House Maternity Home. Vol. III (April, 1919), p. 142.

Plans for prenatal and confinement care and for nine-months' after-care for mother and baby.

News and Coming Events. Vol. III (April, 1919), pp. 145–146.

Presentation to the Local Government Board by the National Council for the Unmarried Mother and Her Child of need of extension of provisions for care of the unmarried mother and her child.

Annotations. Recaptured ideals. Vol. III (July, 1919), pp. 244–245.

A report of discussion on unmarried mothers at the Kingsway Conference, July 3, 1919.

Annotations. Vol. III (July, 1919), pp. 246–247.

Legislation for the child of the unmarried mother; bills proposed.

Maternity and Child Welfare (London)—Continued.

Ballantyne, J. W., M. D.: Antenatal and neonatal factors in infantile mortality. Vol. II (October, 1918), pp. 333–339.

Comparison of neonatal and infantile mortality of children born in and out of wedlock in Edinburgh, 1915–1917, p. 336.

Nevinson, Margaret Wynne: Mother and child in the workhouse. Vol. II (April, 1918), pp. 113–115.

Lying-in ward; foster mothers; paternity orders; "bastardy" laws in England.

–Raimondi, R., M. D.: Four years of infant welfare work during wartime in France. Vol. II (September, 1918), pp. 302–305.

Provision for the unmarried mother by the Assistance Publique, p. 305.

Stacy, Ethel M.: Raising the status of the illegitimate child; a possible solution of the problem. Vol. II (March, 1918), p. 106.

Recommendations for guardianship and supervision.

National Health (London):

Gray, Edwin and Almyra: The law relating to unmarried mothers and illegitimate children. Vol. X (April, 1918), pp. 291–292.

Existing law in England; suggested amendments; extent of assistance given under affiliation orders act.

National Conference on Infant Welfare. "The illegitimate child." Vol. XII (September, 1919), pp. 51–52.

Recommendation for dealing with the problem of the unmarried mother and her baby, made by social workers called in special conference by committee of the Paddington School for Mothers.

National Conference on Infant Welfare. "The illegitimate child." Vol. XII (September, 1919), pp. 54–55.

Notes on discussion of the problem of the unmarried mother and her child.

National Council for the Unmarried Mother and Her Child. "Reform of the bastardy laws," by Mr. F. W. Sherwood. Vol. XII (September, 1919), pp. 65–66; (October, 1919), pp. 90–91.

Framing of bill to present to Parliament; the necessity for improved legislation; the nature of the bill.

ADDENDA.

Child Welfare in Kentucky. National Child Labor Committee, New York, 1919.

Kentucky legislation relating to illegitimacy, pp. 276–278.

Hosford, George Lewis: "The unmarried mother and child." Christian Service. Vol. 7 (January–February, 1920). Published by the Christian Service League of America, Wichita, Kansas.

Report on study of case histories of 285 children.

Racz, Alexandre: "La Croix-Rouge et les enfants illégitimes." Revue Internationale de la Croix-Rouge, 15 Novembre, 1919, pp. 1292–1295.

Society for Helping Destitute Mothers and Infants. Final Report; including a study of the records of the society of five hundred cases, and annual report for the year 1917–18. Boston, 1919.

Study of records of 500 unmarried mothers applying between January, 1914, and October, 1918.

INDEX.

France—Continued.
  Infant mortality, 28.
  Inquiry into paternity, 8, 36.
  Maternal care, payments, 47.
  Napoleonic Code, 36.
  Studies of problem, 8.
  Tours, use of, 43.
  War measures, 46, 54.
  Wards of department of public assistance, 52.
  " Wards of the nation," 54.
Frankfort on the Main :
  Births, per cent illegitimate, 14.
  Infant mortality, 31, 32.

GENERAL REFERENCES, BIBLIOGRAPHICAL MATERIAL, 85.
Georgia, birth-registration law. 19, 20.
German Empire :
  Birth rates, 11, 12.
  Births, per cent illegitimate, 13, 14.
  Cities, births and infant mortality, 14, 15, 31, 32.
  Foundlings, care, 44.
  Guardianship (*see* Public guardians).
  Infant mortality, 28, 29, 31, 32.
  Studies of problem, 8.
  Vital statistics, collection, 8, 10.

Great Britain and Ireland (*see* England and Wales ; Ireland ; Scotland).
Guardian (*see* Public guardians).
" Guardian official," Sweden, 41, 50.
Guardians' Court, Leipzig, 51.
Guardianship, 43.
  Austria-Hungary, 52.
  Berlin, 51.
  France, 43, 53, 54.
  Germany, 33, 51.
  Italy, 54.
  Minnesota, 56.
  State, 50, 52, 55.
  Sweden, 41, 50.
  Switzerland, 52.
Guatemala, births, per cent illegitimate, 18.

HANDICAPS OF ILLEGITIMACY :
  Abandonment, 7, 43, 53.
  Civil rights, deprivation, 36.
  Dangers surrounding birth, 30, 35.
  Ecclesiastical rights, deprivation, 36.
  Economic disadvantages, 36.
  Environment, 8, 28, 36, 56.
  Infant mortality, excessive, 8, 28.
  Measurement, 7.
  Moral influences, 36, 52, 53.
  Physical debility, 8, 28.
  Separation from mother, 8, 30, 43, 44, 56.
  Social stigma, 19, 20, 28, 36, 38, 47.
  Support, inadequate, 8, 39.
Health supervision :
  Austria, 44.
  Birth registration requisite, 18.
  England, 46, 53.
  Foundlings, 49.
  France, 47, 54.

Health supervision—Continued.
  Germany, 51, 52.
  Infant welfare centers, 48, 53.
  Italy, 54.
  Maternity homes and hospitals, 55.
  Minnesota, 48.
  North Carolina, 48.
Heredity, 7, 45.
Home care (*see* Boarding-out ; Foster homes ; Maternity homes).
Home for Destitute Mothers and Infants, Boston, 45.
Home visiting (*see* Supervision).
Hospital (*see* Maternity hospitals).
Hostels for mothers and infants, England, 45.

Hungary :
  Birth rates, 11, 12.
  Births, per cent illegitimate, 13, 15, 17.
  (*See also* Austria-Hungary.)

IDAHO :
  Birth-registration law, 19, 20.
  Workmen's compensation act, 38.
Illinois, birth-registration law, 19, 20.
Indiana :
  Birth rates, 21.
  Births, per cent illegitimate, 23.
  Mothers' pension law, 39.
  Workmen's compensation act, 38.
Infant care (*see* Care of child).
Infanticide, 36, 43, 44.
Infant clinics, France, 47.
Infant mortality :
  Bibliographical material, 59.
  Birth registration, 18, 19.
  Cause of death, 31, 35.
  Early infancy, 29.
  Environment, 28, 30, 35.
  Institutional, 35, 43, 44, 46, 53.
  Prevention, 9, 18, 19, 30, 32, 42, 43, 46, 48, 53.
  Significance, 8, 28, 35.
  Studies of problem, 9.
Infant mortality rates :
  Australia, 30.
  Baltimore, 35.
  Bibliographical material, 59.
  Boston, 35.
  Cities, 31–35.
  Comparison of cities with other units, 33–35.
  Denmark, 34.
  District of Columbia, 35.
  England and Wales, 29, 33, 53.
  European countries, 28.
  Germany, 31, 32.
  Minnesota, 42.
  New South Wales, 30.
  Norway, 29, 34.
  Relative differences, legitimate and illegitimate, 28, 32, 33.
  Sweden, 34.
  United States, 35.
  Victoria, 30.

U. S. DEPARTMENT OF LABOR

W. B. WILSON, Secretary

CHILDREN'S BUREAU

JULIA C. LATHROP, Chief

ILLEGITIMACY
AS A CHILD-WELFARE PROBLEM

PART 2

A STUDY OF ORIGINAL RECORDS IN THE CITY OF BOSTON AND IN THE STATE OF MASSACHUSETTS

By

EMMA O. LUNDBERG

and

KATHARINE F. LENROOT

DEPENDENT, DEFECTIVE, AND DELINQUENT CLASSES SERIES No. 10

Bureau Publication No. 75

WASHINGTON

GOVERNMENT PRINTING OFFICE

1921

CONTENTS.

TABLES.

SUMMARY OF FINDINGS.

SECTION I. THE PROBLEM IN BOSTON.

CHAPTER 1. *The Infant Born Out of Wedlock.*

SECTION II. THE PROBLEM IN THE STATE.

CHAPTER 1. *Illegitimate Births in Massachusetts.*

CHARTS.

SECTION I. THE PROBLEM IN BOSTON.

SECTION II. THE PROBLEM IN THE STATE.

MAPS.

LETTER OF TRANSMITTAL.

U. S. Department of Labor,
Children's Bureau,
Washington, March 18, 1920.

Sir: I transmit herewith the second of two studies on illegitimacy as a child-welfare problem. The previous report presented general information in regard to the extent and significance of the problem in this and other countries. The present report is the result of an intensive study of the histories of children born out of wedlock in a large eastern city and of children under care of social agencies and institutions in that city and in the State whose metropolis it is. The information was gained entirely from public records and from the records of social agencies, and the study is of significance mainly as it throws light upon the relationship between birth out of wedlock and the problems of infant mortality, dependency, neglected childhood, and juvenile delinquency.

It is hoped that this report will help to call attention to the needs of children born out of wedlock and will be of assistance to those endeavoring through legislative action or through work with individual children to mitigate in some measure the hardship of their lot.

The study was made under the direction of Emma O. Lundberg, director of the social service division of the bureau. Katharine F. Lenroot was in charge of assembling and analyzing the data and collaborated with Miss Lundberg in writing the report. Evelina Belden had charge of the field work, assisted in the preparation of the material, and wrote parts of two chapters.

Respectfully submitted.

Julia C. Lathrop, *Chief.*

Hon. W. B. Wilson,
Secretary of Labor.

182299°—21——2

17

ILLEGITIMACY AS A CHILD-WELFARE PROBLEM.

PART 2.

STATEMENT OF PROBLEM AND GENERAL CONCLUSIONS.

PURPOSE OF STUDY.

The importance of illegitimacy as a child-welfare problem has been pointed out in a previous report which dealt with the prevalence and significance of birth out of wedlock, the child's legal status, and the State's responsibility for care and protection.[1] It was shown that at least 32,000 white children are born out of wedlock in the United States each year.[2] Except for four cities it was impossible to secure information in regard to infant mortality among children born out of wedlock in the United States. In three of these cities statistics indicated that the infant mortality rate was at least three times as high among children of illegitimate birth as among other children. European figures showed infant mortality rates among children born out of wedlock almost twice as high as those found among children of legitimate birth.

The previous report also called attention to the fact that in this country the care of children born out of wedlock has been assumed as a part of the general provision for children in need of special care. "Social agencies," the report states, "have become more and more conscious of the large proportion of their work that may be attributed to illegitimacy. They have begun to question whether society has not a peculiar responsibility toward these children who from birth are deprived of normal home life."[3] A multitude of problems are involved in the protection of these children, and knowledge of

---

[1] U. S. Children's Bureau : Illegitimacy as a Child-Welfare Problem, Part 1, by Emma O. Lundberg and Katharine F. Lenroot. Dependent, Defective, and Delinquent Classes Series No. 9, Bureau Publication No. 66. Washington, 1920.

[2] Insufficient data made it impossible to estimate the number of Negro births.

[3] Illegitimacy as a Child-Welfare Problem, Pt. 1, p. 56. See note 1.

19

their histories and the conditions under which they live is essential to constructive work for their welfare.

This study is an attempt to measure the prevalence of illegitimacy in the territory covered, the hazard to life and health, the handicap to the child's welfare which birth out of wedlock constitutes, and the extent to which illegitimacy contributes to the problems of dependency, neglected childhood, and juvenile delinquency.

FIELD AND METHOD OF INQUIRY.

Scope of investigation.

For the purposes of this study the term "child born out of wed-lock" includes any child born to parents who had not been legally married previous to his birth. The Massachusetts law does not recognize the so-called common-law marriage and, therefore, children are included whose parents were living as married, no ceremony having been performed. Children are also included whose parents had been illegally married, the marriage having been void because one or the other had a legal spouse living, or because the ceremony was not performed by a person authorized under the law.

The report is divided into two sections—The Problem in Boston and The Problem in the State. The first section includes a study of infants born out of wedlock in Boston during one year, an analysis of children of illegitimate birth under care of social agencies, and a summary of the Massachusetts law for the support of children born out of wedlock together with a study of the administration of the law in the Boston courts. The second section deals with the number and distribution of births out of wedlock in Massachusetts, children of illegitimate birth under supervision of the State board of charity, adoption cases involving children born out of wedlock, children born out of wedlock who were under the care of State institutions for delinquents and of State institutions for the feeble-minded, and a comparison of the problem in certain sections of the State. The study was based on material secured from public records and from the records of social agencies.

The city of Boston and the State of Massachusetts were selected for the inquiry for the following reasons:

First. The completeness of the registration of births and deaths. Massachusetts was one of the 10 States included in the United States birth-registration area when established in 1915 and one of the 24 included in the death-registration area in 1914.[1] These areas, established by the United States Bureau of the Census, comprise territory in which registration is found to be at least 90 per cent complete

Second. The high degree of development of organized social effort, both public and private, for dealing with problems of child dependency, the awareness of social agencies of the importance of illegitimacy as a child welfare problem, and the comparative com-

---

[1] The District of Columbia, also, was included in these areas.

21

pleteness of their records. The first conference on illegitimacy in this country was established in Boston in 1912, and was composed of representatives of social agencies who felt the need of thoroughgoing discussion of the problems daily met with in their case work. The State has developed a system of caring for children dependent upon the public for support, which is more centralized and on a larger scale than in any other State. The records of the State board of charity, as well as of other agencies, public and private, furnish a mass of very valuable social information.

Third. The activities of the State are to a large extent centralized in Boston, making records easily available. Moreover, Boston is a center of social effort for the State as a whole and, to a lesser degree, for other New England States.

General characteristics of the State.

Massachusetts, in 1910, ranked sixth among the States in population and second in density of population.[2] In 1914 the estimated population of the State was 3,643,863.[3]

The State is divided into 14 counties. Five are entirely inland— Berkshire, Franklin, Hampshire, Hampden, and Worcester. Berkshire and parts of Hampshire and Hampden Counties are to a considerable extent mountainous. Worcester County is the central county of the State and contains the second largest city—Worcester. Six counties border on the sea—Essex, Middlesex, Suffolk, Norfolk, Plymouth, and Bristol. These counties comprise the chief industrial and commercial sections of the State, with Boston as the center. Almost the whole of Suffolk County is included in the city of Boston. Of the three southernmost counties, Barnstable is a peninsula and Dukes and Nantucket are islands. In these counties the population is sparse and the main industries are fishing and cranberry growing.

Twelve cities in the State have 50,000 or more inhabitants, five having populations of 100,000 or more. In 1910 three-fourths of the population of the State lived in cities and towns having a population of over 10,000.[4]

Boston is not only the capital and metropolis of the State but also the commercial center of New England. Its population of 670,585 in 1910 was estimated to have increased to 736,461 in

---

[2] U. S. Bureau of the Census: Statistical Atlas of the United States. Washington, 1914. P. 24.

[3] Estimated as for July 1, 1914, on the basis of the population, Apr. 15, 1910, as given by the U. S. Census, and the population, Apr. 1, 1915, as given by the Massachusetts State census, Seventy-third Annual Report on Births, Marriages, and Deaths for the Year 1914. Boston, 1915. P. 8.

[4] Thirteenth Census of the United States, 1910: Vol. II, Population, p. 855; Vol. IX, Manufactures, p. 489.

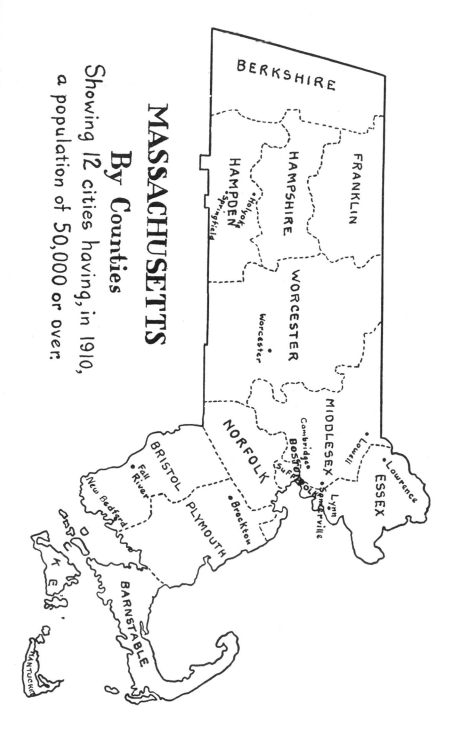

MASSACHUSETTS
By Counties

Showing 12 cities having, in 1910,
a population of 50,000 or over.

BERKSHIRE

FRANKLIN

HAMPSHIRE

HAMPDEN

Holyoke
Springfield

WORCESTER

Worcester

MIDDLESEX

Lowell

Lawrence

ESSEX

Lynn

Cambridge
BOSTON
Suffolk
Somerville

NORFOLK

BRISTOL

Fall River

New Bedford

PLYMOUTH

Brockton

BARNSTABLE

NANTUCKET

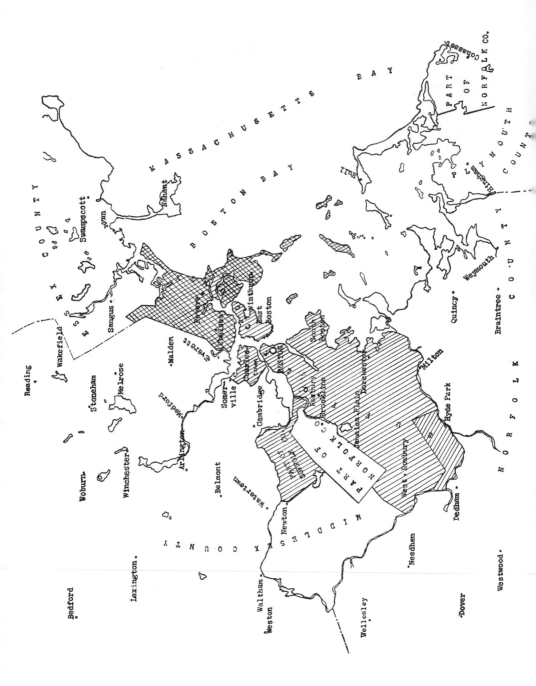

Suffolk Co., City of
Boston

Suffolk Co., outside
Boston

(Hyde Park Township was
annexed to Suffolk County and
to Boston in 1911.)

METROPOLITAN DISTRICT

Arlington	Nahant
Belmont	Needham
Boston	Newton
Braintree	Quincy
Brookline	Reading
Cambridge	Revere
Canton	Saugus
Chelsea	Somerville
Cohasset	Stoneham
Dedham	Swampscott
Dover	Wakefield
Everett	Waltham
Hingham	Watertown
Hull	Wellesley
Lexington	Weston
Lynn	Westwood
Malden	Weymouth
Medford	Winchester
Melrose	Winthrop
Milton	Woburn

1914.[5] A number of neighboring towns and cities are to a considerable ,degree suburban to Boston. Thirty-nine of these towns and cities, together with Boston, belong either to the Metropolitan Water District or to the Metropolitan Parks District.[6] The "metropolitan district" subsequently referred to in this report comprises the cities and towns included in one or both of the metropolitan districts named above. The population of this metropolitan district was 1,429,247 in 1910, and was estimated to be 1,569,171 in 1914.

In 1910, 32.8 per cent of the population of the State were native whites of native parentage; 34.8 per cent were native whites of foreign or mixed parentage; 31.2 per cent were foreign-born white; 1.1 per cent were Negroes, and 0.1 per cent were Chinese. Of the foreign-born white population, 28.1 per cent were born in Canada; 21.2 per cent in Ireland; 11.2 per cent in Russia; and 39.5 per cent in other countries.[7]

In Boston, 23.5 per cent of the population were, in 1910, native whites of native parentage; 38.3 per cent native whites of foreign or mixed parentage, 35.9 per cent foreign-born whites; and 2 per cent, Negroes. Of the foreign-born-white population, 20.9 per cent were born in Canada; 27.4 per cent in Ireland; 17.4 per cent in Russia; 13 per cent in Italy; and 21.3 per cent in other countries.[8]

The female population of Massachusetts between the ages of 15 and 44 years, inclusive, was 871,230 in 1910. Of this population, 47.1 per cent were single, 49.8 per cent were married, and 3.1 per cent were widowed or divorced. The total number of single, widowed, and divorced women of the ages specified was 437,040.[9]

In Boston, the total female population between the ages of 15 and 44 years numbered 181,823 in 1910. The percentage of single women was 49—somewhat higher than for the State as a whole. Married women comprised 47 per cent of the Boston women 15 to 44 years of age, and widowed or divorced women 4 per cent. The total number of single, widowed, and divorced women between the ages of 15 and 44 years, inclusive, was 96,378.[10]

---

[5] Estimated as for July 1, 1914, on the basis of the population, Apr. 15, 1910, as given by the U. S. Census, and the population, Apr. 1, 1915, as given by the Massachusetts State census, Seventy-third Annual Report on Births, Marriages, and Deaths for the Year 1914. Boston, 1915. P. 8.

[6] The Commonwealth of Massachusetts ; 1915. Assessments for Interest, Sinking Funds, Serial Bonds, and Maintenance of the Metropolitan Districts. Boston, 1915. Pp. 7, 14-18. In 1919, as a part of the general reorganization of the executive and administrative functions of the Commonwealth, the metropolitan park commission and the metropolitan water and sewerage board were abolished and their functions transferred to the metropolitan district commission. Acts 1919, ch. 350, sec. 123.

[7] Thirteenth Census of the United States, 1910 : Vol. II, Population, pp. 863–865.

[8] Ibid., pp. 880, 868.

[9] Ibid., p. 867.

[10] Ibid., p. 871.

The total population under 20 years of age in the State of Massachusetts in 1910 was 1,205,253. In Boston, the population under the age of 20 was 115,500.[11]

Massachusetts is primarily a manufacturing State. In 1909, 17.4 per cent of the total population were wage earners employed in manufactures. Of these wage earners, 3.5 per cent were children under 16 years of age, and 29.6 per cent were women 16 years of age and over.[12] Boston, in 1909, ranked eighth among the cities of the United States in value of manufactured products. Of the wage earners in the State, 11.9 per cent were in Boston.[13]

Historical development of the care of dependent, delinquent, and defective children in Massachusetts.

The development of State provision.—The tendency toward State provision for dependent classes has been very marked in Massachusetts. The principal reason for this development lies in the settlement laws. Legal settlement, or residence for purpose of poor relief, is difficult to acquire. In severity of requirements for legal settlement Massachusetts is equaled by only a few States.[14]

The necessity for aid to persons in distress early confronted the colonists of Plymouth and Massachusetts Bay, and the question immediately arose as to who was entitled to receive assistance. During the seventeenth and the greater part of the eigtheenth century the acquirement of settlement was a matter of no great difficulty, a few months' residence constituting a sufficient claim. The town was the unit of local government; and since the rural area surrounding a settlement was included in the town, everyone living in the Commonwealth belonged in some town. Poor relief was a function of the town, not of the county, except that in cases of dispute between towns the county court was empowered to hear and determine complaints and to defray from the county treasury the expense of maintaining persons whose settlement could not be determined. Until 1675 no pauper had received assistance from the general treasury of the Commonwealth. In 1675 the colony of Massachusetts Bay granted aid to refugees from King Philip's War, and this was later regarded as a precedent for the granting of aid to those who could not claim settlement in any town or county.[15]

With the increase of immigration and changing industrial and social conditions, Massachusetts found it necessary to revise her settlement laws. A somewhat stringent law had been passed in 1766,

---

[11] Thirteenth Census of the United States, 1910: Vol. II, Population, pp. 866, 869.
[12] Ibid., Vol. IX, Manufactures, pp. 489–492, 497.
[13] Ibid., p. 500.
[14] U. S. Bureau of the Census: Summary of State Laws Relating to the Dependent Classes, 1913. Washington, 1914. Pp. 322–328.
[15] Cummings, John: "Poor Laws of Massachusetts and New York." Publications of the American Economic Association, Vol. X (July, 1895), pp. 497–502.

and the revision of 1794, instead of making the acquirement of settlement easier, made it a matter of very great difficulty. The present law is based on the law of 1794,[16] though the severity of its provisions have been somewhat modified. During most of the nineteenth century the law provided that a settlement once gained was not defeated by the subsequent acquirement of a settlement outside the Commonwealth. A person removing outside the Commonwealth always retained his settlement and passed it on to his children and his children's children. As a consequence, needy persons outside the State who could claim settlement, even through a remote ancestor, were often sent to Massachusetts for relief.[17]

The present law provides that five consecutive years' residence in a city or town is necessary to acquire a settlement. Settlement can not be acquired or in process of acquirement while a person is receiving relief as a pauper from the State or from a city or town unless the cost thereof is repaid within two years after its receipt. A married woman acquires the settlement of her husband if he has any within the State; otherwise she retains her own. Children of legitimate birth have the settlement of their father if he has any within the State; otherwise they have the settlement of their mother if she has any, and if the father dies they have the settlement of their mother. Children of illegitimate birth have the settlement of their mother if she has any within the Commonwealth. Five consecutive years' absence from a town or city terminates settlement therein. Residence in a public institution within the Commonwealth is not to be counted in computing the time either for acquiring or losing a settlement, except as included above in connection with relief as a pauper and failure to make reimbursement.[18]

With the increasing severity of settlement laws many persons in need of relief could not claim it from the city or town in which they were living. In 1789 a law was passed providing for the reimbursement by the State of cities and towns for expenses incurred in the care of persons without settlement.[19] The administration of relief was left in the hands of the towns, which drew heavily upon the treasury of the Commonwealth. In 1851 the State board of inspectors in regard to alien passengers and State paupers was created. One of its chief duties was the examination of claims brought against the Commonwealth by towns for the support of State paupers.[20] In 1863 the legislature created a more effective central

---

[16] Acts 1794 ch. 34.

[17] Cummings, John: "Poor Laws of Massachusetts and New York." Publications of the American Economic Association, Vol. X (July, 1895), pp. 509–512.

[18] R. L. 1902 ch. 80; Acts 1911 ch. 669, 1913 ch. 266, 1914 ch. 323.

[19] Cummings, John: "Poor Laws of Massachusetts and New York." Publications of the American Economic Association, Vol. X (July, 1895), p. 513.—Acts 1789 ch. 30.

[20] Ibid., p. 517.—Acts 1851 ch. 342.

board—the board of State charities.[21] This board was directed to "investigate and supervise the whole system of public and correctional institutions of the Commonwealth." In 1879 the State board of health, the board of State charities, and the subordinate boards of trustees and inspectors of the several State institutions were abolished and in their place was created a consolidated board of health, lunacy, and charity.[22] In 1886 a separate board of health was established.[23] In 1898 the State board of lunacy and charity was reorganized into two boards, the State board of insanity and the State board of charity.[24] In 1908 a division of State adult poor and a division of State minor wards were established within the State board of charity.[25]

By legislative act of 1919 the executive and administrative functions of the Commonwealth have been reorganized into 20 departments. The department of public welfare takes over the functions of the State board of charity, and has three divisions—aid and relief, child guardianship, and juvenile training. The division of aid and relief includes the functions of the division of State adult poor of the State board of charity, and the division of child guardianship includes the functions of the division of State minor wards. The division of juvenile training consists of the board of trustees of the Massachusetts Training Schools—institutions for juvenile delinquents.[26]

Care of dependent children.—In colonial days the selectmen of the town and later a special board of overseers of the poor provided for dependent children by binding them out as apprentices. Stubborn children were committed to county houses of correction. Later, town workhouses were established to which indigent persons were committed.[27]

By 1832 there were three institutions owned and maintained by the State—a prison, a hospital, and an insane asylum. Several private hospitals and asylums received State aid. In 1847 the first State reformatory for juveniles in this country was established in Massachusetts.[28] In 1848 a State appropriation was made for the education of a limited number of feeble-minded children,[29] and three years later the first State institution in America for the care of this class of children was established.[30] In 1854 the establishment of the

---

[21] Acts 1863 ch. 240.

[22] Acts 1879 ch. 291.

[23] Acts 1886 ch. 101.

[24] Acts 1898 ch. 433.

[25] R. L. 1902 ch. 84 sec. 2 : Acts 1908 ch. 598.

[26] Acts 1919 ch. 350 secs. 87–95.

[27] Cummings, John : "Poor Laws of Massachusetts and New York." Publications of the American Economic Association, Vol. X (July, 1895), pp. 503–505.

[28] Acts 1847 ch. 165.

[29] Resolves 1848 ch. 65.

[30] Resolves 1851 ch. 44.

first separate reformatory for girls in the United States was authorized by law.[31]   Massachusetts was beginning to classify children in
need of public support, and separate provision for the delinquent
and the feeble-minded came before the needs of the destitute and
neglected were recognized.

One of the first acts of the board of State charities was to transfer
children from two of the State almshouses to the third almshouse at
Monson.   These State almshouses had been established in 1852,[32]
and half their inmates were children.   In 1866 the institution at
Monson was designated the State Primary School for Dependent and
Neglected Children, though it was also used as an almshouse until
1872.[33]   This school was the first State institution for dependent
children in the country.   Children were kept in the institution for
longer or shorter periods and were then placed out in families, free
of expense to the State.   Children under 3 years of age were not admitted.

From the first, the board of State charities had recommended care
of children outside institutions.   It engaged an agent to supervise
children placed out from State institutions, and three years later—
in 1869—a State visiting agency was established, reporting to the
board.[34]   The duties of this agency were: To visit all children placed
out from State institutions; to visit and report upon the homes of
applicants for children; to attend trials of juvenile offenders, investigate the circumstances, and advise whether the children should be
committed to a reform school or to the custody of the board of State
charities, to be placed by it with their parents or in other families
or temporarily in the State primary school.   Children could be transferred from the custody of the board to the reform schools.   By
these means, flexibility in dealing with individual children and treatment according to their development and needs were made possible.

Meanwhile, in 1867, the Massachusetts Infant Asylum was incorporated, where public officials and agents could place infants.   The
institution was supported by public funds and private subscriptions,
and it inaugurated a system of boarding out.   In 1880 the boarding
out of children from the State primary school was authorized.[35]
The year previous the legislature instructed overseers of the poor to
place children over 4 years of age in respectable families, and declared it to be unlawful to detain such children in almshouses if possible to care for them in families without inordinate expense.[36]   The

---

[31] Resolves 1854 ch. 52.
[32] Acts 1852 ch. 275.
[33] Acts 1866 ch. 209, 1872 ch. 45.
[34] Acts 1869 ch. 453.
[35] Acts 1880 ch. 208.
[36] Acts 1879 ch. 103.

State visiting agency was abolished [37] and its duties were assigned to the State board, which was given general supervision over all the State charitable institutions, the hospitals for the insane, and the reform schools. In 1882 provision was made for the commitment of neglected children to the custody of the State board,[38] and the board was authorized to place children in families directly without passing them through the State primary school. From time to time laws were enacted extending the classes of children committed to the board's custody. With the development of the boarding-out and placing-out systems it was found possible to decrease the numbers of children in the primary school, and in 1895 this institution was closed.[39] Since that time the State has cared for its dependent and neglected children wholly in private families. In 1900 the State board of charity was authorized to provide for dependent children, without regard to settlement, at the request of parents, guardians, or overseers of the poor.[40]

The city of Boston began a system of special provision for destitute and neglected children in 1877. Previous to that time they had been cared for at the house of industry (city almshouse and workhouse). In that year the boys were removed to the Roxbury almshouse, which became the Marcella Street Children's Home. In 1881 the girls were removed to a building near this home, which was thereafter included as part of the Marcella Street institution. In 1897 the children were placed under a separate board of trustees. The city began in 1889 to board out the younger children, especially the infants, and agents were employed for finding free homes. Nine years later the Marcella Street home was abandoned altogether, all the children being placed out in families.[41]

In the other cities and towns of Massachusetts, dependent children are under the care of the overseers of the poor and are either kept in almshouses, placed in boarding or free homes, or boarded in institutions. A child can not legally be kept in an almshouse longer than two months unless he is under 2 years of age, under 3 years of age if with his mother, or " unless he is a State pauper, an idiot, or otherwise so defective in body or mind as to make his retention in an almshouse desirable." [42] Children supported by cities and towns must be visited at least once a year by agents of the State board of charity. Overseers of the poor turn over large numbers of their cases to the care of the State board, reimbursing the State for the expense involved.

[37] Acts 1879 ch. 291.
[38] Acts 1882 ch. 181.
[39] Acts 1895 ch. 428.
[40] R. L. 1902 ch. 83 sec. 36 ; Acts 1900 ch. 397.
[41] Folks, Homer : The Care of Destitute, Neglected and Delinquent Children. New York, 1911. Pp. 154–156.
[42] R. L. 1902 ch. 81 secs. 5–7 ; Acts, 1905 ch. 303, 1913 ch. 112.

The care of delinquent children.—The development of State provision for delinquent children has already been touched upon. In 1847 the Lyman School for Boys was established, to which boys under 16 years of age could be committed and retained until the age of 21.[43] The present law provides for the commitment of boys under 15 to this institution. In 1854 the establishment of the Industrial School for Girls was authorized, to which girls over 7 and under 16 could be committed and retained until 18.[44] Subsequent changes in the age limits have brought the law to its present form, in which girls under 17 may be committed and retained until 21. In 1869 the State visiting agency began the practice of having a representative at all trials of juveniles and advising as to what disposition should be made. Later, representatives of the State board were present at the trials. In 1870 jurisdiction was vested in the probate courts to try all children under 16 years of age for all offenses except those punishable by imprisonment for life.[45] Four years later a law was passed providing that :[46] " Police, district, and municipal courts shall try juvenile offenders separate and apart from the trial of other criminal cases at suitable times which shall be designated therefor by said courts and shall be called the session for juvenile offenders for which a separate docket and record shall be kept." This was the forerunner of modern juvenile court legislation. In 1879 a single board, known as the trustees of the State primary and reform schools, was given charge of the institutions for delinquent children and of the State primary school.[47] The girls' parole department was established in 1900 in connection with the Industrial School for Girls, and a similar department for boys had been created previously. The Industrial School for Boys was established in 1908,[48] receiving boys between the ages of 15 and 17 years, inclusive. Subsequently the board of trustees, created in 1879, and later changed to the trustees of the Lyman and Industrial Schools, was combined with the trustees of the new Industrial School for Boys to form the trustees of the Massachusetts Training Schools.[49] This board constitutes the division of juvenile training of the new department of public welfare, established by legislative act of 1919.

The Boston House of Reformation for Juvenile Offenders was the second juvenile reformatory in the United States and was established

[43] Acts 1847 ch. 165.
[44] Resolves 1854 ch. 52 ; Acts 1855 ch. 442.
[45] Acts 1870 ch. 359 sec. 7.
[46] Acts 1874 ch. 258 sec. 3.
[47] Acts 1879 ch. 291 sec. 8.
[48] Acts 1908 ch. 639.
[49] Acts 1911 ch. 566.

in 1826.[50] In 1860 the girls were removed to a separate building, and in 1889 the department for girls was closed and the girls were sent to the State industrial school. In 1877 the parental (or truant) school was differentiated from the house of reformation. Later the house of reformation became the Suffolk School for Boys of the City of Boston. During 1914 the parental school was closed.[51]

An exception to the general tendency toward State provision is the existence of five county training schools, maintained by seven counties, to which juvenile offenders may be committed. The Boston parental school, closed in 1914, was also classified as a county training school. The State board of charity in its annual report for 1914 pointed out that this system was " not in accord with the best accepted methods in the care and protection of children, in spite of the efforts of loyal and efficient superintendents to adapt it to their problem." [52]

Provision for the feeble-minded.—The first State institution in the country for the care of the feeble-minded, established in Massachusetts in 1851,[53] was called the Massachusetts School for Idiotic and Feeble-Minded Youth. Later the name was changed to the Massachusetts School for the Feeble-Minded.[54] In 1898 a farm was purchased to be used in connection with the school for the feeble-minded for the employment of adults. This farm became the present Templeton Colony. In 1907 a second State institution for the feeble-minded was established, and in 1915 an appropriation was made for a third institution not yet completed.

In the development of care for the dependent, delinquent, and defective, Massachusetts has taken the lead among American States. Most significant in this development have been the increasing differentiation and classification of those requiring care, together with the tendency toward centralization under State control of provision for these classes, and the use of the family home instead of the institution as a means of providing for dependent, neglected, and certain classes of delinquent children.

Present methods of care.—At the time this study was made the State of Massachusetts provided for dependent and neglected children through the division of State minor wards of the State board of charity, placing them in boarding or free homes; for juvenile delinquents through the division of State minor wards and the three State training schools with their parole departments; and for mentally defective children in the two State institutions for the

---

[50] Acts 1826 ch. 182.
[51] Acts 1914 ch. 738.
[52] Thirty-sixth Annual Report of the State Board of Charity of Massachusetts for the Year Ending November 30, 1914. Boston, 1915. Part I, p. 95.
[53] Resolves 1851 ch. 44.
[54] Acts 1883 ch. 239.

feeblé-minded. However, the accommodations for the care of the mentally defective were far from adequate, and many remained in the community, often constituting serious problems to public and private agencies designed for the care of other classes. In addition to providing for the classes above mentioned, the State also maintained or partly supported institutions for blind, crippled and deformed, and epileptic children, State sanatoria for the tuberculous, and State hospitals for the insane.

The reorganization act of 1919, by which the executive and administrative functions of the Commonwealth of Massachusetts were organized into 20 departments, established two departments of interest in connection with this study—the department of public welfare and the department of mental diseases. The department of public welfare is the successor to the State board of charity and has three divisions—the division of aid and relief, which performs the functions of the former division of State adult poor; the division of child guardianship, which takes over the work of the division of State minor wards; and the division of juvenile training, which consists of the board of trustees of the Massachusetts Training Schools as organized prior to the passage of the act. The department of mental diseases consists of the Massachusetts Commission on Mental Diseases as organized under an act passed in 1916. This commission was the successor to the Massachusetts State Board of Insanity, under whose supervision were the State hospitals for the insane and the State institutions for the feeble-minded.[55]

Alongside the public agencies many private agencies exist for the care and protection of children and are performing valuable functions, both as a stimulus to the public agencies and as a means of working out advanced methods of dealing with special types of problems. The private agencies have utilized the family-home system of caring for their wards to almost as great an extent as the State, placing the children under supervision in boarding or free homes. All private charitable corporations must report to the State board of charity, which also exercises supervision over children under 2 years of age placed in family homes. More detailed descriptions of the work of public and private agencies in Boston and in the State of Massachusetts are given in later sections of this report.

Sources of information and method of analysis.

In the early days of philanthropic effort it was deemed neither necessary nor desirable to keep full records of the circumstances of the individual or family receiving assistance and of the amount and

---

[55] Acts 1919 ch. 350 secs. 79–81, 87–95.

kind of work done in their behalf. Even now some agencies and institutions have not progressed beyond this stage. But with the realization of the need for adequate social information as prerequisite to efficient treatment of the problems presented, social agencies have come to see the value of the systematic recording of the histories of their cases. There is still much to be desired in the way of completeness of information obtained and methods of entering social data. It is generally agreed that the purpose of record keeping is to help the agency to perform its functions with regard to the individuals and families under its care, and to preserve the data obtained in the course of its work for analysis and interpretation which will lead to general measures for social improvement. It is this latter function of record keeping with which this report is mainly concerned. The prime motive in this study was the belief that a wealth of material lies buried in the records of social agencies and institutions which, with little effort, can be made available, and that the subject of illegitimacy is a field in which this method of research is particularly desirable because of the difficulties involved in getting first-hand information from the individuals concerned.

That there are serious difficulties involved in a study based on existing records of agencies and institutions is acknowledged. The greatest obstacle is the lack of completeness and uniformity in case records. One of the reasons for the selection of the city of Boston and the State of Massachusetts for the field of this inquiry was the comparative excellence of the records of social agencies. But the high standards of record keeping maintained by some agencies were not common to all, nor was there general agreement as to the minimum information which should be obtained in the preliminary investigations or as to the method of measuring progress and results obtained after the cases had been definitely assumed. The statistical analyses presented in this study are therefore qualified by the failure to obtain reports as to every item for all the cases included, and the possibility that the cases for which reports were obtained were not entirely representative of the whole group.

It must also be borne in mind that, except for those portions dealing with vital statistics, this study is not representative of the whole problem involved in illegitimate birth, but only of that portion of the problem—the most serious from the point of view of the child and also from that of the burden to the community—with which social agencies come in contact. But it is believed that the data here presented are sufficiently representative to form a basis for general conclusions of value and to furnish a foundation for further studies of special phases of the problem.

The advantages of a study based on existing records are particularly great in a consideration of illegitimacy. They may be summarized as follows:

1. It is not necessary to repeat the delicate and often painful interviews which have already been held by representatives of the agencies and institutions, who make the investigations only for the sake of the service they can render the family.

2. Much information in regard to family history can not be obtained by means of a visit to the family alone. Such data have in many instances been secured by social agencies through many interviews and consultations.

3. Saving of time and expense in the field work required for the investigation.

The study covered the year 1914. This was the last year during which normal conditions prevailed, the succeeding years bringing changes due to the war—the cessation of immigration, for instance.

The material for the inquiry was secured from records of births and deaths, from court records, and from records of public and private agencies and institutions—State and city. Vital statistics gave the data for the first part of the chapter on the infant born out of wedlock, and the chapter on illegitimate births in Massachusetts. The former chapter centers in infants born out of wedlock in Boston during the year 1914, the vital statistics data being supplemented by information secured from the records of social agencies and from court records. The aim was to determine the illegitimate birth rate, the infant mortality among children born out of wedlock as compared with that among children of legitimate birth, the proportion of infants of illegitimate birth coming to the attention of social agencies during the first year of life, and something of the histories of those infants who were more or less dependent upon public or private agencies.

The chapter entitled " Children of Illegitimate Birth under the Care of Social Agencies "—the second chapter of Section I, The Problem in Boston—was based on material obtained from 37 public and private agencies and institutions. These agencies included the State child-caring agency; the public and private child-caring and child-protective agencies of Boston; the State and city infirmaries; maternity homes, health agencies, and hospitals in Boston; the Boston legal aid society; the Boston juvenile court; two State institutions for juvenile delinquents and the reformatory for women; the State institutions for the feeble-minded; and a State hospital, located in Boston, for the first care and observation of mental patients. The State agencies and institutions were included in this chapter only so far as they cared for children whose residence was

Boston at the time of application or commitment. Practically all the social agencies and institutions in Boston whose work touched the problem of illegitimacy were included, except the agencies for family relief and rehabilitation—such as the associated charities and the overseers of the poor—whose work dealt only incidentally with children born out of wedlock. The aim of this part of the study was to determine the proportion the care of children born out of wedlock bore to the total work of the agencies studied, and to secure data in regard to these children which would show how long they had been cared for, why they had come to the attention of the agencies, their circumstances at the time of application for care, where they were living at the end of the period, their physical and mental condition and characteristics, and something of the histories of the mothers and their families and of the fathers. The age limit for inclusion was 21 years.

The third chapter of the analysis of the problem in Boston is a summary of the Massachusetts law for the support of children born out of wedlock and of the administration of the law in the Boston courts. The latter was based on a study of all court cases in Boston initiated in 1914 under the act of 1913, the material having been obtained from court and probation records.

Section II, The Problem in the State, deals principally with children of illegitimate birth under the care of State institutions and agencies caring for dependent, neglected, delinquent, and defective children. The points covered are very similar to those included in the chapter of the Boston section on children under the care of social agencies. The chapter on children under the care of the State board of charity includes studies of children cared for by the division of State minor wards during the year, of infants reported to the board as being cared for apart from their relatives, and of mothers and children at the State infirmary given care by the social service committee of the board. Adoption records of the probate courts of four counties furnished the material for the chapter on the adoption of children born out of wedlock. Infant mortality studies made by the children's bureau in two Massachusetts cities,[56] and a brief field survey of a seacoast rural section made possible the comparative material in the last chapter of the report. Detailed descriptions of the methods used in analyzing and presenting the data are given in each section.

In order to call attention to the most significant findings of the study and to bring together from the different sections of the report the facts that bear on the same topics, a somewhat detailed summary of the whole report is presented as a part of this introductory chapter.

---

[56] Brockton and New Bedford.

Prevalence of birth out of wedlock.

The information secured in this study indicates that in the city of Boston about 1 in every 23 live births is illegitimate, and that for the whole State the proportion is about 1 in 44. During the five years 1910 to 1914 the number of live births registered as illegitimate in Boston ranged from 670 to 867, representing from 3.8 per cent to 4.6 per cent of the total live births in each year; the number of live births registered as illegitimate per 1,000 single, widowed, and divorced women 15 to 44 years of age ranged from 6.9 to 8.7. In the State as a whole in 1914 the number of births registered as illegitimate was 2,108, or 2.3 per cent of the total live births. The rate per 1,000 single, widowed, and divorced women of childbearing age in the State was 4.5. The higher rate for Boston is accounted for largely by the fact that a considerable number of nonresident mothers come to the metropolis to secure maternity care. More than two-fifths of the mothers of infants born in Boston resided elsewhere. Comparison of statistics for communities of various populations in the State indicated that the problem in rural areas and small towns is practically as great as in all cities save the largest.

The year 1914 was selected for intensive study. During this year there were in Boston 752 live births registered as illegitimate and 95 others registered as legitimate, but, as a result of checking through agency and court records, found to be illegitimate. Hence, the total number known to be illegitimate was 847, or 4.4 per cent of all live births in the city, and since there were seven pairs of twins the number of mothers was 840.

Number of children born out of wedlock included in the study.

In addition to the 847 infants born out of wedlock in Boston during the year 1914,[1] the numbers of children dealt with in the various parts of the inquiry are as stated below.

Children under care of Boston agencies.—In this summary the term " children under care of Boston agencies " must be understood to refer to children under care of Boston public and private agencies, and also to children under care of State agencies whose residence was

---

[1] Information analyzed in Sec. I, ch. 1.

Boston at the time of application or commitment. Included in this group are the children who received temporary or prolonged care from Boston agencies whose work included the care of children born out of wedlock, and children under the temporary or prolonged care of the State board of charity or of State institutions for delinquents or mental defectives, if Boston was their residence at the time of application for care or at commitment. During the year 1914 a total of 2,863 children born out of wedlock were under the care of Boston agencies as defined above. The records of 2,178 of these children contained more or less complete social information, and a large part of the analysis relates to them. However, in certain instances the data relate to larger or smaller numbers, according to the varying degrees of completeness of information.

Children under care of the division of State minor wards.—A total of 7,526 children were under the temporary or prolonged care of the division of State minor wards of the Massachusetts State Board of Charity during the year covered by the study, of whom 1,721 were of illegitimate birth. The greater part of chapter 2, Section II, is concerned with their histories. In addition, a comparative study was made of the histories of 1,717 children of legitimate birth and 606 children of illegitimate birth under care of the division during the year whose case records were numbered from 1 to 2000 [2]—a method of selection which may fairly be assumed to give unbiased results.

Children under care of State institutions for delinquents.—A total of 102 children under 21 years of age known to have been born out of wedlock were, during the year covered by the study, under the care of the three State training schools and their parole departments and of the reformatory for women. These children had been committed as delinquents. In addition 80 infants or young children of illegitimate birth were under care with their mothers, who had been committed as delinquents. Chapter 4 of Section II of the report deals with the children under care of these institutions.

Children under care of State institutions for the feeble-minded or awaiting admission.—Seventy-three children under 21 years of age, born out of wedlock, were under care of the two State institutions for the feeble-minded during the year. Sixty-seven children of illegitimate birth under 21 years of age were awaiting admission to these institutions. The facts secured relative to these children are given in Section II, chapter 5.

Other children included in the study.—As part of the chapter dealing with children under the supervision of the State board of charity, there is included a discussion of 1,996 children under 2

---

[2] The case records are filed by families, and the same number is given to all members of the family under care. Many of the cases in the 1 to 2000 group were not current in 1914, the children having been discharged from care before that date.

years of age reported as cared for apart from their relatives in family homes. Of these children, 995 were born out of wedlock. The same chapter also includes a discussion of 211 children of illegitimate birth under the supervision of the social service committee of the State board of charity. This committee makes investigations and gives after care to women and children at the State infirmary.

The chapter on the adoption of children born out of wedlock [3] covers the adoption records of four counties. During 1914 there were 441 adoption cases before the courts of these counties, of which 204 involved children known to have been born out of wedlock.

The third chapter of Section I is concerned with legal action for the support of children born out of wedlock. In 1914 a total of 256 cases were initiated in the Boston courts. These cases involved 239 alleged fathers and 253 children.

The study of the seacoast rural section included 121 children born out of wedlock during a 10-year period.

The background of illegitimacy.

The possibilities of a child's development and the kind of care and protection needed are largely determined by the physical and mental condition and the character of the parents and their families, and by their economic and social status. The study revealed a large proportion of cases in which children deprived by the circumstances of their birth of the advantages of normal homes and parental care carried the additional burden of a heritage in which there was physical weakness or disease, mental subnormality or abnormality, or moral instability.

Ages of parents.—The youth of the parents was an outstanding feature in many cases. Of the 792 mothers of infants born out of wedlock in Boston during the year covered by the study, whose ages were reported, 2 per cent were under 16 years of age—the age of consent in Massachusetts; a total of 13 per cent were under 18 years of age, and 43 per cent were under the age of 21. Of the 285 fathers whose ages were reported, 21 per cent were less than 21 years of age, 4 per cent being under the age of 18. The mothers of 11 per cent of the children under the care of Boston agencies whose histories gave information on this point were under the age of 18 when their children were born; the mothers of 37 per cent were under 21 years of age. The fathers of 17 per cent of the 599 children under care of Boston agencies whose records gave this information were under the age of legal majority.

Physical condition of mother.—For 473 of the 840 mothers of infants born out of wedlock during the year, the information was

---

[3] Sec. II ch. 3.

deemed sufficiently complete to justify classification as to physical condition. Mothers in poor physical condition comprised 24 per cent of the 473 reported, and 14 per cent of the total 840 mothers. Eight per cent of those reported, or 5 per cent of the total 840, had been diagnosed as having venereal infection.

The mothers of 3 per cent of the 2,178 children under care of Boston agencies, whose histories gave social information, were known to have died before the applications for care were made. The mothers of 22 per cent were known to be physically defective or diseased, or in poor physical condition. In 6 per cent of the cases the mother had been diagnosed as having venereal infection.

Mental condition of parents and grandparents.—The facts revealed in the study of infants born out of wedlock and of children of illegitimate birth under care of social agencies throw light on the relationship between low mentality and illegitimacy. The figures secured in the various parts of the inquiry in regard to the mentality of the the mother showed a remarkable similarity. (See Table I.)

TABLE I.—*Mental condition of mothers of children born out of wedlock, as shown by various parts of the inquiry.*

Mental condition of mother.	Per cent distribution.				
	Mothers of infants born out of wedlock during one year.		Children of illegitimate birth.		
	Total (840).	Mental condition reported (488).a	Under care of Boston agencies (2,178).b	Under care of 6 private child-caring agencies in Boston (472).	Under care of division of State minor wards (1,721).
Total..........................	100.0	100.0	100.0	100.0	100.0
Normal, so far as known..................	87.4	78.3	82.6	81.1	82.0
Below normal..........................	12.6	21.7	17.4	18.9	18.0
Subnormal, abnormal, or insane (diagnosed)...............................	2.6	4.5	4.5	5.9	4.6
Feeble-minded (diagnosed).............	5.1	8.8	6.1	4.7	6.5
Probably subnormal or feeble-minded.	4.9	8.4	6.8	8.3	6.9

a The histories of 488 mothers were sufficiently complete to justify their classification according to mental condition.
b Including Boston children under care of State agencies. The total under care was 2,863, but 685 of these were under care of agencies not giving social information.

Thirteen per cent of the mothers of infants born out of wedlock during the year were known to be below normal mentally, 5 per cent having been diagnosed feeble-minded. For each of the three groups of children under agency care the percentage of children whose mothers were below normal was very nearly the same—17 per cent for children under care of Boston agencies, 18 per cent for those under the care of the division of State minor wards, and 19 per cent for the children under care of a selected group of private child-caring agencies in Boston. The percentage whose mothers had been diagnosed feeble-minded ranged from 5 to 7, being highest for children under care of the division of State minor wards and lowest for children under care of the selected group of private agencies.

The fathers of 16 of the 2,178 children under care of Boston agencies whose histories gave social information were reported below normal mentally. One or both maternal grandparents of 65 children—3 per cent—were reported insane or mentally below normal. Considering together the mental condition of the parents and grandparents, 19 per cent of the 2,178 children had a heritage in which there was known to be insanity, feeble-mindedness, or other subnormal or abnormal mental condition, or probable feeble-mindedness or subnormality. In 9 per cent of the 2,178 cases there was definite feeble-mindedness or insanity in the family history. These percentages are understatements because of the large number of cases in which the information was incomplete.

Character of parents and grandparents.—The histories of the mothers, as given in the records of social agencies, contained information of varying degrees of completeness in regard to character. Absence of information was assumed to mean that the mothers were of good character, aside from the sex irregularities connected with these cases of illegitimate maternity. The information secured in various parts of the study in regard to the character of the mother is summarized in Table II.

TABLE II.—*Character of mothers of children born out of wedlock, as shown by various parts of the inquiry.*

Character of mother.	Per cent distribution.			
	Mothers of infants born out of wedlock during one year.		Children of illegitimate birth.	
	Total (840).	Character reported (495).a	Under care of Boston agencies (2,178).b	Under care of division of State minor wards (1,721).
Total....................................	100. 0	100. 0	100. 0	100. 0
Good, so far as known......................	75. 0	57. 6	45. 6	46. 0
Immoral.....................................	18. 7	31. 7	45. 8	47. 0
Otherwise delinquent or of poor character..........	6. 3	10. 7	8. 6	7. 0

a The histories of 495 mothers were sufficiently complete to justify their classification according to mental condition.

b Including Boston children under care of State agencies. The total under care was 2,863, but 685 of these were under care of agencies not giving social information.

One-fourth of all the mothers of infants born out of wedlock during one year were known to have been previously immoral, otherwise delinquent, or of poor character. Considering only those for whom there were social records, more than two-fifths came under this classification.

Repeated violations of the moral code, serious alcoholism, dishonesty, or general worthlessness were reported in the histories of the mothers of 54 per cent of the children under care of Boston agencies, and also for the mothers of the same per cent of the children under care of the division of State minor wards.

The histories of 732 children under care of Boston agencies contained more or less social information about the father. Other immorality besides that connected with the present case was reported in regard to the fathers of 43 per cent of these children. The fathers of 25 per cent were said to be alcoholic. In many instances the father was both alcoholic and immoral. In all, the fathers of 66 per cent of the 732 children were alcoholic, immoral, otherwise delinquent, or of poor character. This high percentage may be partly accounted for by the probability that the histories of fathers who had been repeatedly before the courts or who had other records of delinquency would be known to social agencies to a greater extent than the histories of other fathers.

Considering together the character of the mother, father, and maternal grandparents for the group of 2,178 children under care of Boston agencies, only 38 per cent of the children had parents and maternal grandparents who were of good character, so far as known. The mothers, fathers, or maternal grandparents of 62 per cent were alcoholic, immoral, otherwise delinquent, or of poor character.

Infant welfare.

Infant mortality.—The most significant facts revealed by this study are those relating to the high mortality of infants born out of wedlock. No other data give so definite an index of the hardships and social injustice involved in illegitimate birth. Not only does a high infant mortality rate mean a waste of infant life, but the conditions which result in high mortality also produce lowered vitality and impaired physique among the children who survive.

Infants born out of wedlock in Boston died at a rate three times as high as the rate for infants born in wedlock. The infant mortality rate in 1914, based on the number of births and of infant deaths in that year, was 95 for children born in wedlock and 281 for infants born out of wedlock. In other words, the figures indicate that less than one-tenth of the infants born in wedlock died before they had reached 1 year of age, while between one-fourth and one-third of the infants of illegitimate birth failed to survive the first year of life.

The general infant mortality rate in Boston for the year 1914 was 103.1. The exclusion of births and deaths of infants born out of wedlock reduces the infant mortality rate to 95, a reduction of 8 per cent. The importance of efforts to lower the mortality rate among infants born out of wedlock as a part of the general movement for the reduction of infant mortality is, therefore, evident.

The findings as to age at death indicated that the early separation of the mother and child was a very important factor in the high mortality among infants born out of wedlock. The number of deaths under 1 month per 1,000 illegitimate births was twice as high as in the case of legitimate births. At 1 month the number of deaths per 1,000 illegitimate births was nearly eight times as high, and at 2 months nearly six times as high. Infant mortality statistics in England and Wales show somewhat the same tendency as that shown by the figures for Boston in regard to the relative difference between the number of infant deaths at various ages per 1,000 births among infants of illegitimate birth and among infants born in wedlock. In both cases the difference was less for those under 1 month of age at death than for those dying in the months immediately following. In Boston the difference was greatest at 1 month, while in England and Wales the peak came at 2 months.

According to cause of death, the relative difference between the mortality rate among infants born out of wedlock and among infants of legitimate birth was greatest for the gastric and intestinal diseases, the rate among the former class being nearly six times that among children born in wedlock. The diseases in this group are caused largely by improper feeding. The rate for diseases of early infancy among children born out of wedlock was nearly three times as high as the corresponding rate for children of legitimate birth.

Another and, for some reasons, a more satisfactory method of estimating infant mortality is the following through the first year of life of infants born during a given year, and determining how many died before reaching 1 year of age. On this basis the mortality among the infants born out of wedlock in Boston in 1914 was 251.5 deaths per 1,000 births. This rate is based only on registered deaths, and is an understatement because many of the infants were lost sight of before they reached the age of 1 year. But the rate secured by this method was nearly two and a half times as great as the general infant mortality rate (103.1) for the city in the same year.

Of the 847 infants born out of wedlock in Boston during the year 209 were born at one institution which cares for large numbers of infants, many of whom are separated from their mothers at an early age. Of these 209 infants 74 died at the same institution before they had reached 1 year of age, and 14 were known to have died elsewhere, death certificates having been found. Of the 638 infants of illegitimate birth born elsewhere in the city during the year 125 were known to have died during the first year of life. It would, therefore, appear that 421 out of every 1,000 children born out of wedlock at the institution die before they reach 1 year of age, 354 of them dying in the same institution in which they were born, while the infant mortality among infants born out of wedlock elsewhere than at this institution is 196. Analyzing the figures according to cause of death, it would appear that of every 1,000 infants born out of wedlock at the institution 196 die from gastric and intestinal causes during their first year of life, as compared with a rate of 42 among infants of illegitimate birth born elsewhere in Boston; and that 120 of every 1,000 infants born at the institution die from diseases of early infancy, as compared with 85 of every 1,000 born elsewhere.

Conditions surrounding birth.—More than three-fourths of the 847 infants born out of wedlock in Boston during the year were born in hospitals, maternity homes, or the public infirmary, although less than one-third of all the births in the city during the year occurred in hospitals or other institutions. Of the infants born out of wedlock, 49 per cent were born in hospitals, 25 per cent in maternity homes, 3 per cent in the public infirmary, and 23 per cent in private homes. Hospitals, as a rule, gave care for only a short period following birth, while the maternity homes and the public infirmary often gave care extending over several months before and after the child's birth. Of mothers cared for at the maternity homes, the proportion whose residence was Boston was small. Almost three-fifths of all the mothers out of wedlock were resident in Boston, while less than a third of the mothers cared for in maternity homes were Boston residents. Slightly more than half the mothers confined in hospitals resided in the city.

One-third of the mothers of children born out of wedlock in Boston during the year had received care from child-caring agencies, maternity homes, the public infirmary, or agencies of other types previous to confinement. The child-caring agencies and agencies of other types secured medical care and advice for the mother, provided her with a place where she could live during pregnancy, and arranged for her care during confinement. In two-thirds of the maternity-home cases the mother had been cared for in the home a month or more previous to confinement. These institutions also made a practice of keeping mother and child together for a considerable period following the child's birth. In three-fourths of the maternity-home cases the mother and child remained in the home a month or longer; in a third of the cases they remained two months or longer.

The great advantage of prolonged care, which makes it possible for the mother to keep the child with her under proper conditions and to breast-feed the baby, is indicated by the findings.[4] Twenty-seven per cent of the 847 infants born out of wedlock in Boston were known to have died during the first year of life.[5] Of the 241 infants born in maternity homes or in the public infirmary, 40, or 17 per cent, were known to have died; of the 193 born in private homes, 46, or 24 per cent; of the 201 born in hospitals other than the large institution previously mentioned, 50, or 25 per cent; of the 209 born in that institution, 94, or 45 per cent, were known to have died during the first year of life.

The care of the infant.—Prolonged care by the agencies studied was known to have been given 62 per cent of the children born out of wedlock during the year. Child-caring or child-protective agencies cared for 35 per cent of the children born during the year; maternity homes and the public infirmary cared for 31 per cent, 9 per cent also being under the care of child-caring or child-protective agencies during the year. Of the children not known to have died during the first year of life, 20 per cent were under prolonged care their entire first year.

Of primary importance in the welfare of an infant is the care given him by his own mother, and one of the most serious handicaps to which children born out of wedlock are frequently subjected is the deprivation of a mother's care. Of the infants surviving, so far as known, at the age of 1 month, at least 20 per cent had already been separated from their mothers; and at the age of 3 months, at least 27 per cent had been separated. These are understatements, for there were many cases for which no information was available. Evidence of the hazard to the child's life involved in early separation from the mother is found in information concerning the care of infants of various ages. Of the children definitely known to be surviving at 3 months whose presence with or separation from the mother was reported, 47 per cent were being cared for away from their mothers, while 80 per cent of the infants who had died after reaching the age of 2 weeks but before the age of 3 months, and whose whereabouts previous to death was known, had been separated from their mothers.

The possibilities of parental care.

The physical and mental condition and character of the parents.—Conditions such as extreme youth, low mentality, and bad character, making it difficult to secure for the child care by his own parents, have already been discussed under the heading " The background of

---

[4] See pp. 133–135.

[5] Of the 847 born, 213 died during the first year of life and death certificates were found, and 17 others were reported by agencies to have died, but death certificates were not found because of change of name or because the death had occurred outside the area covered by the study.

illegitimacy." Thirteen per cent of the mothers of infants born out of wedlock in Boston during the year were under the age of 18; the mothers of 11 per cent of the children under care of Boston agencies whose histories gave information concerning age of mother were under the age of 18 when their children were born. The assumption of the responsibility for the physical care of the child is often beyond the powers of these child mothers, even though provision is made for the support of the mother and child. In a considerable number of cases the father was a mere boy, incapable of contributing materially to the child's support.

Almost one-fourth of the mothers of infants born out of wedlock whose histories were deemed sufficiently complete to warrant classification as to physical condition were known to be physically defective or diseased or in poor physical condition; the mothers of almost the same proportion of children under the care of Boston agencies were known to be in poor condition. One-eighth of the mothers of infants born out of wedlock during the year were known to be below normal mentally; the mothers of more than one-sixth of the children under care of Boston agencies and the mothers of about the same proportion of children under the care of the division of State minor wards were reported mentally below normal. One-fourth of the mothers of infants born out of wedlock during the year and the mothers of more than half the children under care of Boston agencies and also of those under care of the division of State minor wards were known to be immoral, otherwise delinquent, or of poor character. Information as to the character of the father was obtained for about one-fourth of the children under the care of Boston agencies. The fathers of 66 per cent of these children were alcoholic, immoral, otherwise delinquent, or of poor character. Conditions such as these usually signify impaired earning capacity, lack of a feeling of responsibility for the welfare of the child, and general unfitness to give the child a proper home or provide adequate support.

Civil condition of mother and father.—Ninety-three per cent of the mothers of infants born out of wedlock during the year for whom this information was obtained were single; 2 per cent were married; and 5 per cent were widowed, divorced, separated, deserting, or deserted. The mothers of 85 per cent of the children of illegitimate birth under care of Boston agencies whose histories gave civil condition were single; of 2 per cent, married; of 4 per cent, widowed; and of 9 per cent, divorced, separated, deserting, or deserted. It is evident that the problem of illegitimate maternity is by no means limited to unmarried women, and that a considerable number of mothers out of wedlock also presumably have children of legitimate birth to care for. The mothers of 251 children under care of Boston agencies whose histories gave social information—12 per cent—were illegally married to the fathers or had been living with the fathers as married prior to the time when the children were born.

Civil condition was reported for only 237 of the fathers of infants born during the year. Twenty-one per cent of these fathers, or 6 per cent of the total 840, were married; 9 per cent of those reported, or 3 per cent of the total, were widowed, divorced, separated, deserting, or deserted. The fathers of about one-third of the children under care of Boston agencies whose histories gave civil condition were presumably responsible for the support of a family, in addition to their obligations for the maintenance of their children of illegitimate birth. The significance of the proportion of cases in which the father probably had family responsibilities is manifest in connection with his ability to contribute to the support of his child born out of wedlock.

Nine per cent of the mothers of infants born out of wedlock during the year were known to have married within a year after the child's birth. Of the 73 known to have married, 31 married the fathers of the children, 24 married other men, and in 18 cases it was not reported whether or not the man was the father of the child.

Economic status of mother and father.—The question of the occupation and earning capacity of the mother is of especial importance in connection with her ability to care for her child. In a large proportion of cases the mother must depend upon her own resources or upon the assistance of social agencies in supporting herself and in caring for the child, and the number of occupations in which she can keep the child with her at her place of employment is limited. Her previous industrial experience is an important factor in planning for her future. The study revealed that a large proportion of mothers of infants born out of wedlock during the year were gainfully employed before their children were born, 86 per cent of those whose occupations were reported being so employed. Considering only the mothers who were 16 to 20 years of age at the time their children were born, 83 per cent were gainfully employed, as compared with 60 per cent of all women in Boston of the same age. Domestic service was the predominant occupation, 47 per cent of the mothers whose occupations were reported having been engaged in domestic or personal service, and 36 per cent of all reported having been employed at housework in private families. Considering only the mothers who were gainfully employed, 55 per cent were engaged in domestic and personal service, though only 25 per cent of all gainfully employed women in Boston in 1910 were in this occupational group. The percentage employed in factories was also considerably higher among the mothers than among all gainfully employed women in Boston—27 per cent as compared with 16 per cent. The percentage of mothers who were classified as clerks and kindred workers was lower than the percentage of all gainfully employed women so classified—11 per cent as compared with 26 per cent.

At the time of application for the care of the children the mothers of 78 per cent of the children under care of Boston agencies whose histories gave information in regard to occupation were gainfully employed. Of the children whose mothers were gainfully employed the mothers of 59 per cent were engaged in domestic or personal service. In 38 per cent of the cases in which the mother was gainfully employed, she was employed at housework.

For 311 of the 840 fathers of infants born during the year of the study, information in regard to occupation was obtained. Twelve per cent of these fathers were engaged in an independent business or profession; 36 per cent were clerks or kindred workers, or skilled workers in various industries; 46 per cent were semiskilled workers, laborers, or servants; 3 per cent were soldiers, sailors, or marines; 3 per cent were not gainfully employed. The occupations of the fathers of 839 children under care of Boston agencies were reported. The distribution was very similar to that found among the fathers of infants born during the year. The information indicates that the father was a man of small income in the majority of cases.

Contributions of the father to the support of the child.—The obligation of the father to give at least a measure of support to his child born out of wedlock has been recognized by the laws of most of the United States. However, the period over which support is required and the maximum amounts frequently specified have in many cases been entirely inadequate. Even though the intent of the law is to require fairly adequate provision, the difficulties of enforcement are very great. The reluctance of the mother to reveal the name of the father and to testify in open court, the absconding of the father to another State, the difficulty in securing evidence and in establishing the facts, compromises out of court for inadequate sums—all these factors have made extremely difficult the establishing of paternity and the enforcement of support. In an effort to provide a more satisfactory means of determining paternity and to establish a higher standard of support Massachusetts enacted a law which went into effect in July, 1913, and which is commonly called the " illegitimate-children act." The provisions of this law are analyzed in Section I, chapter 3 of this report. The father is made liable for reasonable contributions to the support of the child during minority and to this end is made subject to the procedure already established for the support of children born in wedlock.

As a part of this study an analysis was made of the administration of the law in the Boston courts during 1914 and 1915. The law had been in operation for a comparatively short period, and many defects of administration have undoubtedly been remedied since the time covered by the study. In 1914, 256 cases were initiated in Boston under the act; this was less than one-third of the number of children born out of wedlock in Boston during the year. The cases were followed to the end of 1915. By that time less than half the cases initiated in 1914 had actually resulted in an arrangement for the support of the child, for confinement expenses, or for both, which could legally hold the man to his obligation; in a few other cases support was secured as an indirect result of court action. Altogether, only 52 per cent of the cases initiated resulted in provision for the child; in but 7 per cent of the cases was the defendant dismissed as not guilty. The money collected did not as a rule come up to the standard for dependent children who are wards of the State. The marriage of the parents or the death of the child accounted for only a few of the small amounts.

Information obtained through the secretary of the Massachusetts Commission on Probation and from the probation department of the central municipal court indicated that the administration of the act in 1919 differed little from that in the period covered by the Children's Bureau study. Fewer cases came before the courts in 1919 than in 1914—due, in part, it may be assumed, to war conditions. An analysis of dispositions of cases in the largest court showed little variation from year to year in the proportion of cases resulting in an arrangement ordered or sanctioned by the court for the support of the child or for confinement expenses. Probation was more frequently used in the latter period than in the former, and marriages were proportionately less frequent.

Cases involving 99 of the 847 infants born out of wedlock in Boston were initiated in the Boston courts before the end of the first year of life. Agency records gave information in regard to 9 cases in which court action for support had been brought in other places. Hence, for 108 infants—13 per cent—court action was known to have been initiated during the first year of the child's life. As a result of court action, some provision was arranged before the end of the child's first year of life for 60 of the 108 infants—56 per cent. These 60 children comprised only 7 per cent of all the infants born during the year. The father of 1 of these 60 children contributed nothing, the child having been adopted by someone else. The fathers of 59 children not involved in court cases contributed something to the support of the mother or the child during the child's first year of life. Considering together the cases in which contributions were made by the father as a result of court action and the cases in which voluntary contributions were made without court action, the fathers of 118 children—one-seventh of those born during the year—were known to have given more or less financial assistance, though in many cases the amounts were very small.

Undoubtedly the fathers of some of the infants born during the year who did not come to the attention of social agencies contributed to their support without court action. It is impossible to say whether the number of fathers so contributing was large or small.

The fathers of 674 children under care of Boston agencies—not quite one-third of the 2,178 whose histories gave social information—were known to have aided in the support of the children or to have given the mother financial assistance. Often the amount of help was so small as to be practically negligible. In many instances in which the father aided in supporting the child the mother and father had been illegally living as married for a considerable period of time. The fathers of 241 children—11 per cent of the 2,178 for whom social information was obtained—had been involved in court cases for support. It must be borne in mind that the present law did not go into effect until the year before the period covered by the study.

Mother's parental home and mode of living.—The character of the mother's parental home is of significance in a consideration of the possibility of the mother's caring for the child. If the parents are able and willing to take the mother and child into their own home, or to give the mother financial assistance outside the home, the problem of caring for the child is very much simplified.

One or both parents of almost one-third of the 840 mothers of infants born out of wedlock during the year were dead, not living in the United States, or were divorced or separated. Since this information was known only for mothers who had come to the attention of social agencies, this proportion is an understatement. Eight of the 840 mothers were themselves known to be of illegitimate birth. One or both parents of one-eighth of the mothers were reported to be alcoholic, immoral, or otherwise of poor character.

The mode of living previous to the birth of the child was known for 533 of the 840 mothers. Of these mothers, 36 per cent were living in their parental homes, 5 per cent in homes of their own, 9 per cent with relatives or friends, 4 per cent were boarding, and 46 per cent were living in their places of employment. Only 81 per cent of the mothers under 18 years of age were living in homes from which they might expect assistance before the birth of the children or help in caring for their babies. Of the mothers under the age of 18 whose mode of living was reported, 16 per cent were living in their places of employment.

The mothers of 15 per cent of the 2,178 children under care of Boston agencies whose histories gave social information had no parental homes, or none in this country, to which they might look for help. The mothers of 16 per cent lacked normal homes because of the death of one parent or because the parents were divorced or separated, deserting, or deserted. One or both maternal grand-parents of 10 per cent of the children were of poor character, were mentally below normal, or were entirely or partially dependent upon charitable aid. Hence, the mothers of 41 per cent of the 2,178 children under care of Boston agencies did not have normal parental homes, or the character of the grandparents made it impossible for them to provide proper homes for the mothers and children.

Mother's other children.—There are very great difficulties in the way of the mother who attempts to provide for a second child born out of wedlock. If she must depend upon her own resources, it is almost impossible for her to keep more than one child with her. Even though one of the children does not live, or is provided for apart from the mother, it is more difficult for her to secure the assistance needed if she is known to be a " repeater," since some agencies make it a rule to refuse care in such cases.

Seventy-two mothers of infants born out of wedlock during the year—10 per cent of the 730 for whom this information was available, or 9 per cent of all the mothers—were known to have had previous illegitimate births. Sixteen mothers—2 per cent of the total—were known to have become illegitimately pregnant during the first year of life of the child included in the study.

The mothers of 19 per cent of the 2,863 children under care of Boston agencies were known to have had one or more illegitimate births before the children included in the study were born. The mothers of 13 per cent had had such births subsequent to the birth of the child of the study. In all, eliminating duplications, the mothers of more than one-fourth of the children were known to have had other children born out of wedlock.

Child dependency.

Illegitimacy is closely associated with child dependency. Factors, such as poor health, low mentality, bad character, and low economic status on the part of the mother, father, or grandparents, often make it impossible for the child to be provided for without the assistance of social agencies. The failure of the father, in so large a proportion of cases, to contribute amounts at all adequate for the child's support results in placing upon the mother a double burden of care and support. An indication of the extent to which agency care must be provided is furnished by the figures relating to infants born out of wedlock during the year; more than three-fifths of these infants received prolonged care during the first year of life from the agencies studied; more than one-third were under the care of child-caring agencies or of the child-protective agency.

As a part of this inquiry the records of municipal and private agencies in the city of Boston whose work included the care of children born out of wedlock, and of certain State agencies so far as they dealt with Boston children, were studied. The number of agencies included was 37. A separate study was made of the children under care of the division of State minor wards of the State board of charity. Reference has already been made to some of the findings of these studies. The main types of agencies represented were: Child-caring agencies, public and private; a child-protective agency; maternity homes; hospitals; institutions for the care of delinquent children; institutions for the care of mental defectives. Some of the children were given temporary care only—intended to meet emergent situations or to give special types of treatment; a large proportion received prolonged care. Dependent, neglected, delinquent, and defective children were represented, though the proportion of delinquent children was small. All the children, however, were receiving care from social agencies, and, therefore, may be termed " dependent " in the broad sense of the term.

Extent of the problem of illegitimacy in the work of the agencies studied.—In 1914 there were 2,863 children born out of wedlock who were under care of the Boston agencies included in the study and of certain State agencies so far as their work concerned Boston children. Four-fifths of these children had received more or less prolonged treatment from the agencies, their care having been definitely assumed. Cases concerning children born out of wedlock constituted 11 per cent of those dealt with by the public child-caring agency of the city, 17 per cent of the cases dealt with by the private child-caring agencies, and 9 per cent of the cases handled by the child-protective agency. The average for these child-caring and child-protective agencies was 13 per cent. The approximate amount spent during the year for the care of children born out of wedlock by the Boston child-caring and child-protective agencies and for the Boston children by the State child-caring agency was $124,000. This estimate is presumably an understatement of the actual expenditures of these agencies chargeable to illegitimacy, since it is probable that children born out of wedlock presented more difficult problems and required more prolonged and expensive care than other children.

The total number of children receiving prolonged or temporary care from the division of State minor wards during the year was 7,526. Of these children, 1,721, or 23 per cent, were of illegitimate birth. Twenty-two per cent of the children receiving prolonged care were born out of wedlock.

The child's age at time of application.—More than one-fourth of the children under care of Boston agencies had been under care from birth; almost three-fifths had come under care of the agencies studied before they had completed their first year of life. Of the children coming under the care of child-caring and child-protective agencies during the year, more than half were under 1 year of age at the time of application, and more than three-fourths were under the age of 4 years.

The children under the care of the division of State minor wards had also come under care at an early age. Almost half the children born out of wedlock were under 1 year of age at the time they came to the attention of the division; three-fifths were under 2 years of age; more than four-fifths were less than 6 years old.

The comparison of 1,717 children of legitimate birth and 606 children of illegitimate birth under care of the division of State minor wards whose case records were numbered from 1 to 2000 showed that almost half the children born out of wedlock—46 per cent—were less than 1 year of age when application for their care was made to the division, while of the children born in wedlock only 9 per cent were less than 1 year old. A total of 60 per cent of the children born out of wedlock were under 2 years of age, as against 15 per cent of the children born in wedlock. Eighty per cent of the children of illegitimate birth were under the age of 6 years, while only 46 per cent of the children of legitimate birth were under this age. It is evident that children born out of wedlock came under the care of the State at an earlier age than children of legitimate birth.

Previous agency care.—Before coming to the attention of agencies giving care extending into the year studied, many of the children born out of wedlock had been under the care of social agencies for longer or shorter periods. Of the children under the care of Boston agencies giving information in regard to previous history—excluding the children under their care from birth—more than one-third had previously received prolonged care from agencies; many had been cared for by more than one agency. The majority of the children receiving care previously had been under the supervision of other than child-caring agencies. These other agencies included principally maternity homes, public infirmaries, and the child-protective agency. However, one-eighth of the children whose previous histories were known had been wards of child-caring agencies before applications were made to the agencies giving care during the year covered by the study. Almost one-fourth of the children 6 years of age and over at the time of application had been wards of child-caring agencies before coming to the attention of the agencies under whose protection they were at the time of the study.

More than half the children of illegitimate birth under care of the division of State minor wards were under the supervision of agencies at the time of application or commitment. Of the children receiving prolonged care from the division during the year, almost two-fifths had received prolonged care from agencies at some time previous to their coming under care of the division; in many instances care had been given by more than one agency. One-eighth of the children had been under the supervision of child-caring agencies before coming under care of the division of State minor wards.

Source of, and reason for, application or commitment.—The applications or commitments to Boston agencies for 27 per cent of the children under care came from courts or other public agencies, and for 28 per cent from private agencies. The reasons for application or commitment in the cases of children under care of Boston agencies were analyzed only for children first coming under the care of child-caring agencies or of the child-protective agency. Twenty-seven per cent of the applications or commitments were made because the mother was unfit to care for the child or was living in a home in which there existed conditions detrimental to the child's welfare. The largest single group of applications—37 per cent of the total reported—came because of the mother's inability to care for the child. Sixteen per cent of the children came under care because their board had not been paid, they had been definitely abandoned at board, or otherwise deserted.

Almost one-third—32 per cent—of the children of illegitimate birth under the care of the division of State minor wards were committed by courts to the care of the State. Overseers of the poor and other public agencies committed or made application for the care of 27 per cent. Applications for the care of 8 per cent of the children came from private agencies. The mothers applied directly for the care of 21 per cent of the children, and the care of 9 per cent more was applied for by relatives or friends. In the remaining cases the applications came from other sources. The mother's inability to provide for the child was the reason for application for the care of two-fifths of the children; one-fifth came under care because they had been abandoned or deserted. The unfitness of the mother to care for the child, or detrimental conditions in the mother's home, were the reasons given in about one-fourth of the cases.

The comparative study of children born in wedlock and children born out of wedlock who were under care of the division of State minor wards—based on the records of 1,717 children of legitimate birth and 606 of illegitimate birth—showed that less than two-fifths of the children of illegitimate birth were received on court commitments, while almost three-fourths of the children of legitimate birth were committed by courts. In the case of children born out of wedlock the problem appears to be mainly one of dependency, while neglect brings under care the majority of the children of legitimate birth who must depend upon the public for support.

Care given by the agencies studied.—During the year 2,319 children born out of wedlock received prolonged care from Boston agencies. By the end of the year or the close of care, 56 per cent had received care for one year or more. Of the children 6 years of age and over. 49 per cent had been under care for at least six years. The average time under care for the children 1 year of age and over was three years and nine months. Since more than three-fourths of these children remained under care at the end of the year, the time reported under care does not represent the total amount of time over which agency care was likely to be required.

At the end of the year studied or previous to the close of care, 81 per cent of the children receiving prolonged care from Boston agencies were living in family homes, 17 per cent were in institutions, and the place of residence of 2 per cent was not reported. The majority of the children in institutions were in hospitals, infirmaries, or maternity homes.

Of the children under care of child-caring or child-protective agencies, nine-tenths were living in family homes and only one-tenth were cared for in institutions. Two-thirds of the children under care of these agencies were living in boarding, free, or wage homes. Child-caring and child-protective agencies had placed nearly seven times as many children in boarding, free, or wage homes as in institutions. Only 3 per cent of the children had been placed in homes into which they had been adopted or in which they had been placed on trial for adoption. Public child-caring agencies had been able in 1 per cent of their cases to keep mother and child together. Private child-caring agencies had been able to avoid separation in 14 per cent of their cases. It must be borne in mind in this connection that the cases presenting the least possibility of assumption of care by the mother are usually referred to the public agencies.

By the end of the year or the close of care, seven-eighths of the 1,393 children born out of wedlock receiving prolonged care from the division of State minor wards had been under care one year or longer. Of the children 6 years of age and over, more than two-thirds had been under the care of the State for at least six years. Of the children 10 years of age and over, more than half had been under care at least 10 years. The average time under care for the children 1 year of age and over was six years. The figures do not represent the total length of time during which these children will be dependent upon the State, since almost seven-eighths remained under care at the close of the year.

Three per cent of the children receiving prolonged care from the division of State minor wards were with their mothers at the end of the year or the close of care. More than nine-tenths of the children receiving prolonged care—92 per cent—were living in family homes,

7 per cent were in institutions, and the place of residence of 1 per cent was not reported. More than nine-tenths of the children living in family homes were in boarding or free homes.

The comparison of children of legitimate and of illegitimate birth under care of the division of State minor wards showed that the average number of years under care was seven for children of legitimate birth, and eight for children born out of wedlock, though 57 per cent of the former were 14 years of age or over, while only 32 per cent of the latter had reached this age.

Juvenile delinquency.

The conditions frequently accompanying birth out of wedlock—defective heredity; lack of opportunity for normal, healthful living; deprivation of a mother's care and absence of a father's care and support; the social stigma; the mental conflicts caused by knowledge of birth out of wedlock and by the actual or imagined degradation of the parents—these conditions are not conducive to the development of right habits and a sane and normal outlook upon life. Rather may they be expected to lead to restlessness, morbidness, or even to marked delinquency and misconduct. This study has thrown some light upon the effect of bad heredity, unfortunate environment, or the lack of normal conditions of living and the absence of parental care and affection on character development. Some of the findings are here summarized.

Conduct of dependent children born out of wedlock.—During the year 1914 there were 656 children of illegitimate birth 7 years of age and over under care of Boston agencies, excluding 148 under care of agencies not reporting conduct. The conduct of one-fourth of these 656 children was poor; the conduct of more than one-third of the children 14 years of age and over was unsatisfactory. The high percentage among the older children was due partly to the fact that Boston children committed to State institutions for delinquents were included. Of the 29 boys and 59 girls 14 years of age and over whose behavior was reported as unsatisfactory, 3 boys and 37 girls were known to have been sex offenders; 13 boys and 6 girls had been guilty of stealing, stubbornness, or other forms of delinquency; and the remaining 13 boys and 16 girls had given serious trouble at home or at school.

One-fifth of the 849 children of illegitimate birth 7 years of age and over who were under care of the division of State minor wards presented serious problems of conduct. Of those 14 years of age and over more than one-fourth were unsatisfactory in conduct.

Among the children 7 years of age and over who were under care of the division of State minor wards and were included in the comparative study, there were 914 of legitimate birth who were not feeble-minded, concerning whose conduct information was obtained, and 410 born out of wedlock. The conduct of 13 per cent of the former as against 18 per cent of the latter was reported as poor. Considering only the children 14 years of age and over, the conduct of 16 per cent of the children born in wedlock was unsatisfactory, while 28 per cent of the children born out of wedlock were delinquent or presented serious problems of conduct. Hence it is seen that the proportion of children of illegitimate birth under the care of the State who were delinquent or troublesome was considerably higher than of children of legitimate birth who were under care, though children born out of wedlock came under the care of the State at an earlier age than children born in wedlock, and a larger proportion of the former than of the latter were received because of the inability of the mother or other relatives to support the child, and a smaller proportion because of parental neglect, unfit homes, or delinquency. The figures suggest that children cared for during the first years of life in their own homes, even though the homes be of poor character, have an advantage over children cared for from early childhood in boarding or foster homes.

Children of illegitimate birth under the care of institutions for delinquents.—As a part of this inquiry a study was made of wards of State institutions for delinquents who had been born out of wedlock and who were under 21 years of age at the time the study was made. Two State training schools for boys and one for girls, together with their parole departments, were represented, as was also the reformatory for women.

The only figures secured which gave any reliable index of the proportion of wards of institutions for delinquents, who were of illegitimate birth, were those for girls committed to the institutions during the year 1914. In all, 184 girls under 21 years of age were committed, and of these, 17—9 per cent—were of illegitimate birth. This proportion was large in comparison with the proportion of illegitimate births in the State; it was considerably smaller than the proportion—almost one-fourth—of children under care of the division of State minor wards during the year who were born out of wedlock. The conditions accompanying illegitimate birth seem to be more closely associated with dependency and neglect than with delinquency.

The information in regard to age at commitment and time under care suggests that children born out of wedlock come earlier under care of correctional institutions, and remain longer, than do children of legitimate birth. Forty per cent of the children of illegitimate birth under care of the institutions and parole departments were under 14 years of age at the time of commitment; only 25 per cent of the children of legitimate birth committed during the year were under the age of 14. Furthermore, an analysis of offenses indicated that larger percentages of boys and girls born out of wedlock were committed on charges of stubbornness and other undefined delinquencies than were all boys and girls committed during the year. The fact that children of illegitimate birth were committed at younger ages than children born in wedlock probably accounts for the difference in the proportions committed for the less serious offenses.

Somewhat more than one-fourth of the delinquent children born out of wedlock were living with their mothers at the time of commitment; nearly three-fourths were separated from them. Twenty-one per cent of the delinquent children of illegitimate birth were living in adoptive or foster homes, a surprisingly large proportion as compared with the 7 per cent of the children of illegitimate birth 6 years of age and over under the care of the division of State minor wards who were living in adoptive or foster homes at the time of application or commitment.

Almost half the homes from which the delinquent children born out of wedlock were committed were known to be bad. The mothers of almost two-thirds were known to be alcoholic, immoral, or of otherwise poor character. Many of the families had been dependent upon charitable aid for two or three generations. More than two-thirds of the children had been under the care of agencies or had been before the courts previous to the time of commitment. More than one-fifth of the children were very backward or below normal mentally, and one-fourth were in poor physical condition at the time of commitment.

Mental defect.

The heritage of children born out of wedlock.—It has already been shown that one-eighth of the mothers of infants born out of wedlock in Boston during the year were reported to be mentally below normal, and that the mothers of more than one-sixth of the children under care of Boston agencies whose histories gave social information, and about the same proportion of the mothers of children under care of the division of State minor wards, were not normal mentally. The mothers of 6 per cent of the children under care of Boston agencies, and of 7 per cent of those under care of the division of State minor wards had been diagnosed as feeble-minded. [6] In the study of the seacoast rural section the proportion of feeble-mindedness among the mothers appeared to be considerably larger. Nineteen per cent of the children under care of Boston agencies were

---

[6] See pp. 39, 45.

known to have a family history in which there was insanity, feeble-mindedness, or other subnormal or abnormal mental condition. In 9 per cent of all the cases there was a history of definite feeble-mindedness or insanity.

Feeble-minded mothers of children born out of wedlock.—A study of the records of the two State institutions for the feeble-minded revealed that one-eighth of the estimated number of girls and women in the institutions who had reached childbearing age at the time of the study had been illegitimately pregnant. More than one-fifth of the 383 girls and women of childbearing age awaiting admission to the institutions had been illegitimately pregnant, and more than one-third of those who had been mothers out of wedlock had been awaiting admission to the institutions for two years or longer. More than one-fourth of those in the institutions who had been mothers out of wedlock and almost half the mothers awaiting admission had had more than one illegitimate pregnancy.

Mentality of dependent and delinquent children of illegitimate birth.—Excluding children under care of agencies not reporting mental condition, the information in regard to the mental condition of the children under care of Boston agencies indicated that at least 17 per cent of those 7 years of age and over were not normal mentally or were very backward in school. Six per cent had been diagnosed feeble-minded; this was about six times the percentage found in studies of school children made by the United States Public Health Service.

Nineteen per cent of the children of illegitimate birth under care of the division of State minor wards, who were 7 years of age and over, were mentally below normal or were very backward in school; 10 per cent of all reported had been diagnosed feeble-minded. Of the children 7 years of age and over included in the comparative analysis, 10.9 per cent of those of legitimate birth and 11.1 per cent of those born out of wedlock were diagnosed feeble-minded. This finding would seem to controvert an opinion frequently expressed to the effect that dependent children born out of wedlock are more likely to have a sound heritage than are children of legitimate birth for whom public provision has been necessary.

Table III summarizes the data from the various parts of the study in regard to the prevalence of marked retardation, subnormality, or feeble-mindedness among dependent and delinquent children born out of wedlock.

TABLE III.—*Mental condition of dependent and delinquent children born out of wedlock, as shown by various parts of the inquiry.*

Mental condition.	Per cent distribution of children 7 years of age and over under care of—			
	Boston agencies reporting mental condition (656 children).a	Selected group of Boston agencies (305 children).b	Division of State minor wards (849 children).	State institutions for delinquents or parole departments (102 children).
Total........................	100.0	100.0	100.0	100.0
Normal, so far as known................	83.2	89.2	81.4	78.4
Very backward in school...............	5.3	4.9	5.9	3.9
Probably subnormal or feeble-minded, but not diagnosed.......................	2.6	2.3	1.8	4.9
Subnormal or abnormal (diagnosed)........	2.3	2.3	.8	5.9
Feeble-minded (diagnosed).............	6.3	1.3	9.8	5.9
Insane........................	.3	....	.3	1.0

a Including Boston children under care of State agencies.
b Five private child-caring agencies and the child-protective agency.

Children of illegitimate birth under care of State institutions for the feeble-minded or awaiting admission.—In Massachusetts in 1914 a total of 2,553 patients were cared for at the two State institutions for the feeble-minded. Of these, 100—4 per cent—were known to have been born out of wedlock, 73 of them being under 21 years of age.

In 1914 there were 467 applications for admission to the Wrentham State School for persons who could not be received during the year. Thirteen per cent of these applications were for persons of illegitimate birth. The proportion of those born out of wedlock was much smaller among those awaiting admission to the school for the feeble-minded at Waltham; this difference is partly accounted for by the fact that almost half those on the Wrentham waiting list were State wards. Seventy-two feeble-minded persons of illegitimate birth were awaiting admission to the two institutions in 1914, of whom 67 were under 21 years of age.

All but 24 of the 73 in the institutions and 10 of the 67 awaiting admission were known to have been under the care of agencies previous to admission or application. More than three-fifths of the total 140 children had been charges of public child-caring agencies before they were admitted to the schools for the feeble-minded or were placed on the waiting lists.

Half the children in the institutions or awaiting admission were reported as having been delinquent or of otherwise poor character. Four of the girls in the institutions and 2 of those on the waiting lists were themselves mothers of children out of wedlock.

Of the 67 children awaiting admission, 17 had been on the waiting lists for one year, 19 for two years, 11 for three years, and 3 for four years. Three-fourths had been awaiting admission for one year or more. Thirty of the 67 children whose admission had not been secured were delinquent or of otherwise poor character.

The mothers of half the children in the institutions or awaiting admission were known to be immoral, alcoholic, or of otherwise poor character. The mothers of almost one-fourth were reported to be below normal mentally. In 6 of the 140 cases the mother had been diagnosed feeble-minded. The mothers of 43 of the 140 children had had other births out of wedlock.

The histories of many of the children born out of wedlock included in various parts of the study gave evidence of mental subnormality or feeble-mindedness, associated with inefficiency, low standards of living, dependency, and moral laxness, extending through several generations. The relationship between mental defect and such anti-social manifestations as illegitimate maternity or paternity is one which society can not afford to ignore.

The child's point of view.

One of the objects of this study has been to determine the significance to the individual child of birth out of wedlock. The findings have revealed something of the meaning of illegitimate birth in terms of the chance of survival, the absence of normal home life, dependency, defective mentality, and the conditions that handicap normal character development. There is, however, another phase—the psychological factor—which is of very great importance. It is practically impossible to obtain statistical data on this subject, but the stories of several children who were dependent or delinquent charges of society indicated the mental suffering occasioned by uncertainty in regard to the histories or whereabouts of their parents, or by the knowledge that they were of illegitimate birth.[7]

The pyschological effect of such knowledge may be illustrated by the experience of a 16-year-old girl who for seven years had been under the care of the State. Previous to her commitment she lived with her mother and stepfather, who treated her cruelly and wished to be rid of her. While under the care of the State she did well in school and gave satisfaction in the home in which she was placed. However, at the age of 15 she began to realize the facts about her birth and the character of her mother, brooding over these things and insisting that she had inherited her mother's tendencies. As a result of this mental attitude she did little things which she knew were not right. Fortunately the girl was wisely handled by the

---

[7] For discussion of the relation between mental conflicts concerning parentage and misconduct, see Mental Conflicts and Misconduct, by William Healy. Boston, 1917. Pp. 47, 73, 213–217.

family with whom she was living, as well as by the State board, and at the last date of record was reported to be doing well.

The strength of filial affection and the unhappiness and restlessness caused by uncertainty concerning the whereabouts and circumstances of a mother are brought out in the case of a 20-year-old boy who had been under the care of the State from the age of 4 years. At that time his mother, who was boarding him in a private family, failed to meet the payments required, and the authorities committed him to the care of the division of State minor wards. The boy was bright and ambitious, though of a roving disposition and not altogether reliable. His mother visited him occasionally, but there were long periods during which he had no news of her whereabouts. At the age of 17 the boy, not having seen her for three years, wrote for information to the board, which was able to tell him little except the name of a town in a near-by State from which she had come originally. He went there to find traces of his relatives but he was unsuccessful. The next year he met his mother on the street of the town in which he was living. She looked dissipated and her breath smelled of liquor. She would give little information concerning herself and he lost track of her again. The boy continued to worry about her and again wrote to the board asking for assistance in locating her. In one of his letters he said: " I guess she is a pretty slim affair, but just the same she is my mother, and all that is done for her good I shall appreciate."

The instinctive yearning of every child for a mother and father and kin of his own is shown in the appeal of a 17-year-old boy who, after having been a ward of the State from infancy, had been sent at the age of 14 to an industrial school. He wrote to the State board:

I would like to know where I was born and how old I was when I was put on the State, and what for did my Father and Mother die or what was the matter. Have I any brothers or sisters in the world or any friends? I am 17 years old the 25th of this month, just the rite age to learn a trade. Please write and tell me how things are as soon as possible. Your friend.

Another instance is that of a 14-year-old boy who had been under the care of the State for 13 years and whose mother had not been heard from in all that time until the year covered by this study. Then, to his great surprise, he received a letter from her, and his delight was very touching. He wrote the following letter, never received by her, since it was returned from the address she had given:

I was very glad to hear from you. I was so surprised to hear from my mother I didn't know what to do. I didn't know I had a mother. Have I any father, sisters or brothers, aunts, uncles, cousins? I am well. I am almost 14. How old are you? I hope you are well the same as me. Write to me and tell me more about you—what you are doing. From your son.

CONCLUSIONS.

From this study, based upon public records and records of social agencies and institutions in Boston and the State of Massachusetts, certain general inferences may be drawn in regard to the status and care of children born out of wedlock in the United States. However, in connection with the findings of this report, consideration must be given to the fact that conditions differ in the several States, and that children born out of wedlock in one State may be more fortunate than those born in another State in respect to their status under the law and to available care. Massachusetts has taken a leading part in the development of provision for children who are in need of special care. During recent years Boston agencies have given special attention to the problems incident to the care of children born out of wedlock. The Massachusetts law providing for paternal support is comparatively advanced. On the other hand, it may be that the problem of illegitimacy is more serious in States like Massachusetts, where a large proportion of the population lives in cities, than in States having largely rural populations and less complicated social problems.

The conclusions of the study will be dealt with under four topics, concerned with (1) the meaning to the child of birth out of wedlock, (2) the burden upon the public for the care of these children, (3) the measures needed for their better protection, and (4) the lines along which social effort may be so directed as to effect a lessening of the problem.

The handicap of illegitimate birth.

The handicap of illegitimate birth is found chiefly in the defective heritage, the absence of normal home life and parental care, and the other detrimental conditions so frequently accompanying birth out of wedlock. The results of these grave disadvantages may be summarized as follows:

The hazard to life and health.—In Boston, during the year of the study, infants born out of wedlock died at a rate three times as high as the rate for infants of legitimate birth. That many of these deaths might have been prevented is indicated by the differences in the percentages of deaths according to place of birth and kind of care given. A high infant mortality rate implies not only a waste of infant life, but also a high rate of physical disabilities and weaknesses among those who survive.

62

The deprivation of a mother's care.—Separation from the mother at a very early age is a common experience among children born out of wedlock. Sometimes this separation is unavoidable, because of the mother's extreme youth, low mentality, or unfitness to care for her child. Often separation occurs when it might have been prevented, and when it is contrary to the best interests of the child and the mother. Of the infants born in Boston and surviving at 1 month, so far as known, at least 20 per cent had already been separated from their mothers; of those surviving at 3 months, so far as known, at least 27 per cent had been thus separated. Early separation from the mother is shown in this study to be an important contributing factor in the high infant mortality among children born out of wedlock. Those who survive infancy and who do not have the care and affection of their mothers are deprived of that for which they can never be fully compensated.

The deprivation of a father's care and support.—From the information obtained in this study, it would seem probable that a large proportion of children born out of wedlock do not receive any financial assistance from their fathers. In Boston, during the year of the study, the number of court cases initiated under the act relative to the support of children born out of wedlock was less than one-third the number of children born out of wedlock during the same year. Frequently the alleged father can not be located, or the mother's character makes it impossible to determine paternity with certainty. Support is sometimes secured without court action, through the efforts of social agencies or otherwise. However, the records of the agencies studied showed the small proportion of children dependent upon the public whose fathers had assumed any responsibility for their support. That so many children born out of wedlock are deprived of support from their fathers has serious implications in regard to chance for survival, health, and opportunities for normal childhood. Perhaps of almost as great concern is the fact that most children born out of wedlock must grow up without the advantage of a father's affection and guidance.

Hereditary handicaps.—In the heritage of children born out of wedlock are frequently found elements which may seriously affect the child's physical and mental make-up and character development. Almost one-fifth of the children of illegitimate birth under care of Boston agencies were known to have a heritage in which there was insanity, feeble-mindedness, or other subnormal or abnormal mental condition, or probable feeble-mindedness or subnormality. The mothers, fathers, or maternal grandparents of more than three-fifths of the children were known to be alcoholic, immoral, otherwise delinquent, or of poor character. Although it is impossible to determine the extent to which these defects of mentality or character were transmitted, it is significant to note that one-sixth of the children under care of Boston agencies were very backward in school or were not normal mentally, and that 6 per cent were feeble-minded.

Environmental difficulties.—In addition to the deprivation of parental care and support, children born out of wedlock are frequently subjected to other detrimental conditions occasioned by the circumstances under which they live. Many of the children received under care by social agencies had previously lived in homes in which there were alcoholism, immorality, or other delinquencies. The breaking of associations and the readjustment to new conditions involved in frequent shiftings from home to home and from care of one type to care of another, which children of illegitimate birth must often undergo, are likely to deprive them of the advantage of close family and social relationships, and to have injurious effects upon their development.

Legal and social disabilities.—The child born out of wedlock is at a disadvantage in regard to legal rights and social status. In the United States he can usually inherit from the mother but not from the father; his right to care and support from the father is in most cases only partially fulfilled, even though paternity is established through court action. He is frequently excluded from the benefits of such social legislation as workmen's compensation acts and mothers' pensions. His birth record specifically or by implication reveals the fact of his illegitimate birth, and that record is frequently open to public inspection and may be used for malicious purposes; when he goes to school and a copy of his birth certificate is produced, the information concerning the circumstances of his birth is often needlessly revealed; when he goes to work he may be subjected to a similar experience. If he has been cared for apart from his parents from infancy he frequently must suffer from uncertainty as to their whereabouts and condition, and from a longing for knowledge of his heritage. He is sometimes subjected to scorn and undergoes humiliation because of his parentage.

Specific evidence in regard to the psychological effect upon a sensitive child of the knowledge of illegitimate birth is difficult to obtain. Several histories suggested the mental suffering often occasioned children born out of wedlock by the realization of the circumstances of their birth or the character of their parents.

The burden upon the public.

Birth out of wedlock usually implies social maladjustment. This study has shown the large number of cases in which the mothers, for various reasons, were unable to care for their children, and the small proportion of cases in which the fathers contributed to the children's support. The obligations that are not fulfilled by the parents or other relatives must be assumed by the public.

Maternity and infancy care.—More than three-fourths of the infants born out of wedlock in Boston during the year covered by the study were born in hospitals, maternity homes, or the public infirmary. Although no data were compiled in regard to the proportion of cases in which the care was free or was paid for only in part, the indications were that in the majority of instances all or part of the expense was met by these organizations. The necessity for care and supervision of infants born out of wedlock is shown by the fact that more than three-fifths of those born in Boston during one year were known to have been under the prolonged care of agencies for all or part of the first year of life. Almost one-third of the infants born during the year had been cared for by maternity homes or the public infirmary—institutions keeping mother and child together for considerable periods. Child-caring agencies also provided care for a large number of babies.

Child dependency.—One of the most significant aspects of the problem of birth out of wedlock is the burden of child dependency that devolves upon the public. The proportion of children becoming dependent is indicated by the fact that more than one-third of the infants born during one year were given prolonged care by child-caring or child-protective agencies during their first year of life.

The care of children born out of wedlock comprised a considerable proportion of the work of social agencies in Boston and in the State. One-sixth of the cases under care of Boston private child-caring agencies during the year concerned children born out of wedlock, one-ninth of the cases under care of the public child-caring agency of the city, and almost one-fourth of those under care of the division of State minor wards. A comparison of dependent children of legitimate and of illegitimate birth under care of the State showed also that those born out of wedlock came under care earlier and remained public charges longer than those born in lawful marriage.

Antisocial attitude.—The conditions with which many children born out of wedlock must contend often give rise to restlessness, a morbid outlook upon life, or delinquent conduct. There is increasing recognition of the need for careful, expert study, with especial reference to their mental life, of individual children who are not normal in their social reactions. The Judge Baker Foundation is doing pioneer work along these lines, and some of the other agencies in Boston are also giving attention to this important phase of case work.

A comparison of dependent children of legitimate and of illegitimate birth under the care of the State, who were 7 years of age and over, showed that 18 per cent of those born out of wedlock were delinquent or troublesome in their conduct, as against 13 per cent of the children born in wedlock. Among the children 14 years of age and over the corresponding percentages were 28 and 16.

The study of children under care of State institutions for delinquents indicated that the proportion of children born out of wedlock was high in comparison with the percentage of illegitimate births in the State. The figures were too small to warrant definite conclusions, but the findings suggest that children handicapped by birth out of wedlock, and therefore frequently deprived of care by their own parents, are turned over to the care of correctional institutions at an earlier age and for less serious offenses than children whose home ties are more nearly normal.

Measures for the protection of children born out of wedlock.

It has been shown that children born out of wedlock are in special need of protection. This need begins before the child is born, and frequently extends through childhood. The protection of life and health, beginning with the prevention of death in infancy; the safeguarding of the child's right to a mother's care; the securing of support from the father; the closest possible approximation to normal home care for children whose mothers are unable to provide for them; especially wise and understanding care for children handicapped by defective heredity; the equalization, so far as practicable, of the status of the child born out of wedlock with that of the child of legitimate birth; the recognition by the State of its fundamental responsibility for the welfare of these children, who are both the result and the innocent victims of social maladjustment—these are means by which the handicap which has so unjustly been the portion of the child born out of wedlock may be in part overcome.

The prevention of infant mortality.—The means for the reduction of the appalling infant mortality among children born out of wedlock, as revealed by this study, may be summarized as follows:

1. Provision for maternity care, including: Medical advice and supervision during pregnancy and protection of the mother from harmful employment, unfavorable living conditions, financial stress, and mental anguish; confinement in an adequately equipped hospital or maternity home, or, if in a private home, by a properly qualified attendant; and adequate care following confinement. The majority of the mothers of infants born in Boston were confined in hospitals or maternity homes, but the evidence indicated a need for increased care during pregnancy and for convalescent care. Almost half the mothers were confined in hospitals where they usually remained for only two or three weeks following the birth of the child. If they had no homes to which they could go, they were forced to face life with the burden of a child to care for and support before they had

fully recuperated. Under such conditions, the child could neither be properly nourished nor adequately cared for.

2. Care for the mother and infant which will enable the mother to keep her child with her during the nursing period at least. The great advantage to the child of maternal care under proper conditions, either in a maternity home or in a private family, has been shown by the findings of this study. Unless the mother is physically unable to nurse her child, or there is some reason for separation of very great importance, the child should be kept with his own mother during the first few months of life, at least. In order to accomplish this, the most wise and understanding assistance and supervision on the part of social agencies is often necessary.

3. At least as much medical oversight and health supervision for infants born out of wedlock as are deemed necessary for infants of legitimate birth. This can usually be accomplished through general health or infant-welfare agencies; two such private agencies in Boston cared for some of the infants born out of wedlock during the year. Nurses employed by the Boston department of health now visit all infants whose births are registered, if they can be found; during one period they visited only infants of legitimate birth, thus omitting those most in need of supervision.

4. Effective State supervision and licensing of private lying-in hospitals, boarding homes for infants, and agencies and institutions, including the supervision of infants in institutions and of those placed in family homes. In Massachusetts the State board of charity exercises supervision over lying-in hospitals and boarding homes for infants, and nurses employed by the State visit infants reported as cared for apart from their own relatives. The data presented in this report in regard to the mortality of infants born out of wedlock show how necessary it is for the State to gather information in regard to the mortality among infants cared for in the various institutions or under the supervision of agencies and, wherever unduly high rates are found, to take steps to ascertain the reasons and remove the causes.

Insuring a mother's care and a father's support.—Not only during infancy, but also in the years following, is the child entitled to the care of his own mother. In some instances this is impossible, but the child should not be separated from his mother except for urgent reasons. To keep mother and child together often involves prolonged financial and other assistance and careful supervision from social agencies. Several private agencies in Boston and the social service committee of the State board of charity were doing successful work along these lines. In many instances, however, children were being separated from their mothers without due consideration of other possibilities or of the injustice that was being done mother and child. The interests of the child also demand that the father fulfill his obligations, at least to the extent of assisting in the child's support. There would seem to be need in Massachusetts for further development in the practical administration of the law for the determination of paternity and the enforcement of support by the father. Considerable difference of opinion exists among the agencies in regard to the extent to which this act should be uniformly applied and the type of cases which should be brought to court.

The standards adopted by a series of child-welfare conferences held under the auspices of the United States Children's Bureau include the following statement of principles relating to the responsibility of parents for the care of their children born out of wedlock:[1]

Save for unusual reasons both parents should be held responsible for the child during his minority, and especially should the responsibility of the father be emphasized.

Care of the child by his mother is highly desirable, particularly during the nursing months.

No parent of a child born out of wedlock should be permitted to surrender the child outside his own family, save with the consent of a properly designated State department or a court of proper jurisdiction.

Each State should make suitable provision of a humane character for establishing paternity and guaranteeing to children born out of wedlock the rights naturally belonging to children born in wedlock. The fathers of such children should be under the same financial responsibilities and the same legal liabilities toward their children as other fathers. The administration of the courts with reference to such cases should be so regulated as not only to protect the legal rights of the mother and child but also to avoid unnecessary publicity and humiliation.

The care of children whose parents can not provide for them.— For many children born out of wedlock there is no possibility of permanent care by their own parents. For these children provision must be made which compensates as fully as possible for the deprivation of parental care. The essentials of provision for them are in general the same as for children of legitimate birth who must be cared for by agencies or institutions,[2] and may be summarized as follows:

1. Complete investigation of family history and circumstances.
2. The study of the child's physical and mental condition and characteristics.
3. The placing of the child in a properly qualified family home or, if his condition requires, in an institution suited to his needs.

---

[1] U. S. Children's Bureau : Minimum Standards for Child Welfare Adopted by the Washington and Regional Conferences on Child Welfare, 1919. Conference Series No. 2, Bureau Publication No. 62. Washington, 1919. P. 12.

[2] Ibid., pp. 10–14.

4. Careful supervision of the child's health, education, and moral and spiritual development.

5. Complete records of the child's history, and of his development and progress while under care.

6. Vocational training for the child and helpful supervision while he is becoming self-supporting.

7. Particular consideration of the needs of children handicapped by defective heredity.

8. Cooperation between agencies and the fullest utilization of the resources of the community.

The agencies in Boston and in Massachusetts as a rule maintained high standards of work for children under care. Nevertheless, the grade of service was by no means uniform, and in some cases the welfare of the children under care was jeopardized by inadequacy of staff, insufficiency of resources, or lack of emphasis on certain essential features. Proper understanding of the child's needs and of the type of care required was often impossible because of absence of complete information concerning the mother and her family and the father; incompleteness of data in regard to physical condition, only acute illnesses or serious physical handicaps being entered; and failure to secure mental examinations for all children whose development was backward or who presented special problems. Visitors were often too overburdened to give the necessary supervision or to develop the helpful relationships which would be desirable. An unusual amount of cooperation was found among the Boston agencies, but the study indicated the need for still further unification of effort and for utilization of all the community resources available for child welfare. Of great benefit in connection with the handling of cases for the unmarried mother and her child might well be a central application bureau, to which all such cases could first be referred, and which would send applicants to agencies equipped to give the care required.

Safeguarding the rights of the child. —There is much difference of opinion in regard to the extent to which the law should raise the status of the child born out of wedlock to that of the child of legitimate birth in respect to inheritance and the right to the father's name. The matter of inheritance would not seem to be of great practical importance, owing to the relatively few cases in which the father is a man of means. Under many circumstances the bearing of the name of the father might be an actual disadvantage, especially if the mother had the custody of the child. On the other hand, it is argued that as a matter of justice the child of illegitimate birth should be given the same legal rights as though he had been born in wedlock. These questions are of much less practical significance than the insuring to the child of the care and support of his parents, which has already been discussed.

The matter of birth registration is of considerable importance in relation to the rights and welfare of the child born out of wedlock. Birth registration is necessary to the safeguarding of the health of infants and, in later life, to proof of age which is required for various purposes. In Massachusetts, birth registration is fairly complete. However, consideration should be given to the question of whether birth records ought to be safeguarded against improper use or unnecessary publicity. The present law of the State requires that public records shall be open to inspection on demand, and transcripts of birth certificates for various purposes reveal the birth status. In some communities in other States, either by law or by regulation, it is provided that only persons who can show due cause for interest in the information may be permitted access to birth records, and information in regard to parentage is omitted from transcripts for school and employment purposes.[3]

The State's responsibility.—In this country the guardianship or supervision of the State over children born out of wedlock is usually an incidental part of State provision for dependent children or of supervision over agencies and institutions. It is a question as to whether the United States should follow the example of those European countries in which all children born out of wedlock come under public guardianship by virtue of their status, or whether such special protection should be exercised only over those dependent upon social agencies.

The State of Massachusetts not only has some supervision over agencies and institutions caring for children and over infant boarding homes, but it also has under its direct care large numbers of children dependent upon the public, a considerable proportion of whom are of illegitimate birth. The supervisory powers of the State over private agencies and institutions are limited; more effective supervision would promote the welfare of all children under care of these organizations.

One of the weak points in the protection of children born out of wedlock, as well as of children of legitimate birth, is the absence of provision for the investigation of adoption cases before the courts; decrees of adoption are given without adequate consideration of the child's history and circumstances or of the character of the home into which he is to be placed. State officials and leaders in social work in Massachusetts have recognized the need for investigation of

---

[3] For a discussion of the status of the child and birth registration, see U. S. Children's Bureau; Illegitimacy as a Child-Welfare Problem, Pt. 1, by Emma O. Lundberg and Katharine F. Lenroot. Dependent, Defective, and Delinquent Classes Series No. 9. Bureau Publication No. 66. Washington, 1920. Pp. 18–20.

every adoption case by a State department, which would act in an advisory capacity to the court.

In the standards adopted by the child-welfare conferences held under the auspices of the United States Children's Bureau the following principles of State responsibility are set forth :[4]

Upon the State devolves the ultimate responsibility for children who are in need of special care by reason of unfortunate home conditions, physical or mental handicap, or delinquency.

* * * * * * *

A State board of charities or a similar supervisory body should be responsible for the regular inspection and licensing of every institution, agency, or association, incorporated or otherwise, which receives or cares for mothers with children or children who suffer from physical or mental handicaps, or who are delinquent, dependent, or without suitable parental care, and should have authority to revoke such licenses for cause and to prescribe forms of registration and report. This State agency should maintain such supervision and visitation of children in institutions and children placed in family homes as will insure their proper care, training, and protection. The incorporation of private organizations caring for children should be required, and should be subject to the approval of the State board of charities or similar body. State supervision should be conceived and exercised in harmony with democratic ideals which invite and encourage the service of efficient, altruistic forces of society in the common welfare.

General constructive measures.

A consideration of illegitimacy, even though it be from the point of view of the child, would not be complete without mention of measures that may result in a reduction of the problem. This study has dealt with the causative side of illegitimacy only as incidental to the discussion of the child's heritage and the possibilities of parental care. However, the information obtained has thrown some light upon the underlying social and economic conditions leading to illegitimacy.

In a large number of cases included in the study the mother came from a home in which there was poverty, dependency, alcoholism, immorality, absence of parental supervision, or even, in some instances, encouragement of misconduct. In other cases she had no home.

Absence of opportunity for wholesome companionship and recreation, either because of the situation in the home or conditions surrounding employment, and lack of supervision over commercialized recreation, are important factors in moral delinquency. Significant also in this connection are lack of moral training, ignorance of the dangers involved in disregard of the safeguards that have been built up through social conventions, and too great suggestibility or other weaknesses of character. One of the generally recognized factors

[4] U. S. Children's Bureau: Minimum Standards for Child Welfare Adopted by the Washington and Regional Conferences on Child Welfare, 1919. Conference Series No. 2. Bureau Publication No. 62. Washington, 1919. P. 10.

in delinquency of this kind is mental subnormality, which often results in lack of judgment and self-control.

There has been practically no study of the histories of fathers of children born out of wedlock. If the contributing factors in the moral delinquency of the fathers were analyzed, they would probably be found to parallel to some extent the conditions leading to immorality among girls—bad home conditions, unsupervised recreation, lack of moral training, character weakness, and mental subnormality.

Following is a brief statement of some of the measures which will tend toward the reduction of the illegitimate-birth rate through raising the level of family life, developing constructive forces in the community in place of those that are degrading, and affording special protection to individuals who stand in need of such help:

1. Improvement of industrial and economic conditions, resulting in better standards of living.

2. Raising the level of general education, and providing for all children opportunities for moral and spiritual development, including training in standards of morality and conduct.

3. Provision of opportunity for wholesome recreation, properly safeguarded, and supervision of commercialized amusements.

4. Removal of degrading community influences.

5. Adequate provision for the diagnosis and care of the mentally subnormal, including institutional provision for the feeble-minded and the defective delinquent in need of such care, and special training and supervision in the community.

6. Special protection for young people of both sexes who are surrounded by dangerous influences or who show tendencies toward wrongdoing; improved standards of case work with families and children, with special reference to the detection and removal of the influences that menace the welfare of children.

7. Assisting and safeguarding mothers of children born out of wedlock, to the end that they may gain a position of independence and self-respect in the community and that they may not repeat their unfortunate experiences.

SECTION I. THE PROBLEM IN BOSTON.

SECTION I. THE PROBLEM IN BOSTON.

INTRODUCTION.

Boston has long been a center of philanthropic effort for the New England States. Into the metropolis come the unfortunate in need of special help and care, and from it radiate social activities that reach more remote centers of populations as well as near-by towns and cities. As the capital of the State it is the administrative center for State institutions and agencies. Its many organizations for the betterment of social conditions and the amelioration of distress bear witness to the humanitarian ideals of its citizens, while the growing tendency toward coordination and cooperation in social work is gradually eliminating the duplication of effort sometimes occasioned by multiplicity of organizations. The well-developed State provision for dependent classes has allowed the private agencies to select the more promising cases and to specialize in intensive and experimental work.

As indications of the cooperation between agencies and the recognition of the importance of adequate understanding of the problems dealt with, may be mentioned the founding in Boston in 1876 of the first confidential exchange of social information in the United States;[1] the publication in 1880 of a charities directory; the agreement in 1912 between child-caring and child-protective agencies as to the territory which should be covered by the respective societies, the entire State being apportioned among the different agencies; the establishment in 1912 of the Boston Conference on Illegitimacy; the creation in 1915 of the League for Preventive Work, founded and maintained by Boston social agencies for the study and prevention of some of the causes of misery found in their work with families. More recent developments are the Committee of the Permanent Charity Fund, which began operations in 1917, whose functions are to administer an endowment fund in the assistance of such activities as seem to promise the greatest usefulness to the community and to utilize in the same way gifts which may be made to the fund; and the Bureau on Illegitimacy, founded early in 1919 for the study of that problem, the initial support being granted by the Permanent Charity Fund.

Much remains to be accomplished by some of the agencies in the direction of improved methods of case work and greater utilization

---

[1] Byington, Margaret F.: The Confidential Exchange, a Form of Social Cooperation. Charity Organization Department of the Russell Sage Foundation. New York City, 1912. P. 4.

of the available community resources, as well as in further coordination of effort between societies and in elimination of needless duplication and division of endeavor. Forces already set in motion will do much toward the accomplishment of these ends.

The development of municipal provision for dependent and delinquent children has already been discussed, as has the effect of the stringent settlement laws upon the division of responsibility between the State and the city.[2] In 1914, the year covered by this study, the public agencies and institutions of Boston of interest in connection with the inquiry were as follows:

The overseers of the poor.

Public outdoor relief and aid to mothers with dependent children.

The children's institutions department—under the management of the trustees for children.

Care of dependent children, for the most part having settlement in Boston; of neglected children; and of juvenile offenders committed to the Suffolk School for Boys or the Parental School. The latter institution was closed in 1914.

The Boston Infirmary Department—having charge of Long Island Hospital.

For the treatment of chronic cases or cases requiring care for long periods of time. Most of the children received are with their mothers or are wards of the trustees for children.

The Boston City Hospital.

For the treatment of acute diseases.

The Boston Juvenile Court (serving the central district) and courts in other parts of the city hearing children's cases.[3]

Neglected and delinquent children.

Besides these agencies, the department of the city registrar, who keeps the records of births and deaths, was of great importance to this study. The work of this department is described in chapter 1 of this section.

The children's institutions department cared for dependent and neglected children through the placing-out and office division. The children were placed in boarding or free homes under the supervision of visitors. Boys on parole from the Suffolk School for Boys were under the supervision of the placing-out division, as were those on

---

[2] See pp. 25–27, 29–31.

[3] Since the year covered by this study the Judge Baker Foundation has been established in Boston. The principal purpose of this foundation, privately maintained, is to work in cooperation with the juvenile court, serving as a department for medico-psychological study of the children. Thorough physical and mental examinations are given, and information in regard to home conditions, family history, and personal history and characteristics is secured. The foundation also works in cooperation with other agencies in Boston and sometimes gives attention to children who have not come before the court.

parole from the Parental School previous to the close of that institution. A total of 1,537 children, including those in institutions, received prolonged care from the children's institutions department in 1914, and there were 284 applications for care which were not accepted.

There were 36 births in Long Island Hospital in 1914. Expectant mothers often entered the hospital some little time before confinement, and remained in the institution with their babies for several months. The type of care given was akin to that of a private maternity home, in that it included prolonged care before and after the birth of the child. Aside from settlement requirements, there were no limitations as to the women received. The Boston City Hospital reported 77 births during the year, though it had no regular maternity service until October, 1916. In September, 1917, medical-social work for the maternity patients in the hospital was organized.[4] There is also a gynecological out-patient department, in connection with which medical-social work has been inauguarated since the year of this study.

Eleven private child-caring agencies in Boston during the year of this study dealt more or less with the problem of the child born out of wedlock. The Society for Helping Destitute Mothers and Infants [5] placed mothers and babies together, working in close cooperation with hospitals, dispensaries, and other agencies. Its work was limited to Boston. The Children's Aid Society, Children's Friend Society, Children's Mission to Children, Church Home Society,[6] and New England Home for Little Wanderers cared for dependent and neglected children, three of these organizations also providing for delinquent children committed to their care and for mothers who wished to keep their babies with them. Children were supervised in their own homes, placed in boarding or free homes, and given necessary medical care, either by the agencies themselves or by arrangements with hospitals and dispensaries. The Society for Helping Destitute Mothers and Infants and the Children's Aid Society had an arrangement by which the former worked with mothers over 20 and the latter with younger mothers. The Children's Aid Society, Children's Friend Society, Children's Mission to Children, and New England Home for Little Wanderers had an agreement among themselves and with other agencies in the State as to territory covered. All four worked in the city of Boston, but the outlying territory was divided into geographical districts, each district being assigned to one of the agencies entering into the arrangement. The New England Home for Little Wanderers covered also the other New England

---

[4] Russell, Bess Lynde: " A year's study of the maternity ward at the Boston City Hospital." Boston Medical and Surgical Journal, Vol. CLXXX (May 1, 1919), pp. 487–495.
[5] This society discontinued work in 1919.
[6] Formerly the Church Home for Orphan and Destitute Children.

States. The Church Home Society worked throughout Massachusetts, caring for children of Protestant-Episcopal parentage.

The Children's Mission to Children maintained a special service for delicate children, boarding convalescent medical cases for the Massachusetts General Hospital. The New England Home for Little Wanderers opened in 1915 a new home with all modern facilities for medical care and mental diagnosis. To this institution are brought children difficult of diagnosis on the physical side or in need of special medical care and children presenting problems of mentality or behavior. Children remain in the institution as long as their condition requires. The Children's Aid Society in 1915 made special arrangements with the Boston Dispensary for medical care for their wards, placing emphasis upon the preventive side. This work is functioning through a department of the dispensary known as the preventive clinic. The Church Home Society has a similar arrangement with the Boston Dispensary.

The Massachusetts Babies Hospital (formerly the Massachusetts Infant Asylum) provided boarding and convalescent care for babies under 2 years of age. The babies were placed in country homes and visited at least once a week by trained nurses. Under an arrangement with the Boston Dispensary medical care was given by that institution. In 1916 the Massachusetts Babies Hospital was amalgamated with the Children's Aid Society.

The Catholic Charitable Bureau boarded dependent and neglected children and mothers and babies in family homes, and it also conducted a bureau of information for Catholic agencies. It received Catholic children who were residents of Massachusetts. The Home for Destitute Catholic Children cared for children 3 years of age and over, in the Boston diocese, maintaining a temporary receiving home and placing its wards in foster homes. St. Mary's Infant Asylum, maintained in connection with St. Mary's Lying-in Hospital, cared for children under 3 years of age, placing the majority of them in family homes, though caring for some in the institution. Its territory of work was also the Boston diocese.[7]

The court department of the Council of Jewish Women worked with Jewish neglected and delinquent children before the juvenile court and also handled informal cases that had not yet come to court. It gave supervision in the children's own homes and placed children in boarding or free homes.[8]

---

[7] The State is divided into three Catholic dioceses—Boston, Springfield, and Fall River.

[8] Subsequent to the year covered by this study, the Jewish Children's Bureau has been established in Boston for the care of dependent, neglected, and delinquent Jewish children. Its purpose is to care for all Jewish children in the metropolitan district who do not have adequate care in their own homes. Such children are usually placed in carefully selected Jewish homes. A clinic for physical examinations is maintained by the bureau, and mental examinations are given by the Judge Baker Foundation. The work is supported by the Federated Jewish Charities.

The Boston office of the Massachusetts Society for the Prevention of Cruelty to Children was the central office of the society. It dealt mainly with cases in Boston and vicinity but also did special work throughout the State. A temporary home was maintained in connection with the Boston office, where children were kept pending the disposition of their cases in court. In the majority of the towns and cities of the State the society had a representative in court at the hearing of neglect cases, and in these localities neglected children not committed to the State were usually committed to the society on continuances, the society supervising them in their own homes, in homes in which they had been placed, or while under the care of private agencies. The cases handled by this agency were of two types—those brought into court and those given advice, supervision, and assistance, but not brought into court. The society has taken a leading part in general child-welfare movements.

Four maternity homes in Boston gave prenatal and postnatal care to girls and women illegitimately pregnant for the first time and not having venereal infection. Three of them received only mothers who promised to keep their children with them. The Florence Crittenton Home, the Salvation Army Home, and the Talitha Cumi Home received residents of New England. The House of Mercy worked throughout the Episcopal diocese of Massachusetts. The last institution sent girls and women under care to the New England Hospital for Women and Children for confinement, giving care before and after the child's birth. The three other homes had their own maternity wards. Women were often received several months before confinement, and frequently remained with their babies in the homes for four or five months, nursing them and receiving instruction in housework. Places were then found for the mothers where they might keep their children, and supervision and after care were given.

Two health agencies, the Instructive District Nursing Association and the Baby Hygiene Association,[9] did home nursing. The first-named agency, as a part of its work, made a specialty of pregnancy clinics and prenatal and postnatal care, and the second agency of milk stations and well-baby clinics. These societies have done much to reduce infant mortality in Boston.

Four hospitals had large maternity wards and reported illegitimate births during the year studied. These were the Boston Lying-in Hospital, the Massachusetts Homeopathic Hospital, the New England Hospital for Women and Children, and St. Mary's Lying-in Hospital. The Massachusetts General Hospital cared for but few maternity cases. All these hospitals, with the exception of St. Mary's, had out-patient departments.

---

[9] Formerly the Milk and Baby Hygiene Association.

The Boston Dispensary cooperated with other social agencies, giving physical examinations and medical care.

The Boston Legal Aid Society gave legal aid and advice gratuitously or for nominal fees. This agency was important in connection with the prosecution of cases under the law providing for the support of children of illegitimate birth.

The most important private family-care agencies in Boston were the Associated Charities, the Boston Provident Association, the St. Vincent de Paul Society, and the Federated Jewish Charities. The last agency also maintained a home for Jewish children over 5 years of age. The Council of Jewish Women, through its immigrant-aid department, cared for immigrant girls, securing employment for them and assisting them in other ways.[10]

The Boston Society for the Care of Girls and the House of the Good Shepherd dealt with illegitimacy incidentally to their work for the protection of girls. The former society gave care and supervision to girls taken from the juvenile court or received from other sources. The girls were usually placed in boarding or free homes. The House of the Good Shepherd cared for wayward girls and women, either committed by court or received on voluntary application. There were in Boston other agencies and institutions caring for children, most of them having very limited capacity. The ones mentioned are those of most importance to this study.

The psychopathic department of the Boston State Hospital, one of the State hospitals for the care of the insane, gave first care and observation to mental patients, including the feeble-minded, and treated acute and curable mental diseases. It served the metropolitan district; but the out-patient department had no limitations, accepting all who came for diagnosis, advice, and out-patient treatment. The scientific investigation and research work was also State-wide in scope. The purpose of the out-patient department was "to afford free consultation to the poor, and such advice and medical treatment as would, with the aid of district nursing, promote the home care of mental patients."[11] The social service department made investigations and gave supervision and advice. The facilities for diagnosis and out-patient care afforded by the psychopathic department are invaluable to the work of Boston agencies.

---

[10] See note, p. 77, relative to the Jewish Children's Bureau, established subsequent to the year of the study and maintained by the Federated Jewish Charities.

[11] Recommendations of the State board of insanity, quoted in the Second Annual Report of the Psychopathic Department of the Boston State Hospital for the Year Ending November 30, 1913, p. 22.

CHAPTER 1. THE INFANT BORN OUT OF WEDLOCK.

METHOD AND SCOPE OF STUDY.

Of prime importance in a study of illegitimacy is the consideration of the number of illegitimate births each year, the proportion of total births which this number constitutes, the mortality of infants of illegitimate birth as compared with others, and the conditions surrounding their birth and infancy. Vital statistics necessarily form the basis of such a study. The information obtained from birth and death records was supplemented in this study by data secured from the records of social agencies. So far as possible, each child was followed through his first year of life. This investigation was based upon a study of records, and no attempt was made to follow up cases not known to social agencies or to supplement the information secured from records.

The question of registration of illegitimate births has been the subject of much discussion. The method of registering such births varies in different States, but nowhere in this country has a system been put into practice which is thoroughly satisfactory from all points of view. In Massachusetts the fact of illegitimacy is not entered on the birth certificate, and the law forbids the statement in the certificate of the name and other facts relating to the father of a child of illegitimate birth, except at the request, in writing, of both parents. It is, however, in most cases possible to determine the fact of illegitimacy from the birth certificate by the absence of the father's name. This has been considered a basis of selection sufficiently accurate to warrant the issuance of statistics of illegitimate births by the health department of the city of Boston.[1]

Great care is taken by the city registrar to verify and complete all birth-certificate data. As they come in from the physicians, copies of the certificates are sent to the parents for correction. Canvassers are also sent out to secure complete birth registration. The chances of the name of a father of a child of legitimate birth being omitted from the birth record are thus rendered negligible. In checking birth certificates with the records of social agencies, there was no instance in which a child thought to be of illegitimate birth by reason of the evidence on the birth certificate was discovered to be of legitimate birth. The

[1] Forty-fourth Annual Report of the Health Department of the City of Boston for the Year 1915. Boston, 1916. P. 145.

error would appear to lie, rather, in the registration of infants born out of wedlock as though they were of legitimate birth, resulting in an understatement of the number of illegitimate births. A number of instances were found in which this had happened. In some of these cases the parents had been living as married. In others the mother had probably misinformed the doctor as to her civil state.

The name of the father is commonly omitted from the death certificate of a child of illegitimate birth. However, in cases in which the mother was married subsequent to the child's birth, whether to the father or to another man, and kept the baby with her, the name of the mother's husband would probably appear on the death certificate as the name of the child's father.

In order to secure information as to infants born out of wedlock in Boston in the year of the study, all the birth records for 1914 were searched for those that indicated illegitimate birth. Birth certificates indicating that the child had been born out of wedlock were then checked with death certificates indicating illegitimacy, in order that cases in which the child appeared from the death record to be of illegitimate birth, but which had not been found among the birth certificates, might be discovered. Such cases were then traced through the birth registry to determine whether the birth had been registered as illegitimate or legitimate. In some instances the birth and death of the same child were registered under different names, but it was usually possible to check by the first name of the mother and the date and place of birth.

The list of births obtained in the above manner was supplemented by comparison with records of social agencies in Boston. A number of cases were found in which the social agency stated that a child of illegitimate birth had been born in Boston in the year studied, though no birth certificate had been found. These cases were checked through the birth registry and in many instances it was found that the child had been registered as of legitimate birth. These cases were then included in the list of illegitimate births. In the final tabulation of the results only those infants whose births had been registered as either illegitimate or legitimate were included.

As a means of determining how far the year of the study was representative, the total numbers of illegitimate births were secured for each year of the period 1910 to 1914, inclusive. It was not practicable to check the births for the first four years of the period with death records and records of agencies, as was done for the year selected for intensive study. Hence the figures given include only those births registered as illegitimate, and do not include illegitimate births registered as legitimate. The proportions of illegitimate births are, therefore, understatements. The birth registry of Boston includes

182299°—21——6

also records of infants born outside the city whose mothers are residents of Boston, since under the Massachusetts law births to mothers not residents of the place where they are confined are reported to the town of residence.[2] These nonresident births are included in the total births and in the illegitimate births for the first four years of the period, but not for the year 1914. For the purpose of comparison with the first four years of the period, only births registered as illegitimate are included in the 1914 figures.

Two methods were used for measuring the infant mortality among children born out of wedlock. The first method was a comparison of the number of illegitimate births during a given year with the number of deaths during the same year of infants under 1 year of age born out of wedlock. This comparison was made for each year of the five-year period 1910 to 1914, inclusive.

The death certificates were searched for records of infants of illegitimate birth who died under 1 year of age in Boston during the period specified. No distinction was made between deaths of infants born in Boston or outside Boston, or born during the year specified or the year previous. The comparison with births was based on the number of births secured by the method previously described. A more correct rate was obtained for 1914 than for the entire five-year period, because of the greater accuracy in the number of births, obtained through the process of checking. Analyses of age at death and cause of death were made for that year.

The second method used in this study for measuring mortality among infants born out of wedlock was the following, through all available records, of the infants born during the year to determine the number of these infants who died during their first year of life. For this purpose the Boston death certificates of 1914 and 1915 were searched for infants of illegitimate birth born in Boston during 1914 and dying in Boston in 1914 or 1915, aged under 1 year. Where the residence of the mother was a Massachusetts town outside Boston, the death records of the town specified were also searched and death certificates for infants born in Boston in 1914 and dying under 1 year of age were included in the total number of deaths. Deaths reported by social agencies but not verified by death certificates were not included for the purpose of measuring infant mortality. Analyses of age at death and cause of death were made.

A considerable amount of information was available for all these infants from the birth and death certificates. In a large number of cases this was supplemented by information from records of social

---

[2] Copies of all birth certificates are filed in the office of the Secretary of the Commonwealth. Here the returns are checked to avoid duplication in the published statistics. R. L. 1902 ch. 29 sec. 13 as amended by acts 1910 ch. 93; sec. 18 as amended by 1903 ch. 305.

agencies. Material from all sources pertaining to a given case was assembled on one form and the data were then counterchecked.

NUMBER OF ILLEGITIMATE BIRTHS AND PROPORTION TO TOTAL BIRTHS.

During a Five-Year Period.

There are two methods of computing illegitimacy rates. The first gives the percentage of illegitimate births in a given period and is obtained by dividing the number of illegitimate births by the total births. The second method compares the number of illegitimate births with the number of single, widowed, and divorced women of childbearing age in the community, and is obtained by dividing the number of illegitimate births by the number of such women in the population. The first method has to commend it the fact that it emphasizes the extent of the child-care problem involved. The second method is the more valuable if the purpose is to deal with causative factors and to consider the moral and preventive sides of the problem. Both methods are difficult to apply fairly in a city like Boston, which is a center for maternity care and consequently has a large proportion of births to nonresident mothers, particularly mothers of children born out of wedlock.

Table 1 shows for each year from 1910 to 1914, inclusive, the total number of births and the number and per cent of illegitimate births. It must be remembered that these percentages are based upon uncorrected figures, the illegitimate births including only those registered as such.

TABLE 1.—*Per cent of live births in Boston registered as illegitimate, 1910 to 1914.*

Year of birth.	Total live births.a	Live births registered as illegitimate.	
		Number.b	Per cent.
1910	17,831	670	3.8
1911	18,007	757	4.2
1912	18,924	867	4.6
1913	19,288	829	4.3
1914	c 19,462	d 752	3.9

a Unpublished figures, except for the year 1914, secured from the registry department. Except for 1914, includes births outside Boston to Boston mothers, if registered in Boston. These figures are slightly larger than those published in the annual reports, because of additional births that occurred in the years specified but were not registered in time for inclusion in the annual reports.

b Except for 1914, includes births outside Boston to Boston mothers, if registered in Boston.

c Actual births in Boston. Forty-third Annual Report of the Health Department of the city of Boston for the year 1914. Boston, 1915. p. 104.

d Actual births in Boston. This figure does not include births known to be illegitimate but registered as legitimate. It is given in order to be comparable with the preceding uncorrected figures. It is smaller than the corrected figure used later in the report.

The percentage varied during the five years from 3.8 per cent to 4.6 per cent, the lowest percentage being in 1910, and the highest in

1912. The rate for 1914, the year of the intensive study, was 3.9 per cent, the next to the lowest in the five-year period. In the annual report for 1915 the Health Department of the City of Boston published statistics relating to births and deaths of infants born out of wedlock. In that year there were 800 illegitimate births, 4.1 per cent of the total births.[3]

The number of illegitimate births per 1,000 single, widowed, and divorced women 15 to 44 years of age is shown in Table 2 for five years, 1910 to 1914.

TABLE 2.—*Number of live births in Boston registered as illegitimate per 1,000 single, widowed, and divorced women 15 to 44 years of age, 1910 to 1914.*

Year.	Single, widowed, and divorced women 15 to 44 years of age.a	Live births during year registered as illegitimate.	
		Number.b	Rate per 1,000 women.
1910	96,655	670	6.9
1911	97,984	757	7.7
1912	99,313	867	8.7
1913	100,642	829	8.2
1914	101,971	752	7.4

a Estimated as for July 1 of each year, on the basis of U. S. Census figures for 1900 and 1910.
b See notes b and d Table 1.

The rate of illegitimate live births per 1,000 single, widowed, and divorced women of child-bearing age shows a yearly variation similar to that shown by the percentages of illegitimate live births (See Table 1.) The rate estimated on either basis is high in comparison with the illegitimacy rates for the State as a whole. The percentage of illegitimate live births in Massachusetts was 2.3 in 1914,[4] as compared with the percentage of 3.9 for Boston. The number of illegitimate live births per 1,000 single, widowed, and divorced women of child-bearing age in Massachusetts was 4.5 in 1914,[5] as compared with the rate of 7.4 for Boston. The relatively high Boston rates are in part due to the fact that Boston is a center to which many women come from outside the city for the purpose of securing maternity care.

The registration of stillbirths is likely to be less complete than that of live births. The figures obtained, and shown in Table 3, indicate a higher percentage of stillbirths among illegitimate births than among all births. The numbers of stillbirths per 100 births registered range from 3.6 to 3.9 in the period 1910 to 1914. The number of illegitimate stillbirths per 100 births registered as ille-

[3] Forty-fourth Annual Report of the Health Department of the City of Boston for the year 1915. Boston, 1916. Pp. 145, 147.
[4] See p. 270.
[5] Idem.

gitimate range from 6.7 to 5.4, being lower for 1914 than for any other year. Too much importance must not be attached to these figures, however, because of the probable incomplete registration of stillbirths.

TABLE 3.—*Per cent of stillbirths registered in Boston among total births and among births registered as illegitimate, 1910 to 1914.*

| Year of birth. | Total births.a | Stillbirths. | | Births registered as illegitimate.c | Stillbirths registered as illegitimate. | |
		Number.b	Per cent of total births.		Number.	Per cent of all births registered as illegitimate.
1910	18,506	675	3.6	718	48	6.7
1911	18,722	715	3.8	805	48	6.0
1912	19,666	742	3.8	925	58	6.3
1913	20,025	737	3.7	877	48	5.5
1914	20,251	789	3.9	795	43	5.4

a Live births (see Table 1, p. 83) plus stillbirths.
b Forty-third Annual Report of the Health Department of the City of Boston for the Year 1914. Boston, 1915. Pp. 98 and 104.
c Illegitimate live births (see Table 1, p. 83) plus illegitimate stillbirths.

During the Year of the Study.

Considering only the births registered as illegitimate, there were in Boston in 1914, the year selected for intensive study, 752 illegitimate live births. These births were 3.9 per cent of all live births registered in the city.

Through a process of checking with death records and with the records of agencies and institutions, as described above, 95 cases were found in which illegitimate births were registered as legitimate. Hence, there was known to have been a total of 847 illegitimate live births during the year, constituting 4.4 per cent of all live births. [6] This percentage of illegitimate births is still an understatement. Undoubtedly there were other illegitimate births registered as legitimate, which were impossible to trace by the means employed.

During the year there were 43 stillbirths registered as illegitimate—5.4 per cent of all stillbirths—and 5 others registered as legitimate which were known to agencies to be illegitimate. Hence, the total number known was 48, or 6.1 per cent of all stillbirths. In addition, there were 17 stillbirths registered as of unknown parentage.

[6] There were 30 illegitimate births to Boston mothers at the State Infirmary during the year, and 9 other illegitimate births to Boston mothers occurring outside Boston and registered in Boston. These were not included in this study.

The following list gives the distribution of live births and still-births according to the parentage of the child:

Legitimate _____ 18, 614
Registered as illegitimate_____ 752
Registered as legitimate, but known to be illegitimate_____ 95
Of unknown parentage_____ 1

Total live births_____ 19, 462

Legitimate_____ 724
Registered as illegitimate_____ 43
Registered as legitimate, but known to be illegitimate_____ 5
Of unknown parentage_____ 17

Total stillbirths _____ 789

The distribution of illegitimate live births according to month of birth is given in Table 4, in comparison with the distribution of total live births in Suffolk County.

TABLE 4.—*Relative monthly frequency of live births in Suffolk County and of illegitimate live births in Boston, 1914.*

Month of birth.	Live births in Suffolk County.[a]		Illegitimate live births in Boston.	
	Number.[b]	Relative monthly frequency.[c]	Number.	Relative monthly frequency.[d]
Total...	21,794	....	847	....
January..	1,885	102	86	120
February...	1,658	99	65	100
March..	1,929	104	94	131
April..	1,791	100	86	124
May..	1,831	99	80	111
June...	1,777	99	57	82
July...	1,871	101	68	95
August...	1,844	100	64	89
September..	1,870	104	61	88
October..	1,768	96	53	74
November...	1,780	99	60	86
December...	1,790	97	73	102

a The county in which Boston is located. In 1910 Boston included 92 per cent of the population of the county.
b Commonwealth of Massachusetts: Seventy-third Annual Report on Births, Marriages, and Deaths for the Year 1914. Boston, 1915. P. 74.
c The daily average number of live births for the year was 59.71. For each month the number of births that would have occurred at this daily average rate was calculated; the number of births that actually occurred was then divided by the number calculated. The quotient is the relative frequency of births for the month, 100 expressing the average frequency.
d The daily average number of illegitimate live births for the year was 2.32. The relative monthly frequency was computed as described above.

There were no published figures as to month of birth for total births in Boston in 1914. Data in regard to month of birth were available, however, for Suffolk County. Since the population of Boston represents 92 per cent of the population of the county, these figures are fairly comparable with illegitimate births in Boston. The relative monthly frequency of live births in the county was fairly regular, ranging from 96 to 104. In the case of illegitimate births, however, the relative monthly frequencies for the winter and spring months were considerably higher than for the summer and autumn months. In the six months from December to May, inclusive, the relative frequencies were all above the average for the year, rising as high as 131. The frequencies for the six months from June to November were all below the average for the year, falling as low as 74. These figures indicate that a larger number of illegitimate conceptions occur in the months from April through September than at other times of the year, and would seem to show a direct relation to the greater freedom from restraint offered by many forms of recreation prevalent during the spring and summer months.

Accuracy of Registration of Illegitimate Births.

The State of Massachusetts was one of the original States included in the registration area for births established by the United States Bureau of the Census in 1915, on the basis of a registration efficiency of at least 90 per cent.[7] Birth registration in Boston in 1916 was estimated by the Bureau of the Census to be at least 94.6 per cent complete.[8]

It was impossible in the course of this study to make a complete test of the accuracy of the registration of illegitimate births. Only those cases of incorrect registration were found which were disclosed by checking with records of social agencies or with death records. Undoubtedly there were other cases of illegitimate birth registered as legitimate. Even cases which were known to social agencies were sometimes impossible to trace through the registry of births, because of change of name. A number of instances were found in which the mother had assumed several different names, or in which she had married after the birth of the child and was known to agencies only by her married name.

There were 36 cases discovered in which the record stated that the child was of illegitimate birth and had been born in Boston during the year studied, but for which it was impossible to find a birth certificate. It is probable that these were not cases of unregistered birth, but that most of the children had been registered as of legitimate birth under names other than those given in the records. This supposition is borne out by the fact that, of a total of 140 children not registered as of illegitimate birth, 95, or 67.9 per cent, were finally found recorded in the birth registry, though often under other names than those given in the death records or in records of social agencies. Of the remaining 45, 3 were discovered to have been born

---

[7] U. S. Bureau of the Census : Birth Statistics for the Registration Area of the United States, 1915. Washington, 1917. P. 9.

[8] Estimate secured from Division of Vital Statistics, U. S. Bureau of the Census.

outside Boston, though reported by agency or death records to have been born in the city, and 6 were found not to have been born in the year studied. Had complete information been available for all cases, it is highly probable that most of the others actually born in Boston during the year would have proved to have been registered as of legitimate birth. It was considered more conservative to exclude from the study the cases not found in the birth registry, because of the possibility of these births having occurred outside Boston, or outside the year.

It would appear, therefore, that a high percentage of illegitimate births in Boston are registered, but that a considerable number of them are registered as legitimate. It was impossible to ascertain the percentage of illegitimate births actually registered as such, but the figures available indicate that not more than 88.8 per cent are so registered, 752 of the 847 known illegitimate births in Boston being registered as illegitimate.

INFANT MORTALITY.

During a Five-Year Period.

Infant mortality is recognized as an index of social conditions and of child welfare in general. The public has been aroused to a realization of the importance of preventing infant mortality and improving the conditions surrounding infancy and childhood. Those economic and social conditions[9] found to accompany a high infant mortality rate exist to a greater extent among infants of illegitimate birth than among other infants, economic stress and absence of the mother's nursing care being particularly common among the former. The fact that of every 1,000 children born in Boston in 1914 at least 44 were born out of wedlock indicates the importance of a consideration of illegitimacy in efforts for the reduction of infant deaths.

Records of deaths of infants under 1 year of age were searched for the five-year period 1910 to 1914, inclusive, and the deaths of infants of illegitimate birth counted. An intensive study of the death records was made for the year 1914. Infant mortality rates were obtained by dividing the total number of deaths in each year by the number of births in the same year, and the number of deaths of infants born out of wedlock by the number of illegitimate births. For this purpose " illegitimate births " include only births registered as such, since no effort was made to supplement the number of illegitimate births by comparison with records of social agencies, except for the last year of the period.

---

[9] See Infant Mortality reports containing results of field studies in Johnstown, Pa.; Manchester, N. H.; Waterbury, Conn.; Brockton, Mass.; Saginaw, Mich.; New Bedford, Mass.; Akron, Ohio. U. S. Children's Bureau Publications Nos. 9, 20, 29, 37, 52, 68, 72.

TABLE 5.—*Infant mortality rates for all infants and for infants born out of wedlock, 1910 to 1914.*

Year.	Live births registered as illegitimate in Boston.a	Deaths of infants registered as illegitimate in Boston.b	Infant mortality rate for infants of illegitimate birth.c	Infant mortality rate for all infants.d
1910...	670	303	452.2	126.7
1911...	757	302	398.9	125.2
1912...	867	282	325.3	115.7
1913...	829	263	317.2	109.7
1914 e.......................................	752	236	313.8	103.1

a Except for 1914, includes births outside Boston to Boston mothers, if registered in Boston.
b Deaths registered in Boston as for infants of illegitimate birth. Except for 1914, includes deaths outside Boston of Boston residents, if registered in Boston.
c These rates are based only upon births and deaths registered as illegitimate. The 1914 rate here given is somewhat higher than the corrected rate used later in the report, but it is used here in order to be comparable with the preceding uncorrected figures.
d Forty-third Annual Report of the Health Department of the City of Boston for the Year 1914. Boston, 1915. P. 101.
e Only births and deaths registered as illegitimate are included, in order to make this year comparable with the preceding years.

From the figures given in Table 5 it appears that the infant mortality rate among children of illegitimate birth is about three times as high as the general infant mortality rate. There was a steady decrease in the general infant mortality rate during the five-year period, and an even greater decline in the illegitimate infant mortality rate. In 1910 the rate among infants of illegitimate birth was 452 deaths to 1,000 births. In 1914 the rate was 314 deaths to 1,000 births. The illegitimate infant mortality rate in 1910 was three and six-tenths times the mortality rate among all infants. In 1914 the rate was three times the general infant mortality rate. The illegitimate infant mortality rates here given are probably somewhat high, because of inaccuracies in registration. The relative difference between the illegitimate infant mortality rates and the general infant mortality rates (the former divided by the latter) for each of the five years were as follows: 1910, 3.6; 1911, 3.2; 1912, 2.8; 1913, 2.9; 1914, 3.0.

In the 1915 annual report the health department of the city of Boston for the first time published the number of deaths of infants of illegitimate birth that had occurred during the year and the illegitimate infant mortality rate. The illegitimate infant mortality rate in 1915 as given in this report was 300 and the general infant mortality rate was 103.7,[10] a ratio of nearly 3 to 1.

During the Year of the Study.

Rate.

In 1914, the year selected for intensive study, the illegitimate infant mortality rate, based upon the number of illegitimate births

[10] Forty-fourth Annual Report of the Health Department of the City of Boston for the Year 1915. Boston, 1916. Pp. 77, 143.

in that year and the number of deaths in the same year of infants of illegitimate birth, was 281.[11]   The general infant mortality rate during the year was 103.1.   Subtracting the number of illegitimate births from the total births, and the deaths of infants of illegitimate birth from the total infant deaths, the infant mortality rate among infants of legitimate birth was 95.   The rate for infants of illegitimate birth was therefore three times as high as that for infants of legitimate birth.   The exclusion of births and deaths of infants born out of wedlock reduces the infant mortality rate for the city 8 per cent.   (See Table 6.)

Infant deaths per 1,000 live births

CHART I.—Comparative infant mortality rates for infants born in wedlock and born out of wedlock, 1914.

TABLE 6.—*Infant mortality rates for infants of legitimate and of illegitimate birth, 1914.*

Status.	Live births.			Deaths.			Infant mortality rate.		
	Total.	Male.	Female.	Total.	Male.	Female.	General.	Male.	Female.
Total a.........	b 19,462	9,910	9,551	2,007	1,090	917	103.1	110.0	96.0
Legitimate c.........	b 18,615	9,479	9,135	1,769	963	806	95.0	101.6	88.2
Illegitimate d.........	847	431	416	238	127	111	281.0	294.7	266.8

a Forty-third Annual Report of the Health Department of the City of Boston for the Year 1914.   Boston, 1915.   Pp. 108-109.
b Includes 1, sex unknown.
c Obtained by subtracting illegitimate from total.
d Includes 95 births and 2 deaths registered as legitimate, though found to be illegitimate.

The infant mortality rate for males among those of legitimate birth was 101.6, and for females, 88.2.   The infant mortality rate for males among those of illegitimate birth was 294.7, and for females, 266.8.   The ratio of the infant mortality rate for males to the rate for females among the first group was 1.15 to 1, while the corresponding ratio for infants of illegitimate birth was 1.10 to 1.

[11] In Boston, in 1914, there were 847 illegitimate births registered as illegitimate or as legitimate and 238 infant deaths among children born out of wedlock.   The number of deaths of infants born outside Boston is approximately equaled by the number of deaths known to have occurred outside the city among infants of illegitimate birth born in Boston in 1914.   Included in the 238 deaths are those of 36 infants born outside Boston— i. e., deaths among infants who moved into Boston after birth.   On the other hand, among the 847 infants of illegitimate birth born in Boston in 1914, 35 were known to have died outside Boston under 1 year of age (death certificates found in 22 instances), and 2 others probably died outside Boston though the place of death was not definitely reported.

One-fourth of the illegitimate births during the year and more than half the deaths of infants born out of wedlock occurred in one large institution—a maternity hospital and children's institution combined. No estimate could be made for this institution of the infant mortality rate based upon the number of illegitimate births and infant deaths during one year. On the one hand, babies were discharged from the hospital after a few weeks, and on the other hand, infants were received after birth. It is evident, however, from figures given later in this report,[12] that the infant mortality in this institution was disproportionately high.

Age at death.

In order to compare the age at death of infants born in wedlock and out of wedlock, it was necessary to ascertain the number of infants of legitimate birth who died at various ages, by subtracting the deaths of infants of illegitimate birth from the total deaths at various ages as given in the report of the health department. The numbers of deaths at various ages per 1,000 live births, obtained by dividing the number of deaths at each age by the total number of births during the year, are given in Table 7.

TABLE 7.—*Deaths per 1,000 births, 1914, among infants of legitimate and of illegitimate birth, by age at death.*

Age at death.	Total deaths.		Deaths of infants of legitimate birth.		Deaths of infants of illegitimate birth.	
	Number.a	Per 1,000 live births.b	Number.c	Per 1,000 legitimate live births.d	Number.	Per 1,000 illegitimate live births.e
Total....................	2,007	103.1	1,769	95.0	238	281.0
Less than 1 month..............	917	47.1	836	44.9	81	95.6
Less than 1 week..............	655	33.7	610	32.7	45	53.1
1 week.....................	102	5.2	93	5.0	9	10.6
2 weeks....................	87	4.5	74	4.0	13	15.4
3 weeks....................	73	3.7	59	3.2	14	16.5
1 month....................	174	9.0	129	6.9	45	53.1
2 months...................	127	6.5	101	5.4	26	30.7
3–5 months.................	294	15.1	249	13.4	45	53.1
6–8 months.................	261	13.4	232	12.5	29	31.3
9–11 months................	234	12.0	222	11.9	12	14.2

a Forty-third Annual Report of the Health Department of the City of Boston for the Year 1914. Boston, 1915. Pp. 148–149.
b Based on total live births in 1914—19,462.
c Obtained by subtracting deaths of infants of illegitimate birth from total.
d Based on total live births minus the illegitimate—18,615.
e Based on 847 illegitimate live births.

The deaths per 1,000 births in each age group were very much higher for infants of illegitimate than for those of legitimate birth. The relative differences between the number of deaths per 1,000 births for children born out of wedlock and for those of legiti-

[12] See p. 98.

mate birth (the former divided by the latter), according to age at death, were as follows:

All ages_____ 3. 0
Less than 1 month_____ 2. 1 | 1 month _____ 7. 7
    Less than 1 week _____ 1. 6 | 2 months _____ 5. 7
    1 week _____ 2. 0 | 3–5 months _____ 4. 0
    2 weeks _____ 3. 9 | 6–8 months _____ 2. 7
    3 weeks _____ 5. 2 | 9–11 months _____ 1. 2

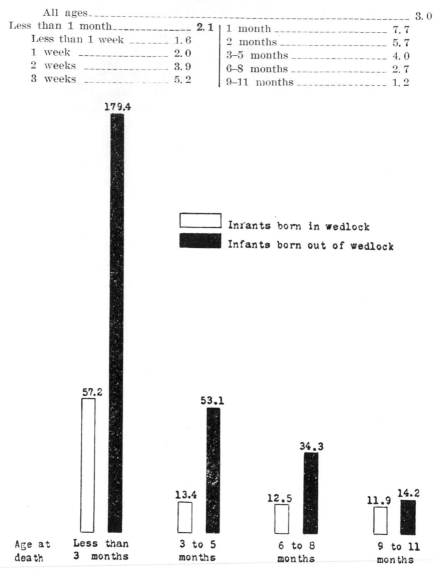

CHART II.—Deaths per 1,000 live births, 1914, among infants born in wedlock and born out of wedlock, by age at death.

The number of deaths per 1,000 births for infants of illegitimate birth less than a week old was 1.6 times that for infants of legitimate birth of the same age. At 1 week of age the rate for infants of illegitimate birth was twice that for infants of legitimate birth. Up to and including 1 month there was a steady increase in the preponderance of deaths per 1,000 births for infants of illegitimate birth. The rate for infants of illegitimate birth 1 month of age, but less than 2 months, was 7.7 times as great as the rate for infants of legitimate birth of the same age group. After this age there was a steady decline in the relative difference, until for infants 9 to 11 months of age the mortality for those of illegitimate birth was only 1.2 times the mortality for those of legitimate birth. The smaller relative difference in the later age groups may be accounted for in part by the increasing probability as the child grows older that his death would be registered as though he were of legitimate birth, because of the marriage of the mother, the child's adoption, or other reasons.

The greater preponderance of the rate for infants of illegitimate birth in the 1-month age group over that for infants of legitimate birth in the same group, and the lesser preponderance in the age groups under 1 month, can probably be accounted for by the separation of mother and child, which occurs in so many cases soon after the mother has recovered from her confinement.[13] Early separation from the mother would seem to have a greater effect upon the infant mortality rate than detrimental prenatal conditions. It might have been expected that the mental stress, the disturbance in economic and social relations, and the absence of proper care to which so many of these mothers were subject during pregnancy would result in an extremely high mortality during the first weeks of the child's life. Although the rate for the period under 1 month is more than twice as high as in the case of infants of legitimate birth, yet the relative difference is not as great as in the later periods of infancy.

Infant mortality statistics in England and Wales show somewhat the same tendency as that shown by the Boston figures in regard to the relative difference between the number of infant deaths at various ages per 1,000 births among infants born out of wedlock and among infants born in wedlock. In the English statistics the comparison is shown in terms of the per cent that infant mortality among children born out of wedlock constitutes of infant mortality among children of legitimate birth (the latter rate being taken as 100). The general infant mortality rate in England and Wales among children born out of wedlock was only twice that among children of legitimate birth, as compared with a relative difference of 3 in Boston. Following are the percentages that the infant mortality rates in 1914 among infants of illegitimate birth were of the

---

[13] See pp. 139–143.

rates for infants born in wedlock, according to age at death, for England and Wales:[14]

Under 1 year_____ 206

Under 1 month_____ 196	6 months _____ 200
1 month _____ 229	7 months _____ 188
2 months _____ 261	8 months _____ 169
3 months _____ 257	9 months _____ 163
4 months _____ 234	10 months _____ 163
5 months _____ 230	11 months _____ 148

Until the end of the third month of life there was an increase in the relative differences between the rates for infants of illegitimate birth and those for infants born in wedlock, the largest difference being at the age of 2 months. The peak thus comes at a later age than was shown in the Boston figures, where the greatest difference came at the age of 1 month. In England and Wales the relative difference at 3 months was almost as great as that at 2 months. There was a steady decline in the later age groups, but not until the age of 7 months was the difference as low as in the age group under 1 month.

Cause of death.

In order to obtain comparative data upon the cause of death among infants of illegitimate and of legitimate birth it was necessary to subtract the number of infants of illegitimate birth dying from specified causes from the total numbers of infant deaths from specified causes as given in the report of the health department. The results are shown in Table 8.

TABLE 8.—*Cause of death for infants of legitimate and of illegitimate birth, 1914.*

Cause of death.	Total infant deaths.[a]	Deaths of infants of legitimate birth.[b]	Deaths of infants of illegitimate birth.
All causes_____	2,007	1,769	238
Principal gastric and intestinal diseases_____	418	329	89
Diseases of the stomach_____	9	8	1
Diarrhea and enteritis_____	409	321	88
Principal respiratory diseases_____	355	330	25
Acute bronchitis_____	29	28	1
Broncho-pneumonia_____	191	175	16
Pneumonia_____	135	127	8
Malformations_____	141	132	9
Diseases of early infancy_____	687	613	74
Premature birth_____	422	387	35
Congenital debility_____	115	82	33
Injuries at birth_____	90	84	6
Other_____	60	60	_____

[a] Forty-third Annual Report of the Health Department of the City of Boston for the Year 1914. Boston, 1915. Pp. 106–107.
[b] Obtained by subtracting deaths of infants of illegitimate birth from total infant deaths.

[14] Seventy-ninth Annual Report of the Registrar-General of Births, Deaths, and Marriages in England and Wales (1916). London, 1918. P. xxxv.

TABLE 8.—*Cause of death for infants of legitimate and of illegitimate birth,*
1914—Continued.

Cause of death.	Total infant deaths.a	Deaths of infants of legitimate birth.b	Deaths of infants of illegitimate birth.
Principal epidemic diseases	183	159	24
Measles	17	17	
Scarlet fever	3	3	
Whooping cough	23	21	2
Diphtheria	13	7	6
Influenza	2	2	
Dysentery	16	16	
Erysipelas	19	18	1
Tuberculosis of the lungs	21	19	2
Tuberculous meningitis	29	25	4
Other forms of tuberculosis	9	6	3
Syphilis	31	25	6
External causes	20	18	2
Causes ill-defined or unknown	13	12	1
All other causes	190	176	14
Meningitis	25	24	1
Convulsions	15	14	1
Organic diseases of the heart	3	2	1
Other	147	136	11

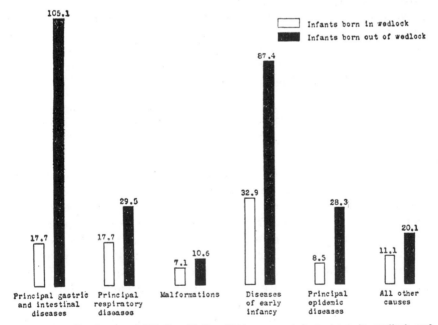

CHART III.—Deaths per 1,000 live births, 1914, among infants born in wedlock and born out of wedlock, by cause of death.

The facts in Table 8 are summarized in Table 9, which also gives the infant mortality rates for the various causes. Specific infant mortality rates were obtained by dividing the number of deaths from each cause by the total number of births during the year.

TABLE 9.—*Specific mortality rates for infants of legitimate and of illegitimate birth, 1914, by cause of death.*

Cause of death.	Total infant deaths.a		Deaths of infants of legitimate birth.b		Deaths of infants of illegitimate birth.	
	Number.	Specific mortality rates.c	Number.	Specific mortality rates.d	Number.	Specific mortality rates.e
All causes...................	2,007	103.1	1,769	95.0	238	281.0
Principal gastric and intestinal diseases........................	418	21.5	329	17.7	89	105.1
Principal respiratory diseases.......	355	18.2	330	17.7	25	29.5
Malformations......................	141	7.3	132	7.1	9	10.6
Diseases of early infancy...........	687	35.3	613	32.9	74	87.4
Principal epidemic diseases.........	183	9.4	159	8.5	24	28.3
All other causes....................	223	11.4	206	11.1	17	20.1

a Forty-third Annual Report of the Health Department of the City of Boston for the Year 1914. Boston, 1915. Pp. 106–107.
b Obtained by subtracting deaths of infants of illegitimate birth from total infant deaths
c Based on total live births in 1914—19,462.
d Based on total live births minus illegitimate live births—18,615
e Based on 847 illegitimate live births.

The specific infant mortality rates were invariably higher for infants of illegitimate birth than for others, though there was a great variation in the proportionate excess of "illegitimate" over "legitimate" rates for the various causes. The relative differences between the mortality rates among infants of illegitimate birth and infants of legitimate birth (the former divided by the latter), according to cause of death, were as follows:

All causes_____ 3.0
Principal gastric and intestinal diseases _____ 5.9
Principal respiratory diseases____ 1.7
Malformations _____ 1.5
Diseases of early infancy____ 2.7
Principal epidemic diseases__ 3.3
All other causes_____ 1.8

The rate for gastric and intestinal diseases was 5.9 times as high for infants of illegitimate birth as for those of legitimate birth. The diseases in this group are largely caused by improper feeding. Hence, early separation from the mother or other circumstances making maternal nursing impossible would be a factor in mortality from this cause. The rate for diseases of early infancy was 2.7 times as great for infants of illegitimate birth as for those of legitimate birth. This group of causes includes premature birth, congenital debility, injuries at birth, and other causes connected with birth. The rate for deaths due to premature birth was 41.3 for children of illegitimate birth, as against 20.8 for children of legitimate birth. The rate for deaths from congenital debility was 39 for infants of illegitimate births, as against 4.4 for infants of legitimate birth, or nine times as high. This rate shows the effect of the detrimental conditions to which the mothers were often subjected during pregnancy. Had stillbirths been included, the comparative importance of the diseases of early infancy would have been considerably greater.

The distribution of deaths of infants born out of wedlock by cause of death was different for the group of 129 deaths occurring in one large maternity hospital and children's institution than for the 109 occurring elsewhere. Of the former group of deaths, 54 per cent were reported as due to gastric and intestinal causes, while among the latter only 17 per cent were so reported. The percentage of deaths of infants of illegitimate birth caused by diseases of early infancy was 22 at the institution specified and 41 elsewhere. The larger proportion of deaths due to gastric and intestinal diseases at the institution under consideration may be accounted for in part by the fact that many of the infants under care were separated from their mothers at a very early age. The comparative distribution of the two groups according to cause of death is given in Table 10.

TABLE 10.—*Cause of death for infants of illegitimate birth who died at a large maternity hospital and children's institution and for those who died elsewhere, 1914.*

Cause of death.	Deaths of infants of illegitimate births, 1914.		
	Total deaths.	Deaths in a large maternity hospital and children's institution.	Deaths elsewhere.
All causes..	238	129	109
Principal gastric and intestinal diseases.............................	89	70	19
Principal respiratory diseases.......................................	25	8	17
Malformations...	9	4	5
Diseases of early infancy...	74	29	45
Principal epidemic diseases...	24	10	14
All other causes..	17	8	9

During First Year of Life of Infants Born in 1914.

Rate.

The more accurate method of estimating the infant mortality rate is to follow all the infants born during a given year through the first year of life, determining how many died before reaching 1 year of age. This has been the method used by the Children's Bureau in its studies of infant mortality. Especially in the case of. infants of illegitimate birth is this method preferable. The mothers of many of these infants are not residents of the city, but come in to secure care at the time of the child's birth. Besides, many infants are brought into the city at the time applications are made for agency care or in the hope that they may be disposed of through adoption. These difficulties are avoided by following infants born during one year through the first year of life. However, many obstacles are encountered in this procedure. The difficulty in investigating the cases in which the mother has endeavored to conceal the situation from her relatives and friends and the numerous cases in which the children, shortly after birth, were taken out of the city by their mothers or by social agencies are serious obstacles in the way of obtaining complete information.

The histories of the 847 infants born out of wedlock during the year were followed throughout the first year of life, so far as was possible by the methods used. No attempt was made to follow up the histories except so far as they were known to social agencies and courts, or where deaths had been registered. Therefore, the number of deaths and the infant mortality rate here reported are considerable understatements. The data are of value only as indicating the minimum infant mortality rate which would be found were all the facts known.

In estimating the rate on this basis only those deaths which had been registered were included. In a number of cases, however, the deaths had occurred outside Boston, and had been registered elsewhere. All birth certificates which indicated that the mother's residence was a Massachusetts town outside Boston were checked with the death records of the towns specified. There were 17 cases in which the child was reported by social agencies to have died, but in which no death certificates were found. Because of the possibility of error in the date of death reported and the lack of accurate information as to the cause of death, these cases were not included in the number of deaths.

Of the 847 infants of illegitimate birth known to have been born in Boston in 1914, 213 were known to have died during the first year of life. The infant mortality rate was, therefore, 251.5. This is lower than the rate of 281 secured by the other method and is to be taken as a considerable understatement of the true rate. Even this minimum rate was 2.4 times as great as the general infant mortality rate of 103.1.

The large number of births and deaths at a single institution— the large maternity hospital and children's institution previously mentioned—make it of interest to consider separately the infant mortality at this institution and elsewhere. Of the 847 illegitimate births in Boston during the year, 209 occurred at the institution specified. Seventy-four of these 209 infants died at the same institution before they had reached 1 year of age, and 14 were known to have died elsewhere, death certificates having been found. On the basis of these figures it would appear that 421 out of every 1,000 children born out of wedlock at the institution die before they reach 1 year of age, 354 dying at the same institution. These infant mortality rates are considerably higher than the rate (251.5) for all infants born out of wedlock in Boston. Eliminating the infants born at the institution mentioned there were 638 infants of illegitimate birth born in the city during the year, of whom 125 were known to have died before they had reached 1 year of age. The infant mortality rate among this group of infants was 195.9—less than half that among infants born at the institution specified.

Age at death.

The number of deaths per 1,000 births for the various ages, based upon births during 1914 and deaths among these same infants during the first year of life, followed the same tendency as the rate based upon the numbers of births and deaths during the same calendar year. The former rates were usually lower than the latter, no doubt largely because of the less complete information secured; but they were consistently higher than the rates for infants of legitimate birth based upon the numbers of births and deaths in the same year, except in the age group of 9 to 11 months. The low rate in this age group was undoubtedly due to the fact that the difficulty in tracing deaths increases with the age of the child, because of migration, legitimation, and adoption. In the age group of less than 1 month and in the 6-to-8-month age group, the infant mortality rate for infants of illegitimate birth was almost twice as high as for infants of legitimate birth. The rate at 1 month was more than 7 times as high as the rate for infants of legitimate birth, at 2 months the rate was 5 times as high, and at 3 to 5 months approximately 4 times the mortality among infants of legitimate birth. (See Table 11.)

TABLE 11.—*Deaths during first year of life of infants born out of wedlock in 1914, and number per 1,000 live births, by age at death.*

Age at death.	Deaths during first year of life of infants born out of wedlock in Boston in 1914.		Infant deaths, 1914, per 1,000 live births.a	
	Number.	Per 1,000 live births.b	Illegitimate.	Legitimate.
All deaths.........................	213	251. 5	281. 0	95. 0
Less than 1 month......................	75	88. 5	95. 6	44. 9
Less than 1 week........................	43	50. 8	53. 1	32. 7
1 week..............................	7	8. 3	10. 6	5. 0
2 weeks.............................	13	15. 3	15. 4	4. 0
3 weeks.............................	12	14. 1	16. 5	3. 2
1 month..............................	43	50. 8	53. 1	6. 9
2 months.............................	23	27. 2	30. 7	5. 4
3–5 months...........................	45	53. 1	53. 1	13. 4
6–8 months...........................	21	24. 8	34. 3	12. 5
9–11 months..........................	6	7. 1	14. 2	11. 9

a See Table *l*, p. 91.
b Based on known number of illegitimate births in 1914—847.

Cause of death.

A comparison of the specific infant mortality rates for deaths from various causes, based upon births during 1914 and deaths among the same infants during the first year of life, with the rates based upon the numbers of births and infant deaths during the same period, gives results similar to those obtained by the comparison of rates for various ages. (See Table 12.)

TABLE 12.—*Deaths during first year of life of infants born out of wedlock in 1914, and specific mortality rates, by cause of death.*

Cause of death.	Deaths during first year of life of infants born out of wedlock in Boston in 1914.		Infant mortality rates based on numbers of births and deaths during 1914.[a]	
	Number.	Specific mortality rates.[b]	Illegitimate.	Legitimate.
All causes	213	251.5	281.0	95.0
Principal gastric and intestinal diseases	68	80.3	105.1	17.7
Principal respiratory diseases	23	27.2	29.5	17.7
Malformations	8	9.4	10.6	7.1
Diseases of early infancy	79	93.3	87.4	32.9
Principal epidemic diseases	19	22.4	28.3	8.5
All other causes	16	18.9	20.1	11.1

a See Table 9, p. 96.
b Based on known number of illegitimate births in 1914—847.

Although the infant mortality rates for deaths from various causes are somewhat lower when based upon births and deaths of the same infants, because of the lack of complete information, they are very much higher than the rates for infants of legitimate birth. The two sets of rates for infants of illegitimate birth show the same general tendency, except that the rate for diseases of early infancy is higher than that for gastric and intestinal diseases when figured according to births and deaths among the same infants, and lower when obtained by the other method. This may be explained in part by the fact that deaths from diseases of early infancy are more likely to occur very early in the child's life than deaths from gastric and intestinal diseases, and that, because of migration or for other reasons, the information concerning infant deaths was more complete for those who died in the early months of life than for those who died in the later periods of infancy. The relative difference between the infant mortality rate for infants of illegitimate birth and that for infants of legitimate birth is very much larger in the group of deaths from gastric and intestinal diseases than in any other group, no matter by which method the rate is estimated.

If the deaths of infants born in the maternity hospital and children's institution previously mentioned are eliminated, the relative importance of deaths from gastric and intestinal diseases becomes very much less, just as in the case of infant deaths in Boston during 1914.[15] Of the 88 infants born out of wedlock at this institution who were known to have died during their first year of life, 47 per cent were reported to have died from gastric and intestinal diseases, while only 22 per cent of the infants born elsewhere who died were so reported. Twenty-eight per cent of the deaths of infants born at the institution were caused by diseases of early infancy, as against 43 per cent of the deaths of infants born elsewhere. The specific infant mortality rate for gastric and intestinal diseases was 196.2 among infants born at the institution, and 42.3 among infants born elsewhere. For diseases of early infancy the specific mortality rate was 119.6 among infants born at the institution, and 84.6 among infants born elsewhere. In other words, the specific infant mortality rate for gastric and intestinal diseases was nearly five times as high among infants born at the institution specified as among other infants, and the rate for diseases of early infancy also was higher in the former case than in the latter. In fact, all the specific mortality rates were higher for infants born in the institution than for infants born elsewhere. (See Table 13.)

TABLE 13.—*Deaths during first year of life of infants born out of wedlock in a large maternity hospital and children's institution, and of infants born out of wedlock elsewhere, in 1914, and specific mortality rates, by cause of death.*

Cause of death.	Deaths during first year of life of infants born out of wedlock in Boston in 1914.					
	Total deaths.		Deaths of infants born in a large maternity hospital and children's institution.		Deaths of infants born elsewhere.	
	Number.	Specific mortality rates.a	Number.b	Specific mortality rates.c	Number.	Specific mortality rates.d
All causes....................	213	251.5	88	421.1	125	195.9
Principal gastric and intestinal diseases.	68	80.3	41	196.2	27	42.3
Principal respiratory diseases..........	23	27.2	6	28.7	17	26.6
Malformations......................	8	9.4	5	23.9	3	4.7
Diseases of early infancy..............	79	93.3	25	119.6	54	84.6
Principal epidemic diseases...........	19	22.4	6	28.7	13	20.4
All other causes....................	16	18.9	5	23.9	11	17.2

a Based on known number of illegitimate births in 1914—847.
b Includes 74 who died at the same institution in which they were born and 14 who died elsewhere. Of those who died elsewhere, 7 died from gastric and intestinal diseases, 2 from respiratory diseases, 1 from a disease of early infancy, 3 from epidemic diseases, and 1 from another cause.
c Based on 209 illegitimate births at the institution in 1914.
d Based on 638 illegitimate births in 1914 elsewhere than at the institution specified.

15 See p. 97.

CONDITIONS SURROUNDING BIRTH.

Place of Birth.

There were known to have been born in Boston during the year of the study 847 infants of illegitimate birth. Among them were seven pairs of twins, hence the number of mothers represented was 840. The places of birth of the 847 children were as follows:

```
        Total children_____  847
Private home_____ 193
        Mother's parental home_____  32
        Mother's own home_____ _____  18
        Other, or not specified_____ 143
Institution_____ 651
        Hospital (including 23 in small private hospitals) 410
        Maternity home_____ 214
        Public infirmary_____  27
Not reported_____        3
```

Only 23 per cent of the children were born in private homes, while 77 per cent were born in hospitals or other institutions. This percentage of institution births was very large. According to figures furnished by the registrar of the city of Boston about 30 per cent of all births during the year studied occurred in hospitals or other institutions.

In the majority of cases in which the child was born in a private home it was impossible to determine whether this was the mother's parental home, her own home, the home of relatives or friends, or a lodging house. This information could be secured only in cases in which it was known to social agencies. Of the 193 births in private homes, 32 were known to have taken place in the mother's parental home, and 18 in the mother's own home. " Own home " is here understood to mean a home established by the mother and her husband or the man with whom she was living as married.

There were 410 infants born in hospitals, almost half the total. In 23 of these cases the place of birth was a small private hospital of very limited capacity. The 214 infants born in maternity homes constituted more than one-fourth of the total. Twenty-seven were born in the city infirmary.

The question arises as to how many of the cases cared for by hospitals and maternity homes were in reality Boston cases, and how many had come from outside the city. Table 14 gives the place of confinement and the residence of the mother.

TABLE 14.—*Place of confinement and residence of mothers of infants born out of wedlock in 1914*

Place of confinement.	Total mothers.	Mothers resident—			
		In Boston.		Elsewhere.	
		Number.	Per cent.	Number.	Per cent.
Total	840	482	57.4	358	42.6
Private home	192	182	94.8	10	5.2
Hospital	407	214	52.6	193	47.4
Maternity home	211	61	28.9	150	71.1
Public infirmary	27	25	92.6	2	7.4
Not reported	3			3	(a)

a Per cent not given because of small number.

Mothers whose residence was Boston constituted 57 per cent of all the mothers. Of those confined at private homes, 95 per cent were Boston residents, but only 53 per cent of those confined at hospitals and 29 per cent of those confined at maternity homes were residents of the city.

Maternity Care.

The 645 mothers who were confined at hospitals, maternity homes, or at the public infirmary received medical and nursing care from the staffs of these institutions. It was impossible to determine in how many of the remaining 195 cases physicians were in attendance. Under the Massachusetts law the practice of midwifery is prohibited, yet the birth-registration law requires the midwife to register all births she attends. In Boston, midwives themselves do not register births, but the cases are reported through doctors, who in many instances are not present at the births.[16] In 45 of the 195 cases in which the birth did not occur in an institution, it was known that hospital externes were in attendance; in 15 of these cases and in 14 others care was known to have been given by visiting nurses.

Complete information was not obtained as to medical examinations and advice given the mother during pregnancy by clinics and hospital out-patient departments. These cases differ from ordinary maternity cases in that mothers illegitimately pregnant require not only medical care and advice but in many cases must be entirely provided for during a considerable period preceding the birth of the child. Private child-caring agencies, maternity homes, the public infirmary, and other social agencies cared for 271 of the 840 mothers previous to confinement. Following are the types of agencies giving care and

16 Report of the Commission on Immigration on the Problem of Immigration in Massachusetts. House No. 2300, 1914. Boston, 1914. P. 193.

the number cared for by each, those cases in which care was given for less than a week preceding confinement being excluded:

Total receiving care previous to confinement_____ 271
Private child-caring agency_____ 25
Other agency _____ 29
Maternity home_____ 167
Public infirmary _____ 19
Private child-caring and other agency_____ 1
Private child-caring agency and maternity home_____ 12
Private child-caring agency and public infirmary_____ 3
Private child-caring agency, maternity home, and public infirmary____ 1
Private child-caring and other agency and public infirmary_____ 2
Other agency and maternity home_____ 7
Other agency and public infirmary_____ 4
Maternity home and public infirmary_____ 1

The work done by child-caring and other agencies in these cases consisted mainly in securing medical care and advice for the mother, providing her with a place in which she could live during pregnancy, arranging for her support, and securing care during confinement. These agencies in most cases continued care and supervision after the child was born. Of the 84 cases cared for by these agencies, 29 were turned over to maternity homes or to the public infirmary for special care.

The maternity homes and the public infirmary in many cases gave care for a considerable period before the birth of the child. There were 188 cases in which care was given by maternity homes, and 30 cases in which the public infirmary gave care. Three of the maternity-home cases and 5 public-infirmary cases were discharged before the child's birth. The length of time the mothers were in the maternity homes previous to confinement is given in the following list for the 185 cases included above, in which the birth occurred in a maternity home, and for 26 others in which the mother was in the home less than a week previous to confinement:

Total cases in which the birth occurred in a maternity home_____ 211

Less than 1 week_____	26	2 months _____	46
1 week, but less than 2_____	14	3–5 months _____	34
2 weeks, but less than 1 month___	32	6 months and over_____	2
1 month _____	57		

In two-thirds of the maternity-home cases the mother had been in the home a month or more previous to confinement. In two-fifths of the cases she had spent two months or more in the home.

The public infirmary also gave care for considerable periods of time. In the 27 cases in which the birth occurred in this institution the length of residence previous to confinement was as follows:

Total cases in which the birth occurred in the public infirmary_____ 27

1 week but less than 2_____	1	2 months_____	6
2 weeks but less than 1 month____	3	3 5 months _____	6
1 month_____	8	Not-reported _____	[17] 3

Of the 24 mothers for whom length of residence in the public infirmary previous to confinement was reported, 20 had been in the institution one month or longer, 12 having been cared for two months or more. Adding together the maternity-home and public-infirmary cases, 159 mothers were cared for by these institutions for one month or more before confinement. These 159 mothers comprised 19 per cent of all the mothers.

The maternity homes and the public infirmary made a practice of keeping mother and child for a considerable period following birth, thus giving the mother a chance to recuperate and to increase her economic efficiency and insuring for the child maternal care under proper conditions. The following list gives the length of time the mother and child remained in a maternity home:

Total cases in which the birth occurred in a maternity home_____ 211

Less than 2 weeks_____	11	3–5 months_____	30
2 weeks but less than 1 month___	34	6 months and over_____	7
1 month_____	87	Not reported_____	8
2 months_____	34		

In three-fourths of the maternity-home cases the mother and child remained in the home a month or more. In a third of all the cases they remained two months or longer.

In the public-infirmary cases the length of residence following the child's birth was as follows:

Total cases in which the birth occurred in the public infirmary_____ 27

Less than 2 weeks_____	2	3–5 months_____	8
2 weeks but less than 1 month___	3	6 months and over_____	6
1 month_____	2	Not reported_____	2
2 months_____	4		

Of the 25 cases in which length of residence was known, 20 remained a month or more, 18 of them remaining two months or more.

THE CHILD'S PARENTAGE.

The Mother.

The primary sources of information in regard to the mother were data from birth certificates. The items covered in the birth records were race and nativity, residence, age, and occupation. This information was supplemented by records of courts, hospitals, and other

---

[17] In one instance the mother was known to have been in the infirmary at least a week previous to confinement and so was considered to have received prenatal care from that institution (p. 104). In the other two instances the mother was not included among those known to have received prenatal care.

social agencies. Fairly complete social information was obtained for 335 of the 840 mothers. Information on individual topics was secured from one source or another for varying numbers of cases.

Race, nativity, and years in the United States.

The racial distribution of the 840 mothers of infants known to have been born out of wedlock in Boston during the year was as follows: White, 787; Negro, 52; American Indian, 1. The percentage of colored mothers was nearly four times as high as in the case of mothers of infants of legitimate birth born during the same period.[18]

Of the 787 white mothers, 453, or 58 per cent, were born in the United States and 327, or 42 per cent, in foreign countries. The nativity of 7 was not reported. Of the 453 native-born white mothers, 80 per cent were born in Massachusetts, 5 per cent in other New England States, and 15 per cent in other parts of the United States. Of the 327 foreign born, 33 per cent were born in Canada, 33 per cent in Ireland, and the remaining 34 per cent in other countries. The following list gives the nativity of the white mothers:

Total white mothers				787
Native born	453	Germany	4	
Massachusetts	363	Ireland	108	
Other New England States	21	Italy	18	
Other parts of the United		Russia and Poland [19]	33	
States	69	Scandinavia	14	
Foreign born	327	Scotland	14	
Canada	109	Other	9	
England and Wales	15	Not reported		7
France	3			

Of the 52 colored mothers, 42 were native born and 10 were foreign born. Twenty of the native-born colored mothers were born in Massachusetts, and 22 in the United States outside New England. The foreign-born colored came chiefly from the West Indies. The Indian mother was born in Massachusetts.

The Health Department of the city of Boston gives in its annual report the distribution of births during the year, according to nativity of mother. Table 15 gives this distribution, together with the distribution of illegitimate births during the year and the distribution of legitimate births obtained by subtracting the illegitimate births from the total.

---

[18] See Table 15, p. 107.

[19] According to classification of the Health Department of the City of Boston.

TABLE 15.—*Race and country of birth of mothers of infants born in wedlock and born out of wedlock in 1914, per cent distribution, and per cent of births illegitimate.*

Race and country of birth of mothers.	Total live births.		Legitimate live births.		Illegitimate live births.		Per cent of births illegitimate.c
	Number.a	Per cent distribution.	Number.b	Per cent distribution.	Number.	Per cent distribution.	
Total....................	19,462	100.0	18,615	100.0	847	100.0	4.4
White..........................	19,087	98.1	18,293	98.3	794	93.8	4.2
United States..............	7,017	36.0	6,561	35.2	d 456	53.8	6.5
Canada.....................	1,610	8.3	1,500	8.1	e 110	13.0	6.8
England and Wales........	353	1.8	338	1.8	15	1.8	4.2
Ireland.....................	2,526	13.0	2,415	13.0	d 111	13.1	4.4
Italy.......................	3,442	17.7	3,424	18.4	18	2.1	.5
Russia and Poland f.......	2,628	13.5	2,594	13.9	34	4.0	1.3
Scandinavia f..............	321	1.6	307	1.7	14	1.7	4.4
Scotland...................	206	1.1	192	1.0	14	1.7	6.8
Foreign, other, and country of birth not reported......	984	5.1	962	5.2	22	2.6	2.2
Negro........................	356	1.8	304	1.6	52	6.1	14.6
Other........................	19	.1	18	.1	1	.1	(g)

a Forty-third Annual Report of the Health Department of the City of Boston for the Year 1914. Boston, 1915. P. 108.
b Obtained by subtracting number of illegitimate live births from total.
c Obtained by dividing the number of illegitimate live births of each nativity group by total live births of each group.
d Includes 3 pairs of twins.
e Includes 1 pair of twins.
f Classification of the Health Department of the City of Boston.
g Rate not computed because of small base.

Of the total births, 98.1 per cent were to white mothers, 1.8 per cent to colored mothers, and 0.1 per cent to mothers belonging to other races. Births to white mothers comprised 98.3 per cent of the legitimate and 93.8 per cent of the illegitimate births, while births to colored mothers comprised 1.6 per cent of the legitimate and 6.1 per cent of the illegitimate. The illegitimacy rate for births to white mothers—that is, the percentage which illegitimate births to white mothers constituted of all births to white mothers—was 4.2, while the rate for births to colored mothers was more than three times as large, 14.6. The very small proportion of colored in the population of the city accounts for the fact that the general illegitimacy rate was only 4.4, as compared with the rate of 4.2 for births to white mothers.

One of the questions of interest in connection with illegitimate birth rates is the influence of the customs and ideals of various nationality groups. Very little reliable evidence as to anthropological factors can be obtained from a statement of comparative numbers of births, especially in view of the complications due to the influence of the new environment upon the various foreign groups. In many cases the situation appears to be the opposite of that found in the native country, probably because of reactions to the new conditions of life. In order to gain an answer to the question as to the part Americanization plays in the problem of illegitimacy it would be necessary to make an intensive study which would include special consideration of mothers who are the children of foreign-born parents. Without such a study no conclusions can be reached as to the effect of the raising of economic standards, the increased freedom, and the lessening of parental restraint.

It was found that 35.2 per cent of the legitimate births were to white mothers born in the United States, while 53.8 per cent of the illegitimate births were to native white mothers. Illegitimate births to white mothers born in the United States constituted 6.5 per cent of all births to native white mothers. This illegitimacy rate is strikingly high as compared with the general illegitimacy rate of 4.4, and suggests that the problem of illegitimacy is more serious among the native born than among the foreign born. However, the factor of immigration from country to city for the purpose of securing maternity care may account in part for the higher rate among the native born.

The percentage of illegitimate births to mothers born in Canada may be considered disproportionately high, because of the number of women coming to Boston from Canada for confinement. Of the legitimate births, 8.1 per cent were to Canadian mothers, while of the illegitimate births, 13 per cent were to natives of Canada. The illegitimacy rate for births to Canadian mothers was 6.8, as compared with 6.5 for births to native white mothers, and 4.4 for all births.

Births to foreign-born white mothers other than Canadian comprised 55 per cent of all legitimate births, while they were only 27 per cent of the illegitimate births. Illegitimate births to white mothers born in the European countries specified in Table 15 constituted 2.2 per cent of all births to white mothers who were natives of these countries. This percentage of 2.2 is strikingly low in comparison with the percentages of 6.5 for illegitimate births to native white mothers and 6.8 for births to Canadian mothers, and it controverts much of the general opinion in regard to the influence of the foreign born upon this social problem.

The illegitimacy rates for births to mothers who were natives of England and Wales, Ireland, and the Scandinavian countries were very similar, ranging from 4.2 to 4.4. The lowest rate was for births to Italian mothers, 0.5. The illegitimacy rate for births to mothers born in Russia and Poland was 1.3. The rate for births to natives of Scotland was 6.8.

Little information was available as to the length of time the foreign-born mothers had been in the United States at the time of the birth of the child. It was known that of the 337 foreign-born mothers, including the colored, 23 were pregnant on arrival in this country. Of these, 14 were Canadians, 5 were Russians, and 4 were from other countries. Eleven were known to have been in this country less than two years, and 63 others less than five years, when their children were born. It is interesting to note that of the 23 mothers pregnant on arrival 4 were under 18 years of age at the time of the child's birth.

Residence.

The proportion of mothers who were not residents of Boston was very much higher in the case of illegitimate than of legitimate births. A large number of women came from neighboring towns and cities, from other States, and from Canada to secure maternity care. The term "residence" as used in this section means usual place of residence at the time of the child's birth. In a number of cases the mother changed her residence during the first months of pregnancy in order to conceal her condition or for other reasons. In these cases her new residence was considered as her residence at the time of the child's birth. If, however, the mother had come to Boston shortly before confinement, and simply for the purpose of securing maternity care, her residence was taken to be the place in which she had last maintained a residence.

The following list gives the residence of the mother:

Total mothers	840
Boston	482
Metropolitan district outside Boston	154
Massachusetts outside metropolitan district	142
Other New England States	38
Other parts of the United States	6
Canada [20]	14
Other countries	2
Not reported	2

The percentage resident in Boston was 57 and the percentage non-resident 43. According to the report of the health department 7 per cent of all births were to nonresident mothers.[21] Three-fourths of the mothers of infants of illegitimate birth—76 per cent—were residents of Boston proper or of the metropolitan district. Residents of Massachusetts outside the metropolitan district comprised 17 per cent of all the mothers, making a total of 93 per cent who were residents of the State.

Age.

The age of the mother at the time of the child's birth was reported on the birth certificates in 684 of the 840 cases. In 393 of these

---

[20] Includes 10 who were pregnant on arrival in this country, 1 of whom was a resident but not a native of Canada; 2 not pregnant on arrival; and 2 for whom time in the United States was not reported. Of the last 2, one was a resident but not a native of Canada. Five Canadian mothers who were pregnant on arrival were considered to have established residence in the United States.

[21] Forty-third Annual Report of the Health Department of the City of Boston for the Year 1914. Boston, 1915. P. 108.

cases and in 108 other instances records of social agencies stated the age of the mother at the birth of the child. The sources from which information as to age of mother was obtained are summarized as follows:

Total mothers _____ 840

Birth certificates only_____ 291	Agency records only_____ 108
Birth certificates and agency records _____ 393	Age not reported_____ 48

In cases in which the reports on age as secured from the two sources did not agree, the age given on the agency records was used in the tabulations.[22] In the cases in which the agency record did not state the age of the mother but the birth certificate gave this information, the age given on the birth certificate was used.

Following are the ages of the mothers as secured by the above process:

Total reported_____ 792

Less than 15 years_____ 6	21–24 years_____ 261
15 years_____ 12	25–29 years_____ 114
16 years_____ 36	30–34 years_____ 50
17 years_____ 54	35–39 years_____ 22
18–20 years_____ 236	41 years_____ 1

These figures indicate that the youth of the mother is a fact of very great importance in a consideration of the problem of illegitimacy. A larger number of mothers were but children themselves, 13 per cent of the total reported being under 18 years of age when their babies were born. An additional 30 per cent were between 18 and 20, thus making a total of 43 per cent who were under 21 years of age. One-third—33 per cent—of all the mothers whose ages were reported were between 21 and 24 years of age; 21 per cent were 25 to 34 years of age, and 3 per cent were 35 years of age and over.

In the 18 cases—2 per cent of the total reported—in which the mother was under 16 years of age, action might have been taken against the father under the law making unlawful intercourse with a female child under 16 years of age a felony punishable by life imprisonment.[23] Another law makes it an offense punishable by three years' imprisonment or by fine, or by both, to induce any person under the age of 18 years of chaste life to have unlawful sexual intercourse.[24] In 3 cases the man was prosecuted on a charge of rape. In the other cases no legal actions under these provisions were reported,

[22] Of the 393 cases, in which information in regard to age of mother was secured both from birth certificates and from agency records, the reports coincided in 76 per cent, differed by one year in 16 per cent, and by more than one year in 8 per cent. The percentage coinciding was higher for the age groups under 21 than for the older age groups.
[23] R. L. 1902, ch. 207, sec. 23.
[24] R. L. 1902, ch. 212, sec. 2, as amended by 1910, ch. 424, sec. 4.

though it is possible that such action was taken in some of the cases concerning which little information was obtained.

Civil condition.

Information in regard to the mother's civil condition at the time the child was born was secured for 718 of the 840 mothers. The distribution was as follows:

Total reported		718
Single	667	Divorced, separated, deserting, deserted
Married	12	... 23
Widowed	16	

The mothers who were single constituted 93 per cent of the total for whom this information was secured. Those who were married and presumably living with their husbands comprised 2 per cent of the total, while 5 per cent were widowed, divorced, separated, deserting, or deserted.

One of the single mothers and one of those separated or deserted were illegally married. A total of 15 mothers were living as married with the fathers of their children. Ten of these mothers were single, four were widowed, divorced, separated, or deserted, and the civil condition of one was not reported.

The histories of the mothers were followed so far as possible through agency records for the first year of the child's life. Information in regard to marriage of the mother after the child's birth is, therefore, limited to the one year. A total of 73—9 per cent of all the mothers—were reported as having married within a year after the child's birth. Considering the fact that there was a large number of cases in which it was not known whether or not the mother had married, her subsequent history being unknown to social agencies, the per cent known to have married during the first year of the child's life was high.

Of the 73 mothers known to have married, 31 had married the fathers of the children; 24 were known to have married other men; and in 18 cases the agencies did not report as to whether or not the men whom the women married were the fathers of the children. It is particularly interesting to note that one-third of the mothers who married during the first year were known to have married men other than the fathers of their children.

Physical condition.

It was possible to secure some information as to the physical condition of the mother during the first year after the birth of the child for 473 of the 840 cases. Considerable attention was paid by many of the agencies and institutions to examination for venereal diseases. Since these diseases are of special importance to this study, the following list gives prominence to them, combining all other diseases and disabilities under one general head.

Total mothers_____ 840
Total reported_____ 473

Physical condition good, so far as known _____ 359	Suspected syphilis_____ 9
Diagnosis of syphilis_____ 14	Suspected gonorrhea _____ 1
Diagnosis of gonorrhea_____ 17	Other diseases or disabilities _____ 62
Diagnosis of syphilis and gonorrhea _____ 8	Died during the year_____ 2
Diagnosis of gonorrhea and suspected syphilis_____ 1	

Hence, poor physical condition was reported for 114 mothers, 24 per cent of those for whom such information was secured, or 14 per cent of all mothers. A total of 40 had been diagnosed as having venereal infection, 8 per cent of those for whom physical condition was reported, or 5 per cent of all the 840 mothers. In 10 cases the mother was suspected of having venereal infection, but diagnoses had not been secured.

Mental condition.

The social histories of 488 mothers—58 per cent of all—were sufficiently complete to justify their classification according to mental condition. Facilities for mental examination are unusually available in Boston, and agencies are aware of the importance of expert diagnosis in all cases in which there is any reason to suspect that the mental condition is not normal.

The following list gives the distribution of the cases according to the mentality of the mothers.

Total mothers_____ 840
Total reported_____ 488

Normal, so far as known_____ 382	Feeble-minded (diagnosed) __ 43
Subnormal or abnormal_____ 16	Probably subnormal or feeble-minded, but not diagnosed_ 41
Insane_____ 6	

The term "subnormal" includes cases diagnosed as high-grade feeble-minded but not committable, or defective or subnormal but not feeble-minded, while the term "abnormal" includes those diagnosed as psychopathic or constitutionally inferior, defective delinquent, or morally defective, and those having mental disorder but not definitely insane. The mothers whose mental condition was diagnosed as subnormal or abnormal constituted 3 per cent of the 488 mothers whose mentality was reported and 2 per cent of the total 840 mothers. Mothers who were insane comprised 1 per cent of those whose mentality was reported. Mothers who had been diagnosed feeble-minded comprised 9 per cent of those whose mentality was reported and 5 per cent of all mothers. In 8 per cent of the reported cases—5 per cent of all cases—the mothers were probably subnormal or feeble-minded, but mental examination had not been made.

Including only those whose mental condition had been diagnosed, a total of 65 mothers—13 per cent of all whose mental condition was reported, or 8 per cent of the total number of mothers—were subnormal, mentally abnormal, insane, or feeble-minded. That more than one-eighth of the mothers whose mentality was known had been diagnosed as not normal mentally indicates the importance of this factor in the problem of illegitimate maternity.

A comparison of the mother's mentality and age at the time of the child's birth is of interest, as indicating whether defective mentality is more prevalent among the younger or among the older mothers.

TABLE 16.—*Mental condition and age of mothers of infants born out of wedlock in 1914.*

Mental condition.	Total mothers.	Age of mother at birth of child.		
		Under 18 yrs.	18 yrs. and over.	Not reported.
Total..	840	108	684	48
Normal, so far as known...........................	382	59	322	1
Subnormal or abnormal.............................	16	5	11	....
Insane..	6	....	6	....
Feeble-minded (diagnosed).........................	43	8	35	....
Probably subnormal or feeble-minded, but not diagnosed......	41	6	35	....
Not reported......................................	352	30	275	47

According to the data in Table 16, 12 per cent of the mothers who were under 18 years of age at the birth of the child were diagnosed subnormal, abnormal, feeble-minded, or insane, as against 8 per cent of the 684 mothers 18 years of age and over. The percentages diagnosed feeble-minded were 7 for the younger age group and 5 for the older. Similarly, the proportion probably subnormal or feeble-minded, but not diagnosed, was higher for the mothers under 18 years—6 per cent as compared with 5 per cent for those over 18 years. In the absence of data on the age of the mother at the birth of the first child out of wedlock, in the cases where the child of the study was not the first, no exact statement can be made as to the relation between defective mentality and illegitimate maternity. However, it would seem evident that defective or disordered mentality was more prevalent among the younger age group, even though the proportion should be discounted to some extent by the fact that agencies were more likely to insist on mental examinations of the younger mothers. This greater prevalence is no doubt partly accounted for by the fact that feeble-minded women who have proved to be in need of custodial care have been removed from the community as far as the capacity of the institutions has permitted.

That the Massachusetts institutions for the care of the feeble-minded are not adequate to the needs is evidenced by the following data showing the dispositions of the mothers diagnosed feeble-minded. This covers treatment during pregnancy or during the child's first year of life.

Of the 43 diagnosed feeble-minded, there were—

    6 admitted to an institution for the feeble-minded.

    13 applications made for admission to an institution for the feeble-minded.

    1 admitted to a hospital for the insane.

    7 provided for in public infirmary (including 4 so provided for pending admission to an institution for the feeble-minded to which application had been made).

    1 placed at housework, under supervision of agency (and 1 other for whom application to an institution was made).

    3 otherwise provided for by agencies.

    12 for whom treatment was not reported.

Hence, one-sixth of the feeble-minded mothers were given permanent custodial care and another one-sixth were provided for temporarily in an institution. In almost one-third of the cases application had been made for admission to an institution; but the crowded condition of the Massachusetts schools for the feeble-minded made it impossible for these women to be given care, and they remained in the community. Of the remaining third, a few were supervised by agencies; and the provision made for the others, if any assistance had been given, was not reported.

Of the 6 insane mothers 3 were admitted to a hospital for the insane during the months of pregnancy or before the child was a year old. Thus, a total of 17 of the 840 mothers became inmates of institutions for the feeble-minded or insane before the end of the child's first year of life, or were temporarily cared for in a public infirmary, and 13 others were placed on the waiting lists of institutions for the feeble-minded.

Character.

The social histories of 495 of the 840 mothers were sufficiently complete to justify their classification according to character. Of these, 285 were reported as good so far as known. Detrimental characteristics were reported as follows:

Total reported as having detrimental characteristics_____ 210

Alcoholism_____ 5

Immorality _____ 140

Other delinquencies _____ 6

Alcoholism and immorality_____ 5

Alcoholism, immorality, and other delinquencies _____ 2

Immorality and other delinquencies _____ 10

Otherwise poor character_____ 42

Under " immorality " were included only sex irregularities other than those connected with the cases of illegitimate maternity included in the study. The number for whom immorality was reported—157, or 32 per cent of those whose character was reported and 19 per cent of all the mothers—implies a high percentage of cases in which there had been infractions of the moral code before the mother became pregnant with this child. Eleven mothers so reported were known to have been professional prostitutes. It is probable that only a minimum of the cases of immorality were reported in the histories of the mothers.

Twelve mothers were stated to be alcoholic, 7 of them also being immoral. In 18 cases other delinquencies were reported; in 12 of these cases the mother was also reported as alcoholic or immoral, or both. In 42 cases no definite delinquencies were reported, but the mother's character was stated to be bad. The histories of a total of 25 per cent of the 840 mothers—42 per cent of those for whom information on this point was obtained—gave evidence of immorality, alcoholism, or otherwise bad character.

The proportion of the mothers under 18 years of age who were reported as being of poor character was greater than the proportion among the women 18 years of age and over, 34 per cent of the younger mothers being so reported, as against 25 per cent of those 18 years of age and over. Alcoholism was negligible among the younger mothers. Immorality, on the other hand, appeared to be as prevalent among the mothers under 18 years of age as among the older women. It is especially significant that 4 of the 11 reported as being professional prostitutes were not yet 18 years of age.

Other children.

The histories of 730 of the 840 mothers gave data, shown in Table 17, in regard to other children or were sufficiently complete to warrant the assumption that absence of information as to other children indicated that there had been none. The proportion of these mothers known to have had other children is a minimum statement.

Seventy-two mothers—10 per cent of those for whom this information was available, or 9 per cent of all the mothers—were known to have had previous illegitimate births.

TABLE 17.—*Age and previous record as to illegitimate births to mothers of infants born out of wedlock in 1914.*

Age at birth of child.	Mothers of infants born out of wedlock in Boston during year.			
	Total.	Who had previous illegitimate births.	Who had no previous illegitimate births, so far as known.	No report as to previous illegitimate births.
Total	840	72	658	110
Under 18 years	108	4	95	9
18 years and over	684	65	539	80
Not reported	48	3	24	21

Four of the 72 mothers having had previous illegitimate births were less than 18 years of age at the time the child of the study was born. These constituted 4 per cent of the mothers under 18 years of age. Each of the 4 mothers had had one previous illegitimate birth.

The 65 mothers 18 years of age or over who were known to have had previous illegitimate births comprised 11 per cent of the mothers of this age group for whom there were reports, or 10 per cent of all the mothers 18 years of age or over.

The number of previous illegitimate births the mothers had were as follows:

```
     Total mothers_____ 840
     Total reported_____ 730
None  _____ 658 | Four _____  1
One _____ 51 | Six  _____  1
Two _____ 18 | Seven _____  1
```

Table 18 gives the civil condition of the mother at the time of the birth of the child of the study, and whether or not there had been previous illegitimate births.

TABLE 18.—*Civil condition and previous record as to illegitimate births to mothers of infants born out of wedlock in 1914.*

Civil condition of mother at time of birth of child.	Mothers of infants born out of wedlock in Boston during year.			
	Total.	Who had previous illegitimate births.	Who had no previous illegitimate births, so far as known.	No report as to previous illegitimate births.
Total..	840	72	658	110
Single..	667	63	592	12
Married, widowed, divorced, deserting, deserted........	51	8	41	2
Not reported...	122	1	a 25	96

a Includes 2 whose civil condition at time of birth of child was not known, but who had had children of legitimate birth.

A total of 63 of the single mothers, or 10 per cent of the 655 whose previous record as to illegitimate births was reported, were known to have been the mothers of children born out of wedlock before the year of the study. Eight of the 51 mothers who were married, widowed, divorced, separated, or deserted were known to have had previous illegitimate births. Of these 51 mothers who had been married, 32 were known to have had children born in wedlock before this child was born, 10 of them having had one; 8, two; 5, three; 5, four; and 4, five or more children of legitimate birth.

The proportion of mothers known to have had previous illegitimate births (see Table 19) was considerably larger among those below normal mentally (including those probably subnormal or feeble-minded, but not diagnosed) than among mothers of normal mentality, so far as known.   Although this may be partly accounted for by the fact that agencies are more likely to arrange for mental examinations in the case of mothers illegitimately pregnant for the second time than in other cases, yet the figures are of considerable significance.   Twenty-six per cent of the 106 mothers below normal mentally had had previous illegitimate births, while only 10 per cent of the 382 mothers whose mentality was normal so far as known had previously been illegitimately pregnant.   Of the 43 mothers diagnosed feeble-minded almost two-fifths had records of previous illegitimate births.

There were 322 mothers 18 years of age and over whose mentality was normal, so far as known.   Of these, 37—11 per cent—were known to have had previous illegitimate births.   Twenty-five of the 87 mothers of the same age group who were mentally below normal—29 per cent—had had previous illegitimate pregnancies.

To state in other terms the relation between mentality and previous illegitimate births, not quite one-eighth of the 658 mothers who had had no previous illegitimate births so far as known were below normal mentally, while more than three-eighths of the 72 who had been illegitimately pregnant previously were mentally below normal. As before stated, these figures are subject to some qualification because of the greater frequency with which mental examinations are given mothers illegitimately pregnant for the second time.

TABLE 19.—*Mentality and previous record as to illegitimate births to mothers of infants born out of wedlock in 1914.*

Mentality of mother.	Mothers of infants born out of wedlock in Boston during year.			
	Total.	Who had previous illegitimate births.	Who had no previous illegitimate births, so far as known.	No report as to previous illegitimate births.
Total....................................	840	72	658	110
Normal, so far as known............................	382	39	341	2
Subnormal or abnormal...............................	16	5	11	....
Insane....................................	6	....	6	....
Feeble-minded (diagnosed)............................	43	17	26	....
Probably subnormal or feeble-minded, but not diagnosed.	41	6	34	1
Not reported...................................	352	5	240	107

The four maternity homes in Boston and at least two of the hospitals included in the study make it a practice to refuse admission to women pregnant out of wedlock for a second or subsequent confinement.   It is felt that the girls who have not had previous illegitimate births are the more promising and warrant the greater amount of constructive effort. It is also believed that the presence in the same institution of girls pregnant for the first time and of repeated offenders against the moral code is demoralizing to the former. The figures as to mentality show that a larger percentage of women illegitimately pregnant for the first time than of women having had previous illegitimate pregnancies are of normal mentality and are therefore capable of benefiting by the type of training given in maternity homes. However, the number of illegitimate pregnancies is not necessarily a test of character, as shown by the fact that 15 per cent of the mothers illegitimately pregnant for the first time were known to have been immoral, alcoholic, or otherwise delinquent, 13 per cent having been immoral. (See Table 20.)

TABLE 20.—*Character and previous record as to illegitimate births to mothers of infants born out of wedlock in 1914.*

Character of mother.	Mothers of infants born out of wedlock in Boston during year.			
	Total.	Who had previous illegitimate births.	Who had no previous illegitimate births, so far as known.	No report as to previous illegitimate births.
Total..	840	a 72	658	110
Good, so far as known.............................	285	....	282	3
Alcoholic...	5	....	5	....
Immoral..	140	64	75	1
Otherwise delinquent.............................	6	....	6	....
Alcoholic and immoral............................	5	2	3	....
Immoral and otherwise delinquent.................	10	3	7	....
Alcoholic, immoral, and otherwise delinquent......	2	2	....	....
Otherwise poor...................................	42	....	42	....
Not reported.....................................	345	1	238	106

a By definition, all those who had previous illegitimate births, and whose social histories were sufficiently complete to justify their classification as to character, were classed as immoral.

Because only a year elapsed between the birth of the child of the study and the end of the period covered, information in regard to subsequent children of these mothers is limited to reports of illegitimate pregnancies that occurred before this child was 1 year old. Sixteen of the 840 mothers—2 per cent—were known to have become illegitimately pregnant before the end of the year. Two of these mothers were under 18 years of age. Of the 14 who were 18 years of age and over or whose ages were not reported, 5 were known also to have had previous illegitimate births. It is interesting to note that 13 of the 16 mothers were single women, 2 were separated, and the civil condition of 1 was not reported. Only one was living as married with the father of the child included in the study. That 2 per cent of the mothers were known to have again become illegitimately pregnant before one year had elapsed after the birth of the infant studied indicates the need for constructive social work in such cases.

Mode of living.

The place in which the mother made her home before the birth of the child was reported for 533 of the 840 mothers. Of these mothers, 193—36 per cent of those reported—were living in their parental homes. The 26 who had been married and were living in homes of their own comprised 5 per cent. A total of 46, or 9 per cent, were living in the homes of relatives or friends, and 21, or 4 per cent, were boarding. One of the mothers had been placed in an institution before the birth of her child. The largest number, 246, or 46 per cent of all whose mode of living was known, were living in their places of employment previous to the birth of the child, 233 of them being employed at housework.

As was to be expected, the largest proportion living in their parental homes or with relatives or friends was in the age group under 18 years. But even among these very young mothers, only 81 per cent of the total reported were living in homes from which they could expect help before the birth of their children and assistance in providing homes for them. Of the mothers 18 to 20 years of age whose mode of living was known, 59 per cent were living in the homes of their parents or with relatives or friends. Of those 21 years of age and over, 28 per cent were living in their parental homes or in the homes of relatives or friends.

Conversely, the proportion living in the place of employment was highest among those 21 years of age and over. Only 16 per cent of the mothers under 18 years of age whose mode of living was reported were living in their places of employment; of those 18 to 20 years, 36 per cent were thus living; while 58 per cent of the mothers 21 years of age and over were living at their places of employment.

Only 1 of the mothers under 18 years of age was living in her own home, and 1 was boarding. Two of the mothers between 18 and 20 years were in their own homes, and 5 were boarding. Among the older women, 22 were in their own homes, 15 were boarding, and 1 was in an institution.

Character of parental home.

The data here given upon the character of the mother's parental home are of interest mainly from the point of view of the possibilities of assistance in the care of the child by the mother's family. Because of the necessary limitations of this study, the facts presented are understatements of the true conditions—to how great an extent can not be determined.

Information in regard to the mother's parental home was available in only a small proportion of cases. It was known that 8 of the mothers were themselves of illegitimate birth. Two of these and 8 others were known to have been brought up by foster parents.

It was known that before the birth of the child both parents of 37 of the 840 mothers had died. In 153 cases, one of the parents had died. In 27 of the cases in which one or both parents were dead, and in 50 others, the mother's parents had never been in the United States. The parents of 21 mothers were divorced or separated. Hence, in a total of 261 cases—31 per cent of the 840 mothers—it was reported that one or both of the mother's parents were dead, were not in this country, or were divorced or separated. Since this information was known only for those mothers who had come to the attention of social agencies, this proportion of almost one-third is a minimum statement.

Reports as to the character of the mother's parents were secured for only 229 mothers. The parents of 122 were of good character so far as known. One or both parents of 107 of the mothers were reported to be alcoholic, immoral, or of otherwise poor character. The probability is that the proportion of cases in which the parents were of bad character was much greater among those known to social agencies than among others. It was, therefore, considered more fair to compare the number of cases in which the character of the parents was reported as poor with the total number of mothers, rather than with the number for whom reports were secured.

The 107 mothers, one or both of whose parents were reported to be of poor character, comprised 13 per cent of the total 840 mothers. In 21 of these 107 cases, one or both parents were reported to be immoral; in 47 cases, alcoholic; in 10 cases, immoral and alcoholic; and in 29 cases the parents were reported as of otherwise poor character.

Almost one-third of the mothers were known to have lost one or both parents, or to lack normal homes because the parents were not in the United States, or were divorced or separated, and at least one-eighth of the mothers had suffered from bad home conditions due to alcoholism, immorality, or otherwise poor character of the parents. These figures indicate how impossible it is in many cases for the mother to rely upon the most natural source of help in the care of the child.

Relation to social agencies.

Through checking with the records of social agencies, it was found that in 112 cases the mother herself, her parents, or her children had been under the prolonged care of social agencies before the birth of the infant born during the year of the study. This number, which excluded cases in which the only care given was on account of the mother's pregnancy, represented 13 per cent of all the 840 mothers. The mother herself had been under care in 58 of the 112 cases. In 11 of these instances the mother's parents had been under care, in 9 cases her children, and in 2 instances care had been given both to the mother's parents and to her children.

The mother's parents had received care in 38 instances, including 15 cases in which the mother or her children had also received care.

The children of 29 mothers, who had not themselves received care and whose parents had not been aided, had been cared for by agencies. In 13 other cases the mother's children had been under agency care, hence there was a total of 42 cases in which the children had received such assistance.

The following is a summary of the cases in which agency care was given before the birth of the child of study:

```
Mother given care _____ 36
Mother's parents given care_____ 23
Mother's children given care_____ 29
Mother and her parents given care_____ 11
Mother and her children given care_____  9
Mother, her parents, and her children given care_____  2
Mother's parents and her children given care_____  2
                                                                  ____
      Total cases in which previous agency care was given_____ 112
```

The agencies that had given care to the 58 mothers were as follows:

```
      Total cases in which the mother was given care_____ 58
Child-caring agency _____ 23 | Child-caring agency and other_  1
Correctional institution or court__ 15 | Correctional institution or
Other_____ 12 |   court and other_____  2
Child-caring agency and correc- |
  tional institution or court_____ 5 |
```

A total of 29 mothers—3.5 per cent of all the mothers—were known to have been wards of child-caring agencies. Twenty-two mothers—2.6 per cent—had been in correctional institutions or had been before the courts.

Occupation previous to birth of child.

As in respect to age, data in regard to the occupation of the mother previous to the child's birth were obtained from two sources—birth certificates and records of social agencies. The numbers of cases in which reports were obtained from these sources were as follows:

```
      Total mothers_____ 840
Birth certificates only_____ 205 | Agency records only_____ 136
Birth certificates and agency rec- |     Occupation not reported_____ 149
  ords_____ 350 |
```

The occupation of the mother was reported on the birth certificate in 555 of the 840 cases. In 350 of these, records of social agencies also stated the mother's occupation. In 136 other cases the birth certificate did not give the occupation, but this information was reported in the records of social agencies. Hence, agency records gave information on the occupations of 486 of the 840 mothers.

In cases in which the occupation of the mother was reported both on the birth certificate of the child and on agency records, and in which the reports did not agree, the occupation given on the agency records was used in the tabulations.[25] "Occupation" refers to the mother's usual occupation previous to the child's birth.

Table 21 gives the occupation of the mother as reported by agencies or, in cases in which agency reports did not give information, as stated on the birth certificate.

TABLE 21.—*Occupation and age of mothers of infants born out of wedlock in 1914.*

Occupation previous to birth of child.a	Total mothers whose occupations were reported.	Age at birth of child.		
		Under 18 yrs.	18 yrs. and over.	Not reported.
Total	691	92	583	16
Not gainfully employed	98	30	66	2
No occupation	38	b 7	b 30	1
Attending school	25	20	5	
Housewives	35	3	31	1
Professional persons	5		5	
Clerks and kindred workers	68	9	59	
Bookkeepers, cashiers, stenographers, typewriters	17	2	15	
Clerks (except clerks in stores)	5		5	
Clerks in stores and saleswomen	32	3	29	
Messenger, bundle and office girls	5	4	1	
Telephone and telegraph operators	9		9	
Semiskilled workers	192	31	158	3
Dressmakers and seamstresses (not in factory)	9		9	
Laundry operatives	13		12	1
Nurses (not trained)	8		8	
Semiskilled factory operatives	159	31	126	2
Other	3		3	
Servants	326	22	293	11
Charwomen, cleaners, laundresses	11	1	10	
Waitresses	50	4	c 43	3
Domestic servants	246	16	c 222	8
Other	19	1	18	
Other	2		2	

a Classification is based on that followed by Alba M. Edwards in "Social-economic groups of the United States." Quarterly publications of the American Statistical Association, Vol. XV (June, 1917), pp. 643–661.

b Includes 1 prostitute.

c Includes 1 also a prostitute.

[25] Of the 350 cases in which information in regard to occupation of mother was secured, both from birth certificates and from agency records, the reports coincided in 74 per cent. The greatest discrepancies between the two reports were in the "no occupation" and the "housewife" groups.

Occupation was reported either by social agencies or on the child's birth certificate for a total of 691 of the 840 mothers. In 98 cases, or 14 per cent of the total reported, the mother was not gainfully employed. Thirty-eight of these mothers—5 per cent of the total— were reported as having no occupation. In 25 cases—4 per cent—the mother was attending school. Mothers who were housewives numbered 35—5 per cent of all reported.

Five mothers were engaged in professional pursuits. Three of these were teachers, 1 was a trained nurse, and 1 an actress. In 68 cases, or 10 per cent, the mother was engaged in clerical or kindred work. A total of 192 mothers—28 per cent of all reported—were semiskilled workers; most of these (159) were employed in factories.

Almost half the mothers reported—326, or 47 per cent—were employed in domestic or personal service. Eleven were charwomen, cleaners, and laundresses; 50 were waitresses in hotels or restaurants; 246 were servants in private families; and 19 were employed in other kinds of personal service. Two mothers were engaged in occupations not specified in Table 21; 1 was a lodging-house keeper, and 1 an agricultural laborer.

The data given in Table 22 shows that a total of 593 mothers—86 per cent of those whose occupations were reported—had been gainfully employed before the birth of the child. This percentage was twice that among all women in the general population aged 14 to 44 years. It would have been more significant to compare the percentage of mothers gainfully employed with the percentage of single, widowed, and divorced women aged 14 to 44 years who were gainfully employed, but these figures could not be obtained. Of the 224 mothers 16 to 20 years of age at the time of the child's birth whose occupations were reported, 83 per cent were engaged in gainful occupations. Only 60 per cent of the women 16 to 20 years of age in the general population were gainfully employed. The percentage of mothers 21 to 44 years of age gainfully employed was 89, as against 41 per cent among all women of this age group in Boston.

TABLE 22.—*Per cent gainfully employed of mothers of infants born out of wedlock in 1914, and of all women of childbearing age, by age periods.*

Age.	Mothers of infants born out of wedlock.						Women in Boston 14 to 44 years of age.		
		Occupation previous to child's birth reported.						Gainfully employed.	
	Total.	Total.	Gainfully employed.		Not gain-fully em-ployed.	Occu-pation not re-ported.	Total.a	Num-ber.b	Per cent.
			Num-ber.	Per cent.					
Total..............	840	691	593	85.8	98	149	187,398	80,388	42.9
14–15 years..............	18	16	7	43.7	9	2	10,850	1,985	18.3
16–20 years..............	326	270	224	83.0	46	56	30,325	18,317	60.4
21–44 years..............	448	389	318	89.5	41	59	146,223	60,086	41.1
Not reported............	48	16	14	....	2	32	....	....	....

a The number of women in Boston in 1910 aged 15 to 19 years was 28,792, and the number aged 20 to 44 years was 153,031. (Thirteenth Census of the United States, 1910: Vol. II, Population, p. 869.) Unpub-lished census figures give the number aged 14 as 5,575, and the number 15 years of age as 5,275. In the figures for school population (Vol. I, p. 1160) the 1910 census gives the number of women in Boston 15 to 20 years of age as 35,600. Subtracting from this the number aged 15 to 19, it was found that the number of women 20 years of age was 6,808. Subtracting the number aged 15 from the 15 to 19 age group, and adding the number aged 20, the number of women aged 16 to 20 was secured. The number aged 21 to 44 was similarly obtained.

b Thirteenth Census of the United States, 1910: Vol. IV, Population, pp. 540–541.

It is impossible to evaluate occupation as a possible causative fac-tor in illegitimate maternity without comparing the occupational distribution of the mothers with the occupational distribution of all the women in the locality studied. Table 23 makes this comparison for women gainfully employed. It must be remembered that the occupations of the mothers refer to occupations previous to the time when the children were born.

TABLE 23.—*Occupational distribution of mothers of infants born out of wed-lock in 1914, and of gainfully employed women in 1910.*

Occupation.	Gainfully em-ployed mothers of infants born out of wedlock.		Gainfully em-ployed women in Boston, 1910.a	
	Number.	Per cent distribu-tion.	Number.	Per cent distribu-tion.
Total..	593	100.0	96,326	100.0
Proprietors, officials, managers........................	1	.2	5,008	5.2
Clerks and kindred workers....................................	68	11.4	24,588	25.5
Bookkeepers, cashiers, stenographers, typewriters..........	17	2.9	10,760	11.2
Clerks (except clerks in stores).............................	5	.8	2,911	3.0
Clerks in stores and saleswomen.............................	32	5.4	8,138	8.4
Messenger, bundle, and office girls.........................	5	.8	635	.7
Telephone and telegraph operators..........................	9	1.5	1,685	1.7
Other..	....	....	459	.5

a Total women 10 years of age and over engaged in each specified occupation in Boston, 1910. Thirteenth Census of the United States, 1910: Vol. IV, Population, pp. 152–164.

TABLE 23.—*Occupational distribution of mothers of infants born out of wedlock in 1914, and of gainfully employed women in 1910*—Continued.

Occupation.	Gainfully employed mothers of infants born out of wedlock.		Gainfully employed women in Boston, 1910.[a]	
	Number	Per cent distribution.	Number	Per cent distribution.
Skilled workers			1,896	2.0
Semiskilled workers	192	32.4	31,137	32.3
Dressmakers and seamstresses (not in factory)	9	1.5	6,568	6.8
Laundry operatives	13	2.2	1,370	1.4
Milliners and millinery dealers	2	.3	1,840	1.9
Midwives and nurses (not trained)	8	1.4	1,797	1.9
Semiskilled factory operatives	159	26.8	15,504	16.1
Other	1	.2	4,058	4.2
Laborers	1	.2	730	.8
Servants	326	55.0	24,319	25.2
Charwomen, cleaners, janitors, laundresses	11	1.9	3,967	4.1
Waitresses	50	8.4	3,239	3.3
Servants (domestic)	246	41.5	} 17,113	17.8
Other servants	19	3.2		
Public officials			68	.1
Semiofficial public employees			5	(b)
Professional persons	5	.8	8,575	8.9

b Less than one-tenth of 1 per cent.

Of mothers of children born out of wedlock the percentage engaged in clerical occupations previous to the birth of their children was less than half the percentage of all women so employed in Boston. Only 3 per cent of the gainfully employed mothers were bookkeepers, cashiers, stenographers, or typewriters, as against 11 per cent of all women wage earners who were so employed. Similarly the clerks in stores and saleswomen represented only 5 per cent of the mothers, while 8 per cent of all women wage earners were so employed.

Almost one-third of the gainfully employed women in the city were classed as semiskilled workers. The percentage of mothers in this group previous to the birth of their children was the same as the percentage of all women. Within this group the most significant comparison is that for factory operatives, 27 per cent of the mothers being so employed, while only 16 per cent of the wage-earning women were reported as engaged in this occupation.

The most striking discrepancy in the percentages of gainfully employed mothers and of all women engaged in gainful occupations occurs in the domestic and personal service group of occupations. More than half the mothers—55 per cent—were so employed before the birth of the children studied, while only one-fourth of all wage-earning women in the city—25 per cent—were engaged in occupations so classified. Within this group the percentage of mothers who were waitresses was 8, as against 3 per cent of all gainfully employed women. The census reports do not classify separately servants in private families. However, only 18 per cent of the gainfully employed women in Boston were employed as servants, exclusive of charwomen, cleaners, janitors, laundresses, and waitresses, while 42 per cent of the gainfully employed mothers were employed in domestic service in private families, a total of 45 per cent being employed as domestics or other servants.

The mother's occupation has great significance in connection with the care of the child. That 86 per cent of those whose occupations were reported had been wage earners before the child's birth, indicates a degree of economic independence which might be considered encouraging from the point of view of the possibilities of providing for the child's support. However, practically all of them had been engaged in occupations paying wages which, at the time the study was made, were at best barely sufficient for the support of the girl herself. The resources of few of the mothers were sufficient to meet the added financial burden of the care of the infant, coupled with the necessity of nursing him. The fact that so large a proportion of mothers were wage earners indicates, too, that they came from families of small or moderate incomes, unable in many cases to provide substantial aid for the mothers.

The Father

Race and nativity.

Because of the absence of any information regarding the father on the birth certificates for children born out of wedlock, definite reports as to race and nativity of father were available in only a small proportion of cases—those in which records of social agencies contained this information. However, in regard to race, it was assumed that both parents were white if the child was white. In 794 of the 840 cases the father was white, in 23 cases the father was known to be colored, and the race of 23 fathers was not known.

Table 24 compares the race of the father and the race of the mother.

TABLE 24.—*Race of fathers and mothers of infants born out of wedlock in 1914.*

Race of mother.	Total fathers.	Race of father.		
		White.	Negro.	Not reported.
Total	840	794	23	23
White	787	786	1	
Negro	52	8	22	22
American Indian	1			1

In 786 of the 840 cases both parents were known to be white; in 22 cases both were colored. In 9 instances it was known that one parent was white and the other colored, there being 1 case of a white mother and colored father, and 8 in which the mother was colored and the father white. The race of the father was not reported in 22 cases in which the mother was colored, and in the 1 case in which she was an Indian.

The records of social agencies gave information in regard to the nativity of only 234 of the 840 fathers. Of these 234, 110 were born in the United States, 28 in Canada, and 96 in other countries. Table 25 compares the nativity of the father with that of the mother for the cases in which the birthplaces of both were known.

TABLE 25.—*Nativity of fathers and mothers of infants born out of wedlock in 1914.*

Nativity of mother.	Total fathers whose nativity was reported.	Nativity of father.		
		United States.	Canada.	Other.
Total..........................	234	110	28	96
United States...........................	116	86	11	19
Canada...........................	34	11	15	8
Other...........................	84	13	2	a 69

a In 56 of the 69 cases the nativity of the father and the mother was the same.

In 157 cases, or 67 per cent of the 234 in which the nativity of both parents was reported, the father and the mother were born in the same country. In 86 instances—over one-third of the known cases— both parents were natives of the United States. Besides these, there were 54 cases in which one parent was born in the United States. Both parents were born in Canada in 15 cases, and one parent in 32 cases. Of those born in other foreign countries, both parents were natives of the same country in 56 cases, and in 13 cases they were from different countries.

Age.

The records of social agencies gave the ages of 285 of the fathers. More than half the fathers whose ages were known—54 per cent— were under 25 years of age. One-fifth of them—21 per cent, were minors, being less than 21 years of age at the time the child was born. In 11 instances—4 per cent—the father was under 18 years of age. The youth of so large a proportion of the fathers of these children is of especial significance in connection with the question of the father's assumption of his duties toward the child.

It is of interest to compare the age of the father and the age of the mother, as shown in Table 26.

TABLE 26.—*Ages of fathers and mothers of infants born out of wedlock in 1914.*

Age of mother.	Total fathers whose ages were reported.	Age of father.							
		Under 18 yrs.	18–20 yrs.	21–24 yrs.	25–29 yrs.	30–34 yrs.	35–39 yrs.	40–49 yrs.	60–69 yrs.
Total	285	11	49	94	71	31	16	11	2
Under 18 years	42	7	13	15	5	1			1
18–20 years	87	3	30	33	15	4	2		
21–24 years	98		4	40	32	13	5	3	1
25–29 years	35	1	2	5	16	5	4	2	
30–34 years	13				1	6	3	3	
35–39 years	7			1		2	1	3	
40 years and over	1						1		
Not reported	2				2			1	

The age of the father was known in 42 of the cases in which the mother was less than 18 years old. In 7 of these cases the father also was under 18, and in 13 he was between 18 and 20 years of age; hence, in 7 per cent of all cases in which the father's age was known the mother was under the age of 18 and the father was under the age of 21 years. In 20 of the 42 cases in which the mother was under 18 the father was between 21 and 29 years of age. In one case the mother was less than 18 and the father between 30 and 34, and in another case of a child mother the father was over 60 years old.

Among the cases of older mothers it is interesting to note 1 in which the mother was between 25 and 29 years of age and the father under 18, and 2 in which the mother was between 25 and 29 years of age and the father between 18 and 20.

In a total of 100 of the 285 reported cases—25 per cent—mother and father belonged in the same age group. In 89 cases—31 per cent—the father was in the age group next higher than that of the mother. Hence, in two-thirds of the reported cases the father and mother were in the same age group or the father was within the group next higher than that of the mother. There were 74 cases—26 per cent—in which the father belonged in a higher age group more than once removed from the mother's age group. The father was in a younger age group than the mother in 20 of 285 reported cases—7 per cent; in some of these cases there was considerable difference in the ages of the parents.

Civil condition of father and social relationship of father and mother.

Civil condition was reported for only 237 of the fathers. Of these 165 were single, 49 married, and 23 widowed, divorced, or separated.

It is probable that the proportion of men in the last two groups would be found to be an overstatement if the civil condition of all the 840 fathers were known. These 72, the majority of whom presumably had other families legally dependent upon them, constituted 30 per cent of those whose civil condition was reported, or 9 per cent of all the fathers. Twenty-one per cent of those reported, or 6 per cent of all, were married. It is a commentary on the general absence of interest in the father that, even in the records of social agencies, there should be so low a percentage of reports on civil condition. The importance of knowledge of the father's status is evidenced by the proportion presumably having legitimate families dependent upon them.

Of especial interest in connection with the causative side of the problem and also as throwing some light upon the probability of future legal marriage, is the social relationship that existed between the mother and the father before the child's birth. Information on this subject was available in only 137 cases. This fact is another illustration of the absence in agency records of information essential to proper understanding of the situation and of the greatest importance in work for the assistance of the mother and child. Following is the distribution of the 137 cases according to the social relationship of the father and mother.

Total reported_____ 137

Illegally married	2	Schoolmates	3
Living as married	15	Father a friend of the mother's family	4
Mother the mistress of the father	12	Members of the same household	13
"Keeping company"	27		
Chance acquaintances	19		
Mother a prostitute	3	Relatives (1 brother, 2 uncles, 4 cousins, 3 brothers-in-law)	10
Father the employer of the mother	8		
Fellow employees	12	Other	9

Occupation.

The occupations of 311 fathers as reported on the records of social agencies are summarized in Table 27. The occupational classification was based upon that used by the Bureau of the Census, so rearranged that occupations of about the same economic status would fall, as far as possible, into the same group.[26] An occupation was not listed separately unless the number reported engaged therein was at least 5.

[26] Rearrangement according to the method followed by Alba M. Edwards in " Social-economic groups of the United States." Quarterly Publications of the American Statistical Association, Vol. XV (June, 1917), pp. 643–661.

TABLE 27.—*Occupation of fathers of infants born out of wedlock in 1914.*

Occupation of father.a	Fathers of infants born out of wedlock, whose occupations were reported.	
	Number.	Per cent distribution.
Total	311	100.0
Proprietors, officials, managers	24	7.7
Professional persons	13	4.2
Clerks and kindred workers	47	15.1
Commercial travelers	11	
Salesmen and clerks in stores	17	
Other	19	
Skilled workers	65	20.9
Carpenters	8	
Electricians	6	
Machinists	10	
Painters and paperhangers	7	
Plumbers and steamfitters	6	
Printers and pressmen	5	
Other	23	
Semiskilled workers	78	25.1
Chauffeurs	19	
Conductors (street railroad)	9	
Factory or mill operatives	23	
Other	27	
Laborers	39	12.5
Draymen, teamsters, expressmen	9	
Other	30	
Servants	26	8.4
Cooks	8	
Janitors and housemen	5	
Waiters	5	
Other	8	
Semiofficial public employees	11	3.5
Soldiers, sailors, marines	10	
Other	1	
Not gainfully employed	8	2.6
Students	5	
Others	3	

a According to Dr. Edward's classification. (See note, p. 129.)

Proprietors, officials, and managers included mainly small dealers, storekeepers, and farmers. In 8 per cent of the reported cases, the father's occupation was so classified; in only a few cases did the information indicate that the income was large. Classifying together proprietors, officials, and managers and professional persons, a total of 12 per cent of the fathers were engaged in an independent business or profession. A total of 36 per cent were clerks or kindred workers or skilled workers in various industries. In 46 per cent of the cases the father was a semiskilled worker, laborer, or servant. The soldiers, sailors, and marines, and those not gainfully employed were probably the least able to assume their responsibilities toward the mother and child. These two groups comprised 6 per cent of the fathers whose occupations were reported.

Very little information as to earnings was available. In only 67 cases was the weekly income reported. Fourteen of these fathers earned from $5 to $9 a week; 27, from $10 to $14; 17, from $15 to $19; 7, from $20 to $29; and only 2 earned $30 or more weekly. This distribution of earnings is not representative of the entire group, for the reason that reports in regard to the larger incomes were probably not secured so frequently as in respect to the smaller. However, both the occupational distribution and the wage data indicate that in most of the instances where the father's occupation was reported he was a man of small income.

Contributions to the support of the child.

As a part of the study of infants born out of wedlock in Boston during the year, the court records were searched in order to secure information in regard to the cases involving the support of these infants. Data were secured from the nine district courts of Boston and from the superior court. A full account of the law under which these cases were brought, the practice in the Boston courts, and the method of obtaining the data is given in the chapter on legal action for the support of children born out of wedlock.[27]

Cases involving 99 of the 847 infants born out of wedlock included in this study were initiated in the Boston courts before the end of their first year of life. In addition, agency records reported 9 other cases in which court action for support had been brought in other places. Hence, for 108 infants, 13 per cent of all infants of illegitimate birth born during the year, court cases for securing support from the father were known to have been initiated before the children had reached 1 year of age. Although there may have been a few court cases outside Boston concerning which information was not obtained, it is probable that this percentage is not a great understatement. That legal steps were known to have been taken to insure the assumption of the father's responsibility for only one-eighth of the infants born during the year shows that the comparatively liberal and advanced Massachusetts law for the support of children of illegitimate birth was directly used only in a minority of cases. Undoubtedly there are a number of cases in which the indirect influence of the law and the fear of its consequences are efficacious without recourse to the court.

As a consequence of court action, some provision for support was arranged before the end of the child's first year of life in 60 of the

---

[27] See pp. 228–264.

108 cases—56 per cent of those brought before the courts. In 3 of these instances the child was adopted; in 4 the parents were married. In the remaining 53 cases cash payments or periodic contributions to the child's support were made by the fathers. In 2 of the adoption cases and in 2 of those in which the parents were married after court action had been initiated cash payments were also made by the father.

The amounts secured from the father during the child's first year of life were known in 40 of the 60 cases in which arrangements for the child's support were made. The total amount of money secured for these 40 children was $5,736.87. The average amount per child was $143.42. This per capita is not large in view of the fact that in some cases the amounts were lump-sum payments, which represented all that was likely to be secured for the support of the child during the years of dependence.

The 60 children for whose support arrangements were made through court action during the first year of life constituted only 7 per cent of all the children born out of wedlock in Boston during the year of the study. In 1 of the 60 cases the father contributed nothing to the support of the child, the child having been adopted by some one else.

In addition to the 59 children for whom arrangements for support by the father were made through court action, there were 59 whose fathers were known to have contributed something to the support of the mother or the child. The manner in which the fathers aided in the support of these 59 children not involved in court cases was as follows:

Total children			59
Parents married each other	9	Irregular contributions	9
Parents living as married	2	Payment toward pregnancy	
Settlement by payment of lump		and confinement expenses	
sum	22	only	8
Regular contributions	9		

The fathers of a total of 118 children—14 per cent of the 847 born out of wedlock during the year—were known to have given more or less financial assistance as a result of court action or otherwise. This is, of course, an understatement, since many of the infants not known to social agencies or courts may have been supported, in part at least, by their fathers.

THE CARE OF THE CHILD.

Extent of Information Secured.

Through data obtained from agencies and from court records and death certificates it was possible to secure some information as to the histories of 796 children born out of wedlock during the year.

In only 51 cases was it impossible to obtain any data. The records of 275 of the 847 infants—32 per cent—showed that the child had survived the first year of life. Agency or death records showed that 230 infants—27 per cent—had died. In 213 of these 230 cases death certificates were found; for 17 the deaths were reported in agency records only, death certificates not having been found because of change of name or because the death had occurred outside the area covered by the study. The histories of 342 infants—40 per cent—did not cover the first year of life, the information being limited to that given on the birth certificate in 51 instances, and extending over a period of less than one year in 291 cases.

Age at Death or at Last Date Known.

The ages at death of the 230 infants known to have died, and the ages of the 617 others at the last record obtained, are given in Table 28.

TABLE 28.—*Age at death, or at last record obtained, of infants born out of wedlock in 1914.*

	Infants born out of wedlock.		
Age at death or at last record obtained.	Total.	At last record obtained.	
		Living.	Dead.
Total	847	617	230
Less than 1 month	a 242	a 165	77
1 month	72	27	45
2 months	40	15	25
3 months	40	17	23
4 months	30	18	12
5 months	20	9	11
6 months	24	15	9
7 months	27	18	9
8 months	26	20	6
9 months	12	9	3
10 months	23	18	5
11 months	16	11	5
1 year	275	275	....

a Including 51 concerning whose histories nothing was known.

One-third of the children were followed to the end of the first year of life and were known to have survived. Not quite half were followed through the first six months and were known to be surviving at the end of that time. The histories of almost three-fifths of the children covered a period of three months or more after birth.

Per cent of Deaths According to Place of Birth.

Although the percentage of infants known to have died before they had completed one year of life is an understatement, for the reason that it was impossible to obtain information concerning all the children, nevertheless a comparative analysis of percentages of deaths according to place of birth is fairly representative. From the information available (see Table 29), it was known that 230 infants,[28] or 27 per cent of all, died during the first year of life. The births of 193 children occurred in private homes; of these children, 46, or 24 per cent, died in infancy. There were 410 infants born in hospitals, of whom 144, or 35 per cent, died during the first year of life. Of the 241 children born in maternity homes or in the public infirmary, 40, or 17 per cent, were known to have died before the end of the first year. The percentage of deaths among infants born in hospitals was considerably higher for the 209 born in one large maternity hospital and children's institution than for the 201 born in other hospitals—45 per cent for the former as compared with 25 per cent for the latter.

TABLE 29.—*Per cent of infants born out of wedlock in 1914, who died during their first year of life, by place of birth.*

Place of birth.	Infants born out of wedlock, 1914.	Deaths known to have occurred in first year of life.	
		Number.	Per cent.
Total	847	230	27.2
Private home	193	46	23.8
Hospital	410	144	35.1
Large maternity hospital and children's institution	209	94	45.0
Other hospital	201	50	24.9
Maternity home or public infirmary	241	40	16.6
Not reported	3		

The highest percentage of deaths occurred among infants born in hospitals, and the lowest among those born in maternity homes or the public infirmary. The large number of deaths among those born in hospitals is probably due to the fact that hospitals usually keep mother and child for only a short period following the child's birth, and that after discharge from the hospital the infant often is separated from the mother. The proportion of mothers who do not keep their infants is probably larger among those who are confined in hospitals than among those confined in the homes of relatives or friends. However, the percentage of deaths among infants born in hospitals other than the large maternity hospital and children's institution specified was very little higher than the percentage among infants born in private homes—25 as compared with 24. The comparatively small number of deaths among infants born in the

---

[28] Total deaths reported from all sources; figures given in discussion of infant mortality, pp. 97–101, based on the 213 cases for which death certificates were found.

maternity homes and the infirmary is a striking proof of the saving of infant life which results from keeping mother and child together under proper conditions during part of or all the nursing period. (See Chart IV, p. 138.)

Physical Condition.

Information as to physical condition was obtained from agency records and from the statements of cause of death on the death certificates. The data thus obtained are incomplete and are of value only as giving an indication of the serious physical disabilities which exist in many cases.

In addition to the 230 infants known to have died, there were 54 reported to be in poor physical condition. This is, undoubtedly, very much of an understatement. The disabilities reported were as follows:

Total reported as having died or as in poor physical condition			284
Deformity	3	Syphilis and gonorrhea	1
Tuberculosis	5	Ophthalmia neonatorum	7
Syphilis	[29] 22	Rachitis	1
Gonorrhea	3	Otherwise poor condition	242

Agency Care.

Number receiving prolonged care from agencies of various types.

Prolonged care was known to have been given 522 of the 847 children—62 per cent—by the agencies studied. Four other children were known to have received such care from agencies not included in the study, and undoubtedly there were others who received care outside Boston and for whom information was not available. The term "prolonged care" signifies the definite assumption by the agency of supervision or provision for the child and does not include care given over a short time or to meet a temporary situation. Hospitals were not considered as giving prolonged care unless the case was followed up and supervised for an extended period. That more than three-fifths of all the children born out of wedlock during the year received prolonged care during their first year of life indicates the extent to which illegitimate birth forecasts dependency.

Most of the children receiving prolonged care were under the supervision of child-caring or child-protective agencies, or of the maternity homes and the public infirmary. Following are the numbers receiving care from agencies of various classes:

Total receiving prolonged care from agencies included in the study	522
Child-caring or child-protective agency	208
Maternity home or public infirmary	176
Other agencies	30

[29] Includes one also deformed and rachitic.

Child-caring or child-protective agency and maternity home or public infirmary _____ 64

Child-caring or child-protective agency, maternity home or public infirmary, and other agency_____ 8

Child-caring or child-protective and other agency_____ 18

Maternity home or public infirmary and other agency_____ 18

Child-caring or child-protective agencies cared for a total of 35 per cent of the children born during the year. Maternity homes and the public infirmary cared for 31 per cent of the children, 9 per cent also being in charge of child-caring or child-protective agencies.

Number of agencies giving care.

Three-fourths of the children receiving prolonged care during the first year of life were under the extended supervision of one agency only; one-fourth received prolonged care from more than one agency. The numbers receiving prolonged care from specified numbers of agencies were as follows:

Total receiving prolonged care from agencies included in the study__ 522

One agency	396	Four agencies	4
Two agencies	97	Five agencies	1
Three agencies	24		

In the large majority of cases in which more than one agency gave prolonged care the agencies were of different classes. In many instances a child was under the care of a maternity home for the first 5 or 6 months of life and then came under the supervision of a child-caring agency. The fact that 29 children were under the prolonged care of three or more agencies may indicate some duplication of effort in these cases.

Age at application.

Most of the cases cared for by maternity homes or the public infirmary came under the care of these agencies before the birth of the child. The only group of cases in which an analysis of age at application is significant is the child-caring and child-protective group. A total of 298 children received prolonged care from these agencies during the first year of life. The ages at which they came to the attention of child-caring and child-protective agencies giving prolonged care were as follows:

Total receiving prolonged care from child-caring and child-protective agencies _____ 298

Unborn	48	3–5 months	24
Less than 1 month	115	6–8 months	8
1 month	43	9–11 months	8
2 months	9	Not reported	43

The age at application was known in 255 cases. The application was made before the child's birth in 19 per cent of these instances. In almost half the cases—45 per cent—the infant was under 1 month of age; in 30 per cent, between 1 and 5 months old; in only 6 per cent of the cases had the child reached the age of 6 months at the time of application for agency care. Thus, in the majority of cases the supervision of the child-caring and child-protective agencies was begun in the early infancy of the child.

Time under prolonged care.

An attempt was made to estimate for the children who had received prolonged care the proportion of time during the first year of life that they had been under such supervision. Of the 847 infants born during the year, there were 522 given prolonged care by the agencies studied and 4 others known to have been under the care of other agencies. No information as to time under care was available for 48 of these 526 cases. In 478 cases it was possible to approximate the proportion of time under the supervision of social agencies. The method of estimating proportionate time under prolonged care was to divide the number of weeks under care by the age of the child at death or at the last record obtained. Table 30 gives the resultant proportions for children of various ages.

TABLE 30.—*Proportion of lifetime spent under prolonged care of agencies, infants born out of wedlock in 1914.*

Age of infant at death or at last record obtained.	Infants born out of wedlock who received prolonged care of known duration at some time during first year of life.						
	Total.	Proportion of time under prolonged care of agencies during first year of life.					
		Entire time.	Four-fifths.	Three-fifths.	Two-fifths.	One-fifth.	Less than one-fifth.
Total....................	478	255	123	24	30	28	18
Less than 3 months............	93	59	12	2	11	9	....
3–5 months....................	51	27	16	6	2	1	2
6–8 months....................	54	29	15	3	2	3	2
9–11 months....................	38	19	10	1	4	3	1
1 year.......................	239	121	70	12	11	12	13

More than half—53 per cent—of the 478 children receiving prolonged care of known duration were under such supervision for the entire period during which the history of the child was known. Care was given for four-fifths of the period to 26 per cent of the children. Hence, 79 per cent were under care at least four-fifths of the time in the first year of life during which their history was known to social agencies.

The histories of 239 children receiving prolonged care covered the entire first year of life. Of these, 51 per cent were under care the whole year and 29 per cent four-fifths of the year.

The 121 children under care the entire first year of life represented 14 per cent of the 847 infants born out of wedlock. These figures indicate that about one-seventh of the children born out of wedlock in a year are agency problems during the entire period of infancy. The extent to which such infants are dependent upon social agencies may be further shown by the fact that the 121 infants receiving care during the entire year constituted 20 per cent of the 617 not known to have died before they were a year old.

	Per cent
Born in maternity homes	16.6
Born in private homes	23.8
Born in hospitals, other than the large maternity hospital and children's institution	24.9
Born in the large maternity hospital and children's institution	45.0

CHART IV.—Per cent of infants born out of wedlock, 1914, who died during first year of life, by place of birth. (See pp. 131–135.)

Care at various ages.

An analysis of the care given the children at various ages is given in Table 31. The earliest age used in this connection was 1 month. At this age hospital care given during the mother's confinement would in most cases have ceased. At the next age period considered—3 months—the mother's living conditions would in many cases have been readjusted and more or less permanent arrangements made for the care of the child. The care given the children at 6 months, at 9 months, and at 1 year is also included. In each case the care reported was that given the child on the date when he attained the age specified. If agencies of more than one type were giving care at the same time, the one most directly concerned with the child's supervision was entered.

TABLE 31.—*Kind of care received at specified ages, infants born out of wedlock in 1914.*

Kind of care.	Infants born out of wedlock, surviving, so far as known, at specified ages.a									
	At 1 mo.		At 3 mos.		At 6 mos.		At 9 mos.		At 1 yr.	
	Number.	Per cent distribution.	Number.	Per cent distribution.	Number.	Per cent distribution.	Number.	Per cent distribution.	Number.	Per cent distribution.
Total	770	100.0	700	100.0	654	100.0	630	100.0	617	100.0
Temporary care only	43	5.6	27	3.8	25	3.8	19	3.0	11	1.8
Prolonged care	394	51.2	350	50.0	286	43.7	237	37.6	211	34.2
Child-caring or child-protective agency	146	19.0	164	23.4	148	22.6	124	19.7	119	19.3
Maternity home or public infirmary	222	28.8	154	22.0	111	17.0	88	14.0	72	11.7
Other agency	26	3.4	32	4.6	27	4.1	25	3.9	20	3.2
Not known whether alive or dead	165	21.4	207	29.6	251	38.4	304	48.3	342	55.4
Known to be alive; no agency care, so far as known	168	21.8	116	16.6	92	14.1	70	11.1	53	8.6

a See Table 28, p. 133. Includes those of whom it was not known as to whether they were alive or dead.

Of those surviving, so far as known, at 1 month, 51 per cent were receiving prolonged care from agencies, while 34 per cent of those surviving, so far as known, at 1 year were receiving such care. Under care of child-caring and child-protective agencies were 19 per cent of the children surviving, so far as known, at 1 month; at 3 months, 23 per cent; at 6 months, 23 per cent; at 9 months, 20 per cent; and at 1 year, 19 per cent. The percentages receiving care from maternity homes or the public infirmary were smaller at the older ages, being 29 at 1 month, 22 at 3 months, 17 at 6 months, 14 at 9 months, and 12 at 1 year.

The proportions under care at various ages are minimum statements. Undoubtedly some of those for whom no information as to whether living or dead was obtained had died outside Boston, but it is very probable that others were receiving agency care in other localities. That one-fifth of all the infants not reported to have died were known to be under the prolonged care of child-caring or child-protective agencies, whether the age specified be 1 month or 1 year, is significant of the relation between illegitimate birth and child dependency.

Time with mother.

The most important single factor in the welfare of an infant is the care he receives from his own mother. In the case of a child of illegitimate birth the chances of being separated from the mother during early infancy are great. Lack of maternal care probably accounts in large part for the very high infant mortality rate among such infants.

A comparison of children of various ages living with and away from their mothers is given in Table 32. The proportion of cases in which the mother and child are together is shown to decrease with the age of the child.

TABLE 32.—*Presence with or separation from mother at specified ages, infants born out of wedlock in 1914.*

Presence with or separation from mother.	Infants born out of wedlock, surviving, so far as known, at specified ages.a				
	At 1 mo.	At 3 mos.	At 6 mos.	At 9 mos.	At 1 yr.
Total..	770	700	654	630	617
Reported......................................	472	405	335	278	247
With mother................................	321	215	168	131	103
Away from mother...........................	151	190	167	147	144
Not reported..................................	298	295	319	352	370
Not known whether alive or dead..............	165	207	251	304	342
Known to be alive, but not reported whether with mother or away from mother.............	133	88	68	48	28

a See Table 28, p. 133. Includes those of whom it was not known as to whether they were alive or dead.

In considering the data given in Table 32, it must be remembered that the cases in which information was obtained were those known to social agencies, and that among those for whom information was not obtained were infants whose mothers found it possible to care for them unaided or with the assistance of relatives. It can not be assumed, however, that in all the " not reported " cases the child and mother were living together. Records of children under 2 years of age reported to the division of State minor wards as cared for in private homes apart from their relatives showed that almost two-fifths of those of illegitimate birth so cared for were under no agency supervision. Most of these children were being privately boarded by relatives or friends.[30]

Twenty per cent at least of all the infants surviving, so far as known, at the age of 1 month had already been separated from their mothers. That this percentage is far lower than that which would be found were all the information available is indicated by the fact that for 39 per cent of the infants surviving, so far as known, at this age, presence with or separation from the mother was not reported. At least 27 per cent of the infants surviving, so far as known, at 3 months, 26 per cent at 6 months, 23 per cent at 9 months, and 23 per cent at 1 year, were separated from their mothers. These percentages are subject to the same qualifications as the percentage at 1 month, except that the increasing percentage of not reported cases—60 per cent at 1 year—makes the statements of the proportions separated from their mothers still more conservative. The

[30] Table 27, Sec. II, p. 320.

slightly lower percentage of infants living apart from their mothers at 9 months and at 1 year than at 3 and 6 months is undoubtedly explained by the increasing percentage of " not reported " cases.

The percentages of the known cases in which the child and mother were together are of interest as indicating the proportion of infants of various ages whom agencies find it possible or practicable to keep with their mothers. At 1 month 68 per cent of the infants whose presence with or separation from their mothers was reported were living with their mothers; at 3 months the percentage was 53; at 6 months, 50; at 9 months, 47; and at 1 year, 42.

The steady decrease in the percentages of children living with their mothers—from 68 per cent at 1 month to 42 per cent at 1 year—indicates the constantly increasing difficulty in keeping mother and child together after the mother is discharged from a hospital or maternity home which has given care during confinement and the first few months of the child's life.

A comparison of the proportion of children surviving at the ages specified who were living away from their mothers with the proportion of the children who died who had been cared for apart from their mothers, based on data given in Table 33, throws some light upon the relation between separation of mother and child and a high infant mortality rate. Deaths under 2 weeks were omitted from the comparison, for the reason that comparatively few infants are separated from their mothers during the first 2 weeks of life.

TABLE 33.—*Comparative percentages living with mother at age specified or prior to death, among survivors and deaths for first 3 months and for first year of life, infants born out of wedlock in 1914.*

Present with or separated from mother at age specified, or immediately prior to death.a	Infants born out of wedlock surviving, so far as known, or dead at specified ages.							
	At 3 mos.—				At 1 yr.—			
	Surviving, so far as known.		Died, aged 2 wks. but under 3 mos.		Surviving, so far as known.		Died, aged 3 mos. but under 1 yr.	
	Number.	Per cent distribution.	Number.	Per cent distribution.	Number.	Per cent distribution.	Number.	Per cent distribution.
Total	700	....	97	....	617	....	83	....
Not reported	b 295	....	11	....	c 370	....	16	....
Total reporting whether or not with mother	405	100.0	86	100.0	247	100.0	67	100.0
With mother	215	53.1	17	19.8	103	41.7	12	17.9
Separated from mother	190	46.9	69	80.2	144	58.3	55	82.1

a In cases in which the child was removed from the mother and taken to a hospital for temporary medical care, the child was counted as "with mother."

b Includes 207 of whom it was not known as to whether they were alive or dead, and 88 known to be alive but of whom it was not known as to whether they were present with or separated from the mother.

c Includes 342 of whom it was not known as to whether they were alive or dead, and 28 known to be alive but of whom it was not known as to whether they were present with or separated from the mother.

Of the 405 children known to be surviving at the age of 3 months whose presence with or separation from the mother was reported by social agencies, 47 per cent were being cared for away from their mothers, while 80 per cent of the 86 infants who had died after reaching the age of 2 weeks but before the age of 3 months, and whose location previous to death was known, had been removed from their mothers. At 1 year, of the 247 known to be surviving whose location was reported, 58 per cent were living apart from their mothers, as compared with 82 per cent of the 67 infants who had died after reaching the age of 3 months but before the age of 1 year and whose location previous to death was reported. The greatest difference between the percentages separated from the mother among those dying and those surviving occurs in the earlier group.

The comparison in favor of infants with their mothers would presumably be strengthened, not weakened, were the facts as to the " not-reported " group known. It is probable that the percentage of children with their mothers would be found to be higher among the " not-reported " group than among the group for which information was obtained, since the latter group comprised cases in which recourse to social agencies was necessary. But assuming, for the present purpose, that half the infants included among those not reported were with their mothers and half were separated from them, the percentages would be changed very little—48 per cent separated from their mothers among those surviving, so far as known, and 76 per cent among those who died. If more than 50 per cent of the ": not-reported " group are assumed to be with their mothers, the percentage separated from their mothers among those surviving, so far as known, is decreased, and a still closer relation between separation from mother and high infant mortality demonstrated. At 1 year a theoretical distribution of the " not-reported " group, on the assumption that half or more than half would be with their mothers, would bring substantially the same results as at 3 months.

Table 34 shows the proportion of time spent with the mother during the first year of life, estimated for those children reported by social agencies as having survived at least 6 months and whose histories gave the length of time the child was with the mother. There were 301 such children, of whom 215 were reported as having survived 1 year, 20 as dying between the ages of 6 and 11 months, inclusive, and 66 as having been lost sight of before they had reached 1 year of age.

TABLE 34.—*Proportion of lifetime spent with mother, infants born out of wedlock in 1914 and surviving to specified ages.*

Proportion of time spent with mother during first year of life.	Known to have survived 6 mos.		Known to have survived 1 yr.		Between 6 and 11 mos. of age at death or at last record obtained.	
	Number	Per cent distribution.	Number.	Per cent distribution.	Number.	Per cent distribution.
Total	301	100.0	215	100.0	86	100.0
Entire time	121	40.2	83	38.6	38	44.2
Four-fifths	27	9.0	18	8.4	9	10.5
Three-fifths	7	2.3	5	2.3	2	2.3
Two-fifths	14	4.7	9	4.2	5	5.8
One-fifth	26	8.6	19	8.8	7	8.2
Less than one-fifth	106	35.2	81	37.7	25	29.0

In 121 of the 301 reported cases in which the infant was known to have lived at least six months—40 per cent—the child had been with the mother the entire period during which the history was known. In 106 cases—35 per cent—the child had been with the mother less than one-fifth of the time.

The histories of 215 children known to have survived the first year of life stated the length of time the child was with the mother. In 83 of these cases—39 per cent—the mother and child had been together the entire year. In an almost equal number of cases—81, or 38 per cent—the infant had been under the care of his mother for less than one-fifth of the year. A total of 109 children—51 per cent—had been with the mother less than three-fifths of the year, a period of about seven months. It must be borne in mind that these figures apply only to cases known to social agencies, and that the proportions spending the entire year or a large part of the year with the mother would probably have been higher had infants of illegitimate birth not known to social agencies been included.

Home or Place of Residence at Various Ages.

Children with their mothers.

The provision which should be made for mother and child in order that they may be kept together at least during the nursing period is one of the most difficult problems in connection with the care of the infant born out of wedlock. In some cases the mother's parents or other relatives are able and willing to take mother and baby into their own home, but a large number must be provided for in other ways. Table 35 gives for the children known to be with their mothers at the ages specified the type of home or institution in which they were living.

TABLE 35.—*Home or place of residence of infants born out of wedlock in 1914, who were known to be with their mothers at specified ages.*

Home or place of residence at specified ages.	Infants born out of wedlock who were with their mothers at specified ages, and whose home or place of residence was known.									
	At 1 mo.		At 3 mos.		At 6 mos.		At 9 mos.		At 1 yr.	
	Number.	Per cent distribution.	Number.	Per cent distribution.	Number.	Per cent distribution.	Number.	Per cent distribution.	Number.	Per cent distribution.
Total	288	100.0	190	100.0	149	100.0	119	100.0	92	100.0
Mother's own home	16	5.6	13	6.8	12	8.1	10	8.4	12	13.0
Mother's parental home	28	9.7	38	20.0	37	24.8	34	28.6	24	26.1
Home of relatives or friends	16	5.6	19	10.0	16	10.8	13	10.9	7	7.6
Boarding or free home	13	4.5	.5	2.6	7	4.7	6	5.0	4	4.4
Mother's place of employment	12	4.2	47	24.8	48	32.2	38	31.9	30	32.6
Hospital	6	2.1			2	1.3				
Maternity home or public infirmary	189	65.6	61	32.1	22	14.8	14	11.8	13	14.1
Other institution	3	1.0	4	2.1	2	1.3	2	1.7	2	2.2
Other	5	1.7	3	1.6	3	2.0	2	1.7		

The number of infants known to be with their mothers, whose home or place of residence was reported, decreased greatly as the age of the child increased. At 1 month, 16 children were living in their mothers' own homes, and at 1 year 12 were so provided for, yet the percentage of the total known who were in this type of home or place of residence increased from 6 to 13. The percentages are representative of the cases known to social agencies, but they must not be taken as representative of the whole group of infants of illegitimate birth in the community, including those not known to social agencies.

At the age of 1 month a total of 21 per cent of the children who were with their mothers were living in the mother's own home or with her family or friends. At the age of 3 months, a total of 37 per cent were thus provided for; while at the age of 6 months, 44 per cent; at the age of 9 months, 48 per cent; and at 1 year, 47 per cent were living with the mother in her own home, in her parental home, or in the home of relatives or friends. The fact that nearly half the children in the older-age groups who were with their mothers were living in their mothers' own homes, their family homes, or with relatives or friends, indicates a considerable extent of assumption of responsibility by those to whom the mother would naturally look for assistance, even in cases in which recourse to social agencies for more or less help was necessary.

A comparatively small number of infants living with their mothers were provided for in boarding or free homes, the percentages so cared for not exceeding 5 at any age specified.

A type of provision increasingly important in the older-age groups is the mother's place of employment. At 1 month 4 per cent of the children with their mothers were in this type of home. The percentage is high, considering the age of the child. The mother would hardly be able to be employed at housework and care for her child at the same time so soon after her confinement. At the age of 3 months 25 per cent of the children living with their mothers were in the mother's place of employment. In the older-age groups nearly one-third were so provided for—32 per cent at 6 months and at 9 months, and 33 per cent at 1 year.

Only a few children were in hospitals at the ages specified—2 per cent at 1 month, 1 per cent at 6 months, and none in the other age groups. Two-thirds of the children with their mothers at 1 month— 66 per cent—were being cared for in maternity homes or the public infirmary. This high proportion may be explained by the fact that information was obtained as to the dispositions at these ages of practically all the infants born in maternity homes or the public infirmary, while a large number of other infants were lost sight of before the age of 1 month. At 3 months, the percentage cared for in these institutions was reduced to 32 per cent, and at 6 months to 15 per cent. Twelve per cent of the children known to be with their mothers at 9 months were in maternity homes or the public infirmary, and 14 per cent of the children with their mothers at 1 year were so provided for.

Children separated from their mothers.

The types of provision for children living away from their mothers are shown in Table 36. The small number of institution cases is significant as indicating the general practice of Boston agencies.

TABLE 36.—*Home or place of residence of infants born out of wedlock in 1914, who were known to be separated from their mothers at specified ages.*

Home or place of residence at specified ages.	Infants born out of wedlock who were separated from their mothers at specified ages.									
	At 1 mo.		At 3 mos.		At 6 mos.		At 9 mos.		At 1 yr.	
	Number.	Per cent distribution	Number.	Per cent distribution	Number.	Per cent distribution	Number.	Per cent distribution	Number.	Per cent distribution
Total	151	100.0	a 189	100.0	167	100.0	147	100.0	144	100.0
Home of mother's parents, other relatives, or friends	1	0.7	3	1.6	5	3.0	4	2.7	6	4.2
Boarding or free home	115	76.1	159	84.2	145	86.8	127	86.4	125	86.8
Adoptive or foster home	5	3.3	5	2.6	9	5.4	10	6.8	8	5.5
Hospital	9	6.0	5	2.6	4	2.4	3	2.0	2	1.4
Other institution	17	11.3	13	6.9	2	1.2	1	.7	1	.7
Other	4	2.6	4	2.1	2	1.2	2	1.4	2	1.4

a Excluding 1 whose location was not known.

The percentages of children separated from their mothers who were living with their grandparents, other relatives, or friends ranged from 0.7 at 1 month to 4.2 at 1 year. From 3 per cent to 7 per cent were living in adoptive or foster homes. By far the greatest number were living in boarding or free homes. At 1 month 76 per cent of the children were so provided for; at 3 months, 84 per cent; at 6 months, 87 per cent; at 9 months, 86 per cent; and at 1 year, 87 per cent. The system of placing children in boarding or free homes, under careful supervision, has been developed to an unusual extent in Massachusetts, while the social agencies are very conservative in the matter of adoptions.

The number of children away from their mothers who were being cared for in institutions was negligible after the first few months of infancy. At 1 month, 6 per cent were in hospitals and 11 per cent in other institutions; at 3 months, 3 per cent were in hospitals and 7 per cent in other institutions; at 6 months, 2 per cent were in hospitals and 1 per cent in institutions of other types; at 9 months, a total of 3 per cent were cared for in hospitals and other institutions; and at 1 year, 2 per cent were so provided for. These figures illustrate the practice in Massachusetts of using institutions only for special cases or as temporary homes, pending placement or replacement in family homes.

Social agencies reported 151 of the children born during the year as living apart from their mothers at the age of 1 month. About one-sixth were in hospitals or other institutions, while five-sixths were being cared for in private homes, chiefly boarding or free homes. The number cared for in boarding or free homes constituted slightly more than three-fourths of the total. Only a few children had been placed out for adoption or taken permanently by foster families.

At the age of 1 year 144 children were known to be living apart from their mothers. All but 3 of these were being cared for in private homes. Seven-eighths of all these children were living in boarding or free homes. The percentage in adoptive or foster homes was slightly larger than at 1 month, but it was still very small.

GENERAL.

Statement of Problem.

This study is principally concerned with the environmental conditions surrounding children born out of wedlock. Aside from considerations of heritage, the handicap of their birth is overcome in proportion to the extent to which normal home life can be supplied. There are several means by which a more or less complete adjustment of the child to society may be made.

1. The parents may marry each other and establish a home for the child. If a normal home life results, the greater part of the handicap of illegitimate birth is removed.

2. The mother may marry another man and the child be accepted as a member of the family. Here, so far as physical care is concerned, the conditions under which the child is brought up closely approximate those surrounding children of legitimate birth. Certain detrimental factors may develop, however, in the " stepfather family," such as a jealous or scornful attitude on the part of the half brothers and sisters, or discrimination on the part of the stepfather in favor of his own children.

3. The mother, though not establishing a home as a result of marriage, may keep the child with her, either in the home of her relatives, in her place of employment, or in an independent home which she maintains. The difficulties are often very great, and the result for the child may be fortunate or unfortunate according to the character of the mother and her ability to support the child. Often the mother is obliged to depend upon social agencies for financial and other assistance. In any case the child lacks the advantages of normal family life.

4. The mother may board the child, paying the board from her own earnings or with the assistance of the child's father or of relatives. The difficulties she frequently encounters in finding the right kind of boarding home and in seeing that adequate care is given are serious. Often the mother is lacking in intelligence, is financially unable to meet her responsibilities, or is careless as to the child's welfare, paying board irregularly and seldom visiting the home.

5. The child may be adopted or taken permanently by relatives or foster parents and brought up as their own child. If the foster home

is a favorable one and the child not difficult to control, conditions of normal family life may be approximated.

6. The child may be taken over by a child-caring agency and placed in a boarding or free home under conditions as nearly normal as possible.

7. The child may be brought up in an institution.

Those cases in which early adjustments are made through the marriage of the mother or the assumption of full or partial responsibility by the mother's relatives are not likely to come to the attention of agencies. The children best provided for are fortunately merged with the general population, and the circumstances of their birth lost sight of. It would be practically impossible, even if it were desirable, to secure full and representative information concerning the children thus successfully absorbed into normal homes at an early age.

This chapter is limited to the study of those cases in which it has been impossible to meet the difficult problems of adjustment without recourse to social agencies. The data secured present only the darker side of the picture, but they give an indication of the relationship between illegitimacy and dependency and the seriousness of the situation both for the child and for the public.

Scope of Study and Sources of Information.

A study of illegitimacy based upon records of social agencies is a study of a section of the problem of child dependency. There is some difference of opinion as to whether the dependent child of illegitimate birth presents a problem differing essentially from that presented by the child of legitimate birth who becomes dependent. An attempt has been made in a later section of this study to compare in certain respects children of legitimate and of illegitimate birth under the supervision of a large child-caring agency. Whether or not differences exist to any considerable extent is, however, of minor importance. The significant facts to be determined are the burden of support, care, and supervision of children born out of wedlock which must be assumed by the public; the reasons for their dependency; and the results for the individual children.

This study of children born out of wedlock who were under the care of Boston agencies and institutions during the year 1914 was an attempt to secure a cross-section of the problem during one year. The aim was to determine, so far as possible, what proportion the care of these children bore to the total volume of children's work of the agencies studied, and to secure data regarding the children born out of wedlock which would show how long they had been in charge of agencies, why they had come to the attention of social agencies, where they were living at the time of application, where they were living at the close of the period studied, what agencies had previously cared for them, the physical condition, mentality, and characteristics of the children, and certain facts regarding the mother and her family and the father, which would have a bearing upon the child's history. All children of illegitimate birth under 21 years of age who were given care during the year by the agencies studied were included in the inquiry.

The study covered the records of municipal and private agencies in the city of Boston whose work included the care of children born out of wedlock and of certain State agencies so far as they dealt with Boston children—that is, children whose residence at the time of application or commitment was Boston. Agencies in the metropolitan district outside the limits of the city proper were not included. The public and private agencies for family relief and rehabilitation were not included, since their work dealt only incidentally with children of illegitimate birth. The agencies studied may be classified as follows:

Public child-caring—2. (Division of State minor wards of the State board of charity, so far as it cared for Boston children; children's institutions department, Boston.)

Private child-caring—11. (Agencies dealing with the supervision and placing of children and with their care in institutions.)

Child-protective—1. (Main office, Boston, of the Massachusetts Society for the Prevention of Cruelty to Children.)

Public infirmary—2. (Boston children at the State Infirmary, Tewksbury, cared for by the social service committee, division of State adult poor; Boston Infirmary Department, Long Island Hospital.)

Maternity homes—4.

Health agencies—2. (Baby Hygiene Association; Instructive District Nursing Association.)

Medical agencies—7. (Hospitals reporting illegitimate births during the year.)

Legal aid—1.

Juvenile court—1.

Correctional institutions—3. (Two Massachusetts training schools and the reformatory for women, so far as they cared for Boston children. A third State training school, the Industrial School for Boys, cared for no Boston children of illegitimate birth during the year. The Suffolk School for Boys, under the control of the children's institutions department, was considered as part of that "child-caring agency.")

Institutions or hospitals for the feeble-minded or for the first care and observation of mental patients—3. (Psychopathic department of the Boston State Hospital and two State institutions for the feeble-minded, so far as they cared for Boston children.)

Many children were under the care of several agencies and several groups of agencies during the year. Records from all agencies caring for a child were combined, in order to make a unified presentation of the child's history and treatment.

The kinds of care given the children were grouped into two main divisions—prolonged care and temporary care. Under "prolonged care" are included all cases in which the problem of supervision or provision for the child had been definitely assumed by the agency. Under "temporary care" are included cases handled by departments of investigation or advice, but not assumed by the agencies; cases in which the care was of a special type to meet a temporary need—such as medical or health care or legal aid, if meeting an emergency situation only, and court care unless the child was put on probation or kept under extended supervision.

EXTENT AND DISTRIBUTION OF THE PROBLEM OF ILLEGITIMACY IN THE WORK OF THE AGENCIES STUDIED.

Number of Cases Dealt With.

During the year covered by this inquiry there were under care of the agencies studied 2,863 children who were known to have been born out of wedlock. Four-fifths of these children had receievd more or less prolonged treatment from the agencies, their care having been definitely assumed. One-fifth had received only temporary care.

Besides the children known to have been born out of wedlock, there were under care 78 foundlings and 26 pseudo-foundlings. By the term "foundling" is meant a deserted child, concerning whose parentage nothing is known, who was abandoned without any provision having been made for his care. "Pseudo-foundlings" include children of unknown parentage abandoned at board or elsewhere after some arrangement had been made for their care. All but 3 of the 104 foundlings and pseudo-foundlings were under the care of public child-caring agencies; these 3 were cared for by private child-caring agencies. All were receiving prolonged care. It is probable that all the foundlings and pseudo-foundlings under the care of the agencies studied had been born out of wedlock, but it was thought best to limit this study to children known to have been of illegitimate birth.

One-fifth of the 2,863 children known to have been born out of wedlock received care from more than one agency during the year. (See Table 37.) A number of them were under the care of three or four agencies, and one child was cared for by six agencies in one year, three giving prolonged and three temporary care.

TABLE 37.—*Kind of care received, by number of agencies giving care during the year.*

Number of agencies from which care was received.	Children born out of wedlock, under care, in 1914.			
	Total.	Receiving specified care.		
		Prolonged.	Prolonged and temporary.	Temporary.
Total..	2,863	1,996	323	544
One agency..	2,268	1,824	....	444
Two agencies......................................	498	162	251	85
Three agencies....................................	78	9	57	12
Four agencies.....................................	14	1	10	3
Five agencies.....................................	4	....	4	....
Six agencies......................................	1	....	1	....

The great majority of these 2,863 children were under the care of city or private agencies. Seven State agencies included in this section of the study cared for 606 children whose residence was Boston, 125 of whom had also been under the care of city or private agencies during the year. An eighth State agency whose field of work was Boston dealt with 29 children. City and private agencies alone cared for 2,228 children.

About half the children (1,447) had been under care before the year covered by the study, their cases having been continued into the year studied. The remaining 1,416 cases were begun during the year. Children who ceased being under care during the year numbered 1,168. Thus, there were remaining under care at the end of the year 1,695 children of illegitimate birth.

Proportion of All Children's Cases under Care.

It was impossible in this study to determine accurately what proportions these 2,863 children born out of wedlock represented of the total number of children cared for by the 37 agencies whose records were studied. With a few exceptions, the total number of children was secured for each separate agency, but it was not practicable to check the cases concerned with children of legitimate birth in order to eliminate duplications between different agencies and avoid counting a child more than once if under care of two or more agencies. However, by adding together the total number of children under care of each agency in a group, and the number of children of illegitimate birth cared for by each, without eliminating duplications, an estimate may be made of the proportionate amount of work devoted by agencies of various types to the care of children born out of wedlock.

Excluding Boston cases handled by State agencies, since the total numbers of Boston cases under care of these agencies were not obtained, a comparison of total and of illegitimacy cases is made in Table 38.

TABLE 38.—*Per cent of cases involving children born out of wedlock, by type of agency.*

Type of agency.	Agencies.a	Children's cases under care in 1914.		
		Total. b	Involving children born out of wedlock.	
			Number.	Per cent.
Child caring and child protective............................	13	16,475	2,145	13.0
Public child caring, city.................................	1	c 1,821	c206	11.3
Private child caring.....................................	11	8,102	1,368	16.9
Child protective..	1	6,552	571	8.7
Juvenile court..	1	d 1,120	d 10	.9
Public infirmary (children under 16 years of age)............	1	93	50	53.8
Maternity homes (infants under care)......................	4	e 267	f 250	93.6
Health agencies..	2	16,200	46	.3
Hospitals (births during year)...............................	g 11	5,327	389	7.3

a Excluding the legal aid society and the hospital for the first care and observation of mental patients, since the number of cases involving children could not be secured. Also excluding State agencies. The total number of children under care of the division of State minor wards during 1914 was 7,526, of whom 1,721, or 22.9 per cent, were of illegitimate birth.

b Sources of information were agency reports and, in some cases, estimates made at the time of the study. The totals were not always for the calendar year 1914, but were, in some instances, for the fiscal year of the agency concerned which nearest approximated the calendar year.

The term "case" as here used represents a unit of work—the care given an individual child by an agency. If two agencies gave care to the same child there would be two cases. Hence the totals do not represent the number of children under care of the agencies in a given group, but the sums of the numbers under care of each constituent agency.

c Includes boys (5 of whom were of illegitimate birth) cared for by the Suffolk School for Boys, since this institution is under the management of the children's institutions department, and boys on parole are supervised by the placing-out division.

d Delinquency cases begun in 1914. Neglect cases were included under "child protective," since that agency does the investigation and follow-up work for all neglect cases brought before the juvenile court.

e Includes 17 cases in which the parents married before the birth of the child, the child, therefore, being of legitimate birth. Does not include those outside the home under supervision if they had not been in the home during the year.

f Includes 29 cases under care at the beginning of the year which were not included in the subsequent analysis, but does not include those outside the home under supervision if they had not been in the home during the year.

g Of the 11, only 6 were included in the later analysis, since no illegitimate births occurred in the other 5. The 11 hospitals mentioned in the table are exclusive of small private hospitals, 1 of which was included in the study but excluded from the table, since total figures could not be secured.

The percentages of cases involving children born out of wedlock varied greatly with the agency groups, according to the class of cases dealt with. The maternity home group naturally showed the highest percentage, since practically all the work of these institutions is concerned with the illegitimacy problem. The public infirmary also showed a high percentage of children of illegitimate birth among all children under 16 years of age given care. The child-caring agencies gave the next highest percentages, 11 for the public and 17 for the private agencies. Had the Boston cases under care of the division of State minor wards been included in the public child-caring group, the percentage of illegitimacy cases would have been considerably higher, since 23 per cent of all the children under care of this agency were of illegitimate birth. The percentage of illegitimacy cases under care of the child-protective agency was considerably lower than in the case of the child-caring agencies. This is probably due to the fact that the former was concerned mainly with family problems involving neglect. The percentage for child-caring and child-protective agencies combined was 13. Of all the births in hospitals exclusive of small private hospitals, 7 per cent were illegitimate.

TABLE 39.—*Estimated expenditures of specified agencies, for children born out of wedlock.*

Type of agency.	Number of agencies.	Total expenditures, 1914.a	Percentage of cases involving children of illegitimate birth.	Estimated expenditures for children of illegitimate birth.
Total..........................	12	....	....	$123,511.01
Public child caring, city..........................	1	$185,424.34	11.3	20,952.95
Public child caring, State..........................	1	(b)	(b)	52,078.40
Private child caring.	c9	267,470.55	16.9	45,202.52
Child protective..........................	1	60,656.74	8.7	5,277.14

a Derived from annual reports of the agencies and, in some instances, from reports of the Massachusetts State Board of Charity, 1914 and 1915, Pt. II, "Charitable Corporations." Boston, 1915, 1916. The expenditures of each agency were those for the fiscal year which nearest approximated the calendar year 1914.

b The total expenditures of this division in 1914 were $693,343.27. The percentage of illegitimacy cases was 22.9, hence the approximate expenditure for illegitimacy cases was $158,775.62. Of the 1,721 children of illegitimate birth under care, 475, or 27.6 per cent, were Boston children included in the Boston study, and 89, or 5.2 per cent, whose residence was not Boston were given care by Boston agencies in 1914, and hence were also included in the Boston study. Thus, 32.8 per cent of the children of illegitimate birth under care of the division of State minor wards were included in the Boston study. The approximate amount expended by the division of State minor wards for the care of these 564 children was $52,078.40.

c No report was secured for the expenditures of one agency, and because of the impossibility in another case of separating the expenditures of a maternity hospital and a children's institution under the same management, the expenditures for this institution were also excluded.

Approximate expenditures during the year for the care of children born out of wedlock were estimated for the child-caring and child-protective agencies. (See Table 39.) The estimates were based on the percentages of cases involving children of illegitimate birth. The approximate amount spent during the year for the care of children born out of wedlock by the Boston child-caring and child-protective agencies and for Boston children of illegitimate birth by the State child-caring agency was $124,000. It is probable that these children, handicapped by the circumstances of their birth, presented the most difficult problems of adjustment and required the most prolonged and expensive care, and that in consequence the estimate here given is an understatement of the actual expenditure chargeable to illegitimacy.

Racial Distribution.

According to the United States Census of 1910,[1] only 2 per cent of the total population of the city were Negroes. The proportion of

---

[1] Thirteenth Census of the United States, 1910: Vol. II, Population, p. 880.

Negroes among children of illegitimate birth—7 per cent—was more than three times that in the general population. Of the 2,863 children born out of wedlock under the care of social agencies, 2,650 were white; 205 pere Negro; 7 were American Indians; and 1 was Chinese.

Proportion of Problem Chargeable to Boston.

In Massachusetts the question of legal settlement is an important factor in the kind of public relief granted, cases of dependency in which settlement can be determined being chargeable to the town of settlement, and other cases being chargeable to the State. No attempt has been made in this study to classify the cases according to settlement. The place of birth and the residence of the child have been taken as indications of what proportion of the problem may properly be considered as belonging to Boston. For this purpose, residence has been defined as the mother's usual residence if the mother had the child with her at the time of application or had the responsibility for his care, and as the child's usual residence if the child was not under the mother's immediate care or supervision.

TABLE 40.—*Residence at application, and place of birth of children under care.*

Residence at time of application for care.	Children born out of wedlock under care in 1914.			
	Total.	Place of birth.		
		Boston.	Elsewhere.	Not reported.
Total..	2,863	1,878	759	226
Boston...	1,785	1,296	369	120
Metropolitan district outside Boston.................	479	274	180	25
Other Massachusetts..............................	386	216	162	8
Other New England...............................	74	49	24	1
Other United States...............................	7	6	1	....
Other..	16	15	1	....
Not reported....................................	116	22	22	72

The following list shows the distribution according to nativity:

Boston _____ 1,878
Metropolitan district outside Boston _____ 221
Massachusetts outside metropolitan district _____ 361
New England outside Massachusetts _____ 79
Other United States _____ 61
Canada _____ 19
Other foreign _____ 18
Not reported _____ 226

　　　　　Total children _____ 2,863

Four-fifths of the children whose nativity was reported (see Table 40) were born within the metropolitan district. The children born in Massachusetts outside this district included 158 born in the State Infirmary, to which institution are sent from all parts of the State persons who have no legal settlement and who must be given hospital care at public expense. The figures indicate a very small proportion coming from outside the United States, only 1 per cent coming from Canada and other foreign countries.

The figures for residence show a greater percentage of the children living within the metropolitan district at the time of application. The children had become Boston problems, and many of them had been under the care of Boston agencies before coming to the agencies giving care during the year studied. However, one-sixth of the children lived outside the metropolitan district at the time of application for agency care. This is due partly to the fact that a number of the Boston agencies cover territory outside the metropolitan district, and partly to the fact that the mothers came into Boston to secure agency care.

THE DEPENDENT CHILD OF ILLEGITIMATE BIRTH.

Status at Time of Application for Agency Care.

Age.

The age of the child at the time of application to the first agency giving care extending into the year studied is significant as indicating the character of the problems which had to be met in providing care for the children, and the time when the care given during the year was first required. However, this does not represent the age at which recourse to the assistance of agencies was first necessary, since the child might have been previously under the care of agencies that did not continue the case into the year studied. Data concerning age and sex at time of application for care are given in Table 41.

More than one-fourth of the 2,863 children had been under care from birth. Almost three-fifths of the children had come under care of the agencies studied before they had completed their first year of life.

TABLE 41.—*Age at application, and sex.*

Age at application.	Children born out of wedlock, under care in 1914.			
	Total.	Boys.	Girls.	Sex not reported.
Total..	2,863	1,459	1,387	17
Under care from birth.........................	766	378	384	4
Less than 1 year.............................	919	463	447	9
1 year......................................	222	127	92	3
2–5 years...................................	503	288	214	1
6–9 years...................................	240	115	125	....
10–13 years.................................	119	56	63	....
14 years and over...........................	74	22	52	....
Not reported................................	20	10	10	....

Of the 2,863 children, 1,459 were boys and 1,387 were girls—72 more boys than girls. Under 1 year the numbers of boys and girls were practically the same, there being 841 boys and 831 girls. From 1 to 5 years the greatest discrepancy between the sexes occurred, there being 415 boys and 306 girls in these age groups. After this age girls predominated.

During the year a total of 1,416 children came under the care of the agencies studied. More than half these children (725) came under the care of child-caring or child-protective agencies. The ages of the children under care of these agencies are of greater significance than the age distribution of all the children under care during the year. Most of the children cared for by maternity homes and hospitals had been under care from birth, and those under care of health agencies were usually infants, hence age distribution would not be of particular interest in these cases. The ages of the children coming under the care of institutions for the delinquent or the mentally defective were relatively high, but the numbers involved were too small to make analysis significant. Following are the ages at time of application of the children coming under the temporary or prolonged care of child-caring or child-protective agencies during the year:

Total coming under the care of child-caring or child-protective agencies during the year [2]_____ 725

Under care from birth_____	63	6–9 years_____	67
Less than 1 year of age_____	308	10–13 years_____	29
1 year_____	65	14 years and over_____	25
2–3 years_____	104	Not reported_____	13
4–5 years_____	51		

More than half the children whose ages were reported—52 per cent—were less than 1 year of age at the time of application. Three-fourths—76 per cent—were less than 4 years old.

Presence with or separation from mother.

Excluding those under care from birth, there were 2,097 children under care of the agencies studied. Presence with or separation from the mother at the time of application was reported for 1,786 of these children. Only 55 per cent were living with their mothers when they came to the attention of the agencies. The percentage was considerably higher for the 1,131 who, previous to application, had not received prolonged care from agencies than for the 655 who were known to have received prolonged care previously—61 per cent as against 45 per cent. Table 42 gives for the former group the propor-

---

[2] Including only cases in which the first application during the year to an agency studied was to a child-caring or child-protective agency.

tions of children of various ages who were living with their mothers at the time of application.

TABLE 42.—*Per cent of children separated from mother previous to application by age—children who had not received prolonged care previously.*

Age at application.	Children born out of wedlock, under care in 1914, who had not received previous prolonged care.						
	Total.a	Whose presence with or separation from mother at application was reported.					Whose presence with or separation from mother was not reported.
		Total.	With mother.		Separated from mother.		
			Number.	Per cent.	Number.	Per cent.	
Total....................	1,382	1,131	687	60.7	444	39.3	251
Less than 1 year...............	716	550	408	74.2	142	25.8	166
1 year......................	131	113	52	46.0	61	54.0	18
2–3 years...................	180	156	69	44.2	87	55.8	24
4–5 years...................	101	88	44	50.0	44	50.0	13
6–9 years...................	139	126	67	53.2	59	46.8	13
10–13 years..................	68	64	30	46.9	34	53.1	4
14 years and over.............	32	31	15	48.4	16	51.6	1
Not reported................	15	3	2	(b)	1	(b)	12

a Excluding 766 who had been under care from birth.
b Less than one-tenth of 1 per cent.

One-fourth of the children under 1 year of age whose presence with or separation from the mother was reported, and who had not been under care previously, had already been separated from their mothers at the time of application to the agencies studied. More than half the children from 1 to 3 years of age, inclusive, had been separated from their mothers. It is interesting to note that the largest proportion living apart from their mothers was found among those 2 and 3 years of age, and that the proportion separated was less for the 6-to-9-year age group than for any other group except that under 1 year. The smaller proportion of children 2 to 3 years of age and the larger proportions of children in the higher age groups who were with their mothers may indicate that if the mother has succeeded in keeping her child with her during his infancy she is able to do so for several years. By the time the child is 4 or 5 years old, however, her resources, either in the form of help from her family or from the child's father, fail her, or the struggle to support the child becomes too difficult and she is forced to apply for help from agencies.

Table 43 gives, for the children who had been under prolonged agency care at some time previous to application, the proportions with their mothers and separated from them.

TABLE 43.—*Per cent of children separated from mother previous to application, by age—children who had received prolonged care previously.*

Age at application.	Children born out of wedlock, under care in 1914, who had received previous prolonged care.						
	Total.	Whose presence with or separation from mother at application was reported.					Whose presence with or separation from mother was not reported.
		Total.	With mother.		Separated from mother.		
			Number.	Per cent.	Number.	Per cent.	
Total....................	715	655	292	44.6	363	55.4	60
Less than 1 year...............	203	190	124	65.3	66	34.7	13
1 year......................	91	85	39	45.9	46	54.1	6
2–3 years...................	144	129	41	31.8	88	68.2	15
4–5 years...................	78	68	24	35.3	44	64.7	10
6–9 years...................	101	93	40	43.0	53	57.0	8
10–13 years..................	51	47	17	36.2	30	63.8	4
14 years and over...............	42	40	6	15.0	34	85.0	2
Not reported..................	5	3	1	(a)	2	(a)	2

a Less than one-tenth of 1 per cent.

For the children who had previously been under prolonged care the percentages separated from their mothers were consistently larger than in the case of the children who had not been under the prolonged care of agencies previous to application. According to age distribution, however, the figures show the same general tendency in both cases. The highest percentage of children under 14 years who were separated from their mothers at the time of application was found among the children 2 and 3 years of age, while the lowest percentages were found among infants, children 1 year of age, and children 6 to 9 years of age.

Home or place of residence.

Of the children whose homes or places of residence at the time of application were known (excluding those under care from birth), 44 per cent were, at the time of coming to the attention of the agencies, in the homes of their mothers, grandparents, other relatives, or friends. Table 44 gives the type of home or place of residence of the child at the time application was made for agency care.

TABLE 44.—*Home or place of residence of children of specified ages at application.*

Home or place of residence of child at application.	Total.a	Children born out of wedlock, under care in 1914.							
		Age at application.							
		Less than 1 yr.	1 yr.	2–3 yrs.	4–5 yrs.	6–9 yrs.	10–13 yrs.	14 yrs. and over.	Not reported.
Total	2,097	919	222	324	179	240	119	74	20
Mother's own home	320	b 62	37	58	b 48	67	34	13	1
Mother's other establishment	42	3	8	3	6	13	6	3	....
Mother's place of employment	51	26	11	9	3	2	......	......	......
Mother's parental home	157	69	18	24	11	20	8	7	......
Other maternal relative's home	73	34	7	7	5	12	7	1	......
Paternal relative's home	31	5	1	5	3	7	4	5	1
Friend's home	30	14	3	4	1	3	2	2	1
Adoptive or foster home	47	2	4	3	4	8	15	11	......
Boarding or free home	403	153	61	82	31	40	23	12	1
Public infirmary or maternity home	97	78	6	8	2	1	......	2	......
Hospital	152	146	2	1	2	......	1	......	......
Other institution	72	10	12	23	10	9	3	5	......
Other	10	8	......	......	......	......	......	2	......
Not reported	612	309	52	97	53	58	16	11	16

a Excluding 766 who had been under care from birth.
b In 1 case the mother was not present in the home.

One of the striking facts brought out by Table 44 is the number of children who were in their mothers' own homes. Twenty-two per cent (320) of the 1,485 children whose homes or places of residence were reported were living in homes of this type at the time of application. By the mother's " own home " is meant a home maintained by the mother and her husband or consort, or a home which had been thus established but which a widowed or deserted mother was maintaining alone. It is interesting to note that half the children living in their mothers' own homes were 4 years of age or over; the mothers who had married or who were living as married had been able in many cases to keep the children a number of years. Some unfortunate crisis in the family, or the discovery of bad conditions in the home, was responsible for the children at last coming to the agencies.

The 42 children—3 per cent of the total reported—living in the mother's " other establishment " included children living with mothers who were proprietors of lodging houses or who were living in lodgings, if the mothers were not married or living as married. A few of the mothers of children included in this group were keepers of disorderly houses. Two-thirds of these children were 4 years of age and over, 9 of them being 10 years of age and over. The conditions under which many of them were living involved extreme moral danger.

A surprisingly small number of children—only 51, or 3 per cent— were living with the mother in her place of employment. In 46 of these cases the mothers were at housework and 5 were in occupations of other kinds. Half the children living under these conditions were less than 1 year of age.

A considerable number—157, or 11 per cent—of the children who came to the attention of agencies and whose homes or places of residence were reported were living in the homes of their mother's parents, either with or away from the mothers. The age distribution shows that more than two-fifths were less than 1 year of age; more than two-thirds were less than 4 years of age. The grandparents had met the situation for a time, but were unwilling or unable to continue care, or the homes were reported unfit. The responsibility for some of these children had been maintained by the grandparents for a considerable number of years.

Besides the children cared for in the homes of their mothers or maternal grandparents, 104, or 7 per cent of the total reported, had been cared for by other relatives previous to application. More than one-third of these were infants under 1 year of age. Of especial interest is the fact that 31 children were in the homes of their fathers' relatives. Most of these children were 4 years of age and over, while in the case of the children who had been cared for by their maternal relatives, the greater number were under 4 years of age. An additional 30 children—2 per cent—had been provided for in the homes of friends.

An interesting group is composed of the children who had been taken over permanently by foster parents, either through legal adoption or otherwise. Of the children who came to the attention of agencies and whose homes or places of residence were reported, 47, or 3 per cent, were under care of foster parents who had found themselves unable to continue caring for these children, or whose homes were reported unfit. As might be expected, more than half these children were 10 years of age and over. That 2 infants had been taken by foster parents whose homes were reported to agencies as unfit before the children were a year old, indicates the necessity for thorough investigations in these cases.

The largest number in any one group were in boarding or free homes, these 403 children representing 27 per cent of the total reported. In some cases the children had been boarded privately by their mothers, who were unable longer to carry the burden of their support. In other cases they had been boarded by agencies, either with or away from their mothers, and their care was transferred from one agency to another. Three-eighths of the children in boarding homes were less than 1 year of age when the applications were made to the agencies studied. Almost three-fourths of them were under 4 years of age. The fact that a change had been made in their care may be partly accounted for by the fact that some of the agencies care only for young children, while others specialize in the care of older children.

A total of 249 children—17 per cent of the total reported— were in public infirmaries, maternity homes, or hospitals previous to application. With the exception of a small number of older children who were receiving medical care, all were under 1 year of age, most of them having been born in these institutions.

Seventy-two children—5 per cent—were living in other institutions, chiefly institutions for children. In many cases these were temporary homes maintained as a part of the work of child-caring societies. Ten children—less than 1 per cent—were living in homes of other types than those specified. The large number of cases in which home or place of residence at application was not reported is due to the fact that the records of some of the agencies did not afford complete information on such points.

The home or place of residence of the 979 children who were with their mothers at the time of application indicates (see Table 45) the ways in which the mother and child had been provided for up to the time of application.

TABLE 45.—*Home or place of residence of children of specified ages, who were with their mothers at application.*

Home or place of residence of child.	Children born out of wedlock, under care in 1914, who were with their mothers at application.					
	Total.	Age at application.				
		Less than 1 yr.	1-3 yrs.	4-9 yrs.	10 yrs. and over.	Not reported.
Total	979	532	201	175	68	3
Mother's own home	318	61	95	114	47	1
Mother's other establishment	42	3	11	19	9	
Mother's parental home	109	61	24	16	8	
Home of relatives or friends	54	37	9	6	1	1
Mother's place of employment	51	26	20	5		
Boarding home	53	37	12	3	1	
Public infirmary or maternity home	71	63	6	2		
Hospital	125	124	1			
Other institution	6	5	1			
Other	1	1				
Not reported	149	114	22	10	2	1

At the time when it was found necessary to apply for care for these children nearly two-thirds—523 of the 830 with their mothers whose home or place of residence was reported—were living in their mothers' homes or in the homes of relatives or friends. Almost one-fourth (196) were in hospitals, maternity homes, or the public infirmary, most of them being under 1 year of age. Only 51 were in the mothers' places of employment and 53 were in boarding homes. Seven children were provided for in other ways than those specified.

Almost two-fifths of the 418 children less than 1 year of age who were with their mothers and whose homes or places of residence were reported were living in their mothers' homes or in the homes of relatives or friends. More than two-fifths were in hospitals, maternity homes, or the public infirmary.

The proportions of children with their mothers who were cared for in their mothers' own homes or by relatives or friends increased in the older age groups. More than three-fourths of those 1 to 3 years of age, and more than nine-tenths of those 4 years of age and over were so cared for.

The percentage of children living in their mothers' places of employment was highest among the children 1 to 3 years of age, 11 per cent of those of this age who were with their mothers being provided for in this way. Six per cent of the children less than 1 year of age were with the mother at her place of employment, the proportion decreasing to 2 per cent among the children 4 years of age and over.

The home or place of residence was known for 650 of the 807 children who were separated from their mothers at the time application was made for agency care. Although deprived of their mothers' care, one-fifth of these children had been provided for in the homes of their maternal grandparents or with other relatives or friends. Over half the children who were away from their mothers were in boarding, free, or wage homes. The homes or places of residence of the children who were away from their mothers were as follows:

```
Total away from their mothers_____ 807
        Total whose home or place of residence was reported_____ 650
Mother's parental home_____  47 | Hospital, maternity home, or
Home of relatives or friends_____  80 |    public infirmary _____  49
Adoptive or foster home_____  47 | Other institution_____  66
Boarding, free, or wage home_____ 350 | Other  _____  11
```

These figures represent a group of children four-fifths of whom had been provided for by other than their natural guardians and who were in need of some other type of care than that which they were receiving. That 47 were in adoptive or foster homes indicates the need for care in the matter of adoptions.

Previous agency care.

Before coming to the attention of agencies giving care extending into the year studied, many of these children had been known to social agencies. Of the 1,625 children (excluding those under care from birth) under the care of agencies giving information on previous history, 595, or more than one-third, had previously received prolonged care from agencies. Many of these had been under the care of more than one agency. Prolonged care does not include hospital care unless it extended over a long period of time. The amount of previous prolonged care known to have been received by the children is shown in Table 46.

TABLE 46.—*Prolonged care received previous to application, by age.*

Age at application.	Children born out of wedlock, under care in 1914.							
	Total.a	Who had received no previous prolonged care.	Who had received previous prolonged care.					
			Total.	From specified number of agencies.				
				One.	Two.	Three.	Four.	Five.
Total	1,625	1,030	595	448	118	20	8	1
Less than 1 year	671	483	188	169	19			
1 year	200	117	83	59	19	5		
2–5 years	362	211	151	107	35	6	3	
6 years and over	385	214	171	111	45	9	5	1
Not reported	7	5	2	2				

a Excluding 766 who had been from birth under care of the agencies studied, and 472 under care of agencies not giving complete information.

Naturally, the proportion who had received previous agency care was larger among the older children than among the younger. Somewhat more than one-fourth of the children under 1 year of age had received previous care. More than two-fifths of the older children had received such care, the percentages for the various age groups above the first year ranging from 42 to 44.

The majority of the children who had been under care previously had been under the supervision of other than child-caring agencies. These other agencies included principally maternity homes, public infirmaries, and the child-protective agency. One reason for the large amount of previous care is that all neglect cases before the courts in Boston are handled by the protective society. Table 47 gives information concerning previous prolonged care by child-caring and by other agencies.

TABLE 47.—*Type of prolonged care received previous to application, by age.*

Age at application.	Children born out of wedlock, under care in 1914.				
	Total.a	Who had received no previous prolonged care.	Who had received previous prolonged care.		
			Total.	From child-caring agencies.	From other agencies.
Total	1,625	1,030	595	b 208	387
Less than 1 year	671	483	188	32	156
1 year	200	117	83	24	59
2–5 years	362	211	151	60	91
6 years and over	385	214	171	91	80
Not reported	7	5	2	1	1

a Excluding 766 who had been from birth under care of the agencies studied, and 472 under care of agencies not giving complete information.
b Including 83 children under care both of child-caring and of other agencies.

It is significant that 208 children—one-eighth of all whose previous histories were known—had been wards of child-caring agencies before applications were made to the agencies giving care during the year covered by the study. In some of these cases the children had merely been transferred from one child-caring agency to another. In most cases they had been discharged from care because relatives or friends had assumed the responsibility for them, or because they had been adopted. These plans for the care of the children had proved not to be permanent solutions, and it had again been necessary for applications to be made for agency help. Only 6 per cent of the children under 2 years of age had been wards of child-caring agencies. The percentage increased with the age of the child, until almost one-fourth of those 6 years of age and over had been under care of such agencies.

A study of the previous histories of these children suggests three things:

First. The fact that a child born out of wedlock is received for prolonged care by a child-caring agency does not indicate that he will always be dependent upon social agencies. Efforts are made by the agencies to secure the assumption of care by those legally responsible as soon as they are able to assume the burden. The histories of many dependent children born out of wedlock show intervals of care by relatives.

Second. In the locality studied there are several agencies engaged in most of the fields of children's work. The same child may have been under the care of two or three agencies of the same type. This does not, however, necessarily imply a criticism of the agencies involved. There is a constantly increasing specialization of work, both territorially and according to types of cases, and a close cooperation among the agencies. The fact that a child has been known to several agencies may imply an effort to secure treatment best adapted to his needs.

Third. Whether or not the shiftings of a child from one type of care to another are unavoidable, or seem to be the best that can be done in the child's interests, the fact remains that change of environment or of supervision, at least in the case of an older child, requires adjustments which are difficult. The severing of old ties and the frequent new situations that he must meet may have a bad effect upon the child's development.

Source of application.

The source of application refers to the person or agency making application for the care of the child to the first agency giving care that extended into the year covered by the study. For the 2,219 children for whom this information was known, the sources of application were as follows:

Total reported_____ 2,219

Court_____	183	Paternal relative_____	21
Public agency_____	408	Friend_____	379
Private agency_____	614	Boarding woman _____	45
Mother _____	377	Other_____	77
Maternal relative _____	115		

In about one-fourth of these cases—27 per cent—the source of application or commitment was a court or other public agency. Applications from public agencies were usually from the overseers of the poor or from the public infirmary.

A slightly larger number of applications—28 per cent—were from private agencies. In some of these cases the applications were made to public agencies, the cases being considered of such a nature as to require public care. In other cases the applications were from one agency which had cared for the child to an agency giving a different type of care, the treatment given by the first agency no longer being appropriate. In a large number of cases the fact that the application came from one agency to another indicated that the mother or other person originally applying for aid had not known which agency was best suited to the needs of the child or which organization would accept the particular type of case.

Seventeen per cent of the applications were made by the mothers and 23 per cent by other relatives or by friends. A small number of applications were made by boarding women. In most of these instances relatives had failed to pay the child's board. In almost all the remaining cases the mother or her family had been under care before the child's birth for other reasons than the mother's need for care during pregnancy.

Reason for application.

It is difficult to classify the social causes which brought these children to the attention of social agencies. The fact of birth out of wedlock usually implies the lack of normal home care and of adequate financial support. The assumption of responsibility by the mother and her family often requires unusual strength of character and willingness to brave public opinion, as well as resources sufficient to bear the burden of support and care. At the same time the background of illegitimacy frequently includes poverty, mental incapacity, moral weakness, and delinquency on the part of the mother or her family. These various factors are so interwoven that no attempt was made to assign to a given case any one cause. The immediate reasons for applications, as distinguished from underlying causes, do, however, throw considerable light upon the types of situations in which recourse to agencies is necessary. These have been classified for the child-caring and child-protective group. For the other agency groups the immediate reasons are self-evident (i. e., maternity homes—maternity care needed; health agencies—nursing care or medical advice needed; correctional agency—child delinquent). In 2,068 instances the first applications were to child-caring or child-protective agencies. The reasons for application were reported for 1,815 of these children, as follows:

	Number.	Per cent distribution.
Total reported	1,815	100.0
Maternity care needed	64	3.5
Mother dead	39	2.1
Mother unfit to care for child or mother's home unfit	486	26.8
Mother feeble-minded or insane	47	
Mother committed to an institution for delinquents	37	
Mother otherwise unfit	166	
Mother's home unfit	236	
Mother unable to care for child	663	36.6
Mother's husband unwilling	16	
Mother physically unable	68	
Mother otherwise unable	579	
Child abandoned or deserted	289	15.9
Board unpaid	24	
Abandoned at board	69	
Otherwise deserted	196	
Child in unfit home (other than mother's)	79	4.4
Boarding home unfit	21	
Custodian's home unfit	58	
Other	195	10.7
Custodian unable or unwilling to care for child	24	
Child neglected, not otherwise specified	51	
Child delinquent or unmanageable	29	
Child sick	29	
Not otherwise specified	62	

In a small number of cases—4 per cent of the total reported—the applications were made before the children were born, because maternity care was needed. In only 2 per cent of the cases did the death of the mother make agency care necessary. More than one-fourth of the applications—27 per cent—were made because the mother was unfit to care for the child, or was living in a home in which there existed conditions detrimental to the child's welfare. This group of 486 cases, because of its size and the nature of the problems involved, represented the most serious condition both for the child and for society. Many of these children had been subjected to abuse and neglect or had lived in homes in which immorality and drunkenness were common. The majority would probably remain under agency care during childhood, and in many cases painstaking and intensive work would be needed to counteract the effect of their early neglect.

In 250 of the 486 cases in which the unfitness of the mother or of her home was the reason for application, the mother herself was mentally incapacitated, delinquent, or immoral. In 236 cases the home conditions under which the mother and child were living were so bad that agency intervention was necessary. In many of these cases, also the mother was delinquent or immoral. Of the 250 mothers whose unfitness was the immediate reason for the application, 47 were feeble-minded or insane, 37 were committed to institutions for delinquents at the time the applications for the children were received, and 166 were otherwise unfit because of delinquency, immorality, or intemperance.

The largest single group of applications came because of the mother's inability to care for the child. This group constituted 37 per cent of the total reported. In 16 of these 663 cases the mother's husband was unwilling to receive the child into his home. In 68 cases the mother's poor health made it impossible for her to retain the responsibility for the child. In the other 579 cases the incompetence of the mother, insufficient means, inability to find employment where she might keep the child with her, and, in a few cases, her unwillingness to make any effort to care for the child, constituted the reasons for application.

In 16 per cent of all the cases in which the cause of application was known, the board of the children had not been paid, they had been definitely abandoned at board, or they had been otherwise deserted; and these were the reasons for the application. Since foundlings, concerning whose parentage nothing was known, were not included in this study, this group of 289 cases is surprisingly large. In the 24 " board unpaid " cases, the boarding women wished to be relieved of the care of the children, as they had received no pay for their services for considerable periods; the mothers or relatives were, however, retaining some connection with the children. In the 69 " abandoned at board " cases the whereabouts of the mothers or relatives was unknown; they had promised to pay for the board of the children and had paid, perhaps, for a time but had then abandoned them. This group of cases is a considerable underestimate of the number of children born out of wedlock received by agencies because they have been abandoned at board. A large number of other cases were found, but the information about parentage was too scant to warrant classifying the children as of illegitimate birth, though the majority of them were probably born out of wedlock. The large group of " otherwise deserted " cases (196) includes foundlings whose parentage was later established by investigation, children who were known to be of illegitimate birth and who were abandoned at other places than at board, and children who were reported as having been deserted but in regard to whose abandonment the details were not given.

Four per cent of the children came to the attention of child-caring or child-protective agencies because of bad conditions in the homes in which they were boarding or in the homes of relatives (other than their mothers) or guardians. Eleven per cent came for miscellaneous reasons, including the inability or unwillingness of the custodian, other than the mother, to retain the care of the child; the neglect of the child, the circumstances of which were not stated; the child's delinquency; the child's illness; the need for aid in securing support from the father; and other unclassified reasons.

In 1,360 cases—66 per cent of the 2,068 in which the first applications were to child-caring or child-protective agencies—the aid requested was that the agency assume full responsibility for the care of the child. In some of those instances the mothers were willing or could be persuaded to contribute something for the support of the children, though they did not wish to keep the children with them or to retain the burden of providing for their welfare. In the remaining 34 per cent of the cases other kinds of aid were requested, such as provision for the care of mother and child, the mother wishing to keep the child with her; assistance in finding the mother employment where she could keep the child; maternity care; assistance in prosecuting the father; investigation and supervision of children who were complained of as neglected; investigation of proposed adoptions; help in settling questions of disputed guardianship; and other assistance of like character.

Following are illustrations of some of the circumstances leading to the application for agency care:

A private child-caring agency in another city asked one of the Boston child-caring agencies to find a place at service for an unmarried mother who wished to keep her child with her. The child had been born in a maternity home and was a little over a year old at the time of application. The mother, a foreign-born colored woman 22 years of age, was described as untidy, sullen, violent tempered, and somewhat abusive, and was said to be of low mentality. The child's father had disappeared. None of the mother's relatives was in this country. The mother was placed, with the child, at service, but did not remain long in any position. After eight months she and the baby went to another city, and the case was referred to an agency there. (Case V 106.)

It was reported to a private agency during the year of the study that a week-old infant was being neglected. On investigation it was found that the mother, 22 years old, and the maternal grandmother had come from Canada three months before the child's birth for the purpose of concealing the situation from the grandfather and from friends. The child was born in a private house. He was very weak and was not properly nourished. The chief concern of the mother and the grandmother was to find a boarding place for the baby that they might return to Canada. The agency secured the cooperation of an infant-welfare society and the baby improved greatly. The grandmother applied to several agencies for help in finding a boarding place for the baby; but she was refused assistance, since all were cooperating with the first agency in impressing upon her and the mother their responsibility for the child. In this the societies were so successful that when the baby was 5 weeks old the mother and grandmother returned to Canada with the child, planning to board him with friends there. (Case V 60.)

During the year of the study complaint was made to a protective agency that two adopted children of illegitimate birth were being neglected by their foster parents. The older child, 3 years old, and the younger, an infant 10 months old, had been legally adopted by the same family, though the children were not related to each other. The foster mother had been very immoral; at the time the complaint was made she was living apart from her husband, who had instituted divorce proceedings. The children were boarded part of the time with a friend of the foster mother. The foster mother died while the children were under supervision and the woman with whom the children had been boarded adopted both the children. A sister of the older child, also of illegitimate birth, was under the care of a child-caring agency. (Case V 576.)

The year previous to the period covered by this study a private agency requested the State child-caring agency to assume the care of a month-old infant. The child had been born in a maternity home in Boston, where the mother and baby were still being cared for. The agency making the application had known the family for a number of years. The child's maternal grandmother was irresponsible and probably feeble-minded and had no control over her children. The home conditions were bad, the grandparents quarrelsome and shiftless. Two of their children were feeble-minded, two were mothers of children of illegitimate birth, and one was an inmate of a reformatory. The family had been under the care of a child-protective society and of the juvenile court.

The child's mother was 19 years of age. She had been given a mental examination and was pronounced a "defective delinquent." Having been promiscuously immoral, she lost her case against the alleged father. The man was colored; the mother, white. He was said to have been married three or four times. The mother had been employed by him in a clerical capacity.

The State child-caring agency investigated the case but refused to assume the care of the child because there was a local settlement. Application was then made to the public child-caring agency of the city of Boston. No definite action was taken for some time by this agency, since the child was being boarded in a near-by town, the maternal grandfather paying the board. When the baby was nearly a year old, the relatives failed to keep up the payments and application was again made to the State child-caring agency. However, a private individual became interested in the case and took mother and baby into his home, the mother doing housework. The man soon became discouraged in his attempts to reform the mother and came to the conclusion that in any case the mother and child should not be kept together, the former being white and the latter colored. He therefore applied to a private child-caring agency, asking that they place the child at board. After investigation, this agency decided not to accept the case, since the child had been placed in a family by a hospital social-service worker, board being paid by the mother's former employer. The latter then applied to another private child-caring agency for assistance in securing the prosecution of the mother and the acceptance of the child by the public child-caring agency in the city. Shortly after, the mother was taken ill and died, and the care of the child was finally assumed by the public child-caring agency of the city. The child was placed in a boarding home, and was reported to be doing well. (Case V 997.)

Care Given by the Agencies Studied.

Length of time children were cared for.

The ages of the children at the end of the year or when agency care ceased were as follows:

Total under care_____ 2, 863

Less than 1 year_____	1, 045	10–13 years_____	241
1 year_____	365	14–17 years_____	203
2–3 years___ _____	319	18 years and over_____	114
4–5 years_____	215	Not reported_____	8
6–9 years_____	353		

The total amount of care given these children by the agencies under whose supervision they were in the year studied could be estimated only for those receiving prolonged care. The time over which the temporary care extended would not have been significant, since the exact amount of work within that time could not have been estimated.

During the year 2,319 children born out of wedlock were under the prolonged care of the agencies included. The amount of care given the children by these agencies by no means represents the total amount of agency care that had been given during their lives. A large number of them had been under agency care before coming to the attention of these agencies; many had received care from agencies not continuing their care until the year studied. The figures given in Table 48 for time under care represent the extent of continuous care from the agencies having charge of the children during the year covered by this study.

TABLE 48.—*Duration of care received by children of specified ages who were under prolonged care.*

Age at end of year or close of care.	Children born out of wedlock, under prolonged care in 1914.								
	Total.	Number of years under care.							
		Less than 1.	1	2–3	4–5	6–9	10–13	14 and over.	Not re- ported.
Total..................	2,319	1,028	383	307	187	241	83	87	3
Less than 1 year............	694	694							
1 year.....................	319	101	218						
2–3 years..................	266	82	73	110					1
4–5 years..................	194	39	30	78	47				
6–9 years..................	319	53	19	65	68	114			
10–13 years................	222	33	21	23	41	70	34		
14–17 years................	188	17	14	22	19	43	31	41	1
18 years and over..........	110	7	6	8	11	14	18	46	
Not reported...............	7	2	2	1	1				1

More than half the children receiving prolonged care—56 per cent—had been under care one year or longer. Of the 1,618 children 1 year of age and over at the end of the period, 80 per cent had been under agency supervision for a year or more. Of the 839 children 6 years of age or over, 49 per cent had been under care of these agencies at least 6 years. One-third of the 520 children 10 years of age and over—33 per cent—had been under care for at least 10 years. Eight children had been under care for 18 years, 5 for 19 years, and 2 for 20 years. Most of the children under care for these very long periods were wards of the State.

Considering only the children 1 year of age and over at the end of the period, and excluding 7 children whose ages were not reported and 2 for whom time under care was not reported, a total of 1,616 children received prolonged care during the year from the agencies included in the study. These 1,616 children received care for an average of about 3 years and 9 months per child. More than three-fourths of these children remained under care at the end of the year; hence the time during which they had received care as reported in this study does not represent the total amount of work these agencies will do in their behalf.

TABLE 49.—*Aggregate and average duration of care received by children of specified ages.*

Age at end of year or close of care.	Children born out of wedlock, under prolonged care in 1914.	Number of years under care.	
		Aggregate.	Average.
Total	a 1,616	6,169.0	3.8
1 year	319	b 268.5	.8
2–3 years	265	368.0	1.4
4–5 years	194	454.5	2.3
6–9 years	319	1,310.5	4.1
10–13 years	222	1,158.5	5.2
14-17 years	187	1,453.5	7.8
18 years and over	110	1,155.5	10.5

a Excluding 694 children under 1 year of age at close of care or at end of period, 7 whose ages were not reported, and 2 for whom time under care was not reported.
b Estimating average for those under care less than 1 year as 6 months—101 children, 50.5 years.

The time under care may be better interpreted in relation to the ages of the children. (See Table 49.) Those between 1 and 2 years of age had been under care an average of 10 months. Those 2 and 3 years of age had spent on an average 1 year and 4 months under the care of agencies. The children 4 and 5 years of age had been under the continuous care of the agencies having charge of them in the year studied for an average of 2 years and 4 months. Those 6 to 9 years of age had been under care for an average of 4 years. Those between the ages of 10 and 13 had been in charge of the societies on an average of five years and two months. The children 14 to 17 years of age had been under supervision for an average of 7 years and 9 months. Those 18 years of age and over had been under the continuous care of these agencies for an average of 10 years and 6 months.

Home or place of residence of children at end of period.

The type of provision made for the child born out of wedlock is of very great interest in considering the kind of care he receives and the degree to which his surroundings approximate those of a child of more fortunate birth. Complete histories of the children would show many expedients adopted for their care and often many shiftings from one disposition to another. The necessary limitations of this report make it impossible to do more than present a cross section of the types of provision made, supplemented by more detailed histories of representative cases. It must be borne in mind that the data here presented refer only to children receiving care from agencies. Those cases in which the most complete adaptation to normal home conditions have been made are not included, since recourse to agency care had not been necessary.

A synopsis is given in Table 50 of data concerning the home or place of residence of the children receiving prolonged care from agencies on the last day of the year studied or, in cases which were closed before that date, immediately previous to the close of care. This furnishes an index of the types of dispositions made by agencies for the children in their care; the ages of the children are significant in this connection.

TABLE 50.—*Home or place of residence, at end of period, of children of specified ages receiving prolonged care.*

Home or place of residence at end of year or immediately preceding close of care.	Children born out of wedlock, under prolonged care in 1914.						
	Total.	Age at end of year or close of care.					
		Less than 1 yr.	1 yr.	2–5 yrs.	6–9 yrs.	10 yrs. and over.	Not reported.
Total..........................	a 2,301	681	316	459	318	520	7
Family home....................	1,875	407	288	426	304	447	3
Mother's own home.............	147	14	17	52	28	35	1
Mother's other establishment...	21	1	2	6	6	6	......
Mother's place of employment...	128	72	28	19	8	1	......
Mother's parental home.........	121	58	20	21	12	10	......
Home of other relatives or friends...	77	27	7	15	11	16	1
Adoptive or foster home........	68	7	12	28	11	10	......
Boarding, free, or wage home...	1,313	228	202	285	228	369	1
Institution....................	379	257	22	28	10	60	2
Hospital, public infirmary, or maternity home..........	199	150	17	18	2	11	1
Institution for the feeble-minded...	19	......	......	......	3	16	......
Institutions for delinquents...	23	6	......	2	1	14	......
Other institution..............	138	101	5	8	4	19	1
Not reported..................	47	17	6	5	4	13	2

a Excluding 18 cases in which the last care received was temporary, though the child had been under prolonged care earlier in the year.

At the end of the year studied or immediately previous to the close of care, family homes were caring for four-fifths—81 per cent—of the 2,301 children received prolonged care at the end of the period. Only 17 per cent were in institutions, and the majority of these children were in infirmaries, hospitals, or maternity homes—institutions not giving permanent care but providing for the children during times of special need. The location of 2 per cent of the children was not reported.

In Massachusetts, perhaps more than in any other State, public and private agencies follow the practice of placing children in family homes rather than caring for them in institutions. Excluding the children who, at the end of the period, were being cared for by relatives, friends, or foster parents and the children receiving special care in hospitals, maternity homes, public infirmaries, or in institutions for the feeble-minded or delinquent, a total of 1,451 children remained. Of these children, 1,313, or 90 per cent, were in boarding, free, or wage homes, while only 138, or 10 per cent, were in institutions. It is probable that most of those 138 children were receiving institutional care only temporarily, pending placement or replacement in family homes.

Although the prolonged care of all the 2,301 children considered had been definitely assumed by the agencies, 168—7 per cent—were living in homes or establishments maintained by their mothers. Advice, supervision, and perhaps financial assistance had to be supplied, but the mothers were succeeding with this aid in keeping their children with them. Only 34 of the children living in homes maintained by their mothers were under 2 years of age. Almost one-fourth of the children cared for in this way were 10 years of age and over. The establishment by the mother of a home of her own in which the child may be brought up seems often to occur a considerable time after the child's birth.

For a mother without means or without relatives able or willing to give shelter to her and the child, placing at domestic service is often the only method by which she can be rendered self-supporting and able to keep the child with her. In some cases employment of other types may be found in which there exist the same possibilities of keeping the child. One of the agencies in Boston placed mothers as wet nurses. Sometimes mothers were employed as institution attendants and allowed to keep their children with them. However, comparatively few children were living at their mothers' places of employment. Only 6 per cent of the children receiving prolonged care were thus provided for at the end of the period. Of the 128 cared for in this manner more than half were under 1 year of age, and more than three-fourths were under 2 years of age; only 9 children were 6 years of age and over. The mothers of 25 of the 128 children were in employments other than housework.

Considering only the children receiving prolonged care from child-caring or child-protective agencies at the end of the period, the distribution according to home or place of residence was as follows:

	Number.	Per cent distribution.
Total receiving prolonged care from child-caring or child-protective agencies at end of period	1,913	100.0
In family homes	1,694	88.6
Mother's own home	139	7.3
Mother's other establishment	20	1.0
Mother's place of employment	82	4.3
Mother's parental home	78	4.1
Home of other relatives or friends	49	2.6
Adoptive or foster home	63	3.3
Boarding, free, or wage [3] home	1,263	66.0
In institutions	189	9.9
Hospital, public infirmary, or maternity home	46	2.4
Institution for the feeble-minded	4	.2
Institution for delinquents	5	.3
Other institution	134	7.0
Not reported	30	1.5

Nearly nine-tenths of these children were in family homes at the end of the period. One-tenth were cared for in institutions. The percentage cared for in family homes was somewhat higher than the percentage of all children studied thus cared for. This is accounted for by the fact that most of the children in charge of other than child-caring or child-protective agencies were cared for by maternity homes and public infirmaries, which gave, in the main, institutional care.

Slightly more than one-fifth of the children under care of child-caring or child-protective agencies were being cared for in the homes of their mothers, in their mothers' places of employment, or in the homes of relatives, friends, or foster parents. Two-thirds of the children were in boarding, free, or wage homes. Child-caring and child-protective agencies had placed nearly seven times as many children in boarding, free, or wage homes as in institutions.

Most of the Boston agencies are very conservative in the matter of adoption. High standards are required, both in the kinds of homes into which children are adopted and in the class of children given for adoption. The adoption of wards of these agencies is not permitted until the homes have been tried for six months or a year and the agencies are convinced that the adoptive homes will be successful. The small number of children—3 per cent of the total—reported to

---

[3] A home in which the child receives wages in return for services.

be in homes into which they had been adopted, or in which they had been placed on trial for adoption, indicates the policy of the agencies in this respect. In Massachusetts the boarding or the free home, in which the child remains under agency supervision, is the preferred method of caring for children who can not remain with relatives.

It had not been necessary to remove from their mothers all the 1,913 children assumed for prolonged care by child-caring or child-protective agencies. In Table 51 are given the facts regarding this phase of the question. Public child-caring agencies had been able in only 1 per cent of their cases to keep mother and child together, but private child-caring agencies had been able to avoid separation in 14 per cent. The most difficult cases, presenting the least possibilities of assumption of care by the mothers, are usually referred to public agencies, while private agencies in accepting applications prefer cases in which there exists the possibility of the mother's cooperation and of constructive work with both mother and child. The child-protective agency deals very largely with neglected children, and in many cases it supervises the children in their own homes, pending final disposition or during a period when constructive work is attempted which will make the removal of the child from his home unnecessary. Therefore, a great many of the children under care of this agency are with their mothers.

TABLE 51.—*Presence with or separation from mother, at end of period—children of specified ages receiving prolonged care—by type of agency.*

Agency caring for child and whether child was present with or separated from mother.	Children born out of wedlock, under prolonged care of child-caring or child-protective agencies in 1914.						
	Total.	Age at end of year or close of care.					
		Less than 1 yr.	1 yr.	2–5 yrs.	6–9 yrs.	10 yrs. and over.	Not reported.
Total................................	1,913	399	279	442	313	476	4
Public child-caring agency....................	538	18	31	162	145	182	....
With mother.............................	7	....	1	2	3	1	....
Separated from mother...................	529	18	30	160	142	179	....
Not reported whether present with or separated from mother..................	2	....	....	....	....	2	....
Private child-caring agency....................	1,003	338	204	172	93	193	3
With mother.............................	136	69	27	26	12	2	....
Separated from mother...................	864	267	176	146	81	191	3
Not reported whether present with or separated from mother..................	3	2	1	....	....	....	....
Child-protective agency......................	372	43	44	108	75	101	1
With mother.............................	214	31	29	72	44	37	1
Separated from mother...................	149	11	13	35	31	59	....
Not reported whether present with or separated from mother..................	9	1	2	1	....	5	....

The detailed histories of the children, the amount of time spent with their mothers, the shiftings from one type of care to another and from boarding home to boarding home, can be shown only for individual cases. A few of these histories are given below, the first two illustrating the very frequent shifting from home to home which sometimes occurs:

Application was made to a private child-caring agency for the care of a 2-weeks-old infant. The mother was living in her parental home, but the maternal grandmother was dead, the mother was obliged to go to work, and there was no one to care for the child. The case was referred to another child-caring agency which had known the family for eight years—having been called in originally by a family-care agency to care for the children, the grandmother being dead and the grandfather in jail. The mother was 19 years of age at the time of the child's birth, and had been earning $6 a week.

The child was placed at board by the second agency mentioned, the mother promising to pay what she could. When the child was 7 months old the case was referred to the agency to which application had first been made, since he was delicate and needed special care. After a few weeks in a hospital he was discharged to the mother, who placed the child at board, but at the end of three weeks hospital care was again necessary. A little later the child was placed at board by the first agency mentioned and remained at board under supervision throughout the year covered by the study. During a period of 15 months the child was in eight different boarding homes. (Case V 1694.)

A little more than a year previous to this study application was made to a private child-caring agency on behalf of a mother who was doing housework in a neighboring city and her child who was being boarded in another State. The friend making the application wished the baby boarded nearer the mother. The mother was of good character, and her employers had stood by her in her trouble. The father, employed by the same family, had disappeared when he learned of the mother's condition. The baby, born in a hospital in another State, was boarded with the mother for two months and then boarded away from the mother under the supervision of a children's agency. She was 3 months old at the time the application was made to the Boston agency. No action was taken for some time, but when the baby was nearly 8 months old she was brought to Boston and boarded near the mother under the supervision of the child-caring agency first mentioned. During the nine months following the child was boarded with seven different families and was placed nine different times, three times in the same family. At the end of that time the mother assumed full responsibility, and the child was discharged from the care of the agency. (Case V 1535.)

Three months before the birth of a child out of wedlock application was made to a private child-caring agency by a medical agency for the care of the mother, a girl of 20 who had no work and no money. The girl's mother had been dead for nine years, and her father had deserted the family five years before the application was made. The girl had worked in a factory, earning $6 a week. From the age of 16 she had been wayward and stubborn. She had lived with the father of her child—a carpenter, earning fair wages—for five or six months; but he had deserted when he discovered her condition. The agency made arrangements for the mother to return to a family with whom she had lived as a young girl. After the baby's birth in a hospital the agency boarded the mother and baby together for six or seven months, and then placed them in a home where the mother did housework. The mother was very fond of the child, and improved wonderfully under agency supervision. She again got in touch with the alleged father, and when the child was nearly 2 years old the parents were married and established a home. The agency helped the mother with the preparations for her marriage. The outlook for the child and the parents seemed very favorable. (Case V 1012.)

Eighteen years before this study was made a child was born out of wedlock in a Boston hospital. The mother, a woman of 28, had been engaged to the father, but refused to marry him because she had found that he was worthless. She was described as very ignorant, but very anxious to support herself and the child. She felt deeply disgraced by the situation. Her occupation was domestic service, and she earned about $6 a week.

When the mother and baby left the hospital the care of the child was assumed by a private child-caring agency. This agency cared only for children under 2 years of age, so when the child reached the age of 2 application was made to another child-caring agency. The mother was paying board regularly, but the child needed supervision. The second agency assumed the care of the child and retained it throughout the period covered by the study. The mother paid part of the child's board, the agency supplementing the amount and paying also a debt of the mother's. When the child was 17 years old she began to work for her board and a few months later was placed in a wage home. She had completed grammar school, but was not very bright, and, after a mental examination, was pronounced probably subnormal. She was neurasthenic and during the year of study had chorea. She was placed in a boarding home for care and then in a convalescent home, but later returned to her place at housework, where she was giving satisfaction. (Case V 1878.)

Occupations of children 14 years of age and over.

Of the 239 children 14 years of age and over under the care of agencies whose records contained more or less complete information, 32 were in institutions. The occupations of 109 of the remaining 207 children were reported and are shown in Table 52:

TABLE 52.—*Occupations of boys and girls 14 years of age and over.*

Occupation at end of period.	Children born out of wedlock, 14 years of age and over, under care in 1914, whose occupations were reported.		
	Total.	Boys.	Girls.
Total	109	53	56
Attending school	48	24	24
Housework	14		a 14
Farm	7	7	
Factory	12	6	6
Store	10	b 6	a 4
Office	1		1
Other	10	9	1
None	7	1	6

a Includes 1 also attending school.   b Includes 4 also attending school.

More than two-fifths of the children 14 years of age and over—24 boys and 24 girls—whose occupations were reported were attending school. Some of the children remained in school after the age of 14 because their previous slow progress had made it necessary; others were being given the opportunity of advanced schooling. It is probable that most of the children of this age who were attending school earned at least a part of their board by helping before and after school hours with the housework and on the farm. In addition to the 48 children included above there were 6 also attending school, of whom 4 boys and 1 girl were employed in stores and 1 girl at housework after school hours or during vacations.

Fourteen of the 56 girls were employed at domestic service, and 12 were employed in other gainful occupations. Seven of the 53 boys were employed at farm work and 21 in gainful occupations of other types.

Disposition of children whose cases were closed during year.

A total of 1,168 children born out of wedlock died or were discharged from care during the year. Of those, 465 were receiving temporary care immediately previous to the close of the case, and 703 were receiving prolonged care. In 264 cases the child had died. Of these children, 52 had received temporary care and 212 prolonged care. The care of the 904 children discharged during the year was assumed by the mothers, other relatives, friends, foster parents, or by other agencies or institutions. (See Table 53.) In a few instances the children were of age or were old enough to take care of themselves and had become self-supporting.

TABLE 53.—*Persons or agencies assuming responsibility for children discharged from temporary and from prolonged care during the year.*

Person or agency assuming responsibility for child.	Children born out of wedlock, discharged from care in 1914.		
	Total.	Who had received temporary care.	Who had received prolonged care.
Total..	904	413	491
Mother..	453	190	263
Relatives or friends..................................	89	29	60
Adoptive or foster parents...........................	42	8	34
Private agency or institution........................	98	58	40
Public agency or institution.........................	74	34	40
Self..	22	....	22
Not reported...	126	94	32

In 58 per cent of the 778 cases in which the person or agency assuming responsibility for the child was reported the child was discharged to his mother. The proportion of children discharged to their mothers from prolonged care was greater than those so discharged from temporary care. Relatives or friends assumed the care of 12 per cent of the children. Adoptive or foster parents took only 5 per cent. These figures again indicate the conservative policy of Boston agencies in regard to adoptions. Twenty-two per cent of the children reported were assumed by other agencies or institutions, more often private than public. Three per cent were of age or were in no further need of supervision, being able to provide for themselves.

Of the 459 children discharged from prolonged care whose histories reported the persons or agencies assuming responsibility, 57 per cent were discharged to their mothers, 13 per cent to relatives or friends, 7 per cent to adoptive or foster parents, 18 per cent to agencies or institutions, and 5 per cent were of age or were in no further need of supervision.

The reasons for the termination of the 465 cases in which the children had received temporary care previous to the close of the case, were as follows:

Total receiving temporary care previous to the close of the case_____ 465
Child dead_____ 52
Mother able to care for child_____ 59
Other relatives or friends able to care for child_____ 21
Home situation improved_____ 46
Care no longer appropriate_____ 163
Other disposition made_____ 72
Child disappeared and impossible to locate_____ 22
Other_____ 22
Reason not reported_____ 8

In a little more than one-tenth of the cases the child had died. In 59 cases—about an eighth of all the temporary cases closed during the year—the mothers were able to assume the responsibiltiy for the care of their children; in 19 of these cases, the mother's family came to her assistance; in 3 cases the mother married the child's father; in 4 cases the mother's husband, though not the father of the child, was willing to provide for him. Relatives or friends assumed the care of 21 children; in 3 of these cases paternal relatives took the child. The 46 cases closed because of improvement in the home conditions had come in as neglect complaints, the situation proving to be less serious than stated or having changed for the better. All but 6 of the 72 cases in which " other disposition " was made were referred to other agencies for care. The 163 cases in which " care was no longer appropriate " were chiefly hospital cases, the patients being ready for discharge. In 22 instances the child had disappeared, and could not be found. The 22 cases closed for other reasons included 7 children placed in adoptive homes, 3 deported, 3 moved from the city, 3 referred to other agencies because of illness, 2 delinquent and

1 feeble-minded referred to other agencies for special care, and 3 discharged for other reasons.

The reasons for terminating the cases of the 703 children receiving prolonged care were as follows:

Total receiving prolonged care previous to the close of the case_____ 703

Child dead_____	212	Child self-supporting_____	6
Mother able to care for child_____	144	Care no longer appropriate___	9
Other relatives or friends able to		Child disappeared and impos-	
care for child_____	47	sible to locate_____	26
Child placed in adoptive home_____	31	Child delinquent, feeble-	
Home situation improved_____	56	minded, or insane_____	12
Child deported_____	18	Other disposition made_____	79
Age limit reached_____	21	Other _____	13
Child of age_____	15	Not reported _____	14

In almost one-third of these cases the child had died. In one-fifth the mothers had become able to assume the care of the children. This proportion is considerably larger than in the case of the children receiving temporary care. In 38 of the 144 cases in which the mother was able to care for the child, the mother's family came to her assistance; in 25 cases the mother married the child's father, and in 3 other cases support was secured from the father; in 17 instances the mother's husband was willing to support the child. In 95 cases—slightly more than one-eighth of all—the child was either deported, reached the age limit set by the agency under whose care he was, became legally of age, was released because he was self-supporting, had disappeared, or the particular kind of care which the agency had been giving was no longer suited to his needs.

Characteristics of the Children.

Physical condition.

Information in regard to the physical condition of the children was limited, since the only sources of information were agency records, and the agencies were not uniform in the completeness of their records. The children's agencies in Boston as a rule make an effort to take the best care of the physical condition of the children in their charge. Physical examinations are given the children on reception. Medical and dental treatment is furnished by consulting physicians and dentists, or by physicians attached to the regular staffs of the agencies. Hospital facilities are excellent and include out-patient and social-service work. The visitors employed by the agencies try to watch carefully the condition of their charges. For infants under 2 years of age some of the agencies have trained nurses as visitors, and visits are made as often as once or twice a day should the child's condition require such frequent attention. Infants reported as boarded in private homes are visited by nurses of the State board of charity, hence all children of this age boarded by agencies have the supervision of the agency and the State board.

Modern child-caring work puts more and more emphasis upon the adequate physical care of the children. Their charges often come to the agencies in poor physical condition because of the circumstances under which they have been living and the neglect to which they have in many cases been subjected. Some of them have a defective heritage and suffer from constitutional weaknesses. The best medical skill and the utmost care are necessary to make possible their development into strong and healthy children.

The New England Home for Little Wanderers, in their home in Boston, has made especially good provision for the physical care of its wards. Facilities for the most efficient medical diagnosis and also for some treatment are provided. Two children's agencies have entered into a special arrangement with the Boston Dispensary for preventive and medical treatment of the children in their care.

Agencies have, however, hardly begun to realize the need for uniform and exact records, filled out at regular intervals, showing the physical condition and development of their charges. Existing records are, in this respect, often haphazard and unscientific. Only serious physical conditions or acute illnesses are entered. The failure to record regular and scientific observations makes it impossible for agencies to check up their work, to determine what treatment is most conducive to the welfare of the children, what homes are providing healthful surroundings and good care, and how much work should be expected from children in free or wage homes who are trying to keep up with their studies. No criteria for measuring results of child-placing work are possible without this primary record of physical condition.

Infants born out of wedlock die, in Boston, at a rate three times as high as that for infants born in wedlock.[4] Lack of proper feeding and care appears to be the chief cause. No information is available in this country as to whether or not those who survive the first year are weaker than children of legitimate birth, or whether more of them suffer from diseases such as tuberculosis, syphilis, and rachitis. It is probable that the handicaps to which so many of the children born out of wedlock are subjected have serious effects upon their physical growth and development.

For 2,288 children the agency records were sufficiently complete to permit the assumption that any serious illness or chronic disease

---

[4] See p. 89.

would have been mentioned in the records. Those children in whose cases no statements as to physical condition were made were assumed to be in good health. The figures as to those in poor condition represent, therefore, only a minimum of those in poor health. The information relates to the end of the year studied or to the time of discharge.

Total children in whose cases records were sufficiently complete to give a basis for statement on physical condition _____ 2, 288
Assumed to be in good physical condition _____ 1, 768
Having very defective vision _____ 9
Having very defective hearing _____ 8
Crippled or deformed (including 1 also rachitic) _____ 23
Tubercular (including 2 also rachitic) _____ 21
Having rachitis _____ 24
Having syphilis or gonorrhea (including 2 also having defective vision, 1 also rachitic and having defective vision, 3 also crippled or deformed, and 1 also rachitic and crippled) _____ 87
Suspected of having syphilis or gonorrhea (including 1 also having defective vision) _____ 10
Epileptic (including 1 also crippled) _____ 2
In otherwise poor condition _____ 336

Slightly more than three-fourths of the children were assumed to be in good physical condition. Almost one-fourth were in poor condition. Many of the children were very seriously handicapped and required special care.

Mental condition.

As in the case of physical condition, the information concerning mentality is fragmentary. Only such data as appeared on existing records were available. Most of the agencies had examinations for mentality only for such of their wards as they had reason to think were not normal. The figures as to subnormal children must, therefore, be considered as minimum. Even school progress was by no means uniformly recorded. Table 54 shows the information obtained in regard to mental condition.

The children assumed to be of normal mentality, no report to the contrary having been made, constituted 83 per cent of the 656 children 7 years of age and over who were under the care of agencies having fairly complete records. Seventeen per cent of the children were not normal mentally or were very backward in school. The proportion below normal increased with the higher age groups.

Of the 110 children who were very backward or mentally below normal, 41 had been diagnosed feeble-minded; 2 were insane; 17 were probably subnormal or feeble-minded, but mental examinations had not been made; 15 were designated subnormal or abnormal; and 35 others were extremely backward in school. The " subnormal or abnormal " group included children diagnosed as borderline feeble-minded, or defective delinquent. The percentage of children who had been diagnosed feeble-minded was high—6 per cent.[5]

TABLE 54.—*Mental condition of children 7 years of age and over.*

Age at end of period.	Children born out of wedlock, 7 years of age and over, under care in 1914.						
	Total.[a]	Mental condition.					
		Normal, so far as known.	Very backward in school.	Probably subnormal or feeble-minded. but not diagnosed.	Subnormal or abnormal (diagnosed).	Feeble-minded (diagnosed).	Insane.
Total....................	656	546	35	17	15	41	2
7-9 years..............	212	185	12	7	1	7	....
10-13 years............	205	171	12	5	5	12	....
14 years and over......	239	190	11	5	9	22	2

a Excluding 148 children under care of agencies not reporting mental condition.

Because of the diversity in the work of the agencies and institutions included in the study, the different classes of children cared for by the various agencies, and the fact that some agencies made more thorough investigations and kept more complete records than others, a separate analysis was made of the mental condition of the children under care of a selected group of private agencies. These comprised five child-caring agencies dealing with children of all ages and the child-protective agency. Table 55 shows the mental condition of the 305 children 7 years of age and over under care of these agencies.

---

[5] An investigation in a rural county in Delaware made by the U. S. Public Health Service and the Children's Bureau showed that 0.94 per cent of the white children 5 to 20 years of age, inclusive, were feeble-minded. The precentage found among white school children, exclusive of placed-out children brought into the county from outside was, 0.95— the same as that previously found by the Public Health Service in the rural schools of a county in Indiana. See Mental Defect in a Rural County. A study made through the collaboration of the U. S. Public Health Service and the Children's Bureau, by Walter L. Treadway, M. D., and Emma O. Lundberg, U. S. Children's Bureau, Dependent, Defective, and Delinquent Classes Series No. 7, Bureau Publication No. 48. Washington, 1919. Pp. 30, 39.

TABLE 55.—*Mental condition of children 7 years of age and over, under care of five private child-caring agencies and a child-protective agency.*

Age at end of period.	Total.	Children born out of wedlock, 7 years of age and over, under care in 1914.				
		Mental condition.				
		Normal, so far as known.	Very backward in school.	Probably subnormal or feeble-minded, but not diagnosed.	Subnormal or abnormal (diagnosed).	Feeble-minded (diagnosed).
Total....................	305	272	15	7	7	4
7–9 years....................	97	92	3	1	1	....
10–13 years....................	112	99	7	4	2	....
14 years and over..............	96	81	5	2	4	4

Eleven per cent of the children 7 years of age and over under care of the five private child-caring agencies and the child-protective agency were not normal mentally or were very backward in school. This percentage was considerably lower than that found among children under care of all agencies included in the study reporting mental condition—17 per cent. Feeble-minded children formed 1 per cent of those under care of the selected group of agencies, as compared with 6 per cent among children under care of all agencies reporting mental condition. These differences may be largely accounted for by the fact that Boston children under care of institutions for the feeble-minded were included in the larger group. The percentages below normal or very backward but not diagnosed feeble-minded or insane were very nearly the same for the two groups—9.5 for children under care of the five child-caring agencies and the child-protective agency and 10.2 for all the children under care of agencies reporting mental condition.

Conduct.

As reported on the records, the conduct of almost one-fourth of the children 7 years of age and over was considered unsatisfactory. A more thorough analysis by the agencies of the personalties and characteristics of the children in their charge would be of the greatest value, both in determining the kind of treatment needed for the individual child and in testing the results of their work. Especially is thorough understanding of character essential to good case work with those children whose reactions toward society are sometimes affected unfavorably by knowledge of the conditions of their birth or by their early experiences.

Absence of information as to conduct in the case histories of agencies who kept records containing more or less complete information concerning the children in their care was assumed to indicate that the child's conduct was satisfactory. It was thought probable that most cases of troublesome behavior would have been recorded. Characteristics were tabulated only for children 7 years of age and over. (See Table 56.)

TABLE 56.—*Conduct of children 7 years of age and over.*

Age at end of period.	Children born out of wedlock, 7 years of age and over, under care in 1914.												
	Boys and girls.				Boys.					Girls.			
	To-tal.	Conduct good, so far as known.		Conduct poor.		To-tal.	Conduct good, so far as known.		Conduct poor.		To-tal.	Conduct good, so far as known.		Conduct poor.	
		Num-ber.	Per cent.	Num-ber.	Per cent.		Num-ber.	Per cent.	Num-ber.	Per cent.		Num-ber.	Per cent.	Num-ber.	Per cent.
Total..........	a656	497	75.8	159	24.2	342	271	79.2	71	20.8	314	226	72.0	88	28.0
7–9 yrs..........	212	188	88.7	24	11.3	111	99	89.2	12	10.8	101	89	88.1	12	11.9
10–13 yrs.........	205	158	77.1	47	22.9	113	83	73.5	30	26.5	92	75	81.5	17	18.5
14 yrs. and over .	239	151	63.2	88	36.8	118	89	75.4	b 29	24.6	121	c 62	51.2	d 59	48.8

a Excluding 148 children under care of agencies not reporting conduct.
b Includes 2 committed from Boston to a State institution for delinquents and not under care of Boston agencies during the year.
c Includes 1 committed from Boston to a State institution for delinquents and not under care of Boston agencies during the year.
d Includes 14 committed from Boston to a State institution for delinquents and not under care of Boston agencies during the year.

As might be expected, a larger percentage of the older children than of the younger were reported as unsatisfactory in conduct. Only 11 per cent of the children from 7 to 9 years of age, inclusive, were so reported, while 23 per cent of the children 10 to 13 years of age, and 37 per cent of those 14 years of age and over were reported as having been delinquent, uncontrollable, or not amenable to discipline. The high percentage among the older children is partly due to the fact that Boston children committed to State institutions for delinquents were included in the study. It must be borne in mind that these percentages are based upon children under care of agencies and are not representative of all children born out of wedlock.

The percentage of boys whose conduct was reported as unsatisfactory was lower than the percentage of girls whose conduct was so reported—21 as compared with 28. Analyzed by age groups, the percentages were very nearly the same among children 7 to 9 years of age—11 for the boys and 12 for the girls. In the age group of 10 to 13 years the percentage of boys whose conduct was poor was much higher than the percentage of girls—27 as compared with 19. Of the children 14 years of age and over, 25 per cent of the boys and 49 per cent of the girls were reported as having been delinquent, uncontrollable, or not amenable to discipline. It must be remembered that Boston children committed to State institutions for delinquents were included in the study. Excluding from the group 14 years of age and over the 2 boys and 15 girls so committed and not under care of Boston agencies during the year, the percentage of boys whose conduct was unsatisfactory is reduced from 25 to 23 and the percentage of girls from 49 to 42. However, the percentage among the girls remains almost twice that among the boys.

Of the 29 boys and 59 girls 14 years of age and over whose behavior was described as unsatisfactory, 3 boys and 37 girls were known to have been guilty of sex offenses, 13 boys and 6 girls of stealing, stubborness, or other forms of delinquency, and 13 boys and 16 girls had given serious trouble at home or in school. Twelve of the girls who were sex offenders were mothers of children born out of wedlock.

Following are some examples of satisfactory and of unsatisfactory character development among the children under care:

An 18-year old girl had been under the supervision of a private child-caring agency from the age of 2 years; before that date she had been cared for by another agency specializing in the care of infants. She had been in the same boarding home from the age of 2 years, her mother paying part of her board regularly. The mother, 32 years of age when the child was born, was described as a self-supporting, self-respecting woman who earned her livelihood as a laundress. Nothing was known of the alleged father except that he was a Canadian and a day laborer. The girl was well liked by her companions and proved to be exceptionally bright. Ambitious to become a school-teacher, she was planning to go to college for at least two years in preparation for that profession. (Case V 1720.)

Three children born out of wedlock—a girl of 6 years, a boy of 4, and a boy of 2—were received by a public child-caring agency 7 years before the period covered by this study. Their mother and father had been living together for 6 or 7 years. At the time of application the father had been sent to prison for perjury, having married a girl of 14 whose age he had misrepresented. Subsequently the mother had, by another man, a fourth child out of wedlock.

The children were all placed in boarding homes, where they did very well. At the time of the study the girl was attending high school and was described as "good, bright, capable, and in good health." The boys were strong, active, and bright, and were doing well in school. (Cases V 816, 817, 818.)

A 16-year- old boy of illegitimate birth had been under the care of a private child-caring agency for 14 years; he had lived in the same boarding home for 9 years. Deserted by his mother when only a few months old, he had been cared for by an infant asylum until he was received by the agency already mentioned. In the year of the study the boy went to work, paying his own board and attending night school. He did poor work, however, and found it impossible to support himself. He refused to follow the plans the agency made for him, and was reported to be fretful, fickle, and somewhat dishonest. (Case V 767.)

A girl of 20 and her 18-year-old half sister, both of illegitimate birth, had been under the care of a private child-caring agency for 10 years. Their mother had been very immoral and had died of tuberculosis before the children were received by the agency. The girls were placed in various family homes. Both sisters were weak and easily influenced, and the older was intemperate; both were very immoral. The elder had a child born out of wedlock during the year of the study. The baby was taken by the girl's foster mother. The year following, the younger sister had a child born out of wedlock. This girl was given a mental examination and was found to be neither insane nor feeble-minded, but very suggestible. (Cases V 2336, 2337.)

A girl of 16 had been under the care of a private agency for two years, having come under care because of her troublesome conduct in school. She had been born out of wedlock, but her parents had later married each other. Her mother had had by another man a previous child born out of wedlock. The girl was wayward and the mother, who worked away from home all day, found it impossible to control her.- At the age of 14 the girl left school and went to work in a factory; she later worked for short periods as a waitress and at housework. Her companions were of bad character, and the girl was very immoral. At the age of 15 she had a child whose paternity it was impossible to determine. The maternity home where the child was born reported the mother untruthful and in need of constant supervision. After leaving this maternity home the mother and baby returned to the home of the mother's parents. The baby died at the age of 3 or 4 months. The girl, though under agency supervision, continued to be a trouble maker in the community. (Case V 1959.)

Nine years previous to this study application was made to a private child-caring agency for the care of a 10-year-old boy of illegitimate birth. The boy's mother died the year after he was born. He had been placed at board when he was 3 days old, the maternal grandparents paying. Later the boarding woman decided to adopt him, but before the adoption was accomplished the woman became ill and made application, through the child's grandmother, to have the care of the boy assumed by the agency. The agency accepted the case but kept the boy in the same home, paying for his board and clothes. A year later the boarding home was changed, since the first woman was unable to keep the child. About this time the boy, who had been apparently a normal child, became nervous, lazy, and troublesome. He was given a mental examination and pronounced mentally subnormal. He was tried in different homes but was unsatisfactory and finally stole a sum of money. He was arrested and sent to a reformatory, where he still was at the end of the period studied. He was reported by the institution as not doing well. (Case V 2285.)

THE CHILD'S HERITAGE AND THE POSSIBILITIES OF THE PARENTS' PROVIDING CARE.

The importance of knowledge of the child's heritage as a necessary preliminary to efficient work is more and more being recognized by child-caring agencies. For children born out of wedlock such information is often difficult to obtain, especially as regards the father and paternal grandparents. Yet from the point of view of heredity, paternal characteristics are of equal importance with maternal. So far as nature is concerned there is no " fatherless child."

The character and capability of the mother and the nature of her relationship to the child are of primary importance in considering the problem of the care of a child born out of wedlock. The fundamental need of childhood is maternal care, no less for children of illegitimate birth than for others. Whether or not the mother can supply this need and what assistance, if any, is necessary depend upon a number of factors, such as her maturity, her physical and mental condition, her ability to earn a livelihood, and the other obligations which she must meet.

The mothers of the children who have come to the attention of social agencies are those whose circumstances are the most pressing— those least able to meet the demands maternity has put upon them. The facts here analyzed are therefore not entirely representative of the whole group of mothers of children born out of wedlock, but only of those most in need of assistance. The purpose of the analysis is to determine the heritage of the children and the conditions surrounding them, and is not intended to be a discussion of the causative factors in the problem of illegitimacy. Therefore, the statistics are based upon the number of children, and not upon the number of mothers. There were 2,863 children included in the study, but in many cases several children in the same family were under care, hence the total number of mothers represented was 2,585. (See Table 57.)

TABLE 57.—*Mothers having specified numbers of children under care.*

Number of mother's children under care.	Mothers of children born out of wedlock, under care in 1914.	Children born out of wedlock, under care in 1914.
Total	2,585	2,863
One	2,388	2,388
Two	140	280
Three	40	120
Four	11	44
Five	5	25
Six	1	6

In cases in which a mother had several children under care, she was counted once for each child. This method of analysis must be borne in mind, especially in the discussions of mental condition, character, and home conditions. The data presented indicate the extent to which the children were subjected to various handicaps and are not intended to show the prevalence of certain conditions among women who are mothers of children born out of wedlock.

Little information was available concerning the fathers of the children studied. It is often very difficult to secure information in regard to the paternity of a child of illegitimate birth because of the natural reticence of the mother. Social agencies have only recently begun to recognize the importance of knowledge of the father's status, not only for the purpose of securing contributions for the support of the child but also as essential to the intelligent handling of the case with justice to all concerned. Social case work is needed with the father as well as with the mother and child, and it must be recognized that he has oftentimes an instinct of affection for his child which may be developed.

The Child's Heritage.

Race and nativity.

Of the 2,863 children under care, 2,650 were white, 205 were colored, and 8 were American Indian or Chinese. (See Table 58.) Miscegenation was known to have occurred in 55 cases in which the children were colored; the mothers of 41 of these children were white and the fathers colored, while in 14 cases the mothers were colored and the fathers white. It is probable that in some cases in which the mother was colored and the paternity was not known the father was white.

TABLE 58.—*Race of children, by race of parents.*

Race of mother and of father.	Children born out of wedlock, under care in 1914.			
	Total.	White.	Negro.	Other.
Total	2,863	2,650	205	a 8
Mother white	2,691	2,650	41	....
Father white	2,650	2,650	....	....
Father Negro	41	....	41	....
Mother Negro	139	....	139	....
Father white	14	....	14	....
Father Negro	54	....	54	....
Father not reported	71	....	71	....
Mother American Indian or Chinese	7	....	....	7
Father white	3	....	....	3
Father not reported	4	....	....	4
Mother not reported	26	....	25	1
Father Negro	3	....	3	....
Father not reported	23	....	22	1

a Includes 7 American Indian and 1 Chinese.

Information as to the nativity of both parents was secured for only 587 of the 2,863 children under care. (See Table 59.) The nativity of the mother only was known in 1,626 cases and of the father only in 21, while in 629 cases the nativity of neither parent was reported. The large number of "not reported" cases is due to the inclusion in the study of certain agencies giving practically no social information.

TABLE 59.—*Nativity of parents.*

Nativity of both parents reported or not reported, and nativity of father if reported.	Children born out of wedlock, under care in 1914.				
	Total.	Whose mothers were of specified nativity.			
		United States.	Canada.	Other.	Not reported.
Total....................................	2,863	1,227	345	641	650
Nativity of both parents reported..................	587	234	93	260	....
Father, United States...........................	200	155	16	29	....
Father, Canada................................	79	23	49	7	....
Father, other foreign..........................	308	56	28	a 224	....
Nativity of mother only reported..................	1,626	993	252	381	....
Nativity of father only reported..................	21	....	....	....	21
United States................................	11	....	....	....	11
Canada.......................................	1	....	....	....	1
Other foreign................................	9	....	....	....	9
Nativity of neither parent reported..............	629	....	....	....	629

a In 147 of these cases the country of birth of the mother and father was the same; in 77 cases, different.

If the cases in which the nativity of the father was known are representative for all the fathers, it would appear that more of the fathers than of the mothers were foreign born. Children whose mothers were foreign born constituted 45 per cent of all children the nativity of whose mothers was reported, while the fathers were foreign born in 65 per cent of the cases in which the nativity of the father was known. Of the 587 children for whom the nativity of both parents was reported, there were 60 per cent whose mothers were foreign born and 66 per cent whose fathers were foreign born.

In 351 cases, or 60 per cent of all in which the nativity of both parents was known, the mother and father had the same country of birth. In 155 of these cases, both were born in the United States; in 49, both in Canada; and in 147, both in some other foreign country.

The fathers and mothers of 236 children were known to have been born in different countries. Of 79 of these children the mothers were born in the United States and the fathers in Canada (23 cases) or in some other foreign country (56 cases). The mothers of 44 children were born in Canada and the fathers in the United States (16 cases) or in a foreign country other than Canada (28 cases). Of the 113 children whose mothers were born in a foreign country other than Canada, there were 29 whose fathers were born in the United States, 7 whose fathers were born in Canada, and 77 whose fathers were born in a foreign country not that of the mother.

Information as to nativity of the mother was secured for 2,213 children. Children of native-born mothers constituted 55 per cent of this total. The mothers of 48 per cent of these children were born in Massachusetts, of 6 per cent in other New England States, and of 46 per cent elsewhere in the United States.

Children, the nativity of whose mothers was reported_____ 2, 213

Mother, native born_____ 1, 227			Mother foreign born—Contd.	
Massachusetts _____ 590			Italy _____	48
Other New England___ 74			Norway _____	3
Other United States___ 563			Poland _____	35
Mother foreign born_____		986	Portugal_____	9
Austria (exclusive of			Russia (exclusive of	
Austrian Poland)____ 12			Finland and Russian	
Canada_____ 345			Poland) _____	52
England and Wales___ 52			Scotland_____	36
Finland _____ 8			Sweden_____	40
France _____ 5			Switzerland _____	5
Germany _____ 9			West Indies_____	15
Greece _____ 9			Other _____	10
Ireland_____ 292			Not reported_____	1

In over one-third of the cases in which the mother was not born in the United States, she came from Canada. The greatest number of those coming from overseas were born in Ireland.

In considering the mother's ability to care for her child, it is of importance to know in the case of foreign-born mothers the length of time they had been in the United States when their children were born. Ignorance of language, custom, and conditions constitutes a serious handicap to the woman who must provide for her child with little or no assistance from the father. Although a large number of foreign-born mothers were of English-speaking nationalities, even with them the disadvantage inherent in recent arrival in a new country was present to a greater or less extent. In many of these cases the situation was made more difficult by the fact that the mother had come to this country alone, and hence there was little possibility of assistance by parents and other relatives.

Information as to length of time in the United States at the time of the child's birth was available in only 518 of the 986 cases in which the mother was foreign born. In 5 per cent of these cases the mother had come to this country after the child was born, in 7 per cent she was pregnant when she emigrated. Some of these mothers had left home for the purpose of concealing their condition from family and friends. The Canadian mothers often came in order to secure the assistance of social agencies. Other cases in which the mother had been in this country less than 5 years at the time of the child's birth constituted 37 per cent of the total reported, while the mothers of 51 per cent had lived in the United States more than 5 years. The place of birth or conception and the length of the mother's residence in the United States are shown below:

Total reported_____ 518
Child born or conceived abroad_____ 62
   Foreign born _____ 25
   Mother pregnant on arrival_____ 37
Child conceived and born in the United States_____ 456
   Mother in the United States less than 2 years_____ 37
   Mother in the United States 2 to 4 years_____ 157
   Mother in the United States 5 years and over_____ 262

In 5 per cent of the cases of foreign-born mothers whose ages were reported they had the additional handicap of extreme youth, being under 18 years of age when their children were born. The proportion under 18 was considerably smaller than that among the native-born mothers—17 per cent.

Native-born mothers whose ages were reported_____ 961
   Native-born mothers under 18 years of age_____ 161
Foreign-born mothers whose ages were reported_____ 723
   Foreign-born mothers under 18 years of age_____ 35

To summarize: More than half the cases involving children born out of wedlock dealt with by the agencies studied, in which the nativity of the mother was reported, concerned children of native-American mothers. More than two-fifths of the cases were complicated by the fact that the mother was foreign born and was probably handicapped by unfamiliarity with American conditions and by the absence of family and friends from whom she might otherwise have received assistance. Children of colored mothers comprised a very small percentage of the total.

Physical condition of mother.

Most of the social agencies studied made efforts to obtain medical examinations whenever there was reason to think that the mother was not in good health. Some of the histories, however, were obtained from agencies making no attempt at social investigation. The information here given pertains only to the mothers of about three-fourths of the children studied, and even for these cases it is undoubtedly an understatement of physical disability. In many instances it was obviously impossible for the agencies to secure complete information in regard to the mothers—for instance, when they could not be located at the time the applications for the care of the children were made.

The histories of 2,178 children were obtained from agencies giving more or less complete social information. The mothers of 59, or 3 per cent, of these children were known to have died before the applications were made for the care of the children. The mothers of more than one-fifth—22 per cent—were known to be physically defective or diseased, or to be in poor physical condition. Following is a statement of the number of cases in which the mothers had disabilities of various types:

```
      Total whose mothers were in poor physical condition_____ 489
Having seriously defective vision_____  10
Having serious deafness_____  13
Crippled or deformed_____  23
Epileptic _____  11
Tubercular _____  61
Having syphilis or gonorrhea__ _ _____ 122
      (Exclusive of 19 cases classed under disabilities previously speci-
   fied; a total of 141 children had mothers diagnosed as syphilitic or
   as having gonorrheal infection.)
Otherwise in poor condition_____ 249
```

The mothers of 6 per cent of the 2,178 children had been diagnosed as having syphilis or gonorrhea. The percentage of cases in which the other specified disabilities existed ranged from less than 1 per cent to 3 per cent, with 11 per cent in which the mothers, though not having the disabilities enumerated, were known to be in poor physical condition.

Mental condition of mother, father, and maternal grandparents.

The importance of knowledge of the mentality of the child's parents as requisite to the intelligent care of dependent children is recognized by child-caring agencies. The New York State Conference of Charities and Correction in the Standards of Placing Out, Supervision, and After Care of Dependent Children, approved in 1915, considers the mentality of the child's parents an important factor in determining the type of home in which the child should be placed and the kind of supervision that should be given.[6] In the case of children born out of wedlock such information is especially difficult to obtain in regard to the father and paternal relatives. Boston agencies caring for unmarried mothers and their children are in general aware of the importance of scientific determination of the mentality of the mother in all cases in which there is a question of abnormal or subnormal mental condition.

The records of 2,178 of the 2,863 children of illegitimate birth under care gave more or less complete social information. Of these 2,178 children, the mothers of 379 were reported not normal mentally. The fathers of 16 children were reported below normal; in all but 4 of these 16 cases the mother was also below normal. So far as the

---

[6] Report of the Special Committee of the New York State Conference of Charities and Correction on Standards of Placing-Out, Supervision, and After-Care of Dependent Children. Submitted to and approved by the Sixteenth New York State Conference of Charities and Correction, Albany, November 16–18, 1915.

histories stated, the mothers and fathers of 1,795 children were of normal mentality, and the parents of 383 were below normal. The 18 per cent having one or both parents below normal was without doubt a minimum. To a very much smaller extent than in the case of the mothers were the fathers known personally to the agencies caring for the children. The mental condition of the fathers would have been known only in the small number of cases in which defective or abnormal mentality was an outstanding factor. So far as the records gave this information, the mental condition of the mothers and fathers of the 2,178 children whose histories gave more or less complete social data was as follows:

```
Total reported _____ 2, 178
Both parents of normal mentality, so far as known _____ 1, 795
One parent of normal mentality, so far as known, other parent
    below normal _____     371
        Mother of subnormal or abnormal mentality _____  65
        Mother insane _____  31
        Mother feeble-minded (diagnosed) _____ 129
        Mother probably subnormal or feeble-minded (not diag-
            nosed) _____ 142
        Father insane _____   3
        Father probably subnormal or feeble-minded (not diag-
            nosed) _____   1
Both parents below normal mentally _____      12
        Mother insane, father probably subnormal or feeble-
            minded (not diagnosed) _____   1
        Both feeble-minded (diagnosed) _____     _____   4
        Both probably subnormal or feeble-minded (not diag-
            nosed) _____   7
```

The mothers of 230 of the 2,178 children, or 11 per cent, were feeble-minded, or mentally subnormal or abnormal as established by mental examination, or were known to have been insane. The mothers of an additional 149, or 7 per cent, were probably subnormal or feeble-minded, but diagnoses had not yet been made.

The cases in which the mother was of subnormal or abnormal mentality, her mental condition having been thus diagnosed, constituted 3 per cent of those in which social information was available, and included 6 cases in which the mother was diagnosed as "high grade feeble-minded, not committable"; 30 in which she was diagnosed as defective or subnormal but not feeble-minded; 3 in which she was diagnosed as "psychopathic" or "constitutionally inferior"; 3 in which the mother had mild mental disorder not amounting to insanity; and 23 in which she was pronounced a "defective delinquent" or "moral defective." In 1 per cent of the cases the mother was insane; in 7 of these 32 cases she had been an inmate of a hospital for the insane previous to her pregnancy, in 4 instances being returned to the institution after the child was born. In addition to these 4, the mothers of 21 children were committed to hospitals for the insane after the children were born; in 4 cases in which the mother was insane she had not vet been admitted to an institution.

The mothers of 6 per cent of the children had been diagnosed feeble-minded. In only 32 cases—less than one-fourth of those in which the mother had been diagnosed mentally defective—had she been committed to an institution for the feeble-minded by the time this study closed. In 6 other cases the mother had been given temporary care in a public institution pending admission to an institution for the feeble-minded.

A separate analysis was made (see Table 60) of the mentality of mothers of children under care of six private child-caring agencies [7] and of the child-protective agency. A total of 472 children born out of wedlock were under care of the six child-caring agencies, while 571 were cared for by the child-protective agency, 37 of these also being cared for by the child-caring agencies.

TABLE 60.—*Mental condition of mothers of children under care of six private child-caring agencies and of a child-protective agency.*

Mental condition of mother.	Children born out of wedlock, under care of 6 private child-caring agencies in 1914.	Children born out of wedlock, under care of a child-protective agency in 1914.
Total..	a 472	b 571
Normal, so far as known.............................	383	474
Subnormal or abnormal..............................	22	25
Insane...	6	7
Feeble-minded.....................................	22	21
Probably subnormal or feeble-minded (not diagnosed)...	39	44

a Includes 37 also under care of the child-protective agency.
b Includes 37 also under care of the child-caring agencies.

The mothers of 11 per cent of the children under care of the six private child-caring agencies were feeble-minded, mentally subnormal or abnormal, or were known to have been insane. The mothers of 39, or 8 per cent, were probably subnormal or feeble-minded, but diagnoses had not yet been made. These percentages are almost identical with the findings for the whole group of 2,178 children whose histories contained more or less complete social information. Among the children under care of the child-protective agency the percentage whose mothers were feeble-minded, mentally subnormal or abnormal, or insane, was slightly lower than in the case of the whole group of 2,178 children—9 as compared with 11. The percentage probably subnormal or feeble-minded but not diagnosed was

[7] The five child-caring agencies included in the group analyzed separately for the mentality of the child, pp. 183–184, and another agency caring for mothers and young children.

8—the same as for the children under care of the child-caring agencies and only slightly higher than the 7 per cent found among the whole group of children.

Little definite information was given as to the mentality of the maternal grandparents. It was known, however, that one or both maternal grandparents of 65 of the children—3 per cent of the 2,178 whose records gave social information—were insane or mentally below normal, the maternal grandmother being thus reported in 44 cases, the maternal grandfather in 13 cases, and both maternal grandparents in 8 cases. Of the 65 cases in which one or both of the maternal grandparents were mentally below normal, there were 25 in which the mother was of normal mentality and 40 in which she was below normal. The mental condition of the maternal grandparents who were known to have been mentally below normal was as follows:

Total children, one or both of whose maternal grandparents were not normal mentally_____ 65
Maternal grandmother:
   Subnormal _____ 2
   Insane _____ 21
   Feeble-minded (diagnosed)_____ 6
   Probably subnormal or feeble-minded (not diagnosed)_____ 15
Maternal grandfather:
   Insane _____ 10
   Probably subnormal or feeble-minded (not diagnosed)_____ 3
Both maternal grandparents not normal:
   Grandmother insane, grandfather feeble-minded (diagnosed)_____ 1
   Grandmother probably subnormal or feeble-minded, grandfather insane _____ 1
   Both probably subnormal or feeble-minded_____ 6

A total of 408 children—19 per cent of the 2,178 whose histories gave social information—had a heritage in which there was known to be insanity, feeble-mindedness, or other subnormal or abnormal mental condition, or probable subnormality or feeble-mindedness. In 195 cases—9 per cent of the total reported—there was definite feeble-mindedness or insanity in the family history.

Total children under care whose histories gave social information__ 2,178
Parents and maternal grandparents mentally normal, so far as known _____ 1,770
Mother or one maternal grandparent mentally subnormal or abnormal_____ 64
One or both parents or maternal grandparents feeble-minded or insane_____ 195
One or both parents or maternal grandparents probably subnormal or feeble-minded (not diagnosed)_____ 149

Character of mother, father, and maternal grandparents.

The information as to the character of the mothers, fathers, and maternal grandparents of the children born out of wedlock under care of social agencies was by no means complete, even in the case of the mother, and was especially fragmentary in regard to the father and the grandparents. The value of such data to the agencies caring for the children is manifest, both for the sake of a better understanding of the child's characteristics and as a basis for decision as to the kind of care needed. Except in the case of abandoned children whose mothers can not be located, there would seem to be no reason why the facts concerning the mother should not invariably be ascertained and recorded. It should also be possible to obtain information in regard to the father's character in all cases in which paternity can be determined. It is often impracticable to secure information as to the character of the maternal grandparents, especially when the mother has immigrated to this country unaccompanied by her family.

The fact of illegitimate maternity or paternity necessarily implies a violation of generally accepted standards of conduct. However, for the purposes of this discussion the character of the mother or father was described as "good" if the infraction of the moral code resulting in the birth of a child out of wedlock was the only known evidence of antisocial conduct.

So far as shown by the records, the mothers of 993 children, or 46 per cent of the 2,178 concerning whom there was more or less complete social information, were of good character. Repeated violations of the moral code, serious alcoholism, dishonesty, or general worthlessness were reported in the histories of the mothers of 1,185 children—54 per cent.

The mothers of 884 children—41 per cent—were reported to have had other illicit sex experiences, while the mothers of 114 more—5 per cent of the 2,178—had lived as prostitutes. Serious alcoholism was also reported in 190 cases in which the mother was stated to have been immoral, while in 45 cases other delinquencies, and in 31 alcoholism and other delinquencies were reported in addition to sex offenses. Not all the mothers stated to have been prostitutes were engaged in prostitution at the time application was made for the care of the children; some had pursued this occupation for a short period only, while with others it had become their regular business. In the majority of cases in which the mother was a prostitute her history indicated that she had been immoral for gain previous to the child's birth. The data did not indicate that there was any considerable number of cases in which this form of immorality had been entered into because of the difficulties and discouragements and temptations that followed upon illegitimate maternity.

The mothers of 267—12 per cent of all—were reported as alcoholic. All but 46 of these were included above among the sexually immoral. The large percentage of cases in which the mothers were addicted to drink indicates the degeneracy into which they had fallen either before or after the births of the children studied. Other delinquencies, such as theft or illegal selling of liquor or drugs, were recorded for the mothers of 98 children, 4 per cent of all. In only 22 cases was such delinquency not combined with the types of misconduct previously described. In 119 cases—5 per cent—the mothers were markedly shiftless, stubborn, uninterested in the welfare of their children or unwilling to make any effort to help themselves, though they had not been guilty of the definite offenses specified above.

It must be borne in mind that the facts here stated relate only to cases in which the mother was forced to apply to an agency for assistance in caring for her child. It is clear, however, that the proportion of children whose mothers were repeatedly sex offenders is large, and that the coincidence of sexual misconduct with failure to conform to the mores of society in other respects is frequent.

The records contained more or less information in regard to the character of the fathers of 732 of the children studied. Undoubtedly these represented to a large extent the men who had come to the personal attention of agencies either in connection with court action to compel support for the children or because they had been involved in other trouble that had brought them into conflict with the law. The data must, therefore, be considered as giving the worst side of the picture rather than as being representative of the whole group.

The fathers of 186, or 25 per cent of the children whose histories gave information as to the character of the father, were said to be alcoholic; in 113 of these cases immorality or other forms of delinquency were also reported. Immorality was reported in 314 cases, or 43 per cent. In 131 cases this form of antisocial conduct was associated with alcoholism or other delinquency. In 72 cases—10 per cent—other forms of delinquency were reported, being in combination with alcoholism or immorality in 46 cases. Hence, in a total of 420 cases—57 per cent of the 732 in which there was information—alcoholism, immorality, or other delinquency was reported. The fathers of 64 children—9 per cent—were otherwise of poor character, being reported markedly unreliable, shiftless, or generally worthless. The fathers of 248 were classified as of good character so far as known, though in 152 of these cases the father had absconded in order to escape his responsibilities toward the child.[8]

Considering together the characters of the mothers and the fathers, and assuming that character was " good " unless otherwise

---

[8] In addition to 54 cases in which the father had deserted and was also reported as alcoholic, immoral, otherwise delinquent, or of poor character.

reported, both parents of 898 of the 2,178 children concerning whom there was social information were of good character so far as known, and one or both parents of 1,280—59 per cent—were of poor character. (See Table 61.) In 389 of these 1,280 cases both parents were of poor character.

TABLE 61.—*Character of mother and of father.*

Character of mother.	Children born out of wedlock, under care in 1914.								
		Whose fathers were of specified character.							
	Total.	Good so far as known.a	Alcoholic.	Immoral.	Otherwise delinquent.	Alcoholic and immoral.	Alcoholic and otherwise delinquent.	Immoral and otherwise delinquent.	Alcoholic, immoral, and otherwise delinquent.	Otherwise poor.
Total......	2,178	1,694	73	183	26	92	7	25	14	64
Good, so far as known.......	993	898	29	18	11	2	3	1	......	31
Alcoholic....................	46	37	5	1	......	......	......	......	......	3
Immoral......................	732	490	11	123	7	49	2	18	11	21
Otherwise delinquent........	22	18	1	......	2	......	......	......	......	1
Alcoholic and immoral......	190	109	14	20	2	34	2	2	3	4
Immoral and otherwise delinquent...................	45	29	1	11	......	3	......	......	......	1
Alcoholic, immoral, and otherwise delinquent......	31	13	5	5	1	4	......	3	......	......
Otherwise poor..............	119	100	7	5	3	......	......	1	......	3

a Includes 1,446 cases in which there was no report on the character of the father.

Although the records in many instances failed to give information as to the character of the maternal grandparents, particularly when they were not living in the United States, or when they had died before the time of application, the information obtained was significant as indicating the minimum proportion of cases in which there were detrimental factors on that side of the child's heritage. A total of 359 children, or 16 per cent of the 2,178 whose records gave social information, were known to have had maternal grandparents one or both of whom were alcoholic, immoral, otherwise delinquent, or otherwise of poor character. The distribution of these 359 cases was as follows:

Total children, one or both of whose maternal grandparents were of poor character_____ 359

Alcoholic_____ 124
Immoral _____ 95
Other delinquent_____ 5
Alcoholic and immoral_____ 33
Alcoholic and other delinquent___ 9

Alcoholic, immoral, and other delinquent_____ 4
Immoral and other delinquent_ 5
Otherwise of poor character__ 84

Of the 2,178 children concerning whom social information was available, 825—38 per cent—had parents and maternal grandparents who were of good character, so far as known. The mothers, fathers, or maternal grandparents of 1,353 children—62 per cent—were alcoholic, immoral, otherwise delinquent, or of otherwise poor character. This 62 per cent must be regarded as a minimum, in view of the comparatively small amount of information available concerning the father and maternal grandparents.

```
        Total children under care whose histories gave social information   2, 178
Mother, father, and maternal grandparents of good character, so
  far as known_____   825
Mother, father, or maternal grandparents reported of poor character 1, 353
    Mother_____ 595
    Father _____  77
    One or both maternal grandparents_____  73
    Mother and father_____ 322
    Mother and one or both maternal grandparents_____ 201
    Father and one or both maternal grandparents_____  18
    Mother, father, and one or both maternal grandparents___  67
```

The most difficult situation to handle, as well as the most tragic from the possible hereditary or social effect upon the child, is found in the cases in which the father was a relative of the mother, either by blood or by marriage. This condition was known to exist in 40 cases—1.4 per cent of the 2,863 studied. Of these cases 16 were known to be cases of incest within the meaning of the Massachusetts law. Following are the cases of relationship between the father and the mother:

```
    Total_____ 40
Father_____  5 | Granduncle_____  1
Stepfather_____  3 | Brother-in-law _____  8
Brother_____  3 | First cousin_____ 10
Half brother_____  1 | Second cousin_____  2
Uncle_____  3 | Degree of relationship not
Step-grandfather_____  1 |   stated_____  3
```

Perhaps the majority of these mothers were the victims of the depraved morals of men who should have been their protectors. In 8 cases the mother was under 18 years of age at the time her child was born; in half the cases she was under 21. With the meager evidence at hand, one can only conjecture as to the vicious circle of low living conditions, abnormal mentality, and moral degeneracy that were the factors. There were 8 cases in which it was reported that the mother was below normal mentally. Situations such as these point the need for preventive and regenerative effort that strikes at the root of such economic conditions, housing, and standards of physical living as are conducive to immorality, as well as at the root of immorality itself.

Illustrations of defective mentality or bad character in the child's heritage.

The following cases are representative of a large number in which the family history indicated defective or degenerate stock or general lack of moral stamina:

Seventeen years before the period covered by this study a child was born to parents who had been married for a very brief period. The child's mother was very immoral, and when the little girl was 3 years old she was placed in charge of a public child-caring agency. After six months, however, she was returned to her home. Five years later her father deserted the family, the record stating that his desertion was due in part, at least, to the mother's misconduct. The mother was later arrested on a sex charge. She had been immoral with several men.

The girl was cared for by various agencies. At the age of 12 she was reported to be running wild and was adjudged neglected and placed in charge of a child-caring agency, the child-protective agency having general oversight of her and her younger brother. She was placed in a home where she said she had to work very hard, and where a man over 80 years of age took advantage of her. Later she and a 17-year-old boy had improper relations, and she was also reported to have been immoral with several others. When she was 15 years old complaint was made that she was a delinquent child, but the case was dismissed for technical reasons. Before her sixteenth birthday she gave birth to a child whose care was assumed by a private child-caring agency. The young mother was placed without the child. Soon she again became illegitimately pregnant. After a mental examination she was diagnosed feeble-minded and was sent to a public infirmary, where her second baby was born during the year covered by the study. The baby had syphilis and was kept at the infirmary with the mother throughout the year. Information subsequent to the period studied showed that the mother had been admitted to an institution for the feeble-minded, the child remaining at the infirmary throughout the first year of life. (Case V 1201.)

At the age of 5 years a little girl, who had been born at the State Infirmary, was abandoned at board by her mother and committed to the care of a public agency. She had been under care about two years at the time covered by the study, and was described as bright and attractive, though very deaf. The agency sent her to a school for the deaf, where she became a good lip reader and tried hard to overcome her handicap.

Both the child's maternal grandparents had been deaf and dumb. The grandmother died of tuberculosis; the grandfather was described as intemperate, a gambler, and a thief. One of the child's aunts had a record for stealing and another was a patient of an institution for the feeble-minded. The child's mother had been committed to the State industrial school at the age of 15 on a charge of stubbornness. At the age of 18 she had a child out of wedlock, who lived only 1 day. After the birth of the child of the study the mother was placed with the baby at housework; later she did home work for a leather factory. Nothing was known of her history subsequent to her abandonment of the child. (Case V 1921.)

During the year covered by the study a child was born out of wedlock to a feeble-minded mother 19 years of age. The mother had been under the guardianship of a private child-caring agency for four years. She had been received by this agency on the application of a family-care agency, because she was morally wayward and had gonorrheal infection. With her mother—the child's grand-mother—the girl had recently come to Boston from another Massachusetts city, where she had worked in a mill. As a child she had been immoral with boys. Later she had been delinquent with several men and was reported to have been a prostitute. She had reached the sixth grade in school. The maternal grand-mother was reported to be a woman of bad reputation; she was separated from the grandfather, who was living with a woman not his wife. A maternal aunt had given birth to a child out of wedlock.

The girl was placed in a boarding home by the agency which had undertaken her guardianship, and was later placed in a wage home. After a time she was sent to the State Infirmary for medical care, and was then placed at housework again, where she earned about $2 a week. She was described as good-natured, easily led, slovenly, untruthful, and slanderous about her employers. Before she had attained the age of 19 she became illegitimately pregnant and was sent to the State Infirmary for maternity care. Meanwhile she had been diagnosed feeble-minded, and application had been made for her admission to an institution for the feeble-minded after the birth of her child. The alleged father of the child, a teamster, was prosecuted and convicted, but the case was appealed and it was reported that a lump-sum payment was finally made.

The child was born at the infirmary, and after a time application was made to the State child-caring agency asking that the child be received, since the mother was awaiting admission to an institution for the feeble-minded. How-ever, the mother grew so fond of her child that she was most unwilling to give it up, and the child and mother were kept together at the infirmary throughout the year covered by the study. Subsequent information showed that the mother was committed to the institution for the feeble-minded, but was so reluctant to give up the baby that they were placed together in a boarding home, and finally a plan was arranged whereby they were both to be sent to a maternal aunt in another State. (Case V 765.)

The information as to the fathers of the children studied was in most cases so meager that it is impossible to present illustrations of defective heritage without overemphasizing maternal traits and giving little mention of paternal. However, the case here presented—that of a 7-year-old boy under care of the child-protective agency—shows bad heredity on both sides of the family.

The boy's maternal grandmother was described as uncertain and rambling in her statements. She owned her own home and had a small canvassing business. She was said to be a disreputable woman, always in trouble. She had divorced her husband years before, the boy's mother having been the only child of this marriage. Subsequently she had had at least one child out of wedlock—according to some statements, three or four. When the mother was 24 years old the grandmother married a man who had worked for her as a hostler for a year. After living with him for two years she found that he had another wife and three children; she left him and petitioned for a divorce, but he had disappeared and could not be found. Before long he induced the woman's daughter—the mother of the child of the record—to live with him in another State as his wife. Four children were born to them, three of whom died; the fourth child was the boy here described. When the boy was nearly 3 years old the father instituted divorce proceedings against the boy's maternal grandmother. He stated that he had lived with the grandmother only because of her money, and that when she transferred some of it to her daughter he had lived with the latter for the same reason. The man went under several dif-ferent aliases.

The boy lived with his mother until her death, the year before application was made to the child-protective agency. He then was cared for by his father's brother. The maternal grandmother was not satisfied with the arrangement and petitioned for guardianship of the child. She did not succeed in attaining this end, and the child lived for a time with his father and then returned to his paternal uncle, the agency giving supervision. (Case V 2104.)

Shortly before her second birthday a little girl whose mother had just been committed to an institution for the feeble-minded was received for care by the public child-caring agency of the city. The child had been born at the public infirmary, and mother and baby had later been cared for by a private agency. The child was placed at board and died of a contagious disease during the year covered by the study.

The mother's family had been known to social agencies for more than 20 years. The maternal grandmother had a court record for intemperance. She had spent a year in a reformatory for women and had subsequently served a sentence for keeping a disorderly house. She died at a public infirmary when the mother was 17 years old. Her death was said to be due to venereal disease and alcoholism. The maternal grandfather had served several sentences for larceny and intemperance. At the age of 10 the mother had been adjudged neglected and placed in the care of a private agency. From that time on she spent most of her life in institutions. She was tried in many different homes, but her conduct was never satisfactory. She spent six years in an institution for wayward girls, was finally placed out, and became illegitimately pregnant with the child whose history is given above. (Case V 270.)

During the year covered by the study twin sisters of illegitimate birth, 19 years of age, and their children, also born out of wedlock, were under the care of the child-protective agency. The mother of the girls had married after their birth, and the twin sisters had been brought up by their mother and stepfather in a home of very low standard. At the time the girls came under the care of the child-protective agency their mother had been arrested for drunkenness on complaint of their stepfather, who was under the influence of liquor when he appeared in court. The mother had intended to secure a warrant against her husband for assault and battery, when he anticipated this action by securing a warrant against her for drunkenness. Subsequently they were evicted from their home for drunkenness, and later the mother was arrested and placed on probation for six months.

At the age of 16 or 17 one of the twins had a child out of wedlock. The baby was cared for by the maternal grandmother, and was reported to be clean and healthy. Later an aunt took the child for a few months, the grandmother paying board, but within a few months the baby was returned to her grandmother. After the child's birth the mother, who had lived at home all her life, secured a position at housework in a near-by town. She was very immoral, finally becoming a professional prostitute.

The other twin was her sister's companion in wrongdoing and was reported to be intemperate and a frequenter of disreputable places. She had two children out of wedlock—the first when she was 18 years old. The father of both children was a peddler. The mother frequently quarreled with him, and shortly after the birth of the second child he disappeared and did not return. When the first child was 3 months old, the mother abandoned her at board and was arrested for abandonment and neglect. The child was placed under care of a private child-caring agency and died at the age of 8 months. When the second child was 2 months old the mother was arrested for drunkenness and was put on probation. She had been immoral with several men, and it was reported that she had left the child with neighbors for days at a time. An alienist examined her and pronounced her subnormal mentally, reporting that her chief characteristics were slowness of mental processes and a high degree of suggestibility. The child was only 3 months old at the close of the period studied. She was subsequently abandoned at board by her mother and was placed in the custody of a private child-caring agency. (Cases V 2865, 2866, 2867.)

The Possibilities of Care by the Parents.

Physical and mental condition and character of the parents.

Among the most important considerations that determine the ability of mothers of children out of wedlock to maintain themselves and their children are their physical condition and their mentality, for the mother's mental and physical fitness and ability to care for her child, as well as her earning capacity, are largely dependent upon these factors. They must be taken into account by any social agency in planning what arrangements can best be made for the child's care and in deciding whether the mother and child are to be kept together or separated. During the child's infancy the primary need is for nursing care and, unless the mother's physical condition is such as to menace the child's health, other considerations may be waived for the sake of securing proper nourishment for the infant. Many mothers whose disabilities make them unfit to care for their children as they grow older, may safely be kept with them during the nursing period, if given supervision and financial assistance.

The mothers of 22 per cent of the 2,178 children whose histories gave more or less complete social information were known to be physically defective or diseased or in such poor physical condition as to be handicapped in caring for their children. The mothers of 3 per cent had died before the applications for the care of the children were made. Children whose mothers had been diagnosed as having syphilis or gonorrhea comprised 6 per cent of the total.[9]

The mothers of 379 of the 2,178 children—17 per cent—were below normal mentally. In 7 per cent of the cases the mother was feeble-minded or insane.[10]

The physical and mental condition of the father is of interest in connection with the possibility of his contributing to the child's support. However, no information as to his physical condition was available and very little as to mentality. The fathers of 16 children were reported below normal mentally, in 7 cases being feeble-minded or insane.[11] The fathers of 51 children—2 per cent—were known to have died before the applications were made.

The mothers of 54 per cent of the children were reported as alcoholic, immoral, dishonest, stubborn, shiftless, lazy, or otherwise of

---

[9] See pp. 192–193.   [10] See pp. 193–195.   [11] See pp. 192–194.

poor character.[12] The difficulties met with by the social agencies in attempting to secure the mother's cooperation and realization of her responsibilities are manifest. In many cases the character of the mother made it unsafe for the child to be kept with her, at least after the period of infancy.

The fathers of 484 of the 2,178 children—22 per cent—were known to be alcoholic, immoral, otherwise delinquent, or otherwise of poor character. That this is an understatement is indicated by the fact that in two-thirds of the cases in which information as to the father's character was obtained, it was reported as bad. The fathers of 206 children were known to have absconded in order to escape their responsibilities toward their children.[13]

Age of mother and of father.

Reports as to the age of the mother when the child was born were obtained for 1,923 of the 2,863 children under care of agencies in the year studied. The age distribution was as follows:

Total reported_____ 1,923	
Less than 16 years_____ 44	21–24 years _____ 590
16–17 years _____ 174	25–34 years _____ 505
18–20 years_____ 496	35 years and over_____ 114

The mothers of 2 per cent of the children were under 16, the age of consent, when the children were born.[14] The mothers of 9 per cent more were under 18 years of age. These young mothers, who were but children themselves, could with the greatest difficulty assume the burdens that maternity laid upon them and were in particular need of assistance in providing care and support for their children. The mothers of 26 per cent were from 18 to 20 years of age, making a total of 37 per cent of the children whose mothers were under the age of 21 years. In almost a third of the cases—31 per cent—the mothers were from 21 to 24 years old.

In 26 per cent of the cases, the mothers were from 25 to 34 years of age, while the mothers of 6 per cent of the children were 35 years of age or over. It is interesting to note that in more than three-fifths of the cases in which the mother was in the last age group, there had been no previous child born out of wedlock.[15]

In only 599 cases was the age of the father stated. Whether or not this number can be taken as representative of all the cases can only be conjectured. It is probable that the exact ages of the younger men would have been reported most frequently and that those of middle age would be represented to a lesser degree. The fathers of 275 children—46 per cent of those whose histories gave this information—were under 25 years at the time the child was born. In 19 cases

---

[12] See p. 221.   [13] See p. 110.   [14] See p. 198.   [15] See p. 197.

the fathers were under 18 years of age, and in 80 others, between 18 and 20 years; the fathers of 17 per cent of all reported being under the age of legal majority when they became fathers of children out of wedlock.

The age group of 21 to 24 years shows the largest number of fathers, the next largest number being in the age group of 25 to 29 years. The fathers of slightly over half of all whose histories were reported were from 21 to 30 years old. The fathers of 18 children were over 50 years of age, in 7 cases being 60 years of age or over.

A comparison of the age of the mother and the age of the father is of interest in the 578 cases in which the ages of both were reported. Table 62 gives this information.

TABLE 62.—*Age of mother and of father.*

Age of mother at birth of child.	Children born out of wedlock, under care in 1914, with age of mother and of father reported.										
	To-tal.[a]	Whose fathers were of specified ages.									
		Un-der 18 yrs.	18–20 yrs.	21–24 yrs.	25–29 yrs.	30–34 yrs.	35–39 yrs.	40–49 yrs.	50–59 yrs.	60–69 yrs.	70 yrs. or over.
Total............	578	19	77	170	128	62	52	53	11	5	1
Under 18 years........	77	11	22	22	9	3	3	1	2	3	1
18–20 years.............	152	4	42	62	23	8	6	6	1	......	......
21–24 years.............	190	3	9	70	62	18	11	16	......	1	......
25–29 years.............	88	1	4	10	31	14	19	7	2	......	......
30–34 years.............	37	......	......	1	2	16	7	9	2	......	......
35–39 years.............	24	......	......	3	......	3	4	11	2	1	......
40 years and over......	10	......	......	2	1	......	2	3	2	......	......

[a] Excluding 21 cases in which the age of the mother was not reported. In 3 of these cases the father was 18–20 years of age; in 6, 21–24; in 8, 25–29; in 2, 30–34; in 1, 35–39; in 1, 60–69.

In almost three-fifths of the cases in which the fathers were reported as between 21 and 29 years the mothers were also in these age groups. This points to a normal condition, the opposite of that indicated by the cases where there was great disparity of ages. Among the abnormal cases are 4 in which the fathers were under 18 years, 3 of the mothers being between 21 and 24 years, and 1 among those 25 to 29 years of age. In 14 cases the fathers were over 40 and the mothers under 20. The fathers of 5 children were between 21 and 24 years of age, 3 of the mothers being from 35 to 39 years, and 2 being over 40 years. Great disparity of ages occurred in 10 cases in which the mothers were under 18—3 of the fathers were between 35 and 39, 1 between 40 and 49, 2 between 50 and 59, 3 between 60 and 69, and 1 was over 70 years old.

The mothers of 40 per cent of the children whose histories gave this information were under 21 years of age. In 17 per cent of the cases in which this information was available the fathers were under 21. It was unlikely that in any considerable number of cases these mothers and fathers who were under the age of majority would be able to meet fully the responsibilities of caring for or contributing to the support of the children.

Civil condition of mother and of father and their relation to each other.

The problem of the child of illegitimate birth is by no means confined to the child of the unmarried mother. The histories of 2,352 children gave information concerning the civil status of the mother at the time of the child's birth. In 85 per cent of these cases the mothers were single. The mothers of 4 per cent were widowed, while in 9 per cent of the cases the mothers were divorced, separated from their husbands, had been deserted, or had themselves deserted their families. The mothers of 2 per cent of the children were married women. In many of the cases in which the mother had been married she had children born in wedlock to care for. The civil status of the mothers at the time the children were born was as follows:

```
Total reported_____ 2,352
Single _____ 2,010 | Divorced,  separated,  de-
Married _____    39  |   serting, or deserted_____ 206
Widowed _____     97  |
```

The problem of the unmarried mother is not limited to the young woman. The mother's age, reported in 1,595 of the 2,010 cases in which she was single at the time of the child's birth, is summarized in Table 63. In 74 per cent of these cases the mother was under 25 years of age, while in 26 per cent she was 25 or over. On the other hand, in 30 per cent of the 250 cases where the mother was married, widowed, divorced, separated, deserting, or deserted, and her age was reported, she was under 25 years. In 3 per cent of the cases in which the mother was single she was 35 years of age or over, as compared with 25 per cent of the cases in which the mother had been married.

TABLE 63.—*Age and civil status of mother.*

Mother's age at birth of child.	Children born out of wedlock, under care in 1914, with age of mother reported.						
			Whose mothers were of specified civil status.				
	Total.		Single.		Married, widowed, divorced, separated, deserting, deserted.		Not reported.
	Number.	Per cent distribution.	Number.	Per cent distribution.	Number.	Per cent distribution.	Number.
Total...................	1,923	100.0	1,595	100.0	250	100.0	78
Under 25 years...............	1,304	67.8	1,186	74.3	74	29.6	44
25–34 years...............	505	26.3	360	22.6	114	45.6	31
35 years and over...............	114	5.9	49	3.1	62	24.8	3

The civil condition of the father was known in only 785 cases. The fathers of 453 children were reported as being single at the time the children were born; in 43 cases the father was widowed, in 99 divorced, separated, deserting, or deserted. In 190 cases the father was living with his legal wife at the time he became the father of a child out of wedlock. Many of these may be presumed to have had children as well as wives dependent upon them for support. Assuming that at least half those in the "widowed, divorced, separated, deserting, deserted" categories also had legal obligations to families, the fathers of about one-third of the children whose histories gave the civil status of the father were presumably responsible for the support of another family in addition to their obligations for the maintenance of their children out of wedlock. However, this proportion might not have held for the total number of cases had the civil condition of all the fathers been reported. Including as single all those whose civil condition was not known, the proportion of children whose fathers had legal families would be about one-tenth of the total. The true proportion of cases in which the fathers had responsibilities for legitimate families, therefore, probably lies somewhere between one-tenth and one-third of the total, 2,863, included in this study. This is an important consideration in connection with the possibility of securing support from the fathers for their children born out of wedlock.

The civil status of the mother and the character of her relations with the father are given in Table 64. The mothers of 251 children— 12 per cent of the 2,178 whose histories gave social information— were illegally married to the fathers or had been living with them as married prior to the time when the children were born. In most of the 28 cases in which a marriage ceremony had been illegally performed some impediment to marriage existed, the father having a wife living, or, in a few cases, the mother having a husband from whom she was not divorced. In some instances the ceremony was illegal because performed by a person not authorized under the law.

TABLE 64.—*Civil status of mother and character of relations with father.*

Civil status of mother at birth of child.	Children born out of wedlock, under care in 1914, whose histories gave social information.			
	Total.	The relations of whose mothers with the fathers were of specified character.		
		Illegally married.	Living as married.	Other.
Total	2,178	28	223	1,927
Single	1,687	22	144	1,521
Married	36			36
Widowed	94		17	77
Divorced, separated, deserted	205	5	60	140
Not reported	156	1	2	153

In almost 10 per cent of the cases in which the mother was single, she and the father were living as married or were illegally married previous to the birth of the child. Of the cases in which the mother was widowed, there were 18 per cent in which the parents were living as married. Of the cases in which the mother was divorced, separated, or deserted, there were 32 per cent in which the parents were living as married or were illegally married.

Table 65 shows that the mothers of 391 of the 2,178 children whose histories gave more or less complete social information had married at some time subsequent to the child's birth. The children were of varying ages when the marriage of the mother occurred. In two-fifths of these cases the mother was known to have married the child's father; but this proportion is probably an understatement, because in many cases where paternity was not known it was uncertain whether or not the man whom the mother married was the father of the child. It is certain, however, that a large proportion of the marriages were to men who were not the fathers of the children.

TABLE 65.—*Subsequent marriage of mother, by character of relations with father.*

Character of relations with father of child.	Children born out of wedlock, under care in 1914, whose histories gave social information.			
	Total.	Whose mothers married after birth of child.		Whose mothers were not reported to have married after birth of child.
		Child's father.	Other man.	
Total..	2,178	160	231	1,787
Illegally married.......................................	28	2	5	21
Living as married......................................	223	53	33	137
Other...	1,927	105	a193	1,629

a Some of these men may have been the fathers, the paternity of the children not being stated on the record.

In one-fourth of the cases in which the parents were illegally married prior to the child's birth, the mother subsequently married legally. In 2 instances she married the father of the child, the obstacles in the way of legal marriage having been removed; in 5 cases she married another man. In almost two-fifths of the cases in which the parents had been living as married, the mother was known to have married after the child was born. Of these 86 cases of subsequent marriage, there were 53 in which the mother married the father of her child and 33 in which she married another man. In only 15 per cent of the cases in which the parents were not known to have been illegally married or living as married was there a record of subsequent marriage of the mother. Of these 298 cases, there were 105 in which the mother was known to have married the father.

Occupation of mother.

The economic status of the mother is of great importance in connection with the need for assistance by agencies in caring for the children. Occupation as given in the records was the only available index of the mother's economic condition. It is evident that the information here given is only a rough approximation of economic status, because of the failure of the records in most cases to report specific employments within the industries and the wages earned. For instance, the wages vary greatly for different types of employment in factories and stores. The data here analyzed pertain to the occupation at the time of application for agency care and not to the occupation before the child's birth, the purpose here being to show the mother's economic condition at the time recourse to agencies was necessary. In cases in which the mother had temporarily ceased work on account of her condition, her usual occupation was given. It would have been impossible to secure any but fragmentary data on the mother's occupation before the birth of the child, since in many cases several years had elapsed between the time of the child's birth and the time of application.

Reports as to the occupation of the mother were obtained in 1,916 of the 2,863 cases studied. Of the remaining 947 cases, there were 75 in which the mother was dead and 872 in which the occupation was not stated. In the cases of 424 children—22 per cent of those for whom the mother's occupation was reported—it was stated that the mother was not gainfully employed at the time application was made for the care of the child. In 38 of the cases—2 per cent of the total—the mother was still in school, and in 289 cases—15 per cent— she was a housewife. In 97 cases—5 per cent—the mother was reported as having no occupation. In 9 cases in which she was a housewife, and in 36 in which she had no occupation, the mother was reported to be a prostitute.

The mothers of 1,492 children—78 per cent of the total reported— were gainfully employed. Their occupations were as follows:

```
        Total reported_____ 1, 492
Proprietors_____   32
Professional persons _____   29
    Actresses_____  15
    Teachers _____   7
    Other _____   7
Clerks and kindred workers_____  125
    Bookkeepers, cashiers, stenographers, and typewriters_____  29
    Clerks (not in stores)_____   9
    Saleswomen and clerks in stores_____  61
    Messenger, bundle, and office girls_____  13
    Telephone and telegraph operators_____  13
```

Semiskilled workers _____ 419
    Dressmakers and seamstresses _____ 24
    Laundry operatives _____ 30
    Nurses, not trained_____ 16
    Semiskilled factory operatives_____ 324
    Other _____ 16
Laborer (farm) _____ 1
Servants _____ 886
    Charwomen, cleaners, laundresses _____ 150
    Waitresses_ _____ 126
    Servants (domestic) _____ 565
    Other servants _____ 45

In 2 per cent of the cases in which the mother was gainfully employed she was classified as a proprietor or manager. In most of these cases she kept a lodging house or was the proprietor of a small store. In 2 per cent of the cases the mother was engaged in a professional pursuit. The mothers of 8 per cent of the children were engaged in clerical occupations as office workers, clerks or other employees in stores, or telephone or telegraph operators.

The mothers of 28 per cent of the children were semiskilled workers, chiefly factory operatives. In almost three-fifths of the cases—59 per cent in which the mother's occupation was reported—the mother was engaged in domestic or personal service. In this group domestic servants predominated, though there were considerable numbers of charwomen, cleaners, and laundresses, and of waitresses.

In 34 cases in which the mother was gainfully employed in a legitimate occupation she was also a prostitute. In 7 of these cases the mother was the proprietor of a lodging house or store; in 2, a clerk in a store; in 2, a seamstress; in 6, a semiskilled factory operative; in 1, a semiskilled worker not otherwise specified; in 5, a charwoman, cleaner, or laundress; in 4, a waitress; in 7, a domestic servant. Adding the 45 cases in which the mother was not otherwise employed, a total of 79 mothers were prostitutes at the time application was made for the care of the child.

One of the most significant bearings of occupation is its relation to the mother's ability to keep her child with her. Eliminating the cases in which the child was less than 6 months of age at the time of application, since these mothers would hardly have had time to re-establish themselves, and the cases in which it was not reported whether the child was with or away from the mother at the time of application, there was a total of 819 children 6 months of age and over the occupations of whose mothers were reported. (See Table 66.) It is probable that the occupation of the mother was more generally reported in the cases where the child was living with the mother than where the child was separated from the mother. Hence the percentages of children living apart from their mothers at the time of application are given, rather than the percentages with their mothers, since the former are very conservative statements. Forty-two per cent of the 819 children 6 months of age and over, the occupations of whose mothers were reported, had been separated from their mothers by the time application for agency care was made.

TABLE 66.—*Occupation of mother at time of application, and child's presence with or separation from mother.*

Occupation of mother at time of application.	Children born out of wedlock, under care in 1914, 6 months of age or over at application, with occupation of mother reported.		
		At time of application.	
	Total.a	With mother.	Separated from mother.
Total..	819	474	345
Not gainfully employed..	272	176	96
No occupation or attending school........................	53	26	27
Housewife..	219	150	69
Proprietors, managers, professional persons..................	42	25	17
Clerks and kindred workers..................................	27	11	16
Semiskilled workers...	116	61	55
Factory and laundry operatives...........................	97	55	42
Others..	19	6	13
Servants..	362	201	161
Charwomen, cleaners, laundresses.........................	117	96	21
Waitresses..	55	26	29
Domestic servants...	167	69	98
Other servants..	23	10	13

a Excluding 311 cases in which it was not reported whether the child was with or away from the mother, 75 cases in which the mother was dead at the time of application, and 1 case in which the child's age was not reported.

In 35 per cent of the cases in which the mother was not gainfully employed the child was living away from the mother at the time of application for care. In 47 per cent of the cases in which the mother was a semiskilled worker the child was separated from the mother. In the domestic and personal service group, 44 per cent of the children were separated from their mothers.

Considering separately the most important occupations, 32 per cent of the children whose mothers were housewives were separated from them; 43 per cent of those whose mothers were factory or laundry operatives; 18 per cent of the children whose mothers were charwomen, cleaners, and laundresses; and 59 per cent of those whose mothers were domestic servants. The children were with the mothers most frequently in the cases in which the mother was a housewife or a day worker employed as a charwoman, cleaner, or laundress. Most of these mothers were maintaining homes, many of them being married, widowed, or separated, or living as married. It is surprising to find that practically three-fifths of the children whose mothers were domestic servants had been separated from their mothers before the present application for agency care.

Economic status of father.

Occupations were reported for the fathers of 839 children. (See Table 67.) They are of significance mainly as an index of economic status, though in the absence of adequate wage data they are only a rough measure of the father's ability to contribute to the support of his child. An occupation was not listed separately unless the number reported as engaged therein was at least 10. Hence, only a few of the occupations included under each class appear.

TABLE 67.—*Occupation of father.*

Occupation of father.	Children born out of wedlock, under care in 1914, with occupation of father reported.	
	Number.	Per cent distribution.
Total..	839	100.0
Proprietors, officials, managers.....................	80	9.5
Professional persons................................	48	5.7
Clerks and kindred workers..........................	87	10.4
Commercial travelers..........................	20	....
Salesmen and clerks in stores.................	37	....
Others..	30	....
Skilled workers.....................................	180	21.5
Carpenters....................................	31	....
Electricians..................................	17	....
Machinists....................................	28	....
Painters......................................	22	....
Plumbers and steamfitters.....................	11	....
Tailors.......................................	12	....
Others..	59	....
Semiskilled workers.................................	193	23.0
Barbers.......................................	21	....
Chauffeurs....................................	28	....
Conductors (street railway)...................	19	....
Factory or mill operatives....................	66	....
Others..	59	....
Laborers..	110	13.1
Draymen, teamsters, expressmen................	37	....
Others..	73	....
Servants..	84	10.0
Cooks...	26	....
Janitors and housemen.........................	11	....
Porters (railroad and hotel)..................	10	....
Waiters.......................................	17	....
Others..	20	....
Semiofficial public employees.......................	36	4.3
Soldiers, sailors, marines....................	32	....
Others..	4	....
Not gainfully employed..............................	21	2.5
Students......................................	20	....
Others..	1	....

In the 10 per cent of the cases in which the father was classified as a " proprietor, official, or manager," he was usually a storekeeper or small dealer, peddler, or farmer. In a few instances the father was a manufacturer or contractor. It is probable that there were only a small number of cases of large incomes.

In 6 per cent of the reported cases, the father was engaged in a professional pursuit. The fathers of one-third of the 48 in this group were engaged in various forms of public entertainment. The fathers of one-fourth were lawyers, doctors, and in 1 case a clergyman. The fathers of the remaining 20 included journalists and newspaper men, teachers, photographers, and other miscellaneous workers.

The fathers of 10 per cent of the total reported were clerks and kindred workers. There were 87 in this group, the fathers of 20 children being commercial travelers. A large number in this class were salesmen and clerks in stores. The remainder included book-keepers and other office employees, shipping clerks, and miscellaneous workers.

In more than a fifth of the cases—21 per cent—the father was a skilled worker. This class included carpenters, electricians, machinists, plumbers and steamfitters, painters, tailors, and, in smaller numbers, engineers and firemen, printers, bricklayers, upholsterers, and workers in like employments.

The fathers of 23 per cent were semiskilled workers, the greatest number being factory and mill operatives. In a considerable number of cases the fathers were chauffeurs, conductors, and barbers. The remainder were in scattered occupations. The fathers of 13 per cent of the total were classified as laborers. In about one-third of these cases they were draymen, teamsters, or expressmen. The fathers of 10 per cent were classed as servants. In almost one-third of these cases they were cooks; in a considerable number they were waiters in restaurants or hotels; the remainder included janitors and housemen, porters, coachmen, bartenders, and elevator men.

In most of the 4 per cent of the cases in which the father was classed as a " semiofficial public employee " he was a soldier, sailor, or marine. Boston, as an important seaport, has always had a considerable number of men from the Army, Navy, and marine services stationed there. It must be remembered, however, that this study covered a period preceding the war.

In 3 per cent of the cases the father was not gainfully employed; in all but one of these cases he was a student. Although none of these fathers was earning anything at the time, some of them had sufficient training to enable them to earn good salaries in the future.

Combining those classified as " professional " and the " proprietors, officials, and managers," the fathers of 15 per cent of the 839 children were engaged in an independent business or in a profession. The fathers of 32 per cent were clerks and kindred workers, or skilled workers in various industries. In almost half the cases—46 per cent—the fathers were semiskilled workers, laborers, or servants. The soldiers, sailors, and marines, because of the small pay they received at the time this study was made, would in most cases have been able to contribute little to the support of their children. These fathers and the students, comprising altogether 6 per cent of the cases, probably represented those least able to assume their responsibilities.

Whether or not the earnings reported for the fathers of 209 of the children studied were representative of all can not be determined. It is probable, however, that the data must be considered as stating more completely the lower rather than the higher range. The information would presumably have been more available in the case of the younger men and for those of lower earning capacity than for older men and those commanding larger earnings.

Of the 209 cases in which information as to earnings was given, 29 reported earnings of $5 to $9 a week; 72, $10 to $14; 62, $15 to $19; 34, $20 to $29; and 12, $30 and over. In only 22 per cent of the cases were the fathers earning weekly $20 or more. In 30 per cent of the total the fathers earned from $15 to $19. At the time the study was made such earnings would have permitted a fairly adequate contribution to the child's support, provided that the father had no other dependents. In almost half the cases—48 per cent—the fathers earned less than $15 a week and were in no position to become responsible for the care of dependents.

Contributions of father to support of child.

In the cases of 758 children—35 per cent of the 2,178 whose histories gave social information—the records indicated that court action for support had been taken or that the father had contributed to the support of the child. Court action had been taken for the support of 241 of these children. In 517 cases no court action had been initiated, so far as known, but the father had made some contributions to the child's support. A discussion of the Massachusetts law relating to the support of children born out of wedlock, and of the cases brought under that law in the Boston courts, occurs in a later chapter.[16] Hence, only a brief summary of the results of court action is given here.

The 241 children whose records gave evidence of court action for support comprised 11 per cent of the 2,178 children for whom social information was available. It must be borne in mind that the present Massachusetts law relating to the support of children born out

---

[16] Sec. I ch. 3.

of wedlock, which is a great advance over the old law, did not go into effect until July 1, 1913. Of the 241 court cases, 39 ended without arrangements having been made for the support of the child. In 50 cases court action was pending at the end of the period. In the remaining 152 cases some provision was made for the child's support. Of the 39 cases in which no arrangement for support was made by the court, there were 5 in which the father had made some contributions to the support of the mother or child before the court action was initiated or after it terminated.

The results of court action were as follows:

```
Total children for whose benefit court action was initiated_____ 241
Parents married_____  21
Certificate of adequate provision filed_____  47
Court order for support_____  74
Sentence imposed_____   7
Payment for pregnancy and confinement expenses_____   3
No arrangement for support_____  39
Case pending at close of period_____  50
```

The fathers of 517 children made some payments for the child's support or for the mother's expenses, though no court action had been taken so far as known. In many of these cases the parents had been living as married following the child's birth, and it was assumed that the father had contributed to the family expenses. The manner in which the fathers aided in the support of the children was as follows:

```
Total children to whose support the fathers contributed, though no
    court action was taken_____ 517
Parents married each other_____ 122
Parents living as married, or illegally married [17]_____ 185
Father adopted child_____   4
Settlement by payment of lump sum_____  58
Regular contributions _____  43
Irregular contributions _____  85
Payment toward pregnancy and confinement expenses_____  20
```

In 122 instances the child was provided for by the marriage of the parents; the parents of 51 of these children had previously lived as married, and the fathers of 10 others had made some contributions toward the support of the children or the mothers. In a total of 185 cases the parents had been living as married at some time following the birth of the child, and the father had presumably contributed more or less to the child's support. In 1 of these cases and in 4 others the father legally adopted the child. The fathers of 58 children settled with the mothers by making lump-sum payments. In 43 cases there were regular contributions; and in 85, irregular pay-

---

[17] In addition there were 51 children whose parents later married, and who were included unde " parents married."

ments to the child's support. In 20 cases no payments were made for the support of the child, but the father assisted the mother in the payment of her expenses during pregnancy or confinement.

Considering together the court and noncourt cases, the fathers of 674 children—31 per cent of the 2,178 whose histories gave social information—were known to have aided in the support of the children or to have assisted the mother in meeting the expenses incurred by her during pregnancy or confinement. It must not be assumed, however, that the amounts contributed were in most cases at all adequate for the care of the child. Frequently, the support covered only a short period of time and amounted to such a small sum as to be practically negligible.

Mother's parental home and present mode of living.

The condition and character of the mother's family are of great importance in considering what arrangements can be made for the care of the child. The mother's parents, though often deeply resenting the humiliation which they considered the mother to have brought upon them, and, as a consequence, sometimes guilty of cruelty and injustice to the mother and her child, in a large number of cases furnished generous help and assistance. Although in only 11 per cent of the cases, in which home or place of residence was reported, were the children living with their maternal grandparents at the time of application,[18] yet it must be remembered that where the grandparents assume full responsibility the children do not usually come to the attention of social agencies.

It is interesting to note that the mothers of 54 children had themselves been born out of wedlock, and that in 8 of these cases the mothers had been brought up by foster parents. The mothers of 26 other children, though themselves of legitimate birth, had been brought up in foster homes.

Both maternal grandparents of 158 children—7 per cent of the 2,178 whose histories gave social information—were known to have died before the time of application for care. The maternal grandparents of 180 children—8 per cent—had never been in the United States. Therefore, in a total of 15 per cent of the cases there was no parental home, or none in this country, to which the mother might turn for assistance.

In 307 other cases—14 per cent—one of the grandparents had died. The maternal grandparents of 52 children, or 2 per cent, had been divorced or separated, or one of them had deserted.[19] Hence, the mothers of 31 per cent of all the children had, in effect, been deprived

---

[18] See p. 160.
[19] Not including 14 cases in which one of the grandparents was dead, having previously been divorced or separated.

of one or both parents, and consequently lacked the protection and help which might otherwise have been theirs. In addition to the cases in which the whereabouts of the maternal grandparents were definitely reported, there were others in which fragmentary information indicated that normal homes did not exist.

Besides the cases in which the maternal grandparents were dead, never in the United States, or separated or deserted, there were 212—10 per cent—in which the maternal grandparents were alcoholic, immoral, otherwise delinquent, shiftless, abusive or of otherwise poor character; insane, feeble-minded, or otherwise not normal mentally; or entirely or partially dependent upon charitable aid. Hence, in a total of 41 per cent of the cases studied in which social information was given, the child's mother had no normal parental home to which she could turn, or the character of the grandparents made it impossible for them to provide mother and child with a suitable home.

Total cases in which mother's parental home was reported not normal _____ 909
Both maternal grandparents dead_____ 158
Maternal grandparents never in the United States_____ 180
One maternal grandparent dead_____ 307
Maternal grandparents divorced, separated, or deserted_____ 52
One or both maternal grandparents not normal mentally, of poor character, or dependent upon charitable aid_____ 212

Besides the cases in which the maternal grandparents were of low mentality or poor character, there were a number of cases in which the brothers and sisters of the mother were reported as feeble-minded, insane, alcoholic, immoral, otherwise delinquent, or generally unsatisfactory as to conduct. If these members of the family were living in the mother's parental home, the home conditions were thereby rendered more or less unsatisfactory, and the maternal grandparents were less able to assist the mother with the care of her child. Since the information in regard to mother's fraternity was very fragmentary in character, no attempt has been made to present these data in detail.

The conditions under which the mother lived at the time of application for agency care for the child—whether or not she was dependent on her own resources or was living with relatives or friends—had an important bearing upon the amount and kind of assistance which had to be provided. In this study her usual mode of living was considered of more significance than her residence on the day the application was made. In many cases the mother had recently left her ordinary place of abode and had come to the city for the purpose of securing hospital care or other assistance from social agencies. In these cases the home which she had left was considered her mode of living.

Information concerning mode of living was obtained for the mothers of 1,656 children, and this is summarized in Table 68. At the time application was made for the care of the child, the mothers of 389 children—24 per cent—were living in their parental homes, and the mothers of 109, or 7 per cent, were in the homes of relatives or friends. In 486 cases—29 per cent—the mother had been established in a home of her own, having been married or living as married. Other establishments of their own were being maintained by the mothers of 56, or 3 per cent. In most of these cases the mother was doing light housekeeping. In only 83 cases—5 per cent—was the mother boarding. The mothers of 20 children—or 1 per cent—were inmates of institutions at the time of application. In the largest number of cases in any one group—513, or 31 per cent—the mother was living in her place of employment, in 481 cases being employed at housework, and in 32 working in a hotel, a hospital, or a similar place.

TABLE 68.—*Mother's age and mode of living at time of application.*

Mother's mode of living at time of application.	Children born out of wedlock, under care in 1914, with mother's mode of living reported.						
	Total.	Whose mothers were of specified ages at time of application.					
		Under 18 yrs.	18-20 yrs.	21-24 yrs.	25-34 yrs.	35 yrs. and over.	Not reported.
Total	1,656	122	270	384	416	181	283
Parental home	389	84	124	95	44	12	30
Home of relatives or friends	109	12	35	26	26	4	6
Own home	486	3	15	37	138	118	155
Other establishment a	56		2	1	19	16	18
Boarding	83	1	15	29	21	5	12
Institution	20	3	2	3	8	2	2
At housework	481	19	75	160	148	23	56
Place of employment other than at housework	32		2	13	12	1	4

a Includes independent lodging, etc.

At the time application was made for aid the mothers of 122 children were under 18 years of age. In more than two-thirds of these cases the mother was living in her parental home. Adding to this number the 12 cases in which she was living with relatives or friends, in more than three-fourths of the cases in which the mother was under 18 years of age she had the protection of her family or of relatives or friends. In 3 cases the mother was established in a home of her own.

In 159, or almost three-fifths of the 270 cases in which the mother was 18 to 20 years of age, she was living in her parental home or with relatives or friends. In more than a fourth—77 cases—she was living at her place of employment, mostly at housework. In 17 cases the mother was living in a home of her own or in another independent establishment.

In the older age groups the proportions living in their parental homes or with relatives or friends naturally decreased, while the proportionate numbers living in their own homes increased. In the 21-to-24-year group the mothers of about one-third of the children were living with their parents or with other relatives or friends; in the 25-to-34-year group the mothers of about one-sixth were so living; in the age group 35 years and over, less than one-tenth. The proportions living in their own homes or in other independent establishments rose from about one-tenth in the lowest of these age groups to three-fourths in the highest. The proportion in domestic service or living in other places of employment was by far the largest in the age group of 21 to 24 years. In more than two-fifths of these cases the mother was living in this way, while in the age group of 25 to 34 years she was thus living in slightly less than two-fifths of the cases, and in the age group of 35 years and over in slightly more than one-eighth.

Mother's other children.

The problems involved in the care of the child born out of wedlock are greatly complicated if the mother has had more than one child of illegitimate birth. It is more difficult for her to secure the assistance needed for the child if she is known to be a " repeater," since certain types of agencies make it a rule to refuse care to such mothers. It is almost impossible for a mother to keep with her more than one child born out of wedlock, if she is at all dependent upon her own resources. Social agencies in arranging for the care of illegitimate families very rarely find it possible to keep more than one child with the mother.

In 2,178 cases more or less social data, including histories of previous children, were obtained by the agencies at the time application for the care of the child was made. If the child was cared for apart from the mother, the mother was often lost sight of; hence it was impossible to determine whether or not she had had subsequent children. On the other hand, where more than one child of the same mother was under care of the agencies studied, the records of the various children were assembled. In this way it was known that the mother had given birth to more than one child in many cases in which social information was not given. It was, therefore, thought best to use all the information secured, from whatever source, and accept it as an understatement of the number of other children born to the mothers of the children studied. The known data on other children previously born out of wedlock to the mothers of the study are given in Table 69.

In 535 cases—19 per cent of the 2,863 children studied—the mother was known to have had one or more previous illegitimate births.[20] In 374 cases—13 per cent—the mother had had such births[21] after the child of the study was born. In 168 of these cases—6 per cent of the total—the mother had both previous and subsequent births. Hence, the mothers of 741 children, or 26 per cent of all, were known to have had other illegitimate births.

In 341 cases the mother had had one previous illegitimate birth; in 125, two; in 34, three; in 20, four; in 15, five or more. Thus the mothers of 194 children—7 per cent of all—were known to have had more than one other previous birth out of wedlock.

In 4 per cent of the cases in which the mother was under 18 years of age at the birth of the child of the study, there had been a previous illegitimate birth. In the age group of 18 to 20 years the percentage was 11; in the age group of 21 to 24 years, 20; in the age group of 25 to 34 years, 35; and in the age group of 35 years and over the mother had had a previous birth out of wedlock in 38 per cent of the cases.

TABLE 69.—*Age of mother at birth of child, and previous record as to illegitimate births.*

Age of mother at birth of child.	Children born out of wedlock, under care in 1914.						
	Total.	Whose mothers had specified number of previous illegitimate births.					
		None, so far as known.	One.	Two.	Three.	Four.	Five or more.
Total....................	2,863	2,328	341	125	34	20	15
Less than 18 years..............	218	209	9	....	....	....	....
18–20 years....................	496	443	49	3	1	....	....
21–24 years....................	590	470	91	25	3	1	....
25–34 years...................	505	328	101	50	12	6	8
35 years and over..............	114	71	15	12	5	6	5
Not reported..................	940	807	76	35	13	7	2

In regard to subsequent children the data may be considered still more of an understatement than in the case of previous children, on account of the large number of mothers lost sight of after the care of the children had been assumed by agencies. In a total of 374 cases, there were reported one or more births out of wedlock[22] after the one included in this study. The proportion of children whose mothers had had subsequent illegitimate births means little unless

---

[20] Counting twins as 1 and including stillbirths.

[21] Counting twins as 1; including stillbirths but not including cases in which the mother was illegitimately pregnant in 1914, but a child was not born until 1915.

[22] Counting twins as 1; including stillbirths but not including cases in which the mother was illegitimately pregnant in 1914, but a child was not born until 1915.

taken in connection with the age of the child of the record at the end of the period or the close of care.   (See Table 70.)

TABLE 70.—*Record of mother as to subsequent illegitimate births, and age of child at end of period.*

Age of child at end of period.	Children born out of wedlock, under care in 1914.					
	Total.	Whose mothers had specified numbers of subsequent illegitimate births.				
		None, so far as known.	One.	Two.	Three.	Four or more.
Total...............................	2,863	a2,489	b239	c79	30	d26
Less than 1 year.....................	1,045	1,043	2	....	....	....
1 year...............................	365	344	21	....	....	....
2–3 years............................	319	258	55	6	....	....
4–5 years............................	215	161	37	17	....	....
6 years and over.....................	911	675	124	56	30	26
Not reported.........................	8	8	....	....	....	....

a Including 22 cases in which the mother was illegitimately pregnant before the end of the year or the close of the case, but in which the child had not been yet born.
b Including 5 cases in which the mother was also illegitimately pregnant before the end of the year or the close of the case.
c Including 2 cases in which the mother was also illegitimately pregnant before the end of the year or the close of the case.
d Including 16 cases of 4 subsequent, 7 of 5 subsequent, 2 of 6 subsequent, 1 of 7 subsequent illegitimate births.

In 1,045 cases the child of the study was less than 1 year of age, but even among these cases there were 2 in which there had been a subsequent illegitimate birth. Of the 365 cases in which the child of the study was 1 year of age at the end of the period or the close of care, 1 subsequent birth was reported in 21 cases—6 per cent. Of the 319 cases in which the child of the study was 2 or 3 years of age, 1 subsequent birth was reported in 55, or 17 per cent; and 2 subsequent births in 6, or 2 per cent. Of the 215 cases in which the child was 4 or 5 years of age, 1 subsequent birth was reported in 37, or 17 per cent; and 2 in 17, or 8 per cent. Of the 911 cases in which the child was 6 years of age or over, 1 subsequent birth was reported in 124, or 14 per cent; 2 in 56, or 6 per cent; 3 in 30, or 3 per cent; and 4 or more in 26, or 3 per cent.

In a total of 741 cases the mothers were known to have had other illegitimate births. The paternity was reported in 526 cases. Table 71 gives the data concerning paternity.

TABLE 71.—*Paternity of mother's other children born out of wedlock.*

Number of other children mother had out of wedlock.a	Children born out of wedlock, under care of agencies in 1914, whose mothers had other children out of wedlock whose paternity was known.					
	Total.	Paternity of other children same as that of child of record.	Paternity of one or more of other children different from that of child of record.			
			Total.	One other father.	Two other fathers.	Three or more other fathers.
Total............................	526	227	299	235	50	14
One other........................	225	85	140	140	....	....
Two others.......................	154	73	81	44	37	....
Three others.....................	54	23	31	11	8	12
Four others......................	46	25	21	15	4	2
Five or more others..............	47	21	26	25	1	....

a Counting twins as 1; including stillbirths but not including pregnacies not terminating until 1915.

In 227 of the 526 cases in which the paternity was known, the father of the child of record was also the father of the other child or children. In 299 cases there were different fathers. In more than three-fifths of the cases where one other child was known to have been born to the mother out of wedlock, there were different fathers. Where there were two other children, the paternity was different in slightly more than half the cases; in almost one-fourth of these cases each of the three children had a different father. In almost three-fifths of the cases where the mother had had three other children out of wedlock, the paternity of one or more of the children was different from that of the child of the record. In more than one-fifth of these cases there were at least three other fathers.

In over half the cases in which the mother had had four other children, the paternity was the same as that of the child of record; the proportionate number of cases in which there were three or more other fathers was much smaller than in the previous group. There were 47 cases in which the mother had had five or more other children out of wedlock; in 21 of these cases the paternity of all the children was the same; in 25 cases there was one other, and in 1 case there were two other fathers. In most of the cases in which several children had the same father the parents were illegally living as married.

The mothers of 373 of the children under care—13 per cent—had had children born in wedlock.[23] In half these cases there was one such child, in almost one-third there were two or three, and in almost one-fifth four or more children of legitimate birth. In 39 per cent of the cases in which there were children born in wedlock, one or

[23] Counting twins as 2; exclusive of stillbirths and pregnancies not terminating until 1915.

more of these children were under the care of the agencies studied during the year.

The characteristics of the brothers and sisters of the children included in this study are of especial interest as showing the prevalence of abnormal mentality, delinquent tendencies, and neglect or other conditions that made them dependent on agencies for care and support. The mothers of 920 of the children studied were reported to have had other children of legitimate or illegitimate birth.[24] In 2 cases one of the other children was insane, in 15 cases one or more had been diagnosed feeble-minded, and in 2 of these cases there was also delinquency among the brothers and sisters. In 30 additional cases one or more had been delinquent.

A considerable amount of dependency and neglect existed among the brothers and sisters of the children studied. In 387 cases dependency was reported; and in 252 neglect, or neglect and dependency. Hence, in a total of 639 cases one or more of the fraternity at one time or another had been dependent upon social agencies by reason of the inability of their relatives to care for them properly.

Mother's agency record.

As a test of the ability of the mothers to meet the difficulties involved in providing for themselves and their children, an analysis was made of the extent to which they themselves had been found in need of care by agencies and institutions before they were brought to the attention of social agencies because of this child. Assistance given to the mother's parents or her family was excluded, as was also care given to other children of the mother. The data secured gave a total of 496 children whose mothers had been under the care of agencies or institutions—23 per cent of the 2,178 whose histories gave social information.

In the greatest number of cases the mother had been an inmate of a correctional institution—198, or 9 per cent of all the cases in which social information was secured. In almost half these cases the mother had also received care from other agencies, in 19 cases having been a ward of a child-caring agency, and in most of the others having been on probation or having had a court record.

The mothers of 86 children—4 per cent—had been on probation. In 41 of these cases the mother had also been an inmate of a correctional institution and in 5 other instances she had received care from agencies of other types. Court records not involving probation or commitment to a correctional institution, though in some instances including short-term commitments to a jail, were reported in 133

---

[24] Counting twins as 2; exclusive of stillbirths and pregnancies not terminating until 1915.

cases—6 per cent. In 80 cases there had been no other type of agency care; in 16 of the court cases there were also probation records or commitments to correctional institutions. In many instances the mother had been before the courts repeatedly. Eliminating duplications involved in more than one type of care being given the same mother, the mothers of 330 children—15 per cent of the cases in which social information was secured—were reported as having court records, some involving commitments or probation and others having different dispositions. This proportion of more than one-seventh is high, considering that no special effort was made to check up the histories of the mothers with court records, and that the sources of the information were the records of agencies dealing with the children.

The mothers of 243 of the children included in the study—11 per cent of the total—had been under care of correctional institutions or on probation from courts; in 84 cases this provision resulted from the offense connected with illegitimate pregnancy. In 13 of these 84 cases the mother had also been under care formerly, and in 6 she subsequently came under care again. In 40 cases the mother had been discharged from correctional care before pregnancy began and had not subsequently come under care. It is interesting to note that in 19 cases the mother became illegitimately pregnant while on probation or parole; in 3 of these 19 cases she had also been under care previously, and in 3 she later came under care again.

The mothers of 89 children had been provided for by child-caring agencies, and of 36 more by child-caring agencies and also by other agencies. Hence the mothers of 6 per cent of the 2,178 children whose histories gave social information had themselves been wards of child-caring societies. By the term " ward " is here meant a child under 21 years receiving prolonged care.

The mothers of 94 children—4 per cent—had been under care of agencies of other types than those specified above. These agencies included almshouses, public infirmaries, and institutions for physical and mental defectives. In 25 of these cases they had also been cared for by the agencies specified above.

In the majority of cases—95 of the 125 in which the mother had been a ward of a child-caring agency—she had been discharged from care previous to the time when she became pregnant with the child of the study. The mothers of 15 children were wards of such societies at the time pregnancy began. In 14 cases the care of the young girl was assumed after pregnancy had begun, in 10 of these instances because of need arising from that situation. In 5 of these 14 cases the mother had also been under care at some former time. In 1 instance the time when the mother had been under care was not reported.

Illustrative cases.

The following cases illustrate some of the conditions making it difficult for the mother to care for the child unaided or to obtain the assistance of relatives:

The youth of the parents and the unwillingness of the mother's family to aid her in caring for the child made it impossible for a baby born during the year covered by the study to be provided for without the assistance of a social agency. The mother was only 16 years old and had recently completed the seventh grade. The father, a schoolboy of 14, was in the sixth grade. Both had good reputations in the community. The mother had always been obedient and truthful and was described as sincere and capable, a reliable worker, and a brave mother. The maternal grandfather was a heavy drinker, abusive, and without affection for his family. The baby—a girl—was born in a hospital, and after six weeks application was made to a private child-caring agency for boarding care for the mother and child. The mother's family was unwilling to keep her at home if she insisted upon caring for her baby. The mother and child were placed in a boarding home and later in a wage home. The maternal grandfather was aided in the prosecution of the baby's father. The boy was adjudged the father and appealed, and the case was pending at the end of the period. When the baby was 5 months old she was found to have syphilis and was admitted to a hospital for treatment. Later the child was boarded apart from the mother, and the mother was placed at housework. (Case V 2602.)

Another type of home conditions is illustrated by the following case:

Although the mother of a baby born during the year covered by the study was only 14 years of age and the maternal grandparents were in very poor circumstances, strong family affection impelled them to assume the care of mother and child after a short period during which a private agency gave supervision and aid. The mother and her family had been in the United States only two years. The mother was bright and attractive and had reached the eighth grade in school. Her teachers were very anxious that she return to school after her baby was born. The alleged father—a peddler, 21 years of age—was the brother of a woman whose children the mother had cared for occasionally. He mistreated her while she was caring for the children. He was prosecuted for rape and given a two-year sentence.

Shortly before the baby was born application was made to a private child-caring agency for supervision and care of the mother. The child was born in a hospital and was soon placed with the mother in a boarding home. When the baby was a little more than 2 months old the private agency giving care applied to a public child-caring agency, asking that the care of the child be assumed on account of the mother's youth and the family's financial inability to carry the burden of providing for the baby. The maternal grandparents, however, decided that they could not give up the child. They thought they could struggle along, and after the father of the baby had served his term they were planning to try to compel him to assist in the child's support. In accordance with this arrangement, the mother and baby went to live with the grandparents, the mother working in a factory and earning $1.50 a week. The plan worked out successfully, and agency care was no longer necessary. (Case V 1420.)

During the period of the study application was made to a maternity home for the care of a pregnant mother. The mother was 26 years old, earned between $25 and $30 a month in a factory, and was helping her younger brothers and sisters to secure an education. The maternal grandfather was dead and the maternal grandmother, a peculiar woman with a violent temper, was a laundress. The mother at first refused to marry the father—a chauffeur—because she felt she must help support her brothers and sisters. Later he declined to marry her, and in consequence she would not accept any help from him. The mother was cared for in the maternity home until the baby was 3½ months old. Mother and child then returned to the home of the maternal grandmother. The mother went to work and the grandmother cared for the child during the day, the maternity home giving supervision. (Case V 556.)

The poverty of the mother's family and the feeble-mindedness of the mother made it impossible for them, unaided, to care for a child born out of wedlock during the year covered by the study. Application had been made to a maternity home nearly three months before the child's birth, asking for confinement care. The family had been under the supervision of a family-care agency for 32 years. The girl's own mother was dead; her stepmother was a well-meaning woman who had tried her best to guard and protect the girl. There had been 11 children in the family, one of whom had been epileptic and feeble-minded. The girl herself, after a mental examination given during the period studied, was diagnosed feeble-minded. She was 28 years old at the time her child was born and had been earning $6 a week in a factory. She had always been very irresponsible. The maternity home gave care before and after confinement. The child was a weak, sickly baby, and died at the age of 2 months. The burial was at public expense. The mother returned to her home and went back to work. (Case V 2828.)

The year previous to the period covered by this study application was made to a private child-caring agency for the care of a 3-day-old infant. The child had been born in the maternal grandparents' home, and was being kept concealed in an upper room, some members of the family not knowing of its existence. The maternal grandparents were honest, self-respecting persons in poor financial circumstances and with six other children besides the mother. They stated that it was all they could do to support their own children, and that they could not assume the care of their grandchild. They felt deeply disgraced by their daughter's trouble.

The baby's mother, 22 years old, had been very sick as a child and was still in poor physical condition. She had been unable to finish grammar school because of weak eyes. She had been employed in a shoe shop. Sixteen months before the birth of the child of the record she had had a child born out of wedlock, whose father was not the father of the second child. The first baby died. The father of the child of the study was the same age as the mother. He had the reputation of being a common street loafer, failed to support his widowed mother, and could scarcely support himself. He was never told of the child's existence, because the mother's family was sure he would not be able to render any assistance.

The baby remained in the home of her grandparents, under agency supervision, until the age of 5 months. She was then boarded by the agency, the mother paying $3 a week. When the child was a little over a year old the mother—whose physical condition had been much improved through the medical care secured by the agency—married and took the child into her own home. (Case V 126.)

CHAPTER 3. LEGAL ACTION FOR THE SUPPORT OF CHILDREN BORN OUT OF WEDLOCK.

INTRODUCTION.

Of great importance in connection with a study of children born out of wedlock is consideration of the extent to which the State is demanding the assumption of parental responsibility by their natural parents. Society has borne a heavy burden in providing for such children not only support but also nurture and training. The responsibilities and privileges of the mother, largely because so closely related to the physical well-being of her child, have been more generally recognized than have those of the father. Other parts of this study have shown how few facts about the father appear to have been known to those who assumed the care of the children. In many instances there was no serious consideration of the father's status and the possibility of securing from him voluntary or forced contributions. Public opinion permits many fathers to shirk their duties; and often from a desire to protect the mothers from publicity and from further association with the man, agencies and individuals ignore the results for the child—and also for the father—of letting the matter lapse.

In order to ascertain what support Massachusetts is expecting from the fathers of children born out of wedlock and how this is being enforced through the courts, an analysis was made of the 1913 act relating to children of illegitimate birth and their maintenance, and of its administration, including a study of all court cases under the act initiated in Boston during 1914, carrying them through 1915. The law had been in operation for a comparatively short period at the time the study was made. A statement of changes in administration since the period covered by the study, based upon figures obtained from court officials, is included in this chapter.

ANALYSIS OF THE MASSACHUSETTS LAW FOR THE SUPPORT OF CHILDREN OF ILLEGITIMATE BIRTH.[1]

General Provisions.

Massachusetts set an advanced standard of parental responsibility for the support of children born out of wedlock through the

---

[1] The analysis of the Massachusetts law and of its administration in the Boston courts in 1914–1915 was prepared by Miss Evelina Belden.

passage of the 1913 act, which came into operation July 1 of that year.[2] Previous to this date, cases had been tried under a civil law which resulted largely in commitments to jail if the defendants were unable to give the sureties required, or in securing inadequate lump-sum settlements.

The new law makes the father " liable to contribute reasonably to the support of the child during minority," and gives the same protection against the lack of such contribution as that provided for failure to support children of legitimate birth under the uniform desertion and nonsupport act.[3] It states that the defendant shall be subject " to all the penalities and all the orders for the support and maintenance of the child provided in the case of a parent who is found guilty of unreasonably neglecting to provide for the support and maintenance of a minor child."

Offense, Jurisdiction, Process.

The present law makes it a misdemeanor to get a woman with child illegitimately, or to fail to support such child reasonably during minority, and subjects the defendant to arrest, trial, and judgment under the criminal law. Jurisdiction is given the police, municipal, or district courts in the locality in which either the man or the woman lives; or if there are none of these courts in that locality, to such courts in the county or to courts presided over by trial justices. This provision permits the choice of a locality in which the case may be tried with the least possible publicity to those concerned. The mother herself or some one else representing the child's interests may make the complaint. If the court deems it wise, especially in cases in which there is no danger of the man's absconding, the man may be summoned to appear to answer this complaint; in other cases he is arrested on a warrant.

Age of Child at Initiation and at Close of Case.

Complaints under section 1 of the act—that making the begetting of a child out of wedlock a misdemeanor—may be entered at any time before or after the child's birth. Complaints under section 7—the nonsupport section—may be entered at any time after the child's birth. In the course of the study of court cases, complaints were found to have been made for 6-year-old children and also for unborn children as early as the third month of pregnancy. Under section 1, if the man pleads guilty, an adjudication may be made as early

---

[2] Acts 1913 ch. 563, an act relative to illegitimate children and their maintenance, as amended by 1918 ch. 199.

[3] Acts 1911 ch. 456, as amended by 1912 chs. 264 and 310, 1914 ch. 520, and 1918 ch. 257 secs. 453–454.

as the court is convinced that a child is to be born. If the man pleads not guilty and objects to a trial, the case must be held over for trial until the mother is at least six months advanced in pregnancy.

Adjudication of Paternity.

A distinct gain over preceding laws is made by the Massachusetts law in its provisions for establishing paternity. The adjudication of paternity, which results from every convicted case, not appealed, under the begetting section of the law, is determined for all time, no matter what the disposition made. The fact of parentage is thus established for all subsequent cases of nonsupport which may be initiated. This type of permanent adjudication follows also a sentence under the nonsupport section of the act, though cases brought in under the nonsupport section do not establish the fact of paternity unless the man is sentenced. If an appeal to an adjudication is taken, it can be granted only if made immediately. Thus, a court completes at the time when evidence can be most easily secured the most difficult part of the trial—that of showing that the defendant is the father of the child and, consequently, is liable for its support.

Section 7—the nonsupport section of the act—was intended to be used for cases in which the child was begotten outside the State or before the act went into effect, or in which an adjudication of paternity had been made in some prior proceeding, disposed of before the new complaint was entered. If a case can be brought under section 1, this proceeding is preferable because of the provison as to adjudication of paternity and also because an order for confinement expenses may be made under section 1 but not under section 7.

Dispositions of Cases and Support Orders.

The primary purpose of the law is to obtain maintenance for the child during its minority and not to punish the man for his misdemeanor. Consequently, provision is made for dismissing the case if such maintenance is secured either by the marriage of the parents or by provision which is satisfactory to the court; or a case may be dismissed if the court finds that no living child will be born or that the child has died. The law aims to protect the child from securing only a small cash settlement, by stating that settlements shall be approved by the court or justice in a " certificate of adequate provision for the maintenance of the child."

Orders for contributions to the child's support through periodic payments are enforced through the probation officer. In case of failure to comply with a probation order, or if the original judgment is a commitment, the man may be sentenced to the house of correction under an order which states that because his dependents are in needy circumstances his wages of 50 cents a day, earned by work in the house of correction, shall be paid to his family. Money is occasionally collected through fines ordered by the court to be paid for the child.

The method of collecting support through the probation office, applicable to payments for children of illegitimate paternity as well as to payments under the uniform desertion and nonsupport act, gives the same officer the duty of collecting the money and also of adjusting the complex social factors in the lives of the persons concerned. The probation office of the central municipal court in Boston does an advanced type of social-service work in connection with the receiving and investigating of complaints and the subsequent treatment of the whole situation.

The probation orders which a court may render include those outlined under the desertion law and the interpretation of its practice as given by a committee of judges:

The disposition of the case, after a plea or finding of guilty, should include an order for weekly payments to the probation officer; a placing on probation until a day certain, not less than six months nor more than two years away; a recognizance, usually with the probation officer as surety; and, unless the court has considerable confidence in the defendant, a sentence, usually of two or three months in the house of correction, and a suspension of the execution of the sentence, conditioned upon performance of the order, and compliance with the usual probation conditions. Where the court has confidence in the defendant, simple probation may be used instead of a suspended sentence. It is of doubtful wisdom to require the defendant to assign his wages to the probation officer, or to give him an order on the employer, as this incites rebellion and is a source of constant irritation. The probation officer should use a systematic method of collections, and should follow up the payments as maturities are followed up in a bank. * * * If any need of increased pressure appears, the probation officer should surrender the defendant and a suspended sentence should be imposed, upon the same conditions, if none has been imposed before.[4]

At any time after an adjudication under section 1 of the act, reasonable confinement expenses in accord with the status of the persons concerned may be ordered paid to the mother or to the probation officer in her behalf.

An order for the child's maintenance may be entered at any time after the adjudication of paternity under the provisions of the law.[5] After the adjudication the court is required to continue the case from time to time until the child is born; but even this does not prevent the making of an order as to confinement expenses, and as to support as well, at any time. Some maintenance orders were found to have been entered before the birth of the child.

---

[4] Association of Justices of District, Police and Municipal Courts of Massachusetts, Committee on Law and Procedure: Report No. 7, Criminal Remedies in Massachusetts for Failure to Furnish Support. August, 1916. p. 36.

[5] Acts 1913 ch. 563 sec. 4.

Period of Support.

The Massachusetts law specifically states that "the defendant shall be liable to contribute reasonably to the support of the child during minority."[6]   This provision is enforced by means of penalties and orders provided by the uniform desertion and nonsupport act for the protection of children of legitimate birth.   That law states :[7]

Before the trial, with the consent of the defendant, or at the trial, on entry of a plea of guilty, or after conviction, if the defendant is placed on probation * * * the court in its discretion, having regard to the circumstances and to the financial ability or earning capacity of the defendant, shall have power to make an order, which shall be subject to change by the court from time to time as circumstances may require, directing the defendant to pay a certain sum periodically, for a term not exceeding two years, to the probation officer.

The exact amount of time within this two-year period is subject to the discretion of the individual justice or court,[8] and definite limits must be fixed in each instance.   The term may be extended from time to time without a new complaint.   There is some difference of opinion in Massachusetts in regard to whether the two-year limitation on the probation period applies to cases brought under the 1913 act.

At the time the study was made, the law had not been in operation a sufficient length of time to show how long cases will be followed— whether until the child becomes of working age and able to be self-supporting, or until he is 21 years old, when legal minority ceases. There appears to be no reason why any man adjudged the father and not dismissed for reasons stated in the statute (certificate, or marriage, or no living child to be born) may not be arrested and ordered to pay as often as he fails to make proper provision.

Thus it is seen that the Massachusetts law purposes to secure reasonable support for the child during its minority.   In general, the provisions and safeguarding of the law are far-reaching.   To what extent this ideal has been realized can be shown only through a study of the actual results obtained in the courts.[9]

ADMINISTRATION OF THE LAW IN THE BOSTON COURTS, 1914–15.

Method of Study and Distribution of Cases.

The study of results obtained under the Massachusetts act was made from records of cases brought before the nine courts in Boston

---

[6] Acts 1913 ch. 563 sec. 6.

[7] Acts 1911 ch. 456 sec. 5 as amended by 1918 ch. 257 sec. 453.

[8] Massachusetts Commission on Probation : Probation Manual, Boston, July, 1916.   P. 16.

[9] For a more detailed analysis of the law see : Manual of Laws Relating to Illegitimacy in Massachusetts, prepared by the Boston Conference on Illegitimacy in 1917.   Also, Report No. 7, Criminal Remedies in Massachusetts for Failure to Furnish Support, prepared by the Committee on Law and Procedure of the Association of Justices of District, Police, and Municipal Courts of Massachusetts.   August, 1916.

trying such cases during 1914. In Boston these and other domestic relations cases were not tried in a centralized court, as in some cities, but in the regular police courts[10] of the several districts of the city or in the Superior Court of Suffolk County. In the superior court were initiated 14 cases in which the defendant or complainant had a Boston residence, and this court also heard 59 cases appealed from the 8 lower courts. Indictments by the grand jury were used as methods of bringing cases to the superior court.

For the purpose of this study, court and probation records were secured for all complaints entered or tried during 1914, and these cases were followed through the dockets to the end of 1915. Complaints for which no warrants were issued were excluded. These court records were checked with records secured for all other parts of the study; and the many additional facts so secured, concerning marriages, adoptions, settlements, and ages and status of children, were used to supplement the court material.

During the year 1914 the courts of Boston issued warrants for 256 cases initiated under the act for the support of children born out of wedlock. In addition 42 cases under the act, held over from 1913, were also pending in the courts in 1914. For purposes of analysis only cases initiated during the year were studied; and these, since many of them were not disposed of until 1915, were followed through 1915 to give time for their closing. (See Table 72.)

TABLE 72.—*Status in 1914 of cases brought under the act relative to the support of children of illegitimate birth, by year of initiation.*

Year of initiation of case.	Cases brought under the act, which were current in 1914.		
	Total.	Closed in 1914.	Pending at end of year.
Total	298	195	103
Prior to 1914	42	37	5
1914	a 256	158	98

a These 256 cases involved 239 fathers and 253 children.

Although the treatment of complaints appeared to be somewhat different in the nine courts, the numbers in each court were too small to warrant comparisons or separate classifications, and all cases for the city were analyzed together. This use of the total number of all cases in the city gives facts which can more readily be compared with other cities which have a centralized court. A case, even though

---

[10] The central municipal court of Boston, one of the district courts, has transferred all cases under this act, as well as domestic relations complaints, to its special domestic relations sessions.

appealed and settled in the superior court, was always considered as belonging to the court in which it originated.

As would be expected, the courts serving the parts of the city where institutions for mothers and babies were located had a large number of cases, quite out of proportion to their total business. The number of cases in the central court of the city was relatively small in comparison with the total number of criminal cases. (See Table 73.)

TABLE 73.—*Total criminal cases initiated and cases initiated under the act relative to the support of children of illegitimate birth, in each court in Boston, 1914.*

Court.	Total criminal cases initiated in fiscal year 1914.a	Cases under the act specified initiated in calendar year 1914.
Boston central municipal	53,247	66
Brighton	1,740	7
Charlestown	5,196	11
Dorchester	3,256	61
East Boston	3,256	15
Roxbury	9,173	48
South Boston	8,666	24
West Roxbury	3,106	10
Superior court and grand jury (Boston residence)	(b)	14

a Fourteenth Annual Report of the Board of Prison Commissioners of Massachusetts, for the year 1914 Boston, 1915. p. 142. Cases begun in fiscal year, Oct. 1, 1913, to Sept. 30, 1914.
b The cases in the superior court could not be compared, because only cases of Boston residence were used, and the court figures are for cases for the whole county of Suffolk.

Since courts usually compute their statistics from the cases initiated and not from the individuals arrested or the children involved in the matter of support, cases were considered in discussing disposition rather than number of fathers or of children. However, in the discussion of the amounts collected, and of ages of children, it was necessary to count children rather than cases; in the discussion of percentages of orders paid, the number of fathers was used. The 256 court cases involved 239 alleged fathers and 253 children.[11]

Ten men were the alleged fathers of more than one child—two being the alleged fathers of three children each, and one being the alleged father of four children.

Court Procedure.

In 1914 and 1915 no uniform and organized method was employed in the Boston courts for receiving, investigating, and prosecuting cases. In general, complaints were made to the regular warrant

[11] An alleged father would be involved in more than one case if he was accused in a second complaint of parentage of a second child, or if a second complaint was made because the first was technically wrong, or if the first had been allowed to lapse before trial. A separate complaint is not necessarily made out for each child.

clerks, who were men. The court did not undertake to have a woman always present to assist with these cases, either at the time of receiving the complaint or later throughout the trial. In Massachusetts it is the duty of the probation officer in all criminal cases to inform the court, so far as possible, whether a person on trial has been previously convicted of crime [12] and, after the defendant's conviction, he may make recommendations as to the desirability of release on probation. Aside from the informal help given to the mother by the probation officers, there was no official in the inferior courts whose duty it was to prosecute each case or to direct its progress. In the superior court, the district attorney represented the State and prosecuted the case for the mother. Social agencies often followed their own cases through the courts with their own attorneys or social workers.[13]

In many instances the mother secured her warrant and brought in her case as best she could alone. Often the judge was obliged to rely merely upon the information produced in court—in many cases only the terrified mother's statement—and was compelled to make a decision of the greatest importance to the child's future without adequate knowledge of the social factors of the situation. The study of records revealed a large number of cases regarding which nothing appeared to have been known except the legal data required on the court forms. Such a method of procedure makes it probable that cases will be dropped after the warrant is issued, or that they will be dismissed at various stages before any real provision has been made for the child. There were 37 [14] of the 256 cases in the Boston courts in which the only entry was the date of the writing of the warrant.

Comparison of Number of Cases Initiated and Number of Illegitimate Births in Boston.

In all Boston courts during 1914 a total of 256 cases (representing 253 children) were initiated. During the same year there were born out of wedlock in the city 847 children. For every 100 births 30.2 court cases were initiated. This ratio of births to court cases is merely suggestive of the relatively small number of cases which are brought to court. It is not an exact ratio, for some of the court children were born before 1914 or were born outside Boston, and support for children born in Boston might have been secured through courts outside the city.

---

[12] R. L. 1902 ch. 217 sec. 84.

[13] Since the time covered by this study, all cases initiated in the central municipal court under the act relative to the support of children of illegitimate birth come to the probation department. In the superior court, also, the probation department handles all these cases.

[14] Including 4 cases in which the child was stillborn or had died before the end of the period.

Philadelphia and Chicago each have a specialized court with an organization equipped to deal with these cases. In Philadelphia in 1916, 38.8 court cases were initiated for every 100 births out of wedlock, a proportion somewhat greater than was the case in Boston. The comparison is only suggestive. The relative proportions of cases brought to court would be affected by the comparative accuracy of birth registration and by other factors. (See Table 74.)

TABLE 74.—*Number of court cases initiated in Boston under the act relative to the support of children of illegitimate birth, and number of court cases of fornication and bastardy in Philadelphia, per 100 illegitimate births in Boston and in Philadelphia, respectively.*

City.	Live births.		Court cases initiated.	
	Total.	Illegitimate.	Number.	Per 100 illegitimate births.
Boston (1914)...	19,462	847	256	30.2
Philadelphia (1916).....................................	a 41,220	982	b 381	38.8

a Reprint from the Annual Report of the Bureau of Health of the Department of Public Health and Charities, Philadelphia, 1916, pp. 54, 70.
b Third Annual Report of the Municipal Court of Philadelphia for the Year 1916, p. 224.

In Chicago, on the other hand, the evidence indicates that the proportion was considerably smaller than in Boston. The Juvenile Protective Association of Chicago stated, in a report of an investigation made by that organization:[15]

It is clearly impossible to estimate the number of children born each year in Chicago out of wedlock, but it is obvious that a minority of cases are brought into court. Last year [1913] the total number of bastardy cases tried in the Court of Domestic Relations was 469—less than a sixth of the number of illegitimate children born in the hospitals alone.

Ages of Children.

The discussion of cases brought into court is mainly concerned with infants, for only 19 of the children involved were 2 years of age or over at the time the case was initiated, and only 1 other child was over this age at the close of the case. More cases were started before the birth of the child than after. The court cases for the 253 children represented were begun at the following times:

```
Total children _____ 253
Before the birth of the child_____ 124
    Third month of pregnancy_____  10
    Fourth to sixth month_____  44
    Seventh to ninth month_____  61
    Month of pregnacy not reported_____   9
```

[15] The Juvenile Protective Association of Chicago: A Study of Bastardy Cases Taken from the Court of Domestic Relations in Chicago. Text by Louise de Koven Bowen. 1914. p. 4.

After the birth of the child_____ 104
   Less than 3 months_____ 54
   3–5 months _____ _____ _____ 8
   6–8 months _____ 6
   9–11 months _____ 5
   12–17 months _____ 6
   18–23 months _____ 2
   2 years or over_____ 19
   Age of child not reported_____ 4
Not reported_____ 25

The cases for 214 of the 253 children were closed by December 31, 1915, the end of the period studied. The cases for 39 were still pending, though 6 of the children concerned had died. Of the 214 whose cases were closed, 36 were unborn and 143 were living at the close of the case, while 4 were stillborn and 19 were dead; in regard to 12 of the children it was not known whether they were born or unborn at the close of the case. All those who died were under 1 year of age at death. Ninety of the living children were under 1 year of age at the close of the case, 36 were 1 year of age or over, and there were 17 whose ages were not reported.

The cases for the 214 children whose cases were closed terminated at the following times:

   Total children_____ 214
Child stillborn_____ 4
Child dead_____ 19
Child unborn_____ 36
Child living, so far as known_____ 143
   Under 3 months of age_____ 45
   3–5 months_____ 16
   6–8 months_____ 16
   9–11 months_____ 13
   12–17 months_____ 10
   18–23 months_____ 6
   2 years or over_____ 20
   Age not reported_____ 17
Not reported whether born or unborn_____ 12

Classification of Cases.

The type and amount of support secured for the children concerned is of greater significance than technical docket information. For this reason the dispositions have been classified not in legal terms but in terms showing the social significance of the court's dealings. All types of dispositions in which the court ordered or sanctioned an arrangement for the child's support are grouped together regardless of the factors of trial or conviction, and in contrast to these are grouped those cases closing perhaps with some sort of provision, but not one which the court could sanction officially under the law or to which it could legally hold the father.

In order to determine how much these arrangements actually accomplished each is related to the provision known to have been seecured. Such information was obtained not only from records of money payments, but from marriage, adoption, and agency records examined in connection with other parts of this study.

Types of dispositions made by court.

As described in the analysis of the law, there are certain dispositions definitely specified by which a case may be closed under this act: Simple probation or probation during a suspended sentence; commitment to the house of correction, usually with an order for payment of wages for the support of the child; dismissal because of certification of adequate provision having been made, or because of the marriage of the defendant and the mother; and imposition of a fine, usually ordered to be paid for the support of the child. These all make some provision for the child. In contrast to these dispositions are those in which the defendant is discharged because found not guilty by the court; cases in which the warrant is returned unserved, usually because the man has completely disappeared; and other cases, including those placed on file, nolle-prossed by the district attorney, dismissed for want of jurisdiction, and withdrawn without prosecution. Cases pending at the close of the period studied include those in which the warrant was still out and waiting to be served, as well as those in which the man, out on bond, had defaulted.

In the analysis of dispositions, cases classified under "order or arrangement for periodic payments or confinement expenses" include all orders for the payment of confinement expenses; orders for periodic payments through the probation officer; and other arrangements made through the court or probation office for periodic payments over a period of time during which a case was continued or a sentence was suspended.

The cases on file after adequate provision was certified include only those for which the judge or district attorney had signed such a statement. Other cash settlements in which the lump sums involved were not officially approved by the court were included in the cases otherwise dismissed—those on file, nolle-prossed, or dismissed for want of prosecution or jurisdiction.

The "dismissed, parents married" cases include not only those in which the marriage was recorded on the court paper as the reason for dismissal but also several without such a statement, in which, from the checking with other records, it was evident that the marriage was taken into consideration by the justice in rendering the judgment.

Types of provisions secured for child's support.

Under the provisions secured for the child during the pendency of the case there were included any definite plans carried out for the child—such as the payment of money, the parents' marriage, or the child's adoption.　These were not necessarily ordered by the court; they were often results of the fear of an order or merely unofficial plans made by persons concerned with the child's welfare.　Agency care was not included as a provision.

Money secured always refers to money paid by the father.　In instances in which there were both money and some other provision, the preference has been given to the most permanent adjustment in the following order: Marriage, adoption, money payments.　In eight of the nine adoption cases and in three of the marriage cases, money was known to have been paid by the father.　These cases, though not appearing under "money secured" in the analysis of the types of provision secured, have been included in the discussion of amounts of money paid.

Analysis of Dispositions and Provisions Made.

Proportion of cases resulting favorably for the child.

Information as to dispositions and provisions made has been summarized in table 75.　Of the 256 cases initiated in the Boston courts during 1914, only 120, less than half, were closed after an arrangement for support or confinement expenses, or for both, which could legally hold the man to his obligation, was ordered or approved by the court. [16]　In six cases the arrangements were not carried out.

In contrast to this, 76 were closed without arrangements for confinement expenses or support, and 42 were pending at the end of the time period.　In 18 other cases, the man was found not guilty, though in 1 of these he married the mother, thus providing for the child.　Since all the pending cases had been open for at least a year, they may justly be considered lost so far as support was concerned, for neither absconders from warrants nor defaulters of bonds are often brought to terms after such a length of time.　Six of these pending cases would never be pressed further, because the children concerned were dead.

---

[16] Of the 120 cases closed after an arrangement for support or confinement expenses had been ordered or approved by the court, there were 118 in which the child was living or unborn at the close of the case, 1 in which the child was dead, and 1 in which it was not known whether the child was living or dead.　Of the 136 in which no provision had been ordered or approved by the court at the end of the period, there were 52 in which the child was living or unborn, 27 in which the child was dead or stillborn, and 57 in which it was not known whether the child was living or dead.

TABLE 75.—*Cases initiated in 1914 under the act relative to the support of children of illegitimate birth, resulting in specified provision for child in 1914 and 1915, and cases pending Dec. 31, 1915, according to disposition of case by court.*

Disposition of case by court.	Total.	Cases initiated in 1914 under the act.				No provision secured or none reported.	Pending, Dec. 31, 1915.
		Provision secured during pendency of case.					
		Total.	Parents married.	Child adopted.	Money secured.		
Total..	256	134	a 29	b 9	96	80	42
Dismissed, not guilty.........................	18	1	1	....	....	17	....
Closed after arrangement for support or confinement expenses was ordered or sanctioned by court..............................	120	114	28	6	80	6	....
Order or arrangement for periodic payments or confinement expenses........	64	58	6	1	51	6	....
Sentence to house of correction with order for assignment of wages..........	5	5	....	....	5	....	....
Dismissed, certificate of adequate provision...................................	28	28	2	4	22	....	....
Dismissed, parents married...............	20	20	20	....	....	....	....
Fine, to be paid for child................	3	3	....	1	2	....	....
Otherwise closed..........................	76	19	....	3	16	57	....
Warrant returned without service......	7	....	....	....	....	7	....
Case otherwise dismissed................	c 69	19	....	3	16	50	....
Pending, Dec. 31, 1915......................	42	....	....	....	....	....	42
Warrant out...............................	37	....	....	....	....	....	37
Defendant defaulted before disposition..	5	....	....	....	....	....	5

a In 3 cases money also was secured.
b In all the cases but 1 (case otherwise dismissed) money was secured.
c Including 6 dismissed for want of jurisdiction.

Although in only 114 cases the court entered judgment which was carried out, in arranging for the support of the child or for confinement expenses, 19 of the cases closed for other reasons and 1 in which the defendant was dismissed as not guilty incidentally resulted in some provision being made during the pendency of the case. Thus, in 134 cases, 52 per cent of the total, some provision was secured as a direct or indirect result of court action. In 17 cases—7 per cent—the defendant was dismissed as not guilty, and no provision was made. In 105 other cases—41 per cent—no provision whatever resulted though in only 18 of these had the child died. To be sure, 42 of the 105 cases were still pending, but, as previously pointed out, there was small probability of favorable action, since they had been open at least a year.

To summarize the 105 cases—41 per cent of the total—lost or closed without results for the child: In 37 instances, the warrants were still out, unserved; 5 others remained open on defaulted bonds; in 7 cases the warrant was returned without service; no money was known to have been paid in 6 cases in which some had been ordered or arranged for; 6 cases were closed because the case was outside the jurisdiction of the court receiving the complaint; and 44 cases, closed in other ways, made no provision so far as could be discovered.

It is probable that in some of these cases great difficulties were encountered in locating the defendant, or the complainant decided not to push the case.

Thus, 256 cases initiated in the nine courts of Boston during one year resulted in provisions being made in only 134 cases, representing 142 children, while there were born into the community during the same year 847 children, three-fifths of whom received prolonged care from agencies during their first year of life.[17] The amount of responsibility placed upon fathers through the courts is evidently not in proportion to that assumed by agencies.

Distribution of cases according to types of dispositions and provisions made.

The dispositions of the cases show the legal orders and judgments rendered or the status of the case on the court docket at the end of the period, December 31, 1915. Of the 120 cases closed after arrangements for support were ordered or sanctioned by the court, 64 were by periodic payments or payment of confinement expenses, 5 by the payment of house of correction wages, 28 by certificates of adequate provision, 20 by the marriage of the parents, and 3 by payment of fines. Except for the fact that the superior court was the only one imposing fines, there was little difference in the various types of dispositions or of provisions made in the inferior courts and in the superior court. A comparison of dispositions in the inferior courts and in the superior court is shown in Table 76.

TABLE 76.—*Dispositions in the inferior courts and in the superior court of cases initiated in 1914 under the act relative to the support of children of illegitimate birth.*

Disposition of case by court.	Cases initiated in 1914 under the act.		
	Total.	Court in which disposition was made.	
		Inferior.	Superior.
Total..	256	183	[a]73
Dismissed, not guilty................................	18	16	2
Closed after arrangement for support or confinement expenses was ordered or sanctioned by court...........................	120	76	44
Order or arrangement for periodic payments or confinement expenses...........................	64	37	27
Sentence to house of correction with order for assignment of wages	5	4	1
Dismissed, certificate of adequate provision....................	28	18	10
Dismissed, parents married..........................	20	17	3
Fine, to be paid for child...........................	3	....	3
Otherwise closed....................................	76	50	26
Warrant returned without service.....................	7	7	....
Case otherwise dismissed............................	69	43	26
Pending, Dec. 31, 1915...............................	42	41	1
Warrant out.......................................	37	37	....
Defendant defaulted before disposition................	5	4	1

[a] Fourteen cases were initiated in the superior court. The others were appealed cases.

[17] See p. 137.

In a total of 134 cases provision of some sort was actually secured for the child. In 96 of these cases money was paid by the father, in 29 instances the parents were married, in 8 money was secured and the child also adopted; 1 child was adopted for whom no money was known to have been obtained.

Periodic payments and cash payments.

An outstanding improvement in the new law over the old civil law is that, in place of dismissing a father after he has made an inadequate cash settlement, which in many instances would be quickly and unwisely spent by the mother, he may be held liable for regular weekly sums of money, to be collected by probation officers, who also can advise upon its expenditure for the child. If the father willfully fails to meet his payments, the probation officer may bring him again before the judge, and he may be committed to the house of correction. Likewise, in approved arrangements for periodic payments during a continuance, the man is held to his agreement because the surety is responsible for his payments.

The need for safeguarding the interests of the child by ordering payments in weekly installments, under the helpful supervision of a probation officer, is borne out by facts discovered in the study of infants born in 1914. This study brought out the frequency of such factors in regard to the mothers as youth, low economic and social status, bad home conditions, absence of home protection, low mentality, and weaknesses of character, which would make them incapable of handling without assistance and supervision a sum of money in trust for the child's future.

In 114 cases closed after arrangement for support or confinement expenses had been ordered or sanctioned by the court, some provision was actually secured during the pendency of the case. Twenty of these cases were dismissed because of the marriage of the parents. Notwithstanding the evident superiority of periodic payments, only 63 [18] of the 94 not dismissed because of the marriage of the parents were closed after orders or arrangements for periodic payments or confinement expenses, while 31 were closed after fines or other cash payments. In 29 of these 31 cases, the child was living or unborn at the close of the case.

Marriages and adoptions.

The social significance of the marriages and adoptions reported for the court cases could not be determined by the method used in obtaining facts for this study. A marriage or an adoption was considered merely as a type of adjustment, regardless of how successful that adjustment had proved to be. In general, social agencies in

---

[18] Including 5 cases in which the defendant was sentenced to the house of correction with order for assignment of wages. See Table 75, p. 240.

Massachusetts discourage adoptions except under most favorable conditions, and the courts do not encourage marriages of the parents brought before them unless they are convinced that such a solution would work for the best interests of all concerned.

Most of the adoptions which were known to have occurred were undertaken through the large maternity hospital and children's institution which cares for unmarried mothers and their children. Adoptions seem to have been agreed to after the payment of sums ranging from $150 to $800, the majority of them being from $200 to $400. In 4 of the 9 adoption cases, adequate provision was certified.[19]

In 29 cases the parents were known to have married during the pendency of the case; in 13, before the child's birth. In a few other cases the parents were known to have married after the court case closed, but only provisions made during pendency of the case were considered. This proportion of marriages, about 1 in 9, is somewhat greater than that in the Philadelphia court in 1914—1 in 12.[20]

Duration of Cases in Court.

It is greatly to the credit of the courts that in cases which terminated after some provision for the child had been arranged, the results were usually accomplished without unreasonable delay between the issuing of the warrant and the conclusion of the case. Some delay is often unavoidable because of the mother's physical inability to be present in court. The fact that 73 cases took less than a month, and 37 others less than three months, implies careful work in pressing trials. (See Table 77.)

TABLE 77.—*Dispositions of cases initiated in 1914 under the act relative to the support of children of illegitimate birth, by length of time between warrant and disposition.*

Length of time between warrant and disposition.	Cases initiated in 1914 under the act.					
	Total.	Disposition of cases in 1914 or 1915.				
		Order or arrangement for confinement expenses or support of child.	Defendant discharged not guilty.	Warrant returned without service.	Otherwise closed.	Pending.
Total......................	256	120	18	7	69	42
Less than 1 month..............	73	52	6	1	14	....
1–2 months....................	37	23	2	....	12	....
3–5 months....................	33	19	1	2	11	....
6–8 months....................	29	14	....	2	13	....
9–11 months...................	14	8	1	....	5	....
12–18 months..................	15	4	1	2	8	....
Not reported or pending........	55	....	7	....	6	42

[19] See Table 75, p. 240.

[20] Second Annual Report of the Municipal Court of Philadelphia for the Year 1915. Pp. 61–63. Fifty-three marriages in 640 cases, or 8.3 per cent; 1 in 6 of the cases legally disposed of and 1 in 12 of all cases handled. Boston—29 marriages in 256 cases, 11.3 per cent.

Amount of Money Secured.

Total amount secured.

The total amount of money known to have been paid during 1914 and 1915 for all cases initiated in the Boston courts during 1914 was $13,143.11. (See Table 78.) Ninety-nine children secured the benefits of this money. In addition, there were 16 children for whom money was secured, though the sum was not known.

Thus, 115 of the 253 children, only 45 per cent, secured money through some one of the methods of payment. In 8 of these cases the money was for confinement expenses only—for the 7 cases for which the amounts were known, a total of $450.[21] Excluding these cases in which the payment was for confinement expenses only, it appears that $12,693.11 was obtained for the support of 92 children. Because of the varying periods of time covered by the amounts paid, the per capita amount would not be significant.

TABLE 78.—*Type of payment and total amount secured in 1914 and 1915, cases initiated in 1914 under the act relative to the support of children of illegitimate birth.*

Type of payment.	Amount secured in 1914 and 1915.	Children involved.[a]
Total	$13,143.11	99
Periodic payments or house of correction wages	6,460.11	63
Cash payments and fines	6,233.00	29
Confinement expenses only	450.00	7

a Excluding 16 for whom amount of money was not reported.

The distribution of the individual sums paid, as shown in Table 79, indicates how few children received amounts of any size and how small the cash payments were. The lump sums represented all that the children would be likely to receive, since new complaints would probably not be entered. These did not appear to be appreciably greater than the sums collected during the time period on continuing payments, whereas they would be expected to be many times greater.

---

21 One of $230, 1 of $100, and the others in sums of $50 or under.

TABLE 79.—*Amounts secured, by type of payment, cases initiated in 1914 under the act relative to the support of children of illegitimate birth.*

Type of payment.	To-tal.	\multicolumn{12}{c}{Children concerned in court cases under the act, for whom money was secured. — Amount of money secured in 1914 and 1915.}
		Less than $10.	$10–$49.	$50–$99.	$100–$149.	$150–$199.	$200–$249.	$250–$299.	$300–$349.	$350–$399.	$400.	$800.	Not reported.
Total	115	5	19	24	15	10	13	5	3	3	1	1	16
Payments on court order or arrangement for periodic payments	59	3	15	15	10	7	4	4	....	....	....	....	1
Court order or arrangement for confinement expenses only	3	1	1	....	1	....	....	....	....	....	....	....	....
Wages from house of correction	5	1	....	3	1	....	....	....	....	....	....	....	....
Fine paid for child	3	....	....	....	1	....	2	....	....	....	....	....	....
Cash settlement	33	....	1	5	2	2	6	1	3	2	....	1	10
Cash settlement with an adoption	7	....	....	....	....	1	....	....	....	1	1	....	4
Cash settlement, confinement expenses only	5	....	2	1	....	....	1	....	....	....	....	....	1

The majority—63 of the payments of all types—were under $150; 34 were between $150 and $400; 1 was $400; only 1 payment was more than $400—a certificate of adequate provision of $800.

The amounts of money paid, however, were so contingent upon whether the child had died, the parents had married, or the payments had ceased that these facts must be taken into consideration before any conclusion can be reached about the adequacy or inadequacy of the amounts secured. Information as to these facts is combined in Table 80.

TABLE 80.—*Amount secured, by status of payment at end of period and whether child was living or dead, cases initiated in 1914 under the act relative to the support of children of illegitimate birth.*

Status of payments at end of period, and whether child was living or dead at close of payments or end of period.	Total.	\multicolumn{9}{c}{Children concerned in court cases under the act, for whom money other than confinement expenses only was secured. — Amount of money secured in 1914 and 1915.}
		Less than $10.	$10–$49.	$50–$99.	$100–$149.	$150–$199.	$200–$399.	$400.	$800.	Not reported.
Total	107	4	16	23	14	10	23	1	1	15
Payments ceased	68	4	10	12	5	5	16	1	1	14
Child living or unborn	62	4	a 9	b 11	2	4	16	1	1	14
Child dead	6	....	1	1	3	1	....	....	....	....
Payments not ceased	39	....	6	11	9	5	7	....	....	1
Child living or unborn	36	....	5	9	9	5	7	....	....	1
Child dead	3	....	1	2	....	....	....	....	....	....

a Includes 2 children whose parents intermarried (payments of $16.50 each), and 2 children whose father was dead.
b Includes 1 child whose parents intermarried (payment of $87).

The payments for almost two-thirds of the children (68 out of 107) had ceased by the end of the period studied, and 30 of these would in all probability never receive more from the father because adequate provision had been certified by the judge (28) or the father had died (2). In the cases in which payments had ceased, contingencies of the child's death or the parents' marriage seem to account for but few of the small payments. In but 2 of the 26 cases in which the money amounted to less than $100, and in but 4 of the remaining cases, could the small amounts be accounted for by the death of the child. In but 3 instances did the parents' marriage explain the small payments; in 2 others they might be accounted for by the death of the father.

For 57 living or unborn children whose parents were not known to have married each other and whose fathers were living, payments had ceased, though 19 of the children had received less than $100, and all but 2 of those for whom the amount of money secured was known had received less than $400. Four of the children received merely nominal sums of less than $10, and 5 others received under $50.

Obviously the sums received were absolutely inadequate to cover the period of minority. The enforcement of the intent of the law would necessitate further complaints, in the cases where such action was possible, to see that the fathers, if they did not voluntarily contribute, are brought again before the court, or that probation periods are renewed.

Amounts ordered and percentages paid.

The amounts of money ordered and the types of orders, as distinguished from the amounts actually paid and the methods by which the payments were finally made, express in a definite way the standards of support set by the courts. That part of the order due by the end of the period studied or by the time of the death of the child or the marriage of the parents was considered, for the purposes of this analysis, the amount ordered. Payments were ordered for 81 children, the amounts of the orders being stated on the records for 77. For these 77 children, a total of $9,806.39 was ordered to be paid during the period covered by the study. In 5 instances, the sums ordered were merely for confinement expenses. (See Table 81.)

TABLE 81.—*Total amount ordered, by type of order, cases initiated in 1914 under the act relative to the support of children of illegitimate birth.*

Type of order.	Total amount ordered.	Number of children concerned.
Total..	$9,806.39	a 77
Periodic payments...	8,669.89	a 64
Wages from house of correction................................	332.50	5
Fine..	500.00	3
Confinement expenses only.....................................	304.00	5

a Four other children were the beneficiaries of orders for periodic payments but were not included here because the amounts of the orders were not given on the records.

To a large degree, however, these orders were not fully met. (See Table 82.) Of the fathers who were ordered to pay in this way, only half paid 100 per cent of the amounts ordered, and almost one-tenth paid nothing at all. The shortage occurred in the periodic payments; all fines and house of correction wages were paid. Considering the leniency of the courts in their original decrees, the percentages secured were notably small.

TABLE 82.—*Per cent paid of amount ordered, by method of payment specified in court order, cases initiated in 1914 under the act relative to the support of children of illegitimate birth.*

Method of payment specified in court order.	Fathers ordered to make payments under the act.									
	Total.	Per cent paid of amount ordered.								
		Over 100.	100	75–99.	50–74.	25–49.	10–24.	Under 10.	None.	Not reported.
Total..........................	74	11	26	14	4	5	2	2	7	3
Periodic payments or confinement expenses........................	a 66	10	19	14	4	5	2	2	7	3
Wages from house of correction........	5	1	4	......	......	......	......	......	......	......
Fine paid for child...................	3	......	3	......	......	......	......	......	......	......

a In previous tables, 2 cases included here were put under "dismissed, adequate provision certified," or under "cash settlements." However, since confinement expenses were ordered and paid before the final dismissal, they are included here, because they started with an order and closed with a lump-sum payment which complied with the order. It must be borne in mind that this table is based on the number of fathers, while Table 81 is based on the number of children.

Periodic payments.

Throughout the discussion of periodic payments the total amounts computed for the period of time covered by the study, rather than weekly orders, were considered. It was evident that the former would be of greater significance in showing results obtained, and since changes of orders occurred from time to time or payments were made in advance or in arrears, no weekly sums could have been stated. Moreover, the method used was the only one which would have shown the percentage paid. In eight cases the judge specified the entire sum which was to be secured from the father before his payments should cease. These amounts ranged from $100 to $300 to be paid in weekly installments. Only that part of the order due by the end of the period studied or by the time of the death of the child or the marriage of the parents was included in this analysis. Periodic payments included in some cases payments for confinement expenses, in addition to weekly installments for the support of the child.

A total amount of $8,669.89 was ordered to be paid periodically during the period studied, for the support of 64 children—an average of $13.92 per month for each child. Four other children were concerned in orders for periodic payments, but the amounts ordered were not given. Following are the total amounts ordered, the average for each child, and the monthly average for the 64 children for whom the amounts of the orders were known:

Total amount ordered for period studied_____ $8,669.89
Number of children concerned in orders_____ 64
Average amount per child_____ 135.47

Total months during period of study covered by orders_____ 623
Average number of months covered by orders_____-_____ 9.7
Average amount ordered per month per child_____ 13.92

Not all the money which was ordered to be paid periodically was secured in that way. The fathers of 4 children made lump-sum payments after the judgment, in order to hasten their release from obligation. The fathers of 5 children paid nothing.

Although 68 children were concerned in orders for periodic payments, only 59 actually received money paid in this way. The amounts of money paid were stated in the case of all but one of these children. A total amount of $6,115.61 was known to have been collected for 58 children through periodic payments or such payments plus confinement expenses, giving an average of $10.60 per month for each child. The following list gives the total amount collected, the average for each child, and the monthly average for the 58 children for whom the amounts collected were known:

Total amount collected during period studied_____ $6,115.61
Number of children concerned_____ 58
Average amount per child_____ 105.44

Total months of collection_____ 577
Average number of months of collection_____ 9.9
Average amount collected per month per child_____ 10.60

The average amount secured for each child, if computed for a year at the average rate per month, would be $127.20. Such a sum is slightly less than the usual amount, $130, paid yearly at the time this study was made, for the board and clothes of each State ward by the State Board of Charity of Massachusetts.[22] It is much less than the standard set by the Federal war risk insurance act[23] for compulsory allotments and Government allowances to dependents of soldiers and sailors. Under the provisions of that act, a child of illegitimate birth, if acknowledged by the father by instrument in writing, or if the father had been judicially ordered or decreed to contribute to the child's support, would receive $240 a year ($20 a month, $15 from the father's pay and $5 from the Government), unless the father had

---

[22] State board of charity, division of state minor wards—Form to be filled out by persons desiring to take children to board.

[23] 40 U. S. Statutes at Large p. 400 sec. 22, p. 402 sec. 201, p. 403 sec. 204, p. 610 secs. 4 and 6.

other dependents, in which case the amount would be proportionately reduced. However, the sum paid for a child to whose support the father had been judicially ordered or decreed to contribute could not under the terms of the act exceed the amount fixed in a previous order or decree of a court.

Even more significant than the average in showing how much the children actually received, month by month, are the numbers of children receiving specified amounts. This information is given in Table 83. Over half the 59 children for whose benefit periodic payments were made had received amounts of less than $100; the small amount may be explained in 4 of these cases by the fact that the child had died. One-third of the amounts under $100 were intended to cover a period of a year or more. One of the 10 children receiving from $100 to $149 had died. In 54 of the 59 cases, the child was living at the end of the period.

Payments had ceased in the cases of 18 children living or unborn at the end of the period and benefiting from money secured through periodic payments. In 3 of these cases, less than $10 was secured; in 8, from $10 to $49; in 4, from $50 to $99. Only 3 of the 18 children received as much as $150, and none received as much as $250. In only 5 of the 15 cases in which less than $100 was secured, could the low amounts be accounted for by the death of the father or the marriage of the parents.

TABLE 83.—*Amount secured by length of time from order to close of payment, cases initiated in 1914 under the act relative to the support of children of illegitimate birth.*

Length of time from order to close of payment or Dec. 31, 1915.	Children for whose benefit periodic payments were made.								
	Total.	Amount of money secured in 1914 and 1915.							
		Less than $10.	$10–$49	$50–$99	$100–$149	$150–$199	$200–$249	$250–$299	Not reported.
Total	59	3	15	15	10	7	4	4	1
Less than 6 months	14	3	5	3	3				
6–11 months	20		4	7	5	2	1		1
12–17 months	18		5	4	2	4	2	1	
18–22 months	5		1	1		1	1	1	
Not reported	2							2	

Payments through house of correction wages and fines.

Orders for fines or wages earned at the house of correction are of less importance than periodic payments. The wages are merely emergency measures. These house of correction wages amounted to—

Less than $10 (length of time covered not reported) _____ 1
$50 to $99 (paid during period of 6 months) _____ 3
$101 (paid during 12 months) _____ 1

In 4 of these cases the child was living or unborn at the end of the period, and the payments had ceased. In 1 case, that in which the highest amount was secured, the child was dead at the end of the period. Fines were for $100 and $200.

Certificates of adequate provision.

A radical provision in the act was that which aimed to protect the child from small cash settlements. The Association of Justices of Massachusetts voted in 1914: "That it is the sense of this meeting that the provision for the dismissal [upon certificate] of complaints * * * should not be employed in place of a continuing order, except in cases where the settlement agreed upon makes adequate provision during the full period of the probable dependence of the child."[24]

Of the 256 cases before the court, 28, involving the same number of children, were dismissed after certificates of adequate provision were signed by the judge or district attorney. The granting of such a certificate would probably preclude any subsequent opening of the case. In all but 8 of the cases in which certificates of adequate provision were signed, arrangements for the care of the child were implied. Fourteen of the children were adopted through, or their care was assumed by, a large maternity hospital and children's institution, 3 others were adopted, 1 was taken permanently by his grandparents, and in 2 cases the parents were married. Three children were unborn at the time certificates were made, and 1 was dead.

The kinds of provision and the amounts of money paid were as follows:

Total certificates of adequate provision granted	28
Parents married	2
Amount paid not reported	2
Grandparents assumed permanently the support of mother and child	1
$300 paid	1
Child adopted through, or care assumed by, a maternity hospital and children's institution	14
$800 paid	1
$350 paid	1
$323 paid	1
$315 paid	1
$225 paid	2
$200 paid	2
$175 paid	1
$150 paid	1
Amount paid not reported (1 child dead)	4

---

[24] Association of Justices of District, Police and Municipal Courts of Massachusetts, Committee on Law and Procedure: Report No. 7, Criminal Remedies in Massachusetts for Failure to Furnish Support. Aug., 1916. P. 44.

Child adopted through other source_____ 3
    $400 paid_____ 1
    Amount not reported_____ 2
Kind of provision not reported_____ 8
    $250 paid_____ 1
    $200 paid_____ 1
    Amount paid not reported_____ 6

The only children receiving as much as $400 directly or indirectly through court action were the two receiving $400 and $800, respectively, on certificates of adequate provision. Both these children were adopted. Half the $400 payment was made before the birth of the child and half after the child was adopted. The $800 payment was made after the adoption of the child, $600 going to the mother and $200 to the agency caring for the child up to the time of adoption.

Two certificates of adequate provision were made for amounts of less than $200. In both these cases an agency was responsible for the care of the child. Amounts paid ranging from $200 to $350 were known for 10 other children.

Judges increasingly refuse to sign certificates for the smaller sums of money. The policy of the association of justices is stated in their report as follows: " * * * that this provision for final dismissal upon certificate was intended for the very rare and exceptional case of a defendant able and willing to make settlement of several thousand dollars upon the child; and it was expected that orders for periodical payments would be used in ninety-nine per cent of all cases." [25] A case brought in since this study closed was known to have been settled in the superior court on a certificate stating that $2,000 was received in trust for the child.

Other cash payments.

Seventeen children, in addition to those concerned in the certificates, received money in lump-sum payments not ordered by the court. In those 17 instances, if the child should later become dependent upon society for support, complaint against the father may again be made, though it might be difficult to find the man. Private settlements between parties would not bar a court complaint, though the court would take all such facts into consideration, especially when a private settlement which seemed fairly reasonable had previously been made. Of the 17 cash settlements, 11 were for sums under $150.

Confinement expenses.

One provision of great importance in the Massachusetts law is that which provides, under penalty, for the payment of a sum deter-

<hr>

[25] Association of Justices of District, Police and Municipal Courts of Massachusetts, Committee on Law and Procedure: Report No. 7, **Criminal Remedies in Massachusetts for Failure to Furnish Support.** Aug., 1916. **P. 44.**

mined by the court for the confinement expenses of the mother. [26]
Such a payment may be ordered only in cases brought under section
1 of the act. It may be collected before or after the child's birth
and may be paid either to the probation officer or to the mother. It
was found in this study that money was paid for this purpose both
before and after the child's birth, and that it was paid in cases in
which the child had died. Several fathers, realizing what the court
would demand, paid these expenses without orders.

Twenty-seven payments for confinement expenses, including those
paid voluntarily, were known to have been received either in connection with another sum for support or as the only payment. This
figure is a minimum, since the purpose of the payment was not always made clear on the records. Some of the probation officers also
made a practice of securing funeral expenses from the father, if the
child died; but because such money was obtained informally it was
not included.

The eight cases in which confinement expenses only were obtained
were all cases in which the child had died or the parents had married.
In one of these cases the amount was for only $6; in one, for $10; in
two other cases, for less than $50; in one, for $50; in one, for $100;
and in one, for $230. In one case the amount was not reported.

SUMMARY OF THE LAW AND ITS ADMINISTRATION IN 1914–15.

The Massachusetts act relative to the support of children born
out of wedlock is an expression of the tendency to render more nearly
normal the lot of the child born out of wedlock. This law provides a standard for support with far-reaching possibilities in the
direction of interpretation and social treatment. Among the fundamental provisions are those which make the father liable for reasonable contributions to his child's support during minority, and those
which safeguard the securing of such support through a procedure
already established in the case of nonsupport of children of
legitimate birth. There are no limitations as to the time when cases
may be brought to court.

The intent of the law is that the father's contributions shall be
paid so far as possible through weekly installments, collected under
the supervision of the probation officer. Thus the money is to be
paid at such times and in such manner as will render it most valuable
to the child. When it appears probable that a father will not
fulfill his obligations under the leniency of probation he may be
sentenced to hard labor; yet this sentence need not thwart the purpose of the law by depriving the child of support, for the father's
wages in the house of correction may be assigned for the support of

---

[26] Acts 1913 ch. 563 sec. 4.

the child. The contributions are collected not for the mother but for the child, though the mother, before or after the child's birth, may receive a reasonable sum for her confinement expenses.

Massachusetts, with its effective State probation commission and its years of experience in probation work, is unusually well equipped to deal with problems of illegitimacy in the courts. Some of the probation work in these cases, especially in the largest courts, was done according to approved methods of social investigation and case treatment and was bringing about most delicate and difficult social adjustments involving father, mother, and baby. In general, too, the courts were found to press these cases with reasonable rapidity and to render judgments without undue delay.

The Massachusetts law had been in operation for a comparatively short period at the time this study was made. Most of the courts had not developed a well-organized method for the reception, investigation, and prosecution of cases under this act. The mothers were often left to shift for themselves in the securing of warrants and the following up of prosecutions. Adequate social information appeared to have been lacking in a considerable number of cases. In fact, in one-seventh of the cases initiated during 1914, the only entry was the date of the writing of the warrant. Often the probation records themselves showed little information about the cases and were too meager to make possible any just estimate of the results obtained.

In 1914 there were 256 cases initiated in the Boston courts. For nearly half the 253 children involved in these cases action was brought before the birth of the child, while for the majority of the others proceedings were begun before the child became a year old. Nineteen children were 2 years of age or more.

The number of court cases initiated under the act was less than one-third of the number of children born out of wedlock in the city during the same year. Of the children born during the year, three-fifths received prolonged care from agencies during their first year of life.

Less than half the cases initiated in the Boston courts during the year actually resulted in an arrangement for the support of the child, for confinement expenses, or for both, which could legally hold the man to his obligation. In a few other instances support was secured as an indirect result of court action. Altogether, but 52 per cent of all the cases initiated resulted in making some provision for the child, though in only 7 per cent of the cases was the defendant dismissed as not guilty. In only two-thirds of the cases resulting in an arrangement for support, where the case was not dismissed because of the marriage of the parents, was the money to be collected through weekly payments, notwithstanding the evident superiority of such a method.

The money collected did not usually amount to sums equal to the standard provided in Massachusetts for dependent children who were wards of the State. But few of the smaller amounts could be explained by the marriage of the parents or the death of the child. Many of the cases in which small amounts were collected had been closed without plans being made by the courts for bringing them in again. The amounts secured through lump-sum payments, including cases in which adequate provision was certified, appeared not to be appreciably greater than the amounts collected during the period on continuing payments, though the lump sums were usually intended to provide for the child's entire minority.

The inadequate results accomplished under the law may be attributed partly to the lack in most of the courts of an organization equipped to deal with the difficult problems involved. The mother, often at a time when she was physically ill-adapted to meet the strain, was attempting to secure support for her child through legal processes which were strange and terrifying to her. The circumstances and means of the father required consideration in making plans. Such facts as these called for more than merely a legal process, if the court was to effect a final disposition of the case which would provide equitably for the child without injustice to either parent.

CHANGES IN ADMINISTRATION SINCE THE PERIOD COVERED BY THE STUDY.

The preceding analysis is based upon the administration of the law in 1914 and 1915. At that time the law was comparatively new, having become effective in July, 1913. During the six years the law has been in force, the Massachusetts Commission on Probation and individual judges and probation officers have been working toward higher standards in administration. It was not practicable to repeat the intensive study for a later period, but an effort was made to obtain some information in regard to the present administration of the act in Boston, as compared with the situation that was revealed by this study. A list of questions was sent by the secretary of the Massachusetts Commission on Probation to the probation officers of seven courts in Boston. Information was obtained direct from the central municipal court, and it was found that no cases under the act are now initiated in the superior court. The questions were as follows:

1. How many cases this year involving children of illegtimate birth?

2. Does the number increase—taking the past four years, for instance?
3. Is there a decline in the proportion of cases in which lump settlements are accepted?
4. Is the certificate of adequate provision as much used as formerly, or is there any change in the policy of the courts as to its use?

The answers to these questions, together with statistics compiled by the probation department of the central municipal court and statistics published in the annual reports of the Massachusetts Commission on Probation, formed the basis for the following brief discussion of the present situation.

Number of Cases Brought into Court.

Although this chapter pertains only to Boston, it may be of interest to note the yearly distribution of probation cases under the act in all the courts of the State. For the six years from October 1, 1913, to September 30, 1919, the number of cases in which the defendants were placed on probation and ordered to make weekly payments for the support of the children were as follows:[27]

1914	71	1917	284
1915	142	1918	262
1916	233	1919	198

The law went into effect in July, 1913, so that 1914 was the first year in which any considerable number of cases were placed on probation under the law. From 1914 to 1917 there was a steady increase in the number of cases placed on probation, the number in 1917 being four times that in 1914. There were fewer probation cases in 1918 than in 1917, and fewer in 1919 than in any year subsequent to 1915. The effect of the war and the difficulty in following up cases of men in camp or overseas probably accounts in large part for this decline. No data are available in regard to the proportion the number of probation cases bears in each year to the total number of cases initiated under the act.

The probation department of the central municipal court of Boston now handles all cases initiated in that court under the act providing for the support of children born out of wedlock. An analysis of the illegitimacy cases handled by the probation department of this court from the time the law became operative until October 16, 1919—a period of a little more than six years—has recently been made by a member of the staff,[28] who has given permission for its use in this

---

[27] Figures are for the fiscal years, Oct. 1 to Sept. 30. Figures for 1914 to 1918 obtained from the Sixth to the Tenth Annual Reports of the Commission on Probation, 1914–1918. Boston, 1915–1919. Figures for 1919 furnished by the deputy commissioner.

[28] Data compiled by Miss Elizabeth A. Lee, of the municipal court of the City of Boston.

report. During this period a total of 511 cases had been initiated in the central municipal court and had been handled by the probation department. During the first part of the period some of the cases initiated were not referred to this department, so that the figures for the first year or two do not represent the total number of cases initiated under the act in the court under consideration. The distribution of cases according to year of initiation was as follows:

Total _____ 511

1913 (6 months) _____	16	1917 _____	90
1914 _____	50	1918 _____	100
1915 _____	87	1919 (9½ months) _____	[a] 86
1916 _____	82		

With the exception of 1916, the figures show an increase from year to year, even through the war period, when the total probation cases under the act in the State as a whole declined. The increases in the first years are so considerable that the correction of the figures by the inclusion in those for the earlier years of cases not handled by the probation department would probably not affect the general tendency. It was estimated in the course of the study made by the Children's Bureau that the total number of cases initiated in 1914 in the central municipal court was 66. The number of cases in the fiscal year ended September 30, 1919, was 107, or 62 per cent higher.

In the Roxbury court the numbers of cases in each year of the period 1915 to 1919 were 52, 37, 35, 35, 30. The Charlestown court reported that the average number of cases under the act remained about the same, the number initiated in 1919 being 13. In East Boston the number of cases in 1919 was 16, showing a slight increase over preceding years. In South Boston the figures showed a decrease from year to year, the number of cases in 1918 and 1919 being 9 and 6, respectively, as compared with 24 in 1914. The Dorchester court reported 13 cases in the last fiscal year, there having been no material change in number over the years immediately preceding. However, the number of cases in the Dorchester court in 1914 was 61; hence, the number of cases in 1919 was only a little over one-fifth of the number in 1914. In West Roxbury the number of cases in 1919 was 4, recent years showing a decrease. In Brighton there were no cases in 1919.

Cases are not now initiated in the superior court of Suffolk County. The court reported an increasing number of appealed cases, though the increase was not very marked.

Table 84 compares the number of cases initiated in Boston under the act in the calendar year 1914 and in the fiscal year ended September 30, 1919.

---

[a] The number of cases during the fiscal year ending Sept. 30, 1919, was 107.

TABLE 84.—*Cases initiated in each court in Boston, 1914 and 1919, under the act relative to the support of children of illegitimate birth.*

Court.	Cases initiated in calendar year 1914.a	Cases initiated in fiscal year ended Sept. 30, 1919.
Total	256	b 189
Boston central municipal	66	107
Brighton	7	
Charlestown	11	13
Dorchester	61	13
East Boston	15	16
Roxbury	48	30
South Boston	24	6
West Roxbury	10	4
Superior court and grand jury (Boston residence)	14	

a See Table 73, p. 234.

b The figures for 1919 included cases in which no warrant was issued; figures for 1914 excluded such cases. In 1919 in the central municipal court there were 13 cases in which no warrant was issued; the figures are not available for the other courts.

Although the number of cases in the central municipal court showed an increase of 62 per cent in 1919 over the number in 1914, the numbers of cases in all but two of the other courts showed a decrease. The decrease was most marked in the court serving the area containing a large maternity hospital and children's institution. It may be that the courts are more careful than formerly about accepting cases on the basis of the mother's residence in a district to which she has come simply for the purpose of securing maternity care. In 1914 only one-fourth of the cases were initiated in the central municipal court of the city; in 1919 the proportion was about five-ninths. The latter ratio is more in accord with the total volume of work done in the central court as compared with the other courts.

The total number of cases initiated under the act in Boston in 1919 was 189, a reduction of 67, or 26 per cent, over the number in 1914. The actual decrease was greater than here indicated, since cases in which no warrant was issued were excluded from the 1914 figures and included in the figures for 1919. In 1914 there were 30.2 court cases initiated for every 100 births out of wedlock. Based on births registered as illegitimate, the ratio was 34. Statistics for illegitimate births are not available for a period later than 1915. However, the average number of births registered as illegitimate for the six years 1910 to 1915 was 779, with no regular tendency to increase or decrease. On the basis of this average the number of court cases initiated in 1919 was only 24.3 per 100 illegitimate births. If illegitimate births registered as legitimate had been included in the number of births, and if cases in which no warrant was issued had been excluded from the number of cases, the proportion would have been still smaller. The lesser number of cases in 1919 as compared with 1914 may be partly accounted for by the fact that many of the alleged fathers were probably in the military or naval service and that in consequence there was difficulty in bringing them before the courts.

Methods of Handling Cases.

Reference has already been made to the change in policy in the central municipal court, whereby all cases initiated under the act are referred to the probation department. In 1914 some of the cases were never dealt with by that department. This change is a great advance over the old policy. As pointed out in the analysis of the Massachusetts law,[29] the probation office of the central municipal court performs a high type of social service work in connection with the receiving and investigating of complaints and the treatment of the whole situation. Complete investigations are made, and physical and medical examinations are given the mothers by women physicians attached to the court in all cases where such examinations are deemed advisable. Arrangements for confinement are made when necessary. A woman probation officer is in charge of cases under the act, and the mother thus has the advantage of a woman's counsel and assistance. The money collected from the fathers by the men probation officers is turned over to the women probation officers, who supervise the expenditure of the money in the interest of the children. The child is supervised, and the mother is brought in for nonsupport if she fails to do her part.

In the superior court, also, all cases under the act are now handled by the probation department. The probation officers of the lower courts report appealed cases and transmit the results of their investigations to the probation department of the superior court.

No information was available in regard to changes in methods of handling cases in the other courts in Boston, but it is probable that the situation in that respect is about the same as in 1914.

Dispositions of Cases.

As a part of the analysis of illegitimacy cases handled by the probation department of the central municipal court over a six-year period, data in regard to dispositions of cases were secured. These data are given in Table 85, rearranged in accordance with the plan followed in the study made by the Children's Bureau.[30] There are several factors which make this analysis not entirely comparable with that made by the bureau for cases initiated in 1914. Table 85 shows the status of the case in October, 1919. Hence, cases initiated in the early years of the period had much more time to be finally dis-

---

[29] See p. 231.   [30] See Table 75, p. 240.

posed of than cases initiated in 1918 or 1919; the latter group of cases therefore includes more pending cases than the earlier group. In the bureau study cases initiated in 1914 were followed to the end of 1915—hence there was not room for as much variation in the period between the initiation of the case and the end of the time covered by the analysis. Moreover, the bureau study followed appealed cases through the superior court, so that the disposition " appealed " did not appear in the analysis, whereas the data given in Table 85 represent only the dispositions in the central municipal court. The figures here given include cases in which no warrant was issued, while such cases were excluded from the 1914–15 analysis.

TABLE 85.—*Disposition of cases initiated in the central municipal court, 1913 to 1919, under the act relative to the support of children of illegitimate birth.*

Disposition of case by court.	Cases initiated in the central municipal court under the act.a							
	Total	Year of initiation.						
		1913b	1914	1915	1916	1917	1918	1919c
Total...................................	511	16	50	87	82	90	100	86
Dismissed, not guilty..........................	22	....	1	3	4	5	4	5
Closed after arrangement for support or confinement expenses was ordered or sanctioned by court....................................	216	7	21	45	35	40	43	25
Placed on probation, with order for periodic payments...........................	d123	3	9	14	19	28	29	21
Sentenced e................................	5	....	....	3	1	....	....	1
Dismissed, certificate of adequate provision.	16	1	3	2	4	3	2	1
Dismissed or on file, parents married........	72	3	9	26	11	9	12	2
Otherwise closed.............................	131	9	18	18	26	18	25	17
Appeal from adjudication of paternity.......	67	5	10	9	12	10	15	6
Dismissed or referred to district attorney or other courts, no jurisdiction...............	37	.....	4	5	8	2	10	8
Otherwise dismissed.......................	f27	4	4	4	6	6	....	3
Pending.......................................	142	....	10	21	17	27	28	39
Warrant out...............................	79	....	5	10	14	21	12	17
No warrant issued..........................	49	....	5	8	2	6	15	13
Defendant defaulted.......................	1	....	....	....	1	....	....	.....
No adjudication............................	9	....	....	2	....	....	....	7
Adjudicated father, case continued.........	4	....	....	1	....	....	1	2

a Includes only cases handled by the probation department. In the early years of the period all the cases did not come to this department.
b Six months of 1913—July 1 (when the law went into effect) to Dec. 31.
c Nine and a half months of 1919—Jan. 1 to Oct. 16.
d Of these 123 cases, the defendant was still on probation Oct. 16, 1919, in 48 cases: in 54, the defendant had defaulted; in 19, the case had been dismissed; and in 2, the defendant had been surrendered and sentenced.
e Presumably with order for the assignment of wages for the support of the child.
f Includes 9 cases closed after agreement to pay (not in court), of which 1 was initiated in 1914, 3 were initiated in 1915, 3 in 1917, and 2 in 1919; 3 cases in which the child was adopted, 1 initiated in 1914, 1 in 1916, and 1 in 1917; 9 cases dismissed for want of prosecution (4 were initiated in 1913, 1 in 1915, 3 in 1916, and 1 in 1919); 3 cases dismissed after the death of the child (1 initiated in 1914 and 2 in 1916); and 3 on file (1 initiated in 1914 and 2 in 1917).

Of the 511 cases handled by the probation department of the central municipal court, the defendant had been dismissed, not guilty, in 4 per cent; in 42 per cent the case had been closed after arrangement for support or confinement expenses had been ordered or sanctioned by the court; and in 3 per cent of the cases money was secured on agreements out of court or the child was adopted. In 13 per cent of the cases the defendant appealed from the adjudication of paternity; in 10 per cent the case was closed for want of jurisdiction or was otherwise dismissed (exclusive of cases in which money was secured informally or the child was adopted), and in 28 per cent the case was pending at the end of the period.

In 123—57 per cent—of the 216 cases closed after arrangement for support or confinement expenses was ordered or sanctioned by the court, the defendant was placed on probation with an order for periodic payments. In these 123 cases 48 defendants were still on probation October 16, 1919, 54 defendants had defaulted, 2 had been surrendered and sentenced, and 19 cases had been dismissed. It must be borne in mind that some of these cases had been initiated within a year of the close of the period, while others had been initiated more than six years before.

Taking the figures year by year and excluding 1913 because of the small number of cases and 1919 because of the short time which had elapsed from the initiation of the cases, there is little variation in the percentages of cases closed after arrangement for support or confinement expenses was ordered or sanctioned by the court. In 1914 the percentage so terminated was 42; in 1915, 52; in 1916, 43; in 1917, 44; in 1918, 43.

The proportion of cases in which the defendant was placed on probation, among those closed after arrangement for support or confinement expenses had been ordered or sanctioned by the court, was much higher in the last years of the period than in the first years. In 1914 three-sevenths of the cases closed after an arrangement for support resulted in the defendants being placed on probation; in 1915 the proportion was somewhat less than a third; in 1916 more than half the cases resulted in probation; in 1917, seven-tenths; in 1918, two-thirds; and in 1919, almost six-sevenths. Hence, in 1919 the proportion of cases in which the defendant was placed on probation among those cases closed after an arrangement for support or confinement expenses had been ordered or sanctioned by the court was twice the proportion in 1914.

In the year 1915, in which the smallest proportion of cases resulted in probation, there was an unusually large proportion of marriages, the cases closed after the marriage of the parents representing almost three-fifths of all those closed after an arrangement for support or confinement expenses which was ordered or sanctioned by the court. The proportion—three-sevenths—of marriages in 1914 was lower than in 1915, but it was higher than in the years following

1915. In 1916, 1917, and 1918 the proportion of cases terminated after the marriage of the parents was less than one-third; in 1919 the proportion was one-twelfth. Hence, there seems to be a marked decline in the proportion of cases terminated by the marriage of the parents.

Only 7 per cent of the cases closed after an arrangement for support or confinement expenses ordered or sanctioned by the court were dismissed after certificates of adequate provision had been granted. These 16 cases represented 3 per cent of the total 511 cases brought before the court. There seems to have been little change in policy from year to year, the number of cases so terminated ranging from 1 to 4 each year.

In the 216 cases closed after arrangement for support or confinement expenses was ordered or sanctioned by the court, the defendant was adjudged father or acknowledged his paternity. In the 67 appealed cases the paternity was adjudicated by the lower court, as well as in the 4 cases continued after adjudication of paternity and included among those pending. Hence, in a total of 287 cases—56 per cent of the total 511—the defendant was adjudged the father by the central municipal court or acknowledged his paternity and made provision for the child which was sanctioned by the court. Analyzing the cases year by year, and excluding 1913 because of the small number of cases and 1919 because of the short time which had elapsed after initiation, the percentages of cases in which the defendant was adjudged father or acknowledged paternity by making provision sanctioned by the court were as follows: 1914, 62 per cent; 1915, 63 per cent; 1916, 57 per cent; 1917, 56 per cent; 1918, 59 per cent. It must be borne in mind that these figures include appealed cases, some of which were lost in the superior court.

Certificates of Adequate Provision and Other Lump-Sum Payments.

As previously stated, a very small number of cases in the central municipal court were closed after adequate provision had been certified, or after agreements to pay, out of court. In the six years from July 1, 1913, to October 16, 1919, there were only 16 cases of adequate provision and 9 cases of agreements to pay, out of court. The yearly distribution of these cases showed no marked change in policy from year to year.

The replies from the other courts in Boston to the questions relating to lump-sum settlements and certificates of adequate provision showed that these methods of disposing of cases are used comparatively infrequently. The Brighton court reported that lump-sum settlements are never accepted, and that the court is not disposed to accept certificates of adequate provision. The South Boston court reported that certificates of adequate provision are never granted. The Charlestown, East Boston, and Dorchester courts reported no change in policy in regard to certificates of adequate provision, the Dorchester court reporting that certificates are sometimes used, but not commonly. In regard to lump settlements, the Charlestown court reported that in only one case—in which the child died—had the court accepted a lump-sum settlement; the Dorchester court reported no change, and the East Boston court stated that "a lump settlement is only accepted when the court is satisfied beyond doubt that the welfare of the child is provided for and it will not become a burden upon the public." The Roxbury court reported no marked change in the method of disposing of cases; in the past five years the certificate has been accepted in only nine cases—in these cases the children were taken by an institution, the father paying a lump sum. The West Roxbury court reported both the certificate of adequate provision and the lump settlement seldom used.

In regard to the superior court, the secretary of the commission on probation states: "The acceptance of the lump settlement is declining, and the certificate of adequate provision is accepted with increasing care."

An analysis of the 16 cases in the central municipal court, in which adequate provision was certified, showed that in 5 instances the child was taken by a maternity hospital and children's institution; in 3 the child was adopted, in 1 case by the mother's husband; in 1 case the child was a ward of the city; in 1 the mother and baby were sent to Scotland; in 4 the child remained with the mother; in 1 case the certificate was granted before the child was born; and in 1 the disposition of the child was not stated.

The amounts in these 16 cases ranged from $164 to $1,000, the sums paid not being reported in 3 cases. In the 5 cases in which the child was taken by a maternity hospital and children's institution the amounts paid were $200, $164, not reported, $265, not reported. The amounts paid in the cases in which the child was adopted were $345, $526, $400. The highest payment, $1,000, was in the case of a child who was a ward of the city; the next highest, $875, was paid for the benefit of the mother and baby who were sent to Scotland. The four payments made in cases where the child remained with the mother were for $200, $400, $300, and $550; in the last 3 cases the mother later applied to the court for further action. Within two months after adequate provision was certified in the case of the mother whose child was unborn, the mother applied to a maternity home for care; the defendant had promised to pay $450, but the mother had only $150 when she applied for care.

Summary of the Present Situation.

From the preceding analysis it would appear that the number of cases brought in the Boston courts under the act relative to the support of children born out of wedlock was considerably smaller in 1919 than in 1914, though there was a redistribution of cases among the courts which resulted in the central municipal court handling a much larger percentage in the later years than in the earlier. There has been improvement in the methods of handling cases in the central municipal court and in the superior court; information was not available for the other courts, though it is probable that in these courts there has been little change in administration. An analysis of dispositions of cases in the central municipal court, made by a probation officer of the court, showed little variation from year to year, except that the proportion of cases placed on probation among all cases closed after an arrangement for support or confinement expenses had been ordered or sanctioned by the court was much higher in the last years of the six-year period, 1913–1919, than in the earlier years of the period, and the proportion of marriages was considerably lower.

In transmitting the replies to the questions sent the Boston courts the secretary of the probation commission said that the statements " indicate that no radical change has come about in recent years, and give warrant for the opinion that the observations made in regard to the operation of the illegitimate children act at the time of the survey [1914–1915] to all intents and purposes are descriptive of the situation as it now exists."

Probation officers and others in Boston familiar with the operation of the act believe that it should be changed in one particular—the provision permitting the granting of certificates of adequate provision should be eliminated. This feature of the law, which was intended to provide for the exceptional case in which the defendant could pay several thousand dollars for the care and maintenance of the child, has not always been fully understood by those administering the act. In a discussion of the act before the Massachusetts Conference of Social Work, December 13, 1919, Mr. Herbert C. Parsons, secretary of the Massachusetts Commission on Probation, stated: " It is true that settlements are arranged for too low amounts. Probation officers feel that the provision for certificates of adequate provision should be eliminated from the law. They feel that it is a continuing limitation against the interests of the mother, the child, and society."

It is also felt by some of those engaged in the administration of the act that the probation period should be extended, so that the order might be renewed from time to time and adjusted as varied circumstances might require. At present there is some uncertainty in regard to whether the probation period can be extended beyond two years. An amendment providing for a judgment of paternity under section 7 of the act (the nonsupport section) as well as under section 1 is also desired by some.

In general, the feeling among those engaged in the administration of the act is that the fullest possibilities of the law have not yet been developed in actual practice, and that no radical changes should be made until the law had been in operation for a longer period.

SECTION II. THE PROBLEM IN THE STATE.

SECTION II. THE PROBLEM IN THE STATE.

INTRODUCTION.

The large city not only creates abnormal conditions of living but also draws to itself many of the unfortunates of small towns and of country districts. Within the larger area of a State the intensified problems of the city become merged with those of small urban and rural communities. In order to secure data of more general application, a part of this study of illegitimacy as a child-welfare problem was made State wide in scope. In fact, it was impossible to make a representative study of the situation in Boston without an analysis of State activities.

The survey of the problem in the State by no means covered all the phases of the subject. Data were obtained in regard to illegitimate births in the State, and a comprehensive study was made of children born out of wedlock who were wards of the State board of charity or of the State institutions for the delinquent and for the feeble-minded. Records of infants under 2 years of age boarded in family homes were consulted, as were the adoption records of four counties. A brief study was made of conditions in a seacoast rural section. Studies of infant mortality previously made by the Children's Bureau in two Massachusetts cities included some data in regard to infants of illegitimate birth which were of value for comparative purposes.

The Massachusetts State Board of Charity has both supervisory and administrative functions. The duties of supervision comprise visitation and inspection of the State hospitals and sanatoria, the State training schools for delinquent girls and boys, the county training schools for juvenile delinquents, wayfarers' lodges and public lodging houses, and the city and town almshouses. The board also has general supervision over children on parole from the State training schools, children supported by cities and towns, and adults supported by cities and towns in families other than their own. Such charitable corporations as ask for or consent to visitation and inspection also come under the supervisory activities of the board, and all applications for the incorporation of charitable organizations are investigated by the board. The work of cities and towns in the relief of mothers with dependent children is under the supervision of the board. Results of visitation and inspection are published, and

266

the board makes recommendations to the legislature for changes in existing laws and for new legislation.

The administrative duties of the board may be classified under two heads—those concerned with the State adult poor and those dealing with the State minor wards. The work with reference to the State adult poor includes the discharge of sane inmates of the State infirmary and the State farm; the investigation of the settlement of persons supported or given aid by cities and towns, and of sane inmates of State institutions; the directing of local aid of persons without settlement; the transfer of paupers from one institution to another or from one place to another; and the management of the hospital for lepers. The work with reference to State minor wards includes the maintenance and care of children coming under the custody of the board, and the execution of the laws concerning abandoned infants, the protection of infants, infant boarding houses, and the licensing of lying-in hospitals.[1]

The board has developed a comprehensive and highly organized service for the care of dependent and neglected children, administered by the division of State minor wards. The board cares for children of all ages, retaining supervision until they reach the age of 21 years, unless previously discharged. Four classes of children are received by the board—dependent, neglected, wayward, and delinquent. Dependent children are not committed through court action but are received by the board from the overseers of the poor of the different towns, from the State infirmary at Tewksbury, or on direct application from parents, relatives, or friends. In certain cases the board itself may take the initiative in removing children from unsuitable boarding homes or homes in which they have been placed for adoption. Neglected, wayward, and delinquent children are committed to the board by the courts. The board must be notified of all neglect proceedings, and agents of the board are present at the hearings and have a right to protest against commitment to the board. A court may request the attendance of one of the board's agents at proceedings involving juvenile delinquency or waywardness if the interests of the child require such protection. Wayward and delinquent children received by the board are those whom the courts consider too young to be committed to an institution for delinquents, or whose behavior does not warrant such treatment, but

---

[1] The functions of the State board of charity have been transferred, by legislative act of 1919, to the newly created department of public welfare. The division of aid and relief is the successor to the division of State adult poor. The board of trustees of the State infirmary (formerly the State infirmary and State farm) is made a part of this division. The functions of the division of State minor wards are taken over by the division of child guardianship, and the board of trustees of the Massachusetts Hospital School is made a part of this new division. The trustees of the Massachusetts Training Schools, together with the institutions and departments under their control, form the division of juvenile training of the new department.

whose home conditions are such that removal of the child is deemed necessary. If, after commitment to the board, these children become incorrigible, they may be transferred to correctional institutions without further action by the court. Besides neglected, wayward, and delinquent children committed to the board, children are sometimes committed to the temporary care of the board pending final disposition of their cases. The treatment of these classes of children is not differentiated. All are placed in family homes, unless exceptional circumstances make other disposition necessary.

A part of the work of the State board of charity is the granting of licenses to maintain boarding homes for infants. The law provides that anyone having under his control for gain or reward at one time two or more infants under the age of 2 years, unattended by a parent or guardian, and not related by blood or marriage, is deemed to maintain a boarding house for infants. Such homes are inspected at least once a year by the State board of charity and local boards of health. Whoever receives under his care or control, and whoever places under the care or control of another for compensation, an infant under 2 years of age, not related by blood or marriage to the person receiving it, is required to give notice within two days to the State board. This notice includes statements of the name, age, and residence of the infant, his parents, and the persons from whom or by whom he was received, together with the terms of placement. Upon the receipt of such notice the board may investigate the case and make such recommendations as it deems expedient. If these are not complied with, the board may apply to a court to make and enforce orders for the care, custody, maintenance, and protection of the infant. Infants reported as cared for apart from their relatives are visited by the nurses who visit infants under care of the board. The board must be notified of the reception for board, or for the purpose of procuring adoption, of an infant of illegitimate birth under 3 years of age. Such children may be taken into the custody of the board if, by reason of neglect, abuse, or other cause, such action is considered necessary to preserve their lives.

The part of the work of the division of State adult poor most concerned with the problem of illegitimacy is the after-care of the women and children discharged by the board from the State infirmary. The majority receiving this care are unmarried women with children. These mothers are helped in finding employment, are given legal assistance in securing support from the father of the child, and are otherwise aided. In certain cases in which the consent of the mother is obtained, the superintendent of State adult poor acts as trustee for the funds collected from the father for the support of the child.

There are three State training schools for juvenile delinquents— the Lyman School for Boys, the industrial school for boys, and the industrial school for girls. These schools are administered by a single board of trustees and are under the general supervision of the State board of charity.[2] The Massachusetts Reformatory for Women receives girls and women 15 years of age and over. Infants under 18 months of age may be provided for with their mothers in this institution.

The two institutions for the feeble-minded—the Massachusetts State School for the Feeble-Minded at Waverley and the Wrentham State School—are under the control of the Massachusetts Commission on Mental Diseases, established in 1916 as the successor to the State board of insanity.[3] An appropriation for a third institution was made in 1914, but the institution has not yet been completed. The State school for the feeble-minded has as an adjunct a farm colony at Templeton. The facilities of the institutions are not at all commensurate with the number of feeble-minded in the State needing care. According to statistics compiled in 1915, there were in April of that year 520 feeble-minded persons in the Massachusetts State hospitals for the insane. This number constituted 3.6 per cent of the total number of patients in these hospitals and equaled 18.9 per cent of the population of the two State institutions for the feeble-minded.[4] Mentally defective patients in hospitals for the insane do not receive proper care and training, and they handicap the work which these institutions are intended to do. A few feeble-minded children are cared for at the Hospital Cottages for Children, Baldwinsville. The State infirmary at Tewksbury maintains a department for mental cases, and a number of mentally defective persons are cared for by this institution until they can be admitted to the schools for the feeble-minded. In 1914 the State board of charity reported 520 persons stated to be mentally defective being cared for in 161 city and town almshouses.[5] A larger number of feeble-minded who are in need of care must remain in the community without the supervision which their condition so urgently requires.

---

[2] By the reorganization of 1919 the board of trustees of the Masschusetts Training Schools becomes the division of juvenile training of the department of public welfare.

[3] By the reorganization of 1919, this commission forms the new department of mental diseases.

[4] League for Preventive Work: Feeble-Minded Adrift. "III. Feeble-minded in State hospitals for the insane." Boston, 1916.

[5] Thirty-sixth Annual Report of the State Board of Charity of Massachusetts for the Year Ending November 30, 1914. Boston, 1915. Pt. III, p. viii.

CHAPTER 1. ILLEGITIMATE BIRTHS IN MASSACHUSETTS.

INCIDENCE IN THE STATE.

Under the Massachusetts law copies of all birth and death certificates are filed in the office of the secretary of the Commonwealth. These records were searched for the year 1914, and a count made of the illegitimate births that had occurred in each town of the State. The results were then classified by county, and also according to size of the community, and compared with the total births in the same areas. By this means it was possible to secure some idea of the distribution of the problem in the State.

During the year studied there were 93,394 live births in the State. Of these, 2,108 were registered as illegitimate. The percentage of illegitimate births was, therefore, 2.3. This proportion is known to be an understatement; it was shown in the Boston study that a number of illegitimate births are registered as legitimate.[1] It was impracticable to correct the State rate by checking with records of social agencies. The percentage of births registered as illegitimate— uncorrected by checking with records of social agencies—was lower for the State as a whole than for the city of Boston, 2.3 as compared with 3.9.[2] This is largely accounted for by the fact that a considerable number of nonresident mothers come to the metropolis to secure maternity care.

The estimated number of single, widowed, and divorced women of child-bearing age—15 to 44 years, inclusive—in the State in 1914 was 468,069.[3] The illegitimacy rate per 1,000 of this population was 4.5 in the year studied. This means that during the year there were between four and five cases of illegitimate maternity to every 1,000 single, widowed, and divorced women of child-bearing age in the State. Here, again, the rate is an understatement.

GEOGRAPHICAL DISTRIBUTION.

The total number of births in each county in the year studied and the number of illegitimate births are given in Table 1. The counties are listed according to geographical location, from west to east.[4]

---

[1] See pp. 85–88.

[2] Uncorrected rate for Boston. See p. 85.

[3] The population of Massachusetts on July 1, 1914, as estimated by the U. S. Bureau of the Census, was 3,605,522. In 1910, the female population between the ages of 15 and 44, inclusive, comprised 12.982 per cent of the total population ; assuming that this proportion would hold for 1914, the number of single, widowed, and divorced women of child-bearing age was estimated to be 468,069. (See Thirteenth Census of the United States, 1910: Vol. II, Population, p. 867.)

[4] See description of counties, p. 22, and map, p. 23.

TABLE 1.—*Per cent of illegitimate births in each county in Massachusetts, 1914.*

County.	Estimated population 1914.[a]	Total live births.[b]	Live births registered as illegitimate.	
			Number.	Per cent.
Total..	[b] 3,643,863	93,399	2,108	2.3
Berkshire...	113,248	2,953	27	0.9
Franklin..	47,553	1,151	8	.7
Hampshire..	68,607	1,666	30	1.8
Hampden..	258,163	7,674	148	1.9
Worcester...	425,995	11,134	203	1.8
Essex...	459,515	11,068	196	1.8
Middlesex...	724,074	16,950	253	1.5
Suffolk...	814,713	21,794	791	3.6
Norfolk...	197,469	3,921	43	1.1
Plymouth..	155,343	3,302	55	1.7
Bristol...	342,639	10,973	227	2.1
Barnstable, Dukes, and Nantucket	36,605	654	13	2.0
State infirmary, Tewksbury (Middlesex County)..........	....	159	114	....

a Estimated as for July 1, 1914, on the basis of the population on Apr. 15, 1910, as given by the U. S. Bureau of the Census, and the population on Apr. 1, 1915, as given by the Massachusetts State census. The estimated population for the State is that given in the Seventy-third Annual Report of the Commonwealth of Massachusetts on Births, Marriages and Deaths for the Year 1914, p. 8.   This estimate is somewhat higher than the estimate of the U. S. Bureau of the Census for the same date, 3,605,522. This is chiefly due to the use of the results of the Massachusetts State census of 1915; the estimates made by the U. S. Census are based on the populations of 1900 and 1910.   The slight discrepancy of 61 between the total figure and the sum of the figures for the various counties is due to the fact that the estimates for the counties are the sums of independent estimates for the towns.

b Seventy-third Annual Report of the Commonwealth of Massachusetts on Births, Marriages and Deaths for the Year 1914, pp. 58–73.

The lowest percentages of illegitimate births were in the western, sparsely populated, and somewhat mountainous counties of Berkshire and Franklin.   Whether these low percentages—0.9 and 0.7— may be attributed to incomplete registration of illegitimate births or to other circumstances can not be determined from the information available.   It is interesting to compare with this section the only other distinctly rural counties of the State—Barnstable, Dukes, and Nantucket.   The percentage for these three counties combined was 2.0, and was exceeded by only two counties—Suffolk and Bristol. The percentages for Hampshire and Worcester Counties were both 1.8, while Hampden had a percentage of 1.9.

The highest percentage for any county was 3.6, that being the rate in Suffolk County, which includes the city of Boston.   Middlesex County, exclusive of the State infirmary, had a percentage of 1.5; Essex County, adjoining Middlesex on the east, had a percentage of 1.8; Norfolk and Plymouth Counties, adjoining Middlesex and Suffolk Counties on the south, had percentages of 1.1 and 1.7, respectively.   Bristol County had a relatively high percentage—2.1.   The births at the State infirmary were not included in the total for Middlesex County, since this institution gives care to persons from all parts of the State.   The average percentage for the State as a whole, exclusive of Suffolk County and of the State infirmary, was 1.7. This is less than half the percentage for the county which includes the city of Boston. It must be remembered, however, that the percentages in the other sections of the State would have been higher had not some of their residents gone to Boston or to the State infirmary to secure maternity care.

DISTRIBUTION ACCORDING TO SIZE OF COMMUNITY.

In addition to the geographical distribution the comparative prevalence of illegitimate births in communities of various sizes is significant. (See Table 2.) In the State there were, in 1914, 14 cities of 25,000 to 50,000 inhabitants, 5 of 50,000 to 100,000, 6 of 100,000 to 500,000, and 1 of more than 500,000 population. The figures may be considered fairly comparable except in the case of the largest city, which is a center for the State and surrounding territory.

TABLE 2.—*Per cent of illegitimate births in Massachusetts, 1914, by size of community.*

Size of community.	Number of communities.	Estimated total population 1914.[a]	Total live births.[b]	Live births registered as illegitimate.	
				Number.	Per cent.
Total....................................	353	3,643,863	93,399	2,108	2.3
Less than 5,000......................	240	393,911	7,305	106	1.5
5,000 but less than 10,000...........	54	373,007	8,186	152	1.9
10,000 but less than 25,000..........	33	509,343	12,386	197	1.6
25,000 but less than 50,000..........	14	531,032	14,129	255	1.8
50,000 but less than 100,000.........	5	391,641	10,178	160	1.6
100,000 but less than 500,000........	6	708,529	21,589	372	1.7
Over 500,000.........................	1	736,461	19,467	752	3.9
State infirmary......................			159	114	....

[a] See note *a*, Table 1, p. 271.
[b] Commonwealth of Massachusetts: Seventy-third Annual Report on Births, Marriages, and Deaths for the Year 1914. Boston, 1915. Pp. 58–73. The number of births in Boston, the only city having more than 500,000 inhabitants, was given in the Report of the Health Department of the City of Boston for 1914 as 19,462, and that figure was used in Sec. I of this report.

The lowest percentage of illegitimate births was found in communities of less than 5,000 inhabitants, and the highest in the city of over 500,000. Within these limits there seems to be no evidence of correlation between size of community and percentage of illegitimate births, the percentages for communities of various sizes being very similar. It is clear that rural areas and small towns have an illegitimacy problem very nearly if not quite as serious as that existing in all but the largest cities.

CHILDREN UNDER CARE OF THE DIVISION OF STATE MINOR WARDS.

Description of the Work of the Division.

The administrative work of the division of State minor wards
may be classified into three main groups—investigation, care of children under 3 years of age, and care of older children. The investigating department has been in existence since 1907, and has
developed a system of intensive investigations of applications for
the reception of dependent children and for the return of children
to their relatives. The activities of this department include constructive social work, which has resulted in a steady decrease in the
proportion of cases received to the number of applications.

The infants' department cares for children under 3 years of age,
boarding them in family homes and supervising their care through
frequent visits by nurses employed by the board. Older children
are usually placed in family homes and regularly supervised by the
board's visitors. As a rule, board is paid for children under 14
years of age and in some cases for children above this age. Whenever
possible, parents are required to contribute toward the support of
their children. Children are sometimes placed with relatives or with
other persons desiring to give them free homes. Wards above the
age of 14 years are usually expected to render services equivalent
to the cost of their room and board, the State consequently being
relieved of this expense. If it is found that a child is unable to do
this and also his school work, the payment of board by the State
is continued.

A quarterly allowance is made by the State for the clothing of each
child, and medical and dental treatment is furnished. The board
itself buys the clothing for the children under 2 years of age. Clothing allowances for older children are paid directly to the families with
whom they are placed.

The policy of the board in regard to adoption of the children under
its care is very conservative. Adoption is desired only for children
whose heredity is good and who have no relatives who might later be
able to provide a home for them. Great care is taken that the persons

desiring to adopt a child are able to provide a good home. In order to insure the suitability of the home and the happiness of the child, no adoption is permitted until the child has been cared for by the family for a year free of charge. In 1914 only 53 children were adopted—less than 1 per cent of the children under the care of the board.[1]

The board does not advocate the general policy of removing a child from school and having him begin work at the age of 14. If a child shows desire and capacity for further education, arrangements are made whereby this may be given. Wards above the age of 14 who have not shown particular promise in school are helped to find a trade and are often given industrial training. At the close of the year of the study 56 per cent of the girls and 40 per cent of the boys over 14 years of age were continuing their education. The State was paying board for more than half the children of this age attending school. Of all the 1,540 children under care who were 14 years of age and over, 151 were attending high school, normal school, or college.[2]

The division of State minor wards maintains no institution for the children under its care. Several boarding homes in Boston and vicinity serve as temporary homes for children coming under the care of the board and for those undergoing special medical treatment. Sick children are sent to the State infirmary at Tewksbury. The board has repeatedly recommended the establishment of a hospital for the care and treatment of sick wards of the State.

The board is constantly confronted with the problem of caring for feeble-minded children. Because of the crowded conditions in the institutions for the feeble-minded, State wards who have been diagnosed mentally defective are compelled to wait long periods for admission. Most of these children are cared for in special boarding homes in which none but feeble-minded children are boarded and in which the compensation paid is greater than for normal children. No more than six feeble-minded children are cared for in any one home. The worst cases are sent to the State infirmary until they can be admitted to the proper institution. State wards who are crippled, epileptic, or suffering from other nervous diseases, and who need institutional care, are provided for at the Massachusetts Hospital School or at the Hospital Cottages for Children—the State institutions designed for the care of these classes of children.

---

[1] Thirty-sixth Annual Report of the State Board of Charity of Massachusetts for the Year Ending November 30, 1914. Boston, 1915. Pt. I, pp. 119, 127.

[2] Derived from the Thirty-sixth Annual Report of the State Board of Charity of Massachusetts for the Year Ending November 30, 1914. Boston, 1915. Pt. I, p. 122.

Method of Securing Data.

In order to secure information in regard to children born out of wedlock under care during the year of the study, all records of children under care during 1914 were searched. Detailed analyses were made of records concerning children born out of wedlock, and a certain amount of comparable material was obtained for children of legitimate birth. With the exception of type of care given and number of families represented, the limitations of the study made it impossible to secure this comparable material for all children born in wedlock, and an arbitrary selection for this purpose was made of children whose case records were numbered from 1 to 2000. The histories of these children of legitimate birth were then compared with the histories of children born out of wedlock whose case records were filed in the same numerical group.

Besides the two main groups of children under care—those of legitimate and those of illegitimate birth—there were two groups of children, foundlings and pseudo-foundlings, whose birth status was not known, though the probabilities were that they had been born out of wedlock. For the purpose of this study, the term "foundling" was defined to mean a deserted child concerning whose parentage nothing was known, abandoned without any provision for care having been made. The term "pseudo-foundling" included children of unknown parentage abandoned at board or elsewhere after some provision for care had been made.[3] All available information concerning these children was obtained from the records.

The State board of charity in its annual report publishes figures concerning the total number of children under care. The total figures obtained in the course of this study are somewhat larger than those given in the annual report of the board for 1914, for the reason that the figures here given included children being investigated but not yet received by the board, while the total figures given in the annual report included only children whose care had been definitely assumed. Also, the difference in the year covered—one, the fiscal year of the board from December 1 to November 30, and the other the calendar year—is a partial explanation of the difference.

Proportion of Work of the Division Concerned with Children of Various Types.

The total number of children under care of the division of State minor wards during the year was 7,526. Of these children, 6,413 were receiving prolonged care—that is, they had been received into the custody of the board—and 1,113 were receiving temporary care only. The total number of children of legitimate birth under care

---

[3] See p. 150.

during the year was 5,590; children born out of wedlock numbered 1,721; foundlings, 144; pseudo-foundlings, 71. On the basis of numerical distribution, 74 per cent of the work of the division was concerned with children of legitimate birth; 23 per cent with those born out of wedlock; and 3 per cent with foundlings and pseudo-foundlings. The distribution according to kind of care and status of child is given in Table 3.

TABLE 3.—*Kind of care received by all children under care, according to status of child.*

Status of child.	Children under care of division of State minor wards, 1914.				
	Total.	Receiving prolonged care.a	Receiving temporary care.		
			Total.	Investigation only.	Temporary commitment.
Total...................................	7,526	6,413	1,113	1,069	44
Born in wedlock......................	5,590	4,805	785	743	42
Born out of wedlock..................	1,721	1,393	328	326	2
Foundling............................	144	144			
Pseudo-foundling....................	71	71			

a Includes 6 children—5 born in wedlock and 1 born out of wedlock—committed to the board temporarily but cared for over long periods of time.

Of the 6,413 children receiving prolonged care, 75 per cent were born in wedlock, 22 per cent were born out of wedlock, and 3 per cent were foundlings or pseudo-foundlings. Children of legitimate birth constituted 71 per cent of those receiving temporary care, while children born out of wedlock constituted 29 per cent. That the percentage of children receiving temporary care who were of illegitimate birth is somewhat larger than in the case of those receiving prolonged care is probably accounted for by the fact that a larger proportion of children of legitimate birth than of illegitimate are committed by courts on neglect complaints, and that these cases are not investigated by the division prior to reception.

The annual report of the State board of charity [4] gives the numbers of children of various classes in custody of the board during the year December 1, 1913, to November 30, 1914. Of the total in custody, 36 per cent had been received as dependents, 55 per cent had been committed as neglected children, and 9 per cent had been committed as delinquent or wayward. Of the 1,393 children born out of wedlock receiving prolonged care during the calendar year 1914, 820—59 per cent—were dependent, 551—39 per cent—neglected, and 22—2 per cent—delinquent or wayward. Of the 215 foundlings and pseudo-foundlings, 189—88 per cent—were dependent, 24—11 per cent—neglected, and 2—1 per cent—delinquent.

[4] Thirty-sixth Annual Report of the State Board of Charity of Massachusetts, for the Year Ending November 30, 1914, Pt. I, p. 128.

Considerably less than two-fifths of all the children had been received as dependents, while nearly three-fifths of the children born out of wedlock had been so received; more than half of all the children in custody had been committed as neglected children, while only two-fifths of the children of illegitimate birth had been so committed; the proportion of children committed as wayward or delinquent was considerably larger among all children than among children born out of wedlock.

For the majority of children born in wedlock care by the State was required because of parental neglect or bad home conditions. For the majority of children born out of wedlock the absence of a home and the inability of the mother to support the child made public provision necessary.

The records of children under care of the division of State minor wards are filed by families and not by individual children, records for all children of the same family being given the same file number. The 7,526 children under care during the year studied belonged to 4,792 families. In some of these families there were children of legitimate and of illegitimate birth. Table 4 gives the distribution of cases according to the number of children of the same family under care.

TABLE 4.—*Family groups represented by all children under care.*

Number of children in each family group under care.	Family groups represented.	Children under care of division of State minor wards, 1914.			
		Total.	Born in wedlock.	Born out of wedlock.	Foundlings and pseudo-foundlings.
Total...............................	4,792	7,526	5,590	1,721	215
One.................................	3,275	3,275	1,774	1,286	215
Two.................................	809	1,618	1,364	254	....
Three...............................	383	1,149	1,046	103	....
Four................................	196	784	736	48	....
Five................................	88	440	429	11	....
Six.................................	29	174	167	7	....
Seven...............................	10	70	58	12	....
Eight...............................	2	16	16	....	....

Not quite one-third of the children born in wedlock—32 per cent—were the only children in their families under care of the division of State minor wards. Three-fourths of the children born out of wedlock were the only members of their immediate families under care. The task of caring for a group of brothers and sisters is more complicated than the care of a single child, since it is the policy of the board to place children of the same family together whenever possible. In this respect, therefore, the care of children born out of wedlock presented less difficult problems than the care of other children. Two-thirds of the children of legitimate birth had near relatives also under care of the board, more than two-fifths having more than one. Only one-fourth of the children born out of wedlock had a near relative under care, one-tenth having more than one.

Status of Children of Illegitimate Birth at Time of Application for Care or at Commitment.

Residence, nativity, and race.

The child's residence at the time he came to the attention of the division of State minor wards was reported for 1,652 of the 1,721 children born out of wedlock who were under care during the year. All but 6 of these children were residents of Massachusetts. About half lived in Boston or the metropolitan district and half in other parts of the State. The 475 whose residence was Boston were also included in the Boston study, Section I, chapter 2. The distribution according to residence was as follows:

```
Total under care_____ 1,721
Massachusetts _____ 1,646
  Boston _____ 475
  Metropolitan district outside Boston_____ 364
  Other Massachusetts (including 38 under care of State
    institutions or agencies, at application)_____ 807
Other _____          6
Not reported_____          69
```

The county of residence of the children who lived in the State is given in Table 5, in comparison with the percentage distribution in 1910 of the population under 18 years of age.

TABLE 5.—*Per cent distribution, by county of residence at time of application or commitment, of children born out of wedlock, compared with per cent distribution, by county, of population under 18 years of age.*

County.	Children born out of wedlock, under care of division of State minor wards in 1914.		Per cent distribution, 1910, of population of Massachusetts under 18 years of age. a
	Number.	Per cent distribution.	
Total..	b 1,606	100.0	100.0
Berkshire..	43	2.7	3.3
Franklin..	13	.8	1.3
Hampshire..	18	1.1	1.9
Hampden..	76	4.7	7.2
Worcester..	130	8.1	12.2
Essex..	225	14.0	12.6
Middlesex..	363	22.6	19.7
Suffolk c..	522	32.6	21.2
Norfolk..	52	3.2	5.3
Plymouth..	62	3.9	3.9
Bristol..	79	4.9	10.4
Barnstable, Dukes, and Nantucket...................	23	1.4	1.0

a Based on population statistics in Thirteenth Census of the United States, 1910: Vol. II, Population, pp. 877, 879.
b Total under care whose residence was Massachusetts, exclusive of 38 under the care of State institutions and agencies, and 2 for whom county of residence was not reported.
c The county in which Boston is located.

The percentages of children born out of wedlock coming to the attention of the division of State minor wards from the western and central counties were low in comparison with the percentage distribution in 1910 of the population under 18 years of age. The percentages coming from the county in which Boston is located and from the two contiguous counties having large centers of population were relatively high. This is due in part to the fact that many of the children had previously been under the care of private agencies, and that Boston is a center for social effort in the State. The Boston agencies, in placing their charges, utilize neighboring territory to a greater extent than more distant localities. However, the percentages of children coming to the attention of the State from the counties immediately to the south of Boston were relatively low.

The nativity of the children under the care of the State was as follows:

Total under care	1,721
Total reported	1,665
Massachusetts	1,543
Boston	563
Metropolitan district outside Boston	224
Other Massachusetts (including 176 born in State institutions)	756
Other United States	98
Canada	15
Other	9

A total of 93 per cent of the children whose nativity was reported were born in Massachusetts—34 per cent in Boston, 14 per cent in the metropolitan district outside Boston, and 45 per cent in other parts of the State.

Of the 1,721 children born out of wedlock who were under care, 1,532 were white, 184 were colored, and 5 belonged to other races. The percentage of colored children was 11. This is higher than the proportion of colored found among children born out of wedlock under the care of Boston agencies during the year, that percentage being 7.

Age and sex.

In the majority of cases the responsibility for care devolved upon the State very early in the lives of these children and was, therefore, likely to be long continued. Almost half the children born out of wedlock were under 1 year of age at the time they came to the attention of the division of State minor wards. Three-fifths were less than 2 years of age, three-fourths were under 4 years of age, and more than four-fifths were less than 6 years old. Mothers and relatives had soon found themselves unable to provide for the children, and private agencies had considered the problems involved so serious and likely to be of such long duration that care by the State was desirable. Table 6 gives the ages of the children at the time of application or commitment, together with their sex.

TABLE 6.—*Sex, and age at time of application or commitment, of children born out of wedlock.*

Age at application or commitment.	Children born out of wedlock, under care of division of State minor wards in 1914.			
	Total.	Boys.	Girls.	Sex not reported.
Total............................	1,721	1,002	714	5
Less than 1 year.....................	794	476	313	5
1 year............................	254	145	109	....
2-3 years.........................	240	151	89	....
4-5 years.........................	134	74	60	....
6-9 years.........................	184	92	92	....
10-13 years.......................	96	54	42	....
14 years and over..................	12	6	6	....
Not reported......................	7	4	3	....

There were 1,002 boys and 714 girls, or 288 more boys than girls. The reasons for this predominance of boys among children of illegitimate birth under the care of the State are not apparent. It seems to occur in the younger age groups, the proportions of boys and girls being practically equal among children 6 years of age and over.

Of the 1,721 children of illegitimate birth under care, 373 came under care during 1914. The ages of these children were as follows:

Total coming under care during year_____ 373

Less than 1 year_____ 190 | 6–9 years_____ 35
1 year_____ 36 | 10–13 years_____ 18
2–3 years_____ 56 | 14 years and over_____ 4
4–5 years_____ 34 |

Half the children were under 1 year of age; three-fourths were under 4 years of age. The distribution was very similar to that among all children under care who had been born out of wedlock.

Presence with or separation from mother.

More than half the children born out of wedlock—56 per cent of the 1,532 reported—had been separated from their mothers before the time of application or commitment to the division of State minor wards. This proportion is large, in view of the fact that three-fifths of the children were under 2 years of age. Of the 924 who, previous to application or commitment, had not received previous prolonged care from agencies, and whose location was reported, 55 per cent were separated from their mothers. The percentage was almost the same—56 per cent—for the 608 who had received previous prolonged care. The percentages of children of various ages who had been separated from their mothers varied considerably for the two groups—a smaller percentage of the younger children who had received prolonged care and a larger percentage of the older children having been separated from their mothers previous to application or commitment to the division of State minor wards. Table 7 gives, for the children who had not previously received prolonged care, the proportions at various ages who had been separated from their mothers.

TABLE 7.—*Per cent of children born out of wedlock not having previously received prolonged care from agencies, who had been separated from their mothers previous to application or commitment, by age.*

Age at application or commitment.	Children born out of wedlock, under care of division of State minor wards in 1914, who had not received prolonged care previous to application or commitment.						
	Total.	Whose presence with or separation from mother at application or commitment was reported.					Whose presence with or separation from mother was not reported.
		Total.	With mother.		Separated from mother.		
			Number.	Per cent.	Number.	Per cent.	
Total...............	a 1,067	924	414	44.8	510	55.2	143
Less than 1 year.........	525	438	218	49.8	220	50.2	87
1 year....................	141	120	40	33.3	80	66.7	21
2–5 years................	227	204	88	43.1	116	56.9	23
6 years and over.........	170	158	68	43.0	90	57.0	12
Not reported.............	4	4	....	....	4	....	....

a Excluding 9 under care from birth.

Half the children under 1 year of age who had not previously received prolonged care had been separated from their mothers, two-thirds of those 1 year of age had been separated, while less than three-fifths of those 2 years of age and over had been cared for apart from their mothers previous to application or commitment. That the largest percentage of children separated from their mothers occurred among those 1 year of age is surprising.

Table 8 gives for the children who had been under prolonged agency care at some time previous to application or commitment the proportions with their mothers and separated from them.

TABLE 8.—*Per cent of children born out of wedlock having previously received prolonged care from agencies, who had been separated from their mothers previous to application or commitment, by age.*

Age at application or commitment.	Children born out of wedlock, under care of division of State minor wards in 1914, who had received prolonged care previous to application or commitment.						
	Total.	Whose presence with or separation from mother at application or commitment was reported.					Whose presence with or separation from mother was not reported.
		Total.	With mother.		Separated from mother.		
			Number.	Per cent.	Number.	Per cent.	
Total...............	645	608	266	43.7	342	56.3	37
Less than 1 year.........	260	242	136	56.2	106	43.8	18
1 year....................	113	110	41	37.3	69	62.7	3
2–5 years................	147	136	54	39.7	82	60.3	11
6 years and over.........	122	117	34	29.1	83	70.9	5
Not reported.............	3	3	1	....	2	....	....

Forty-four per cent of the children under 1 year of age who had previously received prolonged care had been separated from their mothers, as compared with 50 per cent of those who had not previously received prolonged care. The percentage at 1 year was slightly less among the former group than among the latter. Above this age the percentages separated from their mothers were higher among children who had been under agency care than among those who had not received such care—71 per cent for children of the former group 6 years of age and over, as compared with 57 per cent among children of this age who had not received care from agencies.

Table 9 shows the number of children who had been under the supervision of agencies at the time of application or immediately prior to commitment.

TABLE 9.—*Supervision and presence with or absence from mother, at application or commitment, of children born out of wedlock.*

Presence with or separation from mother at application or commitment.	Children born out of wedlock, under care of division of State minor wards in 1914.		
	Total.	At application or commitment.	
		Under agency supervision.	Not under agency supervision.
Total	a 1,712	923	789
With mother	680	413	267
Separated from mother	852	476	376
Not reported	180	34	146

a Exclusive of 9 under care from birth.

Excluding the 9 children who were unborn at the time application was made for care, 923 of the 1,712 children born out of wedlock—54 per cent—were under agency supervision at the time of application or commitment to the division of State minor wards. Of the 680 children who were with their mothers at this time, 413, or 61 per cent, were receiving agency care; of the 852 away from their mothers, 476, or 56 per cent, were under agency supervision. The fact that a greater proportion of those with their mothers than of those away were being cared for by agencies is contrary to what might have been expected.

Home or place of residence.

The home or place of residence of the child at the time of application or commitment is given in Table 10.

TABLE 10.—*Home or place of residence, at time of application or commitment, of children born out of wedlock, of specified ages.*

Home or place of residence of child at application or commitment.	Children born out of wedlock, under care of division of State minor wards in 1914.						
	Total.	Age at application or commitment.					
		Less than 1 yr.	1 yr.	2–3 yrs.	4–5 yrs.	6 yrs. and over.	Not reported.
Total	a 1,712	785	254	240	134	292	7
Mother's own home	207	32	25	42	33	75	....
Mother's other establishment	12	2	1	2	2	6	1
Mother's place of employment	56	29	10	10	3	4	....
Mother's parental home	136	64	15	18	8	31	....
Home of relatives or friends	105	44	7	13	10	31	....
Adoptive or foster home	39	4	7	6	3	19	....
Boarding or free home	473	212	91	77	34	56	3
Public infirmary or maternity home	194	113	32	24	9	16	....
Hospital	53	46	5	1	1	....	....
Other institution	49	15	6	6	4	18	....
Other	19	15	2	....	1	1	....
Not reported	369	209	53	43	26	35	3

a Excluding 9 who were under care from birth.

More than one-third of the children whose residence at the time of application or commitment was reported were living in their mothers' own homes or places of employment, or were being cared for by grandparents, relatives, or friends. The number living in the mothers' places of employment was relatively very small. More than one-third were being cared for in boarding or free homes. Nearly one-fifth were in public infirmaries, maternity homes, or hospitals. Only a small number of children were being cared for in institutions of other types. In 3 per cent of the cases the child had been living in an adoptive or foster home.

As was to be expected, the proportion of children provided for in their mothers' own homes was smaller in the younger-age groups and the proportion in public infirmaries, maternity homes, or hospitals was larger. The smallest proportion in boarding or free homes was found among the children 6 years of age and over.

Previous agency care.

A total of 1,393 children born out of wedlock received prolonged care from the division of State minor wards during the year. Of these, nearly two-fifths had received prolonged care from agencies before coming under the care of the division. In many cases care had been given by more than one agency. Table 11 gives information on this subject.

TABLE 11.—*Prolonged care received previous to application or commitment by children born out of wedlock, according to age.*

Age at application or commitment.	Children born out of wedlock, receiving prolonged care from division of State minor wards in 1914.							
	Total.	Who had received no previous prolonged care.	Who had received previous prolonged care.					
			Total.	From specified number of agencies.				
				One.	Two.	Three.	Four.	
Total......................	1,393	858	535	402	115	12	6	
Less than 1 year................	596	392	204	164	40	....	....	
1 year......................	217	123	94	70	21	....	....	
2–5 years...................	319	192	127	95	27	3	....	
6 years and over..............	254	147	107	71	26	4	1	
Not reported..................	7	4	3	2	1	5	5	

One-third of the children under 1 year of age had received prolonged care previously. More than two-fifths of those 1 year of age at application or commitment, and about the same proportion of those 6 years of age and over, had previously received prolonged care. Prolonged agency care had been given two-fifths of the children between the ages of 2 and 5 years.

In Table 12 will be found information concerning types of agencies giving previous prolonged care. One-third of the children who had previously been under prolonged agency supervision had been cared for by child-caring agencies. Two-thirds had received care from agencies of other types, including maternity homes, public infirmaries, and child-protective agencies. All children committed as neglected had previously been given either temporary or prolonged care by a child-protective agency.

TABLE 12.—*Type of prolonged care received previous to application or commitment by children born out of wedlock, according to age.*

Age at application or commitment.	Children born out of wedlock, receiving prolonged care from division of State minor wards in 1914.				
	Total.	Who had received no previous prolonged care.	Who had received previous prolonged care.		
			Total.	From child-caring agencies.	From other agencies.
Total..........................	1,393	858	535	a 173	362
Less than 1 year.....................	596	392	204	54	150
1 year.............................	217	123	94	17	77
2–5 years...........................	319	192	127	48	79
6 years and over....................	254	147	107	53	54
Not reported.......................	7	4	3	1	2

a Including 94 under care of both child-caring and other agencies.

One-twelfth of the children less than 2 years of age at application or commitment and slightly more than one-sixth of those 2 years of age and over had previously received prolonged care from child-caring agencies. One-eighth of all the children under prolonged care had previously been given prolonged care by child-caring agencies. These agencies had provided for the children for a time, but had found the problems involved of a type with which the State agency was best adapted to deal.

The following cases are representative of a number in which prolonged care had been given by agencies previous to the time of application or commitment to the division of State minor wards:

Two brothers, 5 and 3 years of age, respectively, were committed to the division of State minor wards as neglected children during the year of the study. The elder had been in charge of a private child-caring agency for three years, and the younger for two years. The mother had failed to support the children, and at the time of commitment her whereabouts was not known. The children were healthy, bright, and attractive.

The older child was born in another State. The mother and father had lived as man and wife, and they planned to marry; but the father was not steady— so the mother said—and she left him and came to Boston. The private child-caring agency took charge of the child and sent the mother to a maternity home, where the second child was born. The mother claimed that the children had the same father, but this was questioned. The mother remained at the maternity home with her younger child for some time, acting as cook in the home. Finally discharged because of her intemperance, she was sent to an institution for inebriate women, the child-caring agency assuming the care of the baby. Subsequently the mother served several terms in a correctional institution. She was extremely intemperate and was violent when intoxicated. (Cases W 345, 346.)

Five years before the period covered by this study application was made to the division of State minor wards for the care of an infant less than a month old who was with his mother in a maternity home. The alleged father was a soldier, and the mother refused to give his name. She was ill, and her sister requested that the State assume the care of the child. After investigation the case was closed, because the child had been placed at board by a private child-caring agency. A few months later the boarding woman made application to the State for the care of the child, since the mother was not paying board. This application was also refused, after investigation and conference, since the private agency was willing to continue supervision. However, when the child was not quite 2 years of age this agency came to the conclusion that the mother was too ill to continue to bear any responsibility for the payment of the child's board. She had heart trouble and tuberculosis. The case seemed to involve long-continued care, and the State, therefore, received the child at the request of the private agency. (Case W 350.)

An 8-year-old boy had been received by the division of State minor wards about five years before this study was made, on the application of his maternal aunt. Both maternal grandparents were dead, and the mother had disappeared a few months before the application. The aunt was an actress; and since it was necessary for her to travel frequently, she was unable to care for the child. The mother was reported to have had a previous child of illegitimate birth.

The boy was born in a Boston hospital. When a month old he and his mother were sent by a private child-caring agency to a children's institution, where the latter was employed as a wet nurse. Here they remained until the baby was 7 months old. The child was then boarded in a private family, the mother paying. Two and one-half years later application was made by the mother to the same child-caring agency for a boarding home for the boy. The society sent the child to his aunt, and the mother to the State infirmary, where a third child of illegitimate birth was born. This child was colored. Upon discharge from the infirmary the mother abandoned the baby in a field and was arrested and committed to the reformatory for women. Information in regard to the older child is incomplete, but apparently the aunt provided for him for nearly three years. At the end of that time the mother, who had been released from the reformatory, applied to the agency which had previously been interested in the case, asking that they assume the care of the boy. The agency boarded the child for two years, at the end of which time the aunt again took him. The mother disappeared and the child had been with his aunt for only a few weeks when she again asked the agency to provide for the child. As has been stated, her profession required her to travel a great deal, and it was impossible for her to keep the child longer. The society boarded the boy for two months. Then, realizing that the disappearance of the mother and the inability of the aunt to keep the child made it necessary to provide for him in a more permanent way, the private agency relinquished the child to the care of the State, and the boy became a State ward.   (Case W 1070.)

A boy 18 years of age had been committed to the division of State minor wards at the age of 11, having previously spent six years under the care of a private child-caring agency. Up to the age of 5 years he had been cared for by his maternal grandparents, but they had been unable and unwilling to give him further care. His mother had married a man who was not the child's father. The boy had a tubercular knee, and while under the care of the private agency had spent most of the time in their institution receiving medical treatment. He had also been in a home for crippled children and had spent five months immediately prior to his commitment to the State in a third institution—a children's home—supported by the overseers of the poor. At the time of commitment the boy was in much better physical condition; however, he was placed in a State institution for crippled children, where he improved steadily. He was able to work on the farm, and later was a chauffeur for the institution. At the end of the period covered by this study he was considered able to be placed permanently in a suitable occupation, and his good conduct gave promise for the future.   (Case W 488.)

A boy 18 years of age at the close of the period covered by the study had been committed to the division of State minor wards at the age of 12 years. He had been under the care of agencies since the age of 7 years. His mother and father had been illegally married, the father never having been divorced from his first wife, who was living at the time of his second marriage. In all, three children were born of this illegal union.

When the boy was 7 years old he and his brother and sister were placed under the care of a private child-caring agency. The mother was in a home for incurables and the father in a hospital for the insane. The three children were placed in family homes by the private agency. The boy of the study remained five years in one home, but proving to be unmanageable, revengeful, and dishonest, he was finally removed by the agency and the responsibility for his care was turned over to the town in which the parents had lived. He was placed in the almshouse for a few days and was then committed to the care of the State. His brother and sister remained under the care of the private agency.

The boy was placed by the State in a boarding home, later in a free home, and finally in a wage home. At the end of the period he was working and was reported to be doing very well. (Case W 518.)

Source of application or commitment.

The sources of the applications to the division of State minor wards for the care of the children, or of the commitments of children to the care of the State, were as follows:

Total under care_____ 1,721
Total reported_____ 1,701

Court	542	Paternal relative	8
Public agency	451	Friend	68
Private agency	134	Boarding woman	64
Mother	361	Other	2
Maternal relative	71		

Courts committed 32 per cent of the children to the care of the State. Overseers of the poor and other public agencies committed or made application for the care of 26 per cent. Applications for the care of 8 per cent of the children came from private agencies. The mothers applied directly for the care of 21 per cent of the children, and relatives or friends for 9 per cent more. In 4 per cent of the cases women who had been boarding the children and who had not been adequately paid applied for the assumption of care by the State.

Reason for application or commitment.

The immediate reasons for application or commitment are given below. Although not always the underlying causes of the child's dependency, they indicate the types of situations which made care by the State necessary for these children born out of wedlock:

	Number.	Per cent distribution.
Total under care	1,721	
Total reported	1,690	100.0
Mother dead	39	2.3
Mother unfit to care for child or mother's home unfit	442	26.2
Mother feeble-minded	66	
Mother insane	37	
Mother committed to an institution for delinquents	117	
Mother otherwise unfit	134	
Mother's home unfit	88	
Mother unable to care for child	666	39.4
Mother's husband unwilling	29	
Mother physically unable	86	
Mother otherwise unable	551	

Child abandoned or deserted_____	348	20. 6
Board unpaid _____ 34		
Abandoned at board _____ 193		
Otherwise deserted _____ 121		
Child in unfit home (other than mother's)_____	79	4. 6
Boarding home unfit_____ 28		
Custodian's home unfit _____ 51		
Other _____	116	6. 9
Custodian unable or unwilling to care for child_____ 37		
Child delinquent or unmanageable_____ 28		
Child sick _____ 24		
Not otherwise specified _____ 27		

The mother's inability to provide for the child was the immediate reason for application in nearly two-fifths of the cases. One-fifth of the children came to the attention of the division of State minor wards because they had been abandoned or deserted. The unfitness of the mother to provide proper care or the existence of conditions in the mother's home detrimental to the child's welfare was given as the reason for application or commitment in slightly more than one-fourth of the cases.

The following cases illustrate some of the conditions which lead to application to the State for the care of children born out of wedlock, or to commitments of these children to the care of the State:

The year before the period covered by the study, the mother of a 20-month-old baby girl applied to the State for the care of the child. The mother was not well, and though she worked very hard she was unable to support the baby. She had lived with the father of the child for five years, and they had had three other children, two of whom were living. Just before the baby's birth the mother discovered that the father had a wife living, and for this reason she left him. Two months after the baby's birth at the State infirmary, the mother took the two older children to her parents' home in Canada, placing the baby in the care of a private agency. The grandparents were willing to care for the older children but refused to take the youngest. The agency placed the child in a boarding home, the mother paying board. During the 18 months the baby was under care of this agency she lived in six different boarding homes, having been placed in one of these two different times. Meanwhile, the mother returned to Massachusetts and secured a position at housework, where she earned $6 a week. Out of this amount she paid $2.50 to her parents for the board of the older children, and $2 to the agency for the baby's board; with the balance she had to pay carfare and provide clothing for herself and the children.

The division of State minor wards boarded the baby in a private family. At the end of a year's care she was reported to be a lovable child, in good health, though somewhat backward in her general development. (Case W 1050.)

A baby boy, born in a private hospital, was boarded out from the hospital at the age of 6 weeks. His mother had never seen him. When he was not quite 11 months old application was made for his care to the division of State minor wards, the boarding woman claiming that he had been abandoned at board and that $34 was due her. An investigation was made, and it was found that the mother's relatives were able to continue to support the child, and that the father was a professional man with considerable means. A payment of $500 toward the child's board was obtained from the father, and the responsibility for the child's care was assumed by the mother's relatives, the baby continuing at board. During the first year and a half of the child's life he lived in six different boarding homes, for periods varying in length from two days to six months. (Case W 811.)

A boy 20 years of age at the time of this study was committed to the care of the State at the age of 3 years because of neglect by his foster parents. His mother, a school-teacher, had given him away when he was 2 weeks old. The foster mother proved to be immoral and intemperate and took the child with her to rum shops and questionable places. Her home was filthy, and the boy was badly neglected. The child was placed at board by the State; during the six years next preceding the close of the study, he had remained in the same home. At the age of 17 he was reported to be a good worker; later reports of his conduct were not satisfactory, and he was reported to be shiftless and irresponsible. (Case W 509.)

A 4-month-old baby was received by the State at the age of 1 month, application having been made by a private agency because the mother was ill and unable to care for the child, though she was fond of the baby and anxious to support it. A few days after the application was made the mother was examined at a psychopathic hospital and pronounced syphilitic and feeble-minded, institutional care being recommended.

The mother had applied for help five months before the child was born and was admitted to the State infirmary because she had no home and was in need of treatment for venereal infection. Later she was removed to the almshouse of the town in which she had lived. The baby was born in a private home in the same town. He had sore eyes and was placed in a Boston hospital for treatment, where he remained until received by the division of State minor wards at the age of 1 month. He was boarded out by the State, and at the close of the period was reported to be bright and happy and doing well.

Three years before the child of the study was born the mother had had a previous child out of wedlock, born at the State infirmary. She was 18 years of age at that time. This baby died of pneumonia at the age of 2 months. The alleged father married another woman. The alleged father of the second child denied paternity but said that he was willing to pay board in order to keep the case out of court.

The mother's early history had not been a happy one. At the age of 2 years, when her father deserted his family, she was sent to live with relatives in Canada, where she remained until the age of 10 years. The girl had only a few terms of schooling, having been kept at home most of the time to work on the farm. At the age of 10 years she was placed in a convent school in the United States by her mother—the child's grandmother—and remained there for eight years, spending her vacations with her mother, who worked in a cotton mill. She was reported not to have studied much in school, because she was not in good health. Upon leaving the convent school she went to work in a cotton mill, and before long became pregnant. After her first child was born she drifted from city to city, working for short periods in cotton factories and living at times with her mother and sister, who were out of work much of the time. The girl was intemperate and immoral and was reported to have practiced prostitution for a time. The family history showed tuberculosis, insanity, and excessive alcoholism. (Case W 1151.)

The year before the period covered by the study application was made to the division of State minor wards by the mother of a month-old infant, who desired the State to assume the care of the baby. She had an older child of illegitimate birth whom she could keep with her at her place of employment, but she could not provide for the younger child. After a period of investigation the application was refused, because the mother was under the care of a private agency which was willing to continue supervision. In a few weeks, however, this agency made application to the State for the care of the baby, since it seemed impossible to solve the problem otherwise. At the time the child was received he was suffering from malnutrition, but he improved under the care of the State.

The mother was reported to be in poor physical condition, mentally low grade, and untruthful. She had first come to the attention of agencies at the time her first child was born. She was then 18 years of age and had been in the United States four years, having been employed in domestic service. Her parents had never lived in this country, but her brother—a man of good character—tried to assist her and wished to compel the father of the first child to marry her, but the mother refused to allow this and said her conduct was no more irregular than that of " everyone else." The mother kept the first child with her, obtaining employment at housework; part of the time she was under the supervision of private agencies. When the second child was 5 days old a visiting nurse reported to one of the agencies which had given care previously that the mother was boarding with a woman of doubtful reputation. An investigation was made, advice and supervision were given, and a mental examination arranged for; the mother was diagnosed feeble-minded. At the last report she was again at housework, keeping the older child with her. (Case W 1200.)

Care Given by the Division of State Minor Wards.

Length of time children were cared for.

The ages, at the end of the year or the close of care, of the children born out of wedlock were as follows:

Total under care_____ 1,721

Less than 1 year_____	180	10–13 years_____	264
1 year_____	139	14–17 years_____	183
2–3 years_____	219	18 years and over_____	122
4–5 years_____	228	Not reported_____	1
6–9 years_____	385		

The total amount of care given these children by the division of State minor wards could be estimated only for the 1,393 receiving prolonged care. At the end of the year or the close of care 8 per cent of these children were less than 2 years of age; 26 per cent were from 2 to 5 years old; 26 per cent, from 6 to 9 years of age; 18 per cent, from 10 to 13 years old; and 21 per cent were 14 years of age and over. The number of years they had been under care is given in Table 13.

TABLE 13.—*Duration of care received by children of specified ages, born out of wedlock.*

Age at close of care or at end of year.	Total.	Children born out of wedlock, receiving prolonged care from division of State minor wards in 1914. Number of years under care.							
		Less than 1.	1	2–3	4–5	6–9	10–13	14 and over.	Not reported.
Total	1,393	171	122	256	211	336	176	115	6
Less than 1 year	50	50							
1 year	62	34	28						
2–3 years	169	33	49	87					
4–5 years	199	22	15	75	87				
6–9 years	362	18	15	50	75	201			3
10–13 years	251	12	13	24	28	68	105		1
14–17 years	177	2	2	19	17	39	39	57	2
18 years and over	122				4	28	32	58	
Not reported	1			1					

Seven-eighths of the children who had received prolonged care—88 per cent—had been under care one year or longer. Of the 912 children 6 years of age or over 627, or 69 per cent, had been wards of the State for at least 6 years. Of the 550 children 10 years of age or over, 291—53 per cent—had been under care at least 10 years. Twenty-five children had been cared for by the division of State minor wards for 16 years, 21 children for 17 years, 4 children for 18 years, 7 children for 19 years, and 4 children had been State wards for 20 years.

Excluding 1 whose age was not reported and 6 for whom length of time under care was not given, 1,336 children 1 year of age and over were receiving prolonged care. Up to the end of the year studied the care given these children by the division of State minor wards averaged six years per child. Almost seven-eighths of these children remained under care at the end of the year, hence the figures given in Table 14 by no means represent the total length of time during which they will be dependent upon the State.

TABLE 14.—*Aggregate and average duration of care received by children of specified ages, born out of wedlock.*

Age of child at close of care or at end of year.	Children born out of wedlock, receiving prolonged care from division of State minor wards.	Number of years under care of division of State minor wards.	
		Aggregate.	Average.
Total	a 1,336	b 8,020.5	6.0
1 year	62	45.0	0.7
2–5 years	368	873.5	2.4
6–9 years	359	1,928.0	5.4
10–13 years	250	1,881.0	7.5
14 years and over	297	3,293.0	11.1

a Excluding 50 who were less than 1 year of age, 1 whose age was not reported, and 6 for whom time under care was not reported.
b Estimating average for those under care less than 1 year as 6 months—171 children, 85.5 years.

Children 1 year of age at the end of the period had been under care for an average of about 8 months; children 2 to 5 years of age, for an average of 2 years and 5 months; those 6 to 9 years of age, for an average of 5 years and 5 months. Children between the ages of 10 and 13 had spent on the average 7 years and 6 months under the continuous care of the State, and those 14 years of age and over had been State wards for an average of 11 years and 1 month.

Home or place of residence of children at end of period.

The home or place of residence of the children at the end of the year, or, in the case of those who died or were discharged from care during the year, immediately previous to death or discharge, is an index of the types of provision made by the State for the care of these children. Information was secured as to the various dispositions of the children throughout the period of care by the State, but it is impossible to present all this material in statistical form.

Only 35 of the 1,393 children receiving prolonged care—3 per cent—were with their mothers at the end of the year or the close of the case. Eight of these children were under 1 year of age, 14 were from 1 to 5 years, and 13 were 6 years of age and over.

The home or place of residence of the children is given in Table 15.

TABLE 15.—*Home or place of residence at end of period of children of specified ages, born out of wedlock.*

Home or place of residence at end of year or immediately preceding close of care.	Children born out of wedlock, receiving prolonged care from division of State minor wards in 1914.					
	Total.	Age at end of year or at close of care.				
		Less than 2 yrs.	2–5 yrs.	6–9 yrs.	10 yrs. and over.	Not reported.
Total	1,393	112	368	362	550	1
Family home	1,280	96	351	346	486	1
Home of relatives or friends	a 30	5	10	4	11	....
Adoptive or foster home	47	1	33	9	4	....
Boarding or free home	1,166	90	308	333	434	1
Wage home	36	....	....	....	36	....
Other	1	....	....	....	1	....
Institution	104	16	16	16	56	....
Public infirmary	67	15	15	10	27	....
Institution for the feeble-minded	19	....	....	1	18	....
Institution for delinquents	2	....	....	....	2	....
Other institutions	16	1	1	b 5	9	....
Not reported	9	....	1	....	8	....

a Including 16 in their mothers' own homes, 3 of whom had been adopted by the mother and her husband; 2 in their mothers' places of employment; 4 in their mothers' parental homes; 1 adopted by maternal relatives; 4 in the homes of paternal relatives, 2 of whom had been adopted by their fathers; 3 in friends' homes.
b Including 1 in a hospital.

More than nine-tenths of the children receiving prolonged care—92 per cent—were in family homes. Only 7 per cent were in institutions. The location of 1 per cent was not reported, but it was probable that they were not in institutions.

The prevailing type of disposition was the boarding or free home. Of the 1,280 children in family homes, 91 per cent were in homes of this kind. Many of the older children in free homes were earning their board by assisting in household tasks or on the farm. Children living in wage homes comprised 3 per cent of the total. These were older children, whose services in the home were of sufficient value to merit the payment of wages in addition to room and board. Six per cent of the children were in the homes of relatives or friends or of adoptive or foster parents, under the supervision of the State.

Of the 104 children in institutions, 65 per cent were in the public infirmary. Some of these children were there only temporarily on account of sickness, and others had been in the infirmary for some time, because of prolonged ill health or defective mentality. Children being cared for in institutions for the feeble-minded comprised 18 per cent of the total in institutions; the remaining 17 per cent were in institutions of other types.

Occupations of the children 14 years of age and over.

During the year 305 children 14 years of age and over were under care of the division of State minor wards. All but 6 of these received prolonged care. Twenty-eight of the 299 under prolonged care were in institutions. Information was obtained in regard to the occupations of 174 children—95 boys and 79 girls—who were living in family homes. (See Table 16.)

TABLE 16.—*Occupations of boys and girls 14 years of age and over, born out of wedlock.*

Occupation at end of period.	Children born out of wedlock, 14 years of age and over, receiving prolonged care from division of State minor wards in 1914 whose occupations were reported.		
	Total.	Boys.	Girls.
Total	174	95	79
Attending school	86	41	45
Housework	14		a 14
Farm	13	b 13	
Factory	25	b 15	b 10
Store	7	c 7	
Office	3		3
Other	21	a 17	4
None	5	2	3

a Including 2 also attending school.
b Including 1 also attending school.
c Including 4 also attending school.

Half the children whose occupations were reported were attending school and were not gainfully employed after school hours or during vacations. A few who were gainfully employed part of the time were also attending school. Almost half the children—83 of the 174—were gainfully employed: Twenty-seven were at housework or farm work, 25 were employed in factories, 10 were working in stores or offices, and 21 were engaged in other occupations.

Disposition of children whose cases were closed during year.

During the year studied, 326 children—19 per cent—died or were discharged from care. Of these, 214 had received temporary care and 112 prolonged care. Forty-four children died during the year, of whom 25 had received temporary care and 19 prolonged care.

The 189 children receiving temporary care, whose cases were terminated during the year for reasons other than death, were discharged to the following persons or agencies for the reasons specified:

```
Total receiving temporary care previous to discharge_____ 189
Mother _____  46
       Mother able to care for the child_____ _____ 14
       Mother and her family able_____ 15
       Mother and father married each other_____  2
       Mother married, but not to father_____  2
       Mother's husband willing to care for child_____  2
       Home situation improved_____  1
       Other disposition made_____  5
       Mother and child deported_____  1
       Mother and child disappeared and impossible to locate_____  4
Other relatives or friends_____  43
       Relatives or friends able to care for child_____  38
       Child adopted by relatives_____  2
       Home situation improved _____  2
       Other disposition made _____  1
Adoptive or foster parents_____  18
Private agency or institution_____  53
Public agency or institution_____  22
Not reported to whom discharged_____ _____   7
       Child disappeared and impossible to locate_____  6
       Home situation improved _____  1
```

The care of one-fourth of these children was assumed by their mothers, more than one-fifth were taken by relatives or friends, and the care of one-tenth was assumed by adoptive or foster parents. Private agencies assumed the care of almost three-tenths, and public agencies of more than one-tenth of the children.

The 93 children receiving prolonged care during the year, whose cases were terminated for reasons other than death, were discharged to the following persons or agencies for the reasons specified:

Total receiving prolonged care previous to discharge_____ 93
Mother _____ _____ 12
    Mother able to care for child_____ 3
    Mother and father married each other_____ 4
    Mother married, but not to father_____ 2
    Mother's husband willing to care for child_____ 1
    Mother and child deported_____ 2
Other relatives or friends_____ 8
    Relatives or friends able to care for child_____ 5
    Child adopted by father or other relatives_____ 2
    Other disposition made_____ 1
Adoptive parents_____ 21
Private agency_____ 1
Public agency or institution_____ 21
    Child feeble-minded or delinquent_____ 13
    Child discharged for other reasons_____ 8
Self __ _____ 29
    Of age_____ 22
    Self-supporting _____ 5
    Child disappeared and impossible to locate_____ 2
Not reported_____ 1

One-eighth of this group of children were discharged to their mothers, one-twelfth to other relatives or friends, and nearly one-fourth to adoptive parents. Public agencies or institutions, such as schools for the feeble-minded and institutions for delinquents, assumed the care of almost one-fourth of these children. Nearly one-third were of age or were self-supporting, or had been shifting for themselves for some time.

Characteristics of the Children.

Physical and mental condition.

The division of State minor wards has physicians attached to its staff and pays especial attention to the health of the children under its care. Hence the records contain fairly complete information as to physical condition. At the end of the period studied three-fourths of the children were in good physical condition, so far as known; one-fourth were in poor condition, a considerable number having serious physical disabilities. The proportion in poor condition is practically the same as that found among children born out of wedlock under the care of Boston agencies during the year.

Total children under care_____ 1,721
In good physical condition, so far as known_____ 1,299
Having very defective vision_____ 16
Having very defective hearing_____ 7
Crippled or deformed (including 1 also rachitic and 1 also tubercu-
    lar and rachitic)_____ 37
Tubercular (including 1 also rachitic)_____ 10
Having rachitis _____ 24

Having syphilis or gonorrhea (including 1 also deaf, 4 also crippled
    or deformed, 1 also crippled and rachitic, 1 also rachitic and hav-
    ing defective vision, and 1 also having defective vision)_____   44
Suspected of having syphilis or gonorrhea_____   3
Epileptic (including 1 also crippled)_____   4
In otherwise poor condition_____   277

A total of 1 per cent of the children had seriously defective vision
or hearing and 2 per cent were crippled or deformed. Children having syphilis or gonorrhea comprised 3 per cent of the total.

The division of State minor wards makes a practice of securing
diagnosis of mentality in all cases in which there is reason to believe
that the child is below normal mentally. Children diagnosed feeble-
minded are transferred to the State institutions for the feeble-minded
as soon as there is accommodation for them. However, the limited
capacity of these institutions makes it necessary for the division to
provide for considerable numbers of feeble-minded children either in
private boarding homes or at the State infirmary. Children who are
admitted to the State schools for the mentally defective are usually
not discharged from the division of State minor wards for some time,
the reason being that occasionally after a period of residence at one
of these institutions a child is found not to require permanent custodial care, and it again becomes necessary to provide for him in the
community.

By reference to Table 17 it will be seen that there were under care
during the year 849 children 7 years of age and over who had been
born out of wedlock. Of these 19 per cent were below normal mentally or were backward in school.

TABLE 17.—*Mental condition of children 7 years of age and over, born out of
wedlock.*

Age at end of period.	Children 7 years of age and over, born out of wedlock, under care of division of State minor wards in 1914.						
	Total.	Mental condition.					
		Normal.	Very backward in school.	Probably sub-normal or feeble-minded, but not diagnosed.	Sub-normal (diagnosed).	Feeble-minded (diagnosed).	Insane.
Total.............	849	691	50	15	7	83	3
7–9 years.............	280	236	14	8	1	21	....
10–13 years.............	264	202	22	3	2	35	....
14 years and over.........	305	253	14	4	4	a 27	3

a Includes 1 also insane.

The percentage of children below normal mentally or very backward in school was highest in the 10-to-13-year age group, 23 per cent

of the children of this age being so reported, as compared with 16 per cent of those 7 to 9 years of age and 17 per cent of those 14 years of age and over. The high percentage in the intermediate age group may be explained by the fact that in many cases definite subnormality or abnormality does not manifest itself until the child approaches the age of adolescence, and that in the case of children over the age of 14 there has been opportunity to make some other provision for their care.

Ten per cent of all the children 7 years of age and over had been diagnosed feeble-minded. Of the children 7 to 9 years of age, 8 per cent were known to be mentally defective; of those 10 to 13 years of age, 13 per cent; and of those 14 years of age and over, 9 per cent. The percentage of feeble-mindedness was considerably higher than that found among children under the care of Boston agencies—6 per cent; it was ten times higher than the percentage of feeble-mindedness found among children under the care of a selected group of five private child-caring agencies in Boston.[5] Private agencies, as a rule, turn over their most difficult cases to the State.

The following are illustrations of some of the difficulties involved in giving proper care to children of low mentality, and of the defective heritage frequently found in these cases:

A 10-year-old girl, who had been under the care of the State from the age of 1 month, was backward and very nervous, and progress in school was difficult. She was given a mental examination and pronounced backward but not feeble-minded; it was recommended that she be placed in a special class in school. The child's mother was feeble-minded and deformed—both hands had been amputated when she was a child—and she had served a term in the reformatory for women. At the time of the child's birth, which occurred in an almshouse, she was only 17 years of age. The maternal grandmother was dead and the grandfather was intemperate and unable to care for himself. Three children were subsequently born out of wedlock to this woman by different fathers, the last a resident of the almshouse where she had lived for some time. Two of these children also became wards of the State, but one of them died soon after commitment. The other, a 5-year-old girl, was still under care and was in bad physical condition, having suffered from malnutrition, rachitis, and spinal curvature. The condition of this girl and of her sister—the child first mentioned—necessitated special care and attention. (Case W 582.)

A boy 12 years of age, who had been under the care of the State board from infancy, was the source of considerable trouble at home and at school. He was given a mental examination and pronounced not feeble-minded but hysterical. Although he was in the fifth grade, he was doing third-grade work and was a disturbing element in the class. He was said to have a violent temper.

The boy's mother was committed to a reformatory during the year of the study on a charge of drunkenness. It was her fifth commitment to this institution, the first sentence having been served 17 years before. Sixteen times she had been placed on probation or sentenced to an institution, and she had been arrested several other times. Most of her arrests had been on

[5] See pp. 183–184.

charges of drunkenness, though on two occasions she had been before the court on sex charges. She was diseased and mentally subnormal. Both her parents had been intemperate. The woman was a widow, and had one child of legitimate birth. Since her husband's death she had had two children out of wedlock—the one mentioned above and a child who was placed under the care of a private agency. (Case W 851.)

A 15-year-old girl, who had been under the care of the State for nine years, had been diagnosed feeble-minded four years previous to the period covered by this study. She was repulsive looking and peculiar, had an ugly disposition, and was reported to be a menace to society. One doctor who examined her thought her to be internally paralyzed. She had spells of feeling and acting like a drunken person and at times showed signs of insanity. Application was made for her admission to a school for the feeble-minded, but she had not been admitted at the close of the period studied. She was boarded in a family home for a time, but had been at the State infirmary for three years. Her brother, also of illegitimate birth, had been received by the board at the same time that the girl had been taken. He was described as dreamy and absent-minded, but a fine boy in every respect and making unusually rapid progress at school.

The children's mother was a feeble-minded prostitute, and she was at the State infirmary suffering from tuberculosis at the time that they were received by the State. Her grandfather was the dissolute son of an excellent family; her father was intemperate, and her mother slovenly and inferior mentally. (Case W 303.)

A 19-year-old girl of illegitimate birth had been under the care of the State for 14 years. Nothing was known of her mother, who had not been heard from since the commitment of the child. The girl was boarded until the age of 14, when she was placed in a family who paid wages for her services. She did housework well, but she was very peculiar, one of her characteristics being her strong dislike of children. When 15 years old, she was given a mental examination and pronounced hysterical but not feeble-minded. She grew fault-finding and complaining and was subject to hallucinations. A few months after the first examination she was reexamined and pronounced mentally deranged. She was then placed at the State infirmary. It was finally decided that she was feeble-minded, and application was made to one of the State schools for the feeble-minded. At the close of this study she was still on the waiting list of this institution and was being cared for at the State infirmary, where she had been for three years. About the time when she was suffering from mental disturbance she made inquiries about her people, and was very unhappy when she learned that her mother had never inquired for her. (Case W 378.)

Conduct.

Information regarding the conduct of the children was based on the statements of the visitors of the State board of charity, as given in the records of the children. Absence of a definite statement was assumed to indicate that the child's behavior was satisfactory. Conduct was described as " poor " only if the misbehavior or stubbornness was of such character as to cause serious difficulty in the home in which the child was placed, or in the community, or if it was a menace to his own welfare. Reference to Table 18 will show that one-fifth of the children 7 years of age and over presented serious problems of conduct.

TABLE 18.—*Conduct of children 7 years of age and over, born out of wedlock.*

Age at end of period.	Children 7 years of age and over, born out of wedlock, under care of division of State minor wards in 1914.													
	Boys and girls.				Boys.					Girls.				
	To-tal.	Conduct good, as far as known.		Conduct poor.		To-tal.	Conduct good, as far as known.		Conduct poor.		To-tal.	Conduct good, as far as known.		Conduct poor.	
		Num-ber.	Per cent.	Num-ber.	Per cent.		Num-ber.	Per cent.	Num-ber.	Per cent.		Num-ber.	Per cent.	Num-ber.	Per cent.
Total......	849	678	79.9	171	20.1	527	422	80.1	105	19.9	322	256	79.5	66	20.5
7–9 years.........	280	242	86.4	38	13.6	163	138	84.7	25	15.3	117	104	89.0	13	11.0
10–13 years......	264	216	81.8	48	18.2	173	143	82.7	30	17.3	91	73	80.2	18	19.8
14 years and over.	305	220	72.1	85	27.9	191	141	73.8	50	26.2	114	79	69.3	35	30.7

At the end of the period studied 14 per cent of the children 7 to 9 years of age, 18 per cent of those 10 to 13 years of age, and 28 per cent of those 14 years of age and over were reported unsatisfactory in conduct. Of the 50 boys so described who were 14 years of age and over, 3 were known to have been sexually immoral, 3 alcoholic, 7 otherwise delinquent, and 37 were of otherwise poor character. Of the 35 girls of the same age group 12 were known to have been sexually immoral, 5 of them becoming mothers out of wedlock; 1 had been otherwise delinquent; and 22 were of otherwise poor character.

Among these children troublesome conduct and subnormal mentality appear to be very closely associated. Of the 171 whose behavior was unsatisfactory, 68, or 40 per cent, were below normal mentality or were very backward in school; of the 678 whose conduct was good, only 90, or 13 per cent, were mentally below normal or very backward.

The effect of unfortunate experiences in early childhood before coming under the care of the State, as well as the results of the lack of normal family ties and of shifting from one boarding or foster home to another, are illustrated in the cases studied. Although the division of State minor wards endeavors to place the children in homes in which the relation of parents and child will be approximated as closely as possible, it is extremely difficult, especially with older children, to realize this ideal for all the thousands under care and to insure for each the sympathetic and understanding affection and interest so necessary to right development.

Little information is available as to the psychological effect upon the child of the knowledge of birth out of wedlock. It is certain, however, that very real suffering is entailed upon a sensitive child by lack of information concerning his parentage, or by the feeling that his parents did not care for him or that they had led unworthy and degrading lives. Whether this mental suffering results in a weakening of moral fiber or a dulling of the instincts toward right living depends upon the make-up of the individual and the influences with which he is surrounded.

Instances of successful work on the part of the division of State minor wards are given in the following cases, representative of a large number in which the outcome for the child is favorable.

Fourteen years previous to the period covered by this study a 3-year-old girl was committed to the care of the State on a charge of neglect. Her younger brother was committed at the same time. The children had been living with their mother and maternal grandmother, both of whom were intemperate. There were a number of men boarders in the house, and conditions were very bad. The children had been much neglected. Subsequent to their commitment the mother was arrested fourteen times for drunkenness and once for another offense.

Both children were placed at board in private families, and both did well so far as conduct was concerned. The boy was undersized and not very bright, but he was trustworthy and tried hard to give satisfaction. The girl was sensible, attractive, intelligent. She finished the second year in high school and then became a skilled worker in a factory. She was economical and accumulated a good bank account. She was a credit to the board and to the families with whom she had been placed. (Case W 793.)

A 10-year-old boy was committed to the division of State minor wards as a delinquent child eight years before the study was made. From the age of 2 years he had been living in an institution for children. He was described as a runaway, untruthful, dishonest, and light-fingered. His mother, a widow with one child of legitimate birth, had paid no board for the child for six years and had not seen him for five years. She was reported to have been intemperate. She died while the boy was under the care of the State. The boy was boarded, and later lived for a time with his married sister. At the age of 15 he went to work in a mill and afterwards did farm work. At the end of the period studied he was reported to be a good boy in every way, steady, reliable, and industrious, and doing well in his work. His early tendencies toward wrongdoing seemed to have been entirely overcome. (Case W 52.)

In contrast to the preceding are two illustrations of troublesome conduct on the part of wards of the State who were of illegitimate birth:

Ten years previous to the time covered by this study a 4-year-old boy was received by the State on the application of his mother, who stated that her husband—the boy's stepfather—was out of work, and that they had no home. The mother had been brought up by her stepmother, who treated her well, but was not fond of her; the girl was unruly and was committed to an industrial school on a charge of stubbornness. After a year at the school she was placed at housework, where she did well for a time. Two years later she gave birth to a child out of wedlock—the boy of the study. When the child was less than 2 years of age the mother married, but her husband was worthless and did not support her. Subsequent to the time when the boy was committed to the care of the State, the mother had two other children of illegitimate birth, one of whom did not live long; the other, as well as a child born in wedlock, became wards of the State. The mother continued to live an immoral life.

The boy was placed at board. At the age of 14 he had reached the first year in high school, but his conduct was very troublesome. He ran away to his mother; after he was returned to the family with whom he was boarding, he stole, set fire to a barn, and committed other misdeeds. During the year of the study he was before the court on a charge of arson and was formally committed to the care of the division of State minor wards as a delinquent. Shortly after the close of the period studied he was transferred to an institution for delinquent children. (Case W 632.)

A 19-year-old girl, who had been under the care of the State for 18 years, was thought by the board's physician to be a moral defective. At the time she was received she was in poor physical condition. She had a club foot, which was operated on when she was 8 years old. From the age of 15 she had given trouble by her immoral conduct. The boarding woman's adopted son, also said to be of illegitimate birth, was a partner in her wrongdoing. When the girl was 16 years old she gave birth to a child whose father was a neighbor. The child remained with the mother at the State infirmary for two years, when the mother was placed at housework. The baby had trouble with her foot, but was improving, and it was thought that she would be able to walk.

The girl's mother was, herself, of illegitimate birth; hence, three generations of illegitimate maternity are here represented. The girl had an older sister also born out of wedlock. (Case W 808.)

Status of the Mother.

The same data were obtained in regard to the mothers of the children born out of wedlock under care of the division of State minor wards as in the case of the study of such children under the care of Boston agencies and institutions and of Boston children under the care of certain State agencies. In the section dealing with the problem in Boston the discussion of the child's heritage and the possibilities of the mother's providing care was as complete as the information permitted; hence, only a summary of the outstanding facts is attempted here.

The mothers of 1,570 of the 1,721 children under care were white; of 123 children, colored; of 2, American Indian; the race was not reported in 26 cases. The percentage of children whose mothers were colored was 7.

Information as to the nativity of the mother was obtained in 1,201 cases. In 658 of these instances the mother was native born; in 543, foreign born. The percentage of cases in which the mother was foreign born was 45. In one-fifth of the cases in which the mother was native born her place of birth was Massachusetts. The length of time the mother had been in the United States at the time the child was born was reported in 298 of the 543 cases in which the mother was foreign born. In more that half these cases the mother had been in this country less than 5 years, in a few instances the child being foreign born.

In 1,046 of the 1,721 cases the age of the mother at the time of the child's birth was given. In 14 per cent of these cases she was under the age of 18; in 27 per cent, between the ages of 18 and 20; in 28 per cent, from 21 to 24 years of age; in 25 per cent, between 25 and 34 years; and in 5 per cent, 35 years and over. The mothers of a total of 70 per cent of the children under the care of the division of State minor wards were under 25 years of age. In 1910, 58 per cent of the single, widowed, and divorced women in Massachusetts between the ages of 15 and 44 years were under the age of 25.[6]

Information as to the civil condition of the mother was secured in the cases of 1,459 children under care during the year. In 79 per cent of these cases, the mother was single at the time of the child's birth; in 5 per cent, widowed; in 14 per cent, divorced, separated, or deserted; and in 2 per cent, legally married to a man not the father of the child. The mothers of 10 per cent of the 1,721 children of illegitimate birth, under the care of the State, were living as married at the time of the child's birth; the mothers of 2 per cent were illegally married. In 17 per cent of the cases, the mother was known to have married after the birth of the child. In 3 per cent of all the cases, she was known to have married the child's father.

The mothers of 69 children had died before the application was made to the division of State minor wards for the care of the child. Of the other 1,652 cases, the mother was in poor physical condition in 342, or 21 per cent. In 4 per cent of the cases, the mother was known to have syphilis or gonorrhea. This percentage is somewhat lower than that found among the cases dealt with in section I, The Problem in Boston. The difference may be accounted for by the fact that many children under the care of the division of State minor wards came into its charge years ago, when the importance of information regarding the mother's physical condition was less emphasized.

The mothers of 18 per cent of the children were below normal mentally. In 7 per cent of the cases, the mother was feeble-minded; in 2 per cent, insane; in 2 per cent, subnormal or abnormal mentally, though not definitely feeble-minded or insane; and in 7 per cent, reported as probably subnormal or feeble-minded, diagnoses not having been made. The findings as to mentality are practically identical with those for mothers of children under the care of Boston agencies,

---

[6] Thirteenth Census of the United States, 1910; Vol. II, Population, p. 867.

and also for mothers of children under the care of a selected group of six private child-caring agencies in Boston.[7]

Complete information as to the character of the mother was impossible to obtain in all cases. The proportion described as of poor character, aside from the experience resulting in the birth of the child of the study, must be regarded as a minimum. So far as the records indicated, the mothers of 54 per cent of the children were immoral, alcoholic, otherwise delinquent, or of generally poor character. In 45 per cent of all the cases the mother was reported to have had other illicit sex experiences; in 2 per cent more she had been a prostitute either before or after the child's birth. In a total of 11 per cent of the cases the mother was reported as alcoholic or otherwise delinquent, though in only 3 per cent of the cases was alcoholism or other delinquency not combined with immorality. The mothers of 4 per cent of the children were otherwise of poor character, being shiftless, lazy, abusive, or neglectful of their children.

The mothers of 508 children—29 per cent of all the children of illegitimate birth under care during the year—had been under the care of agencies before the time of application to the division of State minor wards for the care of the child. This excludes the care given the mother's other children or the mother's parents. The mothers of a total of 107 children—6 per cent—had been wards of child-caring agencies. In a total of 332 cases—19 per cent—the mothers had been before the courts. This includes 18 cases—1 per cent—in which the mother had been a ward of a child-caring agency. In 233 of the 322 cases—14 per cent of the total 1,721—the mother had been committed to a correctional institution. In 87 cases—5 per cent—in which the mother had not been a ward of a child-caring agency or before a court she had been given prolonged care by agencies of other types.

The mothers of 416 children—24 per cent of the 1,721 under care— were known to have had illegitimate births before the child of the study was born. In a total of 609 cases—35 per cent—the mother had had one or more such births before or after the birth of the child of the study; in 300 cases—17 per cent—she had had more than one. Of 432 cases in which the mother was under the age of 21 at the time of the child's birth, there were 37, or 9 per cent, in which there had been a previous illegitimate birth. Of 614 cases in which the mother was 21 years of age or over at the time the child of the study was born, there were 227, or 37 per cent, in which she had had one or more previous births out of wedlock. One mother had had 8 previous illegitimate births, and 1 had had 10.

Reports as to the occupation of the mother at the time of application for the care of the child were secured in 1,197 cases. Of these,

---

[7] See p. 195.

the mother was gainfully employed in 820 cases, or 69 per cent. In 4 per cent of the cases in which she was gainfully employed the mother was a proprietor or manager or was engaged in a professional pursuit. In 5 per cent of the cases she was a clerk or kindred worker. In 31 per cent of the cases in which the mother was gainfully employed she was a semiskilled worker, and in 60 per cent she was engaged in domestic or personal service. In regard to specific occupations, in 25 per cent of all the cases in which the mother was gainfully employed she was a semiskilled factory worker and in 43 per cent a domestic servant. In 15 cases in which the mother was gainfully employed—2 per cent—she was a prostitute at the time of application.

Of the 377 cases in which the mother was not gainfully employed there were 247—66 per cent—in which she was a housewife and 16—4 per cent—in which she was attending school. In 5 cases in which the mother was a housewife and in 24 in which she had no occupation the mother was a prostitute. Hence in 8 per cent of the cases in which the mother was not gainfully employed in a legitimate occupation she was earning money through immorality.

In 1,129 cases the mother's mode of living at the time of application for the care of the child was reported. In 33 per cent of these cases she was living in her own home or other independent establishment, in 18 per cent in her parental home, in 6 per cent in the home of relatives or friends, in 6 per cent she was boarding, in 32 per cent living in her place of employment, and in 5 per cent in an institution.

Although complete information was not obtained as to the mother's family, such data as were available indicate that in at least 34 per cent of the cases the mother had no parental home upon which she could rely for assistance or the character or circumstances of her parents made it difficult for her to get help from them. In 6 per cent of the cases both maternal grandparents were dead at the time of application for the care of the child, in 5 per cent they had never been in the United States, in 10 per cent one parent was dead, in 2 per cent the mother's parents were divorced or separated, and in an additional 11 per cent of the cases one or both maternal grandparents were alcoholic, immoral, otherwise delinquent, chronically dependent, mentally below normal, shiftless, abusive, or otherwise of poor character.

In 3 per cent of all the cases one or both of the child's maternal grandparents were feeble-minded or insane or were probably subnormal or feeble-minded. In 13 per cent of the total number of cases one or both maternal grandparents were known to be alcoholic, immoral, or otherwise delinquent, and, in an additional 4 per cent, otherwise of poor character. In 2 per cent of the cases both mental subnormality and poor character were reported. In a total of 19 per cent of the cases one or both of the child's maternal grandparents were alcoholic, immoral or otherwise delinquent, dependent upon charitable aid, mentally below normal, or generally shiftless. The mothers of 44 children—3 per cent of all children of illegitimate birth under care—were themselves known to have been born out of wedlock.

On the whole the mothers of children born out of wedlock under the care of the division of State minor wards seem to be of the same status as the mothers of children under the care of Boston agencies during the year.[8] The mothers of a larger proportion of children under the care of the division of State minor wards had previously received assistance from social agencies; the percentage of children whose mothers had had other births out of wedlock was considerably higher in the " minor-wards " group. With these exceptions, the findings were identical or the differences very minor.

Defective mentality, low moral standards, and dependency—conditions which are found in the family histories of many children born out of wedlock who must rely upon the public for support and care—are illustrated in the following cases:

A 19-year-old girl, a State ward from the age of 3 years, had a heritage of mental defect, dependency, and immorality extending over three or four generations. A great-grandmother and a great-grandfather on her mother's side had been almshouse inmates. The maternal grandmother was an inmate of an almshouse, where she was considered an imbecile; she finally became insane. The girl's mother was born out of wedlock and was brought up by the child's great-grandmother, because of the feeble-mindedness of the grandmother. At the age of 14 the mother was committed to an institution for delinquents, on a charge of having stolen jewelry and money; at the age of 20 she was described as shiftless and incapable of earning her living, and she became an inmate of the almshouse in which the grandmother and great-grandmother had been cared for. Later she was committed on a sex charge to the reformatory for women, and spent 11 months at that institution.

Soon after leaving the reformatory she married and had two children, whose whereabouts were unknown at the time of commitment of the child of the study. After five years the mother was deserted by her husband; four years later he returned to her, but in the meanwhile a child had been born to the mother out of wedlock. The history of that child is also unknown. After two years the husband deserted again, and this time his desertion was final. The mother worked occasionally in private families, and at one of these times the child of the study was born; the father was a reputable business man of good family and was 10 years younger than the mother. Mother and baby were cared for in the almshouse, where the baby remained until she was committed to the care of the division of State minor wards as a neglected child. When the baby was less than 2 years old the mother was sentenced to the reformatory

---

[8] See Sec. I ch. 2. This group also included Boston children under the care of State agencies.

for women for three years on a charge of adultery with an inmate of the almshouse, by whom she had another child of illegitimate birth. A fourth child was born out of wedlock to this woman, but her history did not state when this child was born. After her return from the reformatory she again became an inmate of the almshouse, where she died of pneumonia when the child of the study was 15 years of age. The record described this mother as an undersized woman, not very strong, who could read and talk quite well, and who worked well under supervision, though she had a bad temper and seemed to have no idea of right and wrong.

The child was placed at board by the division of State minor wards. At the age of 17 she was described as poorly nourished, not strong, and suffering from spinal curvature. She was backward in school, though she finally reached the sixth grade and later attended trade school. Because of peculiar lumps on her hands, she was unable to keep long at housework or sewing. A mental examination was given when she was 17 years of age and she was pronounced not feeble-minded. (Case W 578.)

Two little girls, 3 and 7 years of age, had been under the care of the State for nearly two years, having been committed as neglected children from a town in the southeastern part of the State. At the time of commitment the maternal grandmother was in the reformatory for women on a charge of adultery, and the mother was about to be committed to a State institution for the feeble-minded. The home of the maternal grandparents, where the children had always lived, was described as a miserable, filthy hovel. The older child had a weak heart and was very nervous, but while under the care of the State did excellent work in school. The younger child was poorly nourished, pale and anemic, very nervous, and afraid of strangers, but at the close of the period studied she was described as bright and attractive. It was too early to determine whether the children would be able to overcome the handicap of their unfortunate heritage.

The family had been in this country for generations but came from worn-out and run-down stock. The maternal grandfather was feeble-minded and intemperate. The maternal grandmother was feeble-minded and grossly immoral and was committed to the reformatory for women on a charge of adultery just before the children were committed to the division of State minor wards. The grandparents had 11 children, ranging in age, during year covered by the study, from 30 to 9 years. The oldest child was an inmate of a State school for the feeble-minded; the second child was the mother of the children of the study and was committed to a school for the feeble-minded shortly after the children came under the care of the division of State minor wards; the third child—a boy—had been for six years a ward of the State, after which he had returned to his home—he was under indictment for manslaughter at the time his nieces were committed to the State board, but the complaint was dismissed because he was found to be feeble-minded and he was committed to a State institution. The fourth child had been under the care of the State for four years but was not under care at the time the children of the study were committed. The fifth child had been under the care of the State board and was then transferred to a State institution for the feeble-minded. The sixth child was under the care of the division of State minor wards and was of normal mentality. The seventh, eighth, and ninth children had been under the care of the division of State minor wards and had been transferred to institutions for the feeble-minded. The two youngest children were committed to the care of the State board at the same time the children of the study were committed—one of them was of normal mentality and the other was backward.

Hence, of the 11 children of these feeble-minded parents—the maternal grand-parents of the children studied—7 were feeble-minded and were being cared for in State institutions for the feeble-minded, 1 was backward mentally, 2 were normal mentally, and the mentality of 1 was not stated. All but 2 of the 11 had been under the care of the division of State minor wards, and these 2 were in State institutions.

The mother of the children of the study had a third child of illegitimate birth, who died in infancy; she did not know who was the father of this child. The two children committed to the care of the State had different fathers. After the birth of the oldest child the mother married a tramp in an attempt to cover the fact that her child had been born out of wedlock. The man did not support her and deserted her after a short time. (Cases W. 855, 856.)

A boy 12 years of age had been under the care of the State for four years, and previously had received prolonged care from a private agency, having been boarded in family homes. The private agency continued their support; the boy had been in need of a better home than could be found in his native town, especially because he was beginning to suffer from the taunts of the school children—not so much on account of his illegitimate birth as because of the general reputation of his mother in the community. In consequence he was continually fighting with them. At the age of 10 the boy was pronounced a moral defective by the physician who examined him. The year following he caused considerable trouble by setting fires. However, during the year of the study he was reported to be healthy and mentally normal, doing good work in the sixth grade and well liked by his companions.

The boy's maternal grandmother was described as very erratic; she died five years before the boy was received by the State board. The maternal grand-father's relatives were of poor character. At the age of 17 the mother had been committed as a stubborn child to an institution for delinquents. She remained in this institution not quite two years. A year after her return home she married, but she lived with her husband only a short time. Five months after her marriage she was committed to the reformatory for women on a sex charge and remained at the institution 11 months. Seven months after her release she was again committed to the reformatory on a charge of adultery, remaining there about a year and a half. At the age of 25 her first child was born—the boy of the study. Her second child was born out of wedlock, while she was serving her third term at the reformatory. This child, syphilitic and feeble-minded, was a State ward until his death at the age of 6 years. In all, the mother was committed four times to the reformatory on sex charges. While under the care of State institutions, she ran away four times. She was examined for feeble-mindedness and found not committable, and she was twice examined for insanity and found not to be insane. She was described as untruthful, lazy, and immoral, but with strong maternal instincts. A total of five children were born to this woman out of wedlock, each child having a different father. The mother felt no disgrace attached to her immoral conduct, reporting that a cousin had six children of illegitimate birth and that the town had assisted liberally in their support.

Of the five children one was the child of the study, two were dead, one had spent most of her four years of life at the almshouse with her mother, and the fifth was born at the State Infirmary during the year of the study, and was still under the care of that institution at the close of the year. Before the birth of the last child the mother was pronounced insane, and she was to be transferred from the State infirmary to a hospital for the insane. The family was known to a number of social agencies in Boston and elsewhere. (Case W 530.)

A 9-year-old girl of illegitimate birth, received by the State two years before the period covered by this study, had shortly after commitment been found to be feeble-minded. During the two years she had been under care she was provided for in a boarding home. Previous to her commitment to the care of the State the child had been living with her mother, a high-grade imbecile of bad character, and her stepfather, who was reported to be "not bright." A younger brother, also born out of wedlock, was committed to the care of the State at the same time. He appeared to be of normal mentality and did well in the home in which he was boarded.

Both maternal grandparents were reported to be high-grade imbeciles, the grandfather also being epileptic and immoral. The grandmother died when the mother was 5 years old. The grandfather kept the family together with the aid of housekeepers. At the age of 16 or 17 years the mother had her first child of illegitimate birth, her own father being reported as the father of the child. A sister of the mother was reported to have had two children of illegitimate birth by her own father. The mother later married and had eight children born in wedlock, five of whom were living at the time the study was made. Four of these children and the first child of illegitimate birth were committed to th care of the State as neglected; one of them was feeble-minded and was transferred to an institution for the mentally defective. The child not committed to the care of the division of State minor wards was epileptic and was cared for at a State institution for epileptics.

The mother's husband finally secured a divorce on the ground of immorality. She then supported herself for a time through housework, and later she went through a marriage ceremony with a town "bum" who had a legal wife living, though this fact was not discovered by the mother for two years. By this man the mother had two children—the children of the study. When the mother found that her supposed husband had another wife she left him and became a housekeeper for a family, some of whose children were wards of the State. She married the 22-year-old son of this family, who was reported not bright mentally; they had one child.

This imbecile woman, both of whose parents were imbeciles, had in all 12 children, 3 of whom were of illegitimate birth. Nine of these children were living at the time covered by this study. Seven of the 9 were or had been under the care of the division of State minor wards, and another was under the care of a State institution for epileptics. Two of the children were feeble-minded. (Cases W 27, 28.)

The feeble-minded mother of one child born in wedlock and seven born out of wedlock had been married at the age of 17, while a suit was pending to establish the paternity of her unborn child. Her husband deserted on the day of the marriage, and shortly afterwards the mother went to live with another man. They had 6 children; 1 was given away when a baby, 1 died, 1 was adopted, and at the time of the study the other 3 had been under care of the division of State minor wards for five years. They had been committed as neglected, because the parents were held for the grand jury and the home was unfit. Upon release from the institution to which she had been committed, the mother returned to the children's father, and he aided in getting a divorce for her; when this had been procured, he left her and married another woman. The mother went back to her former occupation of domestic service and worked for a third cousin—a widower whose family had been a burden upon charity for years and who had 8 children, two of whom were feeble-minded. The mother became pregnant, and after the birth of the baby both parents were arrested and commited for one year to correctional institutions, the infant being cared for with the mother in the institution.

The oldest child under the care of the division of State minor wards was 13 years of age at the time covered by the study. He was in the seventh grade and was reported to have an excellent mind and to be a good boy in every way. His sister, 10 years of age, had conjunctivitis and tuberculosis and was feeble-minded; she had been in the State Infirmary for two years awaiting admission to an institution for the feeble-minded. The youngest child under the care of the State, 8 years of age, was in good health and was described as bright, though heedless. She did good work in school one year, but during the year of the study she was not doing so well. (Cases W 258, 259, 260.)

The year before the period covered by this study, five children of illegitimate birth having the same mother, but four different fathers, were committed to the care of the State because of unfit home conditions. The home was very dirty, the family had been ordered to vacate the house, the stepfather had been abusive, and the two oldest children had venereal infection for which medical attention had not been provided. The mother had been committed to jail pending a hearing on a charge of neglect, but the stepfather had secured bail and left town with the oldest girl, 12 years of age. Two weeks later the child was found in another State, where she had been abandoned by her stepfather; a private child-caring agency had learned of her abandonment and was taking care of her.

The family had been known to social agencies in three States; at one time some of the children had been wards of another New England State. The family was first known to a Boston agency three years before the period covered by the study; stolen goods had been found in the home and it was frequented by persons of disreputable character. Later there were complaints that the children were going out to beg. At one time the family had resorted to publishing their wants in the newspapers with the hope of securing aid. The maternal grandmother kept a boarding house and received public aid; her immoral conduct caused the public authorities to threaten to withdraw assistance if she did not conform to accepted standards of morality. The mother had eight children in all, two of whom were twins; three of the children, including one of the twins, were dead. The father of the two youngest was a man whose children by his legal wife were wards of the State. Three years after the birth of the youngest child the mother married the man referred to above as the children's stepfather.

The division of State minor wards sent four of the children to the State infirmary; the two youngest had the mumps and the two oldest needed prolonged medical care. The fifth child was immediately placed at board. By the end of the period all the children were in boarding homes. The 16-year-old boy was headstrong and had a bad temper, but he was doing well in the ninth grade in school and was generally satisfactory. The 12-year-old girl was still in poor health, though her physical condition had improved; she had reached only the third grade in school and, though she worked hard, was very backward. The 11-year-old boy was in the fourth grade and was doing very well; he was described as a sensitive child who tried his best to do what was right. The 8-year-old girl was slow and dull. The youngest child, 7 years of age, was also slow and dull, though she was a good girl, well and active. All the children except the oldest boy were placed in the same town, and the three girls were in the same family until it became necessary to remove the oldest on account of her health.   (Cases W 785, 786, 787, 788, 789.)

Comparison of Children of Illegitimate Birth with Those of Legitimate Birth under Care.

Sex, race, and nativity.

There were under care during the year 1,717 children of legitimate birth and 606 children born out of wedlock whose case records were numbered from 1 to 2000—the cases chosen for this comparative study. All but 8 of the children born in wedlock and all but 5 of those of illegitimate birth were receiving prolonged care. Of the children of legitimate birth 1,028 were boys and 689 were girls. Of those born out of wedlock 381 were boys and 224 were girls and the sex of 1 was not reported. The percentage of boys among the children of illegitimate birth was slightly larger than among those of legitimate birth—63 as compared with 60.

There were 1,642 white children of legitimate birth, 74 colored, and 1 of another race. Among the children born out of wedlock were 544 white, 61 colored, and 1 of another race. Colored children comprised 10 per cent of those born out of wedlock, while only 4 per cent of those of legitimate birth were Negroes.

The nativity of the children is given in Table 19:

TABLE 19.—*Comparison, by place of birth, of children born in wedlock and children born out of wedlock.*

Place of birth.	Children under care of division of State minor wards, 1914, whose case records were numbered from 1 to 2000.			
	Born in wedlock.		Born out of wedlock.	
	Number.a	Per cent distribution.	Number.a	Per cent distribution.
Total..	1,669	100.0	591	100.0
Boston..	207	12.4	189	32.0
Metropolitan district outside Boston...............	241	14.4	71	12.0
Other Massachusetts.............................	b 961	57.6	c 289	48.9
Other United States.............................	160	9.6	37	6.3
Canada...	25	1.5	3	.5
Other..	75	4.5	2	.3

a Excluding 48 children born in wedlock and 15 born out of wedlock whose nativity was not reported.
b Including 10 born at State institutions.
c Including 75 born at State institutions.

Almost one-third of the children of illegitimate birth were born in Boston as against one-eighth of the children of legitimate birth. A total of 93 per cent of the former were born in Massachusetts, while only 84 per cent of the latter were born in the State. The proportion of foreign-born was considerably smaller among children born out of wedlock—1 per cent as compared with 6 per cent among children of legitimate birth.

Residence at time of application or commitment.

At the time of application to the division of State minor wards for the care of the child, or—in the case of neglected, wayward, and delinquent children—at the time of commitment, 290 of the 1,717 children born in wedlock were living in Boston, 264 in the metropolitan district outside Boston, 1,143 in other parts of the State (including 11 under the care of State institutions), 1 had just come from another State, and the residence of 19 was not reported. Of the 606 children born out of wedlock, 150 were living in Boston at the time of application, 103 in the metropolitan district outside Boston, 311 in other parts of the State (including 23 under the care of State institutions), and the residence of 42 was not reported. Slightly more than two-fifths of the children born out of wedlock whose residence was known were living in Boston or the metropolitan district at the time of application; not quite one-third of those born in wedlock were residents of Boston or the metropolitan district.

A comparison of the county of residence of children born out of wedlock with the residence of children born in wedlock is made in Table 20 for those children whose residence at the time of application or commitment was Massachusetts.

TABLE 20.—*Comparison, by county of residence, of children born in wedlock and children born out of wedlock.*

County of residence at time of application or commitment.	Children under care of division of State minor wards, 1914, whose case records were numbered from 1 to 2000, and whose residence at time of application or commitment was Massachusetts.			
	Born in wedlock.		Born out of wedlock.	
	Number.	Per cent distribution.	Number.	Per cent distribution.
Total........	1,697	100.0	564	100.0
Berkshire, Franklin, and Hampshire..............	144	8.5	32	5.7
Hampden..........	173	10.2	30	5.3
Worcester........	268	15.8	62	11.0
Essex...........	243	14.3	78	13.8
Middlesex........	273	16.0	93	16.5
Suffolk a.........	317	18.7	168	29.8
Norfolk and Plymouth..................	152	9.0	37	6.6
Bristol...........	81	4.8	36	6.4
Barnstable and Nantucket..............	35	2.1	5	.9
Under care of State institutions or agencies.........	11	.6	23	4.0

a The county in which Boston is located.

The percentage of children born out of wedlock coming from Middlesex, Suffolk, and Bristol Counties was higher than the percentage of children of legitimate birth coming from these counties. In two of these counties—Suffolk and Bristol—the illegitimacy birth rate for the year studied was also high.[9] The percentage of children born out of wedlock who lived in Suffolk County—most of which the city of Boston comprised—previous to application was particularly high—30 as compared with 19 per cent for children born in wedlock. This was to be expected on account of the high illegitimacy rate in Boston and because a number of these children had been under the care of Boston agencies previous to their reception by the division of State minor wards. The percentage of children of illegitimate birth who had been under the care of State institutions or agencies, and whose residence could not properly be assigned to any county, was higher than in the case of children born in wedlock.

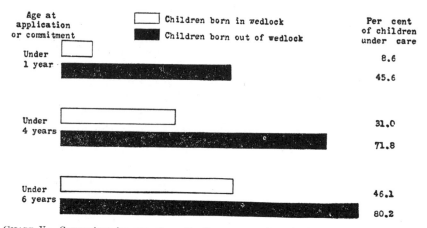

CHART V.—Comparison by age at application or commitment of 1,717 children born in wedlock and 606 children born out of wedlock, under care of the division of State minor wards in 1914.

Age at time of application or commitment.

The ages at which children come under the care of the State are to some extent indicative both of the urgency of the need and of the probable length of time over which care must be given. The children coming under care at the earliest age are those whose natural guardians have been unable to meet their responsibilities even for a short time. Such children probably will be dependent upon the State for the longest period. Table 21 gives the ages at application or commitment, and the comparative numbers of children under care who were born in wedlock and born out of wedlock.

[9] See Table 1, p. 271.

TABLE 21.—*Comparison, by age at application or commitment, of children born in wedlock and children born out of wedlock.*

Age at application or commitment.	Children under care of division of State minor wards, 1914, whose case records were numbered from 1 to 2000.					
	Born in wedlock.			Born out of wedlock.		
	Number.	Per cent distribution.	Cumulative per cent.	Number.	Per cent distribution.	Cumulative per cent.
Total...............	1,717	100.0	....	606	100.0	....
Less than 1 year..............	148	8.6	8.6	276	45.6	45.6
1 year......................	113	6.6	15.2	90	14.8	60.4
2–3 years....................	272	15.8	31.0	69	11.4	71.8
4–5 years....................	259	15.1	46.1	51	8.4	80.2
6–9 years....................	529	30.8	76.9	79	13.0	93.2
10–13 years..................	344	20.0	97.0	35	5.8	99.0
14 years and over.............	49	2.9	99.8	4	.7	99.7
Not reported.................	3	.2	....	2	.3	....

Almost half the children born out of wedlock—46 per cent—were less than 1 year of age when application for their care was made to the division of State minor wards. Only 9 per cent of the children born in wedlock were less than 1 year old. A total of 60 per cent of the children of illegitimate birth were under 2 years of age, as against 15 per cent of the children of legitimate birth. Four-fifths of the children born out of wedlock—80 per cent—were less than 6 years old, while less than half the children of legitimate birth were under this age. The evidence is clear that children born out of wedlock come under the care of the State at an earlier age than children born of parents who are married to each other.

Source of application or commitment.

Almost three-fourths of the children born in wedlock were received by the division of State minor wards from courts, having been committed as neglected, wayward, or delinquent children. Less than two-fifths of the children born out of wedlock were received on court commitments. In the case of children of the latter class the problem is mainly one of dependency, while in the case of children of legitimate birth it is largely one of neglect. Nearly one-third of the children born out of wedlock were received from overseers of the poor or from the superintendent of the State infirmary; only one-ninth of the applications for the care of children born in wedlock came from these sources. The proportion of applications for the care of children of illegitimate birth coming from the mothers was much larger than the proportion of applications coming from parents for the care of children of legitimate birth—more than one-fourth as compared with less than one-eighth. (See Table 22.)

TABLE 22.—*Comparison, by source of application or commitment, of children born in wedlock and children born out of wedlock.*

Source of application or commitment.	Children under care of division of State minor wards, 1914, whose case records were numbered from 1 to 2000.			
	Born in wedlock.		Born out of wedlock.	
	Number.	Per cent distribution.	Number.	Per cent distribution.
Total...............................	a 1,666	100.0	a 593	100.0
Court..............................	1,212	72.8	234	39.4
Public agency......................	185	11.1	173	29.2
Private agency.....................	37	2.2	9	1.5
Parents............................	194	11.6	161	27.2
Relative or friend.................	26	1.6	10	1.7
Other..............................	12	.7	6	1.0

a Excluding 51 cases of children born in wedlock and 13 of children born out of wedlock, in which source of application was not reported.

Home conditions and reason for application or commitment.

The reason for the application for care or for the commitment of the child, as stated on the records, is given in Table 23. Although the alleged reason is not in all cases the underlying cause of the child's dependency, it gives an indication of the situation.

TABLE 23.—*Comparison, by reason for application or commitment, of children born in wedlock and children born out of wedlock.*

Reason for application or commitment.	Children under care of division of State minor wards, 1914, whose case records were numbered from 1 to 2000.			
	Born in wedlock.		Born out of wedlock.	
	Number.	Per cent distribution.	Number.	Per cent distribution.
Total...............................	a 1,696	100.0	a 584	100.0
Death of one or both parents.......................	235	13.9	10	1.7
Desertion or nonsupport........................	491	29.0	102	17.5
Inability of parents or relatives to support.........	109	6.4	228	39.0
Home unfit or parents unfit......................	740	43.6	213	36.5
Child delinquent or unmanageable.................	99	5.8	10	1.7
Child feeble-minded.............................	9	.5	....	....
Child sick......................................	13	.8	9	1.5
Other..	....	....	12	2.1

a Excluding 21 cases of children born in wedlock and 22 of children born out of wedlock in which reason for application was not reported.

The death of one or both parents was the reason given for the application in 14 per cent of the cases of children born in wedlock. Only 2 per cent of the children born out of wedlock came under care because of the death of the mother. Desertion or nonsupport was the reason for application or commitment in 29 per cent of the cases of children of legitimate birth, but in only 18 per cent of those of children of illegitimate birth. Inability of parents or relatives to support the child was given as the reason for application in the cases of only 6 per cent of the children born in wedlock, though in 39 per cent of the cases of children of illegitimate birth the reason stated was the inability of the mother or relatives to care for the child. In 44 per cent of the cases of children of legitimate birth the application was made or the child was committed because of the unfitness of the home or of the parents; in only 37 per cent of the cases of children born out of wedlock was this reason given. The delinquency, defectiveness, or illness of the child was the reason for application in the cases of 7 per cent of the children born in wedlock, but in the cases of only 3 per cent of the children born out of wedlock.

Of greater significance than the immediate reason for application are the home conditions and the character of the parents. The homes of 1,020 children of legitimate birth—59 per cent of the total—had been broken up because of the death or desertion of one or both parents or because the parents were divorced or separated. Practically all the children born out of wedlock lacked normal homes.

One or both parents of 141 children of legitimate birth—8 per cent— had been diagnosed feeble-minded, epileptic, or insane. The mothers of 53 children of illegitimate birth—9 per cent—had been so diagnosed. The percentage for children born in wedlock is very low as compared with the percentage for children born out of wedlock, in view of the fact that both parents of the former are considered and only one parent of the latter. It must be remembered, however, that examinations of mentality probably would not have been made as frequently in the case of parents of children born in wedlock.

Alcoholism, immorality, or other delinquency of one or both parents was reported in the case of 844 children of legitimate birth—49 per cent. The mothers of all the children of illegitimate birth would have been so classified had not this study sought to analyze their character aside from the violation of moral standards resulting in these cases of illegitimate maternity. In 276 cases of illegitimate birth—45 per cent—the mothers were reported as alcoholic, immoral, or otherwise delinquent.

The data indicate that children born out of wedlock are more likely than children born in wedlock to come under the care of the State by reason of the inability of parents or relatives to support them, and less likely to be committed because of parental neglect or improper home conditions. However, the main causes of child dependency—broken homes and low mentality, alcoholism, immorality, and other delinquency on the part of the parents—exist to a much greater degree among children of illegitimate birth.

Length of time cared for.

At the end of the year or, if the child was discharged during the year, at the close of care, 4 per cent of the children of legitimate birth under prolonged care were less than 6 years of age, while 16 per cent of the. children born out of wedlock were under this age. Between the ages of 6 and 13 years were 39 per cent of the children born in wedlock and 52 per cent of the children of illegitimate birth. More than half the children of legitimate birth—57 per cent—were 14 years of age or over, while less than one-third of the children born out of wedlock—32 per cent—had reached the age of 14. The larger proportion of children born in wedlock in the older age groups is due to the later age at which these children are received.

The average number of years the children of various ages had been cared for by the division of State minor wards is given in Table 24.

TABLE 24.—*Comparison of duration of care received by children of specified ages, born in wedlock and born out of wedlock.*

Age at end of period.	Children born in wedlock, under prolonged care, whose case records were numbered from 1 to 2,000.	Number of years under care.		Children born out of wedlock, under prolonged care, whose case records were numbered from 1 to 2,000.	Number of years under care.	
		Aggregate.	Average.		Aggregate.	Average.
Total..............	a 1,705	b 12,402.0	7.3	c 597	b 4,766.5	8.0
1 year....................	3	2.0	0.7	7	5.5	0.8
2–5 years.................	63	193.5	3.1	85	311.0	3.7
6–9 years.................	280	1,420.5	5.1	182	1,117.0	6.1
10–13 years..............	364	2,565.5	6.5	133	1,166.0	8.8
14 years and over........	965	8,220.5	8.5	190	2,167.0	11.4

a Excluding 4 children born in wedlock: 1 less than 1 year of age, 2 whose ages were not reported, and 1, 14 years of age and over, for whom length of time under care was not reported.

b If time under care was less than 1 year, an approximate average of 6 months was used—22 children born in wedlock, 11 years; 7 children born out of wedlock, 3.5 years.

c Excluding 4 children born out of wedlock: 2 less than 1 year of age; 2 for whom length of time under care was not reported, 1 of whom was 11, and the other, 14 years of age.

In spite of the fact that 68 per cent of the children born out of wedlock were under 14 years of age at the close of care or the end of the year, while only 43 per cent of the children born in wedlock were under this age, the average number of years under care was greater for children of illegitimate than of legitimate birth. The children born out of wedlock had been cared for by the State for an average of 8 years, while the children of legitimate birth had been under care for an average of only 7.3 years. The difference is more marked in the older age groups. Children between the ages of 6 and 9 years who had been born out of wedlock had spent an average of 6.1 years under the care of the State, while children of the same age who were of legitimate birth averaged 5.1 years under supervision. The average number of years under care for children 10 to 13 years of age was 8.8 in the case of children of illegitimate birth, and 6.5 in the case of those born in wedlock. Children of illegitimate birth who were 14 years of age and over had spent on an average 11.4 years under the care of the division

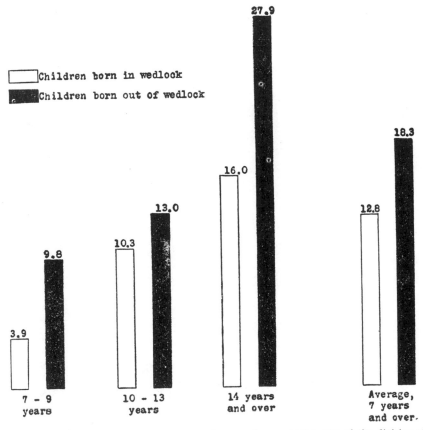

CHART VI.—Per cent of children 7 years of age and over, under care of the division of State minor wards in 1914, whose case records were numbered from 1 to 2,000, whose conduct was poor. (See p. 318.)

of State minor wards, while children of legitimate birth of the same age averaged only 8.5 years under care. These figures indicate the long periods over which children born out of wedlock are dependent upon the public for care and maintenance.

Personal characteristics.

Information concerning the child's mentality and his conduct at the end of the period studied was secured for 1,026 children of legitimate birth who were 7 years of age and over and 461 children of illegitimate birth. Of the children born in wedlock, 112, or 10.9 per cent, had been diagnosed feeble-minded; 51 children born out of wedlock—11.1 per cent—had been so diagnosed. That the percentage of mental defect among children of illegitimate birth under the care of the division of State minor wards is practically the same as that found among children born in wedlock under care of the same agency is worthy of special remark. This controverts an opinion frequently expressed to the effect that dependent children of illegitimate birth are more likely to have a sound heritage than children of legitimate birth who must rely upon the public for support.

There were 914 children born in wedlock and 410 children born out of wedlock, who were not feeble-minded, concerning whose conduct information was obtained. (See Table 25.) The conduct of 13 per cent of the children of legitimate birth was reported as "poor," while the conduct of 18 per cent of the children born out of wedlock was so reported.

TABLE 25.—*Comparison of conduct of children 7 years of age and over born in wedlock and born out of wedlock.*

Age at end of period.	Children 7 years of age and over under care of division of State minor wards, 1914, whose case records were numbered from 1 to 2,000.					
	Born in wedlock.			Born out of wedlock.		
	Total.	Conduct good, so far as known.	Conduct poor.	Total.	Conduct good, so far as known.	Conduct poor.
Total..................	a 914	797	117	b 410	335	75
7–9 years.................	128	123	5	123	111	12
10–13 years................	242	217	25	115	100	15
14 years and over............	544	457	87	172	124	48

a Excluding 112 feeble-minded and 561 concerning whose conduct information was not obtained.
b Excluding 51 feeble-minded.

In each age group the percentage of children born out of wedlock whose conduct was unsatisfactory was higher than that of children born in wedlock. Of those 7 to 9 years of age, 4 per cent of the children born in wedlock were reported poor in conduct, while 10 per cent of those of illegitimate birth were thus described. In the 10-to-13-year age group 10 per cent of the children of legitimate birth and 13 per cent of those born out of wedlock were unsatisfactory. Of the children 14 years of age and over, 16 per cent of the children of legitimate birth were unsatisfactory, while 28 per cent— more than one-fourth—of the children of illegitimate birth presented serious problems of conduct.

The relative importance of heredity and environment as affecting conduct is a moot question. It is impossible to state whether the high percentage of children of illegitimate birth under the care of the State who find it difficult to conform in a fairly satisfactory manner to required standards of behavior may be attributed to innate character defects and lack of stability or to the absence of normal home life and family ties. In this connection it is of interest to note that children born out of wedlock come under the care of the State at an earlier age than children of legitimate birth, and that a larger proportion of the former than of the latter are received because of the inability of the mother or relatives to support the child, and a smaller proportion because of parental neglect, improper home conditions, or their own delinquency. The evidence would seem to indicate that children who have been cared for during the first years of life in their own homes, undesirable though the homes may be, have an advantage over children cared for from early childhood in boarding or foster homes.

INFANTS UNDER TWO YEARS OF AGE REPORTED TO THE DIVISION OF STATE MINOR WARDS AS CARED FOR APART FROM THEIR RELATIVES.

Proportion of Infants Born out of Wedlock.

More than 2,000 infants under 2 years of age are reported each year to the State board of charity under the law requiring notice to the board of the reception of an infant under care or control by a person not related to the child by blood or marriage, or of the placing of an infant under the care and control of another for compensation. Between 40 and 50 per cent of these infants are of illegitimate birth. The number of infants reported and the per cent born out of wedlock are shown in Table 26 for each year of the 10-year period 1905 to 1914. The percentage born out of wedlock decreased between 1905 and 1909 and increased between 1909 and 1914.

TABLE 26.—*Number of infants reported to the State board of charity as cared for apart from their relatives, and per cent born out of wedlock, 1905 to 1914.*

Year.[a]	Infants under 2 years of age reported.[b]						
	Total.[c]	Born in wedlock.		Born out of wedlock.		Of unknown parentage.	
		Number.	Per cent.	Number.	Per cent.	Number.	Per cent.
1905	1,704	876	51.4	784	46.0	44	2.6
1906 [d]	2,037	1,073	52.7	884	43.4	80	3.9
1907	2,002	998	49.9	915	45.7	89	4.4
1908	2,302	1,192	51.8	1,004	43.6	106	4.6
1909	2,264	1,220	53.9	938	41.4	106	4.7
1910	2,164	1,210	55.9	842	38.9	112	5.2
1911	2,078	1,165	56.1	821	39.5	92	4.4
1912	2,169	1,178	54.3	883	40.7	108	5.0
1913	2,339	1,198	51.2	1,036	44.3	105	4.5
1914	2,205	1,033	46.8	1,085	49.2	87	4.0

a Fiscal year of the State board of charity. For 1905 this year was from Oct. 1, 1904, to Sept. 30, 1905; for 1906, the 14-month period, Oct. 1, 1905, to Nov. 30, 1906; for the succeeding years, Dec. 1 to Nov. 30.

b Figures derived from Twenty-seventh to Thirty-sixth Annual Reports of the State Board of Charity of Massachusetts, 1905–1914. Boston, 1906–1915.

c Because of a small amount of duplication on account of transfers of supervision, the actual numbers of infants were somewhat less than the numbers given in the years specified. In 1907 the actual number was 1,925; in 1908, 2,215; in 1909, 2,054; in 1910, 2,099; in 1912, 2,103; in 1913, 2,263; in 1914, 2,136.

d Fourteen-month period.

During the calendar year 1914 a total of 2,104 infants under 2 years of age were reported to the State board of charity as cared for apart from their relatives.[10] Of these, 991, or 47 per cent, were born in wedlock; 1,037, or 49 per cent, were born out of wedlock; and 76, or 4 per cent, were of unknown parentage. Of the total reported, 108 were not cared for in private homes during the year but were in institutions. This analysis is confined to the 1,996 cared for in family homes. The status of the children was as follows:

```
        Total_____ 1,996
Born in wedlock_____ 926
Born out of wedlock_____ 995
Of unknown parentage _____ 75
```

Fifty per cent of the children cared for in private families had been born out of wedlock. Of these 995, 152 were born in Boston during the year studied and were included in the chapter on the infant born out of wedlock. A total of 559 were included in the chapter on children of illegitimate birth under the care of social agencies; 113 of these children and 112 others were under the care of the division of State minor wards during the year.

Type of Supervision.

The kind of supervision the children received while they were cared for apart from their relatives is given in Table 27. In some cases more than one type of supervision was given during the period covered.

TABLE 27.—*Comparison of type of supervision received by infants born in wedlock and born out of wedlock, cared for apart from their relatives in private homes.*

Type of supervision.	Infants under 2 years of age reported to the State board of charity in 1914 as cared for apart from their relatives in private homes.			
	Total.	Born in wedlock.	Born out of wedlock.	Of unknown parentage.
Total...................................	1,996	926	995	75
Agency supervision......................	1,215	544	611	60
State board of charity.......................	365	a 150	b 161	c 54
Other public agency........................	44	c 24	c 18	c 2
Private agency.............................	c 783	d 359	e 420	c 4
State board of charity and other public agency.....	12	5	7	....
Other public agency and private agency...........	4	4	....	....
State board of charity and private agency..........	7	2	f 5	....
No agency supervision (supervision by relatives or friends)...................................	781	382	384	15

```
a Includes 12 under no agency supervision part of the time.
b Includes 26 under no agency supervision part of the time.
c Includes 1 under no agency supervision part of the time.
d Includes 24 under no agency supervision part of the time.
e Includes 55 under no agency supervision part of the time.
f Includes 3 under no agency supervision part of the time.
```

[10] The number reported during the fiscal year of the board, Dec. 1, 1913, to Nov. 30, 1914, was 2,136.

A total of 59 per cent of the children born in wedlock were under agency supervision while cared for apart from their relatives; 61 per cent of the children born out of wedlock were supervised by agencies. Most of those not receiving agency supervision were being privately boarded by their mothers, other relatives, or friends. The State board of charity supervised 16 per cent of the children born in wedlock and 16 per cent of those born out of wedlock. The majority of children given agency supervision were under the care of private agencies or institutions.

Age at End of Period and Length of Time Cared for Apart from Their Relatives.

Somewhat more than one-fifth of the children reached the age of 2 years during 1914. The records of these children automatically closed when they attained their second birthday. The ages of the children at the end of the year, or, if the record closed before that time, at the last date reported, are given in Table 28.

TABLE 28.—*Comparison of age, at the end of year or at last date reported, of infants born in wedlock and born out of wedlock, cared for apart from their relatives in private homes.*

Age attained at end of year or at last date reported.	Infants under 2 years of age reported to the State board of charity in 1914 as cared for apart from their relatives in private homes.			
	Total.	Born in wedlock.	Born out of wedlock.	Of unknown parentage.
Total...	1,996	926	995	75
Less than 6 months..............................	413	177	225	11
6 months but less than 1 year..................	413	194	209	10
1 year but less than 18 months................	377	174	189	14
18 months but less than 2 years...............	314	162	138	14
2 years..	439	202	215	22
Not reported..................................	40	17	19	4

The percentage of children born in wedlock whose ages were reported, and who were less than 6 months of age at the end of the period, was 20; 23 per cent of the children born out of wedlock were under this age. Twenty-one per cent of the children of legitimate birth and 22 per cent of those born out of wedlock were between the ages of 6 months and 1 year; 19 per cent of the children born in wedlock and the same per cent of those of illegitimate birth were 1 year but less than 18 months; 18 per cent of the children of legitimate birth and 14 per cent of those born out of wedlock were between 18 months and 2 years of age; 22 per cent of the former and the same per cent of the latter reached the age of 2 during the year.

The percentage distribution was fairly even and was very similar for the two classes of children.

The total length of time the children had been cared for apart from their relatives, by the end of the year or the date of last record, is given in Table 29.

TABLE 29.—*Length of time infants born in wedlock and born out of wedlock were cared for apart from their relatives in private homes.*

Length of time cared for at end of year or last date reported.	Infants under 2 years of age reported to State board of charity in 1914 as cared for apart from their relatives in private homes.	
	Born in wedlock.	Born out of wedlock.
Total......	926	995
Less than 6 months....	468	380
6 months but less than 1 year....	171	238
1 year but less than 18 months....	143	163
18 months but less than 2 years....	129	192
Not reported....	15	22

Of the children born in wedlock whose ages were reported, 30 per cent had been cared for apart from their relatives in private homes one year or longer. The percentage of children born out of wedlock who had been cared for in this way for that length of time was considerably larger—36. The length of time cared for, together with the age of the child, is given for children born out of wedlock in Table 30.

TABLE 30.—*Length of time infants of specified ages, born out of wedlock, were cared for apart from their relatives in private homes.*

Age attained at end of year or last date reported.	Infants under 2 years of age, born out of wedlock, reported to State board of charity, in 1914, as cared for apart from their relatives in private homes.					
	Total.	Length of time cared for at end of year or last date reported.				
		Less than 6 months.	6 months but less than 1 year.	1 year but less than 18 months.	18 months but less than 2 years.	Not reported.
Total......	995	380	238	163	192	22
Less than 6 months....	225	225				
6 months but less than 1 year....	209	91	118			
1 year but less than 18 months....	189	33	70	84		2
18 months but less than 2 years....	138	16	23	43	56	
2 years....	215	13	26	36	136	4
Not reported....	19	2	1			16

More than half the children born out of wedlock who were between 6 months and 1 year of age had been cared for apart from their relatives in private homes at least 6 months. Four-fifths of the children aged 1 year but less than 18 months had been cared for in this way at least 6 months; more than two-fifths had been cared for at least 1 year. Nearly three-fourths of the children between the ages of 18 months and 2 years had been cared for apart from relatives at least 1 year; two-fifths had been so cared for at least 18 months. Almost two-thirds of the children who reached the age of 2 years had been cared for apart from relatives for at least a year and a half. The majority of the children had been cared for apart from their mothers before they had reached the age of 6 months, and they had thus been deprived of their mothers' care during the time it was most necessary to life and health.

There were a number of instances in which the child was shifted from one boarding home to another, or back and forth from boarding home to relatives. This frequent change in surroundings and in care very probably affected the child's health and development. Some of the worst instances of shifting among the children of illegitimate birth are here given. The records did not state the reasons for the changes.

A little girl was placed at board before she had reached the age of 2 months. After two months she was placed in another home, where she remained for only six days. She was discharged to her aunt, who placed her at board in another family, but after two weeks her boarding place was changed, and after another two weeks it was changed again. She stayed in the last boarding home the remaining four months of the year studied. In a period of seven months this infant had been in five different boarding homes. The child had not been under the supervision of agencies during the period described. (Case BB 10.)

When 11 days old a baby boy was placed at board in a private family by a child-caring agency. He remained in this home for seven months, when he was placed in another family home. Here he remained one month, when he was placed in a third home. After about five weeks the baby was boarded with a fourth family, where he lived for three weeks. At some time during this period the child-caring agency discharged him to relatives, and for the remainder of the period studied he was not under agency supervision. For the period of a little more than two weeks immediately following the child's removal from the fourth boarding home no information was available. He was soon placed with a fifth family, where he stayed for five months. At the end of that time his boarding place was again changed, and a sixth family took him for a period of one month. He was then placed in a seventh home, where he remained for more than six months and where he was still living at his second birthday when reports ceased. (Case BB 11.)

In April of the year studied a 3-months-old infant was placed at board by relatives or friends. He remained in this boarding home two months, when he was placed with a second family. Here he remained two months, when his boarding home was again changed. For the remaining four months of the year he remained with the same family. (Case BB 12.)

An infant boarded throughout the year studied had been placed at board in December of the previous year at the age of 4 months. She was not under agency supervision. During the 12 months and 3 weeks she had been boarded she had been in four different family homes. (Case BB 13.)

SOCIAL SERVICE WORK WITH MOTHERS AND CHILDREN AT THE STATE INFIRMARY.

Description of the Work.

The State infirmary at Tewksbury provides almshouse and hospital care for indigent persons not chargeable for support to any city or town. During the year December 1, 1913, to November 30, 1914, 7,298 persons were under the care of this institution.[11] The maternity department of the infirmary gives confinement and maternity care to women from all over the State who are unable to establish legal settlement, and to a few for whom board is paid by the overseers of the poor of the town of settlement. Expectant mothers from the State institutions for delinquents and for the mentally defective are also sent here for maternity care. During the year studied there were 159 live births at the institution, 119 of which were illegitimate.[12]

The State board of charity has general supervision over this institution and passes upon the discharge of all sane inmates. In 1909 the two women members of the board began special work with the after-care of mothers and children discharged from the infirmary. The purpose of this work, as stated in the 1913 report, was:[13]

Primarily. To protect the welfare of the mothers and children and place them in such environment and under such supervision as will tend to develop them into useful and upright citizens.

Secondly. To segregate the defective who is found to be a menace to the community.

Thirdly. To enforce the responsibility of the husband or father.

The work developed, and a standing committee of the board known as the committee on social service was created to handle it. The visiting and investigating are done by women visitors for maternity cases at the infirmary and by volunteer workers in cooperation with physicians and nurses at the institution. A clerk with legal training is employed to aid in establishing paternity and securing support from the fathers.

---

[11] Thirty-sixth Annual Report of the State Board of Charity of Massachusetts for the Year Ending November 30, 1914. Boston, 1915. Pt. I, pp. 25, 26.

[12] Includes 5 registered as legitimate. The number of births registered as illegitimate was 114. See p. 271.

[13] Thirty-fifth Annual Report of the State Board of Charity of Massachusetts for the Year Ending November 30, 1913. Boston, 1914. Pt. I, p. 124.

The activities of the committee comprise investigation of the cases before admission to the infirmary and during residence therein, securing cooperation from relatives and others, making arrangements for the care of mother and baby, for legal assistance in securing support from the father, and for the follow-up and after-care of the women and children discharged from the institution. The work is not limited to maternity cases. Mothers coming with their children for other than maternity care are also supervised, and many of the pregnant women are accompanied by children. Mothers sent to the infirmary for confinement from State institutions and those who are wards of the State do not come under the supervision of the committee, since they are already provided for. Children at the infirmary unaccompanied by their mothers are not dealt with by the committee, since the division of State minor wards handles all such cases needing assistance.

Overseers of the poor throughout the State are requested to notify the board as early as possible of the case of any pregnant girl or woman before sending her to the State infirmary. It is believed that the younger and less sophisticated women, especially those pregnant for the first time, should be cared for in other ways than at a public hospital, and attempts are made in these cases to secure other provision.

Before discharge from the infirmary, a protective plan is made for the mother and her child. Relatives are communicated with, mental examinations given mothers appearing to be below normal, arrangements for deportation made if the mother has been in this country but a short time, positions in domestic service secured, or other plans made. Every case is investigated from the point of view of legal action to secure support from the father, and all possible steps are taken toward this end.

In the after-care work the cooperation of private societies and of individuals is sought. Advice, counsel, and supervision are given, and every attempt is made to reestablish the mother in the community and to enable her to keep her child.

Proportion of Work Dealing with Children Born Out of Wedlock.

During the year studied a total of 316 women were under the supervision of the social service committee, including those at the infirmary and those given after-care. Of these women, 218 were accompanied by children born out of wedlock or were illegitimately pregnant; during the year, 184 of these were at the infirmary, and 34 were given after-care only. Twenty-five of those at the infirmary were discharged before the birth of the child, the child was not born until 1915, or the infant was stillborn; hence there were no children born out of wedlock under care during the year. Therefore, there were 193 mothers whose children of illegitimate birth were given care during the year studied, 159 mothers receiving care at the infirmary during that period, and 34 given after-care only. These 193 mothers had 211 children of illegitimate birth under care. Of these children, 91 were born at the infirmary during the year,[14] and 84 others were cared for at this institution, while 36 were given after-care only.

Children under Care, Born Out of Wedlock.

About one-third of the children of illegitimate birth under care during the year—71 out of 211—had come under the supervision of the committee previous to the year studied; two-thirds had come under care during the year, though in many of these cases the mother had been admitted during the previous year, the child having been born in the year studied. More than half the children (108) were discharged from care during the year, the others remaining under supervision at the end of the period.

Of the 211 children under care 102 were boys, 107 girls, and the sex of 2 was not reported. There were 194 white children, 16 negro, and 1 American Indian, the percentage of negroes being 8.

Only 2 children were known to be foreign born, 1 having been born in Canada and 1 in the West Indies. The nativity of 1 child was not reported. The other 208 children were born in the New England States, the nativity of 205 being Massachusetts. Seventy per cent of all the children born out of wedlock—148 of 211—were born at the State infirmary. The nativity of the children is summarized as follows:

```
Total under care_____ 211
Massachusetts_____ 205
    Boston_____ 36
    Metropolitan district outside Boston_____ 10
    State infirmary_____ 148
    Other Massachusetts_____ 11
Other New England_____ 3
Foreign_____ 2
Not reported _____ 1
```

The residence of the child at the time of entering the infirmary, or of the mother if the child was unborn, was as follows:

```
Total under care_____ 211
Massachusetts_____ 201
    Boston_____ 83
    Metropolitan district outside Boston_____ 29
    Other Massachusetts_____ 89
Other_____ 9
Not reported_____ 1
```

---

[14] The total number of illegitimate births in the infirmary during the year was 119, but in 28 cases the child was under other supervision than that of the social service committee.

The residence of almost two-fifths was Boston; and of more than half, Boston or the metropolitan district. More than two-fifths lived in other parts of the State. It must be remembered that residence does not imply legal settlement, and that most of, if not all, these cases were not chargeable to any town for poor relief.

The 83 children whose residence was Boston were also included in the study of children born out of wedlock under care of Boston agencies and of State agencies so far as they dealt with Boston children. Twenty-nine other children were also included in the Boston study, having been under the care of Boston agencies during the year. Nine children included in the Boston study and 8 others were under the care of the division of State minor wards during the period studied.

Thirty-five children had brothers or sisters also under care of the social-service committee during the year. The total number of families represented by the 211 children was 193. In 176 of these cases one child only was under care; in 16, two children were being cared for; and in 1, three children were under care.

Most of the children were very young when they were received for care by the infirmary and the social service committee. In 148 of the 211 cases the mother entered the infirmary before the birth of the child. In 38 other cases the child was less than 1 year of age. The ages of the children at the beginning of care were as follows:

Total under care _____			211
Under care from birth _____ [15] 148	2 years_____		7
Less than 3 months_____ 29	3 years_____		6
3–5 months _____ 5	4 years and over_____		3
6–11 months _____ 4	Not reported _____	[16]	1
1 year_____ 8			

In 63 cases the mother and child came under care subsequent to the child's birth. Before entering the infirmary 57 of these children had been living with their mothers, 5 had been provided for away from their mothers, and in one case it was not reported whether or not the child was with the mother. Twenty-five children who had been with their mothers and 2 of those away from their mothers had been under the supervision of agencies.

Of the 57 children who had been living with their mothers before entering the State infirmary, 7 had been living in the mothers' own homes or other independent establishments, 3 in the homes of maternal grandparents, 4 in the homes of other relatives, 8 in homes in which the mothers were employed at housework, 6 in a public in-

---

[15] Includes 1 child 2 years of age who had been born at the infirmary but had been discharged from care. He returned to the institution with his mother when she was again illegitimately pregnant.

[16] Not under care from birth

firmary or maternity home, and 12 in hospitals. The location of 8 was not reported. All but 2 of the children who had been in infirmaries, maternity homes, or hospitals immediately before entering the State infirmary were under 3 months of age. Three of the 5 children who had been away from their mothers were in boarding or free homes, 1 was in an institution, and the location of 1 was not reported.

The application to the infirmary for the care of these mothers and children came in most cases from the overseers of the poor. In 7 instances private agencies made application; and in 8 cases private individuals. The applications for the care of 196 children came from overseers of the poor or other public agencies.

The need for maternity care was the reason given for application in 147 cases—70 per cent of the total. In 20 cases the illness of the mother and in 2 her defective mentality were given as reasons for care being needed. In 42 cases other reasons were assigned, chiefly the mother's inability to provide for herself and her child.

Of the 211 children under care born out of wedlock 30 died during the year and 78 were discharged from care. All but 2 of those who died were under 1 year of age at death, 22 being less than 6 months old. Of the 78 discharged from care, 43 were less than 6 months old; 14, from 6 to 11 months of age; 11, 1 year old; and 10, 2 years of age and over. The length of time under care for the children who died or were discharged was as follows:

Total who died or were discharged		108
Less than 6 months_____ 87	2 years_____	1
6 to 11 months_____ 14	3 years_____	1
1 year_____ 5		

There were 103 children remaining under care at the close of the year. Of these, 28 were less than 6 months of age; 24, 6 to 11 months; 28, 1 year; 16, 2 years; and 7, 3 years and over. The length of time these children had been cared for up to the end of the year studied was as follows:

Total remaining under care		103
Less than 6 months_____ 36	1 year_____	27
6 to 11 months_____ 27	2 years_____	13

At the end of the year or immediately previous to death or discharge from care, 181 of the 211 children—86 per cent—were with their mothers and 30 were away from their mothers. Of the 93 children less than 6 months old at the end of the period, 88 were with their mothers and 5 away; of the 44 children 6 to 11 months of age, 35 were with and 9 were away from their mothers; of the 74 children 1 year of age and over, 58 were living with and 16 had been separated from their mothers.

The homes or places of residence of the children who were with their mothers at the end of the period were as follows:

Total with their mothers			181
Mother's own home	4	Public infirmary	88
Home of maternal grandparents	27	Hospital	1
Home of other relatives or friends	17	Other institution	1
Boarding	4	Not reported	1
Mother's place of employment	38		

Slightly more than one-fourth of the children with their mothers were living in the mothers' own homes, mothers' parental homes, or in the homes of other relatives or friends. A little more than one-fifth were living in their mothers' places of employment. Almost half were still in the public infirmary at the end of the period.

Of the 58 children 1 year of age and over who were with their mothers at the end of the period, 12 were living in the mothers' own homes or parental homes, with other relatives, or with friends; 3 were boarding with their mothers; 23 were living in the mothers' places of employment; and 20 were still at the public infirmary.

Of the 30 children who were living away from their mothers at the end of the period, 7 were living with their maternal grandparents or with other relatives; 1 of these children had been adopted by relatives. Eleven were boarding, 1 had been adopted by others than relatives, 5 were still at the infirmary, 1 was in a hospital, 3 were in other institutions, and the home or place of residence of 2 was not reported.

The care of 108 children terminated during the year, 30 having died and 78 having been discharged from care. The persons to whom discharged and the reasons for closing the cases of the 78 discharged were as follows:

Total discharged from care		78
Discharged to mother		42
Mother able to care for child	8	
Mother and father married each other	4	
Mother married, but not to father	1	
Mother and child deported	27	
Other disposition made	1	
Mother and child disappeared, and impossible to locate	1	
Discharged to maternal relatives		6
Relatives able to care for child	4	
Child adopted by relatives	1	
Other disposition made	1	
Assumed by private agencies		10
Assumed by public agencies		20
Mother and child to be deported	3	
Discharged for other reasons	17	

A total of 30 children—14 per cent of all the children of illegitimate birth under care during the year—were deported. Nine of those deported were returned to Canada, 2 to the West Indies, and 19 to European countries. Five of the mothers who were returned to Canada had been pregnant on arrival in this country. The 2 children returned to the West Indies were brother and sister; one had been born in the West Indies, and the other had been born shortly after the mother's arrival in this country.

Besides the 30 children who died during the year, 23 were reported in poor physical condition; the health of 158 children was good, so far as known. Since all these children had been under the care of the State infirmary, it is probable that any defect or disease would have been reported. The percentage who died or were in poor physical condition was 25. Of the 30 children who died, 7 had syphilis, 1 had gonorrheal infection, 2 were tubercular, 1 was blind, and 19 were in otherwise poor condition. Of the 23 children in poor condition who were living at the end of the period, 7 had syphilis, 1 had gonorrheal infection resulting in blindness, 1 was suspected of having syphilis, 1 was rachitic, and 13 were in otherwise poor condition. Seven and one-half per cent of all the children born out of wedlock under care were syphilitic or had gonorrheal infection, 6.6 per cent of all being syphilitic.

Status of the Mother.

The mothers who come to the State infirmary with children born out of wedlock or to secure maternity care are, in a sense, a residual group. Because of recent arrival in this country or absence of legal settlement in the State, they have been unable to secure care in the towns in which they were living when their need became urgent. Those living in communities well served by private agencies or institutions would probably have been provided for locally had not their physical or mental condition or their general reputation and character discouraged private agencies from assuming responsibility. Maternity homes do not, as a rule, admit women who are venereally diseased or who are illegitimately pregnant for a second time. In Massachusetts it is possible for private agencies to turn over their most difficult cases to the State—both mother and baby cases and cases where the child alone is to be provided for.

As an indication of the extent to which the mothers at the infirmary represent a special group of women who become mothers of children out of wedlock is the comparison, in Table 31, of the 193 mothers of children born out of wedlock who were under the care of the social-service committee of the State board of charity in 1914 and the 840 mothers of infants born out of wedlock in Boston during the same year.[17]

---

[17] See pp. 105–126.

TABLE 31.—*Comparison of characteristics of mothers of children of illegitimate birth under care of the social-service committee of the State board of charity and of mothers of infants born out of wedlock in Boston.*

Item.	Per cent of 193 mothers of children of illegitimate birth under care of social-service committee.	Per cent of 840 mothers of infants born out of wedlock in Boston.
Race: Belonging to Negro race	6.2	6.2
Nativity:		
Foreign born	72.0	40.1
Known to have been in the United States less than 5 years a	39.9	11.5
Age at birth of child: b		
Under 21 years	30.6	41.0
21–24 years	37.3	31.1
25 years and over	32.1	22.3
Not reported		5.7
Civil condition:		
Single	85.0	c 92.9
Married, widowed, divorced, deserted	15.0	c 7.1
Physical condition:		
Poor (including physical defects, diseases, or general poor condition)	48.7	c 24.1
Syphilis or gonorrhea	28.5	c 8.5
Mental condition:		
Diagnosed subnormal, abnormal, or feeble-minded	25.9	c 13.3
Diagnosed feeble-minded	17.1	c 8.8
Character:		
Alcoholic, immoral, d otherwise delinquent, or otherwise poor	63.7	c 42.2
Immoral d	56.0	c 31.5
Other children: Having more than one child of illegitimate birth	39.9	c 9.9
Occupation:		
Gainfully employed	c 95.7	c 85.8
Domestic servants	c 50.0	c 35.6
Semiskilled factory operatives	c 29.3	c 23.0
Mode of living at application: Parental home	c 13.5	c 36.2
Mother's family:		
One or both parents dead, not in the United States, divorced, or separated	84.5	31.1
One or both parents reported of poor character	20.2	12.7

a At birth of oldest child included in the study. Includes 2 mothers whose children were foreign born.
b In case of mothers under care of the social-service committee, age at birth of oldest child included in the study.
c Per cent of total reported.
d Including only sex irregularities other than those connected with the cases of illegitimate maternity studied.

From this comparison it would appear that the proportion of foreign born among the mothers cared for at the infirmary is much larger than among an unselected group of mothers of children born out of wedlock, and that among the former group a larger percentage have been in the United States less than five years. The proportion of women 25 years of age and over is greater, and the percentage under 21 is smaller among the mothers cared for at the infirmary; the proportion of married, widowed, divorced, or deserted women is larger than in the unselected group. The numbers of mothers in poor physical condition, below normal mentally, and of poor character are proportionately great, as is the number having more than one child out of wedlock.

More of the mothers under the care of the social service committee than of the unselected group of mothers were gainfully employed, and larger proportions had been employed as domestic servants and as semiskilled factory workers. Fewer were living in their parental homes. Indeed, most of the mothers at the infirmary or given after-care had no parental homes in this country upon which they could rely for assistance.

Status of the Father and His Contribution to the Support of the Child.

Information as to the status of the father was fragmentary. Age was reported for the fathers of 67 of the 211 children born out of wedlock who were under care. The fathers of 6 were under 21 years of age; of 48, between the ages of 21 and 29; and of 13, 30 years of age and over. The fathers of 86 children were single; of 24, married; of 3, widowed; of 6, separated, deserted, or divorced. Civil condition was not reported in 92 cases.

Data as to occupation were obtained for the fathers of 114 children. Their occupations were as follows:

Total whose histories reported occupation of father_____ 114

Proprietors	5	Servants	14
Clerks and kindred workers	5	Semiofficial public employees	7
Skilled workers	24	Professional persons	5
Semiskilled workers	31	Not gainfully employed	1
Laborers	22		

Court action was known to have been initiated for the support of 34 of the 211 children. Orders for periodic payments were made in 11 cases. Certificates were filed in 4 cases stating that adequate provision for the child's support had been made. The parents of 3 children married each other. In one instance the father was sentenced to the house of correction with an order that his wages earned there should be paid for the child's support. The court case was closed without any provision for the child's support in 9 cases, and 6 cases were pending at the end of the year or the close of care. In a total of 19 of the 34 court cases, support for the child was arranged as a result of court action before the end of the year or the close of care.

In addition to the 19 children for whom provision was made through court action, there were 29 to whose support the father had at some time contributed. In 6 of these cases the father and mother married each other; in 4 they had been living as married or illegally married. The fathers of 4 children contributed regularly to their support; the fathers of 7 made irregular contributions. In 5 cases settlement was made out of court, whereby the father paid a lump sum for the benefit of mother and child. In 3 instances the father paid part of or all the expenses of the mother's pregnancy and confinement, but made no other payments for the child's benefit.

There were 62 cases in which no support from the father was obtained and court action had not been initiated at the end of the year or the close of care. In 86 instances no report was secured as to contributions to support or court action. The 48 children to whose support the fathers were known to have contributed comprised 23 per cent of the total under care.

CHAPTER 3. THE ADOPTION OF CHILDREN BORN OUT OF WEDLOCK.

Adoption is the legal process by which a child is received into the home of the adopting persons as their own child and acquires practically the same status in respect to the adopting parents as that of their natural children. By this means children whose parents are dead or are unable to provide for them are given the advantages of normal home life and natural family and social relationships. Under the right circumstances and conditions this method is probably the ideal way of providing for orphaned children or for children whose parents will never be able to care for them. It is a method which has been widely followed, both by individuals confronted with the problem of provision for homeless children and by organized social agencies and institutions. It has, however, been subject to much abuse. The desire of the unmarried mother to be relieved of the burden of providing for her child—with all the economic and social difficulties involved—and the longing of childless men and women for children whom they may take as their own has been commercialized by unscrupulous persons. Agencies and institutions have placed children for adoption without adequate consideration of their histories, family circumstances, or physical and mental condition, or of the character of the homes into which they were to be adopted. The need for careful and adequate investigation before adoption is decreed by the court is becoming more and more evident.

As has been pointed out in previous chapters of this report, agencies and institutions in Massachusetts have been extremely careful in the matter of adoption. The belief is general that natural family ties should not be completely severed if there is any possibility that in the future the child's own parents may be able to establish a suitable home, and also that adoption should not take place unless the child gives promise of normal development and the adopting parents are in every way able to provide adequately for him. A trial period is usually required before the legal adoption. However, the problem of adoption through private individuals is present. The practice of " adoption through advertisement "—that is, of advertising children for adoption through the newspapers—has attracted considerable attention, and a committee of public and private agencies in Boston, on which the State board of charity is represented, investigates as many such cases as possible and prevents many unsuitable adoptions.

As a part of this study of illegitimacy as a child-welfare problem, the adoption records of the probate courts of four counties, so far as they concerned children born out of wedlock, were consulted. These were Suffolk County—the greater part of which the city of Boston comprises—and the three contiguous counties of Essex, Middlesex, and Norfolk. The population of these four counties constitutes 60 per cent of the population of the State.[1]

ADOPTION LAWS IN MASSACHUSETTS.

Under the adoption laws of Massachusetts,[2] the petition for adoption must be made to the probate court of the county in which the petitioner resides or, if the petitioner is not a resident of the State, of the county in which the child resides. The person petitioning for leave to adopt must be of full age and older than the person he adopts. Adoption by a husband or wife, or by a brother, sister, nephew, or niece, of the whole or of half blood, is forbidden. If the petitioner has a husband or wife living who is competent to join in the petition, the husband or wife must join therein, and upon adoption the person adopted is to all legal intents and purposes the child in law of both.

The written consent of the child himself is necessary if he is above the age of 14 years. If a married woman is to be adopted, the consent of her husband also is required. In all cases other than those expressly excepted written consent must be obtained from the lawful parents or surviving parent; from the parent having lawful custody, if the parents are divorced or living separately; from the guardian of the child, if any; from the mother only of a child born out of wedlock; or from the person substituted for any of the above named by the provisions of the law. The law provides that illegitimacy shall in no case be expressly averred upon the record. The court has held, however, that the entry " Child of M. J., single woman," is not a violation of this provision.[3]

If the child is of full age, no other consent than that of the child, or of the child and her husband, if any, is necessary. The law specifies certain circumstances under which the consent of a parent or other person named, other than the child, is not required. These include: Hopeless insanity; sentence to a correctional institution with more than three years remaining; willful desertion or neglect for two years last preceding the date of the petition; suffering the child to be supported for more than two years continuously, prior to

---

[1] See p. 271.

[2] R. L. 1902 ch. 154 secs. 1, 2 as amended by acts 1904 ch. 302, 3 as amended by acts 1907 ch. 405 and 4 as amended by acts 1915 ch. 53 secs. 5–11.

[3] Purinton v. Jamrock (1907) 195 Mass. 197. Cited in Manual of Laws Relating to the State Board of Charity of Massachusetts. Boston, 1915. P. 272.

the petition, by an incorporated charitable institution, or as a pauper by a city or town or by the State; sentence to imprisonment for drunkenness upon a third conviction within one year and neglect to provide proper care and maintenance; conviction on specified sex charges and neglect to provide proper care and maintenance. Giving up the child in writing, for the purpose of adoption, to an incorporated charitable institution operates as consent to any adoption subsequently approved by the institution. If the child is supported as a pauper by a city or town, notice must be given to the State board of charity and the overseers of the poor, and, if supported by the city of Boston, notice must also be given to the trustees for children of that city. If supported by the State, notice must be given the State board of charity.

If the written consent required is not submitted to the court with the petition, the court orders notice of the petition by personal service, or if the persons are not found within the State, by publication. If the child is of unknown parentage and is a foundling, publication is not required, but notice must be given the State board of charity.[4] If after notice the person whose consent is required does not appear and object to the petition, the court may act without his consent, subject to his right of appeal, or may appoint a guardian at law with power to give or withhold consent.

Before entering the decree of adoption the court must be satisfied of the identity and relations of the persons and that the petitioner is of sufficient ability to bring up the child and provide suitable support and education for it, and that the child should be adopted. Under this clause adequate social investigation could be made and wide discretion used by the court.

The effect of the decree of adoption is: (a) To create between the child and the petitioner and his kindred all rights, duties, and other legal consequences of the natural relation of child and parent, except as regards succession to property; (b) to terminate such rights, duties, and legal consequences between the child and his natural parents or kindred or any previous adopting parent, except as regards marriage, incest, or cohabitation; (c) change of name may be decreed by the court; (d) the person adopted takes the same share of the property which the adopting parent can dispose of by will as he would have taken if born to the parent in lawful wedlock, and stands in regard to the legal descendants, but to no other kindred of the adopting parent in the same position as if born to him; but a person does not by adoption lose his right to inherit from his natural parents or kindred.

---

[4] This provision was not in effect during the year of the study but was added to the law by an amendment in 1915.

Appeal from the decree of adoption may be allowed a parent by the supreme judicial court under circumstances specified in the law.

In regard to the adoption of infants under 2 years of age, the law provides additional safeguards. Whoever receives an infant under 2 years of age for adoption or for giving him a home or for procuring a home or adoption for him must, before receiving the child, ascertain his name, age, and birthplace and the name and residence of his parent or parents, and must keep a record of these facts and of the date of reception. Upon reception of the infant he must give notice in writing to the State board of charity and must give the required information upon the request of the board. Within two days after the child's discharge, notice in writing of the discharge and the disposition made must be given. The board may investigate the case and, at any time previous to a decree of adoption, take the infant into its custody if in the judgment of the board the public interest and the protection of the infant so require.[5]

Still further protection is given children born out of wedlock. The law provides:

Whoever receives an infant under the age of three years for board or for the purpose of procuring adoption shall use due diligence to ascertain whether it is illegitimate, and if he knows or has reason to believe it is, he shall forthwith notify the State board of charity of such reception. The members, officers, or agents of said board may enter and inspect any building where they have reason to believe such illegitimate infant is boarded and remove it, if they believe that, by reason of neglect, abuse, or other cause, its removal is necessary to preserve its life. Such infant shall be in the custody of said board, which shall make provision therefor according to law.[7]

PROPORTION OF ADOPTION CASES INVOLVING CHILDREN BORN OUT OF WEDLOCK.

During the year 1914 there were 441 petitions for adoption before the probate courts of Essex, Middlesex, Suffolk, and Norfolk Counties. (See Table 32.) Almost half the cases—46 per cent—were known to have involved children born out of wedlock. In Middlesex County the percentage was 43, and in Suffolk 49. These percentages must be considered understatements in view of the fact that the law provides that illegitimacy is not to be " expressly averred upon the record."

That almost half the adoption cases involved children born out of wedlock indicates a much higher proportion of such children who are adopted than is the case among children born in wedlock. Only 4.4 per cent of the children born in Boston in the year covered by the

---

[5] R. L. 1902, ch. 83, sec. 11. Manual of Laws Relating to the State Board of Charity of Massachusetts. Boston, 1915. Pp. 102–103.

[7] R. L. 1902, ch. 83, sec. 17. Manual of Laws Relating to the State Board of Charity of Massachusetts. Boston, 1915. P. 104.

study were born out of wedlock.[8] The number of adoption cases involving children of illegitimate birth (204) was about 16 per cent of the number of births registered as illegitimate in the four counties studied.[9] It must be borne in mind that the number of illegitimate births, as well as the number of adoption cases, are understatements.

TABLE 32.—*Adoption cases before the courts of Essex, Middlesex, Suffolk, and Norfolk Counties, 1914.*

County.	Estimated population, 1914.	Adoption cases before the courts of four counties.			
		Total.	Status of child.		
			Born in wedlock, so far as known.	Known to have been born out of wedlock.	Foundlings and pseudo-foundlings.
Total	2,195,771	441	224	204	13
Essex	459,515	94	a 51	39	4
Middlesex	724,074	153	83	66	4
Suffolk	814,713	153	76	75	2
Norfolk	197,469	41	b 14	24	3

a There were 52 children involved in these 51 cases.
b There were 18 children involved in these 14 cases.

AGE OF CHILD AND RELATIONSHIP OF PERSON ADOPTING.

The ages of the children born out of wedlock for whose adoption petitions were filed were as follows:

Total children			204
Less than 1 year	37	4 years	12
1 year	34	5 years	11
2 years	36	6-9 years	23
3 years	29	10 years and over	22

Only 52 per cent of the children were under 3 years of age, the age under which reports of reception for the purpose of adoption of infants born out of wedlock must be made to the State board of charity.[10] Twenty-six per cent were 3 to 5 years of age, inclusive, and 22 per cent were 6 years of age and over.

In 36 cases—18 per cent—the petition was made by relatives. The relationship of the person adopting was as follows:

Total children			204
Father	2	Other relatives	8
Mother and stepfather	19	Not related	159
Maternal grandparents	7	Not reported	9

[8] See p. 85.
[9] See p. 271. The total number of births registered as illegitimate in the counties of Essex, Middlesex, Suffolk, and Norfolk was 1,283.
[10] See p. 336.

The provision of the law which requires the husband or wife of the petitioner to join in the petition makes it necessary for a mother to adopt her own child if the stepfather makes the petition. In 9 per cent of all the cases involving children born out of wedlock the mother and her husband were the petitioners. It is interesting to note that in the year following that in which this study was made a child born out of wedlock was adopted by his own father and mother.

In 30 of the 204 cases involving children born out of wedlock the child had been given temporary or prolonged care by the division of State minor wards during the year. Thirteen of these children and 18 others were included in the study of children under care of Boston agencies.[11]

Sixteen of the children whose adoption was petitioned were born in Boston in 1914. Twenty-one infants born out of wedlock in Boston during that year were adopted in 1915 through the courts of the counties studied, 12 of them being less than 1 year of age at the time of adoption. Adoption was petitioned in the courts studied for a total of 28 infants born out of wedlock in Boston in 1914 and under 1 year of age at the time the petitions were filed. Hence, before they had reached 1 year of age, petitions were filed in the four courts studied for the adoption of 3 per cent of the 847 infants born in Boston during one year. One of the infants born in Boston in 1914 was adopted twice in 1915—first, at the age of 9 months through the Suffolk County court, and, second, at the age of a year and a half in the county of Norfolk. Why the first adopting parents gave the child up was not stated.

The family histories of the children adopted were given only for those children known to Boston or State agencies and for a few other cases in which the adoption record contained fairly complete information. The absence of investigation of cases not known to social agencies and the consequent lack of information in regard to the child and the persons desiring to adopt must result, in some instances at least, in decrees being given when the adoption is not to the best interests of all concerned.

The following cases illustrate defective heritage. The children were so young that it could not be determined whether or not their development would be likely to be normal.

A child of 2 years was adopted in 1914 through one of the courts studied. The record stated that the mother was insane and an inmate of a State hospital. For a long time previous to her commitment to this institution she had been an inmate of a town almshouse. The child had been supported by the town since birth. The petitioners were certified to be of good character, childless, and to have a comfortable home. (Case Nor. 49–7.)

---

[11] See Sec. I, ch. 2. This chapter also included Boston children under care of State agencies.

An infant born in Boston in 1914 was adopted when 11 months old. She had been born at the public infirmary. Her mother was feeble-minded and was later admitted to a State institution for the care of mental defectives; she had served two sentences in a reformatory, had been an inmate of a house of prostitution, and had had a venereal infection. The child's maternal grandmother was reported as "queer," and the maternal grandfather as having been intemperate. One maternal aunt was feeble-minded and one immoral. A cousin was an inmate of an institution for the feeble-minded. The outlook for the child was not promising. (Case B 717.)

CHILDREN COMMITTED AS DELINQUENTS TO STATE INSTITUTIONS.[1]

Introduction.

The adverse environmental conditions which are the lot of so large a number of children born out of wedlock would seem to make difficult the development of normal character. From the preceding chapters of the study it appears that a considerable proportion of these children of unfortunate birth are subject to the types of influences that form the background for delinquency. Children of illegitimate birth are not born into normal homes, and many of them suffer throughout childhood from the lack of natural home life. Often circumstances attendant upon birth out of wedlock involve positive, adverse conditions which undermine moral stamina. A potent but less tangible influence touching children of illegitimate birth is the psychological effect which their peculiar relation to society has upon their attitude toward life.

Children born out of wedlock frequently start life with a heritage of mental subnormality, or of immorality and delinquency, or in their shiftings about are subjected to detrimental influences. Other parts of the study have shown the large amount of alcoholism, sexual irregularity, and other forms of delinquent behavior incident in the heritage and environment of these children.

Children without normal home guidance more often than other children become in need of the strong discipline of the State. Mothers who are obliged to assume double parental responsibility, often working away from home to earn bare livelihoods for themselves and their children, struggle against almost insurmountable difficulties in guiding and training them. A large number of children born out of wedlock are provided for in foster homes. This type of home lacks the strong ties of blood relationship which impel a family to exert every effort to care for and control a difficult child, rather than give him over to a disciplinary agency. Children not living with their parents are frequently subjected to shiftings from one home to another, with consequent disturbance of social relationships and difficulty of adaptation to new surroundings.

---

[1] This section of the chapter was prepared by Miss Evelina Belden.

340

Purpose and Sources of Study.

For the purpose of securing more intensive information regarding the interrelationship of birth out of wedlock and delinquency, a special study was made of the wards of certain State institutions. An attempt was made to estimate the proportion of these wards who were of illegitimate birth, to discover any differences between those born out of wedlock and others, and to analyze some of the conditions in their lives which formed the background of their delinquency. The inquiry was limited to records from the three State schools receiving juvenile delinquents and their parole departments, and to records of girls under 21 years of age in the care of the reformatory for women.

The three schools from which material was secured have the following jurisdiction, as described in a report of the State board of charity:[2]

The Lyman School for Boys at Westborough, the Industrial School for Boys at Shirley, and the Industrial School for Girls at Lancaster are the three industrial schools provided for by the State for juvenile delinquents. They are administered by a single board of trustees. * * * Boys under 15 years of age may be committed to the Lyman School, and under 18 years of age to the school at Shirley. Girls under 17 go to the institution at Lancaster. All persons committed remain under the control of the trustees during minority. For greater efficiency in administration, the Lyman School cares for boys under 15, while those over that age go to Shirley.

The trustees of the training schools also maintain two parole departments, one for boys and one for girls, under whose care children paroled from the three institutions remain during minority. The training schools and parole departments are under the general supervision of the State board of charity, and a history of each case is kept on file in the division of State minor wards. More complete records are kept in the schools and in the girls' parole department.

The Massachusetts Reformatory for Women receives girls and women 15 years of age and over for offenses of all types, under determinate or indeterminate sentences as specified by the judges of the courts. Women paroled from this institution are released to the agent for aiding discharged female prisoners, employed by the board of prison commissioners.

The wards included in the study were those in the four institutions or under the parole departments of the training schools during some part of 1914. The original information for the training-school children was secured from the records of the division of State minor wards. The more complete data for the boys, not being available in

---

[2] Thirty-sixth Annual Report of the Massachusetts State Board of Charity for the Year Ending November 30, 1914. Boston, 1915. Pt. I, p. 33.

Boston, were not secured. The records of the women on parole from the women's reformatory were not examined.

Proportion of Wards of Correctional Institutions Who Were Born Out of Wedlock.

The only figures secured in this study giving any reliable index of the proportion of wards of institutions for delinquents who had been born out of wedlock were those for girls committed to the institutions studied during the year 1914. A total of 184 girls under 21 years of age were committed, of whom 17, or 9.2 per cent, were of illegitimate birth. In the investigations for the girls received during this period special efforts were made to determine parentage, hence the proportion obtained represents a high degree of accuracy. Since the complete records for the boys' cases were not available in Boston, no estimate of the proportion who had been born out of wedlock was attempted. Such information as was secured would seem to indicate either that a smaller proportion of delinquent boys are of illegitimate birth or that the facts of parentage are more often lost sight of. The estimate given for girls should therefore not be considered as indicative of the proportionate number of all delinquents who are of illegitimate birth.

The percentage—9.2—of girls born out of wedlock among the delinquent girls committed during 1914 is very nearly that obtained from a comparison of all girls under care of the industrial school for girls and the girls' parole department in 1914, without regard to the time of commitment. Of these 744 girls 60, or 8.1 per cent, were of illegitimate birth. The fact that this is slightly lower than the first figure is probably due largely to the less complete social information for the earlier commitments.

The proportion of delinquent girls who had been born out of wedlock was large in comparison with the proportion of such children in the community. In 1914, 2.3 per cent of all live births in the State of Massachusetts were registered as illegitimate. In Boston during the same year the percentage of illegitimate births, corrected by information secured from social agencies, was 4.4. The mortality among infants born out of wedlock was shown to be three times that among infants of legitimate birth.[3] Hence the 9.2 per cent of delinquent girls who were of illegitimate birth is considerably in excess of the proportion of children born out of wedlock in the general population.

The factors coincident with illegitimacy are much more closely allied with dependency and neglect than with delinquency. Less

---

[3] See pp. 85, 90, 270.

than one-tenth of the girls committed to institutions for delinquents had been born out of wedlock. In contrast to this is the proportion—almost one-fourth—of children under care of the division of State minor wards during 1914 who were of illegitimate birth. The proportion of delinquents who are of illegitimate birth would thus seem to be materially smaller than the proportion of dependents.

Distribution.

A total of 102 children known to have been born out of wedlock were found to have been under the care of the four institutions and the two parole departments during some part of the year covered by the study. This number represents a minimum, because the number of boys is probably understated. Of the 102 children, 66 were girls, and 36 boys. As before explained this proportion is not a true ratio of boys to girls. There is no reason, however, to think that the boys were in any way a selected group. Three-fourths of the children— 76 out of 102—had been committed to .the institutions previous to 1914, and of these 1 died and 10 were discharged during the year. A third of the children were on parole during the entire year covered by the study, or during that part of the year previous to discharge; 20 others were in the institutions part of the year and on parole the remainder of the year. Of the 10 discharged from care 9 were of age and 1—a boy of 18 on parole—was arrested and committed to another correctional institution.

Although many of the children had been committed previous to 1914—some of them five or more years before—yet their problems need not be considered as in any wise different from those of children admitted during 1914; for there had been no such recent gain or loss in probation work in the State as would cause a difference in the types of cases sent to institutions, and there had been no change of policy in regard to the ages of children committed, their terms of commitment, or the causes of commitments. For this reason comparisons have been made throughout the study between all children committed during 1914 and children born out of wedlock under care during the same year.

Age at Commitment and Time under Care.

Children born out of wedlock appear to be committed to correctional institutions at a much earlier age than other children. (See Table 33.) While but 41 per cent of all children committed in 1914 were under 15 years of age at time of commitment, 59 per cent of the children of illegitimate birth under care were under this age. Twenty-five per cent of all children committed in 1914 were under

14 years of age, as compared with 40 per cent of those of illegitimate birth under care. The difference in age at commitment suggests that children with the handicap of illegitimate birth tend to lose their moral balance earlier, or that because of the lack of properly functioning homes they are earlier turned over to correctional institutions.

TABLE 33.—*Age at commitment of all delinquent children committed to certain State institutions in 1914, and of delinquent children under care who were born out of wedlock.*

Age at commitment.	Delinquent children under care of State institutions or parole departments.			
	Committed, 1914.		Children born out of wedlock, under care in 1914.a	
	Number.	Per cent distribu- tion.	Number.	Per cent distribu- tion.
Total....................................	669	100. 0	102	100. 0
8–11 years....................................	50	7. 5	13	12. 7
12–13 years....................................	114	17. 0	28	27. 5
14 years....................................	109	16. 3	19	18. 6
15–20 years....................................	395	59. 1	42	41. 2
Not reported....................................	1	. 1	....	....

a Includes all under care during the whole or any part of the year.

Since wards of the training schools remain under care until they are 21 years of age,[4] it follows that children born out of wedlock, being received at an earlier age, remain under care for a longer period.

The time under care, from commitment to the end of 1914 or the time of discharge, for the children born out of wedlock was as follows:

Total under care_____	102
Less than 1 year_____	26	2–4 years_____	35
1 year _____	19	5 years and over_____	22

Residence and Nativity.

Cities and large towns are known to contribute proportionately more commitments to correctional institutions than smaller centers or rural sections. This was found to hold true in the residence distribution of the children born out of wedlock. Almost half these children came from Boston or the metropolitan district outside Boston. Those coming from cities having populations of 25,000 or more comprised 72 per cent of the total, though in Massachusetts in 1910 only 64 per cent of all children between the ages of 6 and 21 years lived in cities of this size.[5]   (See Table 34.)

---

[4] Unless care is earlier terminated for exceptional reasons, such as death or transfer to another institution.

[5] Thirteenth Census of the United States, 1910: Vol. II, Population, pp. 866, 881.

TABLE 34.—*Residence, previous to commitment, of delinquent children born out of wedlock.*

Residence previous to commitment.	Delinquent children born out of wedlock, under care in 1914.	
	Number.	Per cent distribution.
Total..	102	100.0
Boston...	24	23.5
Other cities of 25,000 or more *a*...........................	49	48.0
Cities of 5,000 but less than 25,000 *a*......................	14	13.8
Towns of less than 5,000 *a*................................	10	9.8
Not reported..	5	4.9

a In 1910.

The proportion of colored children, 21 out of 102, is strikingly large. Over three times as great a percentage of wards of illegitimate birth were colored as in the case of infants born out of wedlock in Boston in 1914—20 per cent of the wards of correctional institutions, but only 6 per cent of the infants born out of wedlock.[6]

A comparison of the nativity of children of legitimate and of illegitimate birth was possible only for those under care of the three State training schools and of their parole departments. (See Table 35.) The children of illegitimate birth were for the most part born and brought up in the State; only 7 were of foreign birth. The birthplace of 1 was unknown. Of the 87 native born, 67 were born in Massachusetts, 13 in other States of New England, and 7 in other parts of the United States. A slightly smaller proportion of the wards of illegitimate birth under care were foreign born than of all children committed—7 per cent of those born out of wedlock under care and 10 per cent of all committed in 1914.

TABLE 35.—*Nativity of all delinquent children committed to the three State training schools in 1914, and of delinquent children born out of wedlock, under care of the training schools or their parole departments.[a]*

Nativity.	Delinquent children under care of the State training schools or their parole departments.			
	Committed, 1914.[b]		Children born out of wedlock, under care in 1914.[c]	
	Number.	Per cent distribution.	Number.	Per cent distribution.
Total......................	610	100.0	95	100.0
Native.....................	545	89.3	87	91.6
Foreign....................	62	10.2	7	7.4
Not reported...............	3	.5	1	1.0

a Girls at the Massachusetts Reformatory for Women excluded, since the report of that institution did not give nativity according to age.
b From the Fourth Annual Report of the Trustees of the Massachusetts Training Schools for the Year Ending Nov. 30, 1914. Boston, 1915. Pp. 42, 67, 103.
c Includes all under care during the year, without regard to the time of commitment.

[6] See p. 107.

Information about the nativity of the parents, especially of the father, was lacking in a large number of cases. Twenty-two children—slightly more than one-fifth of the total—had mothers known to have been foreign born, and in 9 of these 22 cases the fathers were known to have been of foreign birth also. Ten of the foreign-born mothers were Canadians.

Mentality and Physical Condition.

Owing to insufficient staffs in the institutions, mental examinations were not made for all children. Thus the number who were diagnosed feeble-minded must be considered a minimum. Twenty-two of the 102 children were reported very backward or below normal mentally; 6 of these were definitely diagnosed feeble-minded; 1 was diagnosed insane; 6 were diagnosed subnormal; 5 were considered probably subnormal or feeble-minded, though diagnoses had not as yet been made; and 4 were very backward.

The physical condition of the children at the time of commitment was not reported in all cases. However, 12 were known to have syphilis or gonorrhea or both; 2 were crippled; 2 tubercular; 2 epileptic; and 7 others were in poor condition.

Offenses.

It is of interest to note the specific acts which resulted in the commitments of these children and to compare them with the charges which brought other children into correctional institutions.

In Massachusetts, under the laws relating to juvenile delinquents, a child is usually heard for a specific offense, though the judgment is simply that he is a delinquent or wayward child. The complaint may be for a definite act such as assault, burglary, or larceny, or for being a wayward, stubborn, or delinquent child; and the offenses may range from a minor to a serious one. As in other States in the Union, the Massachusetts courts committing children vary considerably as to the amount and kind of investigations which the judges secure before they dispose of the cases and, consequently, there is a difference in the types of dispositions made throughout the State. There is no reason to suppose, however, that there is either a more or a less detailed investigation made in the cases of children born out of wedlock than of children of legitimate birth. The larger proportion of children of illegitimate birth who do not have suitable homes, or who are cared for by foster parents—less likely than a child's own parents to deal patiently with troublesome conduct—probably results in a larger proportion of commitments to institutions than in the case of children born in wedlock.

The reports of the training schools and the reformatory classify all cases under three headings: (1) Offenses against the person, (2) offenses against property, and (3) offenses against public order.

Offenses against the person include abandonment, assault, rape, and murder. Offenses against property include petty and grand larceny, receiving stolen goods, setting fires, robbery, burglary, and other offenses of like character; such charges often appear far more serious than the actual offenses. Elsewhere in this section, when describing characteristics, offenses against property have been referred to as " dishonesties."

Offenses against public order include all those acts which tend to destroy the social and moral fabric of a community. They include such offenses as soliciting on the streets, illicit sexual relations, vagrancy, idle and disorderly conduct, running away from home, persistent waywardness, stubbornness, or delinquency. Children transferred from the care of the State board of charity to the reformatories are usually classified as wayward, stubborn, or delinquent. Many of the boys' cases had to be classified generally under " stubborn," because no more definite facts were stated in the records. Some of these boys may have committed definite offenses.

In the study of offenses for which the children were committed, and of their characteristics, cases of boys and girls have been analyzed separately. (See Table 36.) A combined analysis would have overweighted the offenses most frequently attributable to girls, since there were more girls than boys. No boys, either of legitimate or of illegitimate birth, were committed for sex offenses and no girls for burglary.

There are several small but suggestive differences between the reasons for the commitments of the wards born out of wedlock and of all children committed during the year. First: Among the children born out of wedlock, none of either sex was committed because of offenses against the person, though a few of both sexes of all committed during the year were committed on this ground. Second: A larger percentage of girls born out of wedlock than of all girls were committed for offenses against property, and a smaller percentage for offenses against public order. For the boys born out of wedlock these differences in percentages were exactly reversed—a smaller percentage for offenses against property and a larger percentage for offenses against public order. Third: Both girls and boys born out of wedlock showed a larger percentage of the less serious offenses of stubbornness and other undefined delinquencies than did all committed during the year. Fourth: Nine per cent fewer girls born out of wedlock were committed for definitely stated sex charges and 6 per cent more for larceny.

TABLE 36.—*Nature of offenses for which delinquent girls and boys were committed to certain State institutions in 1914, and for which delinquent girls and boys born out of wedlock were committed.*

Nature of offense.	Delinquent children under care of State institutions or parole departments.			
	Comitted, 1914.		Children born out of wedlock, under care in 1914.	
	Number.	Per cent distribut.on.	Number	Per cent distribution.
Girls.				
Total............................	184	100. 0	66	100. 0
Against the person......................	2	1. 1	....	....
Against property......................	21	11. 4	11	16. 7
Larceny............................	20	10. 9	11	16. 7
Other............................	1	. 5	....	....
Against public order......................	161	87. 5	55	83. 3
Stubborn, delinquent, wayward...............	70	38. 0	31	47. 0
Sex offenses........................	64	34 8	17	25. 7
Other............................	27	14. 7	7	10. 6
Boys.				
Total............................	485	100. 0	36	100. 0
Against the person......................	14	2. 9	....	....
Against property......................	231	47. 6	16	44. 4
Burglary............................	95	19. 6	7	19. 4
Larceny............................	131	27. 0	9	25. 0
Other............................	5	1. 0	....	....
Against public order......................	240	49. 5	20	55. 6
Stubborn, delinquent, wayward...............	186	38. 4	17	47. 2
Other *a*........................	54	11. 1	3	8. 4

a Includes transfers from State board of charity.

These differences in offenses are largely explained by the differences in the ages of the children when they were committed. Younger children—and the children born out of wedlock have already been shown to be younger when committed—are not usually as serious offenders as older ones, and consequently are much more likely to be committed for waywardness, incorrigibility, and stubbornness than for such causes as assault, robbery, or arson. Also, the fact that there were more children of illegitimate birth in the younger age groups undoubtedly accounts for the smaller percentage of girls who were sex offenders.

The earlier ages alone might not account, however, for these differnces. It is possible not only that children without natural home ties are earlier referred to the discipline of the courts but also that this action is taken for less serious reasons.

The following cases are cited as illustrations of the conditions resulting in commitments of children born out of wedlock for such offenses as stubbornness and larceny:

A girl of 15 was committed to an institution on the charge of stubbornness. As a child she had been neglected in every way. Her mother was immoral and intemperate and had a long court record. The family was known to a number of agencies, public and private. At the age of 10 the child was adjudged neglected and placed in an institution, and later in agency homes. She was described as "profane, vulgar, self-willed, and ill-tempered." At the time of her commitment she had been associating with bad companions and had been immoral. (Case C 55.)

A young girl committed as a stubborn child had been a runaway and a petty thief. She had been adopted by her mother and stepfather. The mother tried hard to care for her children, but the stepfather was abusive and was finally divorced by the mother on statutory grounds. Soon after the mother became insane, and the child was placed out by an agency. She did not do well in her foster home, and her commitment to an institution was deemed necessary. (Case C 63.)

A very young girl committed on a charge of larceny was the child of an immoral woman who was a chronic beggar. After her mother's death the girl went to live with her grandmother, also a beggar and a public charge, who taught the child to beg and steal. Although committed on a charge of larceny, the real reason for her sentence was her need of discipline. She became a self-reliant and capable girl, doing well in the positions in which she was placed. (Case C 17.)

Bad neighborhood and home conditions had always surrounded a young girl whose mother, with whom she lived, was an intemperate and immoral woman, the mother of three children of illegitimate birth by three different men. The home, a boarding house of low character, was a rendezvous for the toughs of the neighborhood. The child was slow in school. She stole money to buy clothes and shoes and was committed to an institution on a charge of larceny. (Case C 80.)

Characteristics.

An analysis of offenses does not give a complete knowledge of the actual delinquencies of the children, for the offenses represent merely the technical charges upon which the commitments were made. For this reason a summary of all known delinquencies, including those embodied in the offenses, was made from the social histories on the case records. Since there are no figures to make possible a comparison in this matter with children born in wedlock, a description of these delinquencies gives merely an idea of the experiences which these children had undergone and of how thoroughly their characters had been undermined. The characteristics described in Table 37 relate to time after commitment as well as before. Half the children were on parole by the end of the year, and half were in the institutions. All but 16 of the 102 children were 14 years of age or over at the end of the period, 48 being 18 years of age or over.

TABLE 37.—*Nature of delinquencies of boys and girls born out of wedlock.*

Nature of delinquencies.	Delinquent children born out of wedlock, under care in 1914.	
	Boys.	Girls.
Total	36	66
Sexual irregularities	3	55
Sexual irregularities alone a	1	25
Sexual irregularities and dishonesties b		10
Sexual irregularities and vagrancy c	2	14
Sexual irregularities and alcoholism		4
Sexual irregularities, dishonesties, and vagrancy		2
All other than sexual irregularities	33	11
Dishonesties	10	5
Dishonesties and vagrancy	11	4
Stubbornness or undefined delinquency d	7	2
Vagrancy and stubbornness	5	

a Sexual irregularities include fornication, common night walking, soliciting or prostitution, keeping a disorderly house, cases of illegitimate pregnancy, and other cases of known immorality.
b Dishonesties include larceny, breaking and entering, burglary, setting fires or arson, and receiving stolen property. If both stubbornness and dishonesty appeared in the same case, the case was included under dishonesties.
c Vagrancy includes being out at night, running away, and being away from home without cause.
d "Stubborness" or "stubborn" covers incorrigibility, waywardness, idle and disorderly disturbing the peace, and undefined delinquency.

An item of significance in the consideration of the interrelation between birth out of wedlock and delinquency appears in the table showing nature of delinquencies. Vagrancy is there shown to be one of the three outstanding traits—sexual irregularities for the girls and dishonesties for both girls and boys being the other two. Half the boys and almost one-third of the girls, or 37 per cent of all, had been vagrants at some time. Vagrancy is usually due to the lack of a normal home, a factor so often connected with birth out of wedlock. This is illustrated by the following case:

The lack of a home and of parental discipline was responsible for the delinquency of a boy committed to a reformative institution at the age of 16 on a charge of vagrancy. His mother was dead, and nothing was known of his father. At the age of 8 he had been placed by his mother under the care of a child-placing agency. After several months in a foster home this society placed him with relatives because he was too hard to manage in a boarding home. His relatives found him so difficult that after a few years they refused to keep him, and he shifted for himself. He was arrested because not working. The agency which had first placed him refused to provide for him further because he needed stronger discipline than they could give. (Case C–62.)

Sexual irregularities are found in the histories of a large proportion of delinquent girls. The histories of five-sixths of the girls born out of wedlock recorded such delinquencies. The proportion would probably have been larger had all the facts been known.

Of the 55 girls who had been sex offenders, 16 had been prostitutes—that is, they had been immoral for money—though 10 of the 16 were not committed on this charge. Nine of the girls had been illegitimately pregnant.

Dishonesty is generally the outstanding delinquency in the case of boys, as immorality is in the case of girls. Nearly three-fifths of the boys had been dishonest, most of them in a serious enough degree to have brought them under discipline other than that of their own homes. A large number of the girls, too—almost one-third—had been dishonest.

Psychological Factors.

If more facts were known of the inner lives of many of these delinquent boys and girls there might be greater evidence of mental conflict occasioned by the realization of the circumstances of their birth or the character of their parents.[7] The histories of several children showed the results of this mental conflict.

A girl who apparently belonged to the white race found in her early 'teens that she was the child of an unmarried colored woman. The knowledge of her colored blood and her illegitimate birth, together with her inability to find her own people, was considered by those caring for her as a contributing cause of her delinquency, which resulted three or four years later in her commitment to an institution.

This child was committed on a charge of stubbornness. The dependency and delinquency record of the girl's family goes back to her maternal grandmother, who received aid from the overseers of the poor and was at one time an inmate of a correctional institution, having been convicted of keeping a disorderly house. The girl's mother became a ward of a child-caring agency, and a few years afterwards became illegitimately pregnant. She placed the baby at board, but after a few years abandoned her. No later trace of the mother was ever found.

The child was placed, by the same agency that had provided for the mother, in a good home where she remained for a number of years. Although a difficult child to manage and having a violent temper, she was fond of her foster parents and they of her. In school her progress was good. She began a commercial course in high school and was eager to become a stenographer. At this juncture, however, she was placed in a new home to work for her board and go to school. Here she was very unhappy and finally ran away, returning to the family with whom she had first lived. She was placed in another family, where she was homesick and lonesome. Three other homes were tried in an effort to place her satisfactorily, but without success. She was described as stubborn, saucy, untruthful, disobedient, and infatuated with boys. It finally became necessary to commit her to a reformative institution.

---

[7] See Healy, William: Mental Conflicts and Misconduct. Little, Brown, and Company, Boston, 1917. Cases showing conflicts concerning parentage, pp. 47, 73, 213–217.

The knowledge of her unfortunate parentage, combined with her removal from a home in which she was happy to one where she was unhappy and lonely, resulted in the moral breakdown of this naturally high-tempered, stubborn girl whose mother and grandmother had also failed to conform to social standards. (Case C 92.)

Analysis of Home and Hereditary Influences.

The very fact that a child is removed from his home and sent to an institution suggests that the home has not been entirely successful. Even though it is true that a judge commits the child because of the offense and not because of the lack of a proper home, yet the offense is usually intimately related to the home conditions. It is therefore of importance to ascertain the kinds of homes from which the children were committed, who had been responsible for the children, the degree to which this responsibility had been shared by agencies, and what were the characteristics of the parents. The histories of children with the handicap of birth out of wedlock show that illegitimate birth, bad home conditions, and delinquency produce and reproduce themselves.

Types of homes.

The homes in which these delinquent children were living before their commitments usually were not temporary but represented attempts at permanent adjustments. For that reason they are particularly worthy of study. From previous figures as to ages it was seen that none of the children was under 8 years of age at commitment, and that three-fourths of them were 14 years or over—64 per cent of the boys and 83 per cent of the girls. The children had all passed their early infancy, when shiftings are likely to occur because of the mother's difficulty in both caring for and supporting a young baby. Years had elapsed during which the mother might have married the father or another man and taken the child into her own home, or during which the child might have been adopted. A child of school age is much less likely to be passed about among various relatives and friends than a younger child. Most of these children, too, had reached an age when, if various other efforts had failed, their care would have been definitely assumed by an agency for a prolonged period. More than three-fourths of the children appeared to be in settled modes of living—either with the mother in her own home, in an adoptive home, in an agency home, or regularly provided for by relatives or friends.

Previous to commitment 29 of the 102 children of illegitimate birth under care were living with their mothers, 70 were separated from them, and in 3 cases presence with or absence from the mother was not reported. Of the 29 children living with their mothers, 25 were in the mothers' own homes; in 4 of these cases the mother had been married to the child's father, in 12 to a man other than the father, and the remaining 9 mothers were maintaining homes separate from their husbands or were living with consorts or with men to whom they had been illegally married.

Of the children who were not living with their mothers, 13 were in homes into which they had been legally adopted; 8 were in foster homes into which they had been received as permanent members of the family; 23 were in agency homes; 15 were cared for by grandparents, other relatives, or friends; 2 were in institutions; 8 were supporting themselves; and in one case the type of home was not reported. A surprisingly large percentage of delinquent children came from adoptive or foster homes as compared with the number of children born out of wedlock under care of the division of State minor wards who came from such homes. Only 7 per cent of children 6 years of age and over under care of the division of State minor wards were in adoptive or foster homes at the time of application or commitment, while 21 per cent of the wards of correctional institutions came from homes of this type. This comparatively large amount of delinquency which comes from adoptive homes occurs in a State where the board of charity pursues the policy of giving very few of its charges for adoption, where it permits no adoption of a ward unless the home has been tried for a year, and where public opinion generally has been educated in advanced theories upon the subject. Yet in this State one out of every eight of the children born out of wedlock who were wards of correctional institutions came from homes into which they had been legally adopted. Local investigations have shown that not all adoptions are accompanied by the careful investigation and safeguarding of the children which obtains in the work of the State board of charity. This amount of delinquency coming from adoptive homes indicates the need of great care in the placement of children for adoption. The following cases of children born out of wedlock who had been brought up in adoptive or foster homes illustrate the difficulties sometimes present:

A child was taken when she was 2 years old from a hospital in a near-by State and brought up by foster parents, though never legally adopted. The home was an excellent one, but the child proved to be a great trial and disappointment. She was backward in school and a truant and she began to lie and steal at the age of 7. At the age of 13 she was sent to a private institution for difficult girls, where she remained for over a year but did not improve. She was then sent to relatives of her foster parents, but she proved to be uncontrollable and was finally committed to a State institution as a stubborn child. She had been under the care of this institution for some time when the study was made. While on parole she had worked in factories but was discharged from several for misconduct. When 18 years old she gave birth to a child out of wedlock. The mother and baby were kept together for a time but finally had to be separated. The mother was unfit physically and mentally to care for the child, and the baby became ill because of the mother's neglect. (Case C 102.)

A boy and a girl born out of wedlock—twin children of a mother who was ill and unable to care for them—were taken by a child-caring agency when a month old, and a little later both were adopted by the same family. The home was a most unfortunate one. The foster mother neglected the children, and the foster father made improper advances to the girl. When the children were 12 years of age, the home was broken up through the misconduct and desertion of the foster father, and the boy was committed to the care of a public agency. A month later his sister was committed to a State institution on a sex charge, having been very immoral. The boy did fairly well, but the girl was nervous, high-strung, and very untruthful. She was immoral while on parole. An examination of mentality was made, and she was pronounced a defective delinquent. (Case C 41.)

A very young boy was committed to an institution on a charge of breaking and entering and larceny. He had been a member of a gang, and he admitted breaking into 15 places. He had been taken when an infant from a midwife by his foster parents, but he had never been legally adopted. The foster parents knew nothing of the mother's history, except that the child had been born out of wedlock. The home was undesirable, and the child had little care. The lack of discipline was undoubtedly largely responsible for his delinquency. While under the care of the institution he made poor progress in school, and his teachers believed him to be defective. (Case C 23.)

A girl born out of wedlock, whose parents were intemperate and immoral and whose home life was most degrading, was adopted when 5 years of age. The adoptive home was not a fortunate one. The family disliked the child and gave her no affection but subjected her to constant criticism. The child was neurotic and unstable and became stubborn, shy, and untruthful. She was finally committed to an institution on a charge of stubbornness. (Case C 60.)

Character of homes.

The descriptions given on the records of the homes where the children lived at commitment (see Table 38) pictured 46 where conditions detrimental to a child's morals existed. Information as to the character of the home was lacking in some cases.

Eleven children were living with immoral mothers, 6 not living with their mothers were in homes where immorality existed, 13 were living in homes of low standards, 11 children were without adequate supervision, and 5 were in homes in which other detrimental conditions existed. Twenty-six of the 29 children who were living with their mothers were living under unfavorable conditions. Five of the adoptive or foster homes, and both the grandparents' homes, were unfavorable. All but one of the agency homes were good, so far as known.

TABLE 38.—*Types and character of homes in which delinquent children born out of wedlock lived before commitment.*

Type of home in which child lived before commitment.	Delinquent children born out of wedlock, under care in 1914.					
	Total.	Character of home.				
		Good, so far as known.	Immorality in household.	Low moral standards.	Lack of supervision.	Otherwise poor.
Total..................................	102	55	17	13	11	6
With mother in own home................	25	2	9	8	5	1
With mother in home of other type.......	4	1	2	a 1	....	....
Grandparents' home.....................	2	....	....	1	1	....
Home of relatives or friends.............	13	9	1	1	1	1
Adoptive or foster home.................	21	b 16	....	1	c 3	1
Home secured by agency or institution (not relatives).........................	23	22	....	....	....	1
Self-supporting home....................	8	1	5	....	....	2
Institution.......'.....................	2	2	....	....	....	....
Not reported...........................	4	2	....	1	d 1	....

a With mother in maternal grandparents' home.
b Seven not legally adopted, though taken permanently by foster parents.
c One not legally adopted.
d Away from mother.

The bringing up of a child of illegitimate birth in the home of the mother and stepfather, along with the half brothers and half sisters, does not always result favorably for the child. Although other factors contributed to the delinquency of the child here described, the scornful attitude and disagreeable treatment of her half brothers and half sisters undoubtedly seriously influenced her conduct.

This girl was committed to a correctional institution at an early age because of sex offenses. She was described as a chronic truant, a runaway, alcoholic, and immoral from the age of 13. At the time of commitment she was leading a life of prostitution, though living in her mother's home.

Her mother felt keenly the disgrace of having a child of illegitimate birth. She was over 40 when the child was born and had a number of children born in wedlock. The home was poor, and the presence of lodgers of questionable character was an unfavorable influence. All the children of legitimate birth, however, were doing well and had exhibited no tendencies toward wrongdoing. Criminal treatment by her own father, who paid irregularly for her support, seems to have been the beginning of her misconduct. (Case C 69.)

A little colored boy born out of wedlock, whose mother had died when he was a baby and who had been brought up by his paternal grandparents, was committed as a stubborn child. His father had never admitted his paternity, though the grandparents were satisfied of it. The grandparents were away all day and the child was left in a cheerless home without companiship or control. (Case C 74.)

The effect of unfavorable home conditions and of unfortunate experiences in early youth is illustrated in the case of a girl committed to a correctional institution in her late 'teens for a sex offense. She had supported a man—sentenced to a penal institution at the same time she was committed—by her earnings as a prostitute. She was of normal mentality and had reached the sixth grade at the age of 12 years. A physical defect seriously marred her appearance. She was alcoholic and had been immoral from an early age.

The mother of the girl was described as "tragically feeble-minded." She had lived with the girl's father for several years when she discovered that their marriage was illegal because he had another wife living. She then left him and soon married a widower with several children. The home thus provided for the mother and her child proved to be most unfavorable. The stepfather was reported to have conducted himself improperly toward the child. At the age of 11 she was forced to improper relations by her stepbrother, who married her under pressure a month before their child was born. The child-mother was but little past her twelfth birthday at the baby's birth. The infant was adopted by the grandparents, and the girl and her husband established a home of their own. The child's efforts at housekeeping were naturally unsuccessful, and she returned to her mother's home.

Her history for the next few years is fragmentary. At the time of commitment she was living in a disorderly house. The lack of chance for normal development in her home, her unhappy early history, and her forced marriage resulted in the delinquent career of this girl who, in spite of the feeble-mindedness of her mother, seemed to have good natural endowments. (Case C 61.

A young boy of illegitimate birth, committed to an institution for juvenile delinquents, was found to have been living on receipts from stolen goods and sleeping in doorways and cellars. His mother—herself born out of wedlock—and his older sister were trying to maintain a home, but the neighborhood was poor, both were employed during the day, and it was impossible to give the boy any attention. The mother, who had never married, had struggled hard to provide for her two children and had succeeded in keeping them with her for a number of years. The alleged father was dead. The lack of home supervision and discipline was disastrous for the boy. (Case C 9.)

Previous agency care.

Almost half the children—50 out of 102—were being supervised by some agency at the time of their commitment. This supervision was being given for 19 children by public child-caring agencies, for 7 by private child-caring agencies, and for 9 by child-protective agencies; 11 were on probation, 3 were under other prolonged care of the courts, and 1 was under supervision of another industrial school. Some of these children had been placed out by the State or by private societies during most of their childhood.

A very large proportion of the children, 70 out of 102, had been under the care of agencies, institutions, or courts at some time previous to commitment. Four of these children had previously been in correctional institutions, 12 had been on probation, and 6 had been given other care by the courts. A total of 56 children had been given prolonged care by other agencies (9 of these also having been before the courts). It is evident that in the majority of cases other methods had been tried before the last measure was resorted to—the reformative institution.

A girl committed to a reformatory at the age of 17 as a stubborn child was one of a family of 13 children born out of wedlock, and had spent the greater part of her childhood in institutions. Her mother and father lived together for a number of years but were never married. The father was intemperate and had a long court record. He deserted the mother several years before the girl's commitment. The mother had been in a correctional institution for intemperance and had lived with a second man to whom she was not married. Little is known of the other children. Some of them died in infancy or early childhood. One is known to have been immoral and to have been an inmate of a reformatory.

At the age of 5 years the girl described was placed in an orphanage and spent the next seven years in this and another institution. She then lived for a time with her parents and was put to work in a factory. After this she kept house for a man with whom she had immoral relations. At the time the study was made she had been for several years under care of the correctional institution to which she was committed. While on parole she failed to do well. (Case C 39.)

A 15-year-old colored girl of illegitimate birth, committed on a charge of larceny, had been living with her two sisters and her aunt. Her mother was dead. The girl had been under the care of agencies for three years previous to commitment,—one child-caring and two family-care agencies had been working on the case. The girl had been put on probation; but she became more delinquent, and it was necessary to send her to an institution. She had stolen from her aunt and from employers and neighbors. The year before this study she was hopelessly paralyzed by a disease of the spine. One of her sisters was later committed to an institution for the feeble-minded. (Case C 2.)

Parental characteristics.

The information concerning the mothers, fathers, and grandparents of the children, though meager, is suggestive. (See Table 39.) Almost two-thirds of the mothers had characteristics sufficiently detrimental to be reported. Fifty of the mothers were known to be sexually delinquent, of whom 8 were prostitutes and 34 had other children of illegitimate birth, 10 of these having four or more other children born out of wedlock. One mother had four other children by four different fathers; each of two mothers who had lived as married with the fathers of their children for long periods had 13 children of illegitimate birth. Twenty-three of the mothers with poor characteristics had the children included in the study living with them previous to commitment.

TABLE 39.—*Character of mothers of delinquent children born out of wedlock.*

Child present with or separated from mother immediately prior to commitment.	Delinquent children born out of wedlock, under care in 1914.					
	Total.	Character of mother.				
		Good, so far as known.	Sexual irregularities.	Alcoholic.	Otherwise poor.	Not reported.
Total............................	102	19	a 50	6	9	18
With mother........................	29	6	17	3	3	....
Separated from mother.................	70	13	32	2	b 6	17
Not reported......................	3	....	1	1	....	1

a Includes 15 who were also alcoholic, 1 of whom was otherwise delinquent as well.
b Represents 5 mothers, as twin sisters were under care.

The 36 mothers who were known to have had more than one child out of wedlock [8] had a total of 141 such children, of whom 74 were dependent, neglected, delinquent, or defective charges of society: Thirty-seven were delinquents included in this study; 8 others were delinquent; 25 were neglected or dependent, 3 of whom were feeble-minded; 4 others were defective.

Full information was not available regarding the mentality and physical condition of many of the mothers. It was known, however, that 13 were reported to be not normal, of whom 3 were diagnosed feeble-minded, 2 were insane, and 8 were probably subnormal or feeble-minded. One mother was epileptic and 8 others were in poor physical condition.

Information regarding fathers of children born out of wedlock is usually lacking, and it is surprising that records of these children, who were received after infancy, contained such facts for half the cases (52). About one-third of the children were known to have fathers who were immoral, alcoholic, or otherwise delinquent. Twenty-six of these men were known either to have been fathers of other children born out of wedlock or to have been otherwise immoral. Several had records of desertion or nonsupport.

Since nothing at all was known of 50 fathers no generalizations can be made concerning the amounts contributed by the fathers toward the support of their children. There were, however, 31 who contributed something, 18 because living as married with or illegally married to the mother, 8 because they married the mother subsequent to the child's birth, and 5 through money payments.

In addition to the evidence in regard to the characteristics of the parents, the maternal grandparents of 16 children were known to have been alcoholic, immoral, otherwise delinquent, or of poor character.

---

[8] Two of these mothers had twin children out of wedlock but no other illegitimate pregnancies, and so were not included in the statement on p. 357.

To sum up the characteristics of the families of these delinquent children of illegitimate birth, the mothers, fathers, or maternal grandparents of 66 of the 102 were alcoholic or immoral, and of 7 others were of otherwise poor character or of abnormal mentality. In only 29 cases was nothing detrimental reported concerning parents or grandparents, and in many of these cases little or nothing was known of the family history. In 17 of the 66 cases in which alcoholism or immorality was reported, the record also stated that one or both parents or maternal grandparents were otherwise delinquent or mentally below normal.

To what extent dependency was present in the homes of these children was difficult to discover. It is known, however, that 21 of the children had mothers who themselves had formerly been wards of agencies; that 34 of the mothers had other children who were, or had been, public responsibilities either as dependent, neglected, delinquent, feeble-minded, or insane; and that the grandparents of 5 children were known to have been dependent upon charitable relief. Thirteen of the children had another member of the immediate relationship under the care of a Massachusetts agency during 1914; in 5 of these cases the children themselves had babies born out of wedlock who were under care during the year. Thus, a considerable number of the children came from families who had contributed largely to the amount of dependency, delinquency, or defect in the community.

A striking illustration of the various factors operating detrimentally in the life of a child born out of wedlock is presented in the following case:

Twin sisters, after 17 years of complete separation, were committed within six weeks of each other to the same correctional institution. The first sister had been duly classified and assigned to work at the institution when one day the receiving matron was called upon to accept a new prisoner. In distress at the apparent escape of one of the inmates, the matron exclaimed to the new prisoner: "How did you get out, and where did you come from?" The matron was not more surprised at the situation than was each of the girls to find her double in the institution.

Both girls were committed for the same offense, vagrancy; both had been sexually delinquent; both were classified as segregable types, though of good native ability; both were epileptic; both had gonorrhea. This was the first commitment for each of them. In both girls, whose early experience had been much the same, but who had later been subjected to somewhat different environmental conditions, the same traits had developed in a strikingly similar manner.

Their mother, the child of an intemperate and pauper family, had been an irresponsible almshouse inmate. She remained in the almshouse with the twin babies for two years after their birth; they were then placed in a private institution and the mother went to an institution in another State. Shortly afterwards the babies were adopted by different families and remained separated until they came together in the reformatory. Both adoptive homes were supposedly good.

After some years the foster parents of one of the girls were forced to place her in an institution because they were unable to care for her. She spent more than six years in this and another institution. Her educational advantages were poor, and she never went beyond the fourth grade in school. A month before commitment she ran away from the institution in which she was living, was immoral with several men in parks and lodging houses, and was finally arrested for vagrancy.

The other sister remained with her adoptive parents until shortly before commitment. Her foster mother was described as an excellent woman, but she failed to make the girl contented. Troublesome, untruthful, and wayward, the girl gave much difficulty in school and at home, though on leaving school at 14 she had attained the ninth grade. After this she worked in a laundry and did kitchen work in an institution, but she was unsatisfactory in both places. She finally ran away from home, and after some immoral experiences was arrested while asking for breakfast at a back door.

The characteristics of both girls seemed to be definitely related to their unfortunate heritage, combined, in one case, with adverse environmental conditions. (Cases C 94, 95.)

Summary.

From this study of wards of correctional institutions, and also from other parts of the inquiry, it is evident that large numbers of children of illegitimate birth are born to and surrounded by conditions which subject them to peculiar moral hazards. Many become delinquent and are placed under reformative influences. These children come earlier to correctional institutions than do children of legitimate birth, and they remain longer. Previous to their commitments they have had a great amount of agency or court care.

Of the children born out of wedlock who were under the care of correctional institutions not only were more than one-fifth below par mentally and one-fourth below par physically at their commitment, but record after record told the story of one or more hereditary or environmental characteristics contributing to their delinquency. Almost half the homes in which the children were living at the time of their commitment were known to be bad. Almost two-thirds of the mothers were known to be alcoholic, immoral, dishonest, or of otherwise poor character, and a considerable proportion of these were mothers who had their children with them at the time of commitment. More than two-thirds of the children had had some previous agency or court care before commitment. Many of the families had records of dependency extending over two or three generations; in several cases other members of the family were under the care of a Massachusetts agency during the year. Children placed out in adoptive homes or with relatives seem not always to have escaped unfavorable environments.

The facts revealed in this study show the extraordinary difficulties which children of illegitimate birth often have to combat, while added to the hereditary and environmental disadvantages are the mental sufferings and abnormal attitude toward life which the knowledge of birth out of wedlock often entails.

INFANTS CARED FOR WITH THEIR MOTHERS.

Number under Care.

Besides the 102 children born out of wedlock committed as delinquents to State institutions and under care during the year, there were 80 young children of illegitimate birth cared for with their mothers. These children were received with their mothers or born while the mothers were under care. The law provides that "if the mother of a child under the age of 18 months is imprisoned in a jail, house of correction, workhouse, or other place of confinement and is capable and desirous of taking care of it, the keeper shall, upon the order of the court or magistrate committing her, or of any overseer of the poor, receive the child and place it under the care and custody of its mother." [9] Of the 80 children under care, 26 were committed with their mothers; 35 were born while their mothers were under care, the mothers having been pregnant when committed; and 19 were born to mothers who had been on parole and who were still under care.

Pregnant women are usually sent to the State infirmary for confinement, and remain as long as special medical services are needed, in most cases for a month or two, though in some instances for a longer time. After this stay, mothers under care of the institution for older girls and women are usually returned to the institution with their babies, though if the mother has been on parole she may be placed again in a private family under supervision. A nursery for babies is maintained by this institution and medical care is given. Mothers and babies under care of the training school for girls are provided for through the parole department. Occasionally children are separated from their mothers, though in most cases the child and mother are kept together.

A law passed in 1918 provides as follows: [10]

Whenever, in the opinion of the physician of any prison or other place of confinement in which is imprisoned a woman who is about to give birth to a child during the term of her imprisonment, the best interests of the woman or of her unborn child require that she be paroled or discharged, he may so certify to the board or officer empowered to grant paroles or discharges from the institution in which she is imprisoned, and such board or officer may, subject to such terms and conditions as appear necessary, grant the parole or discharge.

Seventeen of the 80 infants under care were included in the chapter on children under care of social agencies, since the residence

---

[9] R. L. 1902 ch. 225 sec. 78.
[10] Acts 1918 ch. 79.

of the mother was Boston. Four others were included in that section because they were cared for by Boston agencies during the year. Three children were under the care of the division of State minor wards, one of whom was also included in the Boston study. The birthplaces of the children were: State infirmary, 42; Boston, 9; metropolitan district outside Boston, 5; other parts of the State, 20; other States, 2; not reported, 2. Five children were colored and 75 white. There were 36 boys, 43 girls, and 1 not reported as to sex. Twelve children were under 3 months of age when received; 11 were 3 months but less than 1 year of age; 2 were 1 year old; the age of 1 was not reported; 54 were born while their mothers were under care. Of the 26 committed with their mothers, 21 had been living with them previous to commitment, 4 had been separated from them, and in 1 case it was not reported whether or not the child had been living with the mother.

Care Given the Children by the Institutions and the Parole Department Studied.

Of the 80 children cared for during the year, 54 had been under care from birth. All but 13 of these 54 children had been born at the State infirmary.[11] Most of the mothers and children were kept at the infirmary from one to two months after the child's birth. In 3 of the 41 cases in which the child was born at that institution during a commitment current in the year studied, the infirmary gave care for less than one month; in 24 cases for one or two months; and in 6 cases for three months or more. The time at the infirmary was not reported for 8 children.

Eight children—one-tenth of the total under care—died during the year; 8 others were discharged from care, none of whom was released without his mother. Six of the 8 children who died were under 6 months of age; 2 were more than one year and a half but less than 2 years old. Of the 8 discharged from care, 3 were under 6 months of age, 4 were from 6 to 11 months old, and 1 was 3 years of age.

Twenty-two of the 64 children remaining under care at the end of the year were 1 but less than 2 years of age, 8 children were 2 years of age and over, 33 were less than 1 year of age, and the age of 1 was not reported. The mothers of 8 of the 22 children 1 year of age at the end of the year were still under the care of the institutions, and the mothers of 14 were on parole. The mothers of all but 2 of the 8 children 2 years of age and over were on parole.

---

[11] A total of 42 children had been born at the infirmary, but 1 of them was 1 year of age at the time of the present commitment, having been born while the mother was under care on a previous commitment.

At the end of the year or the close of care 53 of the 80 children had been under care for less than one year, 21 for one year but less than two, and 6 for two years or more. The average number of months under care for all the children included was 11.

Under care of the institutions at the end of the year or previous to death or discharge were 42 of the 80 children, while 38 were under the supervision of the parole departments.[12] Of the former, 37 were with their mothers at one of the institutions, 4 were with their mothers at the State infirmary, and 1 was at the infirmary, though the mother had been returned to the institution to which she had been committed. Of the 38 under the care of parole departments, 28 were living with their mothers, 9 had been separated from them, and in 1 case it was not reported whether or not the child was with the mother. Eleven of the 28 with their mothers were living in their mothers' places of employment, 3 in their mothers' own home, 10 in the homes of grandparents or other relatives, 1 in a boarding home, 2 in a hospital or public infirmary, and the location of 1 was not reported. Of the 9 children separated from their mothers, 5 were boarding, 1 was living with relatives, and 3 were in a hospital or infirmary.

Almost one-fourth of the children—19 of the 80 under care— were known to be in poor physical condition. Three had syphilis, 2 were hydrocephalic, 1 had tuberculosis, 11 were in otherwise poor condition, and no reports as to the physical condition of 2 children were secured. The proportion in poor physical condition was some-what low, in view of the fact that three-eighths of the mothers of these children were in poor physical condition and that more than one-fourth had syphilis or gonorrhea.

THE HERITAGE OF CHILDREN OF ILLEGITIMATE BIRTH WHOSE MOTHERS WERE UNDER CARE OF CORRECTIONAL INSTITUTIONS.

In studying the heritage of children whose mothers were wards of correctional institutions it is of greater significance to consider the whole group of women under care who had been illegitimately preg-nant than to limit the analysis to the mothers of the 80 children cared for during the year. In 1914 the total number of women under the care of the institutions and of the parole department studied was 1,267. Among these were 220—17 per cent—who at some time had been illegitimately pregnant. The girls under the care of one of the insti-tutions and of the parole department were all under 21 years of age.

---

[12]Although records of all under care were secured from only one of the parole de-partments, information was obtained for the mothers on parole from the institution for older women if they had been under care of the institution at some time during the year studied. Of the 42 children under care of the institutions, all but 2 were under care of the institution for older women ; these 2 were at the State infirmary, the mothers not having been paroled previous to the birth of the children.

The percentage illegitimately pregnant among the inmates of the institution for older girls and women was 31.

The offenses for which these girls and women were committed were as follows:

```
       Total who had been illegitimately pregnant_____ 220
Committed for offenses against the person_____       8
    Abandoning infant_____ 5
    Attempt to murder_____ 1
    Murder _____ 1
    Robbery_____ 1
Committed for offenses against property_____      27
    Larceny _____ 27
Committed for offenses against public order_____     183
    Sex offenses:
        Abortion _____ 1
        Adultery _____ 9
        Common nightwalker_____ 17
        Fornication _____ 10
        Keeping disorderly house_____ 2
        Lewdness _____ 60
        Polygamy _____ 1
    Other offenses:
        Concealing death _____ 1
        Drunkenness _____ 15
        Idle and disorderly_____ 16
        Forgery_____ 1
        Neglect of child_____ 2
        Stubbornness or undefined delinquency_____ 37
        Vagrancy _____ 8
        Violating drug laws_____ 3
Not reported_____       2
```

Four per cent of these women had been committed for offenses against the person, 12 per cent for offenses against property, 45 per cent on sex charges, and 38 per cent for other offenses against public order; in 1 per cent of the cases the offense was not reported. The distribution of offenses for which all women received during the year were committed was very similar to the above distribution for women under care during the year who had been illegitimately pregnant.[13]

Nine per cent of the mothers were colored. Native-born mothers comprised 75 per cent of the total, foreign-born mothers 22 per cent, and the nativity of 3 per cent was not reported. These percentages

---

[13] Two per cent against the person, 11 per cent against property, 48 per cent on sex charges, and 39 per cent for other offenses against public order. See Fourteenth Annual Report of the Board of Prison Commissioners of Massachusetts for the Year 1914 (p. 53) and Fourth Annual Report of the Trustees of the Massachusetts Training Schools for the Year Ending Nov. 30, 1914 (p. 102).

correspond closely to those among all women admitted during the year.[14]

One of the institutions studied receives only girls under 17 years of age. During the year studied 59 girls who had been illegitimately pregnant were in this institution or under care of the parole department. Of the 161 mothers under care of the other institution, 42 were under 21 years of age when committed, 117 were over this age, and the ages of 2 were not reported. Hence, of the 220 mothers under care of the two institutions and the parole department, 101—46 per cent—were under 21 when committed. About the same percentage—48 per cent—of all women committed during 1914 were under 21 years of age.[15] However, 98 of the 220 mothers had been under the care of correctional institutions on previous commitments. At the time of the first court commitment to a correctional institution 58 per cent of the mothers were less than 21 years old.

Almost two-thirds of the mothers—64 per cent—were single at the time of commitment, 11 per cent were married, 5 per cent were widowed, and 20 per cent were deserted or separated. Almost one-tenth of all the mothers had been illegally married or living as married.

At the end of the year studied, or, if discharged during the year, at the close of care, 83 of the 220 mothers had been under care less than 1 year; 67, 1 year; 39, 2 to 3 years; 29, 4 years and over; and the time under care was not reported in 2 cases.

The institutions whose records were studied were equipped to give physical and mental examinations; one of the institutions had done special work along the line of scientific research in regard to mentality. Seventy-three of the 220 mothers were found to have venereal infection, and 11 others were suspected of being in this condition though diagnoses had not been completed. Twenty-one had other physical disabilities, making a total of 105 who were in poor physical condition. In 111 cases the physical condition was reported good, and in 4 cases no report was obtained. The data as to physical condition relate to the year of the study. Many of the women had been under care long enough to improve as a consequence of the medical care provided. As was to be expected, the mothers under care of the institution for older women were in worse physical condition than the girls under care of the institution taking younger girls, or on parole therefrom. Of the former, more than half were in poor condition, and nearly two-fifths had syphilis or gonorrhea.

[14] Native born, 72 per cent; foreign born, 27 per cent; not reported, 1 per cent. Derived from Fourteenth Annual Report of the Board of Prison Commissioners of Massachusetts for the Year 1914 (p. 54) and Fourth Annual Report of the Trustees of the Massachusetts Training Schools for the Year Ending Nov. 30, 1914 (p. 103).

[15] See Fourteenth Annual Report of the Board of Prison Commissioners of Massachusetts for the Year 1914 (p. 53) and Fourth Annual Report of the Trustees of the Massachusetts Training Schools for the Year Ending Nov. 30, 1914 (p. 103).

Of the latter, slightly more than one-fourth were in poor condition, one-fifth having venereal infection.

Less than three-fifths of the 220 mothers under care—58 per cent—were reported of normal mentality. Feeble-minded mothers comprised 12 per cent of the total; and mothers who were subnormal mentally, or were reported probably subnormal or feeble-minded but not diagnosed, 29 per cent. In 1 per cent of the cases no report as to mentality was secured. At the institution caring for older women special studies have been made of mentality and grades of efficiency. The results of examinations of 500 inmates, taken in consecutive order, were published in 1915.[16] The resident physician also graded the mothers included in this investigation according to the standards used in the study cited. A comparison of the mentality of the two groups—the first an unselected group and the second a group of women who had been illegitimately pregnant—is given in Table 40.

TABLE 40.—*Comparison of the mental condition of an unselected group of 500 reformatory inmates and of inmates of the same institution who had been illegitimately pregnant and who were under care in 1914.*

Mental condition.	Unselected group of reformatory inmates whose mental condition was diagnosed.a		Women under care o, the same institutionf who had been illegitimately pregnant.	
	Number.	Per cent distribution.	Number.	Per cent distribution.
Total	500	100.0	161	100.0
Imbecile	6	1.2	1	0.6
Moron	74	14.8	b 24	14.9
Subnormal	145	29.0	51	31.7
Dull	102	20.4	19	11.8
Fair	68	13.6	25	15.5
Good	105	21.0	39	24.2
Not reported			2	1.3

a Fifteenth Annual Report of the Board of Prison Commissioners of Massachusetts for the Year 1915. Boston, 1916 (p. 52).
b Includes 19 who were feeble-minded and 5 high-grade mental defectives not classified in this report as feeble-minded.

The distribution of the two groups according to mental condition appears to be very similar, except that a smaller percentage of the mothers were classified as " dull," and slightly higher percentages as " subnormal," and as " fair," and " good."

The reformatory women were also classified by the physician of the institution according to grades of efficiency. Forty-two per cent of the women who had been illegitimately pregnant were classified as " normal," 31 per cent as " subnormal," and 26 per cent as " seg-

[16] Fifteenth Annual Report of the Board of Prison Commissioners of Massachusetts for the Year 1915. Boston, 1916 (p. 52).

regable " types. In 1 per cent of these cases no report on this item was obtained. The findings are practically identical with those for the unselected group of inmates of the same institution.[17]

Of the 220 women who had been illegitimately pregnant, 98—45 per cent—had had previous court records. The percentage was considerably higher for the mothers 21 years of age and over at commitment, 73 of the 117 in this age group—62 per cent—having had previous court records. Some of these mothers had long histories of arrests and commitments.

Sixty-five per cent of the mothers were under 21 years of age at the first illegitimate pregnancy. The age at first illegitimate pregnancy was as follows:

Total mothers			220
Under 18 years	65	25 years and over	32
18–20 years	78	Not reported	8
21–24 years	37		

In 151 of the 220 cases the mother had been illegitimately pregnant once; in 39 cases, twice; in 18 cases, 3 times; in 4 cases, 4 times; in 5 cases, 5 times; in 1 case, 6 times; in 2 cases, 7 times. The total number of illegitimate pregnancies these mothers had had was 344. In 21 instances the mother was pregnant at the close of the year studied. Of the 323 pregnancies terminated before the close of the study 269 resulted in live births and 54 in still births. The percentage of stillbirths was 17.

It was not possible to obtain full information about the children of these mothers. It was known that 187 of the 269 children born alive were living in 1914. Of these 187 children, 127—68 per cent— were known to be under the care of social agencies or institutions during the year studied. Eighty children—43 per cent of those living—were, with their mothers, under the care of the institutions for delinquents and the parole department studied. In 6 of these cases 2 children of the same mother were under care, hence the number of mothers who had children of illegitimate birth also under care was 77.

These 220 mothers represent the most delinquent types of mothers of children out of wedlock. The offenses for which they were committed and their mental condition and grades of efficiency correspond very closely to the findings for unselected groups of reformatory inmates.

---

[17] Unpublished figures for 738 reformatory women. Of these 42 per cent were " normal," 31 per cent " subnormal," and 27 per cent " segregable."

CHAPTER 5. MENTAL DEFECT AND ILLEGITIMACY.

The interrelation between feeble-mindedness and illegitimacy is one of the most serious of problems, both because of its concern to society and because of its individual and racial significance. Manifestly it would be impossible to secure adequate data concerning the proportion of feeble-minded among all persons born out of wedlock. The determination of the prevalence of illegitimate parenthood among persons of defective mentality would be extremely difficult, though estimates and dogmatic assertions are by no means uncommon. Previous chapters of this report have included figures as to the number of mental defectives among the dependent and delinquent children included in the various parts of the inquiry. Because of the absence of mental diagnoses in the majority of cases, these figures have been understatements.

This chapter deals with the feeble-minded children born out of wedlock who were inmates of the two Massachusetts institutions for the feeble-minded or who were awaiting admission. It also includes a discussion of inmates of these institutions or persons on the waiting lists who were mothers of children born out of wedlock. No claim is made that the figures here given are representative of any group other than that forming the basis of the study—those mental defectives who had been so burdensome or so troublesome to society or whose home conditions had been so poor that institutional care was urgently required. Especially under the crowded conditions existing, this qualification applies both to those in the institutions and on the waiting lists.

CHILDREN BORN OUT OF WEDLOCK WHO WERE UNDER THE CARE OF STATE INSTITUTIONS FOR THE FEEBLE-MINDED OR AWAITING ADMISSION THERETO.

Proportion to total number under care or awaiting admission.

During the year studied a total of 2,553 persons [1] were cared for at the two State institutions for the feeble-minded. Of this number, 100—3.9 per cent—were known to have been of illegitimate birth. The percentage was higher for the newer institution at Wrentham

---

[1] Total for the Massachusetts School for the Feeble-Minded at Waltham given in the Sixty-seventh Annual Report of the Trustees of the Massachusetts School for the Feeble-Minded at Waltham for the Year Ending November 30, 1914. Boston, 1915. P. 15. Figures for the Wrentham State School compiled in the course of this investigation for the calendar year 1914.

than for the older one at Waltham—8.2 per cent for the former and 2.3 per cent for the latter.[2] Of the 100 inmates born out of wedlock cared for at the two institutions 73 were under 21 years of age.

The inadequacy of institutional provision for the mentally defective results in large waiting lists for admission to the institutions. In 1914 there were 467 applications for admission to the Wrentham State School for persons who could not be received during the year. Sixty-two of these applications—13.3 per cent—were for persons born out of wedlock, all but 4 of whom were under 21 years of age. The waiting list of the Massachusetts School for the Feeble-Minded at Waltham was almost as large as that of the Wrentham School,[3] but only 12 of those whose admission was sought were known to have been born out of wedlock; applications for two of these were also on file at Wrentham. The difference in numbers is partly accounted for by the fact that almost half those on the Wrentham waiting list were State wards.

The total number of persons known to have been born out of wedlock whose applications were on file at one or both institutions during the year studied was 72, of whom 67 were under the age of 21 years.

The analysis of the social information concerning the inmates of the two schools and those awaiting admission was limited to children under 21 years of age. Although the facts here given are not representative for all feeble-minded children born out of wedlock, they are of interest as showing the nature of the problem the State must meet in providing care for the most helpless of the large group of children compelled by their mental condition and the circumstances of their birth to depend upon the public for support and protection. Information gathered by those interested in securing increased provision for the feeble-minded indicates clearly that many outside the institutions are in as great need of protection as are those whose admission has already been obtained.[4]

The child at time of admission or at application.

There were 73 children of illegitimate birth under 21 years of age, of whom 64 were white and 9 were colored, receiving care in the two institutions during the year. Of the white children 38 were boys and 26 girls. There were only 2 boys among the colored children. Sixty-

---

[2] Total population of the Massachusetts School for the Feeble-Minded in 1914, 1,845; known to have been born out of wedlock, 42. Total population of the Wrentham State School in 1914, 708; known to have been born out of wedlock, 58.

[3] In 1916 there were about 400 applications for admission on file at the Massachusetts School for the Feeble-minded at Waltham, also known as Waverley, and 456 at the Wrentham institution. See Feeble-Minded Adrift, published by the League for Preventive Work, Boston, 1916.

[4] See publications of League for Preventive Work, Boston.

seven children born out of wedlock, of whom 59 were white and 8 were colored, were awaiting admission to the institutions. The numerical relation of the sexes among these children was the reverse of that found among the institution inmates, there being 24 boys among the white children and 35 girls. Only 2 colored boys who had been born out of wedlock were on the waiting lists.

At the time of admission to an institution 14 of the children were under 8 years of age; the waiting lists contained the names of 26 children under 8. Exactly half the children in the institutions were under 12 years of age when admitted; 58 per cent of those on the waiting lists were less than 12 years old when application was made. Table 41 gives the age distribution.

TABLE 41.—*Age on admission or at application of feeble-minded boys and girls born out of wedlock, who were under care or awaiting admission.*

Age on admission or at application.	Children born out of wedlock, under care in 1914.			Children born out of wedlock, awaiting admission in 1914.		
	Total.	Boys.	Girls.	Total.	Boys.	Girls.
Total	73	40	33	67	26	41
Under 8 years	14	8	6	26	15	11
8–9 years	14	11	3	6	5	1
10–11 years	9	4	5	7	3	4
12–13 years	7	4	3	13	3	10
14–15 years	12	3	9	6		6
16–17 years	10	7	3	4		4
18–20 years	7	3	4	5		5

Of the 132 children in the institutions or awaiting admission whose nativity was reported, Boston was the place of birth of 42, or almost one-third, while 73, or more than half, were born in other parts of the State, 5 of them in State institutions. Of the remaining 17, 5 were born in other New England States, 2 in other parts of the United States, 4 in Canada, and 6 in other foreign countries.

Twenty of the children in the institutions and 18 of those on the waiting lists were residents of Boston, while 53 of the former and 49 of the latter were from other parts of the State. Thus, over one-fourth of all these feeble-minded children born out of wedlock came from the metropolis and less than three-fourths from the rest of the State. This is about the proportion that might have been expected, the population of Boston being approximately one-fifth of the entire population of the State.

Seventeen of the 73 children in the institution were included in the study of the problem in Boston,[5] 12 in the study of children under care of the division of State minor wards,[6] and 5 in both studies.

[5] See Sec. I ch. 2.
[6] See Sec. II ch. 2.

Three of the 67 awaiting admission were under the care of Boston agencies during the year, 34 under the care of the division of State minor wards, and 10 were included in both studies.

Of great significance is the fact that only 1 of the 73 children born out of wedlock who had been admitted to the institutions and 1 of the 67 awaiting admission were known to have been with their mothers immediately previous to admission or at the time application was made. Fifty-three of the children in the institutions and 59 of those awaiting admission had been separated from their mothers previous to admission or application. In the cases of 19 in institutions and 7 awaiting admission it was not reported whether or not the children had been with their mothers.

Three of the 73 children in the institutions had been living with relatives previous to admission, 1 had been cared for in a foster home, 30 had been living in boarding or free homes, and 13 had been in institutions—7 of them in public infirmaries. The home or place of residence of 26 was not reported. Of the 67 children awaiting admission, 47 were living in boarding or free homes at the time of application; one child was in the mother's own home, 1 in a foster home, 8 in a public infirmary, and 2 in other institutions. The home or place of residence of 8 was not reported.

The conditions making institutional care necessary are brought out by the fact that only 24 of the 73 who were in the institutions, and 10 of the 67 on the waiting lists were not reported to have been under the prolonged care of agencies previous to admission or application. Table 42 gives the types of agencies giving previous care.

TABLE 42.—*Prolonged agency care received prior to admission or application by feeble-minded children born out of wedlock, who were under care of State institutions or awaiting admission.*

Types of agencies giving prolonged care previous to admission or application.	Children born out of wedlock, under care or awaiting admission in 1914.		
	Total.	Under care.	Awaiting admission.
Total	140	73	67
Public child caring	a 46	20	a 26
Private child caring	7	3	4
Other	b 8	b 7	1
Public child caring and other	29	11	18
Private child caring and other	4	4	
Public and private child caring	8	4	4
Public and private child caring and other	4		4
No previous prolonged care reported	34	24	10

a In 1 of these cases more than one agency had given prolonged care.
b In 3 of these cases more than one agency had given prolonged care.

Public child-caring agencies alone had had charge of 46 of these children, while 41 others had received care from public child-caring and from other agencies. Thus, 62 per cent had been charges of public child-caring agencies before they were admitted to the schools for the feeble-minded, or were placed on the waiting lists. Nineteen children not receiving care from public child-caring agencies had been under the supervision of private child-caring or of other agencies.

Of the 106 children who had been wards of agencies, 49, or 46 per cent, had been given care by more than one agency. The urgent need of custodial care is indicated by the histories of two children awaiting admission who had at the time of application been under care of four agencies. Three of the children in the institutions and 5 awaiting admission had received care from 3 agencies.

At the time of application or admission the records reported physical defects, diseases, or poor physical conditions for 51, or 36 per cent, of the 140 feeble-minded children of illegitimate birth in institutions or awaiting admission. This is undoubtedly a minimum, since the records of 49 contained no statement in regard to physical condition. Thirty-three children were stated to be in general poor condition. In 7 cases there had been a finding of syphilis or gonorrhea, and in 1 case venereal infection was suspected; 1 of these children was also rachitic, and another had seriously defective vision. The following list shows the distribution of physical defects and diseases among these children:

Total children			140
Good physical condition, so far as known	40	Epileptic	1
		Syphilis or gonorrhea (1 also	
Seriously defective vision	1	rachitic; 1 with defective	
Defective hearing	2	vision)	7
Defective speech	1	Syphilis suspected	1
Crippled or deformed	2	General poor condition	33
Tubercular	1	Physical condition not re-	
Rachitic	2	ported	49

Almost half the children born out of wedlock who were in the schools for the feeble-minded and on the waiting lists were of poor character. Thirty-nine of the 73 in the institutions and 30 of the 67 awaiting admission were reported as having been delinquent or of otherwise poor character. For the children in the institutions the proportions of boys and girls who were known to have been of poor character were practically the same—slightly more than half. For the children awaiting admission, on the other hand, only a third of the boys were reported as having been delinquent or extremely troublesome, as against half the girls. Four of the girls in the institutions and 2 of those awaiting admission were themselves mothers of children born out of wedlock.

Length of time under care or awaiting admission.

The length of time the children born out of wedlock had been cared for in the two schools for the feeble-minded is of greatest significance for the older-age groups. (See Table 43.) At the end of the year of this study, 25 of the 73 children under care were between 18 and 21 years of age. Three of those in the oldest group had been in the institutions less than one year; 5, one year; 6, two and three years; 7, four and five years; 3, six to nine years; and 1, ten years. The length of time the institutions had provided care for the children of this age group probably indicates what will continue to be the situation of the majority of these children. Only a negligible proportion had families who would be interested in providing them with homes if it should become practicable for them to leave the institution after a period of training. That most of these children will undoubtedly remain permanent charges of the State is indicated by the fact that only 4 children were discharged from the care of the institutions during the year; 3 of these children were found to be insane and were transferred to hospitals for the insane, and in 1 case the reason for discharge was not reported.

TABLE 43.—*Duration of care received by feeble-minded children of specified ages, born out of wedlock, who were under care of State institutions.*

Age at end of period.	Total.	Children born out of wedlock, under care in 1914.					
		Length of time under care.					
		Less than 1 year.	1 year.	2–3 years.	4–5 years.	6–9 years.	10 years.
Total	73	13	12	25	15	7	1
Less than 8 years	3	1	....	2	....	....	....
8–9 years	7	1	3	1	2	....	....
10–13 years	19	3	2	11	2	1	....
14–17 years	19	5	2	5	4	3	....
18 years and over	25	3	5	6	7	3	1

Conditions surrounding the care of the feeble-minded in Massachusetts are brought out forcibly in Table 44, which shows the length of time the 67 feeble-minded children of illegitimate birth awaiting admission had had their names enrolled on the waiting lists of the two State institutions. The data are probably representative of all children on the waiting lists during the year of the study. And neither the feeble-minded children from normal homes nor those born without the possibility of home care are registered for institutional care to the extent that they would be if there were a hope of their early admittance. Selections from the waiting lists to fill vacancies are made not only according to length of time awaiting admission, but such factors as the urgency of the need are also taken into consideration.

TABLE 44.—*Length of time on waiting list, feeble-minded children born out of wedlock, who were awaiting admission to State institutions.*

Age at end of period.	Children born out of wedlock awaiting admission in 1914.					
	Total.	Length of time on waiting list.				
		Less than 1 yr.	1 yr.	2 yrs.	3 yrs.	4 yrs.
Total...............................	67	17	17	19	11	3
Less than 8 years.........................	8	3	1	1	3	....
8 to 9 years.....................	12	....	6	4	2	....
10 to 13 years.....................	24	7	5	6	4	2
14 to 17 years.....................	15	5	2	6	1	1
18 years and over.....................	8	2	3	2	1	....

Three of these children had been awaiting admission to a school for the feeble-minded for four years. Eleven children had been on the waiting lists for three years and 19 for two years. Three-fourths of all the children born out of wedlock had been on the waiting lists for one year or more.

The child's heritage.

The mothers of 4 of the 140 feeble-minded children of illegitimate birth were themselves known to have been born out of wedlock. For the majority nothing definite was known in regard to the circumstances of birth, and this figure undoubtedly falls short of the truth.

The mothers of 70 of the 86 children for whom this information was given were single at the time of the child's birth. The mothers of 2 were married women; of 2, widowed; and of 12, divorced, separated, or deserted. The mother of 1 child was illegally married, and the mothers of 13 children were living as married with the child's father. After the birth of the child the mothers of 2 children were known to have married the fathers, while the mothers of 19 married other men.

The records gave information as to the place of birth of the mothers of 73 of the 140 children. Almost equal numbers were native born and foreign born. The mothers of only 8 were born in Massachusetts.

The age of the mother when the child was born was reported in only 52 cases. The mothers of 8 children were less than 18 years old; of 10, 18 to 20 years; of 11, 21 to 24 years; of 19, 25 to 34 years; and of 4, 35 years and over.

Very little was known about the physical condition of the mothers at the time the children were admitted to institutions or placed on the waiting lists. As has been seen, only two of the children were with their mothers at this time. It was known that the mothers of

16 of the children were dead. Eleven of the 23 whose physical condition was known had physical ailments.

In slightly over half the cases the mothers were reported as having been delinquent or of unsatisfactory character; assuming that all those not so reported were of good character, the mothers of 51 per cent of the feeble-minded children had records of immorality, alcoholism, or were reported as of otherwise bad character. For a total of 57 children immorality on the part of the mother was reported, in 11 cases the mother being also alcoholic and in 2 otherwise delinquent. In 9 other cases the mother was alcoholic, and she was of otherwise bad character in 5. Thus 41 per cent of these feeble-minded children of illegitimate birth had mothers who were known to have led immoral lives, while the mothers of 14 per cent of the children were reported as alcoholic.

The impossibility of normal home care for many of these children and the hereditary mental defect that placed some of them in need of special protection, are brought out by the facts in regard to the mentality of the mothers. The mothers of 32 of the 140 feeble-minded children—more than one-fifth—were reported to be mentally below normal. Diagnosis would, of course, have been out of the question in the case of a large number of the mothers, and the proportion known to be mentally below normal must be considered a minimum. In 4 of the 32 cases the mother was insane; the mothers of 6 children had been diagnosed feeble-minded, while the mother of 1 child was diagnosed subnormal; the mothers of 21 children were probably subnormal or feeble-minded.

The histories revealed the fact that the mothers of 28 children had themselves been under the care of agencies or institutions. In 14 cases the mother had been committed to a correctional institution, and in 2 others they had been before courts and placed on probation. The mothers of 4 had been cared for as dependents, and the mothers of 8 had received other agency care.

The mothers of 24 children had had one or more illegitimate births before the feeble-minded child of the study was born, and the mothers of 33 had later illegitimate births. Of the 33 children, the mothers of 14 had both previous and subsequent illegitimate births. Hence, the mothers of 43 of the 140 children had other births out of wedlock. In 1 case the mother had 4 previous births; in 7 cases, three; in 4, two; and in 12, one. Of the cases in which the mother had subsequent births out of wedlock, there were 3 in which she was known to have had five or more; 11 more in which there were at least two, and 19 others in which there was at least one illegitimate birth. Something of the history and characteristics of the other children of these mothers who had had more than one child born out of wedlock was known in 27 cases. In 25 instances one or more of the other children were dependent on the public or on private charitable assistance or had been adjudged neglected; in 2 cases there were delinquent children. The mothers of 9 children included in the study were known to have had other children who were feeble-minded.

The following cases illustrate the need which had existed for the protection of the feeble-minded children of illegitimate birth under care or awaiting admission, and the conditions which foster a recurrence of defective mentality and illegitimacy.

A 10-year-old boy of illegitimate birth had been an inmate of a school for the feeble-minded for two years. He had previously been a ward of the State board of charity and had given much trouble because of his dishonesty and untruthfulness. His mother was an inmate of a correctional institution at the time this study was made; she had been committed for a sex offense when the boy was 3 years old, and had been committed again on a similar charge about the time her son was sent to the school for feeble-minded. She was alcoholic and immoral, had syphilis, and was diagnosed subnormal mentally. Her mother also had been immoral, and the whole family were reported to have been drunkards. (Case FM–I 27.)

At the time of this study a 6-year-old child born out of wedlock was awaiting admission to a school for the feeble-minded. She was reported to have congenital syphilis. The girl was in the care of a public child-caring agency and was giving much trouble on account of her mischievous and destructive habits. Her mother had been an inmate at the other State school for the feeble-minded; but she had been removed, much against the superintendent's advice. Before the mother's admission to the institution, she had been a ward of the same child-caring agency which was providing for the child. (Case FM–WL 45.)

A 10-year-old boy—a ward of the State board of charity—had been for three years on the waiting list of one of the institutions. He was untruthful and dishonest and unable to make any progress in school. His mother was an inmate of a hospital for the insane, but she was reported feeble-minded rather than insane. She had married at the age of 17, but after a month she left her husband and went home to her mother. A little more than a year later this child was born, and her husband secured a divorce on grounds of adultery. She was reported to have had a stillborn child before her marriage, and some years afterwards another child was born out of wedlock. The boy's maternal grandmother was reported below normal mentally, as were also an aunt, an uncle, and two cousins. (Case FM–WL 61.)

On the application of a private child-caring agency, a girl 15 years of age with defective sight and hearing was admitted during the year of the study to one of the schools for the feeble-minded. The whereabouts of the mother was unknown, and the child had been living with her grandmother, who, though very good to her, was a woman of low mentality. At this girl's birth the mother was only 14, the alleged father being a man of 70. The mother subsequently had two other children of illegitimate birth by different fathers, and the girl's aunt also had a child born out of wedlock.

At the age of 6 years the girl had a severe attack of scarlet fever, after which the family noticed a change in her mentality. She had reached the fourth grade at the age of 14, but she had spent three years in the third grade. She could not be trusted to do errands; she was mischievous, disobedient, unruly, and quarrelsome. (Case FM–I 64.)

A 12-year-old boy, admitted to one of the institutions during the year of the study, after having been on the waiting list for three years, had been a ward of the State from the time he was 3 years old. His parents, who were never married, were keepers of a disorderly house at the time of the boy's commitment to the State board of charity. They were reported as bad in every way and later became dependent on the city for support. There were two other children of illegitimate birth, one of whom was inferior physically, while the other was peculiar and troublesome.

The boy had been placed by the State in a number of boarding homes. After five years in school, he was only in the second grade at the time of commitment to the school for the feeble-minded. He had given great trouble in the homes in which he had been placed, because of his fondness for handling fire, his stubbornness, and his habits of lying and stealing. (Case FM–I 11.)

Two years previous to the time of this study, at the instance of a private agency in Boston, a 19-year-old girl born out of wedlock was committed to one of the schools for the feeble-minded. She had been arrested for street-walking and was found to be afflicted with both syphilis and gonorrhea. Shortly before, she had given birth to a stillborn child. The court had committed her to the care of the private agency, which sent her to a public infirmary and later gave her a home. All efforts to help her proved futile, and she was finally sent to the institution for the feeble-minded. During the year of the study she was found to be insane and was transferred to a State hospital for the insane. The girl's mother was reported to have been a prostitute. (Case FM–I 32.)

FEEBLE-MINDED MOTHERS OF CHILDREN BORN OUT OF WEDLOCK.

The interrelation between feeble-mindedness and illegitimacy can perhaps be arrived at best through a study from the opposite point of approach to that undertaken in the previous pages, namely, a study of persons of defective mentality who have become parents out of wedlock. Other chapters of this report have shown the results of mental examinations of mothers of children of illegitimate birth, and, to a very much smaller extent, of fathers. In the records of institutions, whether for the delinquent or for the feeble-minded, facts in regard to moral character are emphasized for girls and women and are in much less evidence for boys and men. The fact of illegitimate maternity is usually known and recorded, while illegitimate paternity is not. Emphasis is accordingly placed on the segregation of feeble-minded women of childbearing age, while the relation of the father's mentality to this problem has received very little attention.

As a part of the present study an analysis was made of the records of girls and women in the two institutions for the feeble-minded who had had children out of wedlock. This study can, at best, merely point out tendencies and dangers against which the mentally deficient must be protected. Incidentally there emerge certain facts in regard to the recurrence of mental defect and other results of bad heredity and the conditions under which many unfortunate children are born into the world.

The records of 187 girls and women in the two schools for the feeble-minded and on the waiting lists for admission stated that they had had births out of wedlock. Of the 187, 103 were in the institutions and 84 were awaiting admission at the time of the study.

The total number of girls and women in the two institutions who had reached childbearing age was estimated to be 821.[7] The 103 who had been illegitimately pregnant constituted one-eighth of this population. Had it been possible to base the comparison on the number who had attained childbearing age at the time of admission, the resulting proportion would have been higher.

The total number of girls and women 14 to 45 years of age awaiting admission to the institutions in 1914 was 383. The 84 who had been illegitimately pregnant constituted over one-fifth of this total.

Of the 103 women inmates who had been illegitimately pregnant, 57 were under 21 years of age at the time of admission, 23 of them being less than 18 years old; 34 were between the ages of 21 and 29, inclusive; and 12 were 30 years of age or over. At the time the records were studied, 78 had been in the institutions less than five years; 19, from five to nine years; and 6, ten years and over. One of these women had been cared for by the institution for 17 years, and another for 22 years.

Thirteen of the 84 girls and women awaiting admission were less than 18 years of age when application was made for their care, and 23 were between 18 and 20, making a total of 36 of the 84 who were under 21 years of age. There were 36 between the ages of 21 and 29 years, while 10 were 30 years of age and over at the time of application, and the ages of 2 were not reported.

The length of time these mothers out of wedlock had been awaiting admission to institutions emphasizes the inadequacy of the State's present provision for the feeble-minded who require custodial care. Twenty-nine had been awaiting admission for two years or longer, eight of them having been on the waiting lists for four years or more.

More than one-fourth of the 103 women in the institutions and almost half the 84 awaiting admission had had more than one illegitimate pregnancy. The numbers of illegitimate pregnancies these women had had were as follows:

	In institutions.	Awaiting admission.
Total who had been illegitimately pregnant	103	84
Once	76	45
Twice	17	25

[7] Number of women 14 years of age and over at Wrentham, in 1914, 286; number of women 15 years of age and over at the Massachusetts School for the Feeble-Minded at Waltham, in 1914, estimated to be 535. The latter figure was obtained by applying the percentage of the population on November 30, 1912, represented by women 15 years of age and over, to the total population for 1914, since age figures for that year were not available.

	In insti-tutions.	Awaiting admission.
Three times	6	10
Four times	3	2
Five times	1	2

The ages of the mothers at the time of the birth of the first child, or the only child, were known for 133 in the institutions or awaiting admission. They were as follows:

Total mothers reported _____ 133

Under 21 years	99	Under 21 years—continued.	
12 years	1	19 years	13
14 years	7	20 years	18
15 years	8	21 years and over	34
16 years	20	21–24 years	24
17 years	12	25–29 years	7
18 years	20	30 years and over	3

Three-fourths of these mentally irresponsible girls and women whose ages were reported had become mothers before they were 21 years of age. In Massachusetts the " age of consent " is 16 years, and the law provides a penalty of imprisonment for life or for a term of years for illicit relations with girls under this age.[8] One-eighth of the women whose ages were reported were under 16 when their children were born.

With few exceptions the records stated that the girls and women had been delinquent or difficult to control. As would be expected in these cases, immorality was most frequently reported. A considerable number were said to have been "dishonest," " uncontrollable," " vicious," " irresponsible," " wayward," " stubborn," " destructive," " indolent," with " no idea of right and wrong." Some were described as " man crazy," " having no moral sense," " morally degenerate," "continuously immoral," " depraved," " a danger to the community," " a bad influence to children," while others were " in need of constant protection," " an easy victim," " easily influenced," " childish." In a number of cases there was evidence that the helpless condition of these women had been taken advantage of, often at an early age.

With the exception of 10 of the institution cases and 5 of those awaiting admission, all the records reported the girl or her family as having been known to social agencies. In 58 of the 103 institution cases, and in 59 of the 84 cases awaiting admission, more than one agency had been concerned.

The sources of the applications for care indicate the various kinds of agencies and institutions which had been called upon to deal with these cases, and which had found the girls to be in urgent need of custodial care. It will be noted that in only 6 cases did the applica-

---

[8] R. L. 1902, ch. 207, sec. 23.

tion come directly from a relative or other private individual. The sources of the applications were as follows:

	In institutions.	Awaiting admission.
Total who had been illegitimately pregnant	103	84
State or city infirmary	18	25
Maternity home or hospital	6	8
Public child-caring agency	7	3
Private child-caring or child-protective agency	26	29
Court or institution for delinquent girls	8	1
Other agency or institution	6	12
Relative or friend	1	5
Not reported	31	1

At the time application was made to the schools for the feeble-minded for care for the 84 awaiting admission, 15 of these mentally defective girls and women were living in their parental homes, 2 were in the homes of relatives, and 1 was in an adoptive home. Seven were placed out at service under the supervision of agencies and 7 were being provided for by agencies in boarding homes. Eight were in maternity homes or hospitals, 30 in public infirmaries or in almshouses, 4 in other institutions, 1 was a married woman living in her own home, 1 was boarding, and 1 was at housework without agency supervision, and for 7 the location was unknown.

It is significant of the urgent need that had existed for the protection and safeguarding of these women that 17 of the 103 institution inmates were known to have had venereal infection, and that 22 of the 84 for whom care had not been provided at the time the study was made were reported to have been venereally diseased at the time of application or to have previously suffered from syphilis or gonorrhea. The outlook for the children of these feeble-minded and diseased women was most serious.

Thirteen of the 103 feeble-minded mothers who had been admitted to the institution and 5 of the 84 awaiting admission were known to have been themselves born out of wedlock.

The following histories illustrate the relation between defective mentality and illegitimate maternity.

At the age of 23 a woman, herself of illegitimate birth and the mother of a child born out of wedlock, was committed to a State school for the feeble-minded. She had been 7 years in the institution at the time this study was made. Her mother was reported to have been feeble-minded and immoral, and an older sister was said to have been feeble-minded and mentally deranged. At the age of 7 the girl was subjected to mistreatment by her stepfather and was committed to the division of State minor wards. She lived in 20 or more homes during the 14 years she was under care of that agency. The reasons given by the boarding women for refusing to help her were various—she was unreliable, untruthful, ill-tempered, and irresponsible. Her baby was born at a maternity home and became a ward of the State. The mother was in care of a private child-caring agency at the time of her commitment to the institution for the feeble-minded. (Case FM–I 321.)

Five years before the year covered by this study a 42-year-old woman was admitted to an institution for the feeble-minded. She had had a child born out of wedlock, whose father was a married man with a large family. The woman herself was of illegitimate birth and had been cared for by a children's home for 29 years. She had always been known as mentally deficient. Her mother was said to be a weak-minded woman, who had two other mentally defective children. Her father was the degenerate son of a good family. (Case FM–I 380.)

At the age of 18 a feeble-minded mother of a child born out of wedlock was admitted to a school for the feeble-minded. Soon after admission it was discovered that she was to have a second child of illegitimate birth, and she was sent to the State infirmary for maternity care. The first child had been adopted; the second child died soon after birth. The girl was a paralytic cripple and could not walk without crutches. She had a disagreeable disposition, was dishonest, and her mother had found her impossible to control. Her mother—the grandmother of the children—was reported probably mentally defective. (FM–I 415.)

Some years before the period covered by this study application was made to one of the institutions for the admission of a feeble-minded woman 20 years of age, who was in urgent need of protection. Her admission to the institution was not secured until eight years later; the delay was due partly to difficulty in persuading the girl's mother to sign the commitment papers, but principally to the overcrowded condition of the institution. The woman had had at least one child born out of wedlock before the first application was made and had a second child during the year of the application. Between that time and the date of admission she had two other children of illegitimate birth, the last baby having the same father as the child of another feeble-minded woman who was awaiting admission to the institution during the year studied. (FM–WL x4x.) The woman here described was a prostitute and had served a sentence for idle and disorderly conduct. She received treatment for gonorrhea and erysipelas at one public infirmary; she was cared for by another public infirmary at intervals during a period of four years, her last two babies having been born at this institution. Two of her children were under the care of a private child-caring agency, one was the ward of a public child-caring agency, and the youngest was still at the infirmary at the time covered by this study.

The woman was in poor physical condition, having defective hearing and having lost one eye. She was stubborn and quarrelsome and had a violent temper. She was herself of illegitimate birth and her mother was reported to have been mentally defective, intemperate, immoral, and thoroughly unreliable. (Case FM–I 474.)

The family history of a 26-year-old woman admitted to one of the institutions the year previous to this study showed intemperance, delinquency, immorality, and chronic dependency. The family had been a problem to social agencies from the time of the woman's birth. When she was 8 years old she was placed temporarily in the care of a private agency, and a year later she and her brothers and sisters were adjudged neglected and placed in the care of the same agency. The parents were arrested for keeping a disorderly house. The mother had also been arrested for drunkenness and the father for larceny; both had served sentences in correctional institutions. When the girl was 12 years old, the mother died of venereal infection and alcoholism.

The girl remained in charge of the child-caring agency until she was 17 years old, having been tried in many homes while under its care. None would keep her long, reporting her as unreliable, lazy, and untruthful. At 17, a private institution for girls assumed her care, and by this agency she was later placed in a private family with which she remained less than a year. She returned to the institution and, being illegitimately pregnant, was sent to a public infirmary, where her child was born. Here the mother remained for two years, until admission to the school for the feeble-minded was secured for her. (Case FM-I 449.)

A 12-year-old imbecile girl had been admitted to a school for the feeble-minded on the application of the State board of charity. Her mother was reported as of low mentality, and the family was generally of low grade and unable to control the girl. Some of the children had been committed to the care of the State as neglected. When the girl was 17 years of age her father insisted that she be returned home. Under strong protest on the part of the authorities, she went home on a visit and did not return. Within a few months the mother wrote that the girl was impossible to control when the father was not at home—that she was quarrelsome and wayward and ought to be returned to the institution; but the school was overcrowded and could not receive her. She was then placed at housework by her father with a woman who encouraged her in misconduct. She became illegitimately pregnant and was finally recommitted to the school for the feeble-minded. The girl was found to have gonorrhea, and the baby had ophthalmia neonatorum. (Case FM–I 315.)

Born out of wedlock, the child of a feeble-minded mother and an intemperate father, both of whom were almshouse inmates, a mentally defective child was brought up by her grandparents, who were of low type mentally and morally. She was reported as indolent, destructive, and mischievous. She gave birth to a child out of wedlock, who became a ward of the State board of charity, and the girl herself was committed to a State institution for the feeble-minded, where she had been for 17 years. (Case FM–I 177.)

A 26-year-old woman had been awaiting admission to an institution for the feeble-minded for two years previous to the time covered by this study. She had been at a public infirmary during all this time. It was reported that her return to the community was out of the question. She had congenital syphilis and had lost two children of illegitimate birth. Her mother was in a State hospital for the insane. Her father had been intemperate. (Case FM–WL 3x7.)

During the year of this study application was made by the State board of charity for the care of a 26-year-old inmate of a public infirmary. She had had two children born out of wedlock and two children of legitimate birth. Her mother had been shiftless and weak and unable to control her children; she had been twice committed to a hospital for the insane. The girl's father had been intemperate.

The girl had her first baby when she was only 17 years old, the father of the child being 40 years older. The child was cared for by relatives and private agencies. Four years after the birth of this child the girl married and had two children of legitimate birth. The children were constantly neglected, the mother returning frequently to the father of her first child. One of the children of legitimate birth died of syphilis, and the care of the other was finally assumed by the division of State minor wards. Two years before the period covered by this study the woman's husband died. In a little more than a year thereafter she gave birth to a child whose alleged father was her husband's cousin. The child was born at the infirmary, where the mother was kept awaiting admission to an institution for the mentally defective. She was reported to have both syphilis and gonorrhea. (Case FM–WL 9x0.)

THE MASSACHUSETTS PROGRAM FOR THE CARE OF THE FEEBLE-MINDED.

The Massachusetts Special Commission Relative to the Control, Custody, and Treatment of Defectives, Criminals, and Misdemeanants, in its report to the legislature in February, 1919, emphasized the relationship between feeble-mindedness and illegitimacy. The report states:[9]

To any one dealing with the endless procession of illegitimate children; of disease-breeding prostitutes, who are irresponsible; of inebriates with more than a score of commitments in their record and who, because of mental defect, can not be expected to escape the habit or cease their round of courts and jails; the unrestrained woman married to or cohabiting with the feeble-minded man, and begetting a large family of feeble-minded children to add to the troop of repeaters in the courts and public dependents in almshouses and infirmaries—to those working with these problems it is fully apparent that it does not protect the public to seek out the defective in the latter end of his career of lawbreaking and disease spreading and child breeding—after the fact. The palliative method—catching the defective after the harm is done—tends at its worst to breed the very menace that it seeks to remove. It is only by preventive methods that so grave a menace to the public welfare can be dealt with adequately.

The program presented by the commission included the compulsory mental examination in all courts of all persons found guilty who are repeaters or who are suspected of being mentally deficient and treatment according to their condition, the mental examination of inmates of penal and correctional institutions and of minors and expectant mothers in the State Infirmary, the mental examination of retarded children in the public schools, a centralized system of registration of all feeble-minded, the development of a process of supervising feeble-minded persons in the community, the extension of the Wrentham State School to its capacity, and the completion of the third institution for the feeble-minded.

Laws were passed providing for a census of retarded school children, the establishment of special school classes, and a registry of the feeble-minded to be kept by the commission on mental diseases.[10] With these exceptions, the well-rounded program of the special commission failed of enactment into law.

---

[9] Report of the Special Commission Relative to the Control, Custody, and Treatment of Defectives, Criminals and Misdemeanants. February, 1919. House No. 1403. Boston, 1919. P. 34.

[10] Acts 1919 ch. 277.

Two cities in Massachusetts were included in the series of infant-mortality studies conducted by the United States Children's Bureau. In the course of the inquiries in these cities considerable information was obtained in regard to infants born out of wedlock, though the numbers of illegitimate births were too small to permit any conclusive findings. However, since the periods covered by the infant mortality studies were near the period covered by this study of illegitimacy, and since the figures are of interest as suggesting something of the conditions prevailing in manufacturing cities of medium size as contrasted with the situation in Boston, brief summaries of the findings of these two studies in regard to illegitimacy are included in this report.

Brockton, having a population of approximately 62,000 in 1913, is situated in Plymouth County, 21 miles south of Boston, and is one of the most important shoe-manufacturing cities in the United States. Shoe manufacturing is practically the only industry, and the employees are, in the main, skilled, well-paid workers. The general death rate for each year of the period 1910 to 1913 was lower in Brockton than in any other city in Massachusetts having a population of 50,000 or more. The infant-mortality inquiry covered the year November 1, 1912, to October 31, 1913. During that year the total number of registered births was 1,585, including 60 stillbirths and miscarriages; complete data were obtained, chiefly from the mothers, for 1,247 of these births, including 37 stillbirths. Among the live-born infants there were 117 deaths during the first year of life; the infant-mortality rate was 96.7.[1]

New Bedford, in Bristol County, 57 miles southeast of Boston, had a population of approximately 107,000 in 1913. It is an important textile-manufacturing city, and also has other important industries. In 1910 more than two-fifths of the population were foreign born. The number of women gainfully employed was relatively large. In 1913 the general infant mortality rate for the city was 143, a very high rate in comparison with the infant mortality in other cities in

---

[1] U. S. Children's Bureau: Infant Mortality: Results of a field study in Brockton, Mass., based on births in one year, by Mary V. Dempsey. Infant Mortality Series No. 8, Bureau Publication No. 37. Washington, 1919.

Massachusetts having populations of 50,000 or more. The infant mortality study covered the calendar year 1913. During this period the total number of registered births was 3,633, including 140 still-births and miscarriages. For 2,662 of these births, including 75 still-births, complete information was obtained, principally from the mothers.[2] The number of deaths under 1 year of age among these infants was 337; the infant mortality rate was 130.3. An analysis of infant mortality in the different precints showed five precincts with high rates, and these five were designated as the "unfavorable area." The infant mortality rate for this area was 156.6, while the rate for the rest of the city was 94.6.[3]

Number and Per Cent of Illegitimate Births.

In Brockton, during the selected year, 36 illegitimate live births and 3 illegitimate stillbirths were registered. The total illegitimate births comprised 2.5 per cent of all births registered in the period; the illegitimate live births comprised 2.4 per cent of all live births registered.

The number of registered illegitimate births in New Bedford during the year selected for study was 104, including 101 live births and 3 stillbirths. Of the total registered births, 2.9 per cent were illegitimate; the same percentage of registered live births were illegitimate.

The percentage of illegitimate live births found in Brockton in the period of the study was only slightly higher than the percentage of illegitimate live births in the State as a whole in 1914—2.4 for Brockton and 2.3 for the State as a whole. The percentage of 2.9 in New Bedford was considerably higher than the percentage for the State as a whole. In fact, in 1914 New Bedford had the highest percentage of illegitimate births of any city in the State having a population of 50,000 or more, with the exception of Boston, where the rate was 3.9.

Infant Mortality.

In Brockton, 7 of the 36 infants born out of wedlock during the selected year, exclusive of stillbirths, died before they had reached their first brithday. "It is probable," the report states, "that some of the 12 children who could not be traced till their first birthday died outside the city. At least 19 per cent of the live-born infants died during their first year, indicating, though the basis for the figures is small, a tendency toward a rate twice as high as for legitimate children."[4]

---

[2] All illegitimate births were excluded from the analysis.

[3] U. S. Children's Bureau: Infant Mortality: Results of a field study in New Bedford, Mass., based on births in one year, by Jessamine S. Whitney. Infant Mortality Series No. 10, Bureau Publication No. 68. Washington, 1920.

[4] U. S. Children's Bureau: Infant Mortality: Results of a field study in Brockton, Mass., based on births in one year, by Mary V. Dempsey. Infant Mortality Series No. 8, Bureau Publication No. 37. Washington, 1919. P. 68.

In New Bedford all or part of the information desired was secured for 63 of the 104 illegitimate births. The report states: [5]

Among the 63 births investigated, 2 stillbirths and 18 deaths occurred; in 2 cases it was not reported whether the child survived the first year or not. The infant mortality rate for this group was therefore at least 305. If the entire group of 101 live births is compared with the 35 known deaths in this group, as shown by death certificates, the infant mortality rate was even higher, 347. This rate was over two and a half times as high as the rate for infants of legitimate birth.

Mortality among infants of illegitimate birth would appear to be higher in New Bedford than in Boston, though the relative difference between mortality among infants born in wedlock and among those born out of wedlock does not seem to be as great in the former city as in the latter; the mortality among infants born in wedlock, as well as among infants of illegitimate birth, was much higher in New Bedford than in Boston. The mortality rate among infants born out of wedlock in Boston, based on births and deaths in the same calendar year, was 281, and the rate based on deaths during the first year of life of infants born during the year was 251.5; [6] in New Bedford the rate was 305 among the group of infants for whom information was obtained, and 347 among all infants born out of wedlock. On the other hand, the Boston rate first quoted was three times the rate for infants born in wedlock, while the New Bedford rate for all infants born out of wedlock was 2.7 times as high as the rate found among the infants included in the New Bedford infant mortality inquiry, all of whom were of legitimate birth.

The New Bedford rate of 305 for infants of illegitimate birth for whom information was obtained was almost twice as high as the general infant mortality rate for the so-called "unfavorable area" in the city; it was more than three times as high as the rate for the "favorable area."

The Care of the Child.

The information secured in regard to the care of children born out of wedlock in Brockton was very meager. Complete schedules were obtained from the mothers of 8 infants, and in some instances partial data were secured from social agencies. Of the 35 children who lived at least two weeks, 10 were known to have lived with the mothers; 12 were known to have lived away from the mothers, of whom 4 were boarded in private families, 3 were at a "baby farm," 2 were adopted, 1 was cared for at an infant asylum,

---

[5] U. S. Children's Bureau: Infant Mortality: Results of a field study in New Bedford, Mass., based on births in one year, by Jessamine S. Whitney. Infant Mortality Series No. 10, Bureau Publication No. 68. Washington, 1920.

[6] This rate is known to be an understatement, because of the number of infants concerning whom no information was obtained.

1 was boarded by the division of State minor wards, and 1 was living with relatives; in 13 instances the child's home or place of residence was not reported.

In New Bedford partial or complete information was obtained in regard to 61 of the 101 live-born infants. Four of these 61 infants died before they had reached the age of two weeks. Of the remaining 57, 9 were living with both parents at the time the information was secured or previous to death,[7] 28 were living with their mothers, 2 were supported by the fathers in the homes of the paternal grandparents, and 18 were placed in institutions, boarded out, cared for by relatives, or adopted. Hence, 37 of the 57 infants were living with their mothers, and 20 were separated from them.

Court proceedings for the support of the children were initiated in the cases of 16 of the 104 illegitimate births in New Bedford in 1913, 11 under the old law and 5 under the 1913 act. The proportion of court cases was much smaller than that found in the Boston study, which covered the year 1914. The difference may be due partly to the fact that the new law was not in effect until July, 1913. Of the 16 cases, 5 were not brought to trial because the defendant could not be found. In 9 cases some provision for the child was made.

Nationality, Age, and Occupation of Mother.

Of the 39 illegitimate births in Brockton, including stillbirths, 24 were to native mothers and 15 to foreign-born mothers. In New Bedford, of the 63 illegitimate births, including stillbirths, concerning which information was obtained, 25, or two-fifths, were to native-white mothers and 38, or three-fifths, to foreign-born mothers. The New Bedford report states: " The large proportion of native white among these mothers is noteworthy, since the percentage of native white among the mothers of legitimate births was only 28." [8] This finding is in accord with the 1914 figures for Boston, which showed that 53.8 per cent of the illegitimate births were to white mothers born in the United States, as compared with 35.2 per cent of the legitimate births.[9]

The mothers of more than two-fifths of the 63 infants born out of wedlock in New Bedford for whom this information was secured were under 20 years of age. About the same proportion of mothers of infants born out of wedlock in Boston for whom this information was secured were under the age of 21 years.[10]

---

[7] The information was secured during either the second year of the child's life or the first few months of the third year.

[8] U. S. Children's Bureau: Infant Mortality: Results of a field study in New Bedford, Mass. based on births in one year, by Jessamine S. Whitney. Infant Mortality Series No. 10, Bureau Publication No. 68. Washington, 1920.

[9] See p. 108.

[10] See p. 110.

In New Bedford, as in Boston, a large proportion of the mothers were gainfully employed during the year before the child's birth, but the occupational distribution in the two cities was very different. Of the 63 New Bedford mothers for whom information was obtained, 35, or more than half, worked in cotton mills; only 8 were employed in domestic service. Of the mothers of infants born out of wedlock in Boston for whom this information was obtained, 47 per cent were engaged in domestic or personal service and 23 per cent in factories.

ILLEGITIMACY IN A RURAL SEACOAST SECTION.[11]

Scope and Method of Study.

In order to obtain data in regard to a sparsely populated, largely rural section, which should be in contrast to the study of the problem in Boston, a brief survey was made in Barnstable County (Cape Cod) and in the island counties of Dukes (Marthas Vineyard) and Nantucket.

In 1910 the combined population of these three counties was 35,008, and in 1914 it was estimated to be 36,605.[12] The populations of Barnstable and Nantucket Counties decreased steadily between 1870 and 1910, and the population of Dukes County was less in 1910 than in 1900. However, the State census of 1915 showed slight increases over the 1910 population. Although 44 per cent of the population of Barnstable County was classified in 1910 as urban, living in towns of 2,500 or more inhabitants, the population of the largest town was only 4,676. In Dukes County the entire population was classified as rural, the largest town having in 1910 only 1,196 inhabitants. The county and town of Nantucket are coincident, the population in 1910 being 2,962. More than four-fifths of the inhabitants of these three counties were native-born whites. About one-seventh were foreign-born whites, of whom there were more Portuguese than of any other nationality. Three per cent were Negroes. The principal industries of the district are fishing and cranberry raising.

The study covered illegitimate births in these three counties during the 10-year period 1905 to 1914, inclusive. Birth records filed at the State House in Boston furnished the preliminary data. Information was secured through interviews with relatives, friends, and town officials in regard to the children registered as born out of wedlock and other children discovered in the course of the inquiry to have been born out of wedlock during the period to mothers

[11] The field work for this part of the report was done by Katherine M. Herring, M. D.
[12] See Table 1, p. 271. Estimate based on Thirteenth Census of the United States, 1910, and on Massachusetts State Census of 1915.

living in the district. Some of the children or their families were known to social agencies in Boston or to State institutions and agencies, and information was secured from the records of these agencies and institutions. The field work was done during the late summer and fall of 1915.

Number of Illegitimate Births and Per Cent of Total Births.

During the 10-year period the total number of live births registered in the three counties was 6,508, of which 113 were registered as illegitimate. The percentage of illegitimate births for this time period, 1.7, was slightly lower than the percentage, 2.0, for the year 1914. During that year the percentage for the three counties combined was higher than for any other county except Bristol—the county in which New Bedford is located—and Suffolk, most of which the city of Boston comprises. However, the average percentage for the 10 years for Barnstable, Dukes, and Nantucket Counties was as low as or lower than the 1914 percentages for seven other counties.[13]

In the course of the field study information was obtained for 99 of the 113 children registered as of illegitimate birth. Of the 14 others, 1 was found to have been born in wedlock, 1 was found to have been a stillbirth, and for 12 no information could be secured.

In addition to the 99 children included in the study whose births were registered as illegitimate in the district, 13 children were found to have been born out of wedlock in the district, though their births were not registered as illegitimate, 6 were found to have been born outside the area covered to mothers resident in the district, and 3 children reported on the birth records as stillborn were found to have been live-born children. Hence the total number of children of illegitimate birth included in the study was 121. These 121 children forming the basis of the study were born to 97 mothers. The part of this chapter relating to mothers of children born out of wedlock deals with these 97 mothers and with 6 more who gave birth only to stillborn children during the period.

Mortality of Children Born out of Wedlock.

Twelve of the 121 children born out of wedlock during the period were known to have died before the time of the inquiry. In 16 cases it was not known whether the child was living or dead. Of those who died, 8 died in the first year of life, 3 in the second or third year, and 1 child was 6 years of age. The children who were known to have died in infancy comprised only 7 per cent of the total. This percentage is very low in comparison with the proportion of infant deaths shown in other parts of the report. In Boston in 1914, 27 per cent of

---

[13] See Table 1, p. 271.

the children born out of wedlock were known to have died during the first year of life.[14] In New Bedford 35 per cent of the infants of illegitimate birth died under 1 year of age. It is probable that the proportion of infant deaths among the 16 children in regard to whom it was not known whether they were living or dead was larger than among the whole group. But even assuming, for comparative purposes, that all the 16 died in infancy, the percentage of infant deaths would still have been smaller than that found in Boston or New Bedford—20 per cent for the three counties as compared with 27 per cent and 35 per cent for Boston and New Bedford, respectively.

At the time of the inquiry 77 per cent of the children were surviving, 10 per cent were dead, and in regard to 13 per cent it was not known whether they were living or dead.

Place of Birth.

The place of birth was reported for 99 of the 121 children born during the period. The majority of the children—62 of the 99—were born in the mother's parental home. Twelve were born in the mother's own home, 12 in the mother's place of employment, 2 in the homes of relatives, 4 in private homes of other types, 3 in State institutions, and 4 in hospitals. The number of institution births—7 out of 99—was very small. In Boston 77 per cent of the illegitimate births occurred in hospitals, maternity homes, or the public infirmary.

Only 1 of the institution births occurred in the district studied. The 4 children born in hospitals, 2 of those born in State institutions, and 1 whose place of birth was not reported were known to have been born outside the district comprised of the three counties. Hence, a total of 7 children were known to have been born outside the district. On the other hand, 8 of the births in the district were to nonresident mothers, of whom 1 had come to the home of a relative in order to conceal the birth from her friends in the town where she lived, and 1 had taken a place at housework in the district for the same purpose.

The Care of the Child.

Time with mother.

The children remained with their mothers to a much greater extent than was indicated by the findings for children born out of wedlock in Boston.[15] Of the 93 children known to be living at the end of the period, 66 had lived with their mothers the entire time; of the 81 children 1 year of age and over, 56 had spent their entire lives

---

[14] See p. 134. This per cent is based on the number of infants known to have died, whether or not death certificates were found for them. The percentage is an understatement because of the number of infants for whom no information was secured.

[15] See pp. 139–143.

with their mothers, and all but 5 of the others had lived with their mothers at least a year. The 66 children who had lived with their mothers the entire time comprised 61 per cent of the 109 children who were not known to have died and 71 per cent of the 93 children known to be living at the end of the period. The age of the child at the end of the period and the length of time kept with mother are given in Table 45.

TABLE 45.—*Age of child at end of period and length of time kept with mother.*

Age at end of period.	Children born out of wedlock during period and known to be living at end of period.					
	Total.	Length of time kept with mother.				
		Entire life.	Two years or more.	One year.	Less than one year.	Not reported.
Total..............................	93	66	9	4	7	7
Less than 1 year.......................	11	9	....	....	2	....
1 year................................	9	5	....	1	1	2
2 years...............................	8	6	....	....	a 2	....
3 years...............................	15	13	....	1	....	1
4 to 5 years..........................	18	13	1	1	2	1
6 to 7 years..........................	18	12	5	1	....	....
8 to 9 years..........................	13	7	3	....	....	3
Not reported..........................	1	1	....	....	....	....

a Including 1 whose mother died in childbirth.

Of the 12 children who died 7 had lived with their mothers up to the time of death, 2 had been separated from them at some time prior to death, and in 3 cases the length of time with the mother was not reported.

Last disposition of child, and by whom supported.

At the end of the period, 69 of the 93 children known to be surviving were living with their mothers, 21 were separated from them, and in 3 cases it was not known whether the child was living with or separated from the mother. The proportion of three-fourths living with their mothers is somewhat higher than the proportion—less than two-thirds—found for infants in New Bedford.

The homes or places of residence of the children at the time of the inquiry were as follows:

```
Total known to be living_____  93
With mother _____  69
    Home of mother and father _____   6
    Home of mother and stepfather_____   13
    Mother's independent home _____   6
    Mother's parental home _____   32
    Home of relatives _____   1
    Mother's place of employment _____   4
    State Infirmary_____    1
    Not reported _____    6
```

Separated from mother _____ 21
    Mother's parental home _____ 11
    Boarding home _____ 2
    Adoptive home _____ 1
    Under care of division of State minor wards_____ 7
Not reported _____ 3

More than one-third of the children whose location was reported were living with their mothers in the homes of their maternal grandparents. Almost half were living with their maternal grandparents, either with or away from their mothers. More than one-fifth of the children were living with their mothers and fathers or mothers and stepfathers. It is noteworthy that only one of the children was living in an adoptive home.

Relatives were supporting 74 of the 93 children—in 56 cases without outside assistance and in 18 with the help of public or private relief agencies. Overseers of the poor supported 4 children, and the State provided for 7 through the division of State minor wards and for 1 in the State infirmary. In 2 cases support came from other sources, and in 5 the type of support was not reported.

Court action.

Court action had been brought in connection with 25 of the 121 children born out of wedlock during the period. In 15 of these cases proceedings were brought to secure support from the father—13 under the old law and 2 under the new act. The parents of 6 children were arrested for lewd and lascivious cohabitation; 2 fathers were arrested for rape; 1 mother was brought to court for concealment of birth, and 1 for neglect of the child. Of the 15 children for whose support court action was brought, the fathers of 2 were ordered to support the children; 1 case was dismissed because the parents married and another because the mother died; 7 cases were settled out of court; in 2 cases the defendant was found not guilty; 1 case was dismissed because of lack of evidence; and in 1 case the outcome was not reported.

Agency care.

Of the 121 children born out of wedlock during the period, 48, or 40 per cent, were known to have received prolonged or temporary care from agencies, or to have lived in families receiving relief and other assistance from public or private agencies. Nineteen children received prolonged care from public or private agencies, 7 received hospital or other temporary care, and 22 children not directly under agency care lived in families receiving public or private aid. Only 11 children—9 per cent of the total—were known to have received prolonged care from public or private child-caring agencies. Nine of these children had been under the care of the division of State minor wards. Six children had been under the direct, prolonged care of public relief agencies, and 2 children had been cared for at the State infirmary.

That one-third of the children received prolonged care from public or private child-caring, public relief, or other public agencies, or lived in families receiving public or private aid, is indicative of the poor economic status of the parents and other relatives. Although a large proportion of the children born out of wedlock were cared for in the homes of their mothers or their grandparents, aid was frequently necessary for the families who assumed the responsibility for them. However, the amount of agency care was proportionately much smaller than that found in the study of infants born out of wedlock in Boston. More than three-fifths of those infants were known to have received prolonged care from agencies during the first year of life, and more than a third of the total had been under the care of child-caring or child-protective agencies.[16]

Mothers of Children Born out of Wedlock.

During the 10-year period 1905–1914, 103 mothers residing temporarily or permanently in the counties of Barnstable, Dukes, or Nantucket gave birth to children out of wedlock. Six of these mothers had stillborn children only during the period; 97 were the mothers of the 121 children whose histories were discussed above. Of the 103 mothers 64 lived in Barnstable County, 9 in Dukes County, 22 in Nantucket County, and 8 had come to the district shortly before confinement for the purpose of concealing the birth from friends and relatives at home.

Information in regard to the total number of illegitimate births, including stillbirths, was obtained for 101 of the 103 mothers. These 101 mothers had had 148 illegitimate births. Of these, 140 were live births and 8 were stillbirths. There was one case of plural birth, so that the total number of live-born children was 141. Of the 101 mothers 76 had had one illegitimate birth; 13, two; 6, three; 3, four; 2, five; and 1, six.

Race and nativity.

Of the 103 mothers 81 were white, 11 belonged to the Negro race, and 11 had strains of both Indian and Negro blood. All but 5 of the white mothers were born in the United States; 3 of these 5 were born in Canada, 1 in England, and 1 in Finland. Of the Negro mothers, 5 were native born; 4 were foreign born of Portuguese parentage; 1 was of Portuguese parentage, but the place of birth was not reported; and the nativity and parentage of 1 was not reported.

---

[16] See pp. 135–136.

All the Indian-Negro mothers were born in the United States. The proportion of native-white mothers—almost three-fourths—was lower than the proportion—more than four-fifths—of native white among the total population of the three counties. The proportion of Negro and Indian-Negro mothers was greatly in excess of the proportion of Negroes and Indians in the general population.

Age.

The age at the birth of the first child out of wedlock was reported for 93 of the 103 mothers. Eighteen mothers—19 per cent of those reported—were under the age of 18 years. This percentage is higher than that found among mothers of infants born out of wedlock in Boston, but the two figures are not entirely comparable, because some of the Boston mothers had had previous illegitimate births, so that the age at the birth of the 1914 baby was not always the age at birth of the first child out of wedlock.

Of the mothers in the three counties who were under the age of 18 at the birth of the first child out of wedlock, 1 was 14 years of age; 1, 15; 7, 16; and 9 were 17 years old. Between the ages of 18 and 20 years, inclusive, were 32 mothers, making a total of 50—more than half of all reported—who were under the age of 21. Twenty-eight mothers were 21 to 24 years of age, inclusive; 13 were 25 to 34 years; and 2 had passed the age of 35.

Civil condition.

At the time of the birth of the first child out of wedlock during the 10-year period, 87 of the 103 mothers were single; 1 was illegally married; 5 were married; 3 were widowed, divorced, or separated; 4 were deserted; and the civil condition of 3 was not reported. The proportion of single women was somewhat smaller than that found among mothers of infants born out of wedlock in Boston. The husband of 1 of the 5 married women was serving a long term in prison, and the husband of another was on a sea voyage.

At the time of the inquiry 2 of the 87 single mothers were dead; 27 had been married, 55 were still single, and the marital histories of 3 were not reported. Twelve of the 27 who had married were known to have married the fathers of their children; 9 of these were living with their husbands at the time of the inquiry, and 3 had been deserted. Of the 15 who had married men not known to be the fathers 12 were living with their husbands, 2 had been divorced, and 1 had been deserted. Three of the 5 women who were married at the birth of the first child during the period were later divorced from their husbands. One of these women subsequently married a man not the father of her child.

At the time of the inquiry 55 of the 101 mothers who were living were single; 1 was illegally married; 25 were married; 7 were widowed, divorced, or separated; 8 were deserted; and the civil condition of 5 was not reported.   Thirteen mothers were known to have had legitimate births.

Occupation.

The occupation of the mother before the birth of the first child during the period was reported for 94 of the 103 mothers.   Slightly less than three-fifths of these 94 mothers were gainfully employed.   This proportion is considerably smaller than that found among mothers of infants born out of wedlock in Boston.   Of the 55 who were gainfully employed, 29 were servants in private homes, 13 were employed in hotels or boarding houses, 4 did gainful work at home, 2 went out by the day as cleaners and laundresses, and 7 were employed in occupations of other types.   This occupational distribution is natural in view of the absence of industrial opportunities aside from domestic and personal service in the district covered by the study.

Occupation at the time of the inquiry was reported for 74 of the 101 mothers living at that time.   Of these mothers, 39 were not gainfully employed, 1 of them being an inmate of an institution for the feeble-minded.   Of the 35 who were gainfully employed, 15 were in domestic service in private families, 8 were employed in hotels or boarding houses, 5 did gainful work at home, 2 went out by the day as cleaners and laundresses, and 5 were engaged in occupations of other types.

Mental condition.

Thirteen mothers—13 per cent of all—had been diagnosed feeble-minded.   This percentage is considerably larger than the percentages found in other parts of the study.   Of the mothers of infants born out of wedlock in Boston in one year, 5 per cent had been diagnosed feeble-minded; the mothers of 6 per cent of the children under the care of Boston agencies had been so diagnosed.   The higher percentage in the rural seacoast section may be partly due to the more complete information secured by means of the field study, but the difference is sufficiently great to indicate a larger percentage of feeble-mindedness among the mothers described in this chapter of the report.

Besides the mothers who had been diagnosed feeble-minded, 24—23 per cent of all—were reported probably subnormal or feeble-minded. This percentage is very much higher than the percentages found in other sections of the inquiry and may also be accounted for in part by the completeness of the information secured.

Character and agency record.

Nearly three-fifths of the mothers—60 of the 103—had been the mothers of more than one child out of wedlock or had been immoral repeatedly. This proportion is larger than that found in other sections of the study. Five mothers were professional prostitutes; 27 others had been promiscuous in their sex relations, 4 of whom were feeble-minded women who had been victimized by many men.

More than one-third of the mothers—37 of the 103—had been before the courts or had been known to social agencies. Eighteen mothers had been before the courts; 6 of these mothers had been inmates of correctional institutions. One mother had been an inmate of an institution for the feeble-minded, and another of an institution for the insane. Overseers of the poor had aided 15 mothers, 3 of whom had been under the care of correctional institutions. Agencies of other types had cared for 5 mothers not included above and for 3 who had been before the courts or under the care of overseers of the poor.

Home conditions.

At the time of the inquiry 35 of the 101 mothers who were alive were living in their parental homes; 27 in homes of their own, including 1 living with a man to whom she was not married, 2 with relatives, 12 in their places of employment, 3 in institutions, and the mode of living of 22 was not reported.

The mother's parents were living together in 64 of the 101 cases. In 9 cases the mother's father was dead, and in 2 her mother; the father of 1 was in prison; the fathers of 4 and the mothers of 2 had deserted; the parents of 1 were separated. In 18 cases nothing was known of the mother's parents.

Both parents of five mothers were feeble-minded. The mother of one and the fathers of two had been insane.

Of the 83 cases in which information in regard to home conditions of the mothers was obtained, there were only 23 in which the parental home was good, so far as known, and in three of these cases the father was dead or had deserted his family or the parents were separated. Immoral conditions existed in 21 homes, in 2 of which there was also alcoholism. In six other homes alcoholism existed. Considerably more than one-third of the families—31 of the 83 concerning which information was obtained—were dependent upon public or private aid. In 13 of these cases there was also alcoholism or immorality in the home. Very congested living conditions, a mode of life which was most primitive, or otherwise poor conditions existed in 15 homes. Hence, in a total of 60 of the 83 cases in which information in regard to conditions in the mother's parental home was obtained, immorality, alcoholism, dependency, or otherwise poor conditions existed.

Of the 35 mothers who were living in their parental homes at the time of the inquiry, there were 10 whose home conditions were good so far as known. In seven homes immoral conditions existed. Fourteen families—including four in whose homes immorality existed, were dependent upon public or private aid. In eight other homes, alcoholism or otherwise poor conditions were found.

Summary.

In the rural section studied the problem appeared to be largely chargeable to family degeneracy or to the weak mentality or bad moral character of the mother. Almost three-fourths of the mothers, the character of whose parental home was reported, had lived under poor home influences. More than half, for whom age was reported, when their first child was born illegitimately, were under the legal age of majority. The proportion of mothers who had been diagnosed feeble-minded was more than twice that reported in other parts of the study. More than one-third were definitely known to be feeble-minded, or were reported as probably defective in mentality. The conditions in the parental homes and the mentality of the mothers undoubtedly bore a causative relationship to the proportion—nearly three-fifths—of all the mothers who were reported as having had more than one child out of wedlock or as being repeatedly immoral, and who probably in part accounted for the more than one-third who had been before the courts or were known to social agencies.

In striking contrast to the situation discovered in the metropolis, three-fourths of the surviving children were with their mothers at the time the study was made. Almost half the children whose location was reported were living in the homes of their maternal grandparents. This indicates a different attitude on the part of the parents of these mothers from that oftenest encountered in the city districts. From the standpoint of the physical welfare of the infants this seemed to be a desirable situation; the infant mortality rate was very much lower than in the large city. On the other hand, low standards of family life prevailed in a large proportion of the families of these mothers in the rural section, and the conditions under which the children were being reared were harmful to their development. Only 9 per cent of the children born out of wedlock in the 10-year period, concerning whom information was obtained, were known to have received prolonged care from child-caring agencies. However, a considerable number of the families with whom the children lived received charitable aid.

The problem was found to be largely local. There was neither the influx of unfortunates that is usual in the large centers nor the considerable number of departures of prospective mothers wishing to conceal their condition or to dispose of their infants. The very conditions that helped to create much of the problem were responsible for the smaller proportion of the children thrust upon the public for care, and, by leaving mother and child together, probably kept lower the infant mortality rate. What the situation involved in its broader child-welfare aspects is indicated by the interrelation of bad home influences, poverty or shiftlessness, mental defect, and personal irresponsibility found in so many of the histories of the forbears and guardians of these children.

INDEX.

Except where otherwise stated, *births, birth rates, deaths, mortality rates, children, infants, mothers,* and *fathers* concern children born out of wedlock. *Final* indicates the end of period or close of care; *initial, previous,* at or before the beginning of period or of care; *S. M. W.* stands for division of State minor wards.

CHILDREN AND YOUTH
Social Problems and Social Policy

An Arno Press Collection

Abt, Henry Edward. **The Care, Cure and Education of the Crippled Child.** 1924

Addams, Jane. **My Friend, Julia Lathrop.** 1935

American Academy of Pediatrics. **Child Health Services and Pediatric Education:** Report of the Committee for the Study of Child Health Services. 1949

American Association for the Study and Prevention of Infant Mortality. **Transactions of the First Annual Meeting of the American Association for the Study and Prevention of Infant Mortality.** 1910

Baker, S. Josephine. **Fighting For Life.** 1939

Bell, Howard M. **Youth Tell Their Story:** A Study of the Conditions and Attitudes of Young People in Maryland Between the Ages of 16 and 24. 1938

Bossard, James H. S. and Eleanor S. Boll, editors. **Adolescents in Wartime.** 1944

Bossard, James H. S., editor. **Children in a Depression Decade.** 1940

Brunner, Edmund DeS. **Working With Rural Youth.** 1942

Care of Dependent Children in the Late Nineteenth and Early Twentieth Centuries. Introduction by Robert H. Bremner. 1974

Care of Handicapped Children. Introduction by Robert H. Bremner. 1974

[Chenery, William L. and Ella A. Merritt, editors]. **Standards of Child Welfare:** A Report of the Children's Bureau Conferences, May and June, 1919. 1919

The Child Labor Bulletin, 1912, 1913. 1974

Children In Confinement. Introduction by Robert M. Mennel. 1974

Children's Bureau Studies. Introduction by William M. Schmidt. 1974

Clopper, Edward N. **Child Labor in City Streets.** 1912

David, Paul T. **Barriers To Youth Employment.** 1942

Deutsch, Albert. **Our Rejected Children.** 1950

Drucker, Saul and Maurice Beck Hexter. **Children Astray.** 1923

Duffus, R[obert] L[uther] and L. Emmett Holt, Jr. **L. Emmett Holt:** Pioneer of a Children's Century. 1940

Fuller, Raymond G. **Child Labor and the Constitution.** 1923

Holland, Kenneth and Frank Ernest Hill. **Youth in the CCC.** 1942

Jacoby, George Paul. **Catholic Child Care in Nineteenth Century New York:** With a Correlated Summary of Public and Protestant Child Welfare. 1941

Johnson, Palmer O. and Oswald L. Harvey. **The National Youth Administration.** 1938

The Juvenile Court. Introduction by Robert M. Mennel. 1974

Klein, Earl E. **Work Accidents to Minors in Illinois.** 1938

Lane, Francis E. **American Charities and the Child of the Immigrant:** A Study of Typical Child Caring Institutions in New York and Massachusetts Between the Years 1845 and 1880. 1932

The Legal Rights of Children. Introduction by Sanford N. Katz. 1974

Letchworth, William P[ryor]. **Homes of Homeless Children:** A Report on Orphan Asylums and Other Institutions for the Care of Children. [1903]

Lorwin, Lewis. **Youth Work Programs:** Problems and Policies. 1941

Lundberg, Emma O[ctavia] and Katharine F. Lenroot. **Illegitimacy As A Child-Welfare Problem, Parts 1 and 2.** 1920/1921

New York State Commission on Relief for Widowed Mothers. **Report of the New York State Commission on Relief for Widowed Mothers.** 1914

Otey, Elizabeth Lewis. **The Beginnings of Child Labor Legislation in Certain States;** A Comparative Study. 1910

Phillips, Wilbur C. **Adventuring For Democracy.** 1940

Polier, Justine Wise. **Everyone's Children, Nobody's Child:** A Judge Looks At Underprivileged Children in the United States. 1941

Proceedings of the Annual Meeting of the National Child Labor Committee, 1905, 1906. 1974

Rainey, Homer P. **How Fare American Youth?** 1940

Reeder, Rudolph R. **How Two Hundred Children Live and Learn.** 1910

Security and Services For Children. 1974

Sinai, Nathan and Odin W. Anderson. **EMIC (Emergency Maternity and Infant Care):** A Study of Administrative Experience. 1948

Slingerland, W. H. **Child-Placing in Families:** A Manual For Students and Social Workers. 1919

[Solenberger], Edith Reeves. **Care and Education of Crippled Children in the United States.** 1914

Spencer, Anna Garlin and Charles Wesley Birtwell, editors. **The Care of Dependent, Neglected and Wayward Children:** Being a Report of the Second Section of the International Congress of Charities, Correction and Philanthropy, Chicago, June, 1893. 1894

Theis, Sophie Van Senden. **How Foster Children Turn Out.** 1924

Thurston, Henry W. **The Dependent Child:** A Story of Changing Aims and Methods in the Care of Dependent Children. 1930

U.S. Advisory Committee on Education. **Report of the Committee, February, 1938.** 1938

The United States Children's Bureau, 1912-1972. 1974

White House Conference on Child Health and Protection. **Dependent and Neglected Children:** Report of the Committee on Socially Handicapped — Dependency and Neglect. 1933

White House Conference on Child Health and Protection. **Organization for the Care of Handicapped Children, National, State, Local.** 1932

White House Conference on Children in a Democracy. **Final Report of the White House Conference on Children in A Democracy.** [1942]

Wilson, Otto. **Fifty Years' Work With Girls, 1883-1933:** A Story of the Florence Crittenton Homes. 1933

Wrenn, C. Gilbert and D. L. Harley. **Time On Their Hands:** A Report on Leisure, Recreation, and Young People. 1941